Active Server™ Pages 2.0

Stephen Walther, with

Steven Banick
Aaron Bertrand
Craig Eddy
Christian Gross
Keith McIntyre
Jeff Spotts

SAMS

Unleashed

Active Server™ Pages 2.0 Unleashed

Copyright © 1999 by Sams Publishing

International Standard Book Number: 0-672-31613-7

Library of Congress Catalog Card Number: 98-89981

Printed in the United States of America

First Printing: June 1999

01   00   99   4   3

Trademarks

Warning and Disclaimer

EXECUTIVE EDITOR:
Brad Jones

ACQUISITIONS EDITOR
Chris Webb

DEVELOPMENT EDITOR
Songlin Qiu

MANAGING EDITOR
Jodi Jensen

PROJECT EDITOR
Tonya Simpson

COPY EDITOR
Mary Lagu

INDEXER
Tina Trettin

PROOFREADER
Jill Mazurczyk

TECHNICAL EDITOR
Eric Richardson

SOFTWARE DEVELOPMENT SPECIALIST
Craig Atkins

INTERIOR DESIGN
Gary Adair

COVER DESIGN
Aren Howell

COPY WRITER
Eric Borgert

LAYOUT TECHNICIANS
Brian Borders

Contents at a Glance

Contents

22   Using ASP with Microsoft Message Queue Server   555

PART VI   ADVANCED TOPICS   585

23   SECURING YOUR WEB SITE   587

PART VII ACTIVE SERVER PAGES SAMPLE APPLICATIONS 675

27 CREATING A DISCUSSION FORUM 677

28 CREATING AN ONLINE STORE 695

About the Authors

Stephen Walther is the chief technical officer of CityAuction (www.cityauction.com), one of the Internet's top person-to-person auction Web sites and the exclusive auction provider for both Snap! and CitySearch (CityAuction was recently acquired by Ticketmaster Online-CitySearch). Mr. Walther was past chief technical officer of Collegescape, the leading provider of online college applications that was acquired by Peterson's, North America's largest education and career information company. There, Mr. Walther designed and managed the implementation of the original Collegescape Web site.

Mr. Walther received his Bachelor of Arts from the University of California at Berkeley. He was a Ph.D. candidate in Linguistics and Philosophy at the Massachusetts Institute of Technology when he became involved with the World Wide Web. He can be contacted at Swalther@aol.com.

Contributors

Steve Banick has been a lead and contributing author for several Macmillan publications and is currently a development manager for the consumer Internet division of TELUS Advanced Communications in Alberta, Canada. Steve can be reached at http://www.banick.com.

Aaron Bertrand leads the Web programming effort at Internet startup Bluestreak.com, where he specializes in interface design and database development. After graduating from Nipissing University and running his own consulting company (www.desktop.on.ca) for six years, he has come to play a key role in application development at his new position. Aaron has written technical pieces for online resources such as Microsoft's Sitebuilder Network and www.swynk.com, and has been recognized by Microsoft as a Most Valuable Professional for proficiency in Active Server Pages and Internet Information Server.

Craig Eddy works for Pipestream Technologies, Inc., where he is program manager for Pipestream's Web-based version of its popular customer information management software, Sales Continuum 98 and Continuum 2000. Craig has been a Web, Visual Basic, and Visual C++ developer for several years. He currently resides in Richmond, Virginia, and can often be found surfing the Web or the sands of the Outer Banks in North Carolina. Craig can be reached via email at craig.eddy@cyberdude.com.

Christian Gross is a professional programmer, author, and consultant who speaks regularly at professional developer conferences around the world, including the Visual C++ Developers Conference, Microsoft DevDays, TechEd, and Software Development. You can also find Christian's work in professional journals such as *The Visual C++*

Developer journal. As an IT consultant, Christian has advised such companies as the National Westminster Bank, Magna International, Standard Life, and the Union Bank of Switzerland.

Keith McIntyre has been developing software for two decades. He has watched and participated in the personal computer, local area network, client/server, and Internet evolutions. Keith has contributed to many software products, including those published by Optigraphics, Emerald Systems, Compton's New Media, and Qualcomm, including Eudora versions 3.0 and 4.0. Keith is currently vice president of Engineering for Stellcom's Internet Systems Division. Keith holds a Bachelor of Science in Computer Science.

Jeff Spotts is a senior business systems analyst for Federal Express Corporation and teaches programming courses at State Technical Institute in Memphis. He also creates custom-designed software systems as well as ASP based Web applications for individuals and businesses. He specializes in creating database applications using Visual Basic as a standalone, front-end interface or VBScript as a Web-based interface with a variety of database engines. Jeff may be contacted via email at jspotts@bigfoot.com.

Dedication

This book is dedicated to my grandparents, Edwin and Helyn Orr.

Acknowledgments

I'd like to thank my smarter younger sister, Sue Walther-Jones, for once again reading and commenting on every page of this book when she should have been finishing her novel. I'd also like to thank her husband, Andrew Jones, for reluctantly tolerating the use of his name for the sample scripts in this book.

I am also grateful to my parents, Jon and Judy Walther, who have always been supportive of the strange new twists and turns my life has taken.

I would also like to thank John Pyrovolakis. I owe John a debt of gratitude for convincing me to leave philosophy and become involved with the World Wide Web.

I am also grateful to Andrew Rebele for patiently giving me time to work on this book while we were creating the original CityAuction Web site.

Finally, I want to thank Chris Webb and Songlin Qiu for making the process of writing this book much easier than it should have been.

Tell Us What You Think!

As the reader of this book, *you* are our most important critic and commentator. We value your opinion and want to know what we're doing right, what we could do better, what areas you'd like to see us publish in, and any other words of wisdom you're willing to pass our way.

As an Associate Publisher for Sams Publishing, I welcome your comments. You can fax, email, or write me directly to let me know what you did or didn't like about this book—as well as what we can do to make our books stronger.

Please note that I cannot help you with technical problems related to the topic of this book, and that due to the high volume of mail I receive, I might not be able to reply to every message.

When you write, please be sure to include this book's title and author as well as your name and phone or fax number. I will carefully review your comments and share them with the authors and editors who worked on the book.

Fax:	317-581-4770
Email:	adv_prog@mcp.com
Mail:	Brad Jones Associate Publisher Sams Publishing 201 West 103rd Street Indianapolis, IN 46290 USA

Introduction

Active Server Pages is Microsoft's solution to building advanced Web sites. Many of the largest, most technologically demanding and most successful commercial Web sites running on the Internet today—such as Dell (`www.dell.com`), HotBot (`www.hotbot.com`), barnesandnoble.com (`www.barnesandnoble.com`) and Microsoft (`www.microsoft.com`)— were built using Active Server Pages. In this book, you'll learn everything you need to create a Web site of the same complexity.

Using Active Server Pages, you can:

- Generate dynamic Web pages. An Active Server Page can display different content to different users or display different content at different times of the day.

- Process the contents of HTML forms. You can use an Active Server Page to retrieve and respond to the data entered into an HTML form.

- Create database-driven Web pages. An Active Server Page can insert new data or retrieve existing data from a database such as Microsoft SQL Server.

- Track user sessions. You can use Active Server Pages to store information about users from the moment they arrive at your Web site until the moment they leave.

- Create searchable Web pages. When used with Microsoft Index Server or Microsoft SQL Server Full-Text search, Active Server Pages enable you to create a search engine for your Web site.

- Detect the capabilities of different browsers. An Active Server Page can detect the features that a browser supports and display content that is appropriate to different browsers.

- Send and retrieve email. An Active Server Page can automatically send email to users and retrieve email sent to your Web site.

- Integrate custom components into your Web site. You can extend your Active Server Page scripts with custom server-side components created with Microsoft Script Components, Microsoft Visual Basic, or Microsoft Visual C++.

Why You Should Buy This Book

This edition of *Active Server Pages Unleashed* has been completely revised and updated to cover the latest changes in Microsoft Technology relevant to Active Server Pages.

- This book contains three complete sample applications of Active Server Pages. You learn how to create a discussion forum, an online store, and a job site using nothing but Active Server Page scripts. The complete code for each of these sample applications is included on the CD-ROM that accompanies this book.

- Three chapters are devoted to creating custom Active Server Page components. You learn how to create custom components using Microsoft Script Components, Microsoft Visual Basic, and Microsoft Visual C++.

- This book explains how to use the Active Directory Service Interfaces (ADSI) within your Active Server Pages. You learn how to use ADSI to create Windows NT users and groups and to manipulate security information.

- Four chapters are devoted to the most recent versions of the ActiveX Data Objects (ADO) and OLE DB. For example, you learn how to use native OLE DB providers and create persistent and disassociated Recordsets.

- This book has been updated to cover the new features of Microsoft SQL Server 7.0. For example, you learn how to use the Microsoft SQL Server 7.0 Full-Text Search service within your Active Server Pages.

- You will learn about Microsoft DNA. You learn how to use Microsoft Transaction Server and Microsoft Message Queue Server to make your Web site more scalable and fault-tolerant.

- You will explore the new features of Active Server Pages and Internet Information Server included with Microsoft Windows 2000.

Who Should Read This Book?

This book is written for the professional developer who needs to create or maintain a commercial-quality Internet or intranet Web site. This book is focused on creating dynamic Web sites—primarily database-driven Web sites.

This book assumes that you understand both HTML and VBScript. You should also be familiar with the basics of Windows NT and Microsoft Internet Information Server. Finally, to understand the chapters that explain database access in Active Server Pages, you should have some background with Microsoft SQL Server and the SQL language.

How This Book Is Organized

This book is organized so that you can read it from cover to cover. Earlier chapters cover more basic topics, and later chapters cover more advanced topics. What follows is a brief overview of the topics covered by each part of the book:

- Part I, "Active Server Pages Objects," discusses the built-in objects included with Active Server Pages. For example, you learn how to work with data retrieved from

HTML forms and query strings. You also learn how to store persistent information in Application and Session variables.

- Part II, "Active Server Pages Installable Components," discusses several additional components bundled with Active Server Pages. For example, you learn how to use the CDO for NTS to send and retrieve email, ADSI to manipulate user security information, and the Ad Rotator component to display different banner advertisements at your Web site.

- Part III, "Using Active Server Pages with Databases," discusses how to use the ActiveX Data Objects (ADO) to access databases. You also learn how to use the ADO with Microsoft Index Server and Microsoft SQL Server 7.0 Full-Text Search.

- Part IV, "Active Server Pages Custom Components," discusses how to create server-side components with Microsoft Script Components, Microsoft Visual Basic, and Microsoft Visual C++. You also learn about several valuable third-party components that you can incorporate into your Active Server Pages.

- Part V, "Creating Multitier Distributed Applications," discusses the Microsoft Windows Distributed interNet Applications Architecture (DNA), Microsoft Transaction Server, and Microsoft Message Queue Server.

- Part VI, "Advanced Topics," discusses how to maintain your Web site using Windows Scripting Host and the Task Scheduler. You also learn how to optimize the performance of your Web site by using Profiler and InetMonitor. Additionally, you learn about the new features of Active Server Pages included with Windows 2000.

- Part VII, "Active Server Pages Sample Applications," discusses how to create three complete Web sites using Active Server Pages. You learn how to create a discussion forum, an online store, and a job site.

Conventions Used in This Book

This book uses different typefaces to differentiate between code and regular English, and also to help you identify important concepts.

Text that you type and text that should appear on your screen is presented in monospace type.

```
It will look like this to mimic the way text looks on your screen.
```

Placeholders for variables and expressions appear in *monospace italic* font. You should replace the placeholder with the specific value it represents.

This arrow () at the beginning of a line of code means that a single line of code is too long to fit on the printed page. Continue typing all characters after the ➥ as though they were part of the preceding line.

Note

A Note presents interesting pieces of information related to the surrounding discussion.

Tip

A Tip offers advice or teaches an easier way to do something.

Caution

A Caution advises you about potential problems and helps you steer clear of disaster.

 The CD-ROM icon alerts you to information or items that appear on the CD-ROM that accompanies this book.

Active Server Pages Objects

PART

I

IN THIS PART

CHAPTER 1

Building Active Server Pages

by Stephen Walther

IN THIS CHAPTER

This chapter formally introduces you to Active Server Pages. You will learn how Active Server Pages really work, how to use objects and components with Active Server Pages, and how to configure and troubleshoot the installation of Active Server Pages on your Web server.

Understanding How Active Server Pages Really Work

An Active Server Page is a standard HTML file that is extended with additional features. Like a standard HTML file, an Active Server Page contains HTML tags that can be interpreted and displayed by a Web browser. Anything you could normally place in an HTML file—Java applets, blinking text, client-side scripts, client-side ActiveX controls—you can place in an Active Server Page. However, an Active Server Page has three important features that make it unique:

- An Active Server Page can contain server-side scripts. By including server-side scripts in an Active Server Page, you can create Web pages with dynamic content. To take an extremely simple example, you can create a Web page that displays different messages at different times of the day.

- An Active Server Page provides several built-in objects. By using the built-in objects accessible in an Active Server Page, you can make your scripts much more powerful. Among other things, these objects enable you to both retrieve information from and send information to browsers. For example, by using the `Request` object, you can retrieve the information that a user has posted in an HTML form and respond to that information within a script.

- An Active Server Page can be extended with additional components. Active Server Pages comes bundled with several standard, server-side ActiveX components. These components enable you to do such things as work with databases, send email, and access the file system.

  These standard ActiveX components are very useful. However, you're not limited only to these components. You can buy third-party components or create additional ActiveX components of your own. There's no limit to how you can extend Active Server Pages.

These three features define an Active Server Page. An Active Server Page is a standard HTML page that has been extended with server-side scripts, objects, and components. By using Active Server Pages, you can create Web sites with dynamic content.

The best way to understand how Active Server Pages work is by contrasting the process of retrieving an Active Server Page with the process of accessing a normal HTML page.

The process of serving an HTML page can be broken into the following steps:

1. A user enters the Internet address of an HTML file into the address bar of a Web browser and presses Enter to request a Web page (for example, `http://www.aspsite.com/hello.htm`).

2. The browser sends a request for the Web page to a Web server such as Internet Information Server (IIS).

3. The Web server receives the request and recognizes that the request is for an HTML file because the requested file has the extension .htm or .html.

4. The Web server retrieves the proper HTML file from disk or memory and sends the file back to the browser.

5. The HTML file is interpreted by the user's Web browser, and the results are displayed in the browser window.

Of course, this process is often more complicated (for example, the contents of forms are posted and query strings are passed). But, in broad strokes, these steps outline the moment-to-moment activity of a typical Web server. A server receives requests for particular files and responds by sending the correct file, retrieving it from the hard drive or memory.

> **NOTE**
>
> The discussion of Active Server Pages in this book assumes that you'll be using Active Server Pages with Microsoft's Internet Information Server. However, you can use Active Server Pages with many other Web servers as well. Active Server Pages can be used with Microsoft's Personal Web Server for Windows 95/98 and the Peer Web Server for Windows NT.
>
> You aren't even limited to using Active Server Pages with Microsoft Web servers. By using Chili!Soft's Chili!ASP, you can use Active Server Pages with the Netscape Enterprise and FastTrack servers, the Lotus Domino and Go servers, O'Reilly's WebSite, and many other Web servers (for more information, visit the Chili!Soft Web site at www.chilisoft.com).

Although IIS can be used to serve static HTML pages, Active Server Pages enable IIS to serve dynamic content as well. Using Active Server Pages, you can create pages with new content in response to user requests. The Web server itself becomes active in the process of creating the Web page.

It's important to understand how this process of serving an Active Server Page contrasts with the normal process of serving an HTML page, so we'll break it into steps:

1. A user enters the Internet address of an Active Server Page file into the address bar of a Web browser and presses Enter to request an Active Server Page (for example, `http://www.aspsite.com/hello.asp`).

2. The browser sends a request for the Active Server Page to IIS.

3. The Web server receives the request and recognizes that the request is for an Active Server Page file because the requested file has the extension .asp.

4. The Web server retrieves the proper Active Server Page file from disk or memory.

5. The Web server sends the file to a special program named ASP.dll.

6. The Active Server Page file is processed from top to bottom and any commands it encounters are executed. The result of this process is a standard HTML file.

7. The HTML file is sent back to the browser.

8. The HTML file is interpreted by the user's Web browser, and the results are displayed in the browser window.

> **NOTE**
>
> For clarity's sake, the steps presented here have been slightly simplified. An Active Server Page doesn't need to be recompiled every time it's requested. If an Active Server Page has previously been requested and hasn't been altered, it will be retrieved from the cache instead of being processed again.

From the perspective of the Web server, an Active Server Page is very different from a normal HTML page. A normal HTML file is sent without processing to the browser. All the commands in an Active Server Page, on the other hand, must first be executed to create an HTML page. This allows an Active Server Page to contain dynamic content.

From the perspective of the browser, on the other hand, an Active Server Page is almost exactly the same as a normal HTML page. The only difference is that an Active Server Page typically must end with the extension .asp rather than .htm or .html. When a request is made for an Active Server Page, the browser receives a normal HTML page. This enables an Active Server Page to be compatible with all browsers.

Integrating Objects and Components into Active Server Pages

An Active Server Page is primarily a scripting environment. This book assumes that you will be creating Active Server Page scripts with Microsoft's VBScript. However, you can use other scripting languages with Active Server Pages such as JScript and PerlScript as well. Any scripting language that has a scripting engine compatible with the ActiveX scripting standard can be used in an Active Server Page.

> **NOTE**
>
> If you're familiar with Perl, you'll be happy to know that an implementation of Perl is compatible with Active Server Pages. For more information, see http://www.activestate.com or visit the companion Web site to this book at http://www.aspsite.com.

The easiest way to add a script to an Active Server Page is by using the script delimiters <% and %>. Any text enclosed within these delimiters will be processed as a script. Here's an example:

```
<HTML>
<HEAD><TITLE>ASP Script</TITLE></HEAD>
<BODY>
This is a
<% FOR i=1 TO 10 %>
very,
<% NEXT %>
very long sentence.
</BODY>
</HTML>
```

When this Active Server Page is displayed by a Web browser, the following sentence is displayed:

```
This is a very, very, very, very, very, very, very, very, very, very,
➡very long sentence.
```

The script creates 11 copies of the word very by using a VBScript FOR...NEXT loop.

By default, an Active Server Page assumes you'll be using VBScript as your primary scripting language. This means that you don't need to do anything beyond using the <% and %> script delimiters to use this language. However, there are three ways to explicitly specify a language for use in an Active Server Page.

First, you can use the Internet Service Manager to specify a particular scripting language as the default language for all your Active Server Pages. To do this, perform the following steps:

1. Launch the Internet Service Manager from the Microsoft Internet Information Server program group on the Start menu.

2. Right-click the name of your Web site. If you haven't changed the default configuration, the name of this Web site will be Default Web Site.

3. Choose Properties to open your Web site's property sheet.

4. Click the Home Directory tab.

5. Click the Configuration button. (To do this, you must have an existing application. If you don't, create one now by clicking Create.)

6. In the Application Configuration dialog box, click the App Options tab.

7. In the Default ASP Language text box, enter the name of the scripting language that you want to use as your primary scripting language; for example, enter vbscript or jscript (see Figure 1.1).

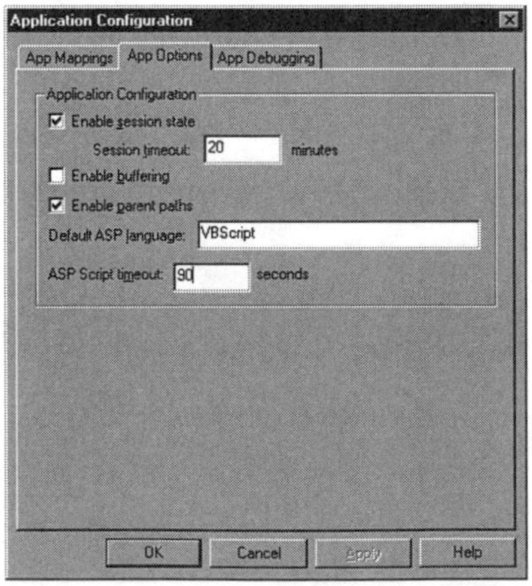

FIGURE 1.1

Using the Internet Service Manager to specify a default scripting language.

After you have specified a particular scripting language as the default scripting language, you can use it in your Active Server Pages simply by using the delimiters <% and %>. If you plan to use JScript for the majority of your Active Server Pages, for example, you should configure this language as your default language.

You can also specify the primary scripting language for a particular page. To do this, place the LANGUAGE directive as the very first line in your Active Server Page file, as shown in this example:

```
<%@ LANGUAGE=JScript %>
<HTML>
<HEAD><TITLE>ASP Script</TITLE></HEAD>
<BODY>
This is a
<% for(i=1;i<11;i++){ %>
very,
<% } %>
very long sentence.
</BODY>
</HTML>
```

The directive in the first line of this script indicates that all the scripts contained in the file should be executed as scripts created with JScript, rather than some other scripting language. When you use this directive, be sure to include a space between the @ character and the keyword LANGUAGE. Furthermore, it's very important that this directive appear before any other commands in your Active Server Page file (otherwise you'll get an error)

A third alternative exists for including scripts in your Active Server Pages. You can use Microsoft's extended <SCRIPT> HTML tag, as in this example:

```
<HTML>
<HEAD><TITLE>ASP Script</TITLE></HEAD>
<BODY>
<SCRIPT LANGUAGE="JScript" RUNAT="server">
function sayhello()
{
response.write("Hello!")
}
</SCRIPT>
<%
sayhello()
%>
</BODY>
</HTML>
```

Here, the <SCRIPT> tags contain a JScript function. The LANGUAGE attribute of the <SCRIPT> tag specifies which scripting language to use. The RUNAT attribute indicates that the script should be executed on the server rather than on the client (the browser).

The function named `sayhello()` is defined in the first script. The second script, marked with the usual `<%` and `%>` tags, is where the JScript function is actually called. This Active Server Page prints the text `Hello!` to the screen.

If you have created client-side JScript or VBScript scripts, you should be familiar with the `<SCRIPT>` tag. Microsoft's extended `<SCRIPT>` tag can be used to specify either client-side or server-side scripts. If you neglected to include the `RUNAT="server"` attribute in the preceding example, the script would be treated as a client-side script. In this case, the server would ignore the script, and the browser would attempt to execute the script. (It would fail miserably because the script isn't a valid client-side script.)

Why would you ever want to use the `<SCRIPT>` tag rather than the `<%` and `%>` script delimiters? Normally, you wouldn't use the `<SCRIPT>` tag. However, there are two significant differences between these two ways of specifying a script.

First, scripts that are contained in the `<SCRIPT>` tag are executed immediately, no matter where they appear in an Active Server Page. For example, consider the following page:

```
<HTML>
<HEAD><TITLE>ASP Script</TITLE></HEAD>
<BODY>
This is the first sentence.
<SCRIPT LANGUAGE="JScript" RUNAT="server">
response.write("This is the second sentence.")
</SCRIPT>
</BODY>
</HTML>
```

Looking at the script, you might be tempted to believe that the sentence `This is the first sentence.` and the sentence `"This is the second sentence."` are printed to the screen in that order. However, when the Active Server Page is displayed in a browser, the order of the two sentences is actually reversed (or worse, nothing is displayed, because an invalid HTML page is generated).

Why does this happen? Whatever is contained in the `<SCRIPT>` tag is executed before anything else in a page. If you use the `VIEW SOURCE` command on your Web browser, you'll see the following results from the preceding Active Server Page:

```
This is the second sentence.<HTML>
<HEAD><TITLE>ASP Script</TITLE></HEAD>
<BODY>
This is the first sentence.
</BODY>
</HTML>
```

This behavior of the <SCRIPT> tag has two implications. First, you can place scripts contained in a <SCRIPT> tag anywhere you want in an Active Server Page. Second, the <SCRIPT> tag, for most purposes, is restricted to containing functions or procedures. The output of any script that's not contained in a function or procedure is displayed immediately and results in an invalid HTML page.

The <SCRIPT> tag has one main advantage over the <% and %> script delimiters. Using the <SCRIPT> tag, you can mix multiple scripting languages within a single Active Server Page. Consider the following example:

```
<%@ LANGUAGE="VBScript" %>
<HTML>
<HEAD><TITLE>ASP Script</TITLE></HEAD>
<BODY>
<SCRIPT LANGUAGE="JScript" RUNAT="server">
function sayhello()
{
response.write("Hello!")
}
</SCRIPT>
<%
FOR i=1 to 10
sayhello()
NEXT
%>
</BODY>
</HTML>
```

This script prints Hello! 10 times in a row. But notice how it does this. The script contained in the <% and %> delimiters is a Visual Basic script. However, this script calls a JScript function. The JScript function is defined within the <SCRIPT> tag. When you want to use one scripting language as your primary scripting language, but you need to call a function from another language, you can use this method. This is useful when one language has particular functions or methods that another language lacks.

To summarize, there are three methods of including a script in an Active Server Page:

- Specify a scripting language for all your Active Server Pages by using the Internet Service Manager to specify a default language.
- Specify a scripting language for a single page by using the Active Server Page directive <%@ LANGUAGE="scripting language" %>.
- Mix multiple scripting languages in a single Active Server Page by using the extended <SCRIPT> tag.

Before ending this section, one final Active Server Pages directive should be discussed.

By using the Active Server Pages' output directive, you can display the value of an expression. Here's an example:

```
<HTML>
<HEAD><TITLE>ASP Example</TITLE></HEAD>
<BODY>
At the tone, the time will be: <%=TIME%>
</BODY>
</HTML>
```

You use the delimiters `<%=` and `%>` to print the value of a variable, method, or function. In the preceding example, the output directive is used to output the value of the VBScript `TIME` function.

There's another way to accomplish the same thing. Consider the following example:

```
<HTML>
<HEAD><TITLE>ASP Example</TITLE></HEAD>
<BODY>
At the tone, the time will be: <% Response.Write(TIME) %>
</BODY>
</HTML>
```

In this example, the value of the VBScript `TIME` function is outputted by using the Active Server Pages `Response` object. The `Write()` method of the `Response` object outputs the value of expressions to the screen. (In the next section, you will learn more about using objects.)

When should you use the `Response.Write()` method rather than the `<%=` and `%>` output directive? It really doesn't matter. Active Server Pages internally represent the output directive as a `Response.Write()` method call in any case. The two methods of outputting the values of expressions are completely interchangeable.

> **NOTE**
>
> When you receive an error using the `<%=` and `%>` output directive, the error will refer to a line of code that uses the `Response.Write()` method. This can be confusing because this line of code actually doesn't exist in your Active Server Page. However, it illustrates that Active Server Pages represents the two methods of outputting the values of expressions in the same way.

Nevertheless, there are situations in which one method of outputting the values of expressions is more convenient than the other. For example, when you need to output the value of an expression within a script, the Response.Write() method is often easier to use. On the other hand, when you want to output the value of an expression within a section of HTML code, the <%= and %> directive is often easier to use. The following illustrates both approaches:

```
<HTML>
<HEAD><TITLE>ASP Example</TITLE></HEAD>
<BODY>
<%
FOR i=1 TO 10
myvar=myvar&"very,"
Response.Write(i&":"&myvar&"<BR>")
NEXT
%>
<HH>
This is a <%=myvar%> long sentence.
</BODY>
</HTML>
```

In this example, the Response.Write() method is used within the loop to display the value of the variable named myvar as it increases in size. The <%= and %> output directive is embedded within normal HTML code. The output directive is used to display the value of myvar (see Figure 1.2).

FIGURE 1.2

Two methods of outputting expressions.

Understanding Objects and Components

Active Server Pages include several built-in objects and installable ActiveX components. These objects and components can be used to extend the power of your Active Server Pages scripts. What are objects and components?

An *object* is something that typically has methods, properties, or collections. An object's *methods* determine the things you can do with the object. An object's *properties* can be read or set to specify the state of the object. An object's *collections* constitute different sets of key and value pairs related to the object.

To take an everyday example, the book *Tom Sawyer* is an example of an object. The object has certain methods that determine the things you can do with it. For example, you can read the book, use it as a doorstop, or even, if you're feeling particularly malicious, tear it into shreds. The object has certain properties. For example, it has a certain number of pages and a particular author. Finally, it has a collection of key and value pairs. Each page number (the key) has a corresponding page of text (the value).

An ActiveX *component* is similar to an Active Server Page built-in object. However, when you are using Active Server Pages, there is one important difference between a component and an object. An instance of a component must be explicitly created before it can be used.

Active Server Pages Objects

Active Server Pages include several built-in objects. These objects enable you to extend the power of your scripts. For example, by using these objects, you can gain access to browser requests and control how the server responds to these requests. The built-in objects also provide you with control over user sessions and Web-server applications.

You have already been introduced to one example of a built-in object—the Response object. You can use the Response object to send output to a browser. However, the Response object also has several other important properties, collections, and methods.

The following chapters explain in detail how to use each of the built-in objects. The following list provides a quick overview of each of the built-in objects:

- The Application object—The Application object is used to store and retrieve information that can be shared among all users of an application. For example, you can use the Application object to pass information between users of your Web site.

- The `Request` object— The `Request` object can be used to access all information sent in a request from a browser to your server. You can use the `Request` object to retrieve the information that a user has entered into an HTML form.

- The `Response` object— The `Response` object is used to send information back to a browser. You can use the `Response` object to send output from your scripts to a browser.

- The `Server` object— The `Server` object enables you to use various utility functions on the server. For example, you can use the `Server` object to control the length of time a script executes before it times out. You can also use the `Server` object to create instances of other objects.

- The `Session` object— The `Session` object can be used to store and retrieve information about particular user sessions. You can use the `Session` object to store information that persists over the course of a visit by a user to your Web site.

- The `ObjectContext` object— The `ObjectContext` object is used to control Active Server Pages transactions. The transactions are managed by the Microsoft Transaction Server (MTS).

The built-in objects differ from normal objects. You don't need to create an instance of a built-in object before you can use it in a script. The methods, collections, and properties of a built-in object are automatically accessible throughout a Web-site application.

> **NOTE**
>
> See Appendix B, "ASP Objects and Components Reference," for a complete list of all the methods, properties, and collections of the built-in objects.

Active Server Pages Components

Like the built-in objects discussed in the preceding section, Active Server Pages components can be used to extend the power of your scripts. Components differ from the built-in objects because they're typically used for more specialized tasks. The following list provides a brief overview of some of the components bundled with Active Server Pages:

- The Ad Rotator component—The Ad Rotator component is used to display banner advertisements on the Web pages of a Web site. You can use this component to specify how frequently different banner advertisements should be displayed.

- The Browser Capabilities component— The Browser Capabilities component can be used to display different HTML content, according to the capabilities of different browsers. For example, you can use this component to display Web pages with frames only to frames-compliant browsers.

- The Content Linking component— Using the Content Linking component, you can link together several HTML pages so that they can be navigated easily. For example, you can use this component to display the pages of an online book.

- The Counters component— The Counters component can be used to keep track of the number of visitors to your Web site. You can use the Counters component to add a hit counter to a Web page.

- The Content Rotator component— The Content Rotator component enables you to rotate through HTML content on a page. For example, you can use the component to randomly display different announcements on the home page of your Web site.

- The Page Counter component— The Page Counter component is exactly like the Counter component, in that it can be used to track the number of visitors and to add a hit counter to a particular Web page.

- The Permission Checker component— The Permission Checker component can be used to display links to Web pages only to those users who have permission to see them. You can use this component to create Web pages that can be viewed only by the administrators of a Web site.

- The Collaboration Data Objects— The Collaboration Data Objects (CDO) enable you to send and retrieve email from within your Active Server Pages. You can use these objects to send email to a new user after the user registers at your Web site.

- The ActiveX Data Objects— The ActiveX Data Objects (ADO) enable you to retrieve and store data in a database such as Microsoft SQL Server. These objects are extremely important. For this reason, they are thoroughly covered in a separate part of this book, Part III, "Using Active Server Pages With Databases."

Part II of this book, "Active Server Pages Installable Components," describes in detail how to use each installable component. Part IV of this book, "Active Server Pages Custom Components," describes how you can extend Active Server Pages with new components by buying them from third-party companies or creating them yourself.

NOTE

See Appendix B, "ASP Objects and Components Reference," for a complete list of all the methods, properties, and collections of the components.

Using Components in Active Server Pages

Before you can use a component, you must first create an instance of it. Although you can automatically access the properties, collections, and methods of the built-in objects on every page, before you can use a component, you must create an instance of the component with a particular scope. In the following three sections, you will learn how to create an instance of a component with page, session, and application scope.

Creating a Component with Page Scope

In most cases, you'll create an instance of a component with *page scope*. A component with page scope is created on a single page and dies when processing on the page ends. You can use a component with page scope only on the page where it is explicitly created. To create an instance of a component with page scope, you can use either the `Server.CreateObject()` method or the HTML `<OBJECT>` tag.

> ### CAUTION
>
> Don't use the `CreateObject` method of VBScript or the new statement of JScript to create an instance of a component. If you use either of these two methods of creating a component, weird and unpredictable things will happen. Always use the Active Server Pages `Server.CreateObject()` method instead.

Here's an example of how you can use the `CreateObject` method to create an instance of the `Dictionary` object with page scope:

```
<%
Set MyDict=Server.CreateObject("Scripting.Dictionary")
MyDict.Add "CA", "California"
MyDict.Add "MA", "Massachusetts"
MyDict.Add "MI", "Missouri"
%>
My dictionary has <%=MyDict.Count %> entries.
<BR>
The first entry in my dictionary is <%=MyDict.Item("CA")%>.
```

When this script is executed, an instance of the `Dictionary` object is created. Next, three key and value pairs are added to the dictionary. Finally, two properties of the dictionary are displayed (see Figure 1.3).

Figure 1.3

An example of the
Dictionary *object.*

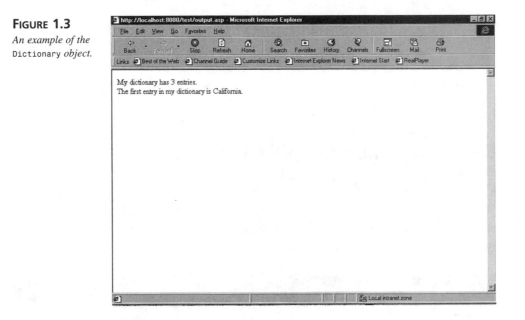

The first statement in this example uses the Server.CreateObject method to create an instance of an object with page scope. In this example, an instance of the Dictionary object is assigned to a variable named MyDict.

After an instance of an object has been created, its methods can be called. In this example, the Add method of the Dictionary object is called to add entries to the dictionary. The first Add method call is used to add the key and value pair CA and California.

After an instance of an object has been created, you can also access its properties. In this example, the Count property of the Dictionary object is read to determine the number of entries in the dictionary. The Item property is also read to return the value of a particular key.

Finally, when you're finished using an instance of an object, you can destroy it. An object created by the preceding method will automatically be destroyed after the server finishes processing the Active Server Page. Therefore, there's usually no reason to explicitly destroy an object. However, you can destroy the MyDict object explicitly by assigning MyDict to a new value or by setting the variable to the value Nothing like this:

```
<% Set MyDict=Nothing %>
```

This example illustrates the most typical method of creating and using ActiveX components in Active Server Pages. You create an instance of an object by calling the Server.CreateObject() method. After you create a new object, you can call its methods and read and set its properties.

> **NOTE**
>
> See Appendix B, "ASP Objects and Components Reference," for examples of
> how to create each ActiveX component.

There exists a second method for creating objects with page scope. Instead of using the
CreateObject method, you can create an instance of an object with the Microsoft
Extended HTML <OBJECT> tag. Here is an example:

```
<OBJECT RUNAT="Server" ID="MyBrow"
PROGID="MSWC.BrowserType"></OBJECT>
```

Because the preceding code is not a script, you should not add it to an Active Server
Page within the <% and %> script delimiters. The <OBJECT> tag is an HTML tag, and it
should appear within the normal HTML content of your page.

This example shows how to use three properties of the HTML <OBJECT> tag. The ID
attribute provides the component with a unique identifier (a name), so you can refer to it
in your Active Server Pages scripts. The PROGID is used to specify the component's registered name. This is the name the server uses to identify the component when it creates an
instance of it. It's the same name you would pass to the Server.CreateObject()
method.

When should you use the <OBJECT> tag, instead of the CreateObject method, to create
an instance of an object? The one advantage of the <OBJECT> tag is that it does not create
an instance of an object until a property or method of the object is actually called. If an
Active Server Page contains objects that might never be called, you should use the
<OBJECT> tag to save some memory.

Microsoft recommends that you create the majority of your components with page scope.
By creating components with page scope, you place less of a burden on the Web server.
A page scope component releases any memory and other resources it requires when the
processing of the page comes to an end.

Creating Components with Session Scope

Instead of creating components that are accessible only within a single Active Server
Page, you can create components that are accessible on multiple Active Server Pages.
One way to do this is to create a component with session scope. A component with session scope is available to a single visitor to your Web site on every page that the visitor
requests. An instance of the component is created for each visitor. The component
instance does not leave memory until the visitor leaves.

Two methods are available for creating components with *session scope*. One method assigns a component to a session variable by using the `Server.CreateObject()` method, as in the following example:

```
<%
Set Session("MyBrow")=Server.CreateObject("MSWC.BrowserType")
%>
```

This script assigns an instance of the Browser Capabilities component to the session variable named `MyBrow`. You can place this script within any Active Server Page or the Global.asa file (You will learn about the Global.asa file in Chapter 4, "Working With Active Server Pages Applications.") Normally, it makes sense to create the object instance in the `Session_OnStart` subroutine of the Global.asa file because you need to create the instance only once for each visitor.

After you have created a component with session scope, you can use its properties and methods by referring to the session variable that contains the component. For example, the following script displays the value of the `Frames` property of the Browser Capabilities component created with the previous script:

```
<%
if session("MyBrow").Frames = TRUE then
  response.write "your browser supports frames!"
end if
%>
```

This method of creating a component with session scope has a significant disadvantage. The `Server.CreateObject()` method immediately creates an instance of a component. Even if the instance of the component is never used, it still drains resources from the server. Because a new instance of a session object is created for each visitor, this can be a significant drain.

Fortunately, there's a second way to create a component with session scope. You can create a component by using the Microsoft HTML <OBJECT> tag, like this:

```
<OBJECT RUNAT="Server" SCOPE="Session" ID="MyBrow"
PROGID="MSWC.BrowserType"></OBJECT>
```

When you create an instance of a component with session scope with the <OBJECT> tag, you should create the instance within the Global.asa file. Create the object instance outside the `Application_OnStart`, `Application_OnEnd`, `Session_OnStart`, and `Session_OnEnd` subroutines.

This example uses four properties of the <OBJECT> tag. The SCOPE attribute indicates that the component created should have session scope. The ID attribute provides the component with a unique identifier (a name), so you can refer to it in your Active Server Pages scripts. The `PROGID` is used to specify the component's registered name. This is the name the server uses to identify the component when it creates an instance of it. It's the same name you would pass to the `Server.CreateObject()` method.

> **NOTE**
>
> Instead of using a component's registered name, you can also use the component's registered number (`CLASSID`) when using the `<OBJECT>` tag, as in this example:
>
> ```
> <OBJECT RUNAT="Server" SCOPE="Session" ID="MyBrow"
>     CLASSID="0ACE4881-8305-11CF-9427-444553540000"></OBJECT>
> ```

When you create an instance of a component with the HTML `<OBJECT>` tag, you can access any of its methods and properties just as if the object were a built-in Active Server Page object. For example, the following script displays a property of the Browser Capabilities component. (It is assumed that an instance of the component was created in the Global.asa file.)

```
<%

if MyBrow.Frames = TRUE then
  response.write "your browser supports frames!"
end if
%>
```

When a component is created with session scope in either of the two ways just described, any of its methods, collections, or properties are available on any page that a particular user requests. However, a particular instance of the component must be created for each user. A component with session scope is created relative to a particular user session.

When would you need to create a component with session scope? In Chapter 9, you will learn how to use the Ad Rotator component. The Ad Rotator component is used to display different banner advertisements with different frequencies. If you want to display banner advertisements on several pages, it makes sense to assign the Ad Rotator component to a session variable.

Creating Components with Application Scope

When you create an instance of a component with *application scope*, you treat it as if it were a built-in object. After it is created, any methods, collections, or properties of the component can be accessed by any user on any page. The component remains available until the server shuts down, the Global.asa file is modified, or the application is unloaded.

> **NOTE**
>
> If a component is created with application scope, its `OnStartPage()` and `OnEndPage()` methods are not called. This might be relevant when you are using custom components.

You can create a component with application scope by using methods similar to those used to create a component with session scope. First, you can create a component with application scope by using the `Server.CreateObject()` method. Look at this example:

```
<%
Set Application("AdRot")=Server.CreateObject("MSWC.AdRotator")
%>
```

Here, an instance of the Ad Rotator component is assigned to an application variable. You could create a component in this way within any of your Active Server Pages. However, normally, you create an instance of an object with application scope only once within the `Application_OnStart` event of the Global.asa file. The object then becomes available to all users of your Web site.

After an instance of the Ad Rotator component has been created with application scope, you can use its properties on any Active Server Page. For example, the following script calls the Ad Rotator's `getAdvertisement` property to display a banner advertisement:

```
<%=Application( "adRot" ).getAdvertisement( "schedule.txt")%>
```

You can also create a component with application scope by using the Microsoft HTML `<OBJECT>` tag, like this:

```
<OBJECT RUNAT="Server" SCOPE="Application" ID="AdRot"
 PROGID="MSWC.AdRotator"></OBJECT>
```

When you create an instance of a component with application scope with the `<OBJECT>` tag, you can only create the instance within the Global.asa file. Create the object instance outside the `Application_OnStart`, `Application_OnEnd`, `Session_OnStart`, and `Session_OnEnd` subroutines.

In this example, four properties of the <OBJECT> tag are used. The SCOPE attribute indicates that the component should have application rather than session scope. The ID attribute provides a name for the component. The PROGID attribute enables the server to identify the component.

> **NOTE**
>
> When creating components with application scope, you must be cautious about the component's threading model. For example, you cannot create an instance of the Browser Capabilities component with application scope because it uses an apartment-threading model. To learn more about threading models, see Chapter 19, "Creating Components with Visual C++."

After creating an instance of an application object in the Global.asa file with the <OBJECT> tag, you can use the component in exactly the same way as you use an Active Server Page built-in object. You can call any of the object's methods and properties on any page without creating another instance of it.

When would you need to create an object with application scope? In the WhosOn Page programming example in Chapter 4, "Working with Active Server Pages Applications," you will learn how to track user page requests. This information is stored in a dictionary created with application scope. This component must be created with application scope. Otherwise, it cannot be accessed by every user on every page.

Troubleshooting Active Server Pages

Before you can use Active Server Pages, make sure that it is properly installed on your system. If you installed Internet Information Server while installing Windows NT Server, Active Server Pages might not be installed. Active Server Pages is included with IIS versions 3.0 and above (the current version is version 4.0 and version 5.0 will be released with Windows 2000). To download the latest version of Active Server Pages, visit the Internet Information Server section of the Microsoft Web site at `http://www.microsoft.com/iis`.

After Active Server Pages is installed, you must configure IIS to use Active Server Pages. Configure at least one directory in your Web site with permissions to execute an Active Server Pages file. Follow these steps:

1. Launch the Internet Service Manager from the Microsoft Internet Information Server program group on the Start menu.

2. In the left pane of the Internet Service Manager, navigate to your default Web site. (If you haven't changed anything, the Web site will be named Default Web Site.)

3. Choose the directory in your Web site where you want to store your Active Server Pages files by navigating to it in the Internet Service Manager.

4. Right-click the name of this directory and choose Properties.

5. Click the tab labeled Directory or Virtual Directory (depending on the type of directory).

6. In the Permissions section, choose either Script or Execute (see Figure 1.4).

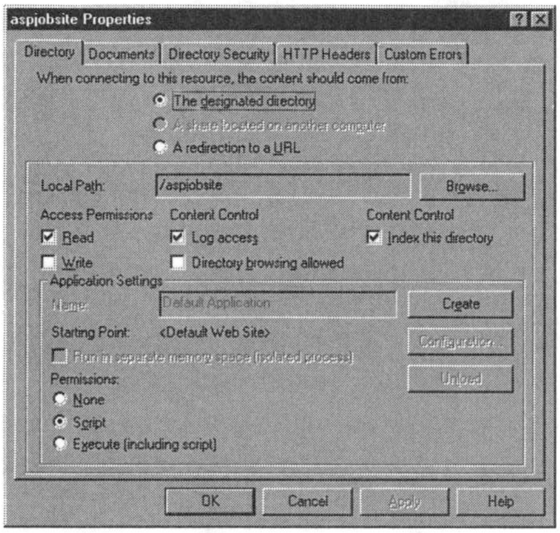

FIGURE 1.4

Setting directory permissions.

Now that you have created a directory with permissions to execute your Active Server Pages, you must store all your Active Server Pages in this directory in order to use them. If the directory is a physical directory, you can simply store your pages in the directory with this name. If the directory is a virtual directory, you must determine the physical path to this directory on your hard drive. You can determine the physical path of a virtual directory by looking at the same tabbed dialog box where you just configured the permissions.

CAUTION

If you're using a browser on the same machine as IIS, be careful how you retrieve an Active Server Page with your browser. When you load an Active Server Page into your Web browser, don't load the page by using your browser's Open command. Using the Open command bypasses IIS, and the Active Server Page won't be processed. You'll see the text of your Active Server Pages scripts instead of the page that these scripts produce. This probably isn't what you want.

To load an Active Server Page into a browser that's located on the same machine as IIS, use the address bar of your Web browser. For example, if the Active Server Page is located in the root directory of your Web site, you can load the page by typing `http://localhost/mypage.asp` into the address bar of your Web browser. This will load the Active Server Page named mypage.asp.

Testing Your Configuration

You can test whether Active Server Pages is configured properly on your system by creating a simple Active Server Page. If you can display this page successfully in your Web browser, you know that everything is set up properly.

To create an Active Server Page, you can use any text editor. For example, you can use Notepad, which is included as an accessory with Windows NT Server. Start Notepad (or your favorite text editor) and enter the following text:

```
<HTML>
<HEAD><TITLE>ASP Page</TITLE></HEAD>
<BODY>
<%
Response.Write("Hello World!")
%>
</BODY>
</HTML>
```

Save the Active Server Pages file as test.asp. Make sure that your text editor doesn't append an extra .txt extension to the filename. Also, make sure that you save the file in a directory with Execute or Script permission (see the preceding section).

> **NOTE**
>
> The file test.asp is available on the CD-ROM that accompanies this book in the Chap01 directory.

Now, launch your favorite Web browser in order to display your new Active Server Page. If you saved your Active Server Page in the root directory of your Web site, you can load the page by typing `http://localhost/test.asp`. If you saved the Active Server Page in a subdirectory of this root directory, include the full path by entering an address such as `http://localhost/mysubdir/test.asp`. If you saved the page in a virtual directory, include the name of the virtual directory in the address. For example, if your virtual directory is named `myvirtualdir`, you should type `http://localhost/myvirtualdir/test.asp`.

If everything works, the Active Server Page should be displayed. The text `Hello World!` should appear in your Web browser's window (see Figure 1.5). If everything doesn't work, see the next section.

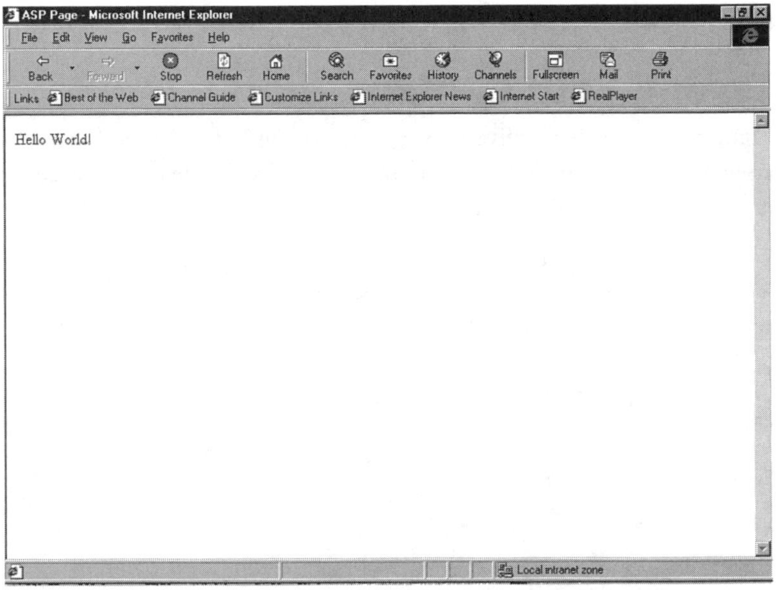

FIGURE 1.5

An Active Server Page.

> **NOTE**
>
> The appearance of the Active Server Page might vary slightly, depending on your browser and its current settings. For example, the size of the text might be larger or smaller than that shown in Figure 1.5.

Troubleshooting Your Active Server Pages Configuration

I sincerely hope that you never need to read this section. However, if you encounter problems displaying an Active Server Page, this section should help. Following are listed both symptoms and possible causes for a number of common problems that you might encounter while attempting to access an Active Server Page.

- Symptom—When attempting to load an Active Server Page, you receive a message complaining that the browser cannot connect to the server. For example, using Netscape Navigator, you receive this message:

```
There was no response. The server could be down or is not responding.
```

Or, using Internet Explorer, you receive this message:

```
Internet Explorer cannot open the Internet site
➥http://localhost/test.asp.
A connection with the server could not be established.
```

Cause—If you're not attempting to connect to your server over the Internet, this problem is almost certainly the result of your Web server being turned off. Make sure that your Web server is running. To do this, launch the Internet Service Manager from the Microsoft Internet Information Server program group on the Start menu. Select the name of your default Web site and check the VCR controls at the top of the window. If IIS isn't running, the VCR Run button will be inactive. Click this button to start the service.

Cause—If you're attempting to connect to your server over the Internet, the error message might result from heavy Internet traffic. Wait a while and try again. If you still can't connect to your server, contact your Internet service provider.

- Symptom—When attempting to load an Active Server Page, you receive the message HTTP/1.0 404 Object Not Found.

Cause—You entered the wrong address for the Active Server Page in your Web browser. If you saved your Active Server Page in the root directory of your Web site, you can load the page by entering http://localhost/test.asp. If you saved the Active Server Page in a subdirectory of this root directory, include the full path by entering an address such as http://localhost/mysubdir/test.asp. If you saved the page in a virtual directory, include the name of the virtual directory in the address. For example, if your virtual directory is named myvirtualdir, you should type http://localhost/myvirtualdir/test.asp.

Cause—Your text editor has appended an extra extension to the end of your Active Server Pages file. Notepad, for example, appends .txt on the end of the name of a file when you save it as a text file. If you save a file as type All Files, however, Notepad won't do this.

- Symptom—When attempting to load an Active Server Page, you receive the message HTTP/1.1 403 Access Forbidden. Execute Access Denied.

Cause—The permissions are improperly configured for the directory or virtual directory where the Active Server Page is stored. See the earlier discussion of configuring permissions in this section.

- Symptom—When the Active Server Page loads, you see the text of your scripts rather than the results of the scripts.

  Cause—You saved the Active Server Page file with the extension .htm or .html instead of .asp. For the Web server to process an Active Server Page, the Active Server Page file must end with the extension .asp.

  Cause—When loading the Active Server Page, you used the Open command on your Web browser. For the Web server to process an Active Server Page, you must load the page using the address bar of your Web browser.

Summary

This chapter introduced you to using Active Server Pages. You learned all the alternative methods for integrating scripts into your Active Server Pages. The chapter also provided an overview of the built-in objects and ActiveX components included with Active Server Pages. Finally, you learned how to configure Active Server Pages and troubleshoot any problems that might arise.

The following chapters explore in detail how to use all the objects and components of Active Server Pages. Whatever your Web project might be, the following chapters will help you accomplish it.

Active Server Pages and the HTTP Protocol

by Stephen Walther

IN THIS CHAPTER

CHAPTER 2

In this chapter, you will learn how to use two of the most important Active Server Page objects: the Response and Request objects. These two objects provide you with complete control over how your Web server communicates with Web browsers. Before we discuss these objects directly, however, you will first be given a brief introduction to the HTTP protocol—the underlying protocol of the World Wide Web.

How does the World Wide Web really work? When you type the address of a Web page in your Web browser, if all goes smoothly, the Web page appears. For example, if you type http://www.yahoo.com into your Web browser, the home page of the Yahoo Web site appears in your browser window. What goes on in the background to make this happen?

When you use a browser to retrieve an HTML page from a Web site, you're using the *Hypertext Transfer Protocol* (HTTP). The HTTP protocol specifies how messages can be transported over the Internet. In particular, the protocol specifies the ways in which a browser and a Web server can interact.

When you retrieve a page from a Web site, your browser opens a connection to a Web server at the Web site and issues a request. The Web server receives the request and issues a response. For this reason, the HTTP protocol is called a *request and response protocol*.

All communication between a browser and a Web server takes place in discrete request-and-response pairs. The browser must always initiate the communication by issuing a request. The Web server's role is completely passive; it must be nudged into action by the request.

A browser request has a certain structure. An HTTP request contains a request line, header fields, and possibly a message body. The most common type of request is a simple request for a Web page, as in the following example:

```
GET /hello.htm HTTP/1.1
Host: www.aspsite.com
```

This is an example of an HTTP request for the Web page hello.htm at the Web site www.aspsite.com. The first line is the request line. The request line specifies the method of the request, the resource being requested, and the version of the HTTP protocol being used.

In this example, the *method* of the request is the GET method. The GET method retrieves a particular resource. In this case, the GET method is being used to retrieve the Web page named hello.htm. Other types of request methods include POST, HEAD, OPTIONS, DELETE, TRACE, and PUT. The POST method, for example, is used to submit the contents of an HTML form.

The second line in this example is a *header*. The Host header specifies the Internet address of the Web site where the hello.htm file is located. In this case, the host is www.aspsite.com.

Typically, a request will include many headers. Headers provide additional information about the content of a message or about the originator of the request. Some of these headers are standard; others are browser-specific.

A request might also contain a *message body*. For example, if the request uses the POST method rather than the GET method, the message body can contain the contents of an HTML form. When you click the Submit button on an HTML form, and the form uses the ACTION="POST" attribute, any data you entered into the form is posted to the server. The form contents are sent within the message body of the request, using the POST method.

When a Web server receives a request, it returns an HTTP *response*. A response also has a certain structure. Every response begins with a status line, contains several headers, and optionally might contain a message body.

You're probably already familiar with the status line. If you have ever requested a Web page and mistyped the address, you've seen an example of a status line (see Figure 2.1). A status line indicates the protocol being used, a status code, and a text message (the *reason phrase*). For example, if a Web server has problems with a request, it returns an error and a description of the error in the status line. If a server can successfully respond to a request for a Web page, it returns a status line that contains 200 OK.

FIGURE 2.1

An example of a status line

HTTP/1.0 404 Object Not Found

Response headers contain information about the content of the response or information about the server providing the response. Some of these headers are standard; others depend on the Web server.

Finally, the message body of a response typically contains the contents of a Web page. For example, if the request was for the Web page hello.htm, the message body of the response would contain the HTML page named hello.htm. However, a message body can contain other types of content as well (text documents, Microsoft Word documents, and so on).

Active Server Pages includes two built-in objects that correspond to the HTTP response and request messages of the Hypertext Transfer Protocol. The Active Server Pages `Response` object corresponds to an HTTP response. The Active Server Pages `Request` object corresponds to an HTTP request. In this chapter, you will learn how to use these objects to control how your server communicates with Web browsers.

Using the Response Object

The Active Server Page `Response` object corresponds to an HTTP response. The methods and properties of this object control how information is sent from your Web server to a Web browser.

In the previous chapter, you were already introduced to the `Write` method of this object. The `Write` method outputs a string to a browser. For example, the following script outputs the string `"Hello World!"`:

```
<%
  Response.Write "Hello World!"
%>
```

The `Response` object has several other useful methods and properties. In the following sections, you will learn how to use the `Response` object to control how a Web page is buffered and cached and how one Web page can be redirected to another.

Buffering Page Output

Normally, when an Active Server Page is processed on the server, the output from the page is sent to the browser immediately after each command in the page is executed. For example, consider the following Active Server Page:

```
<HTML>
<HEAD><TITLE>Buffer Example</TITLE></HEAD>
<BODY>
<%
FOR i=1 TO 500
```

```
   Response.Write(i&"<BR>")
NEXT
%>
</BODY>
</HTML>
```

This script displays the numbers 1 through 500 down the browser screen. The output from the page is sent immediately to the browser after each command in the page is executed. You can watch the numbers appear down the screen in real-time.

In some situations, you might want to buffer the output of an Active Server Page. When you buffer the output of an Active Server Page, none of the page is sent to the browser until the server has finished processing all of the page. Here's a modified version of the preceding script:

```
<% Response.Buffer=True %>
<HTML>
<HEAD><TITLE>Buffer Example</TITLE></HEAD>
<BODY>
<%
FOR i=1 TO 500

   Response.Write(i&"<BR>")
NEXT
%>
</BODY>
</HTML>
```

Only one difference exists between this script and the previous one. In the first line of this script, the Buffer property of the Response object is set to True. When this page is displayed in a Web browser, all the contents of the page are sent to the browser at the same time. The page is *buffered* until the script finishes processing.

TIP

You can use the Internet Service Manager to change the default value of the Buffer property to True. On the App Options page of the Application Configuration dialog box, select the option Enable Buffering.

Any statement that modifies the Buffer property must occur before any HTML or script output. If you attempt to modify the Buffer property after any HTML or script output, you get an error.

Why would you want to buffer an Active Server Page? By buffering a page, you can display two different Web pages, depending on some condition. For example, the following Active Server Page randomly outputs two different HTML pages (included on the CD as buffer.asp):

```
<% Response.Buffer=True %>
<HTML>
<HEAD><TITLE> First Page </TITLE></HEAD>
<BODY>
This is the first page.
</BODY>
</HTML>
<%
Randomize
If INT(2*RND)=1 THEN Response.End
Response.Clear
%>
<HTML>
<HEAD><TITLE> Second Page </TITLE></HEAD>
<BODY>
This is the second page.
</BODY>
</HTML>
```

In this example, two new methods of the Response object are used: the End method and the Clear method. The End method immediately stops the processing of an Active Server Page and outputs the results. You can use the End method whether or not you're buffering the output of a page. In this example, the End method is used to prevent the second page from being displayed when the first page is displayed.

The Clear method empties the current page buffer without outputting the contents of the buffer. You can use the Clear method only when buffering the output of an Active Server Page. In this example, the Clear method is used to prevent the first page from being displayed when the second page is displayed. It clears the first page from the buffer.

One other method of the Response object is used when buffering an Active Server Page. The Flush method immediately outputs the contents of the page buffer. As with the Clear method, an error occurs if you attempt to use this method with a page that isn't buffered. Unlike the End method, after the Flush method is called, the page continues to be processed.

Typically, you won't need to buffer the output of an Active Server Page. It's usually a bad idea. In the case of large HTML pages or long-running scripts, buffering a page delays the appearance of the Web page, which could confuse the user.

If you want to display two different HTML pages conditionally, you can simply use a VBScript conditional. Here's the preceding example, rewritten without using buffering (included on the CD as nobuffer.asp):

```
<%
Randomize
If INT(2*RND)=1 THEN
%>
<HTML>
<HEAD><TITLE> First Page </TITLE></HEAD>
<BODY>
This is the first page.
</BODY>
</HTML>
<% ELSE %>
<HTML>
<HEAD><TITLE> Second Page </TITLE></HEAD>
<BODY>
This is the second page.
</BODY>
</HTML>
<% END IF %>
```

One of the few situations in which buffering is necessary is when you are changing the headers for a page within the body of the page. If you want to change the headers in a page after you have already outputted content to a browser, set the `Buffer` property to `True`. For example, in the next section you learn how to use headers to control how a page is cached. If you modify one of these headers after you have already outputted content to a browser, you should buffer the page. Otherwise, you get an error.

> **NOTE**
>
> If you use the `Response.Redirect` method (see "Redirecting a User to Another Page," later in this chapter), you must buffer the page if you output any content to the browser before calling the method.

Controlling Active Server Page Caching

You might not know this, but your browser could be deceiving you. When you request an HTML page, your browser might decide not to retrieve the page from the Web site where the page is hosted. Your browser could decide to retrieve the Web page from a cached copy on your computer's hard drive instead.

For example, by default, Microsoft Internet Explorer will retrieve a new copy of an HTML page only once any time after the program is started. After the page is retrieved, it is stored in the browser's cache. Every time you revisit the same page, Internet Explorer will redisplay the page from the cache.

Web browsers cache pages to improve performance. A Web page can be retrieved much faster from the local hard drive than from a hard drive located on a Web server somewhere off in the Internet.

> **NOTE**
>
> You can configure how Internet Explorer caches Web pages by selecting View, Internet Options. and selecting Settings under Temporary Internet Files. If you choose to check for newer versions of a page every visit, then Internet Explorer will retrieve a new copy of the page whenever the copy of the page in the browser cache is older than the copy of the page at the Web server. Notice that this does not mean that Internet Explorer will always retrieve a fresh copy of a Web page. It will continue to use a copy of the Web page until the Web server tells it that the cached copy is outdated.

Your browser might not be the only thing caching HTML pages. Proxy servers are also used to cache pages to improve performance. If a proxy server sits between your Web browser and the Web site hosting a page, then the proxy server could provide a stale copy of the Web page instead of a fresh one.

Both proxy servers and browser caches are evil nuisances to Active Server Page programmers. The whole point of an Active Server Page is that it contains dynamic content—content that can change every time you retrieve it. However, page caching could result in stale pages being displayed in Web browsers.

The `Response` object includes three properties for controlling page caching: the `Expires`, `ExpiresAbsolute`, and `CacheControl` properties. The `Expires` and `ExpiresAbsolute` properties are used to control how browsers cache Web pages. The `CacheControl` property is used to control how proxy servers cache Web pages.

Launch your Web browser and request the following Active Server Page from your Web server:

```
<html>
<head><title>The Time</title></head>
<body>
The Time is: <%=TIME()%>
</body>
</html>
```

This page displays the current time. If you repeatedly request this Active Server Page by entering its address in your Web browser and pressing Enter over and over again, the page should keep changing to show the current time. (Depending on your browser and its settings, it might not—that's why you should read this section.)

In order to explicitly tell a browser to retrieve a fresh copy of this page every time it is requested, you can use the Expires or the ExpiresAbsolute property. For example, the following page always expires after 0 minutes (in other words, immediately):

```
<% Response.Expires = 0 %>
<html>
<head><title>The Time</title></head>
<body>
The Time is: <%=TIME()%>
</body>
</html>
```

The value of Expires tells a browser how long it should keep a copy of the page in its cache in minutes. The ExpiresAbsolute property is similar to the Expires property. However, this property is used to set an absolute date when the page should expire.

There might be circumstances when you know that a page will not be changed very often. In these cases, you might want to extend the amount of time that a browser uses its copy of a page. For example, the following page will be cached until January 2, 2000 (included on the CD as absoluteTime.asp):

```
<% Response.ExpiresAbsolute = #JAN 2, 2000 00:00:00# %>
<html>
<head><title>The Time</title></head>
<body>
The Time is: <%=TIME()%>
</body>
</html>
```

If you keep requesting this page by entering its address over and over in your Web browser, the time will not keep changing. The page will remain static until January 2, 2000 (hitting Refresh or Reload in your browser will generally load a fresh copy again).

The Expires and ExpiresAbsolute properties of the Response object can be used to control how browsers cache Web pages. To control how proxy servers cache Web pages, use the CacheControl property of the Response object.

The CacheControl property can have one of two values. By default, CacheControl is set to Private. This setting tells proxy servers that the content of an Active Server Page is private to a particular user and should not be cached. If, on the other hand, you want proxy servers to cache your Active Server Pages, you should set CacheControl to Public as in this example:

```
<% Response.CacheControl = "PUBLIC" %>
<html>
<head><title>The Time</title></head>
<body>
The Time is: <%=TIME()%>
</body>
</html>
```

> **NOTE**
>
> You also can use the Internet Service Manager to control content expiration. Open the property sheet for your Web site and select the tab labeled HTTP Headers. If you check the box labeled Enable Content Expiration, you can specify when a page should expire.

Making Sure the Client Is Still There

Have you ever had a long phone conversation only to discover that the other party had hung up long ago? You might have wasted considerable time and effort. Your server can be caught in the very same situation. Normally, IIS will continue to process an Active Server Page even if the browser that originally requested the page has disconnected. If a user requests a page and then decides to move on to another Web site, your Web server won't know the difference.

To some extent, you can get around this problem by using the isClientConnected property of the Response object. The isClientConnected property has the value TRUE if the client is still connected and the value FALSE otherwise. However, this property can be used only after a string has been outputted to the browser with the Response.Write method. Here's an example:

```
<%
for i = 1 to 1000
  Response.Write i & "<br>"
  if NOT( Response.isClientConnected ) then exit for
next
%>
```

This script outputs the numbers 1 through 1000 in a FOR...NEXT loop. If the client has disconnected at any point while the server is processing this loop, the loop is exited.

Working with Status Codes

Whenever a server responds to a browser request with an HTTP response, the first line it sends is the status line. The status line includes a three-digit status code and a description of the status code (called a *reason phrase*). The following list describes the five classes of status codes:

- 1*xx* Informational—The status codes in this class are mainly experimental.
- 2*xx* Success—The status codes in this class are used to indicate that a request was fulfilled successfully. For example, status code 200 can indicate that the Web page requested was retrieved successfully.
- 3*xx* Redirection—The status codes in this class are used to indicate that some further action must be taken before the request can be fulfilled. For example, status code 301 can indicate that a Web page has been moved permanently to another address. In this case, the browser can be redirected automatically to the new address.
- 4*xx* Client Error— This status code is returned when the browser has made a request that can't be fulfilled. For example, status code 404 indicates that the requested Web page doesn't exist.
- 5*xx* Server Error— The status codes in this class indicate a problem with the server. For example, status code 503 can indicate the server is currently overwhelmed.

2

ASP AND THE HTTP PROTOCOL

> **NOTE**
>
> For a complete list of status codes and their meanings, see the HTTP 1.1 specification at http://www.w3.org.

You can use the Status property of the Response object to specify the status code that should be returned in a response. For example, if someone attempts to retrieve the following Active Server Page on a Wednesday, the status code 401 Not Authorized is returned (this results in a password dialog box appearing):

```
<%
IF WEEKDAYNAME(WEEKDAY(DATE))="Wednesday" THEN
Response.Status="401 Not Authorized"
Response.End
ELSE
%>
<HTML>
```

```
<HEAD><TITLE> Not Wednesday </TITLE></HEAD>
<BODY>
Welcome!  Today is not Wednesday.
</BODY>
</HTML>
<% END IF %>
```

Modifying the `Content-Type` Header

The `Content-Type` header indicates the media type of the body of the response (the MIME type). Common examples are text/HTML, image/gif, application/msword, or text/rtf. You can use the `ContentType` property of the `Response` object to set this header.

NOTE

To view the MIME types that your computer supports, open any desktop folder and select View, Folder Options, File Types. Click on any of the registered file types to view the MIME type.

 One common use of the `ContentType` property is to display the source of an HTML document. If you set the `ContentType` property to text/plain, the body of the response is sent as normal text rather than HTML. Consider the following example (included on the CD as contentType.asp):

```
<%
Response.ContentType="text/plain"
%>
<HTML>
<HEAD><TITLE>HTML Document</TITLE></HEAD>
<BODY>
<H1>This is an HTML document!</H1>
</BODY>
</HTML>
```

When this file is displayed in the Netscape Navigator Web browser, all the text below the script appears exactly as shown here. By setting the `ContentType` property to `"text/plain"`, you prevent this Web browser from interpreting the contents of an HTML page.

Regrettably, this trick works only with the Netscape browser. It will not work with Microsoft's Internet Explorer because Explorer actually checks the page for HTML tags to decide how to interpret the page. If you want to show a text-only page, you must remove all the HTML tags.

Redirecting a User to Another Page

In several situations, you will need to redirect a user to another page. For example, if a user attempts to access a page that requires registration, the user should automatically be redirected to a registration page. Or if the user has entered incomplete form information, he or she should automatically be redirected to the page containing the form in order to complete it.

 It's very easy to redirect a user to a new page using Active Server Pages. The Redirect method of the Response object allows you to redirect a user to a new page. Look at this example (included on the CD as redirect.asp):

```
<%
IF Request.Form("FirstName")="" THEN Response.Redirect "/register.asp"
%>
<HTML>
<HEAD><TITLE> Registration Results </TITLE></HEAD>
<BODY>
Thank you <%=Request.Form("FirstName")%> for registering!
</BODY>
</HTML>
```

Imagine that a user has just completed a registration form and this page is returned. The Response.Redirect method, in this example, is used to redirect the user back to the page with the registration form if the user hasn't entered a first name.

You must use the Response.Redirect method before any text is outputted to the browser. Therefore, it's a good idea to place this method in a script that appears above the <HTML> tag. The only way around this requirement is to buffer the output of your Active Server Page (see the previous section "Buffering Page Output" in this chapter to learn how to do this).

You can use the Response.Redirect method to redirect a user to any valid URL. This could be another page on your Web site or even a page located at another Web site on the Internet.

The Response.Redirect method is potentially a very useful method. Microsoft uses this method extensively in its demonstration applications for Active Server Pages and on its own Web site. Sadly, however, there are problems with it.

The Response.Redirect method works by returning a particular status code. When the Response.Redirect method is called, the status code 302 Object Moved is returned. A location header is also added to the response to give the new location of the page. The status code and location header should automatically redirect the browser to the new page.

> **NOTE**
>
> The `Response.Redirect` method is completely equivalent to the following two lines of code:
>
> ```
> <%
> Response.Status="302 Object Moved"
> Response.AddHeader "Location", "URL"
> %>
> ```
>
> For more information on the `AddHeader` method, see Appendix B, "ASP Objects and Components Reference," at the back of this book.

In reality, however, the user is not always smoothly redirected to a new page. Older browsers in particular have problems with redirection. Worse yet, even relatively recent browsers such as Netscape Navigator 4.0 can have difficulties automatically responding to the redirection status code. When a browser can't respond automatically to a status code, you receive a message like that shown in Figure 2.2.

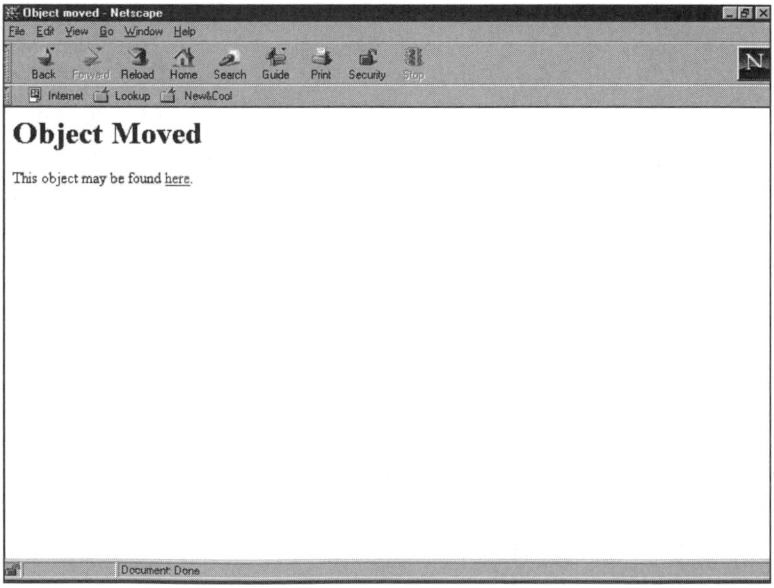

FIGURE 2.2

The results of a server redirect.

This message isn't pretty, and it can lead to confusion. For this reason, you should try to avoid using the `Response.Redirect` method. Use the simulated redirect method discussed in the section titled, "Including Files," at the end of this chapter instead.

> **NOTE**
>
> The new version of ASP included with Windows 2000 has better methods for automatically redirecting users to new pages. To learn more, see Chapter 26, "Future Directions: Windows 2000, IIS 5.0, and Active Server Pages."

Using the Request Object

The Active Server Pages `Request` object contains all the information about the HTTP request performed to retrieve an Active Server Page. The `Request` object includes three collections that correspond to the parts of an HTTP request: the `QueryString` collection, the `Form` collection, and the `ServerVariables` collection.

The `QueryString` Collection

When you include a query string in a request for a Web page, the contents of the query string are retrieved into the `QueryString` collection. A query string is the part of a page request that appears after the `?`. For example, the following request contains the query string `username=Andrew+Jones`:

```
http://www.aspsite.com/hello.asp?username=Andrew+Jones
```

Query strings are used to pass information from a browser to a Web server. In this example, the query string is used to pass a query variable named `username` that has the value `Andrew Jones`. The query string is passed to a page named hello.asp at the Web site located at www.aspsite.com.

Within the Active Server Page named hello.asp, you can retrieve the value of the variable passed in the query string. The following script, for example, outputs the value of the query string to the browser:

```
<html>
<head><title>Query String</title></head>
<body>
Welcome <%=Request.QueryString( "username" )%>!
</body>
</html>
```

Typically, query strings are not entered directly into the address bar of a Web browser. Query strings are most often used in hypertext links to pass information from one Active Server Page to another. Consider the following HTML page (included on the CD as firstpage.asp):

```
<html>
<head><title>A Choice</title></head>
What is your favorite color?
<P>
<a href="nextpage.asp?favcolor=blue">blue</a>
<p>
<a href="nextpage.asp?favcolor=red">red</a>
</body>
</html>
```

This page contains two hypertext links to a page named nextpage.asp. Both links contain a query string variable named favcolor. The value of this variable in the first link is red and the value of this variable in the second link is blue.

 Within the Active Server Page named nextpage.asp (included on the CD as nextpage.asp), you can determine which of the two hypertext links the user clicked to get there:

```
<html>
<head><title>Your Favorite Color</title></head>
<body>
<%
   favColor = Request.QueryString( "favColor" )
%>
Your favorite color is <%=favColor%>!
</body>
</html>
```

This page displays the user's favorite color by retrieving the favColor variable from the QueryString collection. The value of the variable is retrieved from the collection and assigned to a local variable also named favColor. Next, this variable is displayed.

URL Encoding Query Strings

If the value of a query string variable contains non-alphanumeric characters such as quotation marks, spaces, commas, or exclamation points, you must encode the value of the query string before it can be passed. For example, the query string contained in the following link would not be passed properly between pages because it contains a space:

```
<a href="nextpage.asp?username=Andrew Jones">Next</a>
```

Before you can pass the query string in this example, you must first URL encode the query string. You can do this with the URLEncode method of the Server object. Here's an example of how this method is used:

```
<%
  username = Server.URLEncode( "Andrew Jones" )
%>
<a href="nextpage.asp?username=<%=username%>">Next</a>
```

In this script, the URLEncode method replaces all the non-alphanumeric characters in the string "Andrew Jones" with characters that can be passed in a query string. After the string has been URL encoded, it appears like this:

```
Andrew+Jones
```

The space has been replaced with an addition sign.

Active Server Pages does not include a method for URL decoding a query string because, normally, you would have no need to do this. When you retrieve query string variables from the QueryString collection, the variables are automatically URL decoded for you.

Passing Multiple Query String Variables

You are not restricted to passing a single query string variable in a query string. To pass multiple variables, simply separate each variable with the & character. The following query string is used to pass two variables named username and password:

```
<a href="nextpage.asp?username=Fred&password=secret">Next</a>
```

Within the Active Server Page named nextpage.asp, you can refer to the value of each variable by referring to each variable by name. The following script outputs the values of both variables to the browser:

```
<%
Response.Write Request.QueryString( "username" )
Response.Write Request.QueryString( "password" )
%>
```

If you want to assign multiple values to the same variable, you can pass a query string like the following:

```
<a href="nextpage.asp?color=red&color=blue">Next</a>
```

When the query string variable named color is retrieved from the QueryString collection, it will have both the values red and blue separated by a comma. For example, the following script would output the string "red, blue" to the browser:

```
<%=Request.QueryString( "color" )%>
```

Dumping the `QueryString` Collection

You can display all the items in the `QueryString` collection without knowing the names of any of the query string variables in the collection. The following script iterates through the `QueryString` collection and displays each item one by one:

```
<%
for i = 1 to Request.QueryString.Count
   Response.Write Request.QueryString( i ) & "<br>"
next
%>
```

The `Count` property of the `QueryString` collection is used to retrieve a count of the number of items in the collection. If no query string variables are passed, then the count would be `0`.

Instead of using a `FOR...NEXT` loop to walk through the `QueryString` collection, you can also use a `FOR...EACH` loop. The advantage of a `FOR...EACH` loop is that you can use it to display both the name and value of each item:

```
<%
for each thing in Request.QueryString
   Response.Write thing & " " & Request.QueryString( thing ) & "<br>"
next
%>
```

In this example, the value of the variable named `thing` is the name of each query string variable in the collection.

> **NOTE**
>
> Dumping the `QueryString` collection is very useful when debugging an Active Server Page. If you are not sure whether a query string variable is actually being passed to a page, temporarily add one of the scripts in this section to the page.

When Not to Use Query Strings

Query strings are useful when you need to pass small bits of information from one page to another, but there are two situations in which you definitely shouldn't use a query string: when you're passing hidden information and when you're passing large chunks of data.

A query string isn't hidden from view in any way. The query string will always appear in the address bar of a browser. This means that passing the password of a user from page to page with a query string is a very bad idea. Anyone looking over the user's shoulder will immediately know the password.

Query strings are also not a good choice for passing large chunks of data. The exact number of characters that a query string can contain depends on several factors. One of the main factors is the browser being used. Different browsers have different limitations on query string size.

For example, Microsoft Internet Explorer 4.0 can't handle a query string that's larger than about 2,000 characters. A hyperlink with a query string of this size will simply fail to work as a hyperlink with this browser.

You shouldn't conclude from this fact that you can use query strings up to 2,000 characters long. First, the true maximum depends on the length of the URL as well. The combination of the URL and query string—everything in the address bar of the browser—determines the maximum size.

Second, URL-encoding a query string often makes the string considerably longer. For example, periods are converted into three characters (%2E) instead of one. The maximum size of a query string depends on the URL-encoded form of the string.

Third, browsers other than Internet Explorer 4.0 can often handle far fewer than 2,000 characters. After a query string hits a length of 1,000 characters or so, you risk losing compatibility with a number of browsers.

In brief, it's a good idea to keep your query strings short. Query strings aren't an efficient method of passing large amounts of data. Even worse, a page with a large query string can completely fail to function on certain browsers. If you need to pass a large amount of data from one page to another, use a hidden form field. The Netscape browser, for example, can pass form fields with up to 30,000 characters. The HTTP protocol passes form fields in a much more efficient way than query strings.

The Form Collection

Working with the `Form` collection is similar to working with the `QueryString` collection. The `Form` collection is used to store the variables posted within an HTML form. Consider the following simple HTML form:

```
<form method="post" action="nextpage.asp">
<br>Username: <input name="username" type="text" size="30">
<br><input type="submit" value="Go!">
</form>
```

This form contains a text field named Username and a submit button that posts the form to the Active Server Page named nextpage.asp. Within the page named nextpage.asp, you can retrieve the text entered into the form by using the following script:

```
<html>
<head><title>Next Page</title></head>
<body>
<%
  username = Request.Form( "username" )
%>
Your username is <%=username"%>!
</body>
</html>
```

Because working with the Form collection is such an important topic, a complete chapter of this book is devoted to the subject. Chapter 3, "Working with HTML Forms," covers the methods of using the Form collection in depth.

The ServerVariables Collection

 When a browser requests a Web page from a server, the request includes several headers. You can retrieve these headers by using the ServerVariables collection of the Request object. The ServerVariables collection contains both headers and additional items of information about the server. The following Active Server Page (included on the CD as serverVariables.asp) dumps all the contents of the ServerVariables collection to the browser window (see Figure 2.3):

```
<HTML>
<HEAD><TITLE>Server Variables</TITLE></HEAD>
<BODY>
<%
FOR EACH name IN Request.ServerVariables
Response.write("<P><B>"&name&"</B>:")
Response.write(Request.ServerVariables(name))
NEXT
%>
</BODY>
</HTML>
```

FIGURE 2.3

The `ServerVariables` *collection.*

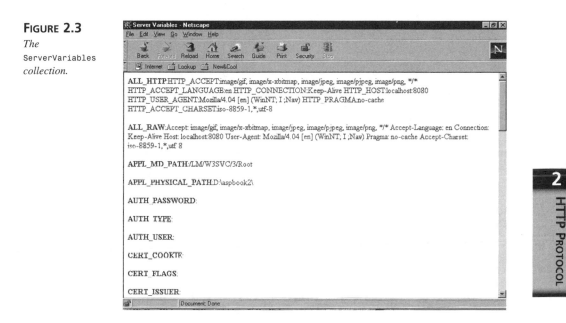

The headers (and server variables) in the `ServerVariables` collection hold a wide assortment of different types of information. Appendix B contains a list of the standard headers and server variables in this collection. The following list explains the more useful ones:

- `HTTP_REFERER`—When someone has arrived at the current page by clicking a hyperlink, this header contains the Internet address of the referring page. The `HTTP_REFERER` header is extremely valuable for determining how the visitors to your Web site arrived there. For example, if you want to know the number of people who arrived at your Web site by using Yahoo!, you could use the `HTTP_REFERER` header to determine this information.

- `HTTP_USER_AGENT`— This header indicates the type of Web browser a visitor to your Web site is using. This information is valuable when you must determine the Web browser used most often by the target audience of your Web site.

- `REMOTE_ADDR`—This header contains the IP address of a visitor to your Web site. The IP address can be interpreted to provide information about the origins of the visitors to your Web site. For example, you can use this header to determine how many people are visiting your Web site from MIT or America Online.

- `QUERY_STRING`—The `QUERY_STRING` server variable contains the portion of the URL after the question mark. This variable contains the complete query string in unparsed form.

- `SCRIPT_NAME`—This server variable contains the virtual path of the current Active Server Page. You can use this variable for self-referencing pages.

- `SERVER_NAME`—This server variable contains the Internet address of the server.

- `PATH_TRANSLATED`—This server variable contains the physical path of the current Active Server Page.

Certain versions of Internet Explorer (such as the Windows 95 version 3.0 and 4.0) contain additional headers in their requests:

- `HTTP_UA_COLOR`—This header indicates the number of colors that the browser can display.

- `HTTP_UA_CPU`—This header indicates the type of machine being used to execute the browser.

- `HTTP_UA_OS`—This header indicates the operating system of the computer executing the browser.

- `HTTP_UA_PIXELS`—This header indicates the screen resolution being used on the computer executing the browser.

CAUTION

You shouldn't rely on these headers; they're supported only by the Windows 95 versions of Internet Explorer.

You can retrieve the contents of a particular header or server variable by passing its name to the `ServerVariables` collection. For example, the following script enables a user to access the page only if he or she arrived from the Active Server Page named origin.asp:

```
<HTML>
<HEAD><TITLE>Server Variables</TITLE></HEAD>
<BODY>
<%
WhereFrom=request.ServerVariables("HTTP_REFERER")
If WhereFrom="http://www.mysite.com/origin.asp" THEN
%>
Welcome to this page!
<%
ELSE
%>
You are not authorized to view this page!
<%
END IF
%>
</BODY>
</HTML>
```

In this script, the HTTP_REFERER header determines the page the visitor used to link to the current page. If the user didn't arrive from the page located at `http://mysite/origin.asp`, he or she isn't allowed to view the contents of the page.

Authorization Headers

When a Web page is password-protected, four headers are useful for retrieving information about the user accessing the page. The AUTH_TYPE header indicates the authentication method used to access the page. The AUTH_USER and LOGON_USER headers contain the name of the Windows NT account of the user. Finally, when Basic authentication is used, the AUTH_PASSWORD header contains the password that was used to access the page.

 For example, the following Active Server Page checks whether the user has used Basic authentication to access the page (see Figure 2.4). This is accomplished by using the AUTH_TYPE header. This header can have only two possible values: Basic for Basic authentication or NTLM for Windows NT Challenge and Response. (The LM stands for *LAN Manager*—Microsoft's pre-Windows NT network operating system.) Next, the Windows NT account of the user is displayed (this Active Server Page is included on the CD as authHeaders.asp):

```
<HTML>
<HEAD><TITLE>Password Protected</TITLE></HEAD>
<BODY>
<%
IF Request.ServerVariables("AUTH_TYPE")="Basic" THEN
%>
You are logged in using Basic Authentication.
Your account is <%=Request.ServerVariables("LOGON_USER")%>.
<% ELSE %>
You are logged in using NT Challenge and Response.
Your account is <%=Request.ServerVariables("LOGON_USER")%>.
<% END IF %>
<BODY>
</HTML>
```

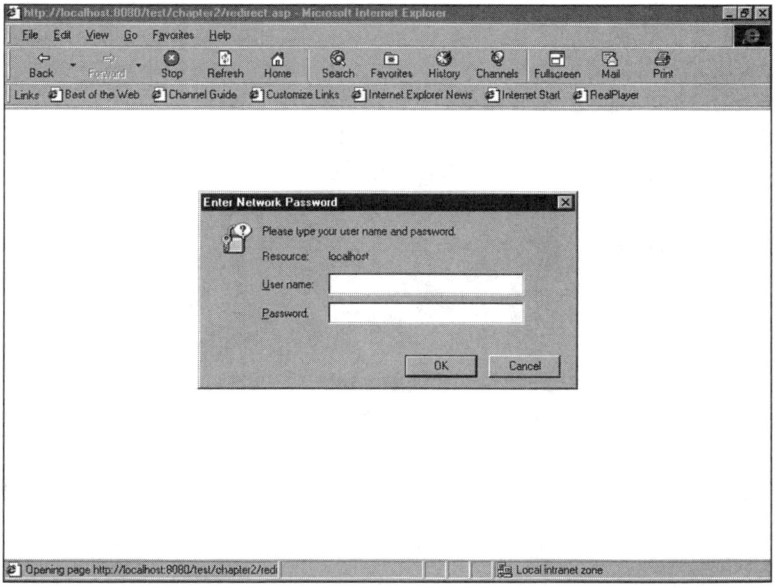

FIGURE 2.4

A password-protected page.

Including Files

You cannot use a function or subroutine located within one Active Server Page within another Active Server Page. If you want to create a library of functions and procedures to use in multiple Active Server Pages, you must place the functions and procedures in a file and include it in each page.

Fortunately, you can easily include one file in another Active Server Page by using a server-side INCLUDE directive. You can use the INCLUDE directive to include a common library of functions and subroutines or to include common HTML content in multiple pages.

A server-side INCLUDE directive shouldn't appear within a script; use it outside a script as part of the HTML code:

```
<HTML>
<HEAD><TITLE> Welcome </TITLE></HEAD>
<BODY>
<!-- #INCLUDE FILE="mybanner.inc" -->
Welcome To Our Web Site!
</BODY>
</HTML>
```

In this example, the file mybanner.inc is inserted into the Active Server Page below the <BODY> tag. When this Active Server Page is processed, any scripts or HTML code in the file mybanner.inc are included in the Active Server Page above.

You can include one file in another in two ways: by providing a physical path to the file, as in the preceding example, or by providing a virtual path to the file. The following is an example of the latter method:

```
<HTML>
<HEAD><TITLE> Welcome </TITLE></HEAD>
<BODY>
<!-- #INCLUDE VIRTUAL="/includes/mybanner.inc" -->
Welcome To Our Web Site!
</BODY>
</HTML>
```

If you supply a physical path to the included file by using the FILE attribute, the file must be located either in the current directory or in a subdirectory of that directory. The path of the file is relative to the current directory. When the VIRTUAL attribute is used, on the other hand, the file can be located within any directory in your Web site. In the preceding example, the included file is located in the subdirectory named /includes located off the root directory.

The included file can have any name and any extension. By convention, included files usually end with the extension .inc, but you can use .asp, .htm, .html, or any other extension you prefer.

> **NOTE**
>
> If the included file contains secret information such as database passwords, you should make the file an Active Server Page file by naming the file with the .asp extension. If someone attempts to view the included file directly by entering its address in a Web browser, the information will be hidden because an Active Server Page is always processed before it is sent to a browser.

Including one file in another is useful in two situations. The first and most obvious use is to display the same content or execute the same script page after page. For example, it's not uncommon for every page at a Web site to have the same header and footer. Instead of repeating the same HTML code over and over, you can simply include a header and footer file as part of every page.

You can also include the same Active Server Page script on multiple pages by using the INCLUDE directive. However, because the INCLUDE directive must occur outside a script, the script you include must be completely contained in script delimiters. You can't include a fragment of a script.

The second situation in which including one file in another is useful is when you want to simulate server redirection. To do this, you include one whole Active Server Page in a second Active Server Page. Consider the following example:

```
<%
IF Request.Form("FirstName")="" THEN
%>
<!-- #INCLUDE VIRTUAL="/register.asp" -->
<%
Response.End
END IF
%>
<HTML>
<HEAD><TITLE> Registration Results </TITLE></HEAD>
<BODY>
Thank you <%=Request.Form("FirstName")%> for registering!
</BODY>
</HTML>
```

This example has exactly the same effect as using the Response.Redirect method. If a user has neglected to enter information into the First Name field of the registration form, he or she is returned to the registration page. However, because including a file takes place completely on the server, this simulated redirection is more reliable than actual redirection.

Notice the use of the Response.End method in this example. The Response.End method is included to prevent the rest of the Active Server Page from being displayed if the registration page is displayed.

It's important to realize that IIS processes any INCLUDE directives before it processes scripts. This means that you can't use a script command to dynamically include one file in another. For example, the following script won't work:

```
<%
IF Request.Form("FirstName")="" THEN
  MyInclude="/register.asp"
```

```
ELSE
  MyInclude="HomePage.asp"
END IF
%>
<!-- #INCLUDE VIRTUAL="<%=MyInclude%>" -->
```

This script won't work because the server will attempt to include any files before the script is executed. This means that the server will attempt to include the file `"<%=MyInclude%>"`, which, of course, doesn't exist.

Summary

In this chapter, you learned how to use the Active Server Page `Response` object to control how information is sent from your Web server. You also learned how to use the `Request` object to retrieve information about browser requests. Finally, you learned how to include a file in an Active Server Page by using the `INCLUDE` directive.

In the next chapter, you will learn several advanced methods for using the `Form` collection of the `Request` object. You will master the methods of working with HTML forms.

CHAPTER 3

Working with HTML Forms

by Stephen Walther

IN THIS CHAPTER

One of the most time-consuming aspects of creating a Web site is the process of constructing and processing the information entered into HTML forms. This chapter provides some tricks and tips to make the task of working with HTML forms easier.

This chapter has three goals. The first goal of this chapter is to provide some general techniques for using different form elements in your Active Server Pages. Text boxes, text areas, radio buttons, check boxes, and select lists all have unique characteristics that pose special problems when you integrate them into your Active Server Pages. The methods for manipulating each of these form elements will be described.

The second part of this chapter is devoted to the important topic of server-side form validation. When users enter data into a form at your Web site, you will want to make sure that the data is entered correctly. In the second part of this chapter, you will learn how to construct a standard INCLUDE file to perform the most common form validation tasks.

Finally, a very special and troublesome HTML form element will be given a part of its own. In this last part, you will master the methods of using the File Upload form element to allow file uploads to your Web site. You learn how to accept and display image uploads using nothing but standard ASP scripts.

Retrieving Form Data

Whenever a user submits an HTML form to your Web site, all the form fields and their values are placed in the Form collection of the Request object. You can retrieve any form fields by name from this collection, or you can move through the complete contents of the Form collection by using a FOR...EACH loop. For example, consider the following simple form:

```
<html>
<head><title>Simple Form</title></head>
<body>

<form method="post" action="result.asp">
<p>Please Enter Your User Name:
<br><input name="username" type="text">
<p>Please Enter Some Comments:
<br><textarea name="comments" cols=40 rows=5></textarea>
<p><input type="submit" value="Save">
</form>

</body>
</html>
```

> **NOTE**
>
> The `Form` collection contains the values of form elements when an HTML form is submitted with the `POST` method. When an HTML form is submitted with the `GET` method, the values of the form elements are placed in the `QueryString` collection.

This HTML form contains two fields: the user is asked to enter a user name into a text box and enter some comments into a text area. When the user clicks the button labeled Save, the contents of the form are submitted to an Active Server Page named result.asp. Within the result.asp file, you can retrieve any of the form fields and their values by accessing the `Form` collection.

For example, you can use the following script to retrieve and display both the form elements by name. This script retrieves the `username` and `comments` items from the `Form` collection, and then it assigns them to the two local VBScript variables of the same name. These two variables are then output to the browser.

```
<%
DIM username, comments
username = Request.Form( "username" )
comments = Request.Form( "comments" )
%>
<html>
<head><title>Result</title></head>
<body>

Your User Name Is: <%=username%>
<p>
Your Comments Are: <%=comments%>

</body>
</html>
```

Instead of accessing each form element by name, you can also simply dump the complete contents of the `Form` collection. The next script outputs the name and value of each element in the `Form` collection to the browser by using a `FOR...EACH` loop to march through the contents of the `Form` collection:

```
<html>
<head><title>Simple Form</title></head>
<body>
<%
DIM formElement
FOR EACH formElement IN Request.Form
```

```
    Response.Write formElement &_
        " = " & Request.Form( formElement ) & "<br>"
NEXT
%>

</body>
</html>
```

This method of iterating through the contents of the Form collection is valuable in two situations. First, you will find it useful when debugging Active Server Pages. If, for some mysterious reason, you are having difficulty retrieving the value of a form field, you can dump the Form collection to determine whether the form field was actually submitted.

Dumping the contents of the Form collection is also useful when you do not know the names of all the form fields. If you want to develop standard scripts that can work with any HTML form, regardless of the names of the form fields, you can use the preceding method to abstract away from the particular characteristics of an HTML form. You will use this method—walking through all the form elements—in the next part of this chapter to develop a standard form validation INCLUDE file that will work with any HTML form.

TIP

Assigning form variables to local variables can be a tedious chore. For each form variable, you must use a statement of the form myvar = Request.Form ("myvar"). In the case of large forms, you might need to type dozens of these statements. Fortunately, using the new VBScript 5.0 EXECUTE statement, you can do this more efficiently. Here is a subroutine that assigns every form variable in the Request.Form collection to a local variable:

```
SUB Form2Local
    for each x in Request.form
        execute x & "="""" & Request( x ) & """"
    next
END SUB
```

Using Text Boxes and Text Areas

In the previous section, you learned how to use the Form collection to retrieve the value of a text box and a text area and assign these values to variables. There are several situations in which you will perform the opposite operation and assign the value of a variable to a text box or text area. For example, suppose you want to include a second form where a user can approve the information entered into the first form. You might want to provide a user with a second chance to change the information before the information is actually entered into a database. Listing 3.1 redisplays the information posted in a previous HTML form within a new form.

LISTING 3.1   A SECOND CHANCE FOR THE USER

```
<%
DIM username, comments
username = TRIM( Request.Form( "username" ) )
comments = TRIM( Request.Form( "comments" ) )
%>
<html>
<head><title>Simple Form</title></head>
<body>

<form method="post" action="result.asp">
Do You Really Want To Save This Information?
<p>Your User Name Is:
<br><input name="username"
type="text" value="<%=Server.HTMLEncode( username )%>">

<p>Your Comments Are:
<br><textarea name="comments" cols=40 rows=5>
➥<%=Server.HTMLEncode( comments )%></textarea>

<p><input type="submit" value="Save">
</form>

</body>
</html>
```

The HTML form just listed redisplays the information that the user entered into the first form. The VALUE attribute of the HTML <INPUT> tag is used to provide the text box with a value. The text area is given a default value by enclosing the comments variable within the <TEXTAREA> start tag and </TEXTAREA> end tag.

Notice two things about this form. First, the VBScript TRIM() function is used to cut away beginning and trailing spaces from the items retrieved from the Form collection. If a user does not provide a value for a text box, a browser will normally add a space character for the empty field when the form is submitted. This behavior can be irritating to someone entering information into a form. The TRIM() function takes care of this problem by stripping away this unwanted space character.

Notice that the form in Listing 3.1 uses the HTMLEncode() method of the Server object. This method is used to encode the two variables before displaying them again within the HTML form. There are certain characters that a user can enter into an HTML form that will corrupt the form if redisplayed. For example, the VALUE attribute of the <INPUT> tag uses quotation marks to indicate the start and end of a string. If a variable that contains quotation marks is assigned to the VALUE attribute, then the variable will be displayed incorrectly and the HTML form will be corrupted. The HTMLEncode() method takes care of this problem by automatically replacing quotation marks with the special HTML character ". A browser correctly interprets this special character and displays it as a normal quotation mark.

Using Radio Buttons and Check Boxes

Radio buttons are useful when you want to force a user to choose among a small number of selections within an HTML form. For example, suppose you want users to indicate their favorite color when registering at your Web site. You can add two radio buttons labeled Red and Blue to an HTML form to allow users to make this selection:

```
<html>
<head><title>Simple HTML Form</title></head>
<body>

<form method="post" action="result.asp">
<b>Please enter your favorite color: </b>
<br><input name="color" type="radio" value="red"> Red
<br><input name="color" type="radio" value="blue"> Blue
<p>
<input type="submit" value="Save">
</form>

</body>
</html>
```

Unlike in the case of a text box, you cannot use the VALUE attribute to provide a radio box with a default value of Checked or Not Checked. If you want the status of a check box to depend on the value of a variable, you must include an additional function in your Active Server Page. The script in Listing 3.2 will correctly display a check mark depending on the value of the variable color.

LISTING 3.2   DISPLAYING A CHECK MARK IN A RADIO BUTTON

```
<%
DIM color
color = "blue"

FUNCTION checked( firstVal, secondVal )
    IF firstVal = secondVal THEN
        checked = " CHECKED"
    END IF
END FUNCTION
%>
<html>
<head><title>Simple HTML Form</title></head>
<body>
```

```
<form method="post" action="result.asp">
<b>Please enter your favorite color: </b>
<br><input name="color" type="radio"
    value="red" <%=checked( color, "red")%>> Red
<br><input name="color" type="radio"
    value="blue" <%=checked( color, "blue")%>> Blue
<p>
<input type="submit" value="Save">
</form>

</body>
</html>
```

Because the color variable has the value of Blue, the second radio button appears with a check mark (see Figure 3.1). The checked() function is used to display the check mark. A radio button appears with a check mark when the CHECKED attribute appears within the radio button's <INPUT> tag. The checked() function has the value CHECKED whenever the value of the color variable is equal to the value of the second argument passed to the function. (The extra space at the beginning of the value returned by the function is used to create a space in the HTML.)

FIGURE 3.1

A form with a check box.

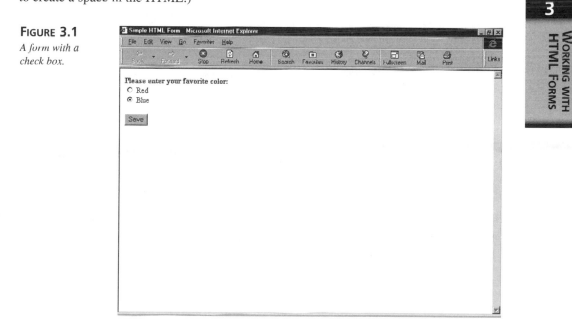

You can use the same function in the case of check boxes. Like a radio button, a check box appears with a check mark when the CHECKED attribute is included in the <INPUT> tag. Listing 3.3 shows an example of a form with a check box that uses the checked() function.

LISTING 3.3   DISPLAYING A CHECK MARK IN A CHECK BOX

```
<%
DIM firstvisit
firstvisit = "1"

FUNCTION checked( firstVal, secondVal )
    IF firstVal = secondVal THEN
        checked = " CHECKED"
    END IF
END FUNCTION
%>
<html>
<head><title>Simple HTML Form</title></head>
<body>

<form method="post" action="result.asp">
<b>Check the box below if this is your first visit here: </b>
<br><input name="firstvisit" type="checkbox"
    value="1" <%=checked( firstvisit, "1")%>> Red
<p>
<input type="submit" value="Save">
</form>

</body>
</html>
```

Using Select Lists

Select lists have a similar function to radio buttons. You can use a select list to display a limited menu of options. Unlike radio buttons and check boxes, however, select lists use the SELECTED attribute to determine which option is selected. Listing 3.4 is an example of a form with a select list.

LISTING 3.4   DISPLAYING A SELECTED OPTION

```
<%
DIM color
color = "blue"

FUNCTION selected( firstVal, secondVal )
    IF firstVal = secondVal THEN
        selected = " SELECTED"
    END IF
END FUNCTION
%>
<html>
<head><title>Simple HTML Form</title></head>
<body>

<form method="post" action="result.asp">
<b>Please enter your favorite color: </b>
<select name="color">
<br><option value="red" <%=SELECTED( color, "red" )%>> red
<br><option value="blue" <%=SELECTED( color, "blue" )%>> blue
</select>

<p>
<input type="submit" value="Save">
</form>

</body>
</html>
```

The SELECTED() function is used in this example to select the option that corresponds to the value of the color variable. Because the color variable has the value Blue, the second option is selected.

Validating Form Data

If you use an HTML form to retrieve data from a user, you will almost always need to validate the information the user has entered. Typical uses of HTML forms include gathering user registration information, performing password validation, or taking product order requests. Constructing the HTML form itself is usually the easy part. The hard part is preventing users from entering incorrect data.

> **NOTE**
>
> To learn how to save form information into a database, see Part III of this book, "Using Active Server Pages With Databases."

3

WORKING WITH HTML FORMS

Typically, there are three requirements for validating data entered into an HTML form. First, you must make sure that all the required fields of the form are completed. If someone submits a product order form at your Web site, but forgets to enter a credit card number or shipping address, you might lose an order.

Second, form validation usually involves checking whether data of the right type has been entered. For example, if someone enters the word cat in the form input field labeled Date Of Birth, you will not retrieve the information you want.

Finally, when incorrect information is entered into an HTML form, an informative error message should be displayed. If the user has made a mistake by overlooking a form field or entering the wrong type of data, he or she should be provided with a graceful method for returning to the original form and making corrections. When the user is returned to the original form, it is important that the data he or she originally entered is not lost.

 In this next section, you will learn how to construct a standard Form Validation INCLUDE file that you can add to your Active Server Pages to make these form validation tasks easier. This standard INCLUDE file will automatically check for required fields, check whether the right type of data has been entered, and display an error message when appropriate. The full code for this INCLUDE file is listed below and can also be found on the CD that accompanies this book (validateform.asp).

Using the Validate Form INCLUDE File

The Validate Form INCLUDE file uses hidden form fields in the form being submitted to indicate which fields are required and their proper data types. By adding the Validate Form INCLUDE file to your Active Server Pages and adding these hidden fields to your HTML forms, you can easily validate your HTML forms without using any additional scripts.

To demonstrate how the Validate Form INCLUDE file works, we'll start by constructing a very simple HTML form. This form, you can imagine, is used to gather user registration information. It consists of only two fields: a field for the user's name and a field for the user's date of birth. The following is the HTML code for this form:

```
<html>
<head><title>Simple HTML Form</title></head>
<body>

<form method="post" action="result.asp">
<b>Please enter your name: </b>
<input name="username" type="text" size=30>
```

```
<p>
<b>Please enter your date of birth: </b>
<input name="birthdate" type="text" size=10>
<p>
<input type="submit" value="Save">
</form>

</body>
</html>
```

 Enter the HTML code for the form into a text editor and save the file with the name form.asp in a directory that can be accessed by your Web server (for example, wwwroot). You can also copy this file from the CD that accompanies this book (form.asp).

 The form is submitted to an Active Server Page named result.asp. The purpose of this page is simply to thank the user for registering. The listing for result.asp is included in Listing 3.5 and can also be copied from the CD that accompanies this book (result.asp). You should save the file in the same directory where you saved form.asp.

LISTING 3.5 RESULT.ASP

```
<html>
<head><title>Result</title></head>
<body>

Thank you for registering!

</body>
</html>
```

If you open form.asp in your Web browser, and click the button labeled Save, you will receive the message Thank you for registering!, regardless of the information you enter into the form. You can even submit this form without entering any data at all. Suppose, however, that you do not want a user to submit the form without completing both of the form fields. By using the Validate Form INCLUDE file, you can specify that both form fields are required fields.

 Copy the file named validateform.asp, from the CD that accompanies this book, into the same directory as the directory where you saved form.asp and result.asp. You will need to make some changes to both form.asp and result.asp in order to take advantage of this file.

First, add the following line at the very top of result.asp:

```
<!-- #INCLUDE FILE="validateform.asp"-->
```

This Active Server Pages directive automatically inserts the contents of the validate-form.asp file into the top of this file.

Next, you must indicate the form fields that are required. Because we do not want a user to submit the form without entering data into both form fields, we want both of the form fields to be required. Add the following two hidden input fields to the HTML form in form.asp:

```
<input name="username_req" type="hidden"
  value="You must enter a user name.">
<input name="birthdate_req" type="hidden"
  value="You must enter your date of birth.">
```

Notice that these form fields have the same names as the previous form fields with the addition of the extension _req. This extension marks both of these fields as required. The VALUE attribute of these hidden form fields is used to store the error message that is displayed if the required information is not entered. You can change this error message to be anything you want.

Next, add an additional hidden form field to form.asp. This form field is used to specify the path of the current page:

```
<input name="formScript" type="hidden"
  value="<%=Request.ServerVariables("SCRIPT_NAME")%>">
```

The server variable named SCRIPT_NAME always has the value of the path of the current Active Server Page. This variable is used to create a link back to the form if there is an error.

Finally, the data should be redisplayed in the original form if an error is encountered. To repopulate the form, we can use the methods described in the previous part of this chapter, "Retrieving Form Data." The VALUE attributes of both form elements need to be assigned to the correct variables.

After you have made all these changes, the script for the finished form.asp page should look like Listing 3.6.

LISTING 3.6   SCRIPT FOR THE FINISHED FORM.ASP PAGE

```
<%
DIM username, birthdate
username = TRIM( Request.Form( "username" ) )
birthdate = TRIM( Request.Form( "birthdate" ) )
%>
<html>
<head><title>Simple HTML Form</title></head>
<body>

<form method="post" action="result.asp">
<input name="formScript" type="hidden"
  value="<%=Request.ServerVariables("SCRIPT_NAME")%>">

<b>Please enter your name: </b>
<input name="username" type="text" size=30
  value="<%=Server.HTMLEncode( username )%>">
<input name="username_req" type="hidden"
  value="You must enter a user name.">
<p>
<b>Please enter your date of birth: </b>
<input name="birthdate" type="text" size=10
  value="<%=Server.HTMLEncode( birthdate )%>">
<input name="birthdate_req" type="hidden"
  value="You must enter your date of birth.">
<p>
<input type="submit" value="Save">
</form>

</body>
</html>
```

3

WORKING WITH
HTML FORMS

   Save the new versions of form.asp and result.asp as form.asp and result.asp
(form2.asp and result2.asp on the CD) and submit the HTML form without
entering any data. When you submit the form, you will receive an error page
complaining that the two fields in the form were not completed (see Figure 3.2). If you
click the button labeled Return, you should be returned to the original form page.

The second aspect of form validation is checking whether the proper type of data has
been entered. The Validate Form INCLUDE file can help here as well. For example, the
Birthdate field should only accept dates and not other types of data. Add the following
hidden form field to the form in form.asp:

```
<input name="birthdate_val" type="hidden" value="date">
```

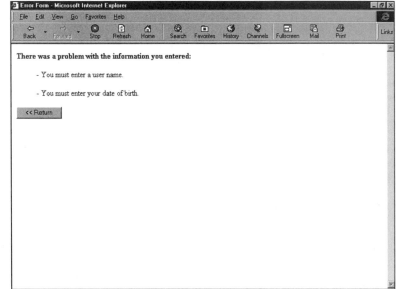

You can add this line anywhere between the <FORM> and </FORM> tags in form.asp. This hidden input field specifies that birthdate should be a date. If you attempt to submit the form with a value other than a date for birthdate, the error page will appear.

As it stands, the Validation INCLUDE file can check for three types of data. You can use the keyword date to check for a date, the keyword number to check for a number, and the keyword currency to check for currency values. However, you can make changes to the Form Validation INCLUDE file to check for any data types that you want. For example, you can check for valid email addresses, social security numbers, or telephone numbers. To check for other data types, simply extend the SELECT CASE statement. For example, the following extension to the SELECT CASE statement checks for valid email addresses:

```
CASE "EMAIL"
IF INSTR( Request.Form( fieldName ), "@" ) = 0
➥OR INSTR( Request.Form( fieldname ), "." ) = 0 THEN
    errorMSG = errorMSG & " - " & fieldName & " must be an email address."
END IF
```

The complete listing for the Form Validation INCLUDE file is included in Listing 3.7.

LISTING 3.7   THE Form Validation INCLUDE FILE

```
<%
'====================================
'  INCLUDE FILE FOR FORM VALIDATION
'====================================


'''''''''''''''''''''''''''''''''''''''''''''''''''''
'  DECLARE GLOBAL VARIABLES
'''''''''''''''''''''''''''''''''''''''''''''''''''''
DIM errorMSG

validateForm
IF errorMSG <> "" THEN errorForm


'''''''''''''''''''''''''''''''''''''''''''''
'  VALIDATE FORM
'''''''''''''''''''''''''''''''''''''''''''''
SUB validateForm
  DIM fieldAttrib, fieldName
    FOR EACH element IN Request.Form
    fieldAttrib   = UCASE( RIGHT( element, 4 ) )
    fieldName = LEFT( element, LEN( element ) - 4 )

    IF fieldAttrib = "_REQ"  AND Request.Form( fieldName ) = "" THEN
        errorMSG = errorMSG & " - " & Request.Form( element ) & "<p>"
    END IF
    IF fieldAttrib = "_VAL" AND Request.Form( fieldName ) <> "" THEN
        SELECT CASE UCASE( Request.Form( element ) )
    CASE "NUMBER"
        IF NOT isNumeric( Request.Form( fieldName ) ) THEN
        errorMSG = errorMSG & " - " & fieldName &
      ➥" must be a number.<p>"
        END IF
    CASE "DATE"
        IF NOT isDATE( Request.Form( fieldName ) ) THEN
        errorMSG = errorMSG & " - " & fieldName &
      ➥" must be a date.<p>"
        END IF
    CASE "CURRENCY"
        IF NOT isNumeric( Request.Form( fieldName ) ) THEN
        errorMSG = errorMSG & " - " & fieldName &
      ➥" must be a money amount.<p>"
        END IF
          END SELECT
    END IF
    NEXT
END SUB
```

continues

3

WORKING WITH
HTML FORMS

LISTING 3.7   CONTINUED

```
'''''''''''''''''''''''''''''''''''''''''''''''''''''
'   ERROR FORM
'''''''''''''''''''''''''''''''''''''''''''''''''''''
SUB errorFORM
    %>
    <html>
    <head><title>Error Form</title></head>
    <body>
    <b>There was a problem with the information you entered:</b>
    <blockquote>
    <%=errorMSG %>
    </blockquote>
    <form method="post" action="<%=Request( "formScript" )%>">
    <% formFields %>
    <input type="submit" value=" << Return ">
    </form>
    </body>
    </html>
    <%
    Response.End
END SUB


''''''''''''''''''''''''''''''''''''''''''''''''''''''''''''''
'   DUMP ALL OF THE FORM FIELDS
''''''''''''''''''''''''''''''''''''''''''''''''''''''''''''''
SUB formFields
    DIM element, fieldAttrib
    FOR EACH element IN Request.Form
        fieldAttrib = UCASE( RIGHT( element, 4 ) )
        IF fieldAttrib <> "_REQ" AND fieldAttrib <> "_VAL" THEN
    %>
    <input name="<%=element%>"
    type="hidden"
    value="<%=Server.HTMLEncode( Request.Form( element ) )%>">
    <%
        END IF
    NEXT
END SUB
%>
```

How the `Validate Form` INCLUDE File Works

The `Validate Form` INCLUDE file works by taking advantage of the `Form` collection of the `Request` object. The script in the INCLUDE file steps through each form element one by one and checks whether each element has the extension _req or the extension val. If the element has the extension _req, we know that the form field with this name, minus the extension, is required. If a form field with this name does not exist in the `Form` collection, an error message is appended to the `errorMSG` variable.

If an element has the extension _val, then we know that the corresponding form field should have a particular data type. A SELECT CASE statement is used to determine whether the value of the form field has the correct data type. If not, an error message is added to the errorMSG variable.

If all goes well, and all the required fields are present and have the correct data type, nothing happens and the rest of the Active Server Page is processed. In the example used earlier, the message Thank you for registering! is displayed.

On the other hand, if the errorMSG variable is not empty, we know that a required field is missing or one of the fields has the wrong data type. In this case, the errorForm subroutine is called. The errorForm subroutine displays the error message contained in the errorMSG variable, and processing of the script is halted with a Response.End statement. The message, Thank you for registering! is never displayed.

When the error form is displayed, the Request.Form collection is dumped into hidden-form variables. This is done so that all the original values of the form data fields can be passed back to the original form—saving the user the trouble of re-entering all the form data.

Accepting File Uploads

Suppose you want to create a Web site where people can advertise houses for sale. It would be nice if people could upload pictures of their homes. Or suppose you want to create a Web site devoted to short stories. It would be nice if people could upload their stories—for example, in Microsoft Word format.

 You can do this with the TYPE=FILE attribute of the <INPUT> tag. Using this attribute, you can create a file upload button on a form (see Figure 3.3). When users of your Web site click this button, they can select a file to upload from their local hard drive. The following is an example (included on the CD as uploadform.asp):

```
<HTML>
<HEAD><TITLE> File Upload </TITLE></HEAD>
<BODY>

<FORM ENCTYPE="multipart/form-data"
ACTION="uploadresult.asp" METHOD=POST>

Please choose a picture to upload:
<BR><INPUT NAME="picture" TYPE=FILE ACCEPT="image/*">
<BR><INPUT TYPE=SUBMIT VALUE="Submit Me!">
</FORM>

</BODY>
```

```
</HTML>
```

FIGURE 3.3

A form with a file

upload button.

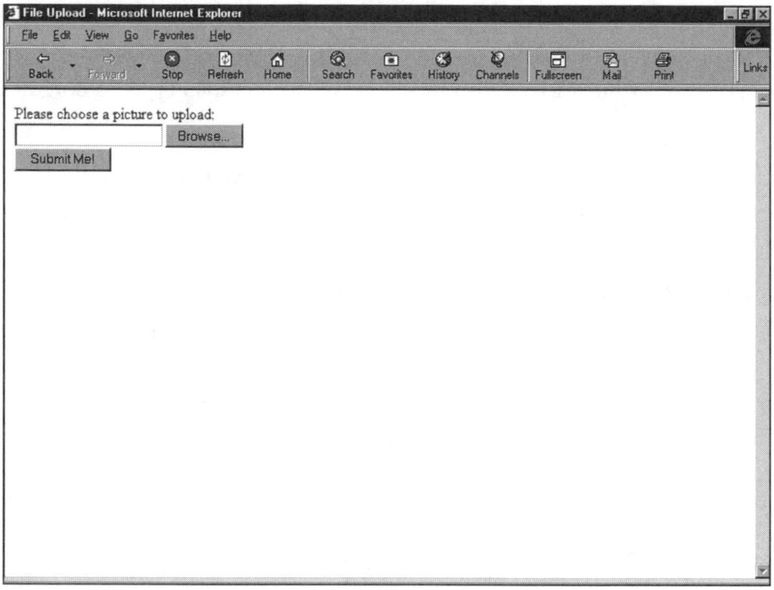

When this HTML file is displayed in Netscape Navigator (version 3.0 or greater) or Internet Explorer (version 4.0 or greater), a normal-looking text box appears next to a Browse button. The user can type the name of the file directly into the text box, or use the Browse button to select a file from a file dialog box. When the form is submitted, the file selected by the user is also submitted.

Notice the addition of the ENCTYPE attribute to the <FORM> tag in this example. The ENCTYPE attribute specifies the type of encoding to apply to the form information when it's submitted. Normally, form information is URL-encoded (spaces are replaced with +, and so on). However, this is a bad encoding format to use with information that isn't text. When uploading files, you must use the ENCTYPE="multipart/form-date" attribute.

The actual file upload button is created using this tag:

```
<INPUT NAME="picture" TYPE=FILE ACCEPT="image/*">
```

Because the value of the TYPE attribute is FILE, the browser should create a file upload button. The ACCEPT attribute restricts the files that will appear in the file dialog box to a particular file type. In this case, the file type is restricted to image files. You can specify any list of MIME types as the value of the ACCEPT attribute.

> **NOTE**
>
> MIME stands for multipurpose Internet mail extension. MIME was originally developed as a means for specifying the file types of email attachments. Browsers use MIME types to associate files with appropriate programs.
>
> Some examples of MIME types are image/gif for GIF images, image/jpeg for JPEG images, application/x-msexcel for Microsoft Excel spreadsheets, and application/msword for Microsoft Word documents.
>
> To view the MIME types that your computer supports, choose View, Options, File Types in Windows Explorer.

Potentially, file upload buttons could be very useful. Regrettably, however, many browsers support file upload buttons only partially—or not at all. For example, Netscape Navigator (versions 3.0 and 4.0) ignores the ACCEPT attribute. Internet Explorer version 3.0 is even worse. It completely fails to interpret file upload buttons, and displays normal text boxes instead. Internet Explorer (versions 4.0 and 5.0), however, does recognize the file upload button. Use file upload buttons with caution.

Using Active Server Pages to Retrieve File Uploads

Creating an HTML form with a file upload button is only the first step in accepting file uploads. If you submit a file with the file upload button, you cannot use the normal methods of the Request object to retrieve the contents of the file. The Request object assumes that a form is submitted with the default encoding type, URL-encoded, but forms submitted with a file upload button do not use this encoding type.

To accept file uploads within an Active Server Page, you must work with the raw data submitted in an HTTP post. Fortunately, Active Server Pages include a special method of the Request object precisely for this purpose. The BinaryRead() method of the Request object can be used to read the raw bytes submitted when a form is posted. You should be warned, however, that after you use the BinaryRead() method in an Active Server Page, you can no longer use the normal Request.Form() method to retrieve form data (or vice versa).

Suppose a user submits a picture named myhouse.gif, using the form described in the previous section. The script in Listing 3.8 can be used to retrieve and display the raw bytes submitted using the BinaryRead() method.

3

WORKING WITH
HTML FORMS

LISTING 3.8 RAW FILE UPLOAD DATA

```
<html>
<head><title>result</title></head>
<body>
<pre>
<%
FormSize = Request.TotalBytes
FormData = Request.BinaryRead( FormSize )
Response.BinaryWrite FormData
%>
</pre>
</body>
</html>
```

This script uses the `TotalBytes` property of the `Request` object to retrieve the total number of bytes sent in the HTTP post. Next, all the form data is assigned to the variable named `FormData`. Finally, the `BinaryWrite()` method of the `Response` object is used to output the contents of the uploaded data. The result of uploading a small image file looks something like this:

```
---------------------------7ce20d227c0232
Content-Disposition: form-data; name="picture"; filename="D:\myhouse.gif"
Content-Type: image/gif

GIF89a"
3ØØØØØØØØØØØØØØØØØØØØØØØØØØØØØØØØØØØØØØØØØØØ!___,"
_APéIgü5'"?__u_…_?ˆ¬?")µ¤uz™Ö®r?£‹1/2å._@(Ç„.'d_áS_:¦\?É8_›Dí_¦šñ\Cˆp_;
---------------------------7ce20d227c0232--
```

Admittedly, the output of the script is not very readable. However, it contains all the uploaded raw data of the file and some important information about the content of the file. For example, the name header contains the name of the form field used to upload the file, the filename header contains the path of the file on the client's hard drive, and the content-type identifies the file as an image file. The raw data of the picture begins with the line that starts with `GIF89a`.

 After you have the data, you can save it to a database, save it to a file, or simply display it. If you are feeling really ambitious, you can even alter the raw image data creating custom images on-the-fly. We are going to do something very simple, however. The following script (uploadresult.asp on the CD) strips the headers and displays whatever file has been uploaded as an image in the browser:

```
<%
FormSize = Request.TotalBytes
FormData = Request.BinaryRead( FormSize )
bnCRLF = chrB( 13 ) & chrB( 10 )
```

```
Divider = LEFTB( FormData,  INSTRB( FormData, bnCRLF ) - 1 )
DataStart = INSTRB( FormData, bnCRLF & bnCRLF ) + 4
DataEnd = INSTRB( DataStart + 1, FormData, divider ) - DataStart
Response.ContentType = "image/gif"
Response.BinaryWrite MIDB( FormData, DataStart, DataEnd )
%>
```

This script extracts the image data from the form data by using the VBScript INSTRB() function to find the start and end of the image data. It is assumed that the image data starts after two carriage return and linefeed characters in a row, and the image data ends with the same divider as the divider at the start of the data. Next, the ContentType of the Response object is used to specify that the content being sent to the browser is a GIF image. Finally, the BinaryWrite() method is used to output the raw image data. The picture is displayed in the browser.

This script assumes that the form being submitted contains only one field and that this one field contains image data. However, an HTML form that contains a file upload element can also contain other standard form elements such as text boxes and text areas. A single HTML form can even contain multiple-file upload elements. For example, here is the raw data posted by a single form that contains both a file upload element named picture and a text area named comments:

```
---------------------------7ce3c1e7c0232
Content-Disposition: form-data; name="picture"; filename="D:\myhouse.gif"
Content-Type: image/gif

GIF89a"
    3    Ø  ØØØØØØØØØØØØØØØØØØØØØØØØØØØØØØØØØØØØØØØØØØØØØØØ!___ _ ,      "
   _APéIgü5'"___u_…_÷^¬'")µ¤uz™Ö®rý£‹1/2å._@(Ç„.'d_áS_:_¦É8_›Dí_¦šñ\Cˆp_  ;
---------------------------7ce3c1e7c0232
Content-Disposition: form data; name-"comments"

This is a picture of my house.
---------------------------7ce3c1e7c0232--
```

Although it is possible to work with these more complicated forms using standard ASP scripts, a better course of action would be to use a third-party ASP component. Using a third-party component, you can work with forms that contain file upload elements in almost the same way as you manipulate a standard HTML form. In Chapter 16, "Third-Party Components," you will learn how to use one of these components to master all aspects of file uploading.

NOTE

For more information on using file uploads, go to the source. See "Form-based File Upload in HTML," E. Nebel and L. Masinter, November 1995 at the World Wide Web Consortium (`http://www.w3.org/MarkUp/Bibliography.html`).

Summary

In this chapter, you learned how to use Active Server Pages to retrieve and manipulate the information entered into HTML forms. In the first part, you learned how to use several advanced techniques to work with HTML text boxes, text areas, radio buttons, check boxes, and select lists. In the second part, you learned how to construct a standard INCLUDE file that can be used to validate form data. Finally, you discovered the secrets of using the file upload form element to enable users to upload files to your Web site.

CHAPTER 4

Working with Active Server Pages Applications

By Stephen Walther

IN THIS CHAPTER

In this chapter, you will learn how to work with Active Server Pages applications. The first section provides an overview of applications. In the second section, you will learn how to use the methods and collections of the `Application` object. Finally, this chapter includes two programming examples: You will learn how to create a simple multiuser chat program and an Active Server Page that displays real-time usage statistics for your Web site.

What Is an Application?

Microsoft wants you to think of Active Server Pages in traditional programming terms. When you create a single Active Server Page, you're creating something like a procedure or subroutine. When you create a group of related Active Server Pages, you're creating an application.

However, an application is something more than a group of pages sitting on a hard drive. When Active Server Pages are joined together in an application, they have certain properties that they would otherwise lack. Following is a list of some features of an Active Server Pages application:

- Data can be shared among the pages in an application, and therefore, among more than one user of a Web site.
- An application has events that can trigger special application scripts.
- An instance of an object can be shared among all the pages in an application.
- Separate applications can be configured with the Internet Service Manager to have different properties.
- Each application can be isolated to execute in its own memory space. This means that if one application crashes, the others won't crash with it.
- You can stop one application (unloading all its components from memory) without affecting other applications.

An Active Server Pages application is not the same as a Web site. A Web site can have more than one application located in multiple directories. Typically, you create separate applications when you have collections of pages related to separate tasks. For example, you might create one application containing all the pages meant for public consumption and another application that's restricted to use by Web site administrators.

An application is defined by using the Internet Service Manager to specify a root directory for the application. An application consists of a particular directory and all its subdirectories. If one of these subdirectories is also defined to be an application, it constitutes a separate application. In other words, no two applications overlap.

When you first install Active Server Pages, a few applications are created by default. For example, an application is created for your default Web site. However, you can create as many additional applications as you need.

Follow these steps to define an Active Server Pages application:

1. Launch the Internet Service Manager from the Microsoft Internet Information Server program group.
2. Click the name of your default Web site in the navigation tree. (If you haven't changed anything, it will be named Default Web Site.)
3. You can select any existing directory, choose the default Web site, or create a new directory for your application. To create a new virtual directory, right-click the name of your default Web site and then choose Create New, Virtual Directory.
4. After you have chosen a directory for your application, you must view its property sheet. You can do this by clicking the Properties icon or by right-clicking the name of the directory and choosing Properties.
5. In the property sheet, click the tab labeled either Virtual Directory or Home Directory.
6. In the Application Settings section, click the Create button.

NOTE

When you create an application, you can provide the application with a name. This name is used only within the Internet Service Manager. It doesn't affect your Active Server Pages scripts.

You have now successfully created a new application. After you create an application, you can set several of its properties by selecting Configuration from the Application Settings panel (see Figure 4.1). For example, you can specify whether the application should use sessions or whether the application should run in its own memory space.

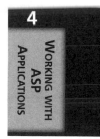

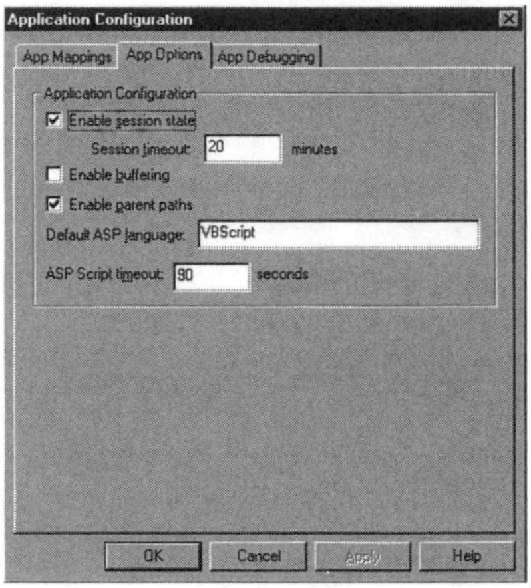

FIGURE 4.1

Creating an application.

Applications and the Global.asa File

Active Server Pages applications can use a special file named Global.asa. Each application can have only one Global.asa file, and the file must be located in the application's root directory. It contains information that's global to your application. The Global.asa file has the following structure:

```
<SCRIPT LANGUAGE=VBScript RUNAT=Server>
SUB Application_OnStart
END SUB
</SCRIPT>

<SCRIPT LANGUAGE=VBScript RUNAT=Server>
SUB Application_OnEnd
END SUB
</SCRIPT>

<SCRIPT LANGUAGE=VBScript RUNAT=Server>
SUB Session_OnStart
END SUB
</SCRIPT>

<SCRIPT LANGUAGE=VBScript RUNAT=Server>
 SUB Session_OnEnd
 END SUB
</SCRIPT>
```

NOTE

A standard Global.asa file is included on the CD with the name Global.asa.

The Global.asa file contains two subroutines that are triggered by application events. The `Application_OnStart` subroutine is executed when an application first starts, and the `Application_OnEnd` subroutine is executed when an application ends. You can associate only one script with each of these two events.

The `Application_OnStart` subroutine is triggered once when the first page located in an application is requested. The event is not triggered again until after the IIS service is stopped, the Global.asa file is modified, or the application is unloaded by using the Internet Service Manager.

Notice that Global.asa uses the Microsoft extended HTML `<SCRIPT>` tag syntax to specify the scripts. You must use this method of indicating a script within the Global.asa file instead of using the normal script delimiters `<%` and `%>`. The Global.asa file in the preceding example uses VBScript as the scripting language, but you can use other scripting languages as well.

You can't include any output within the Global.asa file. In particular, you can't use any HTML tags or the `Response.Write()` method. The Global.asa file itself is never displayed. The file is used only to contain scripts and objects.

To create a script that executes whenever an application is started, you simply add the script to the `Application_OnStart` subroutine, as shown in this example:

```
<SCRIPT LANGUAGE=VBScript RUNAT=Server>
SUB Application_OnStart
    DIM FileName, MyFS, MyFile
    Set MyFS = Server.CreateObject( "Scripting.FileSystemObject" )
    Set MyFile = MyFS.OpenTextFile( "c:\applog.txt", 8, TRUE )
    MyFile.WriteLine NOW() & " - Application Started"
    MyFile.Close
    SET MyFile = Nothing
    SET MYFS = Nothing
END SUB
</SCRIPT>
```

This script simply records the date and time that the application was started to a log file named applog.txt. You can use this log file to track the times when your application requires restarting (for example, after your server crashes).

NOTE

The script in this example uses the File Access Component to write to a text file. To learn more about using the File Access Component, see Chapter 8, "Working with the File System."

The Global.asa file also can be used to declare objects with application scope (To learn more about object scope, see the section titled, "Integrating Objects and Components into Active Server Pages" in Chapter 1, "Building Active Server Pages."). For example, you can declare an instance of a `Dictionary` object that is available to all pages within an application by using the following HTML code:

```
<OBJECT RUNAT="Server" SCOPE="Application" ID="MyDictionary"
PROGID="Scripting.Dictionary"></OBJECT>
```

When you include the HTML code above in the Global.asa file, you should include it outside any of the subroutines or script tags. For example, you can place your object declarations at the very top of the Global.asa file.

CAUTION

Be careful of the threading model when declaring objects with application scope. Declaring an instance of an object that uses the apartment-threading model, such as the `Dictionary` object, can have a severe impact on the performance of a Web site that has heavy traffic (even worse, errors might occur).

After you declare an instance of an object in the Global.asa file using the `<OBJECT>` tag, you can use the object in any Active Server Page just as if the object were a built-in Active Server Page object. You do not need to declare the object again.

Using the Application Object

The `Application` object has all the methods and collections related to applications. In the following sections, you will learn how to use the `Application` object to create application variables and use these variables in the Global.asa file.

Using Application Variables

An *application variable* contains data that can be used on all the pages and by all the users of an application. Application variables can contain any type of data, including arrays and objects. Following are some common uses for application variables:

- An application variable can be used to display transient information on every Web page. For example, you can use an application variable to display a "tip of the day" or a daily news update on every Web page.

- An application variable can be used to record the number of times that a banner advertisement on your Web site has been clicked. (You will learn how to do this in Chapter 9, "Tracking Page Views and Displaying Advertisements.")

- An application variable can hold data retrieved from a database. For example, you can retrieve a list of items for sale at your Web site from a database and display this list on multiple pages using an application variable.

- An application variable can contain a running count of the number of visitors at your Web site. You will learn how to do this in a section of this chapter, "The WhosOn Page."

- An application variable can be used to enable communication among the users of your Web site. For example, you could use application variables to create multiuser games or multiuser chat rooms. An example of a chat page using application variables is provided in a following section of this chapter, "The Chat Page."

Creating and Reading Application Variables

Creating application variables is easy. To create a new application variable, you can simply pass the name of the new variable to the Application object, as in the following example:

```
<HTML>
<HEAD><TITLE> Application Example </TITLE></HEAD>
<BODY>
<%
Application("Greeting")="Welcome!"
%>
<%=Application("Greeting")%>
</BODY>
</HTML>
```

In this example, a new application variable named Greeting is created and assigned the value "Welcome!". Next, the value of the new application variable is outputted to the browser retrieving the page.

After an application variable has been assigned a value, the value can be displayed on all the pages in an application. For example, the following page would also display the greeting, even though the `Greeting` variable hasn't been assigned a value on this page:

```
<HTML>
<HEAD><TITLE> Another Page </TITLE></HEAD>
<BODY>
<%=Application("Greeting")%>
</BODY>
</HTML>
```

After an application variable has been assigned a value, it retains that value until the Web server is shut down or the application is unloaded. If you're lucky, this could be weeks or even months. Because application variables aren't destroyed automatically when a user leaves, you must be careful not to go wild when creating them. Application variables use memory; you should use them sparingly.

NOTE

How do you remove an application variable after it is created? Using IIS 4.0, You can't. Application variables remain in memory until the server is shut down, the Global.asa file is altered, or the application is unloaded. The new version of Active Server Pages included with Windows 2000 contains new methods for removing application variables.

It's also important to understand that an application variable is not relative to a particular user. If one user requests a Web page that assigns one value to an application variable, and another user requests a page that assigns another value, the value of the variable will change for both users. Consider the following script:

```
<%
Randomize
If INT(2*RND)=1 THEN
  Application("FavoriteColor")="Blue"
ELSE
  Application("FavoriteColor")="Red"
END IF
Response.Write Application( "FavoriteColor" )
%>
```

This script randomly assigns the value `Blue` or `Red` to the application variable named `FavoriteColor`. Suppose two users retrieve a page with this script. In that case, the value of the variable would be the same for the two users. The variable would have whatever value was assigned to it when the second user retrieved the page.

Potentially, this can create a problem. Because more than one user can access an application variable at the same time, conflicts can arise. For example, suppose you're using an application variable to record the number of times a banner advertisement has been clicked. Every time the advertisement is clicked, a script like the following is executed:

```
<%
NumClicks=Application("BannerClicks")
NumClicks=NumClicks+1
Application("BannerClicks")=NumClicks
%>
```

The script simply increments the number stored in the application variable BannerClicks by 1. But suppose two users click an advertisement at the same time. The same script would be executed at the same time for both users. If this happens, the value of BannerClicks will be inaccurate. Both users will have incremented the variable to the same value.

Fortunately, the Application object has two methods that can help in precisely this type of situation. The Lock and Unlock methods are used to temporarily prevent other users from changing the value of an application variable. Here's the previous example, rewritten to prevent any potential conflicts:

```
<%
Application.Lock
NumClicks=Application("BannerClicks")
NumClicks=NumClicks+1
Application("BannerClicks")=Numclicks
Application.Unlock
%>
```

The first line in the script locks all the variables in the application object. When the variables are locked, other users can't access or modify them until they're unlocked. The application variables remain locked until the Unlock method is explicitly called (as in the preceding example) or until the end of the page is reached.

Notice that you can't lock application variables selectively; it's an all-or-none choice. The preceding script temporarily prevents other users from modifying all the application variables that might exist.

It's important to understand that locking the application variables doesn't permanently prevent other users from modifying the variables. Locking simply forces any modifications to take place in an orderly fashion. The application variables are modified serially rather than haphazardly.

4

WORKING WITH
ASP
APPLICATIONS

Dumping Application Variables

Most application variables are actually stored in the Contents collection of the Application object. Whenever you create a new application variable, a new item is added to this collection. For example, the following two statements are equivalent:

```
<% Application("FavoriteColor")="Blue" %>
<% Application.Contents("FavoriteColor")="Blue" %>
```

Because application variables are stored in a collection, you can manipulate them by using all the collection properties and methods previously discussed. You can retrieve a count of the number of application variables by using the Count properties. You can display all the items contained in the Contents collection by using either a FOR...EACH loop or a FOR...NEXT loop. Here's an example using a FOR...EACH loop:

```
<%
FOR EACH thing IN Application.Contents
Response.Write("<BR>"&thing&"="&Application.Contents(thing))
NEXT
%>
```

This script displays all the application variables by looping through the Application.Contents collection.

> **NOTE**
>
> The Application object also has a second collection called the StaticObjects collection. This collection contains information about all the objects declared with application scope in the Global.asa file using the HTML <OBJECT> tag.

The Chat Page

In this section and the next, you will learn how to create two Active Server Pages projects by using the Application object—a chat page and a real-time Web site statistics program. These projects are intended to illustrate some of the topics discussed in this chapter, but I hope that you'll also find them useful for your Web site.

The best way to attract users back to your Web site again and again is to create a sense of community. One of the best ways to create a sense of community is to come up with a way for users to interact. The chat page will do this.

The chat page discussed in this section allows real-time interaction between multiple participants. All the users who request the page can view the messages entered by others. Furthermore, they can add their own messages (see Figure 4.2).

FIGURE 4.2

The chat page.

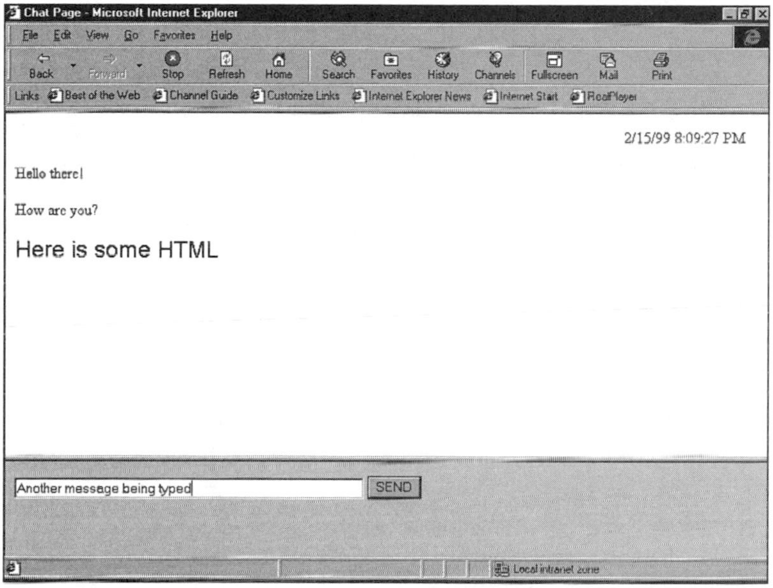

You must create three files to create the chat page. The following list is an overview of the files that need to be created or modified in this project:

- The chat page—The chat page will have two frames; the top frame will display messages from other users and the bottom frame will allow new messages to be entered.
- The display page—This page will display all the messages entered by other users. Every five seconds or so, the contents of the frame will be updated with new messages.
- The message page—This page will allow a user to enter a new message. It contains a single-text input box.
- The Global.asa file—The `Application_OnStart` script will be modified.

Creating the Chat Page

The first page you will create is the chat page. The only purpose of this page is to act as a container for the other two pages. Because it doesn't contain any scripts, you should save it with the name ChatPage.htm, as shown in Listing 4.1.

LISTING 4.1 LISTING FOR CHATPAGE.HTM

```
<HTML>
<HEAD><TITLE> Chat Page </TITLE></HEAD>
<FRAMESET ROWS="*,100">
<FRAME SRC="Display.asp">
<FRAME SRC="Message.asp">
</FRAMESET>
</HTML>
```

Why create frames at all? Because the display page is automatically refreshed every five seconds, a separate page is needed to enter new messages. Otherwise, the page might refresh when a user has entered only half a message (which would be irritating).

Modifying the Global.asa File for the Chat Page

For the chat page to work, the Global.asa file must be modified. The following script is used to initialize the application variables needed for the chat page. The variables must be application variables so that they can be accessed by all users. The first application variable is named Talk. It's an array that holds all the messages. The Talk array is created by assigning the TempArray to it. The second application variable is named TPlace (talk place). It's used to point to the current message in the Talk array. The following script initializes this variable to zero:

```
<SCRIPT LANGUAGE=VBScript RUNAT=Server>
SUB Application_OnStart
 Dim TempArray(5)
 Application("Talk")=TempArray
 Application("TPlace")=0
END SUB
</SCRIPT>
```

Creating the Message Page

The purpose of the message page is to enable a user to enter a new message (see Figure 4.3). The page includes an HTML form with a text input box and a submit button. When the SEND button is clicked, the page reloads itself.

FIGURE 4.3

The message page.

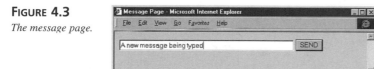

The script does two things. First, it checks whether there are more than four messages. If there are more than four messages, the application variable, TPlace, is reinitialized to zero. This prevents the Talk array from overflowing with too many messages.

 Next, the script adds a new message to the Talk array and increments TPlace. TPlace will always point to the next place in the Talk array where a message can be entered. The complete listing for the message page is included in Listing 4.2 (message.asp on the CD).

LISTING 4.2   LISTING FOR MESSAGE.ASP

```
<%
IF not Request.Form("message")="" THEN
  Application.LOCK
  IF Application("TPlace")>4 THEN
    Application("TPlace")=0
  END IF
    TempArray=Application("Talk")
    TempArray(Application("TPLACE"))=Request.Form("Message")
    Application("Talk")=TempArray
    Application("TPlace")=Application("TPlace")+1
  Application.Unlock
END IF
%>
<HTML>
<HEAD><TITLE> Message Page </TITLE></HEAD>
<BODY BGCOLOR="LIGHTBLUE">
<FORM METHOD="POST" ACTION="message.asp">
<INPUT NAME="message" TYPE="TEXT" SIZE=50>
<INPUT TYPE="SUBMIT" VALUE="SEND">
</FORM>
</BODY>
</HTML>
```

Creating the Display Page

The final page that needs to be created is the display page. This is the page where the messages from all the users are actually displayed (see Figure 4.4).

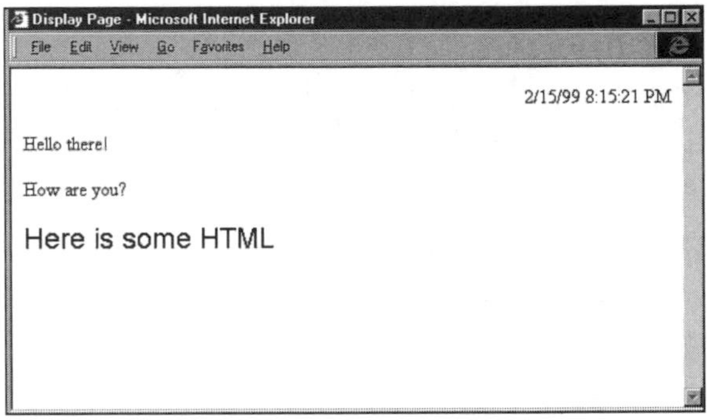

FIGURE **4.4**

The display page.

The page automatically refreshes itself every five seconds. It does this by using client-pull. The HTML <META> tag contains the command to do this. (It adds a REFRESH header to the Active Server Page.)

The first script in the following page is used to identify the current page. The full URL of the current page is retrieved from the ServerVariables collection and assigned to the variable named MySelf. MySelf is used with the <META> tag to indicate the page to be refreshed.

The main script is used to display the contents of the Talk array. The FOR...NEXT loop displays all the current messages. The display page is included in Listing 4.3 (display.asp on the CD).

LISTING 4.3   THE CODE FOR DISPLAY.ASP

```
<%
MyServer=Request.ServerVariables("SERVER_NAME")
MyPath=Request.ServerVariables("SCRIPT_NAME")
MySelf="HTTP://"&MyServer&MyPath
%>
<HTML>
<HEAD>
<META HTTP-EQUIV="REFRESH" CONTENT="5;<%=MySelf%>">
<TITLE>Display Page</TITLE>
</HEAD>
<BODY>
<P ALIGN=RIGHT><%=NOW%></P>
<%
TempArray=Application("Talk")
FOR i=0 to Application("TPlace")-1
  Response.Write("<P>"&Temparray(i))
NEXT
%>
</BODY>
</HTML>
```

Extending the Chat Page Project

There are several ways in which the chat page can be improved. For example, the maximum number of messages that the chat page can display at one time is five. This is inadequate for heavy usage. You can change the maximum number of messages by modifying the size of the `TempArray` in the Global.asa file and by modifying the number at which `TPlace` reinitializes in the message page.

The chat page allows you to enter messages that include HTML formatting. However, it wouldn't be difficult to modify the message page to make this easier. For example, you can have message-formatting check boxes that enable you to specify the font and color of a message.

Finally, the chat page doesn't associate usernames with their messages. Again, this wouldn't be a difficult modification. You can add a logon page before the chat page that requests the username. This name can then be prefixed to all the messages that the user sends.

> **NOTE**
>
> You can see working versions of many of the examples in this book by visiting the companion Web site to this book at `http://www.aspsite.com`.

The WhosOn Page

Good Webmasters have a single purpose in life: They want more users to visit their Web sites. Part of this obsession involves accurately tracking the number of users currently online and determining what they're doing.

The project described in this section allows you to track the visitors to your Web site in real time. You can determine the number of visitors to your Web site at any moment. You can also learn the last page requested by each of your visitors (see Figure 4.5).

4

WORKING WITH ASP APPLICATIONS

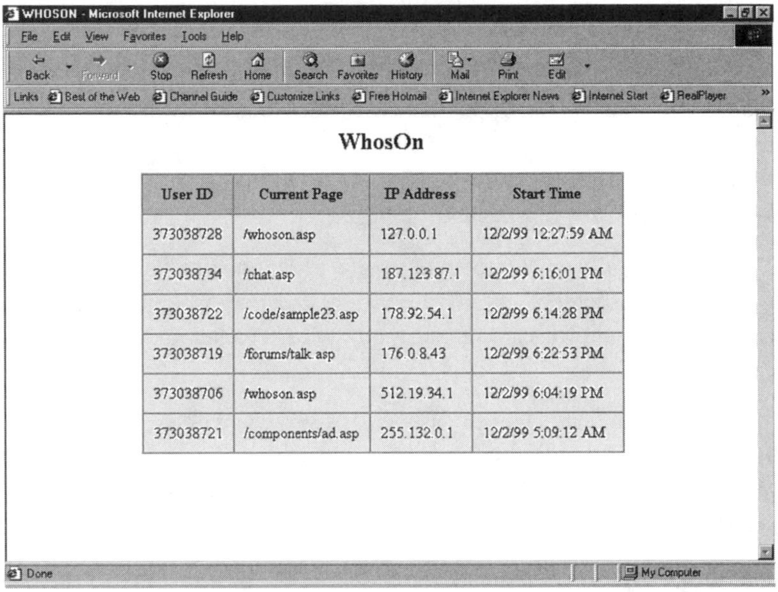

FIGURE **4.5**

The WhosOn page.

This project illustrates how to assign an application array to an application variable. An application array will be used to store information about visitors. Whenever a user requests a page, the information in the application array will be updated. The following files must be created or modified for this project:

- The Global.asa file—Both the Application_OnStart and Session_OnEnd scripts must be modified for this project.

- The GrabStats file—This file updates the application array. You'll need to include this file in every page you want to track.

- The WhosOn page—The WhosOn page displays the users currently at your Web site.

> **NOTE**
>
> In the original edition of this book, the Dictionary object was used to store information about the users being tracked by the WhosOn page. At one time, Microsoft actively encouraged developers to use the Dictionary object with application scope to cache information and improve the efficiency of Web sites (Microsoft used the Dictionary object in this way to improve the performance of its own Web site at www.microsoft.com).

However, users started to experience errors when using the `Dictionary` object with application scope (with heavy traffic, the error "a trappable error has occurred in an external object" appeared throughout a Web site). It turns out that the `Dictionary` object was never designed to be used with session or application scope on the server. Adding to the confusion, the `Dictionary` object was marked with the wrong threading model in the registry.

As I write this, Microsoft has just released a new component called the `LookupTable` component that replaces most of the functionality of the `Dictionary` object. This component was specifically designed to be used with session or application scope.

Nevertheless, in this edition of the book, the WhosOn page has been rewritten using an application array rather than the `LookupTable` component because the `LookupTable` component is read-only. To download or learn more about the `LookupTable` component, visit `http://msdn.microsoft.com`.

Modifying the Global.asa File for the WhosOn Page

To create this project, you must modify two scripts in the Global.asa file. First, you will need to create the application array, which is used to store the information about your visitors. Because this array must be created only once, this is accomplished in the `Application_OnStart` script:

```
<SCRIPT LANGUAGE=VBScript RUNAT=Server>
SUB Application_OnStart
  DIM Stats( 100, 3 )
  Application( "Stats" ) = Stats
END SUB
</SCRIPT>
```

Two lines have been added to the preceding script. The first statement declares a two-dimensional array named Stats. The second statement assigns the array to an application variable with the same name. After it is created, this variable can be used throughout your application.

4

WORKING WITH ASP APPLICATIONS

NOTE

You will learn everything you ever wanted to know about the `Session` object in Chapter 5, "Working with Sessions."

The `Session_OnEnd` script in the Global.asa file also must be modified. The purpose of the following script is to remove a user from the Stats array when the user's session ends (by default, after 20 minutes of inactivity):

```
<SCRIPT LANGUAGE=VBScript RUNAT=Server>
 SUB Session_OnEnd
  Application.Lock
  localStats = Application( "Stats" )
  For i = 0 to UBOUND( localStats, 2 )
    IF localStats( 0, i ) = Session.SessionID THEN
      localStats( 0, i ) = ""
      EXIT FOR
    END IF
  NEXT
  Application( "Stats" ) = localStats
  Application.UnLock
 END SUB
</SCRIPT>
```

Users will be tracked by their session IDs. The first dimension of the Stats array is used to store session IDs. The preceding script checks whether an entry with the session ID of the current user exists in the Stats array. If it does, the entry is removed.

Creating the GrabStats File

To determine the current page of your visitors, you must include a file in every page you want to track. The file consists of the script shown in Listing 4.4.

LISTING 4.4   CODE FOR ADDING GRABSTATS.ASP

```
<%
foundUser = FALSE
Application.Lock
localStats = Application( "Stats" )
FOR k = 0 TO UBOUND( localStats, 2 )
  IF localStats( 0, k ) = Session.SessionID THEN
    localStats( 1, k ) =  Request.ServerVariables( "SCRIPT_NAME" )
    foundUser = TRUE
    EXIT FOR
  END IF
NEXT
IF foundUser = FALSE THEN
FOR k = 0 TO UBOUND( localStats, 2 )
  IF localStats( 0, k ) = "" THEN
    localStats( 0, k ) = Session.SessionID
    localStats( 1, k ) = Request.ServerVariables( "SCRIPT_NAME" )
    localStats( 2, k ) = Request.ServerVariables( "REMOTE_ADDR" )
    localStats( 3, k ) = NOW()
    EXIT FOR
```

```
   END IF
NEXT
END IF
Application("Stats") = localStats
Application.UnLock
%>
```

This script checks whether the session ID of the current user already exists in the Stats application array. If the Stats array already includes the session ID, the information for the current user is updated. Otherwise, if this is the first page that the user has requested from the Web site, a new entry is added to the array

The SCRIPT_NAME and REMOTE_ADDR items from the ServerVariables collection are used to retrieve the name of the current script and the user's IP address. The VBScript NOW() function is used to add the date and time that the new array entry was added.

Save the preceding file with the name GrabStats.asp. You should include this file in every Active Server Page that you want to track. Simply add the following line to the top of every Active Server Page:

```
<!-- #INCLUDE FILE="GrabStats.asp" -->
```

Creating the WhosOn Page

The WhosOn page is used to display the current visitors. The session ID, the last page requested, the IP address, and the start time is displayed for each visitor. Listing 4.5 is the code for the WhosOn page (available on the CD-ROM as WhosOn.asp).

LISTING 4.5   LISTING FOR WHOSON.ASP

```
<!-- #INCLUDE FILE="GrabStats.asp" -->
<%
MyServer=Request.ServerVariables("SERVER_NAME")
MyPath=Request.ServerVariables("SCRIPT_NAME")
MySelf="HTTP://"&MyServer&MyPath
%>
<HTML>
<HEAD>
<META HTTP-EQUIV="REFRESH" CONTENT="20;<%=MySelf%>">
<TITLE>WHOSON</TITLE>
</HEAD>
<BODY>
<%
Application.Lock
localStats=Application("Stats")
Application.UnLock
%>
```

4

WORKING WITH ASP APPLICATIONS

continues

LISTING 4.5   CONTINUED

```
<CENTER>
<h2>WhosOn</h2>
<TABLE BORDER=1 CELLPADDING=10
CELLSPACING=0 BGCOLOR="#eeeeee">
<TR BGCOLOR="#cccccc">
    <TH>User ID</TH>
    <TH>Current Page</TH>
    <TH>IP Address</TH>
    <TH>Start Time</TH>
</TR>
<%
FOR i = 0 TO UBOUND( localStats, 2 )
IF localStats( 0, i ) <> "" THEN
%>
<TR>
    <TD><%=localStats( 0, i )%></TD>
    <TD><%=localStats( 1, i )%></TD>
    <TD><%=localStats( 2, i )%></TD>
    <TD><%=localStats( 3, i )%></TD>
</TR>
<%
END IF
NEXT
%>
</TABLE>
</CENTER>
</BODY>
</HTML>
```

The first line in this file includes the GrabStats.asp file that you created in the previous section. This allows you to know, when you are viewing this page, that you actually are viewing this page. The path of the WhosOn page will appear next to your session ID.

The first script is used to retrieve the path of the current page. The WhosOn page is automatically refreshed, using client pull, every 20 seconds. The path of the current page is needed so the page can be refreshed.

The second script transfers the Stats array stored in the application variable to a temporary local array named localStats. The localStats array is automatically destroyed when the page ends.

The final script loops through all the entries in the localStats array. If an entry has a value, it is displayed (as you saw in Figure 4.5).

Extending the WhosOn Page

As it stands, the WhosOn page provides valuable information about the users of your Web site. By viewing the WhosOn page, you can gather a rough estimate of the number of users currently at your Web site. You can also see the last page each user requested.

There are several ways in which this project can be extended. For example, if your Web site requires users to register, you can display usernames rather than session IDs. To do this, simply add a new element to the Stats array for the username.

The WhosOn page is limited to showing information on no more than 100 users at a time. If your Web site has heavier traffic, you can increase the size of the Stats array in the Global.asa file. For example, to track up to 1,000 users, simply declare the Stats variable in the Application_OnStart event like this:

```
<SCRIPT LANGUAGE=VBScript RUNAT=Server>
SUB Application_OnStart
  DIM Stats( 1000, 3 )
  Application( "Stats" ) = Stats
END SUB
</SCRIPT>
```

> **NOTE**
>
> You can view working versions of several examples in this book by visiting the book's companion Web site at http://www.aspsite.com.

Summary

In this chapter, you learned how to work with Active Server Pages applications. The first section provided an overview of applications. In the second section, you learned how to use the collections and properties of the Application object. Finally, in the third and final section, two programming examples were discussed. You learned how to create a chat page and a page that enables you to track visitors at your Web site.

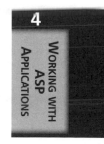

4

WORKING WITH
ASP
APPLICATIONS

CHAPTER 5

Working with Sessions

by Stephen Walther

IN THIS CHAPTER

In this chapter, you will learn how to work with sessions. You will learn how to use session collections, properties, methods, and events. You also will learn how to read and create cookies. Finally, some methods are discussed for retaining state without cookies.

An Introduction to Sessions

A *session* is something that starts the moment a user requests a page from your Web site and ends soon after the user leaves. Each visitor to your Web site is given an individual session.

Sessions can be used to store a visitor's preferences. For example, does the visitor prefer that Web pages have a green background or a blue background? Does the visitor have a strong hostility toward frames? Does the visitor prefer to view a text-only version of your Web site? These preferences can be tracked by using sessions.

Sessions can also be used to create virtual shopping carts. Whenever a visitor selects an item to buy at your Web site, the item can be added to a shopping cart. When the user is ready to leave, he or she can purchase everything in the shopping cart at once. All the information about the items in the shopping cart can be stored in a session.

Finally, sessions can be used to keep track of the habits of your visitors. In the same way in which environmentalists use tracking devices to record the roaming habits of the great white shark, you can use sessions to track the movements of your visitors as they roam from page to page. This information can be used for advertising purposes, to improve the design of your Web site, or simply to satisfy your curiosity.

The Stateliness of Sessions

Sessions were invented to address a limitation of the HTTP protocol. Remember how the HTTP protocol works—whenever a user makes a request, the server supplies a response. All interaction between a browser and a Web server takes place in discrete request and response pairs.

Nothing in the HTTP protocol allows a server to keep track of the users making the requests. After a server has finished responding to a request, the server can't continue to identify the browser that made it. From the perspective of a Web server, each new request is made by a new individual. For this reason, the HTTP protocol is called a *stateless protocol*. The HTTP protocol can't be used to retain the state of a user. This is a very serious limitation because it means that you can't identify a user over multiple Web pages.

Sessions were introduced to fix this problem. By using sessions, you can store information about a user over multiple Web pages. Sessions enable you to do many things that would otherwise be very difficult or completely impossible.

> **CAUTION**
>
> Be warned that Active Server Pages sessions use cookies, and not all browsers support cookies. For details, see the later section "How Sessions Really Work."

Storing Session Information

Session variables are similar to the application variables discussed in Chapter 4, "Working with Active Server Pages Applications." Like an application variable, a session variable can be used in multiple Active Server Pages. However, unlike an application variable, separate copies of a session variable are created for each visitor to your Web site.

Active Server Pages sessions are very easy to use. You can control all aspects of a session by using the Active Server Pages Session object. If you need to store data that will persist throughout a user session, you simply store that data in a collection of the Session object. Here's an example:

```
<HTML>
<HEAD><TITLE> Session Example </TITLE></HEAD>
<BODY>
<%
Session("Greeting")="Welcome!"
Response.Write(Session("Greeting"))
%>
</BODY>
</HTML>
```

When this Active Server Page is displayed in a browser, the greeting Welcome! is displayed. The first line in this script assigns the text "Welcome!" to a session variable named Greeting. The next line in the script outputs the greeting to the screen.

So far, this isn't particularly exciting. You can do the same thing by using a normal VBScript variable. However, imagine that the same user requests another page. For example, imagine that the user requests the following page:

```
<HTML>
<HEAD><TITLE> Another Page </TITLE></HEAD>
<BODY>
<%=Session("Greeting")%>
</BODY>
</HTML>
```

5

WORKING WITH
SESSIONS

When the user views this page, the same greeting `Welcome!` is displayed once again. However, the session variable wasn't assigned a value on this page. The session variable `Greeting` has retained the value it was assigned on the previous page.

You couldn't do this with a normal script variable. The lifetime of a normal variable extends only throughout a single page. A session variable, on the other hand, persists until the user leaves the Web site.

It's important to understand that session variables exist only in relation to a particular user. The values assigned to session variables in one user session don't affect the values of the session variables in another user session. In other words, unlike an application variable, the data stored in session variables isn't shared among different users. For example, suppose the following script appeared in an Active Server Page:

```
<%
Randomize
If INT(2*RND)=1 THEN
  Session("FavoriteColor")="Blue"
ELSE
  Session("FavoriteColor")="Red"
END IF
%>
```

This script randomly assigns the session variable `FavoriteColor` with either the value `"Blue"` or the value `"Red"`. This variable might have a different value in the case of different users. The value of the variable `FavoriteColor` is relative to a particular user session.

Because the value of a session variable is not shared among multiple users, there is not a problem with locking session variables, as there is in the case of application variables. The `Session` object does not have a `Lock` or `UnLock` method. No conflicts can arise because no two users will ever have access to the same session variable.

The Contents of a Session

Most session variables are actually stored in a collection of the `Session` object named `Contents`. For example, the following two statements are equivalent:

```
<% Session("MyVar")="Some data" %>
<% Session.Contents("MyVar")="Some data" %>
```

 As in the collections discussed previously, you can use the `Count` property to determine the number of items in the `Contents` collection. You can also display all the items contained in the `Contents` collection by using either a `FOR...EACH` or a `FOR...NEXT` loop. This example uses both methods (included as sessionContents.asp on the CD):

```
<%
Session("FavoriteColor")="blue"
Session("FavoriteFont")="Comic Sans MS"
%>
There are
<%=Session.Contents.Count %>
items in the Session Contents collection.
<HR>
<%
FOR EACH thing IN Session.Contents
  Response.Write( "<BR>"&thing&"="&Session.Contents(thing))
NEXT
Response.Write("<HR>")
FOR i=1 TO Session.Contents.Count
  Response.Write("<BR>"&Session.Contents(i))
NEXT
%>
```

In this script, two session variables named FavoriteColor and FavoriteFont are created. Next, a count of the number of items in the Contents collection is retrieved. Finally, all the items in the Contents collection are displayed by using both a FOR...EACH and a FOR...NEXT loop (see Figure 5.1).

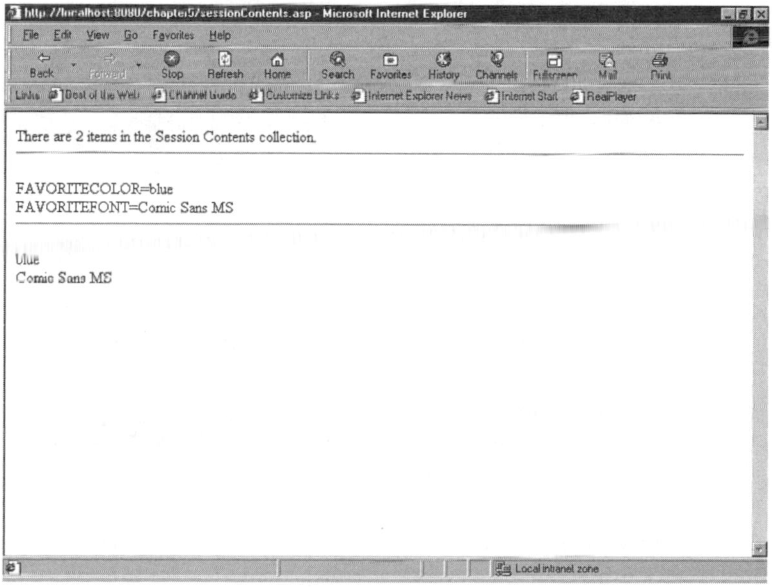

FIGURE 5.1

The contents of the Contents *collection.*

Identifying a Session

 Active Server Pages assigns each user session a unique identifier. This session ID is created when the user session is first created and persists throughout the time the user remains at your Web site. To retrieve the session ID, you use the `SessionID` property of the `Session` object, as in this example (included on the CD as sessionID.asp):

```
<HTML>
<HEAD><TITLE> Session ID </TITLE></HEAD>
<BODY>
Your session ID is: <%=Session.SessionID %>
</BODY>
</HTML>
```

The Active Server Page here simply outputs the value of the `SessionID` property (see Figure 5.2). When different users retrieve the page, a different session ID will be displayed for each. However, if the same user retrieves the page multiple times, the same session ID should be displayed.

FIGURE 5.2

The value of `SessionID`.

One use for the `SessionID` property is to track the movements of your visitors. For example, you can record the pages that a user visits in the log file of your Web site. Simply create the following file and include it in every page:

```
<%
Who=Session.SessionID
CurrentPage=Request.ServerVariables("SCRIPT_NAME")
Response.AppendToLog Who&":"&CurrentPage
%>
```

This script uses the `AppendToLog` method of the `Response` object to append an entry in the server log file. In this example, the string added to the log file contains the session ID that was retrieved from the `SessionID` property. The string also contains the path to the current page, which was retrieved from the `SCRIPT_NAME` server variable.

> **NOTE**
>
> You can use the AppendToLog method of the Response object to append any string under 80 characters to your Web server's log file. Because commas are used to separate fields in the log file, you shouldn't use commas in the string.
>
> The Internet Information Server log file is a text file that contains a log of the activity of your Web server. You can open it by using any standard text editor. By default, it's located in the Winnt/system32/LogFiles directory.

Controlling When Sessions End

How does the server know when a session ends? In other words, how does the server know whether a user has left your Web site for another one or has turned off his or her computer and gone to see a movie?

The server assumes that if someone hasn't requested or refreshed a page for a period of more than 20 minutes, that person has left, and times out that user's session. This strategy enables the server to recover resources that it has been using to track the user's session.

For certain Web site applications, this timeout period of 20 minutes is too short. For example, suppose you have a game site that includes several complicated puzzles, which the user must solve with pen and paper. You might expect the user to be inactive, from the Web server's perspective, for long periods of time.

For other Web site applications, the session timeout period of 20 minutes is too long. If you have a very high-traffic Web site, and you want to ease the burden on your server as much as possible, you might want a shorter session timeout period.

Fortunately, you can control the maximum amount of time for which a user is allowed to be inactive before a session times out. The Session object has a property for this purpose. You can set the amount of time before a session times out by using the Timeout property of the Session object. For example, the following script sets the Timeout property to 60 minutes:

```
<% Session.Timeout=60 %>
```

TIP

You can also specify the session timeout by using the Internet Service Manager. From the Application Configuration dialog box, click the Active Server Pages tab and specify the number of minutes for the Session timeout.

When a user session times out and the user makes a new request, the server treats the user as a new user. The server creates a new session, and all the old session information is lost. You can force this to happen manually by using the Abandon method of the Session object. Consider the following example:

```
<HTML>
<HEAD><TITLE> Abandon Session </TITLE></HEAD>
<BODY>
<BR>The user is <%=Session.SessionID %>.
<% Session.Abandon %>
</BODY>
</HTML>
```

In this example, the session ID of the user is outputted to the screen. Next, the Session.Abandon method is called. When you request a new page, all information in the Session object is lost, and a new ID is assigned to the session. After the Abandon method is called, the server treats the user as a new user.

One situation in which the Abandon method is useful is when you are storing a user's name and password in session variables. You can use these session variables to determine whether a user should have access to a page. If you want to provide a user the option to log out, you can supply a link to a page where the Session.Abandon method is called.

Be aware, however, that the Abandon method does not take effect until after the current page is completely processed. Session variables retain their values anywhere within the page, even in sections of script below where the Abandon method was called.

Sessions and the Global.asa File

In Chapter 4, you were introduced to the Global.asa file. Like an Active Server Page application, a session also has events. Two of them, in fact: the Session_OnStart event, which is triggered when a session begins, and the Session_OnEnd event, which is triggered when a session ends.

The subroutines that correspond to these session events must be located in the Global.asa file for the application. Here is the structure of the Global.asa file once again:

```
<SCRIPT LANGUAGE=VBScript RUNAT=Server>
SUB Application_OnStart
END SUB
</SCRIPT>

<SCRIPT LANGUAGE=VBScript RUNAT=Server>
SUB Application_OnEnd
END SUB
</SCRIPT>

<SCRIPT LANGUAGE=VBScript RUNAT=Server>
SUB Session_OnStart
END SUB
</SCRIPT>

<SCRIPT LANGUAGE=VBScript RUNAT=Server>
 SUB Session_OnEnd
 END SUB
</SCRIPT>
```

To create a script that executes whenever a new session is started, you simply add the script to the Session_OnStart section of the Global.asa file, as in this example:

```
<SCRIPT LANGUAGE=VBScript RUNAT=Server>
SUB Session_OnStart
  Session("UserName")="Unknown"
  Session("UserPassword")="Unknown"
END SUB
</SCRIPT>
```

This script assigns the value "Unknown" to two session variables named UserName and UserPassword. This example illustrates one of the main functions of the Session_OnStart script—initializing session variables.

The Session_OnStart script can be used for other purposes as well. For example, one interesting application of the Session_OnStart script is for redirecting visitors to a new page. Suppose you don't want any visitors to your Web site to go directly to any page other than the home page when they first arrive. You can redirect the first page request to the home page by using the Response.Redirect method. Here's an example:

```
<SCRIPT LANGUAGE=VBScript RUNAT=Server>
SUB Session_OnStart
  MyHomePage="/homepage.asp"
  RequestPage=Request.ServerVariables("SCRIPT_NAME")
IF NOT (STRCOMP(MyHomePage,RequestPage,vbTextCompare)=0)THEN
  Response.Redirect MyHomePage
END IF
END SUB
</SCRIPT>
```

> **NOTE**
>
> Microsoft uses this method of automatically redirecting users to a start page in its Adventure Works sample application, included with the installation of the Windows NT Option Pack.

In this script, the path of the page that the user requests is compared to the path of the home page. If they're not the same, the user is automatically redirected to the home page.

This final example uses both the `Session_OnStart` and `Session_OnEnd` events:

```
<SCRIPT LANGUAGE=VBScript RUNAT=Server>
SUB Session_OnStart
 Response.AppendToLog Session.SessionID&" starting"
END SUB
</SCRIPT>
<SCRIPT LANGUAGE=VBScript RUNAT=Server>
SUB Session_OnEnd
  Response.AppendToLog Session.SessionID&" ending"
END SUB
</SCRIPT>
```

The `Session_OnStart` and `Session_OnEnd` scripts here record the session ID of the user in the log file. Because the `Session_OnStart` script executes when a user first arrives, this `Session_OnStart` script records when the user starts a new session. The `Session_OnEnd` script records when the user leaves. You can use this information to determine the pages that are most often used to enter and exit your Web site.

You can create objects with session scope within the Global.asa file. To do this, use the Microsoft Extended HTML `<OBJECT>` tag. Here is an example that creates an instance of the `Dictionary` object with session scope:

```
<OBJECT RUNAT="Server" SCOPE="Session" ID="MyDictionary"
PROGID="Scripting.Dictionary"></OBJECT>
```

The scope attribute of the `<OBJECT>` tag is used to specify that the instance of the `Dictionary` object named `MyDictionary` should have session scope. After an instance of the `Dictionary` object has been created in this way, it can be treated exactly like an Active Server Page built-in object. You can use any of its methods and properties within any page in the application without declaring the object again.

CAUTION

Be careful of the object's threading model when declaring objects with session scope. Declaring an instance of an object that uses the apartment-threading model, such as the Dictionary object, can have a severe impact on the performance of a Web site that has heavy traffic (even worse, errors might occur).

When an instance of an object is created with session scope, a new instance of the object is created for each user. In general, this means that objects created with session scope demand more memory than objects created with application scope. However, it also means that there will be less access contention over the object because only one user can access each instance of the object.

How Sessions Really Work

Sessions use cookies. (See the following section for details on cookies.) When a user first requests a page from your Web site, the server creates a single cookie in the user's browser to track the session. When the session ends, the cookie expires as well.

The cookie created for each user is named ASPSESSIONID. (You can view it by dumping the ServerVariables collection.) The only purpose of this cookie is to provide a unique identifier for each user.

The session variables themselves are not stored on the user's browser. However, the ASPSESSIONID cookie is needed to use session variables. The server uses the ASPSESSIONID cookie to associate the proper session variables with the proper user. Without the cookie, the server would have no way to identify the same user as he or she moved from page to page on a Web site.

The session ID stored in the ASPSESSIONID cookie is not the same as the SessionID property. Microsoft uses a complicated algorithm to generate the value of the ASPSESSIONID cookie. Microsoft does this in order to prevent hackers from guessing the session ID and pretending to be someone they're not.

> **NOTE**
>
> You can disable sessions in two ways—disable sessions for your entire Web site application, or prevent sessions from being used on a particular page.
>
> To prevent the Web server from creating user sessions entirely, you use the Internet Service Manager. From the Application Configuration dialog box, click the Active Server Pages tab and uncheck the Enable Session State option.
>
> You can also specify that a particular Active Server Page should be sessionless by using the following Active Server Page directive at the top of the file:
>
> ```
> <%@ EnableSessionState=False %>
> ```

Because the Session object uses cookies, the object might be incompatible with both old and recent browsers. Older browsers simply can't use cookies. What's even worse, many recent browsers, such as Netscape 4.0 and Internet Explorer 4.0, provide the option of disabling cookies altogether.

This presents a problem. Because cookies aren't compatible with all browsers, you should be cautious in using the Session object when building your Web site. Although there are certain things that you simply can't do without using sessions, certain properties of a session can be simulated by other means. Some alternatives to using cookies and the Session object are discussed in the later section "Retaining State Without Cookies."

> **NOTE**
>
> Certain browsers, such as Netscape Navigator, use case-sensitive URLs to determine when to send a cookie. This can create problems with sessions. For this reason, Microsoft recommends that you always use the same case when specifying URLs in Active Server Pages. For example, don't use /WWW/mypage.asp and /www/mypage.asp because this might confuse the Netscape browser.

Cookies

Few Internet technologies create greater agitation among Web users than cookies. Cookies have an innocent-sounding name, but many users assume that they have an evil purpose.

Netscape introduced cookies into the world with the first version of its browser. Since then, the World Wide Web Consortium has endorsed a cookie standard. Most browsers now have the capability to use cookies.

What are cookies? Browsers that support cookies maintain one or more special files. These files, called *cookie files* on Windows machines and *magic cookie files* on the Macintosh, are used to store data from Web sites. A Web server can insert pieces of information into these cookie files. This explains the strong negative reaction some Web users have toward cookies. Some people consider a cookie an invasion of privacy. Even worse, some people consider cookies an invasion of their personal space.

Certain cookies are temporary; others are persistent. For example, the cookies used by Active Server Pages to track user sessions expire after a visitor leaves the Web site. Other cookies can remain in the cookie files to be read by the server when a user returns.

It's the cookies that remain in the cookie files that generate the most concern. The fear is that these cookies can be used to track an individual's Web surfing habits. The worry is that if this information falls into the wrong hands, the individual could become the target of multiple bulk-mail advertising campaigns (a fate worse than death).

Recent versions of both Microsoft Internet Explorer and Netscape Navigator have additional options that allow greater control over cookies. You can configure either browser to warn you before accepting a cookie. Additionally, both browsers now provide the option of disabling cookies entirely.

Moreover, various ingenious techniques have been developed to disable cookies even on the browsers that don't provide these options. For example, you can disable cookies on a browser by making the cookie files read-only (see http://www.cookiecentral.com).

Unfortunately, the current state of affairs means that you can't depend on cookies when building your Web site. Cookies work on the majority of browsers, but fail completely when used with certain browsers, and this means that sessions will fail as well.

> **NOTE**
>
> Several Web sites have valuable information on cookies. To view the Netscape specification for cookies, see this site:
>
>   http://home.netscape.com/newsref/std/cookie_spec.html
>
> To view the World Wide Web Consortium's Reference specification on cookies, visit http://www.w3.org. Finally, for general information on cookies, go to http://www.cookiecentral.com.

How Cookies Work

Cookies are passed back and forth between a browser and server through HTTP headers. The server first creates a cookie by using the `Set-Cookie` header in a response. Subsequent requests from the browser will return this cookie in the `Cookie` header.

Suppose you want to create a cookie named `UserName` that contains the name of the visitor to your Web site. To create this cookie, the server would send a header like this:

```
Set-Cookie: UserName=BILL+Gates; path=/; domain=aspsite.com;
 expires=Tuesday, 01-Jan-05 00:00:01 GMT
```

This header instructs the browser to add an entry to its cookie file. The browser adds the cookie named `UserName` with the value `Bill Gates`. Notice that the value of the cookie is URL-encoded.

Furthermore, the header informs the browser that this cookie should be returned to the server regardless of the path used in the request. If the path attribute were set to another value such as `/private`, the cookie would only be returned in requests to this path. For example, the request for the file `/private/mypage.htm` would include the `Cookie` header but not the request `/mypage.htm`.

The `domain` attribute further restricts where the cookie can be sent by the browser. In this example, the cookie can be sent only to the `www.aspsite.com` Web site. The cookie will never be sent to `www.yahoo.com` or any other Web site on the Internet.

Finally, the `Expires` attribute specifies when the cookie should expire. The header in the example tells the browser to store the cookie until the first second of January 1, 2005. Actually, the cookie will probably expire much earlier than that. When a cookie file becomes too large, the browser automatically starts removing cookies.

After the browser has created a cookie, the browser returns the cookie in every request it makes to the Web site—that is, every request that satisfies the path requirement. However, the browser won't send the cookie in requests to a Web site with a different domain name. The browser continues to send the cookie until the cookie expires. The `Cookie` header looks like this:

```
Cookie: UserName: Bill+Gates
```

Creating and Reading Cookies with Active Server Pages

To create a cookie with Active Server Pages, you use the `Cookies` collection of the `Response` object. You can create two types of cookies: a cookie with a single value, or a *cookie dictionary*, which contains multiple name and value pairs.

To create a cookie with a single value, you can use a script like this:

```
<%
Response.Cookies("UserName")="Bill Gates"
Response.Cookies("UserName").Expires="Jan 1, 2005"
%>
```

This script creates a cookie named UserName with the value Bill Gates. This cookie will be returned by a user's browser until January 1, 2005 or until the browser erases it. If you don't specify an expiration date for the cookie, the cookie expires when the user leaves your Web site.

Because the sample script actually creates a header, you must place the script before any output statements in your Active Server Pages file. Alternatively, you can buffer the page (see the section "Buffering Page Output" in Chapter 2, "Active Server Pages and the HTTP Protocol").

The preceding script is a simple example of how you can create a cookie. The example uses only the `Expires` attribute of the `Cookies` collection. However, the `Cookies` collection has several additional attributes. Here's a more complicated example:

```
<%
Response.Cookies("UserName")="Steve Jobs"
Response.Cookies("UserName").Expires="Jan 1, 2005"
Response.Cookies("UserName").Path="/examples"
Response.Cookies("UserName").Domain=".aspsite.com"
Response.Cookies("UserName").Secure=True
%>
```

This script also creates a cookie named UserName. However, this cookie has three additional attributes:

- The Path attribute is used to specify, in a more exact manner, when the browser should send the cookie. In this example, the cookie will be sent only when the path of a requested page begins with /examples. For example, the cookie will be sent with a request for /examples/hello.asp or /examples/chapter5/cookies.asp, but not /hello.asp. By default, the application path is used.

- The `Domain` attribute also specifies when the cookie should be sent. In the preceding example, the cookie will be sent only with requests to the `.aspsite.com` domain. The leading period means that the cookie will be sent to `www.aspsite.com`, `beetle.aspsite.com`, or `cricket.aspsite.com` (any host within the `aspsite.com` domain). If this attribute is not specified, the host and domain of the Web server is used.

- Finally, the `Secure` attribute specifies that the cookie should be sent only in an encrypted transmission. You can use this attribute if you're using the Secure Sockets Layer (Chapter 23, "Securing Your Web Site").

To read a cookie within an Active Server Page, you use the `Cookies` collection of the `Request` object. For example, to output the value of a cookie, you can use the following script:

```
<%=Request.Cookies("UserName") %>
```

This script outputs the value of the cookie named `UserName`. As in all the collections discussed previously, you can use the `Count` attribute to determine the number of items in the `Cookies` collection. You can also use either a `FOR...EACH` or a `FOR...NEXT` loop to iterate through the items in the `Cookies` collection. This example uses a `FOR...EACH` loop:

```
<%
FOR EACH thing IN Request.Cookies
  Response.write("<BR>"&thing&"="&Request.Cookies(thing))
NEXT
%>
```

Creating More Than One Cookie

You can create more than one cookie by simply creating multiple cookies with the `Response.Cookies` collection as in the previous examples. However, many browsers support only three or four cookies from a particular Web site.

An alternative method is available for creating multiple cookies. You can create a *cookie dictionary*. A cookie dictionary is actually a single cookie with multiple name and value pairs. Following is an example of how you can create a cookie dictionary:

```
<%
Response.Cookies("User")("Name")="Bill Gates"
Response.Cookies("User")("Password")="billions"
%>
```

This script creates a cookie dictionary with the name User and the keys Name and Password. When a cookie dictionary is created, a header like the following is sent to the browser:

```
Set-Cookie:User=Name=Bill+Gates&Password=billions
```

A cookie named User is created. However, the value of User is actually two name-and-value pairs. The names and values of each key of the cookie dictionary are joined together into one large cookie.

To retrieve a cookie dictionary, you can use the Request.Cookies collection as in the preceding example. If you simply provide the name of the cookie dictionary, the cookie dictionary is returned in unparsed form. To retrieve particular keys of the cookie dictionary, you pass the name of the key to the collection. Here's an example:

```
<%=Request.Cookies("User")%>
<%=Request.Cookies("User")("Name")%>
<%=Request.Cookies("User")("Password")%>
```

CAUTION

You should be cautious with storing sensitive information such as passwords in a cookie. By default, a cookie is not encrypted when it's sent back and forth between a browser and Web server. If you're using the Secure Sockets Layer (see Chapter 23, "Securing Your Web Site," for details), you can use the SECURE attribute to transmit only encrypted cookies. However, the cookie still will be stored in an ordinary text file on a browser.

To determine whether a cookie is a cookie dictionary, use the HasKeys attribute. For example, the following script returns True if the cookie is a cookie dictionary and False otherwise:

```
<%=Request.Cookies("User").HasKeys %>
```

Retaining State Without Cookies

Using either sessions or cookies is risky because not all browsers support them. The moment you use a cookie at your Web site, you'll receive complaints from countless individuals with obscure browsers who can't use cookies. In this section, you will learn some methods to retain state without cookies. In other words, you will learn how to retain information about a user from page to page. Three methods are compared.

Retaining State with Query Strings

Chapter 2, "Active Server Pages and the HTTP Protocol," explained how to work with query strings. You can add a query string to any hyperlink in your Active Server Pages. By using query strings, you can pass information from page to page, as in this example:

```
<HTML>
<HEAD><TITLE> Query State </TITLE></HEAD>
<BODY>
<%
UserName=Server.URLEncode("Bill Gates")
%>
<A HREF="/nextpage.asp?<%=UserName%>">Click Here</A>
</BODY>
</HTML>
```

This script assigns the name Bill Gates to the variable named UserName. The value of this variable is passed to the page nextpage.asp in the query string when the user clicks the hyperlink.

You can continue to pass the UserName from page to page by retrieving UserName from the QueryString collection. For example, the page nextpage.asp might look like this:

```
<HTML>
<HEAD><TITLE> Next Page </TITLE></HEAD>
<BODY>
<%
UserName=Server.URLEncode(Request.QueryString("Username"))
%>
<A HREF="/nextpage.asp?<%=UserName%>">Click Here</A>
</BODY>
</HTML>
```

The advantage of this method of retaining state is that it works with all browsers. Admittedly, however, it's very cumbersome. If you want to be able to track the user on every page on your Web site, you must include a query string with every hyperlink on your Web site. Every query string must contain the name of the user.

Another disadvantage of this method of retaining state is that it doesn't allow you to pass large amounts of data. Remember, query strings can't be too large. When a query string becomes larger than about 1,000 characters, certain browsers either truncate the query string or fail to create a functioning hyperlink at all.

Retaining State with Hidden Form Fields

If you must pass a large amount of data from page to page without using session variables, you have no choice but to use an HTML form. You can hide the information you're passing by using a hidden form field, as in this example:

```
<HTML>
<HEAD><TITLE> Form State </TITLE></HEAD>
<BODY>
<%
UserName="Bill Gates"
%>
<FORM METHOD="Post" Action="/nextpage.asp">
<INPUT NAME="UserName" TYPE="HIDDEN" VALUE="<%=UserName%>">
<INPUT TYPE="SUBMIT" VALUE="Next Page">
</FORM>
</BODY>
</HTML>
```

This page includes an HTML form. The form has a hidden field named UserName that contains the value of the UserName variable. The form also contains one button. When the button is clicked, the page nextpage.asp is loaded, and the data in the hidden form field is passed to the new page.

You can continue to pass data from page to page in this way indefinitely. On each page, you must use the Form collection of the Request object to retrieve the data in the hidden field. Next, you must create a new hidden field so the data can be passed to a new page again. Here's an example:

```
<HTML>
<HEAD><TITLE> Next Page </TITLE></HEAD>
<BODY>
<%
UserName=Request.Form("Username")
%>
<FORM METHOD="Post" Action="/nextpage.asp">
<INPUT NAME="UserName" TYPE="HIDDEN" VALUE="<%=UserName%>">
<INPUT TYPE="SUBMIT" VALUE="Next Page">
</FORM>
</BODY>
</HTML>
```

Combining Methods

Neither of these two methods of retaining state is particularly elegant. However, these are the only alternative methods of retaining state without using session variables and cookies. By using query strings and hidden form fields, you can preserve compatibility with all browsers.

If you need to track a user through every page on your Web site, you must include either a query string or a hidden form field on every page in your Web site. As soon as a user clicks a naked hyperlink—a hyperlink without a query string—you can no longer track the user.

> **CAUTION**
>
> One significant disadvantage of using either query strings or hidden form fields to retain state is that both methods require information to be passed back and forth between the server and browser. This means that you should be cautious about passing private information such as passwords.

You can combine these two methods of retaining state. For example, on some pages you can use a query string to pass the name of the user, and on other pages you can use a hidden form field. If you do this, you don't need to check both the `QueryString` and `Form` collection on every page. If you call the `Request` method without specifying the collection, both collections are automatically checked. Look at this example:

```
<HTML>
<HEAD><TITLE> Next Page </TITLE></HEAD>
<BODY>
<%
UserName=Request("UserName")
%>
<FORM METHOD="Post" Action="/nextpage.asp">
<INPUT NAME="UserName" TYPE="HIDDEN" VALUE="<%=UserName%>">
<INPUT TYPE="SUBMIT" VALUE="Next Page">
</FORM>
<A HREF="/nextpage.asp?<%=Server.URLEncode(UserName)%>">Click Here</A>
</BODY>
</HTML>
```

In this example, the variable `UserName` is assigned the name of the user regardless of whether the name was passed by a hidden form field or a query string. The call to `Request("UserName")` retrieves the value of `UserName` from either the `Form` or the `QueryString` collection.

Summary

In this chapter, you learned how to work with sessions. You learned how to use the `Session` object to create session variables that can be used to store information over multiple Web pages. You learned how to create scripts that execute when a session starts and ends. You also learned about a close relative of sessions—how to create and read cookies. Finally, some alternative methods for retaining state without cookies were discussed.

Interacting with the Client: ASP and Internet Explorer

by Aaron Bertrand

IN THIS CHAPTER

CHAPTER 6

A very challenging part of building Web applications is making the server and client interact. Traditionally, ASP does its processing on the server side, and then the HTML and client-side script take over. Thanks to many new features in Internet Explorer 4.0, there are several methods by which you can diminish the line between server and client, in order to enhance your applications. In this chapter, you will learn how to implement some of these methods.

There are three sections in this chapter. The first section provides you with information on using ASP to create Dynamic HTML (DHTML). You will learn how to present multiple blocks of information from a database or text file, one block at a time, without making multiple trips to the server. You will also see an example of changing the items in one list box, based on the selection from a previous list box.

The second part of this chapter deals with client-side form validation using VBScript and JavaScript. You will discover how to prevent server-side errors by validating user-entered data on the client side, before a form is submitted. The examples will cover validating data and preventing serious errors. You will also see how to implement an INCLUDE file to reuse common validation functions.

The final component in this chapter revolves around the combination of ASP and Extensible Markup Language (XML). You will learn how to create XML documents on-the-fly from server-side data, such as a database or text file, and then use the XML file to define the structure and content of your Web pages.

Using Active Server Pages with Dynamic HTML

This section delves into methods and reasons for combining Active Server Pages with client-side technologies like Dynamic HTML. Because of Netscape's continued lack of support for certain Dynamic HTML methods, please note that the examples here will work only in Internet Explorer 4.0 and above.

Dynamic Display

When developing with ASP, you will probably encounter situations in which you want to publish data from a database. Typically, a selection of records is returned to the client in one of two formats: first, in a table, where each row represents a record; or second, in a series of pages that the user can navigate through. The problem with the first format is that, depending on the size of the result set, the user may suffer from information overload. With the second method, the user must wait as your application re-queries the database on each successive page.

DHTML can make it very easy to display all this data, one record at a time, without making continuous trips to your database. Like many other bridges between the front end and back end, this reduces traffic on your Web server and also gives the user instantaneous response times.

> **NOTE**
>
> Included on the CD-ROM, in the Chapter06 folder, is a sample Access database called Chapter6.mdb. The Address table contains several fictitious addresses, phone numbers, and email addresses of people whose names are probably familiar. You will be using this database in various examples throughout this chapter; the path to the database is contained in the file called db.inc. When you move this database to your machine for testing, please be sure to edit the path in db.inc to reflect the new location of Chapter6.mdb. Alternatively, you can use a File or System DSN, which are explained in more detail in Chapter 12, "Working with Connections and Data Sources." Here are the contents of db.inc:
>
> ```
> <%
> ' change this path accordingly
> db="drive:\path\Chapter6.mdb"
>
> connStr = "DBQ=" & db & ";Driver={Microsoft"
> connStr = connStr & " Access Driver (*.mdb)}"
> set conn = server.createobject("adodb.connection")
> conn.open connStr
> %>
> ```

In the first example, you will pull several records from the Address table, then use DHTML to enable the user to cycle through them, without re-querying the database. To do this, you must extract all the records, loop through them one by one, and build corresponding table and script code that will make the DHTML possible. Listing 6.1 can be found in the script file ch6_1.asp in the CD's Chapter06 folder.

LISTING 6.1   EXAMPLE OF DATABASE-DRIVEN DHTML

```
<html>
<head>
<%
sel=""
tables=""
scripts=""
datum=""
%>
```

continues

LISTING 6.1   CONTINUED

```
<!--#include file="db.inc"-->

<%
sql = "select fname,lname,address,city,phone,email"
sql = sql & " from Address order by lname"
set rs = conn.execute(sql)
if not rs.eof then
    cn = 1
    do while not rs.eof
    ' extract each field into local vars
        fn = rs("fname")
        ln = rs("lname")
        ad = rs("address")
        ct = rs("city")
        ph = rs("phone")
        em = rs("email")
    ' build the name, address and phone string
        datum = "<b><a href=""mailto:" & em & """>"
        datum = datum & ln & "</b>, " & fn
        datum = datum & "</a><br>" & ad & "<br>"
        datum = datum & ct & "<br>Phone: " & ph
    ' build the select list
        sel = sel & "<option value=""div" & cn & """>" & fn
        sel = sel & " " & ln & chr(10)
    ' set display = none for all but the first record
        if cn > 1 then
            dis = " style=""display:none"""
        end if
    ' build the <div> code
        tables = tables & "<div id=div" & cn & dis & ">"
        tables = tables & datum & "</div>" & chr(10)
    ' build the script code that will make all divs invisible
        scripts = scripts & "    document.all(""div" & cn & """)"
        scripts = scripts & ".style.display=""none""" & chr(10)
    ' increase the counter
        cn = cn + 1
        rs.movenext
    loop
    rs.close
    set rs = nothing
    conn.close
    set conn = nothing
%>

<script language="vbscript">
sub show(el)
    ' make all elements invisible
<%=scripts%>
    ' make the current selection visible
```

```
        document.all(el).style.display=""
end sub
</script>

<%
    response.write("</head><body bgcolor=#ffffff><center>")
    response.write("<table border=1>")
    response.write(chr(10) & "<tr valign=top><td width=205>")
    response.write(chr(10) & "Choose:<p><select ")
    response.write("onChange=""show(sel1.value)""")
    response.write(" class=i1 id=sel1>" & chr(10) & sel)
    response.write("</select></td><td width=285>" & chr(10))
    response.write(tables & "</td></tr></table>")
    response.write("</center>")
else
    response.write("</head><body>No records.")
end if
%>
</body></html>
```

This produces a two-celled table with a select box and a display cell (see Figure 6.1). The DHTML involved uses a simple trick of disabling the display of all elements, then enabling it for the item chosen from the select list. You do this so that the only address visible at any one time is the one most recently selected. Each address is made invisible through the document.all collection; then the chosen item is made visible by reference. If you view the source of the output, you will see the code from Listing 6.2.

LISTING 6.2   SAMPLE OUTPUT FROM LISTING 6.1

```
<html>
<head>

<title>Create DHTML with ASP</title>

<script language="vbscript">
sub show(el)
    ' make all elements invisible
    document.all("div1").style.display="none"
    document.all("div2").style.display="none"
    document.all("div3").style.display="none"
    document.all("div4").style.display="none"

    ' make the current selection visible
    document.all(el).style.display=""
end sub
</script>
```

continues

LISTING 6.2   CONTINUED

```
</head><body bgcolor=#ffffff><center><table border=1>
<tr valign=top><td width=205>
Choose:<p><select onChange="javascript:show(sel1.value)"
 class=i1 id=sel1>
<option value="div1">Aaron Bertrand
<option value="div2">Charlie Chaplin
<option value="div3">Bill Gates
<option value="div4">Jimi Hendrix
</select></td><td width=285>

<div id=div1><b><a
 href="mailto:abertrand@9thsquare.com">Bertrand</b>,
 Aaron</a><br>1 Test St.<br>Newport<br>Phone:
 (213) 555-5555</div>

<div id=div2 style="display:none"><b><a
 href="mailto:cchaplin@warner.com">Chaplin</b>,
 Charlie</a><br>44 Apple Lane<br>Detroit<br>Phone:
 (905) 440-4400</div>

<div id=div3 style="display:none"><b><a
 href="mailto:billg@microsoft.com">Gates</b>,
 Bill</a><br>1 Gates Drive<br>Redmond<br>Phone:
 (555) 555-5555</div>

<div id=div4 style="display:none"><b><a
href="mailto:jimi@music.net">Hendrix</b>,
 Jimi</a><br>100 E Street<br>Los Angeles<br>Phone:
 (702) 333-9999</div>

</td></tr></table></center>
</body></html>
```

The next example of DHTML will make your coworkers label you "genius" because it demonstrates a technique that is rarely applied effectively. You will learn how to dynamically update one select list based on the selection made in a different select list.

FIGURE 6.1

Changing the displayed address with DHTML.

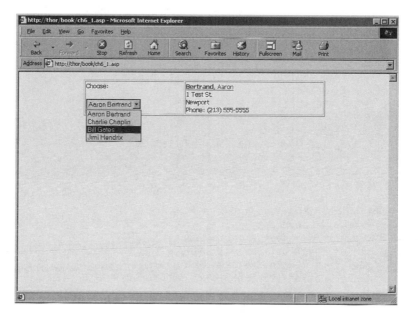

Dynamic Select Lists

In this example, you will learn how to use dynamically generated select lists. First, start with the client-side code required to perform this action. (This code is found in the file ch6_2.htm.) Listing 6.3 shows the code that enables you to select a music category and, when you do so, presents you with a group of artists to choose from.

LISTING 6.3   DYNAMICALLY GENERATED SELECT LISTS

```
<html>
<script language="javascript">
function fixSelect(val) {
    if (!pause) {
        // update select
        document.write("<option>"+val);
    } else {
        // repopulate
        var gr = document.artists.groups;
        var valOption = new Option(val);
        var valLen = gr.length;
        gr.options[valLen] = valOption;
    }
}
```

continues

LISTING 6.3   CONTINUED

```javascript
function InitOptions() {
    if (style1=="Alternative") {
        // add Alternative options to listbox
        fixSelect("Green Day");
        fixSelect("Korn");
    }
    if (style1=="Country") {
        // add Country options to listbox
        fixSelect("Conway Twitty");
        fixSelect("Kenny Rogers");
    }
}
function reInitOptions() {
    var val = document.styles.style;
    var gr = document.artists.groups;
    style1 = val.options[val.selectedIndex].text;
    for (i=gr.length;i>0;i--) {
        gr.options[0] = null;
    }
    pause = true;
    InitOptions();
    gr.options[0].selected = true;
    return false;
}
function go() {
    var gr = document.artists.groups;
    var g = gr.options[gr.selectedIndex].text;
    alert('You chose '+g+'!');
}
</script>

<body bgcolor=#ffffff>

<b>Select a style:</b>
<form name="styles">
<select name=style onChange="reInitOptions()"
 style="width:200">
<option>Alternative
<option>Country
</select>
</form>

<b>Select an artist:</b>
<form name='artists'>

<script language="javascript">
var pause = false;
var style1 = document.styles.style.options[0].text;
document.write("<select name='groups' style='width:200'>");
```

```
InitOptions();
document.write("<\/select>");
</script>
<p>
<button width=100 style='cursor:hand'
 onClick="go()">Choose</button>
</form>
</body></html>
```

 As you can see, the function InitOptions() writes the content of the second select list as the page is loaded, and the function reInitOptions() writes them dynamically when the first select list is changed. Now to make this page server-driven, only a few changes have to be made. Let's suppose that the information on categories and artists is found in the same Chapter6.mdb database used in the first example; this time, it is found in a table called Music. You will need to loop through the records in the Music table to extract two types of information:

- The distinct categories (in the field Style)

- The distinct artists relevant to each of those categories (in the field Artist)

 The database code that will make this possible can be seen in the new source file, as displayed in Listing 6.4. As you step through the code, you will see the basic structure of Listing 6.3, with the added code for pulling the options and conditional statement from a database.

LISTING 6.4 EXTRACTING CATEGORIES AND ARTISTS

```
<html>
<!--#include file="db.inc"-->
<script language="javascript">

function fixSelect(val) {
    if (!pause) {
        document.write("<option>"+val);
    } else {
        var gr = document.artists.groups;
        var valOption = new Option(val);
        var valLen = gr.length;
        gr.options[valLen] = valOption;
    }
}
function InitOptions() {
<%
s1 = "select distinct style from Music order by style"
set r1 = conn.execute(s1)
if not r1.eof then
```

continues

LISTING 6.4 CONTINUED

```
    do while not r1.eof
        ' Loop through distinct styles
        st = r1("style")
        sels = sels & chr(10) & "<option>" & st
        ' Prepare re-population function per style:
%>
        if (style1=="<%=st%>") {
<%
        s2 = "select artist from Music where style='"
        s2 = s2 & st & "' order by artist"
        set r2 = conn.execute(s2)
        if not r2.eof then
            do while not r2.eof
                ' Loop through artists for this style
                rt = r2("artist")
%>
                fixSelect("<%=rt%>");
<%
                r2.movenext
            loop
        end if
%>
}
<%
        r1.movenext
    loop
end if
%>
}
function reInitOptions() {
    var val = document.styles.style;
    var gr = document.artists.groups;
    style1 = val.options[val.selectedIndex].text;
    for (i=gr.length;i>0;i--) {
        gr.options[0] = null;
    }
    pause = true;
    InitOptions();
    gr.options[0].selected = true;
    return false;
}
function go() {
    var gr = document.artists.groups;
    var g = gr.options[gr.selectedIndex].text;
    alert('You chose '+g+'!');
}
</script>
```

```
<body bgcolor=#ffffff>

<b>Select a style:</b>
<form name="styles">
<select name=style onChange="reInitOptions()"
 style="width:200">

<%=sels%>
</select>
</form>

<b>Select an artist:</b>
<form name='artists'>

<script language="javascript">
var pause = false;
var style1 = document.styles.style.options[0].text;
document.write("<select name='groups' style='width:200'>");
InitOptions();
document.write("<\/select>");
</script>

<p>
<button width=100 style='cursor:hand'
 onClick="go()">Choose</button>
</form>
<%
r1.close
set r1 = nothing
r2.close
set r2 = nothing
conn.close
set conn=nothing
%>
</body></html>
```

 The preceding ASP script can be found in the file ch6_2.asp, also in the Chapter06 folder on the CD-ROM. Notice that only a few changes have been made to this HTML file. The most notable change is that the function InitOptions() has been built with a loop through the database. The only other significant change is that the initial select list has been built from a variable, sels, which represents each option corresponding to a unique category found in the Music table.

Client-Side Form Validation

A decision you'll have to make as an ASP developer is where to validate form data. There are certainly advantages to validating data on the server; for example, you can be confident that your data is validated regardless of the browser being used by the client. However, when you know that your user is using a newer browser like IE 4.0, you can perform this validation on the client. Among the reasons for performing validation on the client are that this will reduce the workload on the server and reduce wait time for the client if a correction needs to be made.

Validating Data Formats on the Client

One of the biggest headaches ASP developers have to deal with is the dreaded database error. Most data format-dependent errors—such as trying to insert a string into a numeric field—can be prevented. In this section, you will learn many techniques that will help you to predict and handle almost every user-driven database error conceivable.

TIP

 Some of the validation routines introduced in this section are quite verbose. In most cases, it is both easier and more efficient to include a separate file that can be called from any ASP script, as opposed to reproducing the entire file in every ASP script that requires it. The validation file validate.vbs, found in the Chapter06 folder on the CD-ROM, can be included in two ways:

As an ASP include:

```
<script language="vbscript">
<!--#include file="validate.vbs"-->
</script>
```

Or as a linked VBScript file:

```
<script language="vbscript" src="validate.vbs">
</script>
```

The performance difference between these two options is negligible. However, you might want to exercise the latter option, if it is important to make your logic a bit more secure. (An ambitious scripter will need to take one more step to view the source code.)

The following validation routines will aid in verifying several data types, including dates, credit card numbers, credit card expiration dates, and even email and URL formats. You will be introduced to each routine individually. Then you will see how you can use any combination of them for a multifield form.

isLength()

This function ensures that the data entered in that field is not empty. It does this by obtaining the length of the field's value with VBScript's built-in len() function. If a length of 0 is returned, the user is alerted that the field must have a value. This function is the first listed because it is used in several other functions, where an empty string could cause unexpected errors.

```
function isLength(val)
    if len(val.value)>0 then
        isLength = true
    else
        msgbox "This value can't be empty."
        val.select
        isLength = false
    end if
end function
```

isNumber()

The isNumber() function checks to see whether that field's value is numeric, using VBScript's isNumeric() function. If the data is anything but numeric, the user is informed with a MsgBox.

```
function isNumber(val)
    if isNumeric(val.value) then
        isNumber = true
    else
        msgbox "This value must be numeric."
        val.select
        isNumber = false
    end if
end function
```

isCCnumber()

This function uses a checksum algorithm to verify that the field's data contains a possible credit card number (although certain oddball combinations will falsely pass the test, such as 0000000000000000). Please be advised that this function does not establish whether the card is valid, nor does it determine whether it is actually registered to the person filling out the form. This function was adapted from VB Code by John Anderson (the original function can be found at http://www.planet-source-code.com/vb/scripts/ShowCode.asp?txtCodeId=902).

```
function isCCnumber(val)
    if isLength(val) then
        ccnumber = false
        val.value = trim(replace(val.value," ",""))
        if isNumeric(val.value) then
            ccnum = val.value
            for i = len(ccnum) to 2 step -2
                total = total + cint(mid(ccnum,i,1))
                tmp = cstr((mid(ccnum,i-1,1))*2)
                total = total + cint(left(tmp, 1))
                if len(tmp)>1 then
                    total = total + cint(right(tmp,1))
                end if
            next
            if len(ccnum) mod 2 = 1 then
                total = total + cint(left(ccnum,1))
            end if
            if total mod 10 = 0 then
                ccnumber = true
            end if
        end if
        if ccnumber then
            isCCnumber = true
        else
            msgbox "Please use a valid credit card number."
            val.select
            isCCnumber = false
        end if
    end if
end function
```

You can see this code in action in Figure 6.2.

FIGURE 6.2

*Entering an
invalid credit card
number.*

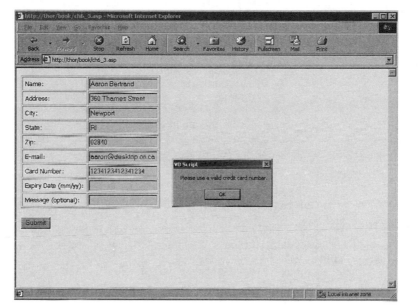

isCCdate()

The isCCdate() function ensures that the field's data is a valid expiration date, both in terms of date format (mm/yy) and in relation to the current month. This routine, the longest of all the validation functions, solves two difficult issues surrounding credit card dates. One is the need to see whether the year on the credit card is the same as the current year; if so, you must check that it is at least this month or later (otherwise the card has already expired). The other issue is to effectively eliminate years that are too far in the future; this was a much more complex task in years prior to 1999 because the year 2000 caused multiple problems. Thankfully, it is already 1999, so any year after the current year can simply be subtracted from the cutoff date (for example, 2003–2000 = 3). In this example, you use four years out, which is typically the longest period of time any credit card is valid. You can change this time period in the 17th line of this routine (if yr<currYear+4 then).

```
function isCCdate(val)
    if isLength(val) then
        ccdate = false
        if len(val.value)>=3 and len(val.value)<=5 then
            if instr(val.value,"/")>0 then
                tCC = split(val.value,"/")
                if isNumeric(tCC(0)) and isNumeric(tCC(1)) then
                    mn = cint(tCC(0))
```

```
            yr = cint(tCC(1))
             currYear = cint(right(year(date()),2))
             if mn>0 and mn<13 then
                 if yr = currYear then
                     if mn >= month(date()) then
                         ccdate = true
                     end if
                 else
                     if yr<currYear+4 then
                         ccdate = true
                     end if
                 end if
             end if
         end if
     end if
 end if
 if ccdate then
     isCCdate = true
 else
     msgbox "Please enter a valid expiry date."
     val.select
     isCCdate = false
 end if
     end if
 end function
```

isProperdate()

This routine checks that the value entered is a valid date, using VBScript's native
`isDate()` function. Note that it is not bound to regional settings, so dates like 12/25/98,
25/12/98, and even February 2, 2000 will all be accepted. If the date entered is not in an
acceptable date format, the user is prompted to try again.

```
function isProperdate(val)
    if isDate(trim(val.value)) then
        isProperdate = true
    else
        msgbox "Please enter a valid date."
        val.select
        isProperdate = false
    end if
end function
```

isPositive()

The `isPositive()` function compares the field's value with zero. If it is greater than
zero, `isPositive()` returns `true`, otherwise the user is alerted to enter a positive number.
This test is conducted, of course, after the value is confirmed to be a number.

```
function isPositive(val)
    if isNumber(val) then
        if val.value>=0 then
            isPositive = true
        else
            msgbox "Please enter a positive number."
            val.select
            isPositive = false
        end if
    end if
end function
```

isNegative()

Like isPositive(), the isNegative() routine first verifies that the value it is passed is numeric. If it is, it is compared to zero. If it is not a negative number, the user is prompted.

```
function isNegative(val)
    if isNumber(val) then
        if val.value<0 then
            isNegative = true
        else
            msgbox "Please enter a negative number."
            val.select
            isNegative = false
        end if
    end if
end function
```

isAlpha()

The isAlpha() routine tests whether a field's value is alphanumeric; for example, that it does not contain characters such as quotes and apostrophes (both of which can wreak havoc on ASP-created SQL statements). This function is designed to be quite customizable because your definition of alphanumeric might overlap the next person's. For example, you might want to allow spaces and the @ symbol, whereas the next person doesn't want those, but chooses to allow braces. The third line shows the list of characters which, by default, are not allowed; if there are any characters there that you want to allow, remove them from the isNot variable. Note that the quote symbol (") is not listed within the third line, but on the fifth line. It is tested with the built-in instr() function and the quote's ASCII equivalent, chr(34). If you want to allow quotes, simply comment out lines five through seven.

```
function isAlpha(val)
    if isLength(val) then
        isNot=" `~!@#$%^&*()-_=+[{]}\|;:'',<.> /?"
        invalid = false
```

```
        if instr(val.value,chr(34))>0 then
            invalid=true
        else
            for i = 1 to len(val.value)
                for x = 1 to len(isNot)
                    if mid(val.value,i,1)=mid(isNot,x,1) then
                        invalid = true
                    end if
                next
            next
        end if
        if not invalid then
            isAlpha = true
        else
            msgbox "Please use alphanumeric characters."
            val.select
            isAlpha = false
        end if
    end if
end function
```

isEmail()

The name of the isEmail() function is slightly misleading. It does not actually determine that an email address is valid; it only ensures that it contains both an @ symbol and
a period, and that it has at least six characters. The only reliable way of ensuring that the
users are entering their own valid email addresses is to email them a confirmation code
and ask for it   a process which can't be accomplished with client-side VBScript, and
which is outside the realm of this discussion.

```
function isEmail(val)
    if isLength(val) then
        e = val.value
        if instr(e,"@")>0 and instr(e,".")>0 and len(e)>5 then
            isEmail = true
        else
            msgbox "Please enter a proper email address."
            val.select
            isEmail = false
        end if
    end if
end function
```

isZip()

The isZip() routine checks to see that the entered ZIP code is in a valid format (for example, 11111 or 11111-1111). Like the isEmail() function, it can't actually determine that the ZIP code entered is, in fact, a valid one; It can only determine that it is in the proper format. Similar to possible in-depth solutions for verifying an email address, there are databases of zip codes available (from companies like UPS) that will enable you to map ZIP ranges with states or even counties.

```
function isZip(val)
    isZip = false
    tVal = trim(val.value)
    if len(tVal)=5 then
        if isNumeric(tVal) then
            isZip = true
        end if
    elseif len(tVal)=10 then
        l5 = left(tVal,5)
        r4 = right(tVal,4)
        m1 = mid(tVal,6,1)
        if isNumeric(l5) and isNumeric(r4) and m1="-" then
            isZip = true
        end if
    end if
    if not isZip then
        msgbox "Please enter a valid Zip code."
        val.select
    end if
end function
```

isPath()

This routine is useful when your users are asked to enter the local path to a file or folder. It ensures that the path entered contains the typical drive/slash notation (:\) and uses a similar isNot variable to eliminate certain non-alphanumeric characters. Characters that are allowed are those typically found in local paths, such as underscores, hyphens, and periods. Like the isAlpha() routine, this can be customized as you see fit. You can also dictate a particular drive letter by editing the :\ in the fourth line to be c:\ or any other drive letter.

```
function isPath(val)
    if isLength(val) then
        path = false
        if instr(val.value,":\")>0 then
            isNot=" `~!@#$%^&*()=+[{]}|;'',<> /?"
            path = true
            if instr(val.value,chr(34))>0 then
                path = false
```

```
        else
            for i = 1 to len(val.value)
              for x = 1 to len(isNot)
                if mid(val.value,i,1)=mid(isNot,x,1) then
                     path = false
                end if
              next
            next
          end if
      end if
      if path then
          isPath = true
      else
          msgbox "Please enter a valid local path."
          val.select
          isPath = false
      end if
    end if
end function
```

isURL()

This function is used to verify that the value entered by the user is in fact a URL. It demands the colon/slash/slash notation we're all familiar with (which can be extended to http:// or ftp:// if necessary, by editing the fourth line). The characters allowed include question mark, equals sign, hash mark, underscore, and period. Like the other routines that use an isNot string, you can dictate which characters are permissible by editing the fifth line of the isURL() function.

```
function isURL(val)
    if isLength(val) then
        url = false
        if instr(val.value,"://")>0 then
            isNot=" `!@$^*()[{]}\¦;'',<> "
            url = true
            if instr(val.value,chr(34))>0 then
                url = false
            else
                for i = 1 to len(val.value)
                  for x = 1 to len(isNot)
                    if mid(val.value,i,1)=mid(isNot,x,1) then
                         url = false
                    end if
                  next
                next
            end if
        end if
        if url then
            isURL = true
```

```
        else
            msgbox "Please enter a valid URL."
            val.select
            isURL = false
        end if
    end if
end function
```

Putting It All Together

In the file ch6_3.asp, you will see how you can use any combination of these validation routines to step through a multifield form with little difficulty. Specifically, this example tests eight fields, using the following functions:

```
isLength()
isZip()
isEmail()
isCCnumber()
isCCdate()
```

Notice that the form on that page actually has nine fields; the final field is optional, demonstrating how you can leave fields not validated when they can be empty or do not have to conform to any specific data format. Also, notice that when all the data is accepted as valid, a MsgBox is displayed instead of actually submitting the form. Listing 6.5 shows the source of ch6_3.asp.

LISTING 6.5   USING GENERIC VALIDATION ROUTINES

```
<html>
<head>
<script language=vbscript>
<!--#include file="validate.vbs" -->
</script>
</head>

<body bgcolor=#ffffff>
<form name="f">
<table border=1>
    <tr><td> Name: </td>
        <td><input name="aname" type="text"></td></tr>
    <tr><td> Address: </td>
        <td><input name="address" type="text"></td></tr>
    <tr><td> City: </td>
        <td><input name="city" type="text"></td></tr>
    <tr><td> State: </td>
        <td><input name="state" type="text"></td></tr>
    <tr><td> Zip: </td>
        <td><input name="zip" type="text"></td></tr>
```

continues

LISTING 6.5   CONTINUED

```
    <tr><td> E-mail: </td>
        <td><input name="email" type="text"></td></tr>
    <tr><td> Card Number: </td>
        <td><input name="ccnum" type="text"></td></tr>
    <tr><td> Expiry Date (mm/yy): </td>
        <td><input name="ccdate" type="text"></td></tr>
    <tr><td> Message (optional): </td>
        <td><input name="msg" type="text"></td></tr>
</table>
<p>
<input type=button onClick='check()'
 value="Submit">
 </form>
</body>
</html>

<script language=vbscript>
function check()
    if not isLength(document.f.aname) then
        exit function
    elseif not isLength(document.f.address) then
        exit function
    elseif not isLength(document.f.city) then
        exit function
    elseif not isLength(document.f.state) then
        exit function
    elseif not isZip(document.f.zip) then
        exit function
    elseif not isEmail(document.f.email) then
        exit function
    elseif not isCCnumber(document.f.ccnum) then
        exit function
    elseif not isCCdate(document.f.ccdate) then
        exit function
    end if
    msgbox "Data is good; submit the form."
    'document.f.submit()
end function
</script>
```

Of course, there are other data formats you might want to build functions for. You might want to test phone numbers, postal codes, or state abbreviations, all of which can be easily built using validate.vbs as a base.

Validating Server-Side Data on the Client

This section shows you how to prevent annoying database or other server-side errors, by intercepting them before the form is even submitted. This specific example, found in the file ch6_4.asp, prevents a duplicate entry from being inserted into an Access database with a "no duplicates allowed" indexed field. In this case, you will use Chapter6.mdb again, and the Music table. The indexed field is artist, so you will prevent an artist from being inserted a second time. Without this validation, entering a duplicate artist would result in this nasty error:

```
[Microsoft][ODBC Microsoft Access 97 Driver] The changes you
 requested to the table were not successful because they would
 create duplicate values in the index, primary key, or
 relationship. Change the data in the field or fields that
 contain duplicate data, remove the index, or redefine the index
 to permit duplicate entries and try again.
```

To avoid this error, you will pull all the possible conflicting values into a client-side validation routine at runtime. This is accomplished by looping through the Recordset and building an if/then routine for each unique record. At the small expense of a slightly longer page load time, the user will be spared an ODBC error and instead will be informed immediately, before submitting the form, that he is attempting to insert a record that already exists.

Listing 6.6 shows how this is done.

LISTING 6.6 PREVENTING ODBC ERRORS WITH CLIENT-SIDE VALIDATION

```
<html>
<head>
<!--#include file="db.inc"-->
<%
sql = "select artist from music"
set rs = conn.execute(sql)
%>
<script language="javascript">
<!--
function check(frm) {
art = frm.art.value.toLowerCase();
art = art.replace("'","\'");
   if (art=='') {
    alert('Please enter a name.');
    frm.art.select();
    return false;
   }
<%
if not rs.eof then
```

continues

LISTING 6.6   CONTINUED

```
  do while not rs.eof
    sart = replace(lcase(rs("artist")),"'","\'")
    response.write("   if (art=='" & sart & "') {" & chr(10))
    response.write("     alert('""" & sart & """ exists.\n")
    response.write("Please enter a different name.');")
    response.write(chr(10) & "     frm.art.select();")
    response.write(chr(10) & "     return false;")
    response.write(chr(10) & "   }" & chr(10))
    rs.movenext
  loop
end if
rs.close
et rs = nothing
conn.close
set conn = nothing
%>
    alert('submit()');
    // frm.submit();
}
//-->
</script>
</head>

<body bgcolor=#ffffff>
<form name="f1" onSubmit="check(document.f1);return false">
Enter an artist: <input type="text" name="art"><p>
<input type=submit value="Check name >> ">
</form>
</body>
</html>
```

Notice that on both the server side and the client side, you convert the value of the artist to lowercase. This prevents case ambiguity; if someone enters all uppercase or a mixture of upper and lower, they are still considered equal because they are converted to lowercase before they are compared (for example: Unconverted, Korn would be evaluated as NOT EQUAL TO KORN). Another thing you do is precede any single quote character (') with an escape sequence (\'), so that a quote in a name like Stompin' Tom is not wrongly interpreted by the client-side script as an end of string marker (or, if you use VBScript on the client, as a comment delimiter). Listing 6.7 is a portion of the resulting script (also see Figure 6.3).

LISTING 6.7   SAMPLE RESULT FROM LISTING 6.6

```html
<html>
<head>
<script language="javascript">
<!--
function check(frm) {
art = frm.art.value.toLowerCase();
art = art.replace("'","\'");
   if (art=='korn') {
    alert('"korn" exists.\nPlease enter a different name.');
    frm.art.select();
    return false;
   }
   if (art=='tiffany') {
    alert('"tiffany" exists.\nPlease enter a different name.');
    frm.art.select();
    return false;
   }
   if (art=='') {
    alert('Please enter a name.');
    frm.art.select();
    return false;
   }
   alert('submit()');
   // frm.submit();
}
//-->
</script>
</head>
<body bgcolor=#ffffff>
<form name="f1">
Enter an artist: <input type="text" name="art"><p>
<input type=button onClick="check(document.f1);"
 value="Check name >> ">
</form>
</body>
</html>
```

The applications for validation are endless; any time you are allowing a user to enter data, there exists the potential for errors, and hence, the need for validation. Although this validation can occur on the client or on the server, it is often beneficial to run it on the client—mainly to eliminate unnecessary server load and to keep client wait times at a minimum.

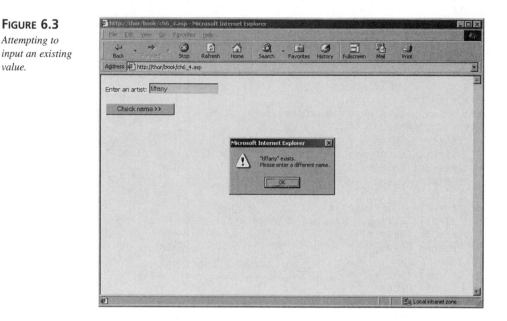

Active Server Pages and XML

You've heard of XML. If you've created a CDF channel for Internet Explorer 4.0, you've used XML. But until now, have you used it to do anything extraordinary? This section will show you how you can combine ASP and XML to create a dynamic, database-driven page from an XML file that is reusable in any other application.

 As a quick overview, here is the basic thought process for this example. You have a database table called Phonebook with a listing of phone numbers for fictitious employees (this table is, once again, found in Chapter6.mdb). This Phonebook table provides the data for the XML file, phonebook.xml, which is used in various applications throughout the office. When the ASP script you build is requested (meaning someone wanted to view the phone directory through a Web browser), it checks the timestamp of the Chapter6 database. If it has been updated since phonebook.xml was last modified, the ASP script loops through the phonebook Recordset and re-creates the XML document on-the-fly. If the database has not been updated since the XML document was last
modified, it skips to the next step: inserting the content of the XML file into the current document.

Well, that was a mouthful, wasn't it? Let's proceed with this example one step at a time. First, here is a relevant portion of the XML document you will be working with. Essentially, it is just a list of people, within their various departments, and their respective telephone extensions. For the purposes of this discussion, this XML document is well-formed, but does not conform to any defined document type definition (DTD).

```xml
<?xml version="1.0"?>
<PHONEBOOK>
 <DEPT VALUE="Accounting">
   <PERSON VALUE="Aaron, Hank">
     <EXT VALUE="4419"/>
   </PERSON>
   <PERSON VALUE="Bench, Johnny">
     <EXT VALUE="2639"/>
   </PERSON>
   <PERSON VALUE="Jackson, Bo">
     <EXT VALUE="4403"/>
   </PERSON>
 </DEPT>
</PHONEBOOK>
```

This is a fairly simple XML document that can define the data structure of this phone directory in a variety of applications. One such application is getting this data to display properly in a Web browser. As an ASP developer, you can probably envision immediately that you could use the File System component (discussed in detail in Chapter 8, "Working with the File System") to load the XML document's contents into a local variable, parse its contents, and build an HTML string from it. Thankfully, Internet Explorer 4.0 comes with an object called MSXML that makes this task much easier. Listing 6.8 demonstrates how to load the XML document into a Web page.

LISTING 6.8 LOADING AN XML INTO A WEB PAGE

```html
<html>
<body onLoad="xmlGet();" bgcolor=#ffffff>

<b>Simple company phonebook, generated from XML.</b>
<p id="xmlP"><b>Getting data from XML, please
 wait...</b></p>
</body>

<script language="javascript">
<!--
var xml; p = self.location.href;

function xmlGet() {

  xml = new ActiveXObject("msxml");
```

continues

LISTING 6.8   CONTINUED

```
// ASSUMING THE XML FILE IS IN THIS SAME FOLDER:

for (var s=p.length;p.charAt(s)!="/";s--);
var pPath = p.substring(0,s+1);
xml.url = pPath + "Phonebook.xml";

// OTHERWISE USE A DIRECT PATH:
//
// xml.url = "http://yourserver/folder/file.xml";
//

window.setTimeout("xmlDone();",200);

}

function xmlDone() {

  var xmlReady = xml.readyState;
  if (xmlReady==4) { xmlWrite(); }
  else { window.setTimeout("xmlDone();",200); }

}

function xmlWrite() {

  var tab = "<table border=1 bgcolor=#dedede width=350>";
  tab = tab + "<tr><th align=left> Name</th>";
  tab = tab + "<th align=left> Extension</th></tr>";
  var rt = xml.root;
  var depts = rt.children.item("DEPT");dl = depts.length;
  for (x=0;x<dl;x++) {
    var dept = depts.item(x);
    tab = tab + "<tr><th colspan=2 bgcolor=#ffff00>"
    tab = tab + dept.getAttribute("VALUE") + " Dept.";
    tab = tab + "</th></tr>";
    var names = dept.children.item("PERSON");pl = names.length;
    for (y=0;y<pl;y++) {
        var staff = names.item(y);
        tab = tab + "<tr><td> "+staff.getAttribute("VALUE");
        var ext = staff.children.item("EXT");
        tab = tab + "</td><td> "+ext.getAttribute("VALUE");
        tab = tab +"</td></tr>";
    }
  }
  tab = tab + "</table>";
  document.all("xmlP").innerHTML=tab;

}
//-->
</script>
</html>
```

Not exactly a cakewalk, but the preceding script gets the job done. It opens the file phonebook.xml, extracts the data, and places it into an HTML table. The XML file is retained so that it can still be used in any other applications. How can you make sure that the data inserted into the HTML stream is the most current? If the XML data comes from a database, whenever you access this file, you can use the File System component to compare the timestamp of that database to the timestamp of the XML file. If the database has been modified more recently than the XML file, chances are you should re-create the XML file from that new data.

> **TIP**
>
> Given that Phonebook is not the only table in the database, there might be times when the timestamp on the MDB file is newer because a different table has been updated. Although no harm is done in this situation (an identical XML file simply replaces the old one), you might find it inefficient to have the server re-create that file for nothing. If so, you could add a record to Phonebook that contains all other fields, plus a value in a new field called lastUpdate. You could add the variable now() to that record any time you insert, update, or delete records from Phonebook. Then, instead of comparing the MDB file date with the XML file date, you could compare the lastUpdate field with the XML file date.

Listing 6.9 shows the code for comparing file dates and re-creating the XML if necessary. This is a self-maintaining ASP page that always shows the most up-to-date data from the XML file (see Figure 6.4). You'll certainly want to change the path of the variable xmlPath to reflect the correct location of the XML file on your server.

LISTING 6.9 COMPARING FILE DATES AND RE-CREATING THE XML

```
<!--#include file="db.inc"-->
<%
' !NOTE! CHANGE THIS PATH ACCORDINGLY:
xmlPath = "drive:\path\phonebook.xml"

set fso = server.createobject("scripting.filesystemobject")

set XMLfile = fso.getFile(xmlPath)
lastXMLupdate = XMLfile.dateLastModified
set XMLfile = nothing
```

continues

LISTING 6.9 CONTINUED

```
set DBfile = fso.getFile(db)
lastDBupdate = DBfile.dateLastModified
set DBfile = nothing

if lastDBupdate > lastXMLupdate then
  set f = fso.createTextFile(xmlPath,true)
  f.writeline "<?xml version=""1.0""?>"
  f.writeline "<PHONEBOOK>"
  sql1 = "select distinct department from phonebook"
  sql1 = sql1 & " order by department"
  set rs1 = conn.execute(sql1)
  do while not rs1.eof
    dept = rs1("department")
    f.writeline " <DEPT VALUE=""" & dept & """>"
    sql2 = "select lastname,firstname,extension from "
    sql2 = sql2 & "phonebook where department='" & dept & "'"
    sql2 = sql2 & " order by lastname,firstname"
    set rs2 = conn.execute(sql2)
    do while not rs2.eof
      fullname = rs2("lastname") & ", " & rs2("firstname")
      f.writeline "  <PERSON VALUE=""" & fullname & """>"
      f.writeline "   <EXT VALUE=""" & rs2("extension") & """/>"
      f.writeline "  </PERSON>"
      rs2.movenext
    loop
    f.writeline " </DEPT>"
    rs1.movenext
  loop
  f.writeline "</PHONEBOOK>"
end if
conn.close
set conn = nothing
set f = nothing
set fso = nothing
%>
<html>
<body onLoad="xmlGet();" bgcolor=#ffffff>

<b>Simple company phonebook, generated from XML.</b>
<p id="xmlP"><b>Getting data from XML, please
 wait...</b></p>
</body>

<script language="javascript">
<!--
var xml; p = self.location.href;

function xmlGet() {

  xml = new ActiveXObject("msxml");
```

```
  // ASSUMING THE XML FILE IS IN THIS SAME FOLDER:

  for (var s=p.length;p.charAt(s)!="/";s--);
  var pPath = p.substring(0,s+1);
  xml.url = pPath + "Phonebook.xml";

  // OTHERWISE USE A DIRECT PATH:
  //
  // xml.url = "http://yourserver/folder/file.xml";
  //

  window.setTimeout("xmlDone();",200);

}

function xmlDone() {

  var xmlReady = xml.readyState;
  if (xmlReady==4) { xmlWrite(); }
  else { window.setTimeout("xmlDone();",200); }

}

function xmlWrite() {

  var tab = "<table border=1 bgcolor=#dedede width=350>";
  tab = tab + "<tr><th align=left> Name</th>";
  tab = tab + "<th align=left> Extension</th></tr>";
  var rt = xml.root;
  var depts = rt.children.item("DEPT");dl = depts.length;
  for (x=0;x<dl;x++) {
    var dept = depts.item(x);
    tab = tab + "<tr><th colspan=2 bgcolor=#ffff00>"
    tab = tab + dept.getAttribute("VALUE") + " Dept.";
    tab = tab + "</th></tr>";
    var names = dept.children.item("PERSON");pl = names.length;
    for (y=0;y<pl;y++) {
      var staff = names.item(y);
      tab = tab + "<tr><td> "+staff.getAttribute("VALUE");
      var ext = staff.children.item("EXT");
      tab = tab + "</td><td> "+ext.getAttribute("VALUE");
      tab = tab +"</td></tr>";
    }
  }
  tab = tab + "</table>";
  document.all("xmlP").innerHTML=tab;

}
//-->
</script>
</html>
```

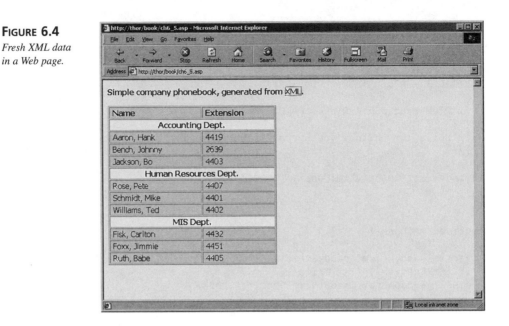

FIGURE 6.4

Fresh XML data in a Web page.

The preceding file moves through two distinct loops to create the XML data from the database and writes that to the file, line by line, reproducing the structure with updated data. Only then is the XML file accessed from JScript to insert the data into the HTML stream.

Summary

This chapter explored some advanced methods of using ASP to create great Web sites for Internet Explorer 4.0 and above. You learned how to create Dynamic HTML from ASP and server-side data. You also learned valuable form validation techniques, including how to predict and prevent database errors before they happen. And finally, you learned how to pull data from an XML file and insert it into an HTML stream, as well as to ensure that the XML file is synched with its counterpart data in an Access database.

At this point in the book, you have learned the fundamentals of ASP, the `Response` and `Request` objects, HTML forms, the `Application` object, the `Session` object, and advanced techniques for Internet Explorer. In the next part of this book, you will learn about several components and services that can be used with IIS to enhance your applications and Web sites.

Active Server Pages Installable Components

IN THIS PART

CHAPTER 7

Generating Dynamic Content from the Server

by Stephen Walther

IN THIS CHAPTER

In this chapter, you will learn how to work with three ActiveX components that can be used in your Active Server Pages to create dynamic content. In the first part, you will learn how to use the Browser Capabilities component to automatically detect the features of a visitor's Web browser. In the second part, you will learn how to use the Content Rotator component to randomly display different HTML content. Finally, in the last part, you will learn how to use the Content Linking component to easily add links between your Active Server Pages.

> **NOTE**
>
> The Browser Capabilities component and the Content Linking component are included with the Windows NT Option Pack. You can download the Content Rotator component from Microsoft at `http://www.microsoft.com/iis` or buy the component as part of the Internet Information Server Resource Kit.

Detecting Browser Properties

One explanation for the explosive growth of the Internet is the openness of its standards. HTML was designed to be platform- and browser-neutral. In theory, a Web page should appear the same way, regardless of the browser and the computer being used. In reality, however, this was never the case. From the beginning, Netscape introduced proprietary HTML tags. For example, Netscape Navigator version 1.0 could interpret an HTML tag for blinking text. To this day, the majority of non-Netscape browsers can't interpret this tag. Frames are another example of a Netscape extension to HTML.

As competition between Netscape and Microsoft heated up, the situation only worsened. Microsoft has introduced its fair share of proprietary tags. For example, the `<BGSOUND>` tag, which plays background sounds, and the `<MARQUEE>` tag, which displays a scrolling marquee, were originally introduced by Microsoft and could be interpreted only by the Microsoft browser.

HTML has been fragmented steadily into multiple standards. With each new version of the Microsoft and Netscape browsers, the gap between what might be called "Netscape HTML" and "Microsoft HTML" widens. Also, users persist in using obscure and trendy browsers such as Lynx and Opera. This creates a serious problem for the Web page designer.

On the one hand, there's pressure on the Web page designer to include the newest HTML tags. Never underestimate the "coolness factor." If you want users to return to your Web site, you need to push the limits of HTML. On the other hand, there's pressure on the Web page designer to make Web pages universally accessible. No one appreciates a Web page that they can't see. As soon as you use proprietary HTML tags, you risk losing whole populations of potential users.

Caught between these contradictory pressures, what should a good Web page designer do? Microsoft's answer is to use the Browser Capabilities component, as described in the following section.

Using the Browser Capabilities Component

You can use the Browser Capabilities component to display different Web pages, depending on the capabilities of a browser. For example, some browsers support frames; others don't. Using the Browser Capabilities component, you can detect whether a browser supports frames, and consequently, you will display a framed version of a page only when appropriate.

> **NOTE**
>
> Depending on the version of the browscap.ini file installed on your computer, the Browser Capabilities component may detect more browser features than listed here. For details, see the later section "How the Browser Capabilities Component Really Works."

> **NOTE**
>
> You can also detect certain browser and computer features such as screen resolution and color depth by using the ServerVariables collection. This works only with some versions of Microsoft Internet Explorer. For more information, see Chapter 2, "Active Server Pages and the HTTP Protocol."

By default, the Browser Capabilities component can detect the following features of a Web browser:

- browser—The type of the browser; for example, Internet Explorer or Netscape
- version—The complete version of the browser
- majorver—The major version of the browser (the number before the period)
- minorver—The minor version of the browser (the number after the period)
- frames—Indicates whether the browser supports frames
- tables—Indicates whether the browser supports tables
- cookies—Indicates whether the browser supports cookies
- backgroundsounds—Indicates whether the browser supports the <BGSOUND> tag

- vbscript—Indicates whether the browser supports client-side VBScript scripts

- javascript—Indicates whether the browser supports client-side JavaScript scripts

- javaapplets—Indicates whether the browser supports Java applets

- ActiveXControls—Indicates whether the browser supports client-side ActiveX controls

- beta—Indicates whether the browser is still a beta version

- platform—Indicates the operating system of the browser; for example, Windows 95, Windows NT, or Mac PowerPC

- Win16—Indicates whether the browser runs on Windows 3.x rather than Windows 95 or Windows NT

Unlike the objects discussed in previous chapters such as the Request and Response objects, the Browser Capabilities component is an installable component. This means that you must create an instance of the component with a particular scope before you can use it (for more information about creating components with different scope, see Chapter 1, "Building Active Server Pages").

 After an instance of the component has been created, you can simply append the name of the feature you want to detect to the name of the component instance. For example, the Active Server Page contained in Listing 7.1 displays several browser features (browserFeatures.asp on the CD):

LISTING 7.1   DISPLAYING BROWSER PROPERTIES

```
<HTML>
<HEAD><TITLE> Browser Capabilities Example </TITLE></HEAD>
<BODY>
<%
Set MyBrow=Server.CreateObject("MSWC.BrowserType")
%>

Your browser has the following properties:
<P>
<TABLE BORDER=1 CELLPADDING=10>
<TR>
<TD>Browser Type</TD><TD><%=MyBrow.Browser%></TD>
```

```
</TR>
<TR>
<TD>Cookies</TD><TD><%=MyBrow.Cookies%></TD>
</TR>
<TR>
<TD>Frames</TD><TD><%=MyBrow.Frames%></TD>
</TR>
<TR>
<TD>Platform</TD><TD><%=MyBrow.Platform%></TD>
</TR>
<TR>
<TD>VBScript</TD><TD><%=MyBrow.vbscript%></TD>
</TR>
</TABLE>
</BODY>
</HTML>
```

This script detects and displays several browser features. Different results will be displayed for different browsers. Figure 7.1 shows sample output using Microsoft Internet Explorer 4.0; Figure 7.2 shows sample output using Netscape Navigator 4.5. Finally, for perspective, Figure 7.3 shows sample output using Opera 3.51.

FIGURE 7.1

Sample Browser Capabilities component output using Internet Explorer 4.0.

Your browser has the following properties:

Browser Type	IE
Cookies	True
Frames	True
Platform	Unknown
VBScript	True

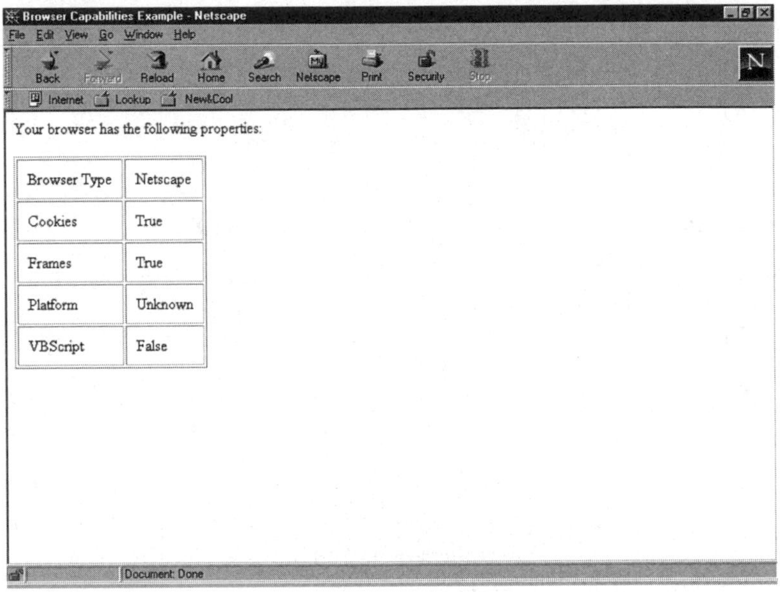

FIGURE 7.2

Sample Browser Capabilities component output using Netscape Navigator 4.5.

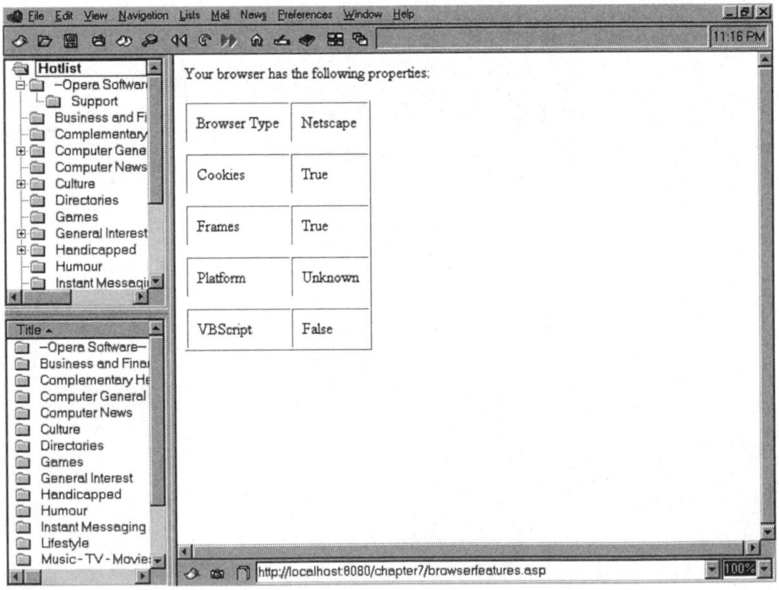

FIGURE 7.3

Sample Browser Capabilities component output using Opera 3.51.

How the Browser Capabilities Component Really Works

It's important to understand how the Browser Capabilities component really works so you can understand some of its serious limitations. The component detects the features of a browser by using an HTTP request header and by using a special text file that contains browser information.

Whenever a browser makes a request, it includes a USER AGENT header in the request. This header contains information about the type of browser being used and its version number. You can retrieve this header directly by using the ServerVariables collection of the Request object, like this:

```
<%=Request.ServerVariables("HTTP_USER_AGENT")%>
```

When used with Netscape Navigator 3.0 for Windows NT, for example, the value of the USER-AGENT header would be as follows:

```
Mozilla/3.0 (WinNT; I)
```

It's important to understand that this is the only information passed between the browser and the server. The Browser Capabilities component depends on the information in this header. The component doesn't detect any of the features of a browser directly.

The Browser Capabilities component retrieves the value of the USER-AGENT header and attempts to match it with a browser definition in a special file named browscap.ini. The browscap.ini file is located on the server, typically in the directory named Winnt/ system32/inetsrv. When you install Active Server Pages, this file is automatically installed as well.

The browscap.ini file is nothing more than a normal text file. It contains a list of browsers and their features. For example, this is the browser definition in the browscap.ini file for Netscape Navigator version 2.0:

```
[Netscape 2.0]
browser=Netscape
version=2.0
majorver=2
minorver=0
frames=TRUE
tables=TRUE
cookies=TRUE
backgroundsounds=FALSE
vbscript=FALSE
javascript=TRUE
javaapplets=TRUE
beta=False
Win16=False
```

7

GENERATING DYNAMIC CONTENT

The Browser Capabilities component uses this definition when it reports the features of Netscape Navigator 2.0. You can modify this text file directly. For example, contrary to reality, you could specify that Netscape Navigator 2.0 can use the <BGSOUND> tag by changing backgroundsounds from FALSE to TRUE.

There are several browser features that the Browser Capabilities component should detect but doesn't. For example, it would be extremely useful if you could use the component to detect whether a certain browser can use the Secure Sockets Layer or Cascading Style Sheets. Because this information isn't included in the browscap.ini file, however, you can't use the Browser Capabilities component to detect these features. However, you can add this information to the browscap.ini file yourself. For example, you can add the following two lines to the definition entry for Netscape Navigator 2.0:

```
SSL=TRUE
CSS=FALSE
```

After these two lines are added, the Browser Component will report these features for Netscape Navigator 2.0. Whenever the component detects that a browser is Netscape Navigator 2.0 (using the USER-AGENT header), the component will assume that the browser has these properties. For example, the following script returns TRUE when included in a page retrieved by Netscape Navigator 2.0:

```
<%=MyBrow.SSL %>
```

You might notice that many of the browser definitions in the browscap.ini file look like this:

```
[Mozilla/2.0 (Win95; U)]
parent=Netscape 2.0
platform=Win95
```

When a browser definition has a parent parameter, the definition will inherit all the features of its parent. The preceding definition inherits all the features of the Netscape Navigator 2.0 browser. For example, even though the definition doesn't specify whether the Windows 95 version of Netscape can use frames, the Browser Capabilities component will report that this version of Netscape Navigator can use frames because its parent can.

With the parent parameter, the same information doesn't have to be entered over and over. You can make one parent definition, and create several smaller child definitions that contain more specific information. Any browser feature specified in the child definition that conflicts with the parent definition will take precedence.

The Browser Capabilities component is only as accurate as the browscap.ini file. If someone is using a browser or a version of a browser that isn't included in the browscap.ini file, the Browser Capabilities component won't be able to report its features accurately. When the Browser Capabilities component doesn't recognize a browser, it reports the features specified for the default browser. This is an example of the default browser definition:

```
[Default Browser Capability Settings]
browser=Default
Version=0.0
majorver=#0
minorver=#0
frames=False
tables=True
cookies=False
backgroundsounds=False
vbscript=False
javascript=False
javaapplets=False
activexcontrols=False
AK=False
SK=False
AOL=False
beta=False
Win16=False
Crawler=False
CDF=False
```

Again, if you don't like the default properties specified in the browscap.ini file, you can modify them directly. For example, you might not want to assume that all browsers can use tables. To change this assumption, simply change the value of the tables property in the definition for the default browser.

NOTE

You should check for updates to the browscap.ini file at the Microsoft site; Microsoft frequently updates this file. Check at http://www.microsoft.com/iis.

Several third-party updates to this file are also available. One example is at BrowsCap Central, located at http://www.cyscape.com/asp/browscap/.

A Sample Application of the Browser Capabilities Component

This section presents a possible application of the Browser Capabilities component. The purpose of this example is not only to show how to use the component, but also to show its limitations.

 In the Active Server Page contained in Listing 7.2 (checkFrames.asp on the CD), the Browser Capabilities component is used to detect whether a browser can use frames. If the browser can use frames, a framed version of the page is displayed. If the browser can't use frames, the user is warned that he or she must have a frames-compliant browser to visit the Web site.

LISTING 7.2 DETECTING WHETHER A BROWSER SUPPORTS FRAMES

```
<%
Set MyBrow=Server.CreateObject("MSWC.BrowserType")
IF MyBrow.Frames THEN
%>
<HTML>
<HEAD><TITLE> Framed Page </TITLE></HEAD>
<FRAMESET COLS="100,*">
<FRAME SRC="menu.asp">
<FRAME SRC="body.asp">
</FRAMESET>
</HTML>
<% ELSE %>
<HTML>
<HEAD><TITLE> Frameless Page </TITLE></HEAD>
<BODY>
We have detected that your browser is incapable of using frames.
You are using a <%=MyBrow.browser%> browser
(version <%=MyBrow.version %>).
To download a more recent browser, please visit:
<P> <A HREF="http://www.microsoft.com">Microsoft</A>
<P> OR
<P> <A HREF="http://www.netscape.com">Netscape</A>
</BODY>
</HTML>
<% END IF %>
```

This Active Server Page conditionally displays two pages. If the Browser Capabilities component detects that a user's browser can interpret the frame tags, the first page is displayed. This page displays two frames. Otherwise, the second page is displayed. Notice how the Browser Capabilities component is also used to report the name and version of the browser being used.

This example not only illustrates how the Browser Capabilities component can be used, it also illustrates why the component normally should not be used for this purpose. It demonstrates a serious problem with the Browser Capabilities component.

The problem with this Active Server Page is that it will always display the second page when it doesn't recognize a browser. In other words, even if a browser can support frames, the second page will be displayed because, according to the browscap.ini file, browsers cannot display frames by default.

The major shortcoming of the Browser Capabilities component is that it must depend on the information placed by Microsoft or you in the browscap.ini file. The speed at which new technologies and new browsers are introduced on the Internet undermines its usefulness.

 When possible, it's much better to use HTML itself to display different content, depending on the capabilities of a browser. For example, a better way to detect whether a browser can use frames is by using the standard <NOFRAMES> HTML tag as in Listing 7.3 (checkFramesHTML.asp on the CD):

LISTING 7.3   USING HTML TO DETECT WHETHER A BROWSER SUPPORTS FRAMES

```
<HTML>
<HEAD><TITLE> Framed Page </TITLE></HEAD>
<FRAMESET COLS="100,*">
   <FRAME SRC="menu.asp">
   <FRAME SRC="body.asp">
<NOFRAMES>
   We have detected that your browser is incapable of using frames.
   You are using a <%=MyBrow.browser%> browser
   (version <%=MyBrow.version %>).
   To download a more recent browser, please visit:
   <P> <A HREF="http://www.microsoft.com">Microsoft</A>
   <P> OR
   <P> <A HREF="http://www.netscape.com">Netscape</A>
</NOFRAMES>
</FRAMESET>
</HTML>
```

The advantage of this approach is two-fold. First, using the <NOFRAMES> tag complies with the World Wide Web Consortium's specifications for HTML 4.0. The World Wide Web Consortium is the organization entrusted with keeping a common standard for HTML (see http://www.w3.org). The second advantage of this approach is that it will work with any obscure browser, either old or new.

If a browser does not support frames, the frameless version of the page contained within the <NOFRAMES> tag will be displayed. This happens even when a browser does not explicitly recognize the <NOFRAMES> tag. When a browser doesn't recognize an HTML tag, it simply ignores it. So all the frame-related tags will simply be ignored, and the frameless content will be displayed instead.

Using the Content Rotator Component

The *Content Rotator component* is used to randomly display different HTML content on a Web page. Here are some ideas for how this component can be used:

- Tip of the day—You can use this component to randomly display different tips for using your Web site. For example, Visit our news group to exchange messages with other users.

- News flash—This component can be used to rotate through a list of news events. For example, *Active Server Pages 2.0 Unleashed* now available in stores!

- Random link— You can use this component to display a random link drawn from a list of your favorite Web sites.

- Banner advertisement— Like the Ad Rotator component (discussed in Chapter 9, "Tracking Page Views and Displaying Advertisements"), this component can be used to display banner advertisements. However, using this component, you have greater flexibility as to how the advertisement is displayed. For example, you can use the Content Rotator component to display rich media ads (ads with dynamic HTML).

> **NOTE**
>
> This component isn't officially supported by Microsoft, and it is not included with the Windows NT Option Pack. Getting your hands on this component might be difficult. Occasionally, Microsoft has the component posted at its Web site for download (see http://www.microsoft.com/iis). If you cannot find the component at the Microsoft Web site, then you have no choice but to buy the Microsoft Internet Information Server Resource Kit (available, for example, from Amazon.com).

To use this component to display an HTML content string, you use the component's `ChooseContent()` method. The `ChooseContent()` method retrieves an HTML string from a special file called the content schedule file and displays it in an Active Server Page, as shown in the following example:

```
<HTML>
<HEAD><TITLE> Home Page </TITLE></HEAD>
<BODY>
<%
Set MyContent=Server.CreateObject("IISSample.ContentRotator")
%>
<%=MyContent.ChooseContent("content.txt") %>
</BODY>
</HTML>
```

In this example, an instance of the component is first created by calling the `CreateObject()` method. Next, an HTML content string is retrieved from the content schedule file named content.txt and displayed on the Web page. Whenever the page is requested, a different HTML string may be displayed.

The Content Schedule File

The content schedule file is used to contain all the HTML content strings. This file is a normal text file, which can be created and edited with any text editor. It can also be given any name. Listing 7.4 shows an example.

LISTING 7.4 THE CONTENT.TXT FILE

```
%%#2 // Here is the first entry
<FONT COLOR="RED"> Visit Our News Group! </FONT>
%%#3 // Here is the second entry
<B> Don't Forget To Bookmark This Web Site. </B>
%%#5 // Here is the third entry
Download the following free software from our Download Page:
<UL>
<LI> ActiveX Components
<LI> Link Checker
<LI> HTML Validator
</UL>
```

This content schedule file contains three entries. The beginning of each entry is marked by a double percent sign (`%%`). Whenever the `ChooseContent()` method is called, one of these entries is retrieved.

In this example, each entry is given a certain weight. This determines the relative frequency at which a particular entry will be chosen by the ChooseContent() method. You indicate a weight by providing a number after the number sign (#). For example, the first entry is given a weight of 2.

The weight of an entry can be any number between 0 and 65,535. If an entry has a weight of 0, it's never shown (this is useful for temporarily disabling an entry). The higher the weight, the more likely an entry will be retrieved by the ChooseContent() method. If you don't specify a weight for an entry, the entry will have a weight of 1.

In this example, the first entry will be displayed 2 out of every 10 times that the ChooseContent() method is called. The second entry will be displayed 3 out of 10 times, and the third entry will be displayed 5 out of 10 times. To determine how often an entry will be displayed, divide the weight of that entry by the sum of the weights of all the entries.

Each entry also includes a comment. For example, appropriately enough, the first entry includes the comment Here is the first entry. To include a comment, simply use the characters // before the comment. The comment won't be displayed on the page when the HTML content string is retrieved.

Finally, each entry contains an HTML content string. This string can span multiple lines. It can include any HTML tags. For example, the first entry displays the string Visit Our News Group! in red. The last entry contains a list of software that can be downloaded from the Web site.

Both comments and weights are optional. A minimal content schedule file would contain nothing but HTML content strings that are separated with the %% characters. In that case, every content string would be displayed with the same frequency.

Dumping the Contents of the Content Schedule File

The Content Rotator component includes one additional method. By using the GetAllContent() method, you can retrieve all the HTML content strings from the content schedule file. Here's an example of how this method is used:

```
<HTML>
<HEAD><TITLE> Content Schedule File Contents </TITLE></HEAD>
<BODY>
<%
Set MyContent=Server.CreateObject("IISSample.ContentRotator")
%>
<%=MyContent.GetAllContent("content.txt") %>
</BODY>
</HTML>
```

When this Active Server Page is displayed, all the entries in the content schedule file named content.txt are included in the page. Entries are automatically separated by horizontal rules with the HTML <HR> tag.

Why would you want to do this? This method can prove useful in several situations. For example, if you're using the Content Rotator component to randomly display links to Web sites, you might want to give the user an option to view all the links.

The GetAllContent() method is also useful for debugging a content schedule file. If you want to test the appearance of all the entries in this file, you can use this method to view its contents before the entries are displayed to the world.

The Content Linking Component

The *Content Linking component* is useful in situations where you have a series of pages you must link together. For example, you can use this component to link the pages of an online book, a slide show, or even the messages in a newsgroup.

> **NOTE**
>
> The Content Linking component is included with the Windows NT Option Pack. It should have been installed automatically when you installed the Internet Information Server. The component is named NEXTLINK.dll and, by default, it is located in the Winnt/system32/inetsrv directory.

Normally, to link a series of pages, you must insert a hypertext link in each page. The Content Linking component simplifies this process. Using this component, you can create a list of pages in a single file. After this file is created, you can use the methods of the component to display appropriate links in each page.

The Content Linking component has the following methods:

- GetListCount*(Content Linking List File)*

  Returns the total number of pages contained in the Content Linking List file.

- GetListIndex*(Content Linking List File)*

  Returns the position of the current page in the Content Linking List file.

- GetNextDescription*(Content Linking List File)*

  Returns the description of the next page in the Content Linking List file.

- GetNextURL*(Content Linking List File)*

Returns the path of the next page in the Content Linking List file.

- GetNthDescription*(Content Linking List File, Number)*

  Returns the description for a page with a particular index in the Content Linking List file.

- GetNthURL*(Content Linking List File, Number)*

  Returns the path of the page with a particular index in the Content Linking List file.

- GetPreviousDescription*(Content Linking List File)*

  Returns the description for the previous page in the Content Linking List file.

- GetPreviousURL*(Content Linking List File)*

  Returns the path of the previous page in the Content Linking List file.

For example, suppose you want to create a step-by-step guide to cooking pasta. You want to devote a distinct Active Server Page to each step and display the steps in order. The Content Linking component makes this easy to do.

 First, you must create a special file called the Content Linking List file. The Content Linking List file is a normal text file that you can create with any text editor. It simply contains a list of the pages you want to link. Listing 7.5 contains an example (included on the CD as pasta.txt).

LISTING 7.5 STEPS FOR COOKING PASTA

/pasta/grabpot.asp	Grab a pot from the cupboard.
/pasta/boilwater.asp	Boil some water in the pot.
/pasta/openbox.asp	Open box of pasta.
/pasta/dumpcontents.asp	Dump contents of box in pot.
/pasta/wait.asp	Wait ten minutes.
/pasta/home.asp	Return to home page.

After you create the Content Linking List file, you can save the file with any name. For example, you could save the file as pasta.txt.

This sample file has two columns. The first column contains a list of the files to link. These can be Active Server Pages files or normal HTML files. The second column contains descriptions of these files. These two columns must be separated by a single tab character rather than spaces. The Content Linking component won't be able to distinguish the two columns otherwise.

> **NOTE**
>
> Any special formatting applied to the Content Linking List file, such as bold or italics, is ignored. The Content Linking List file is nothing more than a text file.

 After you have created the Content Linking List file, you can use the Content Linking component to add navigational links to your Active Server Pages. For example, you might want to display a list of all the steps involved in preparing pasta on the home page of your Web site. You could do this with the Active Server Page in Listing 7.6 (included on the CD as pastaMenu.asp).

LISTING 7.6 MENU FOR COOKING PASTA

```
<HTML >
<HEAD><TITLE> Home Page </TITLE></HEAD>
<BODY>
<H2>Welcome To The Pasta Web Site!</H2>
<%
Set mylinks=Server.CreateObject("MSWC.NextLink")
%>
Here are the
<%=mylinks.GetListCount("pasta.txt")-1%>
steps for preparing pasta:
<OL>
<%
FOR i=1 TO mylinks.GetListCount("pasta.txt")-1
%>
<LI><A HREF="<%=mylinks.GetNthURL("pasta.txt",i)%>">
<%=mylinks.GetNthDescription("pasta.txt",i)%></A>
<%
NEXT
%>
</OL>
</BODY>
</HTML>
```

This Active Server Page displays a list of the links in the Content Linking List file (see Figure 7.4). This is accomplished by creating an instance of the Content Linking component. An instance of this component is assigned to the variable named `mylinks`.

FIGURE 7.4

*The Pasta
Web site.*

Three methods of the component are used:

- First, the GetListCount() method retrieves a count of the number of entries in the Content Linking List file. Whenever you call a method of the Content Linking component, you must pass the name of the Content Linking List file. In this example, the method is called by using mylinks.GetListCount("pasta.txt").

> **NOTE**
>
> The last FOR loop goes from 1 to GetListCount()-1, leaving out the last list item. That's correct and intended (the last item in the list file is Return to home page).

- Second, the GetNthURL() method retrieves the *n*th URL entry in the Content Linking List file. This method has two parameters. The first parameter indicates the name of the Content Linking List file. The second parameter indicates which entry to retrieve from this file. For example, if you call GetNthURL("pasta.txt",2), the URL listed as the second entry in the pasta.txt file is returned.

- Third, the GetNthDescription() method is called to retrieve the page descriptions from the Content Linking List file. This method also takes two parameters. The first parameter specifies the name of the Content Linking List file. The second parameter indicates which entry to retrieve from this file. For example, if you call GetNthDescription("pasta.txt", 2), the description in the second entry in the pasta.txt file is returned.

The GetNthURL() and GetNthDescription() methods are used within a FOR...NEXT loop to display all the entries in the Content Linking List file. All the entries are displayed except the final one. This last entry is excluded because it points back to the home page.

In the preceding example, the methods of the Content Linking component are used to list a series of pages. You can also use the methods of this component to link the individual pages together, as in Listing 7.7 (included on the CD as pastaStep2.asp).

LISTING 7.7 STEP TWO FOR COOKING PASTA

```
<HTML>
<HEAD><TITLE> Step Two </TITLE></HEAD>
<BODY>
<H1>Step 2: Boil Water </H1>
<H3>Boil some water in a pot.</H3>
<HR>
<%
Set mylinks=Server.CreateObject("MSWC.NextLink")
IF mylinks.GetListIndex("pasta.txt")>1 THEN
%>
<A HREF="<%=mylinks.GetPreviousURL("pasta.txt")%>">
Previous Step</A>
<% END IF %>
<P>
<A HREF="<%=mylinks.GetNextURL("pasta.txt")%>">
Next Step</A>
</BODY>
</HTML>
```

Two methods of the Content Linking component are used in this Active Server Page. The GetPreviousURL() method retrieves the path of the previous page. The GetNextURL() method retrieves the path of the next page. These methods create a link to the previous page and a link to the next page.

The GetPreviousURL() and GetNextURL() methods return different results depending on the current page. When these methods are called, the path of the current page is compared to the entries in the Content Linking List file. The GetPreviousURL() method returns the entry that's above the entry for the current page. The GetNextURL() method returns the entry that's below the entry for the current page.

If the current page isn't included in the Content Linking List file, the `GetPreviousURL()` method returns the first entry in the Content Linking List file. The `GetNextURL()` method retrieves the last entry.

The Content Linking Component does not do anything that you could not do manually by entering each hypertext link in each page yourself. The component simply makes it easier to maintain the links between a series of pages by doing it automatically for you.

Summary

In this chapter, you learned how to use three components for creating dynamic content in your Active Server Pages. In the first part, you learned how to use the Browser Capabilities component to detect browser features, and you discovered some of this component's limitations. In the second part, you learned how to dynamically display different HTML content with different frequencies by using the Content Rotator component. Finally, you learned how to make your Web site easier to navigate by using the Content Linking component.

Working with the File System

by Stephen Walther

IN THIS CHAPTER

CHAPTER 8

This entire chapter is devoted to the Active Server Pages File Access component. By using this component within your Active Server Pages, you can gain complete control over your computer's file system. The first section of this chapter presents an overview of the objects used by this component. In the second section, you will learn how to read and write to a text file. The third section shows how to work with the methods, properties, and collections of files. The final section investigates the methods for manipulating folders and drives.

Overview of the File Access Component

Active Server Pages includes a rich set of methods, properties, and collections for working with files. By using Active Server Pages scripts, you have complete control over almost all aspects of the file system.

To work with files, you use the File Access component. This component uses the following objects:

- `FileSystemObject`—Includes all the basic methods for working with the file system. For example, you can use the methods of this object to copy and delete folders and files.

- `TextStream`— Used for reading and writing to a text file.

- `File`— The methods and properties of this object enable you to work with individual files. For example, you can use this object to discover the date that a file was last modified or the path to a file.

- `Folder`— The methods and properties of this object enable you to work with file folders.

- `Drive`— Represents a disk drive or network share. You can use the properties of this object to retrieve information such as the amount of disk space available or the type of file system being used on a drive.

The File Access Component also has three collections:

- `Files` collection— Represents a set of files in a folder.

- `Folders` collection— The items in this collection represent the individual subfolders in a folder.

- `Drives` collection— This collection represents either drives located on the server or remote network shares.

The File Access object has close to one hundred properties and methods (more than can be covered in a single chapter). After reading the following pages, you'll understand how to use the most valuable methods and properties of these objects in your Active Server Page scripts. For a complete list of the methods, properties, and collections of these objects, see Appendix B, "ASP Objects and Components Reference," at the back of this book.

Reading and Writing to a File

This section describes the most important file access activities: reading and writing to a text file. There are many uses for a text file, including these common ones:

- A custom log—Use a text file to record the activities of the visitors to your Web site. You can record such information as their IP addresses, the browsers they used, and the amount of time they spent at your Web site.

- Form data— Use a text file to store the information collected from an HTML form. For example, if a user enters registration information into an HTML form, you can store that information in a text file.

- Tip of the Day— Use a text file to store a list of tips for using your Web site in a text file and randomly retrieve and display them on a Web page.

Writing to a Text File

Before you can create a file in a folder, you must have permission to write to the folder. Anonymous Internet users access your Web server under the security context of the IUSER_*MachineName* account. To check whether this account has permission to write to a folder, right-click the name of the folder on your computer desktop, choose Properties, and then select the tab labeled Security. Next, click the button labeled Permissions and examine the permissions for the IUSER_*MachineName* account. The IUSER_*MachineName* account, or a group that includes this account, must have Write access in order to write a new file (see Figure 8.1).

8

WORKING WITH
THE FILE SYSTEM

> **NOTE**
>
> If you receive the following error when executing the following script, the IUSER_*MachineName* account does not have the correct permissions set to write the file:
>
> ```
> Writing file...
> Server object error 'ASP 0177 : 800a004c'
> Server.CreateObject Failed
> /mydir/test.asp, line 7
> The operation completed successfully.
> ```

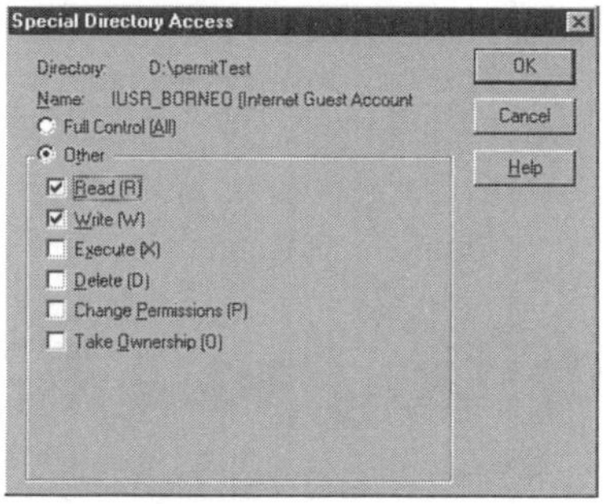

FIGURE 8.1

Setting user permissions.

To create and write to a text file, you can use the `FileSystemObject` and `TextStream` objects. First, you must create an instance of the `FileSystemObject`. Next, call the `CreateTextFile()` method of the `FileSystemObject` to return an instance of a `TextStream` object. Finally, use the `WriteLine()` method of the `TextStream` object to write data to the file. Here's an example:

```
<html>
<head><title>Write File</title></head>
<body>
Writing file...
<%
Set MyFileObject=Server.CreateObject("Scripting.FileSystemObject")
Set MyTextFile=MyFileObject.CreateTextFile("c:\mydir\test.txt")
MyTextFile.WriteLine("Hello There!")
MyTextFile.Close
%>
</body>
</html>
```

This example creates a file named test.txt with the path c:\mydir\test.txt. The `WriteLine()` method is used to send the single line of text `Hello There!` to the file. Finally, the instance of the `TextStream` object is closed to preserve system resources. Each of these steps is described in more detail in the following paragraphs.

> **NOTE**
>
> If you need to map the virtual path of a file to its physical path, you can use the `Server.MapPath()` method, as in the following example:
>
> ```
> PhysicalPath=Server.MapPath("/private/test.txt")
> ```
>
> If the virtual directory named /private has the physical path c:\private, this call to MapPath() would return c:\private\test.txt.

The CreateTextFile() method is used to create the new text file. When this method is called, a TextStream object is returned. This method has one required parameter and two optional ones:

- *FileSpecifier*— Specifies the path of the file to create. If a directory in the path doesn't exist, the error File not found is returned.

- Overwrite— This parameter is optional. By default, it has the value TRUE. A call to CreateTextFile() automatically overwrites any preexisting file with the same name. If this parameter is set to FALSE, an error occurs if the file already exists.

- Unicode— This parameter is optional. By default, it has the value FALSE, which indicates that a file using the ASCII character set should be created. If set to TRUE, a file using the Unicode character set will be created.

After a file has been created with the CreateTextFile() method, you can use the TextStream object to write to the file. When using the TextStream object for writing, you can use the following methods:

- Write*(string)*—This method writes a string to the file.

- WriteLine*([string])*—This method writes a string to the file and adds a newline character. The *string* argument is optional. If no string is specified, a newline character is written to the file.

- WriteBlankLines*(lines)*—This method writes the specified number of blank lines (newline characters) to the file.

- Close—This method is used to close an open TextStream file and free up resources.

For example, to create a text file containing the text Hello World! 32 times in a row, you would use the following script:

```
<%
Set MyFileObject=Server.CreateObject("Scripting.FileSystemObject")
Set MyTextFile=MyFileObject.CreateTextFile("c:\mydir\test.txt")
FOR i=1 to 32
  MyTextFile.WriteLine("Hello World!")
NEXT
MyTextFile.Close
%>
```

Reading and Appending Data from a Text File

To read from a text file, you must create an instance of the `FileSystemObject`. Next, use the `OpenTextFile()` method to return an instance of the `TextStream` object. Finally, you can use the `ReadLine` method of the `TextStream` object to read from the file. Here's an example:

```
<%
Set MyFileObject=Server.CreateObject("Scripting.FileSystemObject")
Set MyTextFile=MyFileObject.OpenTextFile("c:\mydir\test.txt")
WHILE NOT MyTextFile.AtEndOfStream
  Response.Write(MyTextFile.ReadLine)
WEND
MyTextFile.Close
%>
```

This script reads everything from the text file named test.txt. It outputs the contents of this file to the browser. If the file doesn't exist, the error `File Not Found` is returned. (In the next section, you learn how to detect whether a file exists.)

The `WHILE...WEND` loop in this example moves through the contents of the file until the end of the file is reached. The `AtEndOfStream` property has the value `FALSE` until the loop moves to the end of the file.

The following properties of the `TextStream` object are useful when reading from a text file:

- `AtEndOfLine`—This property indicates whether the end of a particular line in a text file has been reached. When the newline character is detected, this property has the value `TRUE`.

- `AtEndOfStream`—This property indicates whether the end of the entire text file has been reached. It can have the value `TRUE` or the value `FALSE`.

- `Column`—This property indicates the current character position in a line. The property returns an integer value.

- `Line`—This property indicates the current line in a file. The property returns an integer value.

Instead of using the `ReadLine` method to read through the contents of a file, you can use the `Read()` method. The `Read()` method returns a specified number of characters from an open text file. Following is an example of how to use this method:

```
<%
Set MyFileObject=Server.CreateObject("Scripting.FileSystemObject")
Set MyTextFile=MyFileObject.OpenTextFile("c:\mydir\test.txt")
WHILE NOT MyTextFile.AtEndOfLine
```

```
   Response.Write(MyTextFile.Read(1))
WEND
MyTextFile.Close
%>
```

This script retrieves the first line from a text file, one character at a time. The `AtEndOfLine` property detects when the end of the first line of the text file has been reached. The `Read()` method reads one character at a time from the text file.

The following methods are useful when reading data from a text file:

- `Read(characters)`—This method reads the specified number of characters from the text file.
- `ReadLine`—This method reads a single line from the text file. (The newline character is not returned.)
- `ReadAll`—This method retrieves the entire contents of the `TextStream` file.
- `Skip(characters)`—This method skips the specified number of characters in an open text file.
- `SkipLine`—This method skips a single line in an open text file.
- `Close`—This method closes an open `TextStream` file and frees up resources.

Normally, the `OpenTextFile()` method is used for retrieving data from a text file. However, you can also use this method to append new data to a text file, like this:

```
<%
Set MyFileObject=Server.CreateObject("Scripting.FileSystemObject")
Set MyTextFile=MyFileObject.OpenTextFile("c:\mydir\browser.log", 8, TRUE)
MyTextFile.WriteLine(Request.ServerVariables("HTTP_USER_AGENT"))
MyTextFile.Close
%>
```

This script creates a log of the browsers being used at a Web site. Whenever the script is executed, the type of browser used to request the page is recorded in a text file. This browser information is retrieved from the `ServerVariables` collection.

8

WORKING WITH
THE FILE SYSTEM

> **NOTE**
>
> For more information about the `ServerVariables` collection, see Chapter 2, "Active Server Pages and the HTTP Protocol."

The preceding script appends the browser type to the end of the text file named browser.log. If the file browser.log doesn't exist when this script is first executed, the file is created automatically. This is accomplished by using two parameters of the OpenTextFile() method: the IOMode and the Create parameters.

The following list describes all the parameters of the OpenTextFile() method:

- *FileSpecifier*—Specifies the path to the file to open for reading or appending.
- IOMode—Optional parameter indicating whether the file should be opened for reading, writing, or appending. The default value is 1 for reading. To open a file for writing, set this value to 2. To open a file for appending, set this value to 8.
- Create—Optional parameter indicating whether the file should be created if it doesn't exist. By default, the value of this parameter is FALSE.
- Format—Optional parameter that specifies the format of the file. By default, a file uses the ASCII character set. However, you can use the Unicode character set by passing the value -1, or the system default by passing the value -2.

> **NOTE**
>
> You can't use constants with the OpenTextFile() method in the current release of Active Server Pages. For example, you must use the value 8 rather than the constant ForAppending with the IOMode parameter.

Sample Application

This section provides a sample application of the methods used for reading and writing to files. A few years ago, before it became a multibillion dollar company, Amazon held a competition to write a collaborative online story. The first part of this story was entered by John Updike. Each day, visitors to the Amazon.com Web site submitted new sentences to add to the story. One sentence was selected every day, and the winner received $1,000. The story was written collaboratively.

This competition was a great idea. It attracted repeat visitors to the Amazon.com Web site, and it generated a tremendous amount of publicity. (During some days of the six-week competition, Amazon received 10,000 story submissions—and this was in 1997.) You might want to add something similar to your Web site. Listing 8.1 shows a simple example of how you could do this.

LISTING 8.1 THE SCRIPT FOR STORY.ASP

```
<%
IF NOT Request.Form("NextLine")="" THEN
Set MyFileObject=Server.CreateObject("Scripting.FileSystemObject")
Set MyTextFile=MyFileObject.OpenTextFile("c:\mydir\TheStory.txt",
➡8, TRUE)
MyTextFile.WriteLine(Request.Form("NextLine"))
MyTextFile.Close
END IF
%>
<HTML>
<HEAD><TITLE> Online Story </TITLE></HEAD>
<BODY>
<HR>
<%
Set MyFileObject=Server.CreateObject("Scripting.FileSystemObject")
Set MyTextFile=MyFileObject.OpenTextFile("c:\mydir\TheStory.txt")
WHILE NOT MyTextFile.AtEndOfStream
  Response.Write("  "&MyTextFile.ReadLine)
WEND
MyTextFile.Close
%>
<HR>
<H3>Enter a new line for the story: </H3>
<FORM METHOD="POST" ACTION="story.asp">
<INPUT NAME="NextLine" TYPE="TEXT" SIZE=70>
<INPUT TYPE="SUBMIT" VALUE="Submit Sentence">
</FORM>
</BODY>
</HTML>
```

This Active Server Page contains two scripts. The first script executes when a new sentence has been submitted. If a new sentence exists, it's appended to the file named TheStory.txt.

The second script is used to display the contents of the TheStory.txt file. Each line in the file is outputted (see Figure 8.2). The lines are separated by two nonbreaking space characters, so that the sentences will be divided by spaces when displayed.

The rest of the Active Server Page contains an HTML form for submitting the next line in the story. The Active Server Page posts the form contents to itself. For this to work, you must name the Active Server Page story.asp.

Before you use this Active Server Page for the first time, you need to create a text file named TheStory.txt. The first sentence of the story must be entered into this file. If you want to restart the story, simply clear this file and enter a new first sentence.

FIGURE 8.2

*An online collabo-
rative story.*

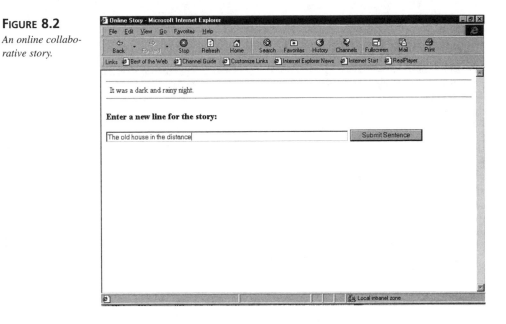

Working with Files

This section covers how to work with files—how to copy, move, and delete files; how to detect whether a file exists; and how to retrieve the attributes of a file.

Copying, Moving, and Deleting Files

There's more than one way to copy, move, or delete a file. To do any of these, you can use the methods of the FileSystemObject or the methods of the File object. The methods of the FileSystemObject are slightly more flexible because you're not restricted to working with a single file.

The following list describes the methods of the FileSystemObject for manipulating files:

- CopyFile *source*, *destination*, [Overwrite]—This method copies a file from one location to another. You can use wildcards in the *source* parameter to copy more than one file at a time. The optional Overwrite parameter indicates whether to overwrite an existing file. It can have the value TRUE or the value FALSE.

- MoveFile *source*, *destination*— This method moves a file from one location to another. You can use wildcards in the *source* parameter to move more than one file at a time. If the file already exists at the destination, an error is generated.

- DeleteFile *FileSpecifier*— This method deletes the specified file. You can use wildcards to delete more than one file at a time. If you use wildcards and no matches are made, an error is generated.

Before you can use any of these methods, you must create an instance of the FileSystemObject. The next example shows how each of the methods are used:

```
<%
'  Create an instance of the FileSystemObject object
Set MyFileObject=Server.CreateObject("Scripting.FileSystemObject")
'  Create a file to manipulate
Set MyFile=MyFileObject.CreateTextFile("c:\test.txt")
MyFile.Writeline("Hello")
MyFile.Close
' Copy the file
MyFileObject.CopyFile "c:\test.txt","c:\test2.txt"
' Move the file
MyFileObject.MoveFile "c:\test2.txt","c:\test3.txt"
' Delete both files
MyFileObject.DeleteFile "c:\test.txt"
MyFileObject.DeleteFile "c:\test3.txt"
%>
```

Instead of using the FileSystemObject to copy, move, or delete files, you can also use the File object. These are the equivalent methods you can use with the File object:

- Copy *newcopy*, [Overwrite]—This method creates a new copy of the current file. If the optional Overwrite parameter is set to TRUE, any preexisting file is overwritten.

- Move *newcopy*— This method moves the current file. The current file will now refer to this file.

- Delete—Deletes the current file.

Before you can use these methods, you must first create an instance of the File object. To create an instance of the File object, you can use the GetFile() method of the FileSystemObject. Here's the preceding script, rewritten to use the methods of the File object:

```
<%
'  Create an instance of the FileSystemObject object
Set MyFileObject=Server.CreateObject("Scripting.FileSystemObject")
'  Create a file to manipulate
Set MyFile=MyFileObject.CreateTextFile("c:\test.txt")
MyFile.Writeline("Hello")
MyFile.Close
'  Create an instance of the File object.
Set afile=MyFileObject.GetFile("c:\test.txt")
```

8

WORKING WITH
THE FILE SYSTEM

```
' Copy the file
afile.Copy "c:\test2.txt"
' Move the file
afile.Move "c:\test3.txt"
' Delete the original file
afile.Delete
%>
```

Detecting Whether a File Exists

To detect whether a file exists, you can use the FileExists() method of the FileSystemObject. Simply pass the physical path of a file to this method and it will return either TRUE or FALSE. Here's an example of how this method is used:

```
<HTML>
<HEAD><TITLE> FileExists Example </TITLE></HEAD>
<BODY>
<%
MySelf=Request.ServerVariables("PATH_TRANSLATED")
'   Create an instance of the FileSystemObject object
Set MyFileObject=Server.CreateObject("Scripting.FileSystemObject")
If MyFileObject.FileExists(Myself) THEN
  Response.Write("I exist!")
ELSE
  Response.Write("I do not exist.")
END IF
%>
</BODY>
</HTML>
```

This Active Server Page checks whether it exists. The server variable PATH_TRANSLATED is used to return the physical path of the current file. The FileExists method checks whether this file exists. In this example, necessarily, the method must always return TRUE. (In other words, the file checks its own existence, verifies that it exists, and returns TRUE.)

Retrieving the Attributes of Files

The File object includes several properties that are useful when working with files. The following list explains these properties:

- Attributes—This property returns the attributes of the current file (like the DOS ATTRIB command). For example, you can use this property to determine whether a file is hidden or read-only.

- DateCreated— This property returns the date and time the file was created.

- DateLastAccessed— This property returns the date and time the file was last accessed.

- `DateLastModified`— This property returns the date and time the file was last modified.

- `Drive`— This property returns the drive where the file is located.

- `Name`— This property returns the name of the file.

- `ParentFolder`— This property returns the folder in which the file is contained.

- `Path`— This property returns the path of the file.

- `Size`— This property returns the size of the file in bytes.

- `Type`— This property returns the type of the file—for example, `Text Document`, `ASP File`, or `Internet Document (HTML)`.

 To use any of these properties, you must first create an instance of the `File` object. The next example (fileProperties.asp on the CD) displays all the properties for a file with the path c:\test.txt (see Figure 8.3):

```
<HTML>
<HEAD><TITLE>File Properties</TITLE></HEAD>
<BODY>
<%
'  Create an instance of the FileSystemObject object
Set MyFileObject=Server.CreateObject("Scripting.FileSystemObject")
'  Create an instance of the File object.
Set afile=MyFileObject.GetFile("c:\test.txt")
%>
<BR>Name: <%=afile.Name%>
<BR>Path: <%=afile.Path%>
<BR>Drive: <%=afile.Drive%>
<BR>Size: <%=afile.Size%>
<BR>Type: <%=afile.Type%>
<BR>Attributes: <%=afile.Attributes%>
<BR>Date Created: <%=afile.DateCreated %>
<BR>Date Last Accessed: <%=afile.DateLastAccessed%>
<BR>Date Last Modified: <%=afile.DateLastModified%>
</BODY>
</HTML>
```

The `Attributes` property requires some explanation. This property returns a number corresponding to the sum of the file attributes that have been set. Table 8.1 lists the file attribute values.

FIGURE **8.3**

File properties.

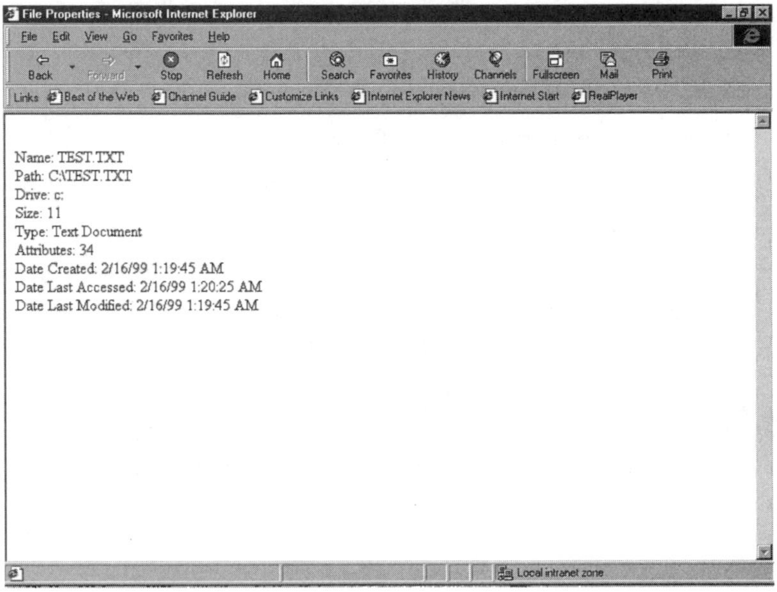

TABLE **8.1**   FILE ATTRIBUTES

Attribute	Value
Normal	0
Read-only	1
Hidden	2
System	4
Volume	8
Directory	16
Archive	32
Alias	64
Compressed	128

The file shown in Figure 8.3 has its hidden and archive attributes set. The combination of the values 2 (for hidden) and 32 (for archive) equals 34. There's no danger of ambiguity because every combination of attribute values yields a unique number.

Some of these properties not only can be read, but also can be set. You can set the read-only, hidden, system, and archive properties. For example, to make the file c:\test.txt hidden, you could use the following script:

```
<%
' Create an instance of the FileSystemObject object
Set MyFileObject=Server.CreateObject("Scripting.FileSystemObject")
' Create an instance of the File object.
Set afile=MyFileObject.GetFile("c:\test.txt")
' Make it hidden
afile.attributes=2
%>
```

Working with Drives and Folders

This section explores the methods for working with drives and folders. It shows you how to retrieve information about the drives on the current machine and how to create, copy, move, delete, and list the contents of folders.

Working with Drives

There are two objects that you can use to retrieve information about the drives on the local machine: the `FileSystemObject` and the `Drive` object. For example, the following Active Server Page (driveList.asp on the CD) displays a list of all the drives on the server, their total sizes, and their available sizes (see Figure 8.4):

```
<HTML>
<HEAD><TITLE>Drive List</TITLE></HEAD>
<BODY>
<%
' Create an instance of the FileSystemObject object
Set MyFileObject=Server.CreateObject("Scripting.FileSystemObject")
' Loop through the Drives collection
FOR EACH thing in MyFileObject.Drives
%>
<BR>Drive Letter: <%=thing.DriveLetter%>
<BR>Drive Total Size: <%=thing.TotalSize%>
<BR>Drive Available Space: <%=thing.AvailableSpace%>
<HR>
<%
NEXT
%>
</BODY>
</HTML>
```

> **NOTE**
>
> If you run the script in this section, and you do not have a disk in your floppy drive or a CD in your CD drive, you will receive an error. You can get around this problem by using the `isReady` property to check whether media is present in the drive.

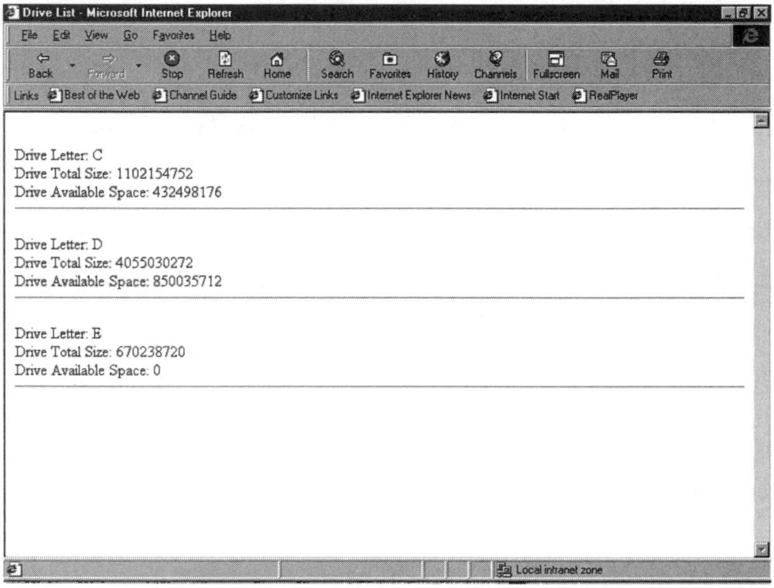

FIGURE 8.4

Displaying drive properties.

FIGURE 8.4

Displaying drive properties.

The `Drives` collection of the `FileSystemObject` contains the collection of all the available drives on the server. However, it contains only those drives that have been mapped to a drive letter. These are the methods of the `FileSystemObject` related to drives:

- `DriveExists`*(DriveSpecifier)*—This method returns TRUE if the specified drive exists.
- `Drives`—Returns the collection of drives for the local machine.
- `GetDrive`*(DriveSpecifier)*— Returns a `Drive` object that represents the drive specified.
- `GetDriveName`*(Path)*— Returns a string that contains the drive for the path specified.

Not surprisingly, the `Drive` object also contains several methods and properties that are useful for working with drives:

- `AvailableSpace`—Returns the space available on the drive in bytes.
- `DriveLetter`— Returns the letter of the drive—for example, C:, D:, or E:.
- `DriveType`— Returns a number corresponding to the type of the drive, for example, a CD-ROM or removable drive.
- `FreeSpace`— The amount of free space on the drive in bytes (normally the same as `AvailableSpace`).

> **TIP**
>
> You might wonder when `FreeSpace` and `AvailableSpace` would differ. Windows 2000 will enable the system administrator to allocate hard drive space to each user of the server. If a user were allocated a limited amount of space on the server, the `FreeSpace` and `AvaliableSpace` values would differ.

- `IsReady`— Indicates whether a volume is ready to be used. This property is useful for indicating the state of removable drives.
- `Path`— Indicates the path of the drive.
- `RootFolder`— This property returns a `Folder` object representing the root folder on the drive.
- `SerialNumber`— Returns the serial number of the drive.
- `ShareName`— Returns the share name of the drive.
- `TotalSize`— Returns the total size of the drive in bytes.
- `VolumeName`— Returns a string representing the volume name of the drive.

To use these properties and methods, you must create an instance of the `Drive` object. You can do this by using the `GetDrive()` method of the `FileSystemObject`. The following example returns the volume name of the C: drive:

```
<%
'  Create an instance of the FileSystemObject object
Set MyFileObject=Server.CreateObject("Scripting.FileSystemObject")
'  Create an instance of the Drive object
Set MyDrive=MyFileObject.GetDrive("c;")
Response.Write(MyDrive.VolumeName)
%>
```

Working with Folders

This section shows how to manipulate folders and display their contents. To work with folders, you can use either the `FileSystemObject` or the `Folder` object. This example displays all the files in a folder with the path c:\myfolder:

```
<HTML>
<HEAD><TITLE>Folder Contents</TITLE></HEAD>
<BODY>
<%
'  Create an instance of the FileSystemObject object
Set MyFileObject=Server.CreateObject("Scripting.FileSystemObject")
'  Create a folder object
```

8

WORKING WITH THE FILE SYSTEM

```
Set MyFolder=MyFileObject.GetFolder("c:\myfolder")
'   Loop through the Files collection
FOR EACH thing in MyFolder.Files
  Response.Write("<P>"&thing)
NEXT
%>
</BODY>
</HTML>
```

In this example, a `Folder` object is created by using the `GetFolder()` method of the `FileSystemObject`. After the `Folder` object is created, the `FOR...NEXT` loop is used to loop through its `Files` collection. The page displays all the files in this collection (see Figure 8.5).

FIGURE 8.5

Folder contents.

The `FileSystemObject` object includes several methods for working with folders. The following list provides a brief explanation of how these methods can be used:

- `CopyFolder source, destination, [Overwrite]`— This method copies a folder from one location to another. You can use wildcards in the *source* parameter to copy multiple folders at the same time. By default, if the folder already exists, it will be overwritten. Set `Overwrite` to `FALSE` to prevent this from happening.

- `CreateFolder FolderSpecifier`— Creates the specified folder.

- `DeleteFolder FolderSpecifier`— Deletes a folder and all its contents. You can use wildcards to delete multiple folders at the same time.

- `FolderExists(FolderSpecifier)`— Returns TRUE if the folder exists, FALSE otherwise.

- `GetFolder(FolderSpecifier)`— Returns a Folder object that represents the folder specified.

- `GetParentFolderName(Path)`— Returns a string containing the path of the parent folder.

- `MoveFolder source, destination`— Moves a folder from one location to another. You can use wildcards in the source parameter to move more than one folder at a time.

To use any of these methods, you must first create an instance of the `FileSystemObject` object. The following example creates a folder, moves it, and then deletes it:

```
<%
'  Create an instance of the FileSystemObject object
Set MyFileObject=Server.CreateObject("Scripting.FileSystemObject")
'  Create a new folder
MyFileObject.CreateFolder "c:\newfolder"
'  Move the folder
MyFileObject.MoveFolder "c:\newfolder", "c:\oldfolder"
'  Delete the folder
MyFileObject.DeleteFolder "c:\oldfolder"
%>
```

The methods and properties of the Folder object can also be used to manipulate folders. Here's a brief explanation of the properties and methods of the Folder object:

- `CopyFolder newcopy, [Overwrite]`—Copies the current folder to a new location. If Overwrite is set to FALSE, an error occurs if the folder already exists.

- `DeleteFolder` Deletes the current folder and any of its contents.

- `Files`— Returns the collection of Files contained in the folder. Hidden files are not revealed.

- `IsRootFolder`— Returns TRUE if the folder is a root folder.

- `MoveFolder FolderSpecifier`— Moves the folder from one location to another.

- `Name`— Returns the name of the folder.

- `ParentFolder`— Returns the parent folder.

- `Size`— Returns the size of a folder and all its subfolders in bytes.

- `SubFolders`— Returns the collection of subfolders of the current folder.

To use any of these methods, you must first create an instance of the `Folder` object. This example (folderContents.asp on the CD) returns a list of all the sub-folders of the folder with the path c:\myfolder:

```
<%
'  Create an instance of the FileSystemObject object
Set MyFileObject=Server.CreateObject("Scripting.FileSystemObject")
'  Create an instance of the Folder object
Set MyFolder=MyFileObject.GetFolder("c:\myfolder")
FOR EACH thing IN MyFolder.SubFolders
 Response.Write(thing)
NEXT
%>
```

The `FOR...EACH` loop in this script loops through all the items contained in the `SubFolders` collection, showing the name of each item one by one.

Summary

This chapter described how to use the objects of the File Access component. You learned how to read and write to text files and how to work with the methods and properties of the `File` object. Finally, you learned how to use the `Folder` and `Drive` objects to manipulate folders and retrieve information about the drives on your server.

CHAPTER 9

Tracking Page Views and Displaying Advertisements

by Stephen Walther

IN THIS CHAPTER

This chapter explores three ActiveX components that you can use to track visitors and display banner advertisements. In the first part, you will learn how to use the Page Counter component to track how many times a particular Active Server Page has been requested. Next, you will learn how to use the Counters component, which can be used to track page views or anything else. The final part of this chapter explains how the Ad Rotator component can be used to display banner advertisements at your Web site.

Counting Visitors with the Page Counter Component

If you randomly surf around the Internet, you will discover that the home pages of many Web sites contain a hit counter. These hit counters normally appear toward the bottom of the home page and are used to display the number of times that a Web page has been visited. Microsoft provides a component that can be used to easily create a hit counter: the Page Counter component.

> **NOTE**
>
> The Page Counter component is not officially supported by Microsoft, and it is not included with the Windows NT Option Pack. During certain seasons of the year, Microsoft has this component available for download at http://www.microsoft.com/iis. If you cannot find the component at the Microsoft site, then you have no choice but to buy Microsoft's Internet Information Server Resource Kit (available, for example, at Amazon.com).

Because the Page Counter component is intended for a very particular purpose, it is a simple component. The component has the following three methods:

- Hits(*path*)—Returns the number of times a page with the specified path has been opened. If no path is provided, the method returns this value for the current page.
- PageHit()—Updates the number of times the current page has been opened. You *cannot* supply a path to another page.
- Reset(*path*)—Resets the count to 0 for the page with the specified path. If no path is provided, the value for the current page is reset.

Because the Page Counter component is not a built-in object like the Request or Response objects, you must create an instance of it before it can be used. Listing 9.1, for example, creates an instance of the component and displays the number of times that the page has been viewed.

LISTING 9.1 PAGECOUNTER.ASP

```
<HTML>
<HEAD><TITLE> Page Counter Example </TITLE></HEAD>
<BODY>
<%
Set MyHits=Server.CreateObject("IISSample.PageCounter")
MyHits.PageHit()
%>
This page has been viewed
<%=MyHits.Hits%>
times.
</BODY>
</HTML>
```

This Active Server Page simply displays the number of times the current page has been requested. The PageHit() method is used to increment the hit count for the current page. The Hits method is called without any parameters, which results in the hit count for the current page being returned (see Figure 9.1).

FIGURE 9.1

Output from the Page Counter component.

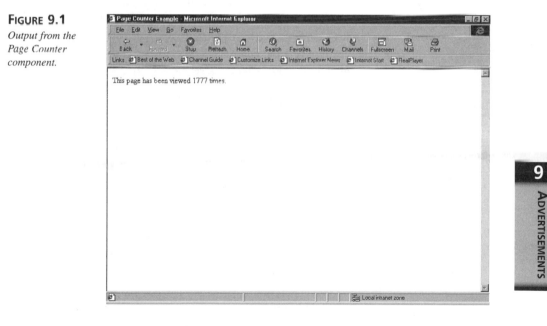

Admittedly, the counter in Figure 9.1 is a little boring. Most hit counters you see on Web sites use images to display the number of times that a page has been viewed. There are two ways that you can use the Page Counter component to display images. In Chapter 16, "Third-Party Components," you will learn how to create JPEG images on-the-fly, using the ShotGraph component. Alternatively, you can simply create a set of 10 images, representing the numerals 0 through 9, and use the Page Counter component to display these images with the script in Listing 9.2.

LISTING 9.2   PAGECOUNTERIMAGE.ASP

```
<%
Set MyHits=Server.CreateObject("IISSample.PageCounter")
MyHits.PageHit()
SUB ShowImageCnt(TheNum)
    CntStr=CSTR(TheNum)
    FOR i=1 TO LEN(CntStr)
    CntPart=MID(CntStr,i,1)
    %>
    <IMG SRC="<%=CntPart%>.gif" ALT="<%=CntPart%>">
    <%
    NEXT
END SUB
%>
<HTML>
<HEAD><TITLE>Some Page</TITLE></HEAD>
<BODY>
This page has been requested
<%
ShowImageCnt MyHits.Hits
%>
times.
</BODY>
</HTML>
```

This Active Server Page also displays a hit counter. However, the hit count is displayed by using images rather than text (see Figure 9.2). The procedure named ShowImageCnt first converts the page count to a string. Next, a FOR...NEXT loop is used to walk through each numeral in the string and display a corresponding image.

FIGURE 9.2

A page counter with images.

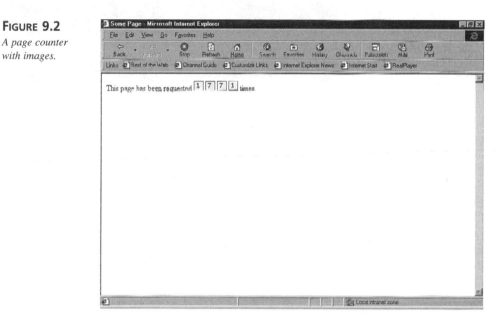

To use this example, you'll need 10 images named 0.gif, 1.gif, 2.gif, and so on. You can create these images yourself. However, several Internet sites have libraries of counter images that you can download freely (check the graphics section at your favorite Internet directory).

Tracking Page Views with the Counters Component

The *Counters component* can be used to count the number of times a page has been requested, but it can also be used to count anything else. For example, you can use it to count the number of visitors to your Web site, the number of times an advertisement has been clicked, or even the number of times someone has requested a Web page with the Netscape 2.0 browser.

9

PAGE VIEWS AND
ADVERTISEMENTS

You can create only one instance of this component. However, after you create an instance of the component, you can create as many individual counters as you need. The single Counters component can contain many individual counters with different names.

> **NOTE**
>
> The Counters component is not officially supported by Microsoft, and it is not included with the Windows NT Option Pack. Every so often, Microsoft has this component available for download at http://www.microsoft.com/iis. If you cannot find the component at the Microsoft site, you have no choice but to buy Microsoft's Internet Information Server Resource Kit (available, for example, at Amazon.com).

Because you can create only one Counters component, it's a good idea to create the component within the Global.asa file. This will guarantee that only one instance of the Counters component is created when your Web server starts.

> **NOTE**
>
> For more information on using the Global.asa file, see Chapter 4, "Working with Active Server Pages Applications."

Here's an example of how you can create the component within the Global.asa file:

```
<OBJECT RUNAT="Server" SCOPE="Application" ID="MyCount"
PROGID="MSWC.Counters"></OBJECT>
```

The Microsoft extended HTML <OBJECT> tag is used here to create an instance of the Counters component named MyCount with application-wide scope. Remember to use the <OBJECT> tag outside any scripts within the Global.asa file. After an instance of the Counters component has been created in this way, you can access its methods from any page within your application just as you can for a built-in Active Server Page object.

The Counters component has four methods. The following list details how each method is used:

- Get*(counter name)*—This method returns the current value of a counter. If the counter doesn't exist, it is created and set to 0.

- Increment*(counter name)*—This method adds 1 to the current value of a counter. If the counter doesn't exist, it is created and its value set to 1.

- Remove*(counter name)*—This method destroys a counter.
- Set*counter name, integer*—This method accepts two arguments. The first argument is the name of a counter, and the second argument is an integer value. The method adds the integer to the counter. If the counter doesn't exist, it is created with the specified value.

After an instance of the Counters component has been created in the Global.asa file, you can increment and decrement individual counters within any Active Server Page. A counter created in one page can be incremented, decremented, set or removed in another page. The following is an example of how you can use the Counters component to keep track of the number of times a particular page has been requested:

```
<HTML>
<HEAD><TITLE>Some Page</TITLE></HEAD>
<BODY>
This page has been requested
<%=MyCount.Increment("PageCnt") %>
times.
</BODY>
</HTML>
```

The first time this page is requested, a counter named PageCnt is created and set to the value 1. Subsequent requests increment the value of this counter by 1. The PageCnt counter reflects the number of times the page has been requested.

What happens if your server is unexpectedly shut down? The counters you create with the Counters component are persistent. They're saved in a file named counters.txt. If the server shuts down, the counters still exist when it starts again. They retain their values and pick up where they left off.

 As previously mentioned, the Counters component can be used to track any values you choose. For example, you can use the component to track and display the number of times that a visitor has requested a page using the Netscape or the Microsoft Browser. Listing 9.3 provides an example.

LISTING 9.3 NSORIE.ASP

```
<%
theBrowser = UCASE( Request.ServerVariables( "HTTP_USER_AGENT" ) )

if instr( theBrowser, "MSIE" ) > 0 THEN
  MyCount.Increment( "Microsoft" )

else
```

continues

9

PAGE VIEWS AND
ADVERTISEMENTS

LISTING 9.3 CONTINUED

```
  MyCount.Increment( "Netscape" )
end if
%>
<HTML>
<HEAD><TITLE>Some Page</TITLE></HEAD>
<BODY>
<p><b>Microsoft Visitors:</b><%=MyCount.Get( "Microsoft" ) %>
<p><b>Netscape Visitors:</b><%=MyCount.Get( "Netscape" )%>
</BODY>
</HTML>
```

This Active Server Page uses the USER-AGENT header to determine the type of browser used to request the page. If the header contains the string "MSIE", then the page was requested with Microsoft Internet Explorer. Otherwise, it is assumed that the Netscape browser was used to request the page.

The two counters named Microsoft and Netscape are used to store the data about the relative popularity of the two browsers. The values of the counters are incremented by using the Increment method and displayed by using the Get method of the Counters component (see Figure 9.3).

FIGURE 9.3

Pages requested with Internet Explorer versus pages requested with Netscape.

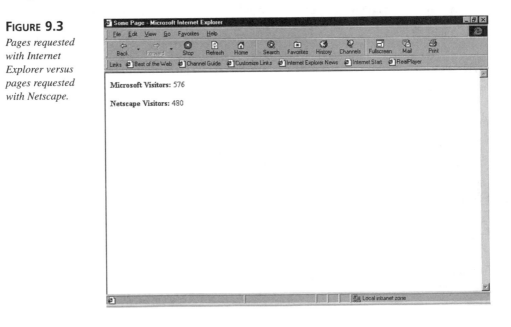

Displaying Advertisements

Many commercial Web sites are built on the assumption that they'll make money through banner advertisements. The assumption is that a Web site is very much like a magazine or a television show. Like a TV show, a Web site with compelling content attracts a population of viewers. Where viewers go, it's assumed, advertisers will soon follow with advertising dollars.

So far, however, this strategy hasn't worked for most Web sites. The problem is that very few corporations are paying for advertisements on the Internet. Even worse, the few corporations willing to advertise on the Internet tend to advertise only on the same select group of Web sites. Netscape and the other Internet portals such as Yahoo!, Lycos, Infoseek, and Excite tend to draw all the advertising money. This leaves very few advertising dollars for the little guys.

> **NOTE**
>
> One way to easily get started selling banner advertisements for your Web site is to join an advertising network such as flycast (http://www.flycast.com) or LinkExchange (http://www.linkexchange.com).

Nevertheless, selling banner advertisements is the primary way to make money on the Internet. Unless you plan to generate revenue directly from your Web site's visitors by offering a product or service—an even riskier proposition because users must offer up their credit cards—you'll need to use banner advertisements. In this section, you will learn how to incorporate banner advertisements into your Web pages.

Using the Ad Rotator Component

Using the *Ad Rotator component*, you can create a Web page that displays a different banner advertisement every time it's viewed. You can assign advertisements different weights so that they're displayed at different frequencies. You can also record the number of times an advertisement has been clicked to determine the advertisement's click-through rate.

The Ad Rotator component is included with the Windows NT Option Pack. When you installed Internet Information Server, this component should have been installed automatically as well (look in the Winnt/system32/inetsrv directory for a file called ADROT.dll).

The Ad Rotator component has a single method. The GetAdvertisement() method is used to retrieve information about a banner advertisement. Here's an example of how it's used (included on the CD as adrot.asp):

```
<HTML>
<HEAD><TITLE> Home Page </TITLE></HEAD>
<BODY>
<CENTER><H1>Welcome to our web site!</H1></CENTER>
<HR>
<%
Set MyAd=Server.CreateObject("MSWC.AdRotator")
%>
<CENTER><%= MyAd.GetAdvertisement("adrot.txt") %></CENTER>
</BODY>
</HTML>
```

This Active Server Page displays a banner advertisement below all of the content of the page (see Figure 9.4). The script creates an instance of the Ad Rotator component by using the Server.CreateObject() method. Next, the banner advertisement is actually displayed by calling the GetAdvertisement() method.

Notice that the GetAdvertisement() method takes a parameter. This parameter specifies a file that contains the information about the advertisement to be displayed. In this example, the name of this file is adrot.txt. You will learn how to create this file in the next section.

Ad Rotator Properties

The Ad Rotator component has three properties. Before calling the GetAdvertisement() method, you can set these properties to control how an advertisement is displayed. The following list explains each property:

- Border—This property overrides the BORDER parameter specified in the rotator schedule file. You can use this property to indicate the size of a banner advertisement's border (in pixels) for a particular page.

FIGURE 9.4

Banner advertise-ment example.

- Clickable— This property specifies whether the banner advertisement should function as a hyperlink. It can have the value True or False.

- TargetFrame— This property indicates the name of the frame into which the banner link should be loaded.

The TargetFrame property is particularly useful. If you set the TargetFrame property to the name of a new frame, when a user clicks a banner advertisement, the advertiser's page loads into the frame (see Figure 9.5). By doing this, you prevent the user from permanently leaving your Web site. Here's an example of how this property is used:

```
<HTML>
<HEAD><TITLE> Home Page </TITLE></HEAD>
<BODY>
<CENTER><H1>Welcome to our web site!</H1></CENTER>
<HR>
<%
Set MyAd=Server.CreateObject("MSWC.AdRotator")
```

```
MyAd.TargetFrame= "TARGET=""AdFrame"""
%>
<CENTER><%= MyAd.GetAdvertisement("adrot.txt") %></CENTER>
</BODY>
</HTML>
```

NOTE

Notice that you must include the actual expression "Target=" in the value of the TargetFrame property. This is a bug in the current implementation of the Ad Rotator component for IIS 4.0.

FIGURE 9.5

Using the TargetFrame *property.*

The Rotator Schedule File

Before you can use the Ad Rotator component, you must create a special file called the rotator schedule file. The rotator schedule file contains all the information about the banner advertisements. It's a normal text file that you can create and edit with any text editor.

 The rotator schedule file has two sections. In the first section, you provide general information about all the advertisements you want to display. In the second section, you specify the information for each advertisement. Listing 9.4 shows an example of this file.

LISTING 9.4   THE ADROT.TXT FILE

```
REDIRECT adredir.asp
WIDTH 468
HEIGHT 60
BORDER 0
*
aspsitead.gif
http://www.aspsite.com
The Active Server Pages Site
80
cityauctionad.gif
http://www.cityauction.com
CityAuction
20
```

The two sections of information in this file are divided by an asterisk (*). The first section contains four parameters that affect all the advertisements in the file. Here's an explanation of what these parameters do:

- REDIRECT—Specifies a redirection file for the advertisements. When a banner advertisement is clicked, the user is redirected to this file.
- WIDTH— The width of the banner advertisement image, specified in pixels. If you omit this parameter, the value of this parameter defaults to 440 pixels.
- HEIGHT— The height of the banner advertisement image, specified in pixels. If you omit this parameter, the value of this parameter defaults to 60 pixels.
- BORDER— The size of the border around the banner advertisement image. By default, the advertisement has a border that's one pixel thick.

In the adrot.txt file shown in Listing 9.4, the REDIRECT parameter points to the Active Server Page named adredir.asp. The WIDTH and HEIGHT parameters specify that the width of the banner advertisement image should be 468 pixels and the height should be 60 pixels. Finally, the BORDER parameter is set to 0, which results in no border being displayed.

The second section contains information specific to each advertisement. Here, the rotator schedule file contains information on two advertisements. The first banner advertisement is for the Active Server Pages Site (the companion Web site to this book). The second advertisement is for a Web site named CityAuction.

For each advertisement, you provide four lines of information. The first line gives the path to the image for the advertisement. This image may be located on the local computer or anywhere else on the Internet.

9

PAGE VIEWS AND
ADVERTISEMENTS

The second line contains the URL for the advertiser's home page. When users click an advertisement, they can be redirected to this page (see the next section). If you place a hyphen (-) on this line, the advertisement won't function as a hyperlink.

The third line indicates alternative text to display when a browser doesn't support graphics. It's equivalent to the ALT attribute of the HTML <IMAGE> tag. You can place any non-HTML text here that you want.

> **NOTE**
>
> You cannot use the Ad Rotator component to display rich media advertisements (banner advertisements that include dynamic HTML). To display this type of advertisement, use the Content Rotator component discussed in Chapter 7, "Generating Dynamic Content from the Server."

Finally, the fourth line specifies how often a particular advertisement should be shown. It indicates the *relative weight* to be given to the advertisement. In the example, the first advertisement will be displayed 80% of the time, and the second advertisement will be displayed 20% of the time.

> **NOTE**
>
> By specifying different weights for each advertisement, you can sell advertisements at different rates. Normally, Web sites sell advertisements according to their cost per thousand impressions (CPM). In other words, buyers are charged a certain amount depending on the number of times their banner advertisements are viewed. The formula used to determine the cost of displaying an advertisement is
>
> cost = (number of impressions/1,000) $\times$ CPM
>
> For example, suppose you want to sell banner advertisement space on your Web site at a CPM of $10.00 (a typical rate for smaller sites). If a buyer purchases 100 dollars worth of advertisement impressions, the advertisement should be displayed 10,000 times. If your Web site averages 100,000 visitors a month, the banner advertisement should be shown 10% of the time. Using the rotator schedule file, you can specify that an advertisement should be shown at this frequency by indicating the relative weight of the advertisement.

The Redirection File

You can specify a redirection file that applies to all the advertisements in a particular rotator schedule file. When users click a banner advertisement, they're brought to this file. Normally, this file is an Active Server Pages file, but it can be an HTML file as well.

The main function of this file is to record the number of times a particular banner advertisement has been clicked. After this information is recorded, the user is typically redirected to the advertiser's home page. Listing 9.5 shows an example.

LISTING 9.5 THE adredir.asp FILE

```
<%
Response.AppendToLog Request.QueryString("url")
Response.Redirect Request.QueryString("url")
%>
```

This redirection file contains a two-line Active Server Page script. The first line records information about which advertisement has been clicked in the server log. Next, the script uses the Redirect method to send the user to the advertiser's home page.

Whenever the redirection file is called, two query strings are passed. The url query string contains the path to the advertiser's home page. This is the same path that you entered as the path for the advertiser's home page in the rotator schedule file.

The second query string is named image. The image query string contains the path of the banner image. The value of this query string indicates the path you entered for the banner image in the rotator schedule file.

 You actually can place anything you want in the redirection file. For example, you could make the redirection file a normal HTML file that displays your Web site's advertisement rates. Listing 9.6 is an example (see Figure 9.6).

LISTING 9.6 ADRATES.ASP

```
<HTML>
<HEAD><TITLE> Ad Rates </TITLE></HEAD>
<BODY>
<H1> Advertisement Rates </H1>
To advertise at this Web site, please contact
<A HREF="mailto:admaster@mysite.com"> Ad Info </A>.
<P>
By advertising at this Web site, you will reach
thousands of developers a day.
```

continues

LISTING 9.6   CONTINUED

```
We offer a number of advertising packages:
<OL>
<LI>The Gold Package: $30 CPM
<LI>The Silver Package: $20 CPM
<LI>The Bronze Package: $10 CPM
</OL>
</BODY>
</HTML>
```

FIGURE 9.6

Advertisement information.

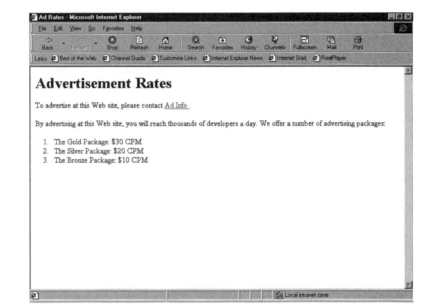

Normally, however, the redirection file is used to track the click-through rate for a banner advertisement. There are several different methods of doing this. First, you can store this information in Application variables. The redirection file in Listing 9.7 (adredirApp.asp on the CD) creates a new Application variable for each advertisement URL.

LISTING 9.7   TRACKING ADS WITH APPLICATION VARIABLES

```
<%
  ' Get The Ad URL
  theURL = UCASE( Request.QueryString( "url" ) )
  ' Replace periods with addition signs
  theURL = "AD_" & REPLACE( theURL, ".", "+" )
  ' Increment the click-through count
  Application( theURL ) = Application( theURL ) + 1
```

```
  ' Redirect to the advertiser's page
  Response.Redirect Request.QueryString( "url" )
%>
```

The script retrieves the `"url"` query string that contains the address of the advertiser's page. Next, the URL is converted into a valid VBScript variable by replacing all the periods in the URL with addition signs (+) and prefixing the string `"AD_"` to the variable name. This variable is then used to store a count of the advertisement click throughs.

NOTE

Valid VBScript variables must begin with an alphabetic character, can be no more than 255 characters long, and cannot contain periods.

After the information has been stored in Application variables, a report on the number of times each advertisement has been clicked can be generated with the Active Server Page in Listing 9.8 (see Figure 9.7).

LISTING 9.8 ADREPORTAPP.ASP

```
<html>
<head><title>Ad Report</title></head>
<body>
<h1>Banner Advertisement Report</h1>
<%
for each x in Application.Contents
  if LEFT( x, 3 ) = "AD_" then
  url = Replace( x , "!", "." )
  url = RIGHT( url, LEN( url ) - 3 )
  clicks = Application( x )
  %>
  <p>
  The banner advertisement that links to <%=url%>
   has been clicked <%=clicks%> times.
  <%
  end if
next
%>
</body>
</html>
```

9

PAGE VIEWS AND ADVERTISEMENTS

The Advertisement Report page iterates through the contents of the Application collection to find all the Application variables that start with the string `"AD_"`. The value of each of these variables, which contains the number of times the advertisement was clicked, is outputted to the browser.

This approach to tracking advertisement clicks is convenient, but it has a significant drawback. If the Internet service is shut down, the Global.asa file is modified, or your Web site crashes, then all the information stored in the Application variables will be lost. If you must report advertisement statistics to your advertisers, the loss of this information would be disastrous.

As a better alternative to storing information about the number of times an advertisement has been clicked, consider using the Counters component instead (see "Tracking Page Views with the Counters Component" earlier in this chapter). If your server crashes, and the information is stored in a counter, then you will not lose as much information because the counters are automatically written to a text file (you might lose some information if the counter values cannot be written to the file in time).

Listing 9.9 is a sample redirection file that uses the Counters component (it is assumed that an instance of the Counters component named "myCount" was created in the Global.asa file).

LISTING 9.9   ADREDIRCOUNTERS.ASP

```
<%
  ' Get The Ad URL
  theURL = UCASE( Request.QueryString( "url" ) )
  ' Replace  colons with addition signs
  theURL = "AD_" & REPLACE( theURL, ":", "+" )
  ' Increment the click-through count
  myCount.Increment( theURL )
  ' Redirect to the advertiser's page
  Response.Redirect Request.QueryString( "url" )
%>
```

This redirection file is exactly the same as the one in Listing 9.8 except a counter instead of an Application variable is used. Unfortunately, the Counters component does not include a method for returning the names of all the counters, which makes it more difficult to automatically display an advertisement report. To retrieve the values of the counters, you must use the File Access component (see Listing 9.10).

> **NOTE**
>
> To learn more about the File Access Component see Chapter 8, "Working With The File System."

LISTING 9.10   ADREPORTCOUNTERS.ASP

```
<%
Const counterFile = "c:\winnt\system32\inetsrv\counters.txt"
SET fs = Server.CreateObject( "Scripting.FileSystemObject" )
SET ts = fs.OpenTextFile( counterFile )
%>
<html>
<head><title>Counters Ad Report</title></head>
<body>
<h1>Banner Advertisement Report</h1>
<%
'  Retrieve each counter
WHILE NOT ts.AtEndOfStream
  textLine = ts.ReadLine
  counterName = LEFT( textLine, INSTR( textLine, ":" ) - 1 )
  counterValue = RIGHT( textLine, LEN( textline ) -
➥INSTRrev( textLine, ":" ) )
  if LEFT( counterName, 3 ) = "AD_" then
  url = Replace(  counterName , "+", ":" )
```

9

PAGE VIEWS AND
ADVERTISEMENTS

continues

LISTING 9.10   CONTINUED

```
  url = RIGHT( url, LEN( url ) - 3 )
  clicks = counterValue
  %>
  <p>
  The banner advertisement that links to <%=url%>
   has been clicked <%=clicks%> times.
  <%
  end if
WEND
%>
</body>
</html>
```

This script uses the File Access component to open the text file named Counters.txt. The Counters component automatically writes the name and value of each counter to this file. Next, each line in the file is read and the name and value of each counter is extracted. If the name of the counter begins with "AD_", then the name and value of the counter are outputted to the browser.

> **NOTE**
>
> Before you can use the File Access component to read the Counters.txt file, you might have to first provide the IUSER_*MachineName* account with the right permissions to read the file. See Chapter 8, "Working with the File System," to learn how to do this.

Summary

In this chapter, you learned how to track visitors and display banner advertisements. You were shown how to track visitors to your Web site by using the Page Counter component and the Counters component. You also learned how to incorporate advertisements into your Web pages with the Ad Rotator component. Finally, two methods for tracking advertisement click-throughs were discussed. You learned how to track clicks with Application variables and how to track clicks with the Counters component.

CHAPTER 10

Working with Email

by Stephen Walther

There are many situations in which you need to send email from your Web site. For example, after a user registers, you might want to automatically send the user an email message that contains his or her registration information. Or, if a user buys software from your Web site, you might want to email the software as a file attachment.

In this chapter, you will learn how to send and retrieve email messages from within your Active Server Pages. In particular, you will learn how to use the Collaboration Data Objects for Windows NT Server (CDO for NTS) to communicate with the Microsoft SMTP Service.

In versions of the Internet Information Server prior to version 4.0, sending email from an Active Server Page was difficult. You really had no choice but to buy a third-party ASP component or to write a custom email component of your own. Fortunately, Microsoft has bundled both an SMTP server and a collection of objects for communicating with mail servers with IIS 4.0 in the Windows NT 4.0 Option Pack.

In the first part of this chapter, you will learn how to configure and use the Microsoft SMTP Service. The SMTP Service does all the actual work of exchanging email with the outside world.

The second part of this chapter covers the methods of using the CDO for NTS to send email. You will learn how to build a simple subroutine that enables you to send email with a single statement in an Active Server Page script. You also will learn how to use several advanced properties of the CDO for NTS that enable you to send email with attachments, different priorities, and HTML formatting and images.

In the third part, you will learn how to access the Drop directory to retrieve email that has been sent to your Web site. In this section, you will learn the methods for retrieving and sorting through delivered email messages.

Finally, in the last part of this chapter, you will learn how to use the CDO for NTS and the SMTP Service to create a simple list server. You can use this list server to create and maintain an email-based discussion group.

The Microsoft SMTP Service

The Microsoft SMTP Server does the very basic job of sending and retrieving email in accordance with the Simple Mail Transport Protocol. In some ways it is very limited. The service does not support the Post Office Protocol (POP). This means that you cannot use the service to create mailbox accounts for multiple users or retrieve email from the service using an email client such as Outlook Express or Eudora. If you need to create a full-blown email system that goes beyond support for basic SMTP, you will need to invest in additional software such as Microsoft Exchange Server, Internet Shopper's NTMail (see `http://www.ntmail.co.uk`) or Software.com's Post.Office (see `http://www.software.com`).

On the positive side, the Microsoft SMTP Service is very valuable for sending automated email messages from your Web site. The service can support sending thousands of email messages a day. For example, you can use it to conduct mass email advertising campaigns. You can also use the service to create multiple SMTP sites that support multiple domains on a single server.

Configuring the Microsoft SMTP Service

To check whether the SMTP Service is installed and running on your server, open the Internet Service Manager and see whether an icon labeled Default SMTP Site appears within the Internet Information Server folder (see Figure 10.1). If the icon does not appear, you should install the service by running the Windows NT Option Pack Setup program. If the service is installed but not running, you can start the service by selecting Action, Start.

FIGURE 10.1
The Microsoft SMTP Service accessed via the MMC.

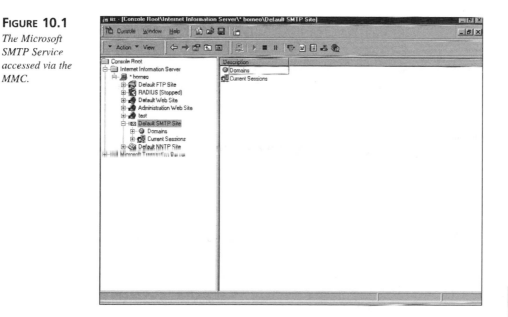

When the SMTP Service is installed, a single default local domain is created. The name of the default local domain determines how the service delivers messages. If the service receives an email message that is addressed to the same domain as the default local domain, it is delivered locally; otherwise the service attempts to send it somewhere else. The default local domain has the same domain name as your Web site.

You can also create additional alias domains for a single SMTP site. Alias domains are useful when your Web site itself has multiple domain names. To create an alias domain, open the Internet Service Manager, right-click on your default SMTP site and choose New, Domain. These additional alias domains must all share the same Drop directory (see the next section) as the default local domain.

You can even create multiple SMTP sites on the same server. To do this, you will need to verify whether you have the latest version of the Microsoft SMTP Service. The Windows NT Option Pack currently includes Microsoft SMTP Server version 1.0. A new version of the SMTP Service is included with Windows NT 4.0 Service Pack 4.0. To learn how to install the new version and create additional SMTP sites on the same server, search for the Microsoft Knowledge Base Article ID Q183476 at `http://www.microsoft.com/search`.

After you have the SMTP Service installed, you can monitor its performance by examining its log files. By default, the service keeps a log of its activity in the \WINNT\System32\LogFiles directory. This directory can be changed by clicking on the SMTP site's property sheet and editing the entry labeled Log File Directory. You can open and examine the SMTP Service's log files in any standard text editor such as Notepad.

How the Microsoft SMTP Service Works

From a user's perspective, the SMTP Service is a very simple component. The service uses two main directories, named Pickup and Drop, to process email. Both of these directories are located under the InetPub/MailRoot directory.

The Pickup directory is used to send email. The service constantly monitors the Pickup directory for new email messages. Whenever it finds an email message, the service attempts to send it. If the service is unable to immediately deliver the message, it is kept in the Queue directory while the service attempts to keep delivering the message. If the email message cannot be delivered and cannot be returned to the sender, the message is moved to the Badmail directory.

The Drop directory is used to receive email. When email messages are received by the SMTP Service, the service writes the messages out to the Drop directory. It doesn't do anything else with them; they just stay there. Again, the Microsoft SMTP Service does not support multiple mail boxes.

The email messages in these two directories are nothing more than text files. For example, you can send an email message by opening Notepad, entering the following text, and saving the file in the Pickup directory (Inetpub/mailroot/pickup):

```
To: webmaster@aspsite.com
From:  someone@somewhere.com
Subject:  Testing SMTP Service

Here is the message!
```

As soon as you save the file, the file should disappear from the Pickup directory because the SMTP Service is attempting to send it.

In theory, you could use the File Access component from within your Active Server Pages to write messages to the Pickup directory and send email (for information about the File Access component, see Chapter 8, "Working with the File System."). In practice, however, this is not a good strategy for two reasons. First, occasionally only partial messages are sent using this method (the SMTP Service appears to get ahead of itself and sends the email before the whole file has been written to the directory). Second, it is not easy to use this method when working with advanced email features such as message priorities and file attachments.

The most dependable and easiest method of using the SMTP Service to send email is by using the Collaboration Data Objects (CDO). This is the strategy explored in the rest of this chapter.

Sending Email with the CDO for NTS

It is very easy to use the CDO to send an email message from within an Active Server Page. This can be accomplished with a subroutine that contains only eight statements. Here is an example:

```
SUB sendMail( fromWho, toWho, Subject, Body )
    DIM myMail
    SET myMail = Server.CreateObject("CDONTS.Newmail")
    myMail.From = fromWho
    myMail.To = toWho
    myMail.Subject = Subject
```

10

WORKING WITH EMAIL

```
    myMail.Body = Body
    myMail.Send
    SET myMail = Nothing
END SUB
```

This subroutine accepts four parameters that correspond to the following:

- The email address of the sender of the message
- The email address of the recipient of the message
- The subject of the message
- The body of the message

An instance of the NewMail object is created, the appropriate properties are set, and the Send method is used to actually send the email message.

When sending email messages, you will need to set the From address to an email address with your domain name. Otherwise, email servers might automatically reject your messages.

Listing 10.1 is a simple ASP page that includes a form for sending email. The form appears in Figure 10.2.

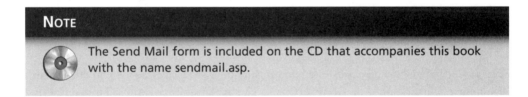

NOTE

The Send Mail form is included on the CD that accompanies this book with the name sendmail.asp.

LISTING 10.1 THE SEND MAIL FORM

```
<%
SUB sendMail( fromWho, toWho, Subject, Body )
    DIM myMail
    SET myMail = Server.CreateObject("CDONTS.Newmail")
    myMail.From = fromWho
    myMail.To = toWho
    myMail.Subject = Subject
    myMail.Body = Body
    myMail.Send
    SET myMail = Nothing
END SUB

fromWho = TRIM( Request.Form( "fromWho" ) )
toWho = TRIM( Request.Form( "toWho" ) )
Subject = TRIM( Request.Form( "Subject" ) )
```

```
Body = TRIM( Request.Form( "Body" ) )

IF toWho <> "" THEN
     sendMail fromWho, toWho, Subject, Body
END IF
%>
<HTML>
<HEAD><TITLE>Email Form</TITLE></HEAD>
<BODY BGCOLOR="#eeeeee">

<FORM METHOD="POST" ACTION="<%=Request.ServerVariables("SCRIPT_NAME")%>">
<BR>TO: <INPUT NAME="toWho" TYPE="text" SIZE=40>
<BR>FROM: <INPUT NAME="fromWho" TYPE="text" SIZE=40>
<BR>SUBJECT: <INPUT NAME="subject" TYPE="text" SIZE=40>
<BR><TEXTAREA NAME="Body" COLS=40 ROWS=5></TEXTAREA>
<BR><INPUT TYPE="SUBMIT" VALUE="Send Mail">
</FORM>

</BODY>
</HTML>
```

FIGURE 10.2

The Send Mail form.

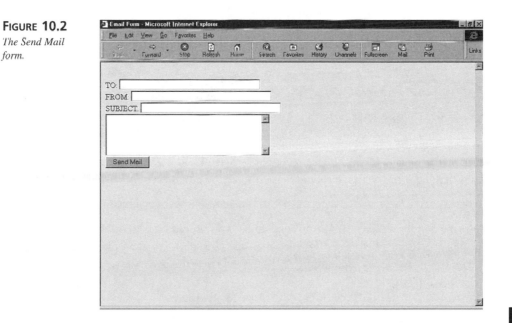

TIP

Instead of setting each property of the `NewMail` object one by one, you can also set them in a single statement within the `Send` method. For example, the following statement sends an email message:

```
myMail.Send( "sender@somewhere.com", "recipient@somewhere.com",
➥"Here is the subject", "Hello!")
```

If you are sending a long message, you will probably need to include line breaks in the message body. To create a line break, you can use the VBScript constant, `vbCRLF`, which adds a carriage return and a line feed. For example, here is an email message with multiple lines:

```
DIM theMessage
theMessage = "This is the first line." & vbCRLF &_
                    "This is the second line." & vbCRLF &_
                    "This is the third line."
SET myMail = Server.CreateObject("CDONTS.Newmail")
myMail.MailFormat = 0
myMail.BodyFormat = 0
myMail.From = "server@yourdomain.com"
myMail.To = "user@somewhere.com"
myMail.Subject = "Welcome to our Web site!"
myMail.Body = theMessage
myMail.Send
SET myMail = NOTHING
```

When sending email, you can send the same message to multiple email accounts by separating the email address of each recipient by a semicolon. The following statement specifies that the same message should be sent to all the email accounts listed:

```
myMail.To = "user1@somewhere.com;user2@somewhere.com;user3@somewhere.com"
```

When using the `NewMail` object to send email, you should be warned that a new instance of this object must be created for each message you send. For example, the following script fragment results in an error:

```
DIM objMail, k
SET myMail = Server.CreateObject("CDONTS.Newmail")
FOR k = 1 TO 50
    myMail.From = "sender@somewhere.com"
    myMail.To = "recipient@somewhere.com"
    myMail.Subject = "message #" & k
    myMail.Body = "Test Message"
    myMail.Send
NEXT
```

If you need to send multiple email messages from within a single Active Server Page, you must create and destroy multiple instances of the object to avoid receiving the error. The following script correctly sends multiple messages by creating new `NewMail` objects and then destroying each object by setting it to `Nothing`:

```
DIM objMail, k
FOR k = 1 TO 50
    SET myMail = Server.CreateObject("CDONTS.Newmail")
    myMail.From = "test@somewhere.com"
    myMail.To = "test@somewhere.com"
    myMail.Subject = "message #" & k
    myMail.Body = "Test Message"
    myMail.Send
    SET myMail = NOTHING
NEXT
```

This limitation is not really a limitation. A single Active Server Pages script can send thousands of individual email messages by creating and destroying the `NewMail` object over and over again.

Sending Email with Attachments

A file attachment can be added to an email message by using the `AttachFile()` method of the `NewMail` object. The `AttachFile()` method accepts three parameters: the full file path of the file to send and, optionally, the name of the file as it will appear in the email message, and the encoding method that should be used to encode the file:

objNewMail.**AttachFile(***Source* **[,** *FileName***] [,** *EncodingMethod***])**

In this code, *Source* is the full file path of the file to attach to the message. *FileName* is the name of the file as it will appear in the email message—if this parameter is not supplied, the file path will be used instead. *EncodingMethod* is either 0 for UUEncoded or 1 for Base 64 Encoded.

For example, the Active Server Page in Listing 10.2 automatically sends its own ASP source as an attachment if you enter your email address and click the button labeled Send Source.

LISTING 10.2   SEND THE SOURCE OF A FILE (SENDSOURCE.ASP)

```
<%
DIM myMail, thisPage, email
thisPage = Request.ServerVariables( "PATH_TRANSLATED" )
email = TRIM( Request.Form( "email" ) )
IF email <> "" THEN
    SET myMail = Server.CreateObject("CDONTS.Newmail")
    myMail.From = "source@yourdomain.com"
```

continues

LISTING **10.2** CONTINUED

```
        myMail.To = email
        myMail.Subject = "Source for " & thisPage
        myMail.Body = "This email has the source for file " & thisPage
        myMail.AttachFile ThisPage, "Source"
        myMail.Send
        SET myMail = NOTHING
END IF
%>
<HTML>
<HEAD><TITLE>Some Page</TITLE></HEAD>
<BODY>
<FORM METHOD="POST" ACTION="sendsource.asp">
Email Address: <INPUT NAME="email" TYPE="TEXT" SIZE=40>
<INPUT TYPE="SUBMIT" VALUE="Send Source">
</FORM>
</BODY>
</HTML>
```

Setting Email Message Priorities

Most, but not all, email clients support message priorities. For example, using Microsoft Outlook, you can send a message with Low, Normal, or High priority. When a High priority email is received, it appears as shown in Figure 10.3.

FIGURE **10.3**

An important message has been received.

Indicates a
High priority
message

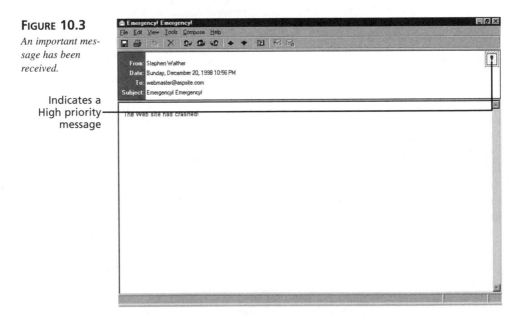

You can use the `Importance` property of the `NewMail` object to set the priority of a message. You can set the property to the following values:

0 Low Importance

1 Normal Importance (default value)

2 High Importance

The following script sends an email message of high importance:

```
<%
DIM myMail
SET myMail = Server.CreateObject("CDONTS.Newmail")
myMail.From = "server@yourdomain.com"
myMail.To = "administrator@yourdomain.com"
myMail.Subject = "Web Site Crashed!!!"
myMail.Body = "The Web Site has crashed!"
myMail.Importance = 2
myMail.Send
SET myMail = NOTHING
%>
```

Sending Carbon Copies and Blind Carbon Copies

When you send an email message, you can indicate that a copy of the message should be sent to another email address. There are two ways that you can send a copy of a message. When you send a message with a carbon copy, the main recipient of the message is able to view the email address of the recipient of the carbon copy. Here is an example of a script that sends a normal carbon copy:

```
<%
DIM myMail
SET myMail = Server.CreateObject("CDONTS.Newmail")
myMail.From = "fred@aol.com"
myMail.To = "alice@yahoo.com"
myMail.Subject = "Confidential Information"
myMail.Body = "Alice, I haven't sent any email to Bob."
myMail.Cc  = "bob@ix.netcom.com"
myMail.Send
SET myMail = NOTHING
%>
```

In this example, the `Cc` property of the `NewMail` object is used to send a carbon copy of the email message to the `alice@yahoo.com` email account.

Alternatively, you can send a blind carbon copy. If you send a blind carbon copy, the main recipient of the message will not know that another copy of the message has been sent. To send a blind carbon copy, you use the Bcc property of the NewMail object:

```
<%
DIM myMail
SET myMail = Server.CreateObject("CDONTS.Newmail")
myMail.From = "fred@aol.com"
myMail.To = "alice@yahoo.com"
myMail.Subject = "Confidential Information"
myMail.Body = "Alice, I haven't sent any email to Bob."
myMail.Bcc  = "bob@ix.netcom.com"
myMail.Send
SET myMail = NOTHING
%>
```

Sending blind carbon copies is very useful for monitoring the email activity that occurs at your Web site. For example, suppose that your Web site automatically sends an email message with registration information to each new user. You can send a blind carbon copy of the message to a separate email account to check whether the email is actually being sent or to automatically keep a copy of all the registration information.

You can list more than one email account as the recipient of either a normal carbon copy or blind carbon copy. To do this, simply separate each email account by a semicolon like this:

```
myMail.Bcc ="user1@somewhere.com;user2@soemwhere.com;user3@somewhere.com"
```

Sending Email with HTML Formatting and Images

You can use the CDO to send messages that include HTML formatting and images. For example, you can include text with particular fonts and colors, custom background images, and HTML links.

You should be warned, however, that most email clients do not fully support email with either HTML formatting or images. Although Microsoft Outlook supports these features, sending email with HTML formatting to other email clients can result in completely unreadable gibberish (the HTML source itself appears).

By default, the CDO sends email messages as plain text. To send email that contains HTML, you must set two properties of the NewMail object: the MailFormat property and the BodyFormat property:

```
myMail.MailFormat = 0
myMail.BodyFormat = 0
```

When the `MailFormat` property is set to `0`, the email is sent in MIME format. When the `BodyFormat` is set to `0`, the email message can contain HTML. After these two properties are set, you can send email with HTML formatting like this:

```
<%
DIM myMail, HTML
HTML = "<CENTER><FONT SIZE=+2 FACE=""Arial""> " &_
       "Come visit our Web site!" &_
       "<p><a href=""http://www.yourdomain.com"">
       ➥Click Here To Visit</a>" &
       "</FONT></CENTER>"
SET myMail = Server.CreateObject("CDONTS.Newmail")
myMail.MailFormat = 0
myMail.BodyFormat = 0
myMail.From = "server@yourdomain.com"
myMail.To = "user@somewhere.com"
myMail.Subject = "Welcome to our Web site!"
myMail.Body = HTML
myMail.Send
SET myMail = NOTHING
%>
```

This script sends an email message where the body of the message appears in a large Arial typeface. A hypertext link is included in the message that links back to the Web site at www.yourdomain.com (see Figure 10.4).

FIGURE 10.4

Email with a hypertext link.

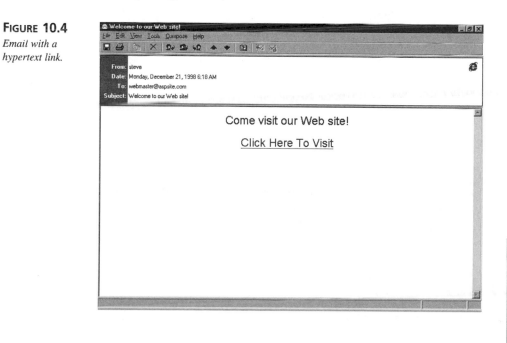

10

WORKING WITH EMAIL

When including links in your email, you will need to include the absolute path of the link (otherwise, the email client won't have enough information to find the proper Web site). In other words, you must use an address of the form `http://www.yourdomain.com/thepage.asp` rather than the shorter relative address `thepage.asp`. You can get around this limitation by using the `ContentLocation` property of the `NewMail` object. Here is an example:

```
<%
SET myMail = Server.CreateObject("CDONTS.Newmail")
myMail.MailFormat = 0
myMail.BodyFormat = 0
myMail.ContentLocation = "http://www.yourdomain.com/"
myMail.From = "server@yourdomain.com"
myMail.To = "user@somewhere.com"
myMail.Subject = "Welcome to our Web site!"
myMail.Body = "<a href=""thepage.asp"">Visit Our Web Site!</a>"
myMail.Send
SET myMail = NOTHING
%>
```

There are two methods that you can use to include images in your email. The simplest method is to include the HTML `<IMG>` tag in the body of your message. The following script uses this method to display a GIF image of a dinosaur (see Figure 10.5):

```
<%
SET myMail = Server.CreateObject("CDONTS.Newmail")
myMail.MailFormat = 0
myMail.BodyFormat = 0
myMail.ContentLocation = "http://www.yourdomain.com/images/"
myMail.From = "server@yourdomain.com"
myMail.To = "user@somewhere.com"
myMail.Subject = "Welcome to our Web site!"
myMail.Body = "<IMG SRC=""dinosaur.gif"">"
myMail.Send
SET myMail = NOTHING
%>
```

When someone views this email message, the actual image is fetched from the Web server. If your Web server goes down, or you delete the image file off your server's hard drive, the image can no longer be viewed. To get around these problems, you can send the image file itself with the email message. To do this, you use the `AttachURL()` method of the `NewMail` object:

```
<%
SET myMail = Server.CreateObject("CDONTS.Newmail")
myMail.MailFormat = 0
myMail.BodyFormat = 0
myMail.AttachURL "d:\inetpub\wwwroot\images\dinosaur.gif", "dinosaur.gif"
myMail.ContentLocation = "http://www.yourdomain.com/images/"
```

```
myMail.From = "server@yourdomain.com"
myMail.To = "user@somewhere.com"
myMail.Subject = "Welcome to our Web site!"
myMail.Body = "<IMG SRC=""dinosaur.gif"">"
myMail.Send
SET myMail = NOTHING
%>
```

In this script, the `AttachURL()` method is passed the full path of the image and image name. Because the image is included with the email, it is rendered immediately. You can attach additional images by calling the `AttachURL()` method as many times as you need.

FIGURE 10.5

Email with an image.

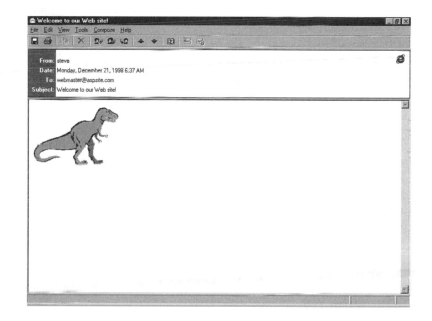

Retrieving Email with the CDO for NTS

When email messages arrive at your Web site, the SMTP service places them in the Drop directory. If you want to view these messages, there is nothing to prevent you from using Notepad to open and read them. The email messages are nothing more than normal text files.

You can use the CDO for NTS to retrieve the messages from the Drop directory within your Active Server Page scripts. In order to do this, you must first log on to the SMTP Service by using the CDO `Session` object. The following script fragment demonstrates how to log on using the display name Administrator and email address `administrator@yourdomain.com`:

```
SET mySession = Server.CreateObject( "CDONTS.Session" )
mySession.LogonSMTP "Administrator", "administrator@yourdomain.com"
```

You must call the `LogonSMTP()` method to initialize the `Session` object before you can use any of the other properties and methods of the CDO (with the exception of the `NewMail` object). After you have finished using the CDO, you should log off:

```
mySession.Logoff
```

After you have logged on, the next step for retrieving mail is to get a reference to the Inbox folder. In the case of the Microsoft SMTP Service, the Inbox folder corresponds to the Drop directory. This step can be accomplished with the `Inbox` property of the `Session` object:

```
SET myInbox = mySession.Inbox
```

Next, to retrieve an object that represents all the messages in your Inbox folder, use the `Messages` property:

```
SET myMessages = myInbox.Messages
```

Finally, you have an object with which you do something useful. The `Messages` object contains a collection of all the messages in the Drop directory. Because this object is a collection, you can use `Item` and `Count` to loop through all the individual messages in the collection:

```
FOR k = 1 TO myMessages.Count
    SET myMessage = myMessages.Item( k )
    Response.Write myMessage.Sender & " - "
    Response.Write myMessage.Subject & "<br>"
NEXT
```

This script iterates through all the messages in the `Messages` object and displays the sender and subject of each email message. Notice that each message in the `Messages` collection is itself an object. The `Message` object has several useful properties, as shown in Table 10.1 (this is not a complete list, but includes the most important ones).

TABLE 10.1 MESSAGE OBJECT PROPERTIES

Property	Description
Attachments	A single Attachment object or collection of Attachment objects representing all the attachments to the email message.
ContentBase	Returns the Content-Base header in the case of MIME HTML email messages.
ContentID	Returns the Content-ID header in the case of MIME email messages.
ContentLocation	Returns the Content-Location header in the case of MIME email messages.
HTMLText	Returns the content of the body of an email message in HTML form.
Importance	Returns the message priority. This property can have three values: 0: Low Importance 1: Normal Importance 2: High Importance
Recipients	A single Recipient object or collection of Recipient objects representing all the recipients of an email message.
Sender	Returns an AddressEntry object that represents the sender of the email message.
Size	Returns the approximate size of the message in bytes including the size of any attachments.
Subject	Returns the subject of the email message. This is the default property of the email object.
Text	Returns the content of the body of an email message in plain text format.
TimeReceived	Returns the date and time the email message was received or, if that information is not available, returns the data and time the message was sent.
TimeSent	Returns the date and time the email message was sent.

The Message object also contains a useful method for working with messages in your Drop folder. You can use the Delete() method to delete an individual message:

```
myMessage.Delete
```

10

WORKING WITH
EMAIL

If you are feeling really destructive, you can even call the `Delete()` method on the `Messages` collection. This will result in all the messages in the Drop folder being permanently removed.

Using these properties of the `Message` object, you can easily create a simple Web-based email client (see Figure 10.6). The script in Listing 10.3 enables you to retrieve the messages in the Drop directory and view each message one by one.

FIGURE 10.6

A simple email client.

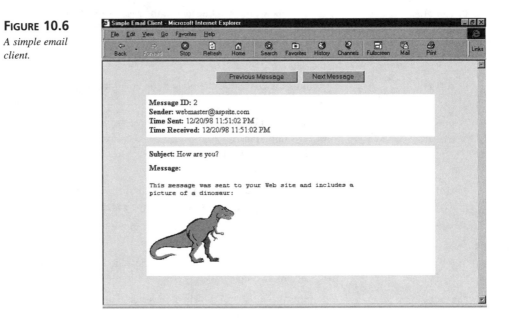

LISTING 10.3 SIMPLE EMAIL CLIENT (EMAILCLIENT.ASP AVAILABLE ON THE CD)

```
<%
DIM displayName, emailAddress
DIM mySession, myInbox, myMessages, myMessage
DIM messageIndex
displayName = TRIM( Request( "displayname" ) )
emailAddress = TRIM( Request( "emailAddress" ) )
messageIndex = Request( "messageIndex" )
IF messageIndex = "" THEN messageIndex = 1
messageIndex = cINT( messageIndex )

IF displayName = "" OR emailAddress = "" THEN
    %>
    <HTML>
    <HEAD><TITLE>Login</TITLE></HEAD>
    <BODY BGCOLOR="#EEEEEE">
    <FORM METHOD="POST" ACTION="emailclient.asp">
```

```
        <P>Display Name:  <INPUT NAME="displayName" TYPE="TEXT" SIZE=20>
        <P>Email Address: <INPUT NAME="emailAddress" TYPE="TEXT" SIZE=40>
        <P><INPUT TYPE="SUBMIT" VALUE="Login">
        </FORM>
        </BODY>
        </HTML>
        <%
        Response.End
END IF

SET mySession = Server.CreateObject( "CDONTS.Session" )
mySession.LogonSMTP displayName, emailAddress
SET myInbox = mySession.Inbox
SET myMessages = myInbox.Messages
%>
<HTML>
<HEAD><TITLE>Simple Email Client</TITLE></HEAD>
<BODY BGCOLOR="#EEEEEE">
<CENTER>
<%
IF myMessages.Count = 0 THEN
%>
You do not have any messages.
<%
ELSE
SET myMessage = myMessages.Item( messageIndex )
%>
<% IF myMessages.Count > 0 THEN %>
<TABLE CELLPADDING=4>
<TR>
<% IF messageIndex > 1 THEN %>
    <FORM METHOD="POST" ACTION="emailclient.asp">
    <INPUT NAME="displayName" TYPE="HIDDEN"
     VALUE="<%=displayName%>">
    <INPUT NAME="emailAddress" TYPE="HIDDEN"
     VALUE="<%=emailAddress%>">
    <INPUT NAME="messageIndex" TYPE="HIDDEN"
     VALUE="<%=messageIndex - 1%>">
    <TD>
    <INPUT TYPE="SUBMIT" VALUE="Previous Message">
    </TD>
    </FORM>
<% END IF %>
<% IF messageIndex < myMessages.Count THEN %>
    <FORM METHOD="POST" ACTION="emailclient.asp">
    <INPUT NAME="displayName" TYPE="HIDDEN"
     VALUE="<%=displayName%>">
    <INPUT NAME="emailAddress" TYPE="HIDDEN"
     VALUE="<%=emailAddress%>">
```

10

WORKING WITH
EMAIL

continues

LISTING 10.3   CONTINUED

```
     <INPUT NAME="messageIndex" TYPE="HIDDEN"
      VALUE="<%=messageIndex + 1%>">
     <TD>
     <INPUT TYPE="SUBMIT" VALUE="Next Message">
     </TD>
     </FORM>
<% END IF %>
</TR>
</TABLE>
<P>
<% END IF %>
<TABLE WIDTH=600 BGCOLOR="#FFFFFF" CELLPADDING=4>
<TR>
     <TD>
     <B>Message ID:</B> <%=messageIndex%>
     <BR><B>Sender:</B> <%=myMessage.Sender%>
     <BR><B>Time Sent:</B> <%=myMessage.TimeSent%>
     <BR><B>Time Received:</B> <%=myMessage.TimeReceived%>
     </TD>
</TR>
</TABLE>
<P>
<TABLE WIDTH=600 BGCOLOR="#FFFFFF" CELLPADDING=4>
<TR>
     <TD><B>Subject:</B> <%=myMessage.Subject%></TD>
</TR>
<TR>
     <TD>
     <B>Message:</B>
     <br>
     <PRE><%=myMessage.Text%></PRE>
     </TD>
</TR>
</TABLE>
</CENTER>
</BODY>
</HTML>
<%
END IF
SET myMessages = Nothing
mySession.Logoff
SET mySession = Nothing
%>
```

Creating a Simple List Server

 In this final part of this chapter, you will learn how to apply all the information you learned in previous parts to create a simple list server (see Figure 10.7). You can use the simple list server to create an email-based discussion group. The complete code for the simple list server is included on the CD that accompanies this book with the name listserver.asp.

FIGURE 10.7

The simple list server.

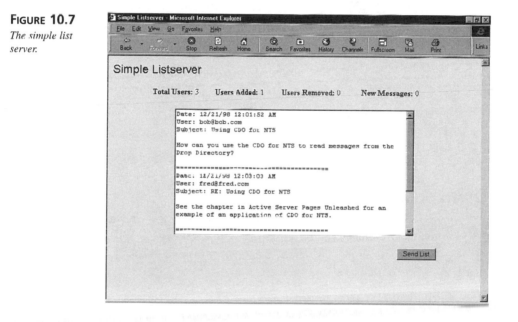

The simple list server has three main functions. First, it enables new users to join the list by sending an email message with the single word Add in the subject line of the message. After someone has joined the list, the person will receive the compiled email messages from the other users.

Second, the simple list server allows users to automatically remove themselves. Anyone can stop participating in the list by sending an email with the single word Remove in the subject line of the message.

Finally, the list server compiles all the email messages sent to it into a single email and broadcasts the email back to all the members of the list. You can send the compiled messages whenever you choose by clicking the button labeled Send List (see Figure 10.8).

FIGURE 10.8

*Send a list to all
the list server
members.*

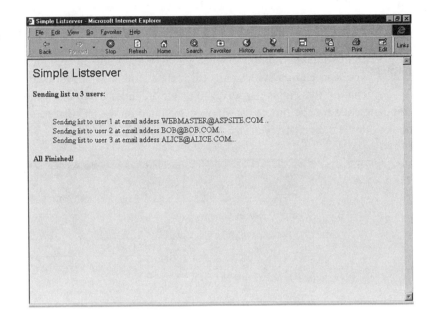

Using the Simple List Server

To use the simple list server, you will need to copy the file named listserver.asp from the CD that accompanies this book to a directory accessible to your Web server (for example, wwwroot). Next, you will need to change two constants that appear at the top of this file.

First, the constant `listServerEmail` is used to specify the email address of the list server. Members of the list send their email messages to this address. You should change this email address to an address within your domain (for example, `listserver@yourdo-main.com`).

Second, the constant `userListDir` provides the path to the directory where the messages and user list are stored. This can be any directory on your server (but it needs to exist!). Also, to use the list server, the Web server will need permission to write to this directory. (See Chapter 8.)

Whenever you execute the simple list server by opening the page listserver.asp in your Web browser, the simple list server automatically updates its list of users and messages. The current members of the list are kept in the file named userlist.txt. The compiled list of messages are kept in a file named messages.txt.

How the Simple List Server Works

The simple list server maintains its list of messages and users by iterating through all the email messages addressed to it in the Drop directory of your Web site. For example, the following subroutine is used to add new users to the list:

```
SUB addUsers
    DIM mySession, myInbox, myMessages, myMessage, k
    addUsersCount = 0
    SET mySession = Server.CreateObject( "CDONTS.Session" )
    mySession.LogonSMTP "listserver", listServerEmail
    SET myInbox = mySession.Inbox
    SET myMessages = myInbox.Messages
    IF myMessages.Count > 0 THEN
    FOR k = 1 TO myMessages.Count
        IF UCASE( TRIM( myMessages.Item( k )  ) ) = "ADD" THEN
            SET myMessage = myMessages.Item( k )
            addUser myMessage.Sender
            myMessage.Delete
            addUsersCount = addUsersCount + 1
        END IF
    NEXT
    FND IF
    SET myMessages = NOTHING
    mySession.Logoff
    SET mySession = NOTHING
END SUB
```

This subroutine logs on to the SMTP server and iterates through all the email messages with a FOR...NEXT loop. When an email message with the word ADD in its subject line is encountered, the user is added to the list with the addUser subroutine. Also, the email message is deleted from the Drop directory so that the user will not be added more than once.

When a user is added to the list, the File Access component is used to append the email address of the user to a file named userlist.txt. Here is the subroutine that adds a user:

```
SUB addUser( ByVal theUser )
    DIM fs, ts
    IF NOT userExists( theUser ) THEN
        Set fs = Server.CreateObject( "Scripting.FileSystemObject" )
        Set ts = fs.OpenTextFile( userlistDIR & "userlist.txt", 8, TRUE )
        ts.WriteLine UCASE( theUser )
        ts.Close
        SET fs = Nothing
        SET ts = Nothing
    END IF
END SUB
```

10

WORKING WITH EMAIL

The simple list server uses similar subroutines to manage the list of messages. New email messages are pulled from the Drop directory and appended to a file named messages.txt. After each message is added to this file, the message is automatically deleted from the Drop directory.

When you click Send List, the messages in the messages.txt file are sent to each email address contained in the userlist.txt file. The list of users is loaded with the following subroutine:

```
SUB loadUserList
    totalUsersCount = 0
    DIM fs, tf
    DIM userlistFile
    SET fs = Server.CreateObject( "Scripting.FileSystemObject" )
    IF fs.FileExists( userlistDir & "userlist.txt" ) THEN
    SET tf = fs.OpenTextFile( userlistDir & "userlist.txt" )
        userlistFile = UCASE( tf.ReadAll )
        userList = SPLIT( userlistFile, vbCRLF )
    tf.Close
    SET tf = Nothing
    totalUsersCount = UBOUND( userlist )
    IF totalUsersCount = 0 THEN totalUsersCount = 1
    END IF
    SET fs = Nothing
END SUB
```

This subroutine uses the File Access component to load the userlist.txt file. The complete contents of the file are retrieved with the ReadAll method and assigned to the variable named userlistFile. The VBScript SPLIT() function is then used to create an array of all the users by splitting the contents of userlistFile wherever a carriage return and line feed are encountered. The end result of the loadUserList subroutine is this array of all the users.

The following script is used to actually send the list of messages to all the users in the userlist array:

```
IF totalUsersCount > 0 THEN
FOR i = 0 TO UBOUND( userlist )
IF userlist( i ) <> "" THEN
 %>
<br>Sending list to user <%=i + 1%> at email address <%=userlist( i )%>...
<%
sendMail listServerEmail, userlist( i ), listServerSubject,  messages
END IF
NEXT
```

This script uses a FOR...NEXT loop to move through all the users. The sendMail subroutine (discussed in the second part of this chapter, "Sending Email with the CDO for NTS") emails the message.

Summary

In this chapter, you have learned all the secrets of using email with your Web site. In the first part, you learned how to configure the Microsoft SMTP Service. In the second and third parts, you learned how to use the CDO for NTS to interact with the SMTP Service to send and receive email from within your Active Server Pages scripts. Finally, an example of an application of the SMTP Service and CDO for NTS was discussed. You learned how to create a simple list server.

CHAPTER 11

Working with the Active Directory Service Interfaces

by Keith McIntyre

IN THIS CHAPTER

ADSI is an acronym that stands for Active Directory Services Interface. So what does that mean? From the name, you can derive that ADSI is probably an interface. Indeed, ADSI is a collection of COM objects that provides methods and properties through which an application can interface with a service. From the name, you might glean that ADSI has something to do with the Active Directory. Indeed, ADSI can be used as an interface to the Active Directory. Then again, from the name you might infer that ADSI is an active interface to a directory service.

This chapter will help you examine ADSI from several angles. You will look at the generic model of a directory service. You will also look at what Microsoft's Active Directory promises to be. But most of your time will be spent looking at the interfaces (objects) that make up ADSI.

This chapter will not be able to provide exhaustive details and examples regarding all aspects of ADSI. The topic is too large for a single chapter. The goal of this chapter is to provide a clear understanding of what ADSI is, as well as provide some clear, simple, and useful examples of how ADSI can be leveraged within your ASP code.

Also, the examples shown in this chapter are meant to show the "Zen" of using ADSI. The examples purposefully exclude error detection logic. They also avoid code that would beautify the output. Instead, the examples are meant to cut to the quick and demonstrate the use of the ADSI programmatic interface.

A special note regarding the examples in this chapter. The examples were developed using ADSI version 2.0 and require the ADSI SDK to be installed on the IIS machine where these examples are executed. The ADSI SDK is available for download from Microsoft's Web site. Also, some of the examples shown require that other Microsoft products such as Exchange Server 5.5 and Site Server 3.0 be installed before they will execute properly. A final note, the examples have been made generic by replacing specific server names with the string `"server"`. Specific server references must be supplied based on your development environment.

What Is a Directory?

Life is full of examples of directories. The phone book is one example that quickly comes to mind. A phone book provides a central store where information about people and/or services is stored. The white pages are a directory of people's names, addresses, and phone numbers. The entries of the directory are easily found because they are sorted by last name. Additional information can be gleaned from the white pages for certain entries. Is the person male or female? Is the person a doctor? Are multiple people associated with a single address?

The yellow pages are a different type of directory. It is organized by services. Although it still provides the name, address, and phone number information associated with each entry, it also provides a slew of additional information (attributes) about the service being offered.

Directories are usually organized for efficient searching by at least one parameter. The white pages are organized to efficiently find people by last name. The yellow pages require the user to know the type of product or service desired.

What Is a Directory Service?

In the world of computers, a directory service is used to keep track of entities of importance to the Information Systems (IS) or the Information Technology (IT) departments. Directory services keep track of things such as which computers belong to which domain, which printers exist and where they reside, which users exist within a system, and what access rights are to be granted each user. The model extends to keeping track of ancillary information regarding users, such as email addresses, phone numbers, and addresses.

As organizations grow larger than a single LAN, it becomes harder to manage and keep track of all the resources (including people) associated with the organization. Consider a worldwide organization that wants to have a single directory of all employees so that mail can be easily addressed to one or all members of the organization.

The computer industry has developed several solutions to help solve these problems. Novell developed the Bindary back in the NetWare 3.x days. The Bindary provided directory services for a LAN environment. The Bindary allowed for naming networking resources such as printers and file systems.

Novell increased the scope of the Bindery when it introduced the Directory Services as part of NetWare 4.0. The improved Directory Services were intended to support very large enterprises. It was appropriate for wide area networks (WANs) built of many dispersed LANs.

Another solution to the management of an organization's networking resources was developed in the form of the X.500 standard. X.500 was developed by the Open System Foundation as the solution for the OSI model. The X.500 standard provided an extremely robust specification for an enterprise-level directory service. Unfortunately, the X.500 specification is so open it requires implementations to support many data formats and transformations, communications protocols, and so on.

The X.500 standard was overkill for many organizations. The need for a simple directory service led to the development of the Lightweight Directory Access Protocol (LDAP) specification. The IETF developed the alternative LDAP specification (RFC 1777) that defined a subset of the X.500 standard. LDAP was designed around TCP/IP and provided support for just the basic interfaces required to implement a useful directory service.

Microsoft has embraced the LDAP specification and has leveraged it to provide membership and personalization services for Site Server 3.0, Microsoft's toolkit for developing Internet sites including intranets and commerce sites. Microsoft has also embraced LDAP as a store for Exchange Server address and contact information. This chapter will cover LDAP in more detail a bit later.

Microsoft will more fully embrace directory services with the release of Windows 2000, a suite of operating system offerings that will unify and replace Win98 and Windows NT. The Active Directory will be a central and foundational component of the Windows 2000 product and will indeed replace the existing PDC/BDC/domain model.

In general, a directory service is a global store for information about objects maintained in a network or organization. The specific objects and information about those objects can typically be extended. The directory service represents a persistent store that ties together heterogeneous environments.

What Is the Active Directory?

Microsoft Window NT 4.0 security is based on a domain model and a Security Access Manager (SAM) that keeps track of users and groups. Unfortunately, the practical limits on a Windows NT-based domain is around 20,000 users. Larger installations can be created by using multiple domains joined together via trust relationships, but they can be cumbersome to administer. To date, Windows NT has been a great platform for building LAN environments but has lacked the capability to support very large enterprises. (I'm sure Microsoft would argue these points.)

Another shortcoming or barrier to the adoption of Windows NT as an enterprise operating system has been the preeminence of Novell and its directory service.

Microsoft hopes to change all this by replacing the existing PDC, BDC, and SAM architecture with a new LDAP-based infrastructure dubbed the Active Directory (AD). The AD will solve the scalability issues that have plagued Windows NT 4.0 as well as fully embrace Novell's directory service solution. Moving forward, Windows NT 5.0, (also known as Windows 2000) will enable Microsoft products to take over the day-to-day management tasks of existing Novell networks. Of course, when new servers are required Microsoft hopes Windows NT will be the platform of choice.

One of the major goals of the AD is to allow for very large organizations consisting of millions of objects spread over a large and often disperse environment. AD promises the highly desirable capability to support a single username and password across multiple LANs comprised of dissimilar operating system environments. Single logons to file servers, email systems, and extranets will reduce the cost of ownership associated with enterprise-wide networking environments. (AD will also reduce hair loss and premature graying for IT professionals and users alike.)

The active directory is built on the concept of forests, trees, and domains. A forest is a collection of one or more trees that share in a trust relationship. Each tree is a collection of one or more domains that share a common schema. A domain is broken into one or more organizational units that are logical, self-administering entities.

The top of each tree is typically identified by an organizational name (O) that acts as a collection for other organizational units (OU). An organizational unit is traditionally a standalone entity that maintains its own users, groups, administrators, and resources. OUs are often self-managed. For example, an organizational unit might be geographical in nature: San Diego, Los Angeles, Phoenix, and Denver. Each OU could have an administrator group that maintained the member objects of the OU.

The AD is one of many namespaces supported by ADSI. Others include the current WinNT address space, NetWare Bindary, NetWare Directory Service, LDAP, and NFS. The AD namespace is constructed of Distinguished Names (DN). A DN starts with the specific and proceeds through the namespace to the general. AD names are comprised of keywords borrowed from the X.500 (and LDAP) model. Table 11.1 describes the entities from which AD names are created.

TABLE 11.1 ACTIVE DIRECTORY ENTITIES

Key	Description
O	Organization
DC	Domain Component
OU	Organizational Unit
C	Country Name
ST	State/Province
L	Locality
CN	Common Name

The following are examples of well-formed AD names.

CN=Keith McIntyre, OU=Engineering, OU=Stellcom, O=Microsoft Solution Providers

CN=Color Laser Printer, OU=Sales, OU=Stellcom, O=Microsoft Solution Providers

LDAP and the AD share many of the same object-naming conventions such as organization, organizational unit, and domain component. In fact, AD is based upon LDAP and represents another case where Microsoft has embraced a standard and gone one better. The AD will be a specialization of the generic schema model that LDAP supports.

The ADSI documentation supplied by Microsoft actually claims that ADSI is "X.500 compliant for LDAP and Novell Directory Services (NDS)." Certainly the namespace organization of these two ubiquitous directory services is adopted and promoted by both ADSI and AD.

The current state-of-the-art is that each directory service offering maintains its own namespace syntax. AD promises to unify the world of namespaces so that an IT manager or programmer will only need to deal with a single namespace syntax in order to maintain an enterprise comprised of dissimilar systems. AD will mollify the pains of working with NFS, NetWare, Windows NT, and other dissimilar networking environments within a single enterprise. (In these days of mergers and acquisitions, such collections are commonplace.)

Overview of the ADSI Object Model

ADSI implements an object model that supports representing many directory services that are available today. There are currently ADSI service providers for Windows NT 4.0, Windows NT 5.0, NetWare 3.x, NetWare 4.x, LDAP, and NFS. ADSI provides a flexible environment in which these current namespaces can be modeled. ADSI also allows for the creation and extension of schema, which allows for extensibility. For example, if an organization unit decides it is important to track a user's Social Security number or credit card information, those fields can be added to the schema of the User object.

If you spend time downloading and looking through the documentation for ADSI, you will find additional information about accessing ADSI via C++, Java, VB, and so on. As an ASP programmer, the only interfaces you need to be focused on are those that start with IADs*XXX*. These are the automation COM interfaces that are accessible via ASP applications.

ADSI provides three object interfaces that are ubiquitous to the ADSI object hierarchy. They are IADs, IADsContainer, and IADsPropertyList objects.

The IADs interface is fundamental to all ADSI objects and is responsible for object identification. It is like a base class that is inherited by all other ADSI classes. The IADs interface supplies access methods to properties. The properties differentiate one ADSI object from another. The IAD's interface also provides access to the schema that describes the metadata of an ADSI object. All leaf objects in the ADSI directory tree are derivations of IADs. Table 11.2 describes the properties and methods associated with the IADs interface.

TABLE 11.2   IADs PROPERTIES AND METHODS

Property/Method	Description
Name	The object's relative name
Class	The object's schema class name
GUID	The object's globally unique identifier
AdsPath	Path that uniquely identifies the object within the namespace
Parent	The AdsPath for the object's parent
Schema	AdsPath of the schema associated with this node
SetInfo()	Saves changes made to the object and its dependents
GetInfo()	Reloads the properties associated with the object from the underlying data store
Get()	Gets the value for a specific property
Put()	Sets the value for a specific property
GetEx()	Gets the value for a specific multivalue property
PutEx()	Sets the value for a specific multivalue property
GetInfoEx()	Reloads the properties associated with the object from the underlying data store

IADsContainer is the required interface for ADSI objects that create, delete, copy, move, and enumerate other ADSI objects. IADsContainer objects are used to create branches of the directory tree. IADsContainer enhances all the properties and methods of IADs, but they also add additional properties and methods to supplement the core functionality. Table 11.3 describes the additional properties and methods associated with the IADsContainer.

TABLE 11.3   IADsContainer PROPERTIES AND METHODS

Property/Method	Description
Count	The number of objects in the container
Filter	The filter used when enumerating a container's contents
Hints	The properties to load (suggested)
GetObject()	Gets an interface to the named object
Create()	Creates the specified object
Delete()	Deletes the specified object
CopyHere()	Copies the specified object to another location within the namespace
MoveHere()	Moves the specified object to another location within the namespace

IADsPropertyList is an interface that allows access to an object's properties. Table 11.4 describes the IADsPropertyList interface.

TABLE 11.4   IADsPropertyList PROPERTIES AND METHODS

Property/Method	Description
PropertyCount	The number of properties in the list
Next()	Gets the next property in the list
Skip()	Advances past *n* items in the list
Reset()	Starts over at the beginning of the list
Add()	Adds a property to the list
Remove()	Removes a property from the list
Item()	Gets the property that is named
GetPropertyItem()	Gets the value of a named property
PutPropertyItem()	Sets the value of a named property
PurgePropertyList()	Deletes all properties from the list

From these base interfaces, ADSI implements many specializations, as you will see later in the chapter.

ADSI uses these interfaces to build a hierarchical representation of all available namespaces. In fact, the root of the tree is an IADsCollection called IADsNamespaces. IADsNamespaces allows for iterating through each available namespace. (Each namespace is supported by a service provider.) The root, or top-level, ADSI namespaces object is given the name ADS:. In order to iterate all namespaces, one must bind to the root and then iterate through all member namespaces.

 The example in Listing 11.1 demonstrates enumeration of all the namespaces available on your network. The code is available on the companion CD in the file Namespaces.asp.

LISTING 11.1 ENUMERATING NAMESPACES

```
<%
On Error Resume Next

Dim oNameSpaces
Dim oNameSpace

Set oNameSpaces = GetObject("ADS://")
if Err = 0 Then
    Response.Write oNameSpaces.name & "<BR>"

    For each oNameSpace in oNameSpaces
        Response.Write "   " & oNameSpace.name & "<BR>"
    Next
Else
    Response.Write "ADSI error - " & Hex( Err )
End if

%>
```

ADSI implements a schema hierarchy in conjunction with the namespace hierarchy. Each namespace provides a description of itself via a schema that is attached to the root of the namespace. The schema consists of IADsClass, IADsProperty, and IADsSyntax interfaces. The schema itself is an IADsCollection that enables iteration through the class, property, and syntax objects that define the namespace. (Different branches of a namespace, for example, Organizational Units, can have different schemas that override the namespace schema defined in the root of the namespace tree.)

A requirement of a directory service, and hence of ADSI, is that each entity in the namespaces managed by the directory service be uniquely identifiable. ADSI uses the AdsPath to uniquely identify each node in the directory. The AdsPath is built of two main components—the ProgID of the namespace provider and the provider-specific string that uniquely identifies the node within the namespace. Examples of the ProgID portion of an AdsPath are WinNT and LDAP. The ProgID is separated from the namespace-defined portion by ://. The following are a few sample AdsPaths:

```
WinNT://Stellcom1/Uranus/HP Color Printer 3rd floor
```

```
LDAP://O=Stellcom ,OU=Engineering,CN=HPLJ5
```

```
LDAP://CN=HPLJ5,OU-Engineering,O=Stellcom
```

Note that LDAP names can be formed in specific-to-general or in general-to-specific terms. The preferred method is to form LDAP distinguished names (DN) from specific-to-general.

ADSI provides other interfaces that typify the objects abstracted and managed within a directory service environment. These objects include the IADsUser, IADsDomain, and IADsOU interfaces. These interfaces are provided particularly to support LDAP and AD namespaces.

Additional interfaces are also provided to support security and authentication. These interfaces include IADsAccessControlEntry, IADsAccessControlList, IADsSecurityDescriptor, and IADsOpenDSObject. You will learn about these interfaces a bit later in this chapter.

Property Caching

A very important feature of ADSI, both from an efficiency and operational vantage, is the property caching provided by the IADs interface. As identified earlier in this chapter, IADs has several methods associated with retrieving and setting properties associated with the various ADSI interfaces. These methods are listed here again in Table 11.5 for easy reference.

TABLE 11.5   IADs PROPERTY CACHE-RELATED METHODS

Property/Method	Description
SetInfo()	Persists the property cache
GetInfo()	Loads the property cache from the persisted store
Get()	Retrieves a specific property from the cache
Put()	Stores a specific property to the cache
GetEx()	Loads a multivalued property from the cache
PutEx()	Stores a multivalued property to the cache
GetInfoEx()	Loads the property cache from the persisted store

ADSI maintains a property cache that keeps the low-level implementation software from having to revisit the persisted data store each time a property is read or written. The caching logic can greatly improve performance when you are changing several properties associated with the same object. A good example of this is creating and specifying the configuration of a new user. Unfortunately, the caching of properties must also be diligently considered when writing ADSI code to ensure that logic errors do not occur.

The basics of ADSI's property cache are fairly straightforward. The cache is filled when GetInfo() or GetInfoEx() is called. If GetInfo() or GetInfoEx() has never been called and a Get() or GetEx() call is made, then the cache is automatically filled. Implicit loading of the cache will occur only the first time a Get() or GetEx() call is performed.

The cache is written (persisted) when SetInfo() is called. The Put() and PutEx() calls only write data to the cache. The cache will not be persisted until SetInfo() is called.

Be careful when setting and retrieving properties to make sure that a call to SetInfo() is made in order to save the cache before reading values from the cache. Calling GetInfo() will reload the cache with values from the persisted store. Any values modified via Put() or PutEx() that have not been persisted via SetInfo() will be lost when GetInfo() or GetInfoEx() is called.

Another interesting feature (or side effect) of caching is the behavior that is displayed when multiple applications attempt to change the same set of properties. After the cache is loaded, changes made to the underlying persisted store are not visible via any automatic mechanism. An application must call GetInfo() again in order to see changes made by other applications. The last application to call SetInfo() will win. It is easy to accidentally overwrite changes made to an object by another application. (This problem would typically be solved via record locking. ADSI does not support record locking.)

A final issue to be aware of when setting properties is the fact that SetInfo() does not guarantee that all properties will be saved when SetInfo() is called (SetInfo() is not transactional). Typically, all properties are persisted when SetInfo() is called. But it is possible for a failure to occur partially through saving the properties, in which case some property values could be lost.

Some of these ADSI shortfalls will be improved during subsequent releases. Despite these issues, ADSI is still a powerful tool that should (must) be embraced.

The property cache also affects the operation of IADsContainer. Objects added to the container are not persisted until SetInfo() is called. Objects deleted, however, are immediately reflected in the persisted data store. (The persisted data store is typically SQL Server, but can be Access, another database system, or any other persisted data store supported by the namespace service provider.)

The code in Listing 11.2 demonstrates how to access properties using ADSI. You can find the code on the companion CD in the file Properties.asp.

Listing 11.2 Accessing Properties via ADSI

```
<%@ Language=VBScript %>
<HTML>
<HEAD>
<META NAME="GENERATOR" Content="Microsoft Visual Studio 6.0">
</HEAD>
<BODY>

<%

Dim oContainer
Dim oRecipient
Dim oProperty
Dim idx

Set oContainer = _
    GetObject("LDAP://server/o=organization/ou=site/cn=Recipients")
oContainer.GetInfo()    'load the property cache

For Each oRecipient in oContainer
    Response.Write oRecipient.Name & "<BR>"

    For idx = 1 to oRecipient.PropertyCount
        Set oProperty = oRecipient.Next
        Response.Write "   "
        Response.Write oProperty.Name
        Response.Write " - "
        Response.Write oRecipient.Get(oProperty.Name)
        Response.Write "<BR>"
    Next
Next

%>

</BODY>
</HTML>
```

This example lists all the recipients belonging to an Exchange Server. The name of the recipient is displayed followed by a list of properties associated with the recipient. (Properties of a recipient include information such as phone numbers, fax numbers, addresses, and so on.)

The previous example requires access to an Exchange Server. (Testbox was the server used in the example.) The script should be run while logged in as the Exchange Server administrator to ensure sufficient privilege level exists.

Examining a Domain

ADSI provides an interface for a domain object that supports controlling many system-level policies. One of the beauties of ADSI is that you can use the schema interfaces to determine what the domain object looks like. The ASP code in Listing 11.3 queries the WinNT namespace schema in order to determine the types of objects it contains, as well as the mandatory and optional properties associated with each.

 The following code can be found on the companion CD in the file WhoAmI.asp.

LISTING 11.3   QUERYING AN ADSI SCHEMA

```
<%@ Language=VBScript %>
<HTML>
<HEAD>
<META NAME="GENERATOR" Content="Microsoft Visual Studio 6.0">
</HEAD>
<BODY>

<%

Dim oMe
Dim oMySchema
Dim oProperty
Dim oMember

On Error Resume Next

' bind to a domain object
Set oMe = GetObject( "WinNT://stellcom1" )

' properties of the domain object
Response.Write "Domain's definition -<BR>"
Response.Write "Name = " & oMe.name & "<BR>"
Response.Write "ADsPath = " & oMe.ADsPath & "<BR>"
Response.Write "Class = " & oMe.Class & "<BR>"
Response.Write "GUID = " & oMe.GUID & "<BR>"
Response.Write "Parent = " & oMe.Parent & "<BR>"
Response.Write "Schema = " & oMe.Schema & "<BR>"

' the domain's schema
```

continues

LISTING **11.3** CONTINUED

```
Response.Write "<BR>Schema's definition -<BR>"
Set oMySchema = GetObject( oMe.Schema )
Response.Write "Schema Name = " & oMySchema.Name & "<BR>"
Response.Write "Schema ADsPath = " & oMySchema.ADsPath & "<BR>"
Response.Write "Schema Class = " & oMySchema.Class & "<BR>"
Response.Write "Schema GUID = " & oMySchema.GUID & "<BR>"
Response.Write "Schema Parent = " & oMySchema.Parent & "<BR>"

' the schema is a container
if oMySchema.Container Then
    Response.Write "A WinNT domain contains -<BR>"
    Response.Write "    derived from " & oMySchema.DerivedFrom
    For Each oProperty in oMySchema.Containment
        Response.Write "   " & oProperty & "<BR>"
    Next

    Response.Write "Domain Required Properties -<BR>"
    For Each oProperty in oMySchema.MandatoryProperties
        Response.Write "   " & oProperty & "<BR>"
    Next
    Response.Write "Domain Optional Properties -<BR>"
    For Each oProperty in oMySchema.OptionalProperties
        Response.Write "   " & oProperty & "<BR>"
    Next
    Response.Write "Domain Naming Properties -<BR>"
    For Each oProperty in oMySchema.NamingProperties
        Response.Write "   " & oProperty & "<BR>"
    Next
End if

Response.Write "Members of the domain...<BR>"
For Each oMember in oMe
    Response.Write "   " & oMember.Name & "<BR>"
Next

%>

</BODY>
</HTML>
```

The code first binds to a known domain, in this case Stellcom1. (If you attempt to run this script you will need to supply an appropriate domain name as a replacement.) Next, the standard properties defined by IADs are retrieved and displayed. One of those standard properties is the AdsPath of the schema tied to the domain. The code uses the schema path to bind to the actual schema.

The schema is itself a container. The code verifies this fact and then proceeds to use the `Containment`, `MandatoryProperties`, and `OptionalProperties` collections to ascertain details about the domain interfaces. Figure 11.1 represents the output of the previous ASP page.

You might have noticed that the sample code contains an `ON ERROR RESUME NEXT` statement, as do most of the examples in this chapter. This statement is required because many properties are optional within the ADSI object model. Attempting to access optional properties that don't exist in a specific implementation will cause errors that should be ignored.

FIGURE 11.1

Displaying a schema.

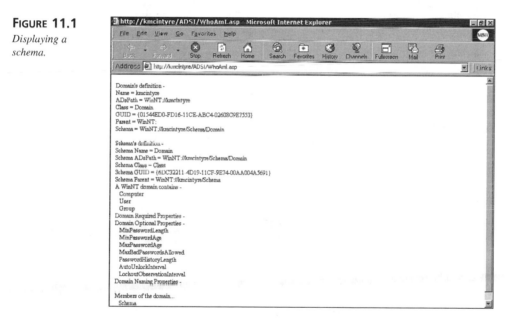

Based on this output, you can see that the ADSI support for a `WinNT` domain includes the following optional properties as shown in Table 11.6.

TABLE 11.6   PROPERTIES ASSOCIATED WITH A DOMAIN

Property	Description
MinPasswordLength	Passwords must be at least this number of characters
MinPasswordAge	Number of seconds a password must exist before it can be changed

continues

TABLE 11.6   CONTINUED

Property	Description
`MaxPasswordAge`	Number of seconds a password can exist before it must be changed
`MaxBadPasswordsAllowed`	Number of bad logon attempts to be made within `LockoutObservationInterval` seconds prior to an account lockout being invoked
`PasswordHistoryLength`	Number of unique passwords required prior to reuse of a password
`AutoUnlockInterval`	Number of seconds to lock out an account if `MaxBadPasswordsAllowed` has been exceeded
`LockoutObservationInterval`	Number of seconds in which `MaxBadPasswordsAllowed` attempts must be attempted before an account is locked out

Using some of the properties of a WinNT namespace domain, you can write some simple ASP code to change a password aging policy.

 The code in Listing 11.4 demonstrates one possible scenario. The code can be found on the companion CD in the file AgePasswords.asp.

> **NOTE**
>
> The Active Server Page in Listing 11.4 must be password protected for the script to work. To learn how to password protect an Active Server Page, see Chapter 23, "Securing Your Web Site." You will also need to replace Domain with the name of your Windows NT domain.

LISTING 11.4   A PASSWORD AGING POLICY

```
<%@ Language=VBScript %>
<HTML>
<HEAD>
<META NAME="GENERATOR" Content="Microsoft Visual Studio 6.0">
</HEAD>
<BODY>

<%

Dim oDomain
```

```
On Error Resume Next

Response.Write "Invoking strict password security...<BR>"

'bind to a domain object
'need to be a domain admin to execute this script
Set oDomain = GetObject( "WinNT://Domain" )

'cache up the changes
oDomain.MinPasswordLength = 8
oDomain.MinPasswordAge = 60 * 60 * 24 ^ 2
oDomain.MaxPasswordAge = 60 * 60 * 24 * 30

'flush the changes
oDomain.SetInfo

Response.Write "All done...<BR>"

%>

</BODY>
</HTML>
```

Manipulating Users and Groups

The previous example established a password policy that was global to the domain. Another common task for a system administrator is the creation and management of groups. ADSI provides for creating applications that can automate these necessary (but sometimes mundane) tasks.

The example in Listing 11.5 demonstrates listing the users on a domain by binding to the users' group associated with a WinNT domain. The code can be found on the companion CD in the file ListUsers.asp.

> **NOTE**
>
> The Active Server Page in Listing 11.5 must be password protected for the script to work. To learn how to password protect an Active Server Page, see Chapter 23. You will also need to replace server with the name of your Windows NT server.

LISTING 11.5 LISTING THE MEMBERS OF A GROUP

```
<%@ Language=VBScript %>
<HTML>
<HEAD>
<META NAME="GENERATOR" Content="Microsoft Visual Studio 6.0">
</HEAD>
<BODY>

<%

Dim oUsersGroup
Dim oUser
Dim oMember

Set oUsersGroup = GetObject("WinNT://server/Users")

Set oMembers = oUsersGroup.Members()
For Each oUser in oMembers
    Response.Write oUser.Name & "<BR>"
Next

%>

</BODY>
</HTML>
```

This example displays the usernames as HTML text. Using ASP, one could as easily create a drop-down list box of users via an HTML SELECT statement.

ADSI can be used to manage user accounts. In order to create a new user, you must bind to a machine or PDC and then use the Create method provided by IADsContainer.

 The example in Listing 11.6 creates a user and initializes the initial logon password to 12345678. The code can be found on the companion CD in the file CreateUser.asp.

> **NOTE**
>
> The Active Server Page in Listing 11.6 must be password protected and executed with sufficient rights to allow for user account creation for the script to work. To learn how to password protect an Active Server Page, see Chapter 23. You will also need to replace server with the name of your Windows NT server.

LISTING 11.6   CREATING A USER

```
<%@ Language=VBScript %>
<HTML>
<HEAD>
<META NAME="GENERATOR" Content="Microsoft Visual Studio 6.0">
</HEAD>
<BODY>

<%

Dim oDomain
Dim oUser

Response.Write "Creating a new user...<BR>"

'bind to a computer or PDC
Set oDomain = GetObject("WinNT://server")

'create the user need to be a domain admin to execute this script
Set oUser = oDomain.Create("User", "newADSIuser")

'persist the user
oUser.SetInfo

'assign a default password
oUser.SetPassword("12345678")

'persist the password
oUser.SetInfo

Response.Write "Done...<BR>"

%>

</BODY>
</HTML>
```

The preceding code fragment utilizes another interface ADSI makes available to the programmer. That interface is the User object. The User object is an attempt to standardize the kinds of information maintained by a directory service on a per-user basis. Of course, the schema is extensible. The ADSI User abstraction does not require use of any of the available properties. They are all optional. Table 11.7 lists the properties and methods available via the ADSI User interface.

TABLE 11.7 IADsUser PROPERTIES AND METHODS

Property/Method	Description
BadLoginAddress	Address of last node considered an intruder (RO)
BagLoginCount	Number of bad login attempts since last reset (RO)
LastLogin	Date and time of last login (RO)
LastLogoff	Date and time of last logoff (RO)
LastFailedLogin	Date and time of last failed login (RO)
PasswordLastChanged	Date and time of last password change (RO)
Description	Text describing the user account (RW)
Division	The division within an organization (RW)
Department	The organizational unit within an organization (RW)
EmployeeID	User's employee identification (RW)
FullName	User's full name (RW)
FirstName	User's first name (RW)
LastName	User's last name (RW)
OtherName	User's additional name (nickname, middle name) (RW)
NamePrefix	User's prefix (Mr., Mrs., Ms.) (RW)
NameSuffix	User's suffix (Jr., III, Esquire) (RW)
Title	User's title (RW)
Manager	User's manager (RW)
TelephoneHome	User's home telephone number (RW)
TelephoneMobile	User's mobile telephone number (RW)
TelephoneNumber	User's work telephone number (RW)
TelephonePager	User's pager number (RW)
FaxNumber	User's fax number (RW)
OfficeLocations	Array of office addresses (RW)
PostalAddresses	Array of post office addresses (RW)
PostalCodes	Array of zip codes (RW)
SeeAlso	Array of AdsPaths to associated objects (RW)
AccountDisabled	User account status (RW)

AccountExpirationDate	Date and time when the user will be blocked from subsequent logins (RW)
GraceLoginsAllowed	Number of times a user can log in after password has expired (RW)
GraceLoginsRemaining	Number of grace logins remaining (RW)
IsAccountLocked	User account locked status (RW)
LoginHours	Time periods during day and week when user can log in (RW)
LoginWorkstations	List of workstations the user can log in at (RW)
MaxLogins	Number of concurrent user logins allowed (RW)
MaxStorage	Maximum amount of disk space allowed (RW)
PasswordExpirationDate	Date and time the user's password expires (RW)
PasswordMinimumLength	Minimum characters allowable for the user's password (RW)
PasswordRequired	Shows whether a password is required for the user (RW)
RequireUniquePassword	Shows whether a new password must be different from others in the password history list (RW)
EmailAddress	User's email address (RW)
HomeDirectory	User's home directory (RW)
Languages	Array of languages for the user (RW)
Profile	Path to user's profile (RW)
LoginScript	Path to user's login script (RW)
Picture	Array of bytes that contain a picture of the user (RW)
HomePage	URL for the user's home page (RW)
Groups()	Returns the groups to which the user belongs
SetPassword()	Sets the user's password
ChangePassword()	Changes the password from the specified old value to the new value

You can see there is a very complete set of properties available to describe the user within the standard ADSI implementation.

Another common task of a system administrator is that of adding and removing users from groups. ADSI makes it easy for programmers to develop Web-based administration tools to assist in performing these tasks. Listing 11.7 demonstrates how to use ADSI to manage groups. The code is available on the companion CD in the file GroupLogic.asp.

LISTING 11.7 MANAGING GROUPS

```
<%@ Language=VBScript %>
<HTML>
<HEAD>
<META NAME="GENERATOR" Content="Microsoft Visual Studio 6.0">
</HEAD>
<BODY>

<%


Dim oDomain
Dim oGroup
Dim oMember
Dim oMembers
Dim bMember
Dim strGroup

On Error resume next
Set oDomain = GetObject("WinNT://server")

Set oGroup = GetObject("WinNT://server/Engineers")

If err <> 0 Then
    ' create a new group called Engineers
    Set oGroup = oDomain.Create("group", "Engineers")
    oGroup.SetInfo
End If

' add members to the group
oGroup.Add("WinNT://server/user1")

' remove members from the group
bMember = oGroup.IsMember("WinNT://server/Users/user1")
If bMember Then
    oGroup.Remove("WinNT://server/Users/user1")
End If

' list all members of the group
Response.Write "Members of the Engineering group...<BR>"
set oMembers = oGroup.Members()
For Each oMember in oMembers
```

```
        Response.Write "   " & oMember.Name & "<BR>"
Next

' delete the group - assumes a group call lackies...
' construct a possible ADsPath based on computer/domain and group name
strGroup = oDomain.AdsPath & "/" & "Lackies"

'attempt to bind to the group
Set oGroup = GetObject(strGroup)
if Err Then
    Response.Write "Group not found...<BR>"
Else
    ' Get parent of group
    Set oParent = GetObject(oGroup.Parent)
    if Err Then
        oParent.Delete "group", oGroup.Name
    End if
End if

%>

</BODY>
</HTML>
```

The preceding example checks to see whether a group called Engineers exists. If it does not exist, it is created. When the group exists a user named user1 is added to the group. The script verifies that user1 has been added to the group and immediately removes the user from the group. (This is sample code. It is not particularly useful to add and remove a user in this fashion other than to demonstrate the capability.)

Next the listing shows how to iterate through all members of a group and display their names. Finally, the example demonstrates how to delete a group through its parent's Delete() method.

Remember, you must supply a valid server name and execute the script with sufficient privilege in order to successfully manipulate users and groups.

Controlling NT Services

ADSI can be used to start and stop NT services. This enables you to create custom Web interfaces that do everything from controlling operations of a server farm to stopping an FTP service on your home-based NT workstation.

> **CAUTION**
>
> Controlling NT services can be a dangerous pastime. Using ADSI, you could easily write an ASP page that stops all services. Worse yet, you could write a script that changes the default startup property of one or more services so that the next time you reboot your machine nothing will work properly. Be careful. Only attempt to control services if you know what you are doing.

ADSI provides the capability to perform almost any task available via the Services Control Panel applet. The key to controlling NT services is found in the IADsService interface. Table 11.8 identifies the properties and methods of IADsService.

TABLE 11.8 IADsService PROPERTIES AND METHODS

Property/Method	Description
Dependencies	A list of other services that must be running in order to start this service
DisplayName	The service name displayed to the user
ErrorControl	The security level assumed if the service fails to start
HostComputer	AdsPath of the host computer
LoadOrderGroup	The load order for this service
Path	The file path of the service's executable file
ServicesAccountName	The name of the account used to run the service
ServiceAccountPath	The AdsPath of the account used to run the service
ServiceType	One of four types of service
StartType	One of five values describing how the service will start
StartupParameters	Parameters passed to the service on startup
Version	The version of the service

IADsService exposes all the properties typically set via the Services applet. A second ADSI interface provides the capability to actually control the operational state of the services. The IADsServiceOperations interface should be used to start, stop, pause, and resume services. Table 11.9 defines the methods exposed by IADsServiceOperations.

11

TABLE 11.9 IADsServiceOperations PROPERTIES AND METHODS

Property/Method	Description
Status	Returns the current status of the service
Start	Starts the service
Stop	Stops the service
Pause	Pauses the service
Continue	Resumes the service
SetPassword	Sets the password associated with the service

Controlling services is fairly simple using ADSI. The example in Listing 11.8 shows how to stop and start a service. Essentially, the script checks the status of the W3SVC service and then toggles the service to the opposite state. If the service is running, the script stops it. If the script is stopped (or paused), it is restarted.

 The code for Listing 11.8 is available on the companion CD in the file Services.asp.

NOTE

The Active Server Page in Listing 11.8 must be password protected for the script to work. To learn how to password protect an Active Server Page, see Chapter 23. You will also need to replace server with the name of your Windows NT server,

---

LISTING 11.8 CONTROLLING A WINDOWS NT SERVICE

```
<%@ Language=VBScript %>
<HTML>
<HEAD>
<META NAME="GENERATOR" Content="Microsoft Visual Studio 6.0">
</HEAD>
<BODY>

<%

Dim oService

'Warning this will shut off your www service,
'causing early termination of script
Set oService = GetObject("WinNT://server/W3SVC")
```

continues

LISTING 11.8   CONTINUED

```
Response.Write oService.name &",  "& oService.class &"<BR>"

Select Case oService.Status
    Case 1:  'stopped
        oService.Start
    Case 4:  'running
        oService.Stop
    Case 7:  'paused
        oService.Continue
End Select

%>

</BODY>
</HTML>
```

Controlling Printers

ADSI also gives you programmatic control over the management of printers and print queues. Using ADSI you can determine what printers are available and what their print queue status is. The print queue can be started, stopped, and paused. ADSI also enables print jobs to be individually manipulated. Table 11.10 outlines some of the properties and methods associated with the IADsPrintQueue.

TABLE 11.10   IADsPrintQueue PROPERTIES AND METHODS

Property/Method	Definition
PrintPath	The AdsPath of a shared printer
Model	Name of the printer driver associated with queue
Description	Text description of the print queue
Location	Text string describing where the queue is maintained
DefaultJobPriority	Default priority assigned to each print job
BannerPage	File system path to a divider page
PrintDevices	Array of BSTRs defining the print devices associated with the queue
NetAddress	Array of network addresses fields
Status()	Gets the print queue status
PrintJobs()	Returns a list of IADSPrintJobs in the queue

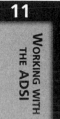

Property/Method	Definition
Pause()	Pauses processing the print queue
Resume()	Resumes processing the print queue
Purge()	Clears the print queue

Table 11.11 highlights some of the properties and methods associated with the
IADsPrintJob object.

TABLE 11.11   IADsPrintJob PROPERTIES AND METHODS

Property/Method	Description
HostPrintQueue	AdsPath of the associated print queue
User	Username of person who submitted the job
UserPath	AdsPath of the user who submitted the job
TimeSubmitted	The time the job was submitted
TotalPages	The number of pages in the job
Size	Job size in bytes
Description	Text describing the job
Priority	Priority for the print job
StartTime	The earliest the job can be started
UntilTime	The latest the job can be started
Notify	The name of the person to notify when the job is done
NotifyPath	The AdsPath of the person to notify when the job is done
Status()	Job status
TimeElapsed()	Seconds since job started
PagesPrinted()	Number of pages printed
Position()	Numeric position of the job in the print queue
Pause()	Pauses processing of the print job
Resume()	Resumes processing of the print job

As you can see, ADSI provides a lot of control over the various print jobs and printer
resources available in a network environment.

The code in Listing 11.9 demonstrates using ADSI to control printing resources.
The code is also available on the companion CD in the file Printers.asp.

LISTING 11.9   CONTROLLING PRINTING RESOURCES

```
<%@ Language=VBScript %>
<HTML>
<HEAD>
<META NAME="GENERATOR" Content="Microsoft Visual Studio 6.0">
</HEAD>
<BODY>

<%

Dim oServer
Dim oPrintQueue
Dim strFilter

'prepare to iterate through all printers
strFilter = Array("PrintQueue")
Set oServer = GetObject("WinNT://server")
oServer.Filter = strFilter

'purge all the print queues
Response.Write "Printers on " & oServer.Name & "<BR>"
For Each oPrintQueue in oServer
    Response.Write "   " & oPrintQueue.Name & "<BR>"
    oPrintQueue.Purge
Next

%>

</BODY>
</HTML>
```

The preceding example iterates through all print queues maintained on the specified server. (Remember to specify your server name when running this script.) The name of each printer is echoed to the client browser. The print queue is then purged of all print jobs.

Managing Exchange Server

Microsoft Exchange 5.5 uses LDAP to keep track of recipients (user accounts). ADSI can be used to programmatically access the Exchange LDAP store. This enables a programmer to read and write many parameters associated with a recipient, including information such as the name, address, work and home phone numbers, pager, fax, and mobile phone number of an Exchange user.

The LDAP interface also provides access to public folder hierarchies, groups, and distribution lists, as well as HTTP, IMAP, NNTP, and POP3 settings. Essentially, almost anything you would set via the user interface of Exchange can be accessed via the LDAP schema and associated interfaces and objects.

A bit later in this chapter, you will see a simple example of accessing recipient information from Exchange server via ADSI.

ADSI and Site Server

Another example of how ADSI and LDAP have been embraced by Microsoft can be seen in Site Server 3.0. Microsoft Site Server is an industrial-strength platform for developing Internet systems including intranets, extranets, and commerce sites. The membership and personalization components of Site Server are based on LDAP. (Actually, Site Server Membership can use either Windows NT or LDAP Membership authentication.) Regardless of authentication method, LDAP can be used to maintain many aspects of Site Server including site vocabularies, schema information about groups and members, application-specific settings and parameters, and distribution lists used by Direct Mail.

The advantage to using LDAP is that it scales nicely to millions of users. When used in an Internet application, it enables you to write secure Web applications that are not limited to the relatively small authentication capabilities of a Windows NT domain.

Another advantage of LDAP is the capability to use ADSI to programmatically query and modify the contents of the directory. Additionally, the Active User Object (AUO) interface provides another programmatic interface to the directory tree. AUO uses ADSI, and, in fact, exposes the IADs and IADsContainer interfaces in a simplified access mechanism to the directory tree.

Site Server implements a specific directory tree through which many aspects of a site can be controlled. The tree starts with an organization name at the root. Under the organization are several organizational units: Admin, Groups, Members, Applications, and DistributionLists. The Admin organizational unit contains several subordinate organizational units including the Schema organizational unit.

The LDAP organizational tree can be displayed, browsed, modified, and enhanced using the Microsoft Management Console (MMC) application. Figure 11.2 shows a partial expansion of the Site Server personalization and membership LDAP store.

FIGURE **11.2**

Using MMC to access Site Server's LDAP Directory.

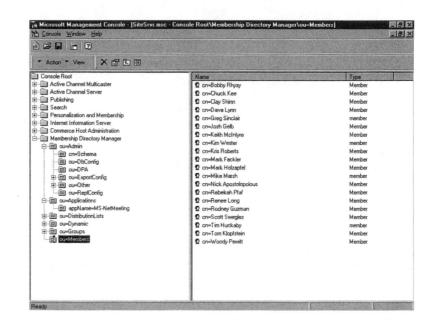

The Members organizational unit contains a subordinate organizational unit called AnonymousUsers. This container is used to keep information about users who are not members of the site yet but allow cookie authentication.

Personalization information about such users can be collected and maintained in the o=XXX, ou=Members, ou=AnonymousUsers container until they sign up to the site. The personalization information can then be copied to leaf objects that represent site members.

The ou=Members container is used to store all member information. Every member is represented by a leaf node within the Members container. The cn (common name) field of the member object is used to distinguish each user. Hence the distinguished name for a member is cn=username, ou=members, o=organization. A specialization of this general syntax might be cn=kmcintyre, ou=members, o=stellcom.

The Site Server LDAP configuration supports the following ADSI interfaces: IADs, IADsContainer, IADsClass, IADsProperty, and IADsOpenDSObject. You have seen all these classes with the exception of IADsOpenDSObject, which will be discussed a bit later in the chapter. These basic interfaces allow an application to discover the specific properties associated with a user (via IADsClass and the schema), enumerate and find users (via the IADsContainer interface), open a user's object (via IADsOpenDSObject), and access the properties that define the user profile (via IADsProperty).

 The code sample in Listing 11.10 demonstrates accessing a member's object in the directory tree and subsequently iterating through all the properties associated with the member. The code is available on the companion CD in the file SiteServer.asp.

LISTING 11.10 ACCESSING SS3 MEMBERSHIP PROPERTIES VIA ADSI

```
<%@ Language=VBScript %>
<HTML>
<HEAD>
<META NAME="GENERATOR" Content="Microsoft Visual Studio 6.0">
</HEAD>
<BODY>

<%

Dim oNamespace
Dim oMember

'bind to the namespace
Set oNamespace = GetObject("LDAP:")

'open the member object using authentication credentials
'credentials must be meaningful in terms of the service being provided
'i.e. fully qualified path to the admin user
Set oMember = oNamespace.OpenDSObject( _
    "LDAP://server/cn=user, ou=Members, o=organization", _
    "cn=adminUser,ou=Members, o=organization", _
    "password", 0)

'now access some of the members' properties
curBalance = oMember.AccountBalance
If CurBalance > 1000 Then
    oMember.bHighRoller = 1
Else
    oMember.bHighRoller = 0
End if

%>

</BODY>
</HTML>
```

Using ADO with ADSI

Searching directory services can be accomplished in many ways. The most simple search technique is to enumerate all objects in an IADsContainer and sequentially examine each entry to see whether it meets the desired criteria. Such a brute force approach will possibly lead to very poor performance, but it is simple to implement and can be useful if the number of entries is known to be small.

An alternative to this brute force technique is to apply an ADSI filter to the enumeration of an IADsContainer. The filter is an array of BSTRs that specify which types of objects you want to have returned.

 Listing 11.11 shows how to use the IADsContainer::filter property to reduce the scope of enumerations. The code is available on the companion CD in the file Filter.asp.

LISTING 11.11   USING IADsContainer's Filter PROPERTY

```
<%@ Language=VBScript %>
<HTML>
<HEAD>
<META NAME="GENERATOR" Content="Microsoft Visual Studio 6.0">
</HEAD>
<BODY>

<%

Dim oContainer
Dim oRecipient

'bind to the exchange server
Set oContainer = _
    GetObject("LDAP://server/cn=Recipients,ou=site,o=organization")

'apply a filter
oContainer.Filter = Array("OrganizationalPerson")

'load the cache
oContainer.GetInfo

For Each oRecipient in oContainer
    'do something with the recipient\
    If oRecipient.postalCode = "92121" Then
        Response.Write oRecipient.Name & "<BR>"
    End if
Next

%>

</BODY>
</HTML>
```

The preceding example accesses an Exchange Server and iterates through all recipients that are also members of the OrganizationalPerson group. The postalCode property of each recipient is checked to see whether it matches a specific zip code. If the recipient's zip code matches 92121, the name of the recipient is echoed to the client browser.

Another way to improve efficiency of searches is to use the `IADsContainer::hints` property to inform ADSI and the service provider of the items you will be interested in accessing. The `hints` property lets the service provider know which properties the application will be accessing. The service provider can hold off loading the property cache with values for those properties that are not of interest to the application. The service provider can subsequently load properties from the persisted store when specifically requested. If an application intends to iterate through lots of objects and examine only a particular property of each object, letting the service provider know which property will be accessed via the hints can increase efficiency of the total search. (Not all service providers honor hints.)

Perhaps the best method of querying a directory service is to use ADO. ADSI includes an OLE DB provider through which ADO can perform queries against the underlying directory service. This is a powerful way to find specific leaf objects within a namespace. It can be much faster than enumerating the entire directory information tree. ADO only provides read-only access to the underlying datastore. The ADSI OLE DB provider does not support writing values into the directory via ADO. Chapter 12 deals with using ADO and OLE DB. Use it as a reference if you don't readily understand the following code.

Using ADO to access a directory tree is similar to using ADO against any other datastore. The biggest hurdle is simply connecting to the ADSI OLE DB provider.

The code in Listing 11.12 demonstrates how to perform a simple query using ADO. The code is available on the companion CD in the file ADOExample.asp.

LISTING 11.12 USING ADO TO QUERY ADSI

```
<%@ Language=VBScript %>
<HTML>
<HEAD>
<META NAME="GENERATOR" Content="Microsoft Visual Studio 6.0">
</HEAD>
<BODY>

<%

Dim oADOConnection
Dim oRecordSet
```

continues

LISTING 11.12   CONTINUED

```
Dim oMember
Dim bstrQuery

'establish the ADO connection
set oADOConnection = Server.CreateObject("ADODB.Connection")
oADOConnection.Provider = "ADSDSOObject"
oADOConnection.Open "ADs Provider"

'specify a query
bstrQuery = "<LDAP://server/cn=Recipients,ou=site,o=organization>;"
bstrQuery = bstrQuery & "(objectClass=*);adspath,cn;subtree"

'execute the query
set oRecordset = oADOConnection.Execute( bstrQuery )
if err.number <> 0 Then Response.Write "error<BR>"

'access the records
Response.Write "Returned members <BR>"
Do While Not oRecordset.EOF
    Set oMember = GetObject( oRecordset.Fields(0).Value )
    Response.Write "   " & oMember.Name & "<BR>"
    oRecordset.movenext
Loop

%>

</BODY>
</HTML>
```

Security Considerations

So far, you have been using `GetObject()` to bind to ADSI objects. This works as long as the directory service being accessed is not protected by security ACLs. ADSI provides several interfaces to support and promote security. In this section, you will take a quick look at these interfaces.

ADSI provides the `IADsOpenDSObject` interface as a means of supplying credentials when requesting access to a directory service. `IADsOpenDSObject` contains one method that will be useful to automation clients such as an ASP application. That is the `OpenDSObject()` method.

`OpenDSObject()` requires four parameters as follows:

`OpenDSObject( DN, UserName, Password, Flags )`

where

DN is the AdsPath for the object you want to bind to. *Username* and *Password* specify the user account to be used when binding, and *Flags* can be either ADSI_USE_SECURE_AUTHENTICATION or ADSI_USE_ENCRYPTION.

A typical invocation of OpenDSObject() is demonstrated in Listing 11.13.

LISTING 11.13 AUTHENTICATION USING OpenDSObject()

```
Set oNamespace - GetObject("WinNT:")
Set oDomain = oNamespace.OpenDSObject("WinNT://stellcom1", _
    "kmcintyre", "passthis", 0)

' use oDomain as we have before
Response.Write "Name = " & oDomain.name & "<BR>"
```

The current version of ADSI does not include an object for working with file permissions that can be used within an Active Server Page. If you want to manipulate a file's permissions by changing its access control list (ACL), you must either use the DOS Cacls.exe command-line utility or a custom component.

Cacls.exe is a DOS utility that can be used to modify a file's ACLs. The script in Listing 11.14 uses Cacls.exe and the Run method of the Windows scripting host Shell object to change the permissions of a file named test.txt. (This example is a modified version of the script presented in a Microsoft Web Workshop article by Jeff Sanquist and Tom Moran entitled "Create a Virtual Directory Automatically with ADSI, ASP, and a Couple of Magic Tricks, Part II" at http://msdn.microsoft.com).

LISTING 11.14 SETTING FILE PERMISSIONS WITH CACLS.EXE

```
<%
currentUser = TRIM( Request.ServerVariables( "LOGON_USER" ) )
if currentUser = "" then
  Response.Status = "401 Not Authorized"
  Response.End
end if
acls = "cmd /c echo y¦ CACLS d:\test.txt "
acls = acls & " /g " & currentUser & ":f"
set objWSH = Server.CreateObject( "WScript.Shell" )
result = objWSH.Run( acls, 0, True )
if result = 0 then
  Response.Write "Changed Permissions!"
else
  Response.Write "Problem"
end if
%>
```

The preceding script forces a password dialog box to appear, and then assigns full access permissions for test.txt to the user who logs in. The Cacls.exe /g parameter grants user rights to the specified file. For more information on using Cacls.exe, see the entry for Cacls.exe in Windows NT Help.

 Using Cacls.exe to change file permissions is not particularly elegant or scalable. A much better solution is to use a custom component. The CD that accompanies this book includes a fully functional version of the Software Artisan's SA-FileManager component. This component includes methods for changing permissions for a file and for returning information about the ownership of a file.

As another alternative, Persits Software produces a component named AspAccessControl that not only allows you to change a file's permissions, but also allows you to display the current permissions for a file. For more information on this component, see http://www.persits.com.

Using ADSI with the IIS Metabase

Internet Information Server includes a collection of objects—the IIS Admin Objects—that together implement an ADSI namespace provider for IIS. These objects enable you to programmatically configure properties of your Web server such as its applications, file and directory permissions, virtual directories, and default documents. In fact, just about anything you can do with the Internet Service Manager you can do with the IIS Admin Objects. (The HTML version of the Internet Service Manager that Microsoft includes with IIS uses the IIS Admin Objects in the background.)

When you use the IIS Admin Objects to configure properties of your Web server, you are actually changing values in the IIS metabase. IIS uses the metabase rather than the Windows registry to store configuration information. The paths of the keys in the metabase correspond to ADSI paths.

For example, the script in Listing 11.15 returns a list of the names and paths of the virtual and physical directories located under the Default Web Site. It uses the ADSI path IIS://Server/W3SVC/1/Root to retrieve the root virtual directory of your Default Web Site (Web site number 1).

 The code for Listing 11.15 is available on the companion CD in the file IISListVDirs.asp.

LISTING 11.15 LISTING DIRECTORIES OF THE DEFAULT WEB SITE

```
<%@ Language=VBScript %>
<HTML>
<HEAD>
<META NAME="GENERATOR" Content="Microsoft Visual Studio 6.0">
</HEAD>
<BODY>

<%

ON ERROR RESUME NEXT

myServer = Request.ServerVariables( "SERVER_NAME" )
Response.Write "Server = " & myServer
ADSIPath = "IIS://" & myServer & "/W3SVC/1/ROOT"
Set defaultSite = getObject( ADSIPath )
for each thing in defaultSite
  Response.write "<p><b>" & thing.Name & "</b>"
  Response.write "<br>" & thing.Class
  Response.write "<br>" & thing.Path
next

%>

</BODY>
</HTML>
```

The script in Listing 11.15 automatically creates the ADSI path to the virtual root directory of the Default Web Site by retrieving the SERVER_NAME item from the
ServerVariables collection. Next, a FOR...EACH loop is used to display all the virtual
and physical directories located under the Default Web Site's virtual directory.

You also can use the IIS Admin Objects to create a new virtual directory and set its properties. The script in Listing 11.16 creates a physical directory named testdir and associates it with a new virtual directory named StellcomScripts.

The code for Listing 11.16 is available on the companion CD in the file
IISCreateVDir.asp.

LISTING 11.16 CREATING A NEW VIRTUAL DIRECTORY

```
<%@ Language=VBScript %>
<HTML>
<HEAD>
<META NAME="GENERATOR" Content="Microsoft Visual Studio 6.0">
</HEAD>
```

continues

LISTING 11.16   CONTINUED

```
<BODY>

<%

' Create the Physical Directory
Set FS = Server.CreateObject( "Scripting.FileSystemObject" )
FS.CreateFolder "c:\testdir"

' Create the Virtual Directory
myServer = Request.ServerVariables( "SERVER_NAME" )
ADSIPath = "IIS://" & myServer & "/W3SVC/1/ROOT"
Response.Write "ADSIPath = " & ADSIPath
Set defaultSite = getObject( ADSIPath )
Set vDir = defaultSite.Create( "IISWebVirtualDir", "StellcomScripts" )
vDir.Path = "c:\testdir"

' Set Virtual Directory Properties
vDir.AccessRead = TRUE
vDir.AccessScript = TRUE
vDir.DefaultDoc = "index.asp"
vDir.SetInfo
Response.Write "Virtual Directory Created!"

%>

</BODY>
</HTML>
```

The script in Listing 11.16 uses the File Access component (discussed in Chapter 8, "Working with the File System") to create a new physical directory named testdir. Next, an object representing the root virtual directory is retrieved by using the ADSI path `IIS://Server/W3SVC/1/ROOT`. A new virtual directory named StellcomScripts is created with the ADSI container Create method. Read permissions, script permissions, and a default document for this new virtual directory are set. Finally, the new virtual directory and its properties are saved to the IIS metabase by calling the ADSI SetInfo method.

Summary

In this chapter, you looked at some of the reasons why ADSI was created. You learned how to use ADSI to perform tasks often performed by a system administrator. You examined many of the most commonly used ADSI automation interfaces; those available for use in an ASP environment. You have seen examples of code that can manage users, groups, services, printers, and print jobs. You also briefly looked at how ADSI and LDAP have become central to the programmatic control of Exchange Server and Site Server. The chapter also covered the security interfaces available via ADSI and how to use ADSI to configure IIS from within Active Server Page scripts.

Using Active Server
Pages with Databases

PART

III

IN THIS PART

CHAPTER 12

Working with Connections and Data Sources

by Stephen Walther

IN THIS CHAPTER

In this chapter, you will be introduced to the methods for working with databases within your Active Server Pages. You will learn how to create a connection to a database and how to use this connection to store and retrieve data. Finally, some advanced methods for working with connections will be discussed.

An Alphabet Soup of Data Access Terms

I quickly get a headache when reading Microsoft's White Papers on database access. The problem is that acronym is piled upon acronym. To understand Microsoft's strategy for database access, you must understand the meaning and importance of such technologies as the MDAC, ADO, ADOX, ADOMD, RDS, OLE DB and ODBC. To spare you, gentle reader, from experiencing the same headache, this section will clarify some of these terms:

- MDAC—The Microsoft Data Access Components contain all Microsoft's software components for database access. It's the actual collection of software components that you can download from the Microsoft site and install on your computer. Currently, MDAC 2.1 is the latest version. The MDAC can be downloaded from `http://www.microsoft.com/data`. The MDAC includes all the software components discussed next.

- ADO—The ActiveX Data Objects provide an application-level interface to data providers such as Microsoft SQL Server or Microsoft Access. You use the ADO directly within your Active Server Pages to communicate with databases. The ADO is the primary subject of this chapter and the following ones.

- ADOX—The ADO Extensions for DDL and security comprise a collection of objects used to manage database objects and security. You can use these objects within your Active Server Pages to create databases and tables and retrieve their properties. The ADOX is also included in MDAC.

- ADOMD—The ADO Multidimensional is a collection of objects used to work with multidimensional data. Unless you are working with the Online Analytic Processing (OLAP) service system included with Microsoft SQL 7.0, you can safely ignore these objects.

- RDS—The Remote Data Service is a collection of objects that enable you to communicate with data providers located on remote machines or in separate processes. For example, you can use an RDS component within Microsoft Internet Explorer to retrieve data from a database over the Internet. The RDS is not covered in this book.

- OLE DB—OLE DB is a system-level interface to data providers such as Microsoft SQL Server or Microsoft Access. For example, the ADO uses the set of interfaces provided by OLE DB to communicate with Microsoft SQL Server. You never use OLE DB directly in your Active Server Pages. Instead, you use the ADO as a higher-level interface to OLE DB.

- ODBC—Once upon a time, the Open Database Connectivity Interface was used as the standard for communicating with databases. Almost all databases on the market today are compatible with ODBC. However, Microsoft is gradually replacing ODBC with OLE DB. Currently, Microsoft has OLE DB providers for such databases as Microsoft SQL Server, Oracle, and Microsoft Jet. Microsoft has also developed an OLE DB provider for ODBC to use with databases that do not have their own OLE DB providers.

In general, after you have your database connection configured, you can ignore all these software components except the ADO. The ADO contains all the objects that you will normally use within your Active Server Pages. Here's a brief overview of the three main objects contained in the ADO:

- Connection object—The Connection object represents all the features of a connection to a data source. You must open a connection with the Connection object before you can communicate with a data source. Typically, a Connection object is used to communicate with a database such as Microsoft SQL Server or Microsoft Access. However, you can open a connection to other data sources such as a normal text file, Microsoft Excel, Microsoft Exchange, Microsoft Index Server, or even—through ADSI—the file system. The Connection object will be discussed extensively in this chapter.

- Recordset object—A Recordset object represents the rows of data returned from a data source. For example, if you query a database, the rows of data returned from the database are returned in a set of records represented by the Recordset object. The Recordset object will be discussed in detail in Chapter 13, "Working with Recordsets."

- Command object— The Command object represents a command that can be executed against a data source. Typically, the Command object is used to execute a SQL stored procedure. The Command object is covered in detail in Chapter 14, "Working with the Command Object."

> **NOTE**
>
> The discussion and examples in this chapter and the following ones assume that you are using the version of ADO included with MDAC 2.1 (ADO version 2.1). You can determine the version of ADO installed on your computer by executing the following script:
>
> ```
> <%
>     Set Con = Server.CreateObject( "ADODB.Connection" )
>     Response.Write "ADO Version=" & Con.Version
> %>
> ```
>
> You can download the latest version of the ADO by visiting http://www.microsoft.com/data.

Creating Connections with OLE DB and ODBC

To access a database within your Active Server Pages, you use the ADO. The ADO contains the actual collection of objects that you use in your scripts to create a connection to a database and read the records from a database table. The ADO provides an application-level interface to data sources such as databases.

The ADO, however, does not communicate directly with a data source. Instead, the ADO communicates through an intermediary interface called OLE DB. OLE DB provides a system-level interface to a data source such as Microsoft SQL Server or Microsoft Access.

In general, after you have created a connection to a database, you can ignore the existence of OLE DB because it does all its work in the background. You never access OLE DB directly within your Active Server Pages. However, when you create your initial database connection, you must be aware of the existence of OLE DB because you can choose to access a database through different OLE DB providers.

There are two ways that an OLE DB provider may provide access to a database: either indirectly, through an ODBC driver; or directly, if it's a native OLE DB provider. Why is this so complicated?

The traditional method of communicating with a database was through the Open Database Connectivity (ODBC) interface. ODBC provides a common standard for communicating with databases using the SQL language. Whenever database vendors develop a new version of a database, they typically release a new set of ODBC drivers so that existing applications can communicate with the new database. The ODBC standard has made life easier for database developers by creating a common standard.

> **NOTE**
>
> SQL stands for Structured Query Language. It's the standard language for communicating with databases. See Appendix D, "SQL Reference," for a quick list of the most important SQL commands and their syntax.

However, Microsoft is gradually replacing the ODBC standard with OLE DB. The problem with ODBC is that it was developed with the narrow purpose of working with databases that support the SQL language. OLE DB, on the other hand, was designed to work with a much wider range of data sources. For example, Microsoft has developed OLE DB providers for such diverse data sources as Microsoft Exchange, Microsoft Index Server, and ADSI.

To accelerate the adoption of OLE DB, Microsoft created an OLE DB provider that works with traditional ODBC drivers. The OLE DB provider for ODBC drivers maps the OLE DB methods and interfaces to the ODBC API. By using this provider, you can use OLE DB to communicate with databases that do not yet have a native OLE DB provider.

Therefore, there are currently two methods for using the ADO to create a connection to a database. On the one hand, you can create a connection using the OLE DB provider for ODBC drivers. This type of connection will work with any database that has an ODBC driver (which means almost any database on the market today). On the other hand, you can create a connection using a native OLE DB provider.

Which provider should you use? When possible, you should use native OLE DB providers because they provide more efficient access to data. Microsoft, and several other companies, have developed native OLE DB providers for many of the most popular databases, including Microsoft SQL Server, Oracle, and Microsoft Access. You should use ODBC only when a native OLE DB provider for the data source is not available. The following sections provide examples of how to use both types of connections with Microsoft SQL Server and Microsoft Access.

Connecting to Microsoft SQL Server

Before you can communicate with a database such as Microsoft SQL Server, you must first open a connection to it. This is accomplished by opening the ADO `Connection` object with a *connection string*.

The connection string contains such information as the location of the data source and the security credentials of the user opening the connection. There are two general methods of providing this information: You can provide all the information in the connection string itself, or you can use the connection string to refer to an external file (or registry entry) that contains the information.

Connecting to SQL Server with OLE DB

The preferred method to connect to a Microsoft SQL Server database is to use the native OLE DB provider for SQL Server. The following example opens a connection to a Microsoft SQL Server named `yourServer`:

```
<%
Set Con = Server.CreateObject( "ADODB.Connection" )
Con.Open "PROVIDER=SQLOLEDB;DATA SOURCE=yourServer;
➡UID=sa;PWD=secret;DATABASE=Pubs "
%>
```

This script creates an instance of the ADO `Connection` object. Next, a connection to SQL Server is opened with a connection string that contains five parameters: the OLE DB provider, the data source, the database, the user ID, and the password.

The `PROVIDER` parameter is used to specify the name of the OLE DB provider to use for the connection. This example uses the native OLE DB Provider for SQL Server. If you don't supply this parameter, the OLE DB provider for ODBC drivers is used by default. For faster database access, you should always use this parameter to specify the OLE DB provider for SQL Server.

The `DATA SOURCE` parameter is used to provide the name of your SQL Server. For example, if SQL Server is located on a machine named `Plato`, then you should provide this parameter with the value `Plato`. If your database server is located on the same machine as your Web server, then you can supply the value `LocalServer` for this parameter.

The `UID` parameter indicates the SQL Server login that should be used with the connection. This example uses the sa login to connect to the database. Normally, however, you will want to use a different login with more restricted security permissions.

The UID parameter is optional. If you leave it out, a connection will be made with the IUSER_*MachineName* account. If your database does not have an IUSER_*MachineName* login, then the connection will fail.

The PWD parameter contains the SQL login's password. You can set this password within the SQL Enterprise Manager. The database connection will fail unless the correct password is provided.

The DATABASE parameter is used to specify a particular database located on your database server. This parameter is also optional. If you do not indicate a database, the SQL login's default database will be used (a login's default database can be configured within the SQL Server Enterprise Manager).

Instead of manually creating the connection string yourself, you can use Microsoft Data Link to automatically create a file that contains the connection information. After this file has been created, you can refer to it within your connection string.

To create a new Data Link, follow these steps:

1. Right-click your Windows desktop and choose New, and select Microsoft Data Link. You are provided with the opportunity to give your new Data Link a name (for example, myDataLink).

2. Double-click the new Data Link. This will launch the Data Link applet.

3. Next, choose the data provider by choosing the Microsoft OLE DB provider for SQL Server from the tab labeled Provider(see Figure 12.1). Click Next.

FIGURE 12.1

Creating a new Data Link for SQL Server.

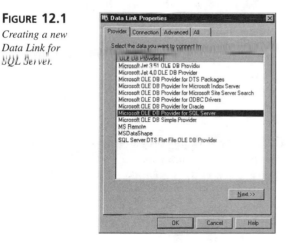

4. From the Connection tab, enter your server name, provide your authentication information, and select a particular SQL database to access.

5. Click OK to save your new Data Link.

After you have created a Data Link, you can open a database connection with a script like the following:

```
<%
Set Con = Server.CreateObject( "ADODB.Connection" )
Con.Open "File Name=C:\myDataLink.UDL;UID=sa;PWD=secret"
%>
```

This script assumes that you created a Data Link named myDataLink and saved it to the root directory of your C Drive.

One advantage of using a Data Link is that you can save the user ID and password within the file. To do this, choose the option labeled Allow Saving Password. When the password is saved in this way, you can open a connection with the following script:

```
<%
Set Con = Server.CreateObject( "ADODB.Connection" )
Con.Open "File Name=C:\myDataLink.UDL"
%>
```

> **NOTE**
>
> Notice that most of the programming examples in this book use a Data Link that includes the user ID and password to open a database connection.

Connecting to SQL Server with ODBC

The traditional method of connecting to a SQL Server database is through ODBC. When you open a connection without explicitly specifying an OLE DB provider, the connection uses the OLE DB provider for ODBC drivers.

There are three methods of opening a connection with this provider. The three methods correspond to different locations where the connection information is stored. You can store the information in the Windows registry, a text file, or within the connection string itself.

Creating a System DSN for Microsoft SQL Server

To store the connection information in the Windows registry, you create a System Data Source Name (DSN). Here is an example of a script that opens a connection to a database with a System DSN:

```
<%
Set Con = Server.CreateObject( "ADODB.Connection" )
Con.Open "DSN=MyDSN;UID=sa;PWD=secret;DATABASE=Pubs"
%>
```

This script creates an instance of the ADO Connection object with the CreateObject method. Next, the Connection object is opened by passing a connection string that contains four parameters: a System DSN, a user ID, a password, and a database name.

The user ID and password should correspond to a valid SQL Server login and password. You can use any login that you have created for your database. However, you must make sure that the login has the correct permissions to access whatever database you are connecting to.

The database parameter is optional. If you do not include it, a connection will be opened to the login's default database.

Before you can execute this script, you must create the System DSN in the Windows registry. Here are the steps for creating a System DSN:

1. Launch the ODBC Data Source Administrator. This applet is located in the Windows Control Panel and is labeled ODBC Data Sources (see Figure 12.2).

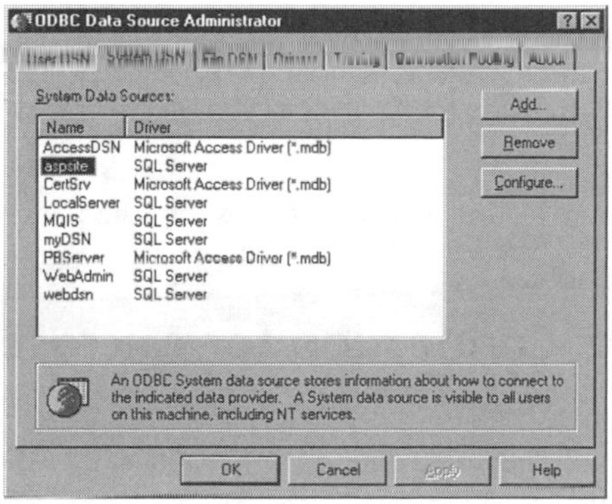

FIGURE 12.2

ODBC Data Source Administrator.

2. Within the ODBC Data Source Administrator, choose the tab labeled System DSN.
3. Click Add, select the SQL Server Driver, and click Finish.

4. Enter a name (for example, MyDSN) and description, and then choose the server to which you want to connect. If SQL Server is located on the same machine as IIS, choose Local. If the server is located somewhere on the Internet, you can enter an IP address or domain name. Click Next.

5. Choose a method of authentication. The authentication information is used only while creating the System DSN, not when the System DSN is actually used in your Active Server Pages. Click Next three times to skip the next two screens.

6. Finally, you are given the opportunity to test your new connection. If all goes well, the new System DSN is created.

You create a System DSN only once. After it has been created, you can use it within any of your Active Server Page scripts located on the same machine. If you ever migrate your Web site to another server or change the location of your database server, you must create a System DSN with the same name again.

Creating a File DSN for Microsoft SQL Server

Instead of storing the connection information in the Windows registry, you can store it in a text file by creating a File DSN. To create a File DSN, launch the ODBC Data Source Administrator and choose the tab labeled File DSN. Click Add and you will be given the opportunity to specify the name and location of the file used to store the connection information. The remaining steps are the same as the steps that you would follow to create a System DSN.

If you give your File DSN the name myFileDSN, you can open a database connection with the following script:

```
<%
Set Con = Server.CreateObject( "ADODB.Connection" )
Con.Open "FILEDSN=myFileDSN;UID=sa;PWD=secret;DATABASE=Pubs"
%>
```

Notice that this script is the same as the previous one, except the parameter FILEDSN is used rather than DSN.

Creating a DSN-less Connection for Microsoft SQL Server

Finally, if you want to include all the connection information within the connection string itself, you can open a DSN-less connection. In this case, you do not need to configure anything with the ODBC Data Source Administrator. The following script has exactly the same effect as the previous two scripts:

```
<%
Set Con = Server.CreateObject( "ADODB.Connection" )
Con.Open "DRIVER={SQL Server};SERVER=yourServer;UID=sa;PWD=secret"
%>
```

Instead of using the DSN or FILEDSN parameter, this connection string uses the DRIVER and SERVER parameters. To use this script, replace the expression yourServer with the name of your database server.

Opening a Database Connection Across the Internet

You can use any of the connection methods discussed in this section to communicate with a SQL Server database server no matter where it is located. For example, you can retrieve all the records from a database table located in England within an Active Server Page running on a computer in California. If you want to communicate with a database server across the Internet, you must configure both the client and server to use the TCP/IP protocol.

To configure your Web server to use the TCP/IP protocol, launch the Client Network Utility from the Microsoft SQL Server program group. Next, enable the TCP/IP network library. If the Client Network Utility is not installed on your Web server, you can install it by running the Setup program from your SQL Server installation CD.

To configure your SQL Server 7.0 database server to use the TCP/IP protocol, use the Server Network Utility located in the Microsoft SQL Server 7.0 program group (the TCP/IP library is enabled by default). To enable your SQL 6.5 database server to use TCP/IP, run the Setup program from the Microsoft SQL Server 6.5 program group.

If your database server is located at host.domain.com, you can connect to it with the following script:

```
<%
Set Con = Server.CreateObject( "ADODB.Connection" )
Con.Open "PROVIDER=SQLOLEDB;DATA SOURCE=host.domain.com;
➥UID=sa;PWD=secret;DATABASE=Pubs "
%>
```

After you have your database server and client configured to use TCP/IP, you also can use all the SQL client utilities across the Internet. For example, you can use both the Enterprise Manager and Query Analyzer to manage your SQL Server databases remotely.

Connecting to a Microsoft Access Database

If you expect many people to use your Web site, you should not use Microsoft Access for your Web site's database. Microsoft Access is a desktop database and not a client/server database. This means that it was not designed to support the number of simultaneous users that even a modest public Web site receives. For example, Microsoft Access does not support advanced multiuser locking, transaction logs, or efficient indexing.

> **NOTE**
>
> Unless explicitly stated otherwise, all the examples in this book assume that you are working with a Microsoft SQL Server database.

With these warnings in mind, this section discusses how to open a connection to an Access database within your Active Server Pages. You will learn how to create a connection by using both the native OLE DB provider for Access and by using ODBC. Finally, you will learn how to create a new Access database within your Active Server Pages by using the ADOX.

Creating a Microsoft Access Connection Using OLE DB

The preferred method for creating a connection to an Access database is by using a native OLE DB provider. There are two native OLE DB providers for Microsoft Access: MICROSOFT.JET.OLEDB.3.5 and MICROSOFT.JET.OLEDB.4.0. The two providers work with different versions of the Access database. Here's an example of how a connection can be opened by using the 4.0 provider:

```
<%
Set Con = Server.CreateObject( "ADODB.Connection" )
Con.Open "PROVIDER=MICROSOFT.JET.OLEDB.4.0;DATA SOURCE=c:\myAccess.mdb"
%>
```

Notice that the DATA SOURCE parameter is used to provide a path to the Access database (the mdb file).

Instead of providing all the connection information in the connection string, you can store the information in a Data Link. Here are the steps for creating an Access Data Link:

1. Right click on your Windows desktop and choose New, and select Microsoft Data Link. You will be provided with the opportunity to give a name to your Data Link file (for example, myDataLink).

2. Double-click the new Data Link. This will launch the Data Link applet.

3. Next choose the data provider by choosing Microsoft Jet OLEDB Provider from the tab labeled Provider (see Figure 12.3).

FIGURE 12.3

Creating a Data Link for Microsoft Access.

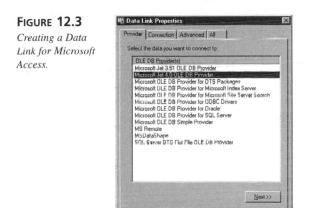

4. From the Connection tab, enter the path to your Access database (the mdb file).

5. Click OK to save your new Data Link.

After you have created a new Data Link, you can refer to it in your connection strings like this:

```
<%
Set Con = Server.CreateObject( "ADODB.Connection" )
Con.Open "File Name=C:\myDataLink.UDL"
%>
```

Creating a Microsoft Access Connection Using ODBC

If you prefer to create a connection to an Access database using ODBC, you have three choices. You can store the connection information in the Windows registry, a file, or in the connection string itself.

Creating a System DSN for Microsoft Access

In order to store the connection information in the Windows registry, you must create a System DSN. Here are the steps for creating an Access System DSN:

1. Launch the ODBC Data Source Administrator. This applet is located in the Windows Control Panel and is labeled ODBC Data Sources.

2. Within the ODBC Data Source Administrator, choose the tab labeled System DSN.

3. Click Add, select the Access Driver, and click Finish.

4. Enter a Data Source Name (for example, AccessDSN), and a description for the connection. You are given the choice to create a new Access database or you can click the button labeled Select to choose an Access database that already exists on your server. (Notice that by clicking Advance, you are presented with several advanced options. For example, you can supply a default directory for your Access databases or provide a default login name and password.) Click OK to finish.

After the System DSN has been created, you can use it within any of the Active Server Pages located on the same computer. For example, the following script opens a connection to an Access database using a System DSN named AccessDSN:

```
<%
Set Con = Server.CreateObject( "ADODB.Connection" )
Con.Open "DSN=AccessDSN"
%>
```

This script creates an instance of the ADO Connection object and opens it with a connection string. Notice that no authentication information is included in the connection string (it's not required when using Microsoft Access). If you want to include authentication information, you can supply the UID and PWD parameters like this:

```
<%
Set Con = Server.CreateObject( "ADODB.Connection" )
Con.Open "DSN=AccessDSN;UID=admin;PWD=secret"
%>
```

Creating a File DSN for Microsoft Access

The procedure for creating a File DSN is similar to the procedure for creating a System DSN. To create a File DSN, launch the ODBC Data Source Administrator and choose the tab labeled File DSN. Click Add and you will be given the opportunity to specify the name and location of the file used to store the connection information. The remaining steps are the same as the steps that you follow to create a System DSN.

After you have created a File DSN, you can open a connection to an Access Database with the following script:

```
<%
Set Con = Server.CreateObject( "ADODB.Connection" )
Con.Open "FILEDSN=AccessDSN"
%>
```

This script opens a connection by including the name of the File DSN in the connection string. You can supply authentication information by including the UID and PWD parameters in the connection string.

Creating a DSN-less Connection for Microsoft Access

Finally, if you do not want to create either a System DSN or File DSN, you can create a DSN-less connection. To create a DSN-less connection to an Access database, you must include two additional parameters in the connection string: the DRIVER and DBQ parameters:

```
<%
Set Con = Server.CreateObject( "ADODB.Connection" )
Con.Open "DRIVER={Microsoft Access Driver (*.mdb)};DBQ=C:\myDatabase.mdb"
%>
```

The DRIVER parameter is used to specify the Microsoft Access driver. The DBQ parameter supplies the path to your Microsoft Access database file (the mdb file). In this case, the database is located in the root directory of the C: drive.

Creating Access Databases Within an Active Server Page

You do not need to purchase Microsoft Access in order to use an Access database with your Web site. You can create a new Access database by using the ODBC Data Source Administrator, the Data Link applet or, programmatically, within an Active Server Page script.

 The ADO itself does not include a method for creating a new Access database. To create a new database within an Active Server Page, you must use the ADOX (the ADO Extensions for DDL and security). The ADOX is included with the MDAC 2.1 download from Microsoft (see http://www.microsoft.com/data). The following script creates a new Access database and opens a connection to it (it's included on the CD as newAccess.asp):

```
<%
DBName = "c:\myAccessDB.mdb"
Set myCat = Server.CreateObject( "ADOX.Catalog" )
```

```
myCat.Create "Provider=Microsoft.Jet.OLEDB.4.0;Data Source=" & DBName

Set Con = Server.CreateObject( "ADODB.Connection" )
Con.Open "PROVIDER=MICROSOFT.JET.OLEDB.4.0;DATA SOURCE=" & DBName
%>
```

This script creates an instance of the ADOX `Catalog` object and uses the object's `Create` method to create a new Access database. Next, a connection is opened to the new Access database using the native OLE DB provider.

Closing an Open Connection

You never need to explicitly close an open database connection within your Active Server Pages. An open connection is automatically closed when an Active Server Page finishes processing.

However, it is good practice to explicitly close a connection when you are no longer using it. A database can handle only a certain number of connections at a time. By explicitly closing a connection, you free up resources on your database server.

To explicitly close a connection, use the `Close` method of the `Connection` object like this:

```
<%
Set Con = Server.CreateObject( "ADODB.Connection" )
Con.Open "FILE NAME=C:\myDataLink.UDL"
'...Do Some Database Work...
Con.Close
Set Con = NOTHING
%>
```

This example opens a database connection and, after the connection has been used, closes it with the `Close` method. The final statement in the script removes the `Connection` object from memory.

Executing a SQL Statement with the Connection Object

After you have opened a database connection, you can actually do something useful with it. With the `Execute` method of the `Connection` object, you can execute any SQL statement. In the following sections, you will be provided with examples of how to create a new database table with Microsoft SQL Server. You will learn how to insert, update, delete, and select data from a database table.

Creating a New Database Table

The following script creates a new database table named Webusers in the sa login's default database:

```
<%
MySQL="Create Table Webusers(username VARCHAR(20), password VARCHAR(20))"
Set Con = Server.CreateObject( "ADODB.Connection" )
Con.Open "FILE NAME=c:\myDataLink.UDL"
Con.Execute MySQL
%>
```

The SQL Create Table statement is used to create the new table. The table is created with two columns named Username and Password. Both columns are VARCHAR columns with a maximum length of 20 characters.

> **NOTE**
>
> To remove a table after you have created it, you can use the SQL Drop Table statement. The following statement removes the table named Webusers:
>
> ```
> Drop Table Webusers
> ```

Inserting Data into a Database Table

To insert a new row of data into a database table, you use the SQL Insert statement. Here is an example:

```
<%
MySQL = "Insert Webusers ( username, password )
▶values ( 'Andrew Jones', 'secret' )"
Set Con = Server.CreateObject( "ADODB.Connection" )
Con.Open "FILE NAME=C:\myDataLink.UDL"
Con.Execute MySQL
%>
```

This script inserts the username Andrew Jones and the password secret into the Webusers table. Notice that single quotes are used around the strings being inserted.

> **NOTE**
>
> When inserting data into an Access database rather than a SQL Server database, you must use Insert Into instead of Insert.

The SQL statement that is executed is just a string. You can manipulate the string however you want to insert different values. Listing 12.1 demonstrates how you can retrieve data from an HTML form and insert the data into the Webusers table (see Figure 12.4).

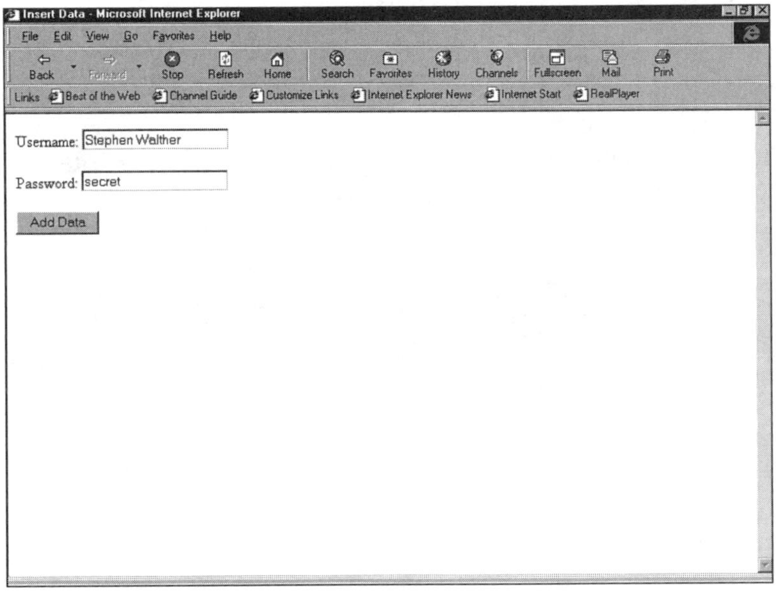

FIGURE **12.4**

Inserting data with an HTML form.

```
Insert Data - Microsoft Internet Explorer
File   Edit   View   Go   Favorites   Help
Back  Forward   Stop  Refresh  Home   Search  Favorites  History  Channels  Fullscreen  Mail  Print
Links  Best of the Web   Channel Guide   Customize Links   Internet Explorer News   Internet Start   RealPlayer

Username: Stephen Walther

Password: secret

   Add Data
```

LISTING **12.1**   INSERTDATA.ASP

```
<%
FUNCTION fixQuotes( theString )
  fixQuotes = Replace( theString, "'", "''" )
END FUNCTION
username = TRIM( Request( "username" ) )
password = TRIM( Request( "password" ) )
IF username <> "" AND password <> "" THEN
  mySQL = "INSERT Webusers (username, password ) VALUES "
  mySQL = MySQL & "('" & fixQuotes( username ) & "','" &
➥fixQuotes( password ) & "')"
  Set Con = Server.CreateObject( "ADODB.Connection" )
  Con.Open "FILE NAME=C:\myDataLink.UDL"
  Con.Execute mySQL
END IF
%>
<html>
<head><title>Insert Data</title>
<body>
<form method="post" action="insertData.asp">
```

```
<P>Username: <input name="username" size=20>
<p>Password: <input name="password" size=20>
<p><input type="submit" value="Add Data">
</form>
</body>
</html>
```

This Active Server Page retrieves the values from two HTML form fields named user-name and password. Next, a valid SQL Insert statement is constructed using these values. When the Execute method of the Connection object is called, the username and password are inserted into the Webusers table.

Notice that this Active Server Page includes a function named fixQuotes(). The fixQuotes() function replaces every occurrence of the apostrophe character with two apostrophe characters. If someone uses this Active Server Page to insert a name or password that includes a single apostrophe, an error is generated because SQL uses the apostrophe character to mark the beginning and end of a string value. You should use the fixQuotes() function whenever you need to insert data into a database by executing a SQL statement with the Connection object.

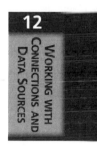

Updating Data in a Database Table

To modify existing data in a database table, you use the SQL Update statement. You can use the Update statement to modify all the rows in a table or only a particular row. Here is an example that changes every password in the Webusers table:

```
<%
MySQL = "UPDATE Webusers SET password = 'apple'"
Set Con = Server.CreateObject( "ADODB.Connection" )
Con.Open "FILE NAME=C:\myDataLink.UDL"
Con.Execute MySQL
%>
```

This script changes every password to apple. Normally, you will not want to change every row in a database table. To change only particular rows, you can include a WHERE clause in your SQL statement:

```
<%
MySQL="UPDATE Webusers SET password='apple'
➥WHERE username='Andrew Jones'"
Set Con = Server.CreateObject( "ADODB.Connection" )
Con.Open "FILE NAME=C:\myDataLink.UDL"
Con.Execute MySQL
%>
```

This script changes the password only if the username is equal to Andrew Jones. By default, SQL Server is not case-sensitive. This means that the preceding script will change the password when the username is equal to andrew jones, ANDREW JONES, or AnDrEw JoNeS.

Deleting Data in a Database Table

To remove a row from a database table, use the SQL Delete statement. The following script deletes every row from the Webusers table:

```
<%
MySQL = "DELETE Webusers"
Set Con = Server.CreateObject( "ADODB.Connection" )
Con.Open "FILE NAME=C:\myDataLink.UDL"
Con.Execute MySQL
%>
```

This script removes all the rows from the Webusers table. However, it does not remove the table itself.

> **NOTE**
>
> Normally, you should not use the SQL Delete statement to delete all the rows from a database table because it places too much work on SQL Server (it fills up the transaction log). To remove all the rows from a table, use the Truncate Table statement as in this example:
>
> ```
> Truncate Table Webusers
> ```

If you want to remove only a particular row from a database table, you can use a WHERE clause in your SQL statement. The following script removes only those rows where the password is equal to secret:

```
<%
MySQL = "DELETE Webusers WHERE password='secret'"
Set Con = Server.CreateObject( "ADODB.Connection" )
Con.Open "FILE NAME=C:\myDataLink.UDL"
Con.Execute MySQL
%>
```

Selecting Data from a Database Table

To retrieve rows from a database table, you use the SQL Select statement. For example, to retrieve all the rows from the Webusers table, you can use the following script:

```
<%
MySQL = "SELECT * FROM Webusers"
Set Con = Server.CreateObject( "ADODB.Connection" )
Con.Open "FILE NAME=C:\myDataLink.UDL"
Set RS = Con.Execute( MySQL )
While Not RS.EOF
  Response.Write RS( "username" ) & " = " & RS( "password" ) & "<br>"
  RS.MoveNext
WEND
%>
```

This script retrieves all the columns and rows from the table named Webusers into a Recordset object named RS. Next, all the rows from the Recordset are output to the browser within a WHILE...WEND loop.

> **NOTE**
>
> You'll learn everything you ever wanted to know about the Recordset object in Chapter 13, "Working with Recordsets."

If you want to retrieve only certain columns from a database table, you can list the columns that you want to retrieve in the Select statement. Here is an example that only retrieves the values from the password column in the Webusers table:

```
<%
MySQL = "SELECT password FROM Webusers"
Set Con = Server.CreateObject( "ADODB.Connection" )
Con.Open "FILE NAME=C:\myDataLink.UDL"
Set RS = Con.Execute( MySQL )
While Not RS.EOF
  Response.Write RS( "password" ) & "<br>"
  RS.MoveNext
WEND
%>
```

To select only certain rows to return from a database table, you can include a SQL Where clause. For example, the following script returns only those rows where the password column has the value apple:

```
<%
MySQL = "SELECT * FROM Webusers WHERE password='apple'"
Set Con = Server.CreateObject( "ADODB.Connection" )
```

```
Con.Open "FILE NAME=C:\myDataLink.UDL"
Set RS = Con.Execute( MySQL )
While Not RS.EOF
  Response.Write RS( "username" ) & " = " & RS( "password" ) & "<br>"
  RS.MoveNext
WEND
%>
```

Finally, if you want to retrieve only a set number of rows from a database table, you can use the TOP keyword. The following example retrieves no more than 10 rows from the Webusers table:

```
<%
MySQL = "SELECT TOP 10 * FROM Webusers"
Set Con = Server.CreateObject( "ADODB.Connection" )
Con.Open "FILE NAME=C:\myDataLink.UDL"
Set RS = Con.Execute( MySQL )
While Not RS.EOF
  Response.Write RS( "username" ) & " = " & RS( "password" ) & "<br>"
  RS.MoveNext
WEND
%>
```

> **NOTE**
>
> The TOP keyword does not work with SQL Server version 6.5. You can only use TOP when working with Microsoft SQL Server 7.0 or Microsoft Access.

Advanced Methods and Properties of the Connection Object

In the following two sections, you will learn about some of the advanced features of the Connection object. You will learn how to execute a series of SQL statements as a single transaction. You will also learn how to use the Connection object to retrieve information about the databases and tables that exist on your database server.

Using Transactions

When a series of SQL statements are executed within a transaction, you are provided with the guarantee that either all the statements will execute or none of them will. For example, suppose you have a script that moves all the rows from one table to another:

```
<%
Set Con = Server.CreateObject( "ADODB.Connection" )
Con.Open "FILE NAME=C:\myDataLink.UDL"
Con.Execute "INSERT Webusers2 SELECT * FROM Webusers"
Con.Execute "Delete Webusers"
%>
```

The first statement executed in this script copies all the rows from the table named
Webusers into a table named Webusers2. Next, all the rows from the Webusers table are
deleted.

Now suppose that something horrible happens while this script is being executed. For
example, imagine that the first SQL statement is executed, but a comet hits your database
server and the second SQL statement is never executed. In this case, all the rows are
copied from one table to the other, but the rows in the original table are not deleted. The
two tables are now thrown out of sync.

To prevent this result, you can execute a series of SQL statements within a single transaction. Here's how the previous script can be modified to use a transaction:

```
<%
Set Con = Server.CreateObject( "ADODB.Connection" )
Con.Open "FILE NAME=C:\myDataLink.UDL"
Con.BeginTrans
Con.Execute "INSERT Webusers2 SELECT * FROM Webusers"
Con.Execute "Delete Webusers"
Con.CommitTrans
%>
```

This script wraps the two SQL statements within a transaction. The BeginTrans statement starts the transaction, and the CommitTrans statement ends the transaction. If any of
the statements within the transaction fail, none of the statements are executed.

If you want to abort a transaction in the middle of a transaction, you can use the
RollBackTrans method. Here is an example:

```
<%
Set Con = Server.CreateObject( "ADODB.Connection" )
Con.Open "FILE NAME=C:\myDataLink.UDL"
Con.BeginTrans
Con.Execute "INSERT Webusers2 SELECT * FROM Webusers"
Con.Execute "Delete Webusers"
Con.RollBackTrans
%>
```

If you execute this script, absolutely no changes are made to the database. The rows are not copied between the tables and the rows in the Webusers table are not deleted. The RollBackTrans method prevents any of the statements included within the transaction from executing.

> **NOTE**
>
> You have two other alternatives for including transactions within your Active Server Pages. You can create transactional Active Server Page scripts by using Active Server Pages with Microsoft Transaction Server (see Chapter 21, "Using ASP With Microsoft Transaction Server"). Also, you can create transactions within Microsoft SQL Server stored procedures.

Working with Database Schemata

The Connection object includes a very useful method for retrieving information about the properties of your database. By using the OpenSchema method, you can retrieve information about the names of your databases, the tables contained in your databases, and their column and index properties.

> **NOTE**
>
> As an alternative to using the OpenSchema method to retrieve database information, you can use the ADOX (the ADO Extensions for DDL and security). To learn more, consult the ADOX documentation included with the MDAC download.

The OpenSchema method accepts two parameters: a query type and a criteria. The query type parameter specifies the type of database object about which you want to return information. The criteria parameter restricts the results returned from the query. The OpenSchema method returns a Recordset.

 For example, to return a list of all the user-created tables contained in the Pubs database (the sample database included with Microsoft SQL Server), you can use the following script (included on the CD as openSchema.asp):

```
<!-- #INCLUDE VIRTUAL="/adovbs.inc" -->
<%
Set Con = Server.CreateObject( "ADODB.Connection" )
Con.Open "FILE NAME=C:\myDataLink.UDL"
queryType = adSchemaTables
```

```
criteria = Array( "Pubs", Empty, Empty, "TABLE" )
Set RS = Con.OpenSchema( queryType, criteria )
While NOT RS.Eof
  Response.Write RS( 2 ) & "<br>"
RS.MoveNext
Wend
%>
```

This script has several features that need to be explained. Notice that the first line in the script includes a file named adovbs.inc. This file is included in the page by using the Active Server Pages #INCLUDE directive. Whenever you use ADO constants, such as the adSchemaTables constant in the script above, you must include this file.

> **NOTE**
>
> The adovbs.inc file was installed on your server when you installed Active Server Pages. The file contains a long list of ADO constants and their values. To make it convenient to include this file in your Active Server Pages, you should copy it to your Web server's root directory.

The script assigns the variable named queryType the value of the constant adSchemaTables. When the OpenSchema method is called with this query type, a list of tables is returned. This list of tables includes user-created tables, system tables, and table views.

The criteria variable is used to restrict the results from the query. It has an array for its value. The array has four elements that correspond to the database owner, name, and type of table to return. In the preceding script, the list of tables is returned from the Pubs database. The TABLE value is used to restrict the query results to user-created tables and not system tables or views.

Finally, the WHILE...WEND loop is used to actually display the list of tables (see Figure 12.5). The second column of the Recordset is displayed to show the names of the tables.

The OpenSchema method has many different query types and criteria. Consult Appendix B, "ASP Objects and Components Reference", to view the full list of the types of database information that you can retrieve with this method.

 To demonstrate some of the other query types that can be used with the OpenSchema method, a more complicated sample application is included in Listing 12.2. This Active Server Page is named DBSummary.asp and it's included on the CD.

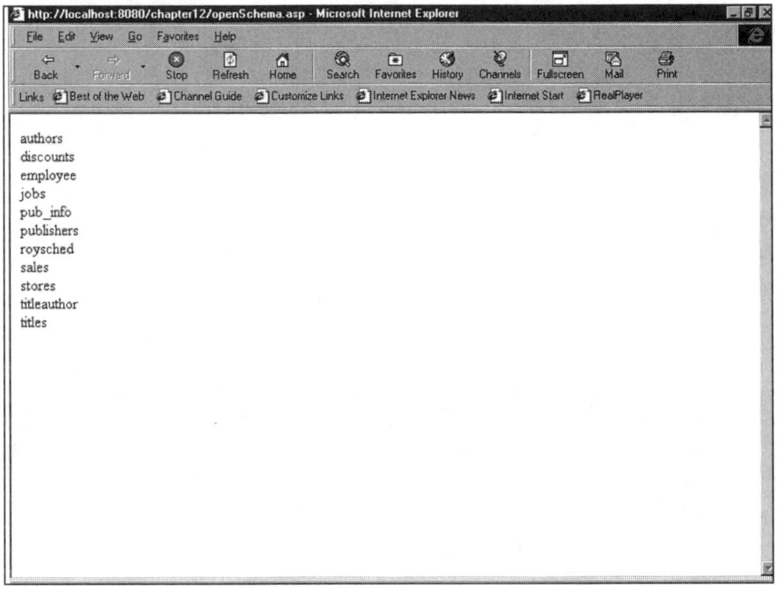

FIGURE 12.5

Using the
OpenSchema
method.

LISTING 12.2   DBSUMMARY.ASP

```
<!-- #INCLUDE VIRTUAL= "/adovbs.inc" -->
<%
On Error Resume Next
' Show All Tables In A Database
SUB showTables( byVal theDatabase, byRef theCon )
  Constraints = Array( theDatabase, Emtpy, Empty , TABLE )
  SET tableRS = Con.OpenSchema( adSchemaTables, Constraints )
  IF tableRS.Eof Then
    Response.Write "None"
  Else
  While NOT tableRS.Eof
    Response.Write tableRS( 2 ) & "<br>"
    tableRS.MoveNext
  Wend
  End IF
END SUB

' Show All Procedures In A Database
SUB showProcedures( byVal theDatabase, byRef theCon )
  Constraints = Array( theDatabase, Emtpy, Empty , Empty )
  SET procRS = Con.OpenSchema( adSchemaProcedures, Constraints )
  IF procRS.Eof Then
    Response.Write "None"
  Else
```

```
    While NOT procRS.Eof
      Response.Write procRS( 2 ) & " " &  "<br>"
      procRS.MoveNext
    Wend
    End IF
END SUB


UID = TRIM( Request( "UID" ) )
PWD = TRIM( Request( "PWD" ) )
DBServer = TRIM( Request( "DBServer" ) )
IF UID <> "" and DBServer <> "" THEN
  conString - "DRIVER-{SQL Server}"
  conString = conString & ";SERVER=" & DBServer
  conString = conString & ";UID=" & UID
  conString = conString & ";PWD=" & PWD
  Set Con = Server.CreateObject( "ADODB.Connection" )
  Con.Open conString
  IF Err <> 0 THEN
    conString = ""
  End IF
END IF
%>
<html>
<head><title>DB Summary</title></head>
<body>
<form method="post" action="DBSummary.asp">
<table bgcolor="#eeeeee" width="100%">
<tr>
  <td>UID: <input name="uid" size=20 value="<%=UID%>"></td>
  <td>PWD: <input name="pwd" size=20 value="<%=PWD%>"></td>
  <td>Server: <input name="DBServer" size=20 value="<%=DBServer%>"></td>
  <td><input type="submit" value="Connect">
</tr>
</table>
<hr>
<% IF conString = "" then %>
  No database specified or error while trying to connect.
<% else%>
<%
SET dbRS = Con.OpenSchema( adSchemaCatalogs )
While NOT dbRS.Eof
  DBName = dbRS( 0 )
  %>
  <h2><%=dbRS( 0 )%></h2>
  <b>Tables:</b>
  <blockquote><% showTables DBName, Con  %></blockquote>
  <b>Stored Procedures:</b>
  <blockquote><% showProcedures DBName, Con  %></blockquote>
```

continues

LISTING 12.2 CONTINUED

```
<%
dbRS.MoveNext
WEND
%>
<% end if %>
</body>
</html>
```

DBSummary.asp displays a list of all the databases, tables, and stored procedures located on a database server. You connect to the database server by supplying a SQL login, a password, and the name of the database (see Figure 12.6).

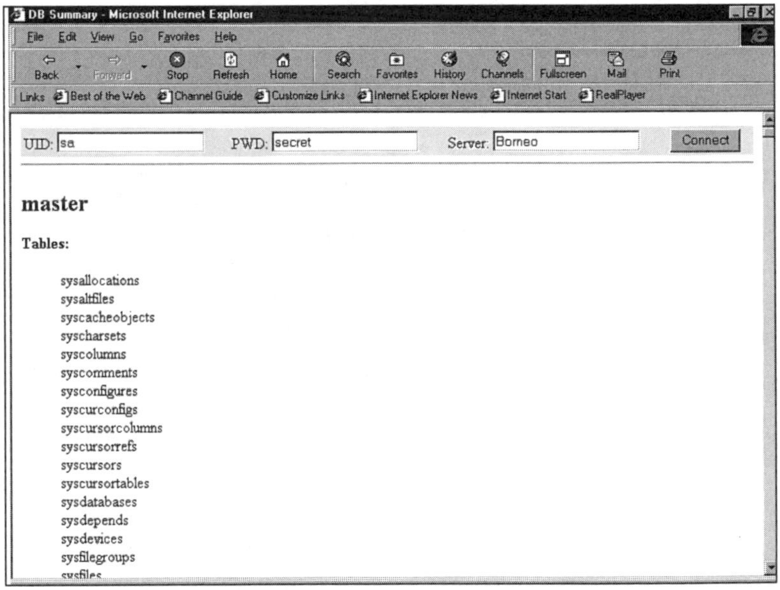

FIGURE 12.6

Displaying a database summary.

This Active Server Page will connect to a database no matter where it is located. You can even use it to connect to a database and retrieve information about it when the database is located across the Internet. It creates a DSN-less ODBC connection on-the-fly to connect to the database server.

Understanding Session and Connection Pooling

It takes significant time and effort for an Active Server Page to open a database connection. If hundreds of people are simultaneously accessing an Active Server Page that opens a database connection, this can significantly drain the resources of your server.

Fortunately, Microsoft has added a feature to both OLE DB and ODBC to reduce this strain. OLE DB supports session pooling, and ODBC supports connection pooling.

When connections are pooled, database connections remain open, even after the Active Server Page that requested the connection has finished processing. When a new connection is requested, the connection can be drawn from the pool. The time-consuming step of opening a new connection is avoided.

You do not have to do anything special to use connection pooling. Connection pooling is enabled by default when using either the OLE DB provider for SQL Server or the OLE DB provider for ODBC drivers. The only situation in which you must explicitly enable connection pooling is when you are using Internet Information Server 3.0 with an ODBC connection (consult your IIS 3.0 documentation to learn how to enable connection pooling in this situation).

12
WORKING WITH CONNECTIONS AND DATA SOURCES

> **NOTE**
>
> You can manage ODBC connection pooling within the ODBC Data Source Administrator located in the Windows Control Panel. After opening this applet, choose the tab labeled Connection Pooling.

There are three things that you must keep in mind to get the most out of connection pooling.

First, after you open a connection within an Active Server Page, you should close the connection as quickly as possible to release the connection back to the connection pool. Until a connection is closed, it cannot be reused. Use the `Close` method of the `Connection` object to close a connection after you have finished with it.

Second, connections can be pooled only when they share the same connection string. For example, if you open a connection with a new value for the `UID` parameter, then the new connection cannot be pooled with connections that use a different value for the `UID` parameter.

To ensure that different Active Server Pages are using the same connection string to open connections, you should assign the connection string to an `Application` variable. To do this, modify the `Application_OnStart` subroutine in the Global.asa file to contain the following statement:

```
Application( "conString" ) = "FILE NAME=C:\myDataLink.UDL"
```

Whenever you open a connection in your Active Server Pages, open the connection with the `Application` variable that contains the connection string like this:

```
Set Con = Server.CreateObject( "ADODB.Connection" )
Con.Open Application( "conString" )
```

Finally, you should be aware that connection pooling can cause problems when using certain connection-specific properties of SQL Server. For example, temporary stored procedures and temporary tables created in SQL Server are created relative to a particular connection. When a connection is closed, they are supposed to be automatically deleted. When connection pooling is enabled, however, these temporary objects might not be properly deleted. This may result in your TempDB database being filled up with ghost temporary stored procedures and tables (objects that no longer function but continue to occupy memory).

This problem is especially acute when using an ODBC connection rather than a native OLE DB provider. When creating a new data source with the ODBC Data Source Administrator, do not choose the option to create temporary stored procedures for prepared SQL statements. If you select this option, temporary stored procedures may be created that never go away.

Summary

In this chapter, you learned how to open a connection to a database such as Microsoft SQL Server or Microsoft Access. You learned how to open connections using both native OLE DB providers and the OLE DB provider for ODBC drivers. You also learned how to execute SQL statements with the `Connection` object. Finally, you learned how to use several advanced properties of the `Connection` object.

CHAPTER 13

Working with Recordsets

by Stephen Walther

In this chapter, you will learn how to work with the records that you retrieve from a database. You will learn how to use the ADO `Recordset` object to display a list of records within an Active Server Page. You will also learn how to work with Recordsets that use different cursor and locking types. Finally, you will learn about some of the advanced properties and methods of the `Recordset` object.

Retrieving a Recordset

In the previous chapter, you learned how to use the ADO `Connection` object to execute a SQL statement. If you execute a SQL statement that returns rows from a database table, the rows are returned with an ADO `Recordset` object. A `Recordset` can be used to represent the rows returned from a SQL query within an Active Server Page script.

A `Recordset` object can be used to represent only a single row or it can be used to represent dozens or even millions of rows. The same object is used no matter how much data is returned by a query.

 For example, the Active Server Page in Listing 13.1 (included on the CD as showTable.asp) retrieves all the rows from a database table named Authors and outputs the rows, one by one, to the browser window (see Figure 13.1).

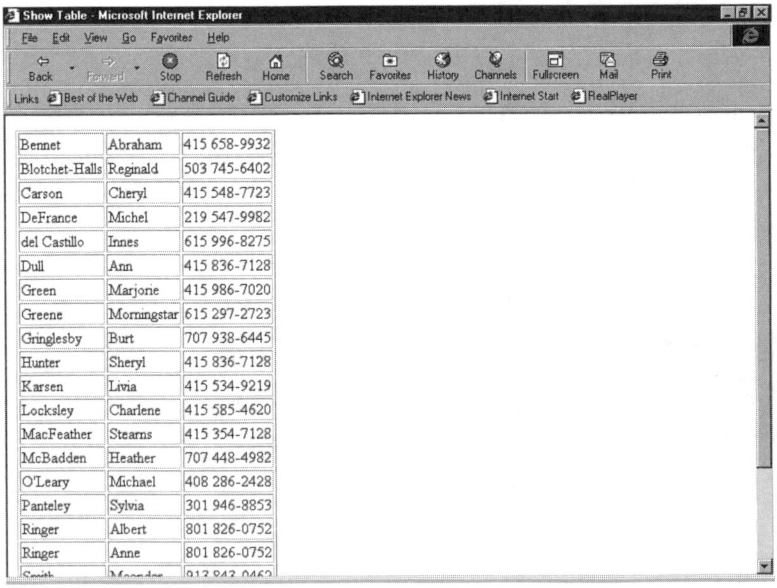

FIGURE 13.1

Displaying a Recordset.

Bennet	Abraham	415 658-9932
Blotchet-Halls	Reginald	503 745-6402
Carson	Cheryl	415 548-7723
DeFrance	Michel	219 547-9982
del Castillo	Innes	615 996-8275
Dull	Ann	415 836-7128
Green	Marjorie	415 986-7020
Greene	Morningstar	615 297-2723
Gringlesby	Burt	707 938-6445
Hunter	Sheryl	415 836-7128
Karsen	Livia	415 534-9219
Locksley	Charlene	415 585-4620
MacFeather	Stearns	415 354-7128
McBadden	Heather	707 448-4982
O'Leary	Michael	408 286-2428
Panteley	Sylvia	301 946-8853
Ringer	Albert	801 826-0752
Ringer	Anne	801 826-0752
Smith	Meander	913 843-0462

LISTING 13.1   SHOWTABLE.ASP

```
<html>
<head><title>Show Table</title>
<%
Set Con = Server.CreateObject( "ADODB.Connection" )
Con.Open "FILE NAME=c:\myDataLink.UDL;DATABASE=Pubs"
Set RS = Con.Execute( "select * from Authors ORDER BY au_lname" )
%>
<table border=1>
<% While NOT RS.EOF %>
  <tr>
    <td> <%=RS( "au_lname" )%> </td>
    <td> <%=RS( "au_fname" )%> </td>
    <td> <%=RS( "phone" )%> </td>
  </tr>
<%
RS.MoveNext
Wend
RS.Close
%>
</table>
</body>
</html>
```

This Active Server Page opens a database connection by using a Data Link file named
myDataLink.UDL. After the connection has been opened, a SQL SELECT query is executed that retrieves all the rows from the table named Authors located in the pubs database
(the sample database included with SQL Server). The rows are retrieved into a Recordset
named RS and displayed one-by-one within a WHILE...WEND loop.

Notice that an instance of the Recordset object is never explicitly created. The Recordset
is automatically returned from the Connection object when the SQL query is executed.

NOTE

There are certain situations in which you will need to explicitly declare a
Recordset object, for example, when working with updateable Recordsets. See
"Recordset Cursor and Locking Types," later in this chapter.

After the table rows have been retrieved into the Recordset, the au_lname, au_fname, and phone columns of each row are displayed by using a WHILE...WEND loop. The EOF property of the Recordset object is used to detect when the last row in the Recordset has been reached. After the last row has been displayed, the EOF property has the value TRUE and the WHILE...WEND loop is exited.

Within the WHILE...WEND loop, the MoveNext method of the Recordset object is used to move to the next row. When a Recordset is first opened, the Recordset object represents the first row returned from the query. Each time the MoveNext method is called, the Recordset object represents a new row.

Finally, after all the rows have been displayed, the Recordset is closed by calling the Recordset object's Close method. A Recordset is automatically closed when an Active Server Page finishes processing, but closing a Recordset early releases server resources.

> **NOTE**
>
> You must be careful when retrieving text columns with a Recordset. To prevent blank records from being returned, you must list the text column as the last column in your SELECT statement, or you must open a cursor other than the default forward-only cursor. For more about cursors, see "Recordset Cursor and Locking Types," later in this chapter.

Recordset Fields

Every Recordset contains a Fields collection. The Fields collection contains individual Field objects. The fields in the Field collection represent the columns returned from a database query. You can use the Fields collection in a number of different ways to display a column value.

First, and most typically, you can display the value of an individual Field by using the name of the Field. For example, the following script displays a column named phone by name:

```
<%
Set Con = Server.CreateObject( "ADODB.Connection" )
Con.Open "FILE NAME=c:\myDataLink.UDL;DATABASE=pubs"
Set RS=Con.Execute( "SELECT phone FROM Authors WHERE au_lname='Green'" )
Response.Write RS( "phone" )
%>
```

This script retrieves a single column and row from the pubs database table and displays the column's value. It retrieves the phone number of the author who has the last name Green and displays it.

The value is displayed with the last line in the script:

```
Response.Write RS( "phone" )
```

This statement displays the value of the Field by passing the name of the field to the Recordset object. However, you can display the same value by using any of the following statements:

```
Response.Write RS( "phone" )
Response.Write RS.Fields( "phone" )
Response.Write RS.Fields( "phone" ).Value
Response.Write RS( 0 )
Response.Write RS.Fields( 0 )
Response.Write RS.Fields( 0 ).Value
```

The Fields collection is the default collection of the Recordset object. This means that you can refer to an individual Field by explicitly referring to the Fields collection or by simply referring to the Recordset object that contains the Fields collection. The latter method is suggested because it saves typing.

The last three statements display the value of the Field by referring to its position in the Field collection. In this case, because only one column was retrieved in the SQL query, the value of the Phone column is displayed.

Why would you ever want to retrieve the value of a Field by its position rather than by its name? Using the position of a Field is useful when you do not know the names of the columns in a database table. For example, the Active Server Page in Listing 13.2 (included on the CD as anytable.asp) uses an HTML form field to accept the name of a table. When the name of the table is submitted, all the columns and all the rows of the table with the name submitted are automatically displayed (see Figure 13.2).

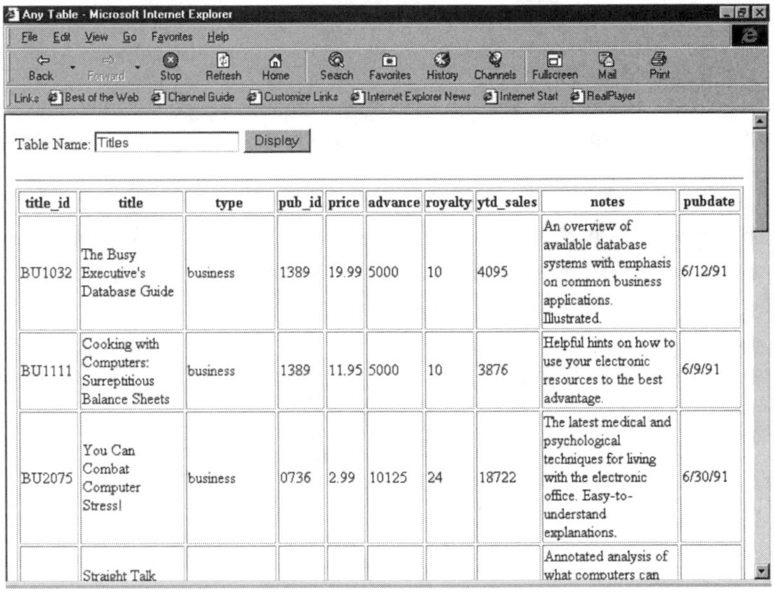

FIGURE **13.2**

Automatically displaying any Recordset.

LISTING **13.2** ANYTABLE.ASP

```
<html>
<head><title>Any Table</title></head>
<body>
<form method="post" action="AnyTable.asp">
Table Name: <input name="tablename" size=20>
<input type="submit" value="Display">
</form>
<hr>
<%
tablename = TRIM( Request( "tablename" ) )
if tablename <> "" then
  Set Con = Server.CreateObject( "ADODB.Connection" )
  Con.Open "FILE NAME=c:\myDataLink.UDL"
  Set RS = Con.Execute( "SELECT * FROM " & tablename )
%>
  <table border=1>
    <tr>
    <% for i = 0 to RS.Fields.Count - 1 %>
    <th><%=RS( i ).name%></th>
    <% next %>
    </tr>
  <% while not RS.EOF %>
    <tr>
    <% for i = 0 to RS.Fields.Count - 1 %>
    <td><%=RS( i ).value %> </td>
```

```
    <% next %>
    </tr>
  <% RS.MoveNext %>
  <% wend %>
  </table>
<%
end if
%>
</body>
</html>
```

When the name of a table is submitted, the script displays the name of each column within a FOR...NEXT loop. Each column's name is returned by using the Name property of the Field object.

Next, the value of each column in each row is displayed by using a second FOR...NEXT loop. This loop iterates through each column and displays the column value. By referring to Recordset Fields by their position, all the data in a table is displayed without knowing anything about the structure of the table.

The Field object has several other useful properties that you can use in your Active Server Page scripts to retrieve information about the columns returned by a database query. These are shown in Table 13.1

TABLE 13.1 PROPERTIES OF THE Field OBJECT

Property	Use
ActualSize	When used with columns that have variable length data types, such as VARCHAR columns, this property returns the actual length of the data stored in the column.
Attributes	Includes several different properties of a column. For example, you can use this property to determine whether a column can contain NULL values or whether the column has a variable or fixed length data type. See Appendix B, "ASP Objects and Components Reference," for more information.
DefinedSize	The maximum number of bytes (or characters) that a column can contain. For example, a VARCHAR column may have a DefinedSize of 500, but an ActualSize of 2.
Name	The name of a column.
NumericScale	For numeric and decimal columns, returns the scale of a column (the maximum number of digits that can appear to the right of the decimal point).

continues

13

WORKING WITH
RECORDSETS

TABLE 13.1 CONTINUED

Property	Use
OriginalValue	When a Field is updateable, this column contains the original value of the Field in the Recordset before it was changed. You'll learn more about updating Recordsets later in this chapter in the section titled "Updating Records with Native ADO Methods."
Precision	For numeric and decimal columns, this property returns the precision of the column (the maximum number of digits that can appear to the left and right of the decimal point).
Type	The data type of a column—for example, whether the column is a date or VARCHAR column.
UnderlyingValue	Contains the current value of the column in the database table. The value of this property can differ from the Original value property because the column in the database might have been updated after the Recordset was retrieved.
Value	The value of the column. You never need to explicitly use this property because it is the default property of the Field object.

Recordset Cursor and Locking Types

Whenever you open a Recordset, the Recordset is opened—either implicitly or explicitly—with a particular cursor and locking type. Understanding cursor and locking types is important for two reasons.

- First, using different cursor and locking types can have a dramatic effect on the performance of your Active Server Page scripts. If you make the wrong choices, it can take forever for your Active Server Page to retrieve and display a list of database records.

- Second, certain properties of the Recordset object are available only when you use the correct cursor and locking types. For example, you must open the Recordset with the right cursor and locking type to retrieve a count of the records in a Recordset or to create a Recordset that contains updateable records.

Choosing the correct cursor and locking type for a Recordset is a matter of balancing these two considerations: the need for performance and the need for particular Recordset properties. After reading the following two sections, you should have a better idea of how to do this.

Understanding ADO Cursors

When you execute a SQL query that returns a set of rows, the rows are delivered to your ADO application through a cursor. There are four different types of cursors that determine how the results of a query are delivered:

- Forward-only cursor—This is the default cursor and provides the fastest performance. When a Recordset is opened with a forward-only cursor, all the results are fetched serially, from start to finish. Forward-only cursors do not support backward scrolling, allowing only a single pass through the result set.

- Static cursor—A static cursor reflects the state of the data in a table when the cursor is first opened. The cursor cannot detect whether rows in the underlying table have been updated or deleted or whether new rows have been added. Unlike a forward-only cursor, however, a static cursor can be used to scroll back and forth through the result set.

- Keyset-driven cursor—A keyset-driven cursor can detect certain changes made to the underlying rows in a table, but not all changes. In particular, a keyset-driven cursor can accurately reflect data that has been updated. However, it cannot detect whether rows have been inserted or deleted by other users (deleted rows create holes in the Recordset). A keyset-driven cursor supports scrolling.

- Dynamic cursor—A dynamic cursor is the richest cursor type. It can detect any changes made to a table by other users while the cursor is open. It also fully supports scrolling.

13

WORKING WITH
RECORDSETS

When you open a Recordset without specifying the cursor, as in the case of all the previous programming examples in this chapter, the Recordset is opened with a forward-only cursor. When this default cursor is used with SQL Server, the cursor is opened in *firehose* mode. It's called firehose mode because the connection is kept open and the results of the query are blasted to your application as fast as possible.

To use a richer cursor type, you must explicitly create an instance of the `Recordset` object and set its cursor type before you execute the query. Here is an example that opens a dynamic cursor:

```
<!-- #INCLUDE VIRTUAL="/adovbs.inc" -->
<%
Set Con = Server.CreateObject( "ADODB.Connection" )
```

```
Con.Open "FILE NAME=c:\myDataLink.UDL;DATABASE=pubs"
Set RS = Server.CreateObject( "ADODB.Recordset" )
RS.CursorType = adOpenDynamic
RS.Open "SELECT * FROM Authors", Con
%>
```

> **NOTE**
>
> The adovbs.inc file was installed on your server when you installed Active Server Pages. The file contains a long list of constant definitions to use with the ADO.

The script explicitly creates an instance of the `Recordset` object. This is necessary so that the `CursorType` property can be set. After the `CursorType` has been set to a dynamic cursor, the Recordset is opened by passing a SQL string and the name of the `Connection` object.

Notice that this script includes the adovbs.inc file with the Active Server Pages `INCLUDE` directive. This is necessary because the `adOpenDynamic` ADO constant is used within the script. Here is a list of all the ADO constants for the cursor types:

    adOpenForwardOnly

    adOpenStatic

    adOpenKeyset

    adOpenDynamic

Now that you understand the four cursor types, how do you decide which cursor to use when opening a Recordset? In general, you should use the default forward-only cursor, because it provides the best performance. You should only consider a different cursor type when working with one of the advanced properties of the ADO `Recordset` object discussed later in this chapter.

Client- and Server-Side Cursors

There is one additional option when working with ADO cursors. You can choose to open a client-side or a server-side cursor. When a client-side cursor is used, the cursor is opened and managed on the machine hosting the Active Server Page. When a server-side cursor is used, the cursor is opened and managed on the machine hosting the database.

By default, when you create a Recordset, a server-side cursor is used. To indicate that you want to work with a client-side cursor, you must use the `CursorLocation` property like this:

```
<!-- #INCLUDE VIRTUAL="/adovbs.inc" -->
<%
Set Con = Server.CreateObject( "ADODB.Connection" )
Con.Open "FILE NAME=c:\myDataLink.UDL;DATABASE=pubs"
Set RS = Server.CreateObject( "ADODB.Recordset" )
RS.CursorLocation = adUseClient
RS.CursorType = adOpenDynamic
RS.Open "SELECT * FROM Authors", Con
%>
```

In this example, the `adUseClient` constant is assigned to the `CursorLocation` property to specify that a client-side cursor should be used. The Recordset is opened with a dynamic, client-side cursor.

The advantage of using a client-side cursor is that it removes work from your database server. All the results from the query are sent to the machine hosting your Active Server Page application.

Using a client-side cursor may also increase the performance of your Active Server Page application. Because the cursor is located on the same machine as your application, you can scroll through the rows of the cursor very quickly.

You should use a client-side cursor when you are worried about placing too much work on your database server. On the other hand, you should use the default server-side cursor when you do not want to place too much work on your Web server or cause too much network traffic.

13

WORKING WITH
RECORDSETS

> **NOTE**
>
> When you use a keyset-driven cursor with a client-side cursor, the data itself is not sent to the client. A keyset-driven cursor represents a result set with a set of keys that uniquely identify each row. When a particular cursor row is fetched, the key is used to retrieve the correct row from the underlying database table.

Understanding ADO Locking Types

A database-driven Web site might need to support hundreds of users accessing the same database tables at the same time. When more than one user is updating and reading data in a database table at the same time, conflicts will occur.

For example, suppose that your Web site contains a table that is used to record the number of times that the Web site's home page has been visited. When Sue—the 1,888th visitor to your Web site—arrives at your home page, the value 1,887 is retrieved from the table. At the same time, Andrew arrives at your Web site and the same value is retrieved from the table. If the value is updated for both users at the same time, an incorrect value will be recorded in the database table.

To control how these conflicts are resolved, you can use the Recordset's LockType property. The LockType property can have the values explained in Table 13.2.

TABLE 13.2 THE LockType PROPERTY VALUES

Value	Definition
adLockReadOnly	This is the default locking type. Read-only locking is used to allow multiple users to read the same data at the same time. However, when you open a Recordset with this locking type, you cannot alter the data.
adLockPessimistic	When a Recordset is opened with pessimistic locking, other users are prevented from accessing the data as soon as you begin editing the record.
adLockOptimistic	When a Recordset is opened with optimistic locking, other users can access the record until the changes are actually committed.
adLockBatchOptimistic	This locking type is used when performing batch updates (see the section titled "Batch Updating Records," later in this chapter).

If your Active Server Page is used only to display data from a database table, you should not change the default locking type. However, if you are going to use the native methods of the ADO to update data, then you will need to choose a different locking type. In general, you should choose optimistic locking because it causes the least interference with other users, and it is least likely to cause database deadlock.

NOTE

When executing SQL statements to perform changes in a database, you do not need to worry about the locking type. The LockType property is relevant only when using native ADO methods, such as AddNew, to update a database table.

Here's an example that sets the locking type to optimistic locking:

```
<!-- #INCLUDE VIRTUAL="/adovbs.inc" -->
<%
Set Con = Server.CreateObject( "ADODB.Connection" )
Con.Open "FILE NAME=c:\myDataLink.UDL"
Set RS = Server.CreateObject( "ADODB.Recordset" )
RS.LockType = adLockOptimistic
%>
```

Advanced Methods and Properties of the Recordset Object

In the following sections, you will learn how to use several of the advanced features of the Recordset object. You will learn how to perform such tasks as retrieving a count of records in a Recordset, scrolling and paging through a Recordset, and creating persistent Recordsets.

Retrieving a Count of Records

After a Recordset has been opened, you can determine the number of records that exist in the Recordset by using the RecordCount property. The RecordCount property is not supported by forward-only or dynamic cursors. When used with either of these cursor types, it always returns the value -1.

Here is an example that correctly uses the RecordCount property with a static cursor:

```
<!-- #INCLUDE VIRTUAL="/adovbs.inc" -->
<%
Set Con = Server.CreateObject( "ADODB.Connection" )
Con.Open "FILE NAME=c:\myDataLink.UDL;DATABASE=pubs"
Set RS = Server.CreateObject( "ADODB.Recordset" )
RS.CursorType = adOpenStatic
RS.Open "SELECT * FROM Authors", Con
Response.Write "This Recordset contains:"
Response.Write RS.RecordCount
Response.Write " records"
%>
```

You should avoid using the RecordCount property whenever possible because it always demands a rich cursor type. If you are only interested in determining whether a Recordset is empty, use the EOF property instead:

```
<!-- #INCLUDE VIRTUAL="/adovbs.inc" -->
<%
Set Con = Server.CreateObject( "ADODB.Connection" )
```

```
Con.Open "FILE NAME=c:\myDataLink.UDL;DATABASE=pubs"
Set RS = Server.CreateObject( "ADODB.Recordset" )
RS.CursorType = adOpenStatic
RS.Open "SELECT * FROM Authors", Con
if RS.EOF
  Response.Write "No records retrieved"
else
  Response.Write "Records retrieved!"
end if
%>
```

Scrolling Through a Recordset

The ADO Recordset object includes a number of methods and properties for moving back and forth through the rows of a Recordset. For example, the following script opens a Recordset, moves to the last record, and then displays all the records in the Recordset—moving backward from the last record to the first record:

```
<!-- #INCLUDE VIRTUAL="/adovbs.inc" -->
<%
Set Con = Server.CreateObject( "ADODB.Connection" )
Con.Open "FILE NAME=c:\myDataLink.UDL;DATABASE=pubs"
Set RS = Server.CreateObject( "ADODB.Recordset" )
RS.CursorType = adOpenStatic
RS.Open "SELECT * FROM Authors ORDER BY au_lname", Con
RS.MoveLast
While not RS.BOF
  Response.Write RS( "au_lname" ) & "<br>"
RS.MovePrevious
Wend
%>
```

This script uses the MoveLast method to move to the last record, the MovePrevious method to move to the previous record, and the BOF property to detect when the first record has been reached.

When scrolling through a Recordset, you can use the properties explained in Table 13.3.

TABLE 13.3 PROPERTIES USED WITH A RECORDSET

Property	Use
AbsolutePosition	Sets or returns the current ordinal position of the current record in a Recordset.
Bookmark	Sets or returns a bookmark that uniquely identifies the current record in a Recordset.

Property	Use
BOF	This property has the value TRUE when the current record is positioned before the first record.
EOF	This property has the value TRUE when the current record is positioned after the last record.

The AbsolutePosition property enables you to move directly to any record according to its position. For example, the following script retrieves and displays the record that appears in the middle of the Recordset:

```
<!-- #INCLUDE VIRTUAL="/adovbs.inc" -->
<%
Set Con = Server.CreateObject( "ADODB.Connection" )
Con.Open "FILE NAME=c:\myDataLink.UDL;DATABASE=pubs"
Set RS = Server.CreateObject( "ADODB.Recordset" )
RS.CursorType = adOpenStatic
RS.Open "SELECT * FROM Authors ORDER BY au_lname", Con
RS.AbsolutePosition = RS.RecordCount / 2
Response.Write RS( "au_lname" )
%>
```

You can use the Bookmark property to return a unique identifier for a record so that you can return to it later. For example, the following script creates a Bookmark for a record, and then repositions the Recordset cursor to the Bookmark:

```
<!-- #INCLUDE VIRTUAL="/adovbs.inc" -->
<%
Set Con = Server.CreateObject( "ADODB.Connection" )
Con.Open "FILE NAME=c:\myDataLink.UDL;DATABASE=pubs"
Set RS = Server.CreateObject( "ADODB.Recordset" )
RS.CursorType = adOpenStatic
RS.Open "SELECT * FROM Authors ORDER BY au_lname", Con
While not RS.EOF
  if RS( "au_lname" ) = "Locksley" then
    ' Set the Bookmark
    myBookmark = RS.Bookmark
  end if
RS.MoveNext
Wend
' Return to the Bookmark
RS.Bookmark = myBookmark
Response.Write RS( "au_lname" )
%>
```

13

WORKING WITH
RECORDSETS

In this example, a Bookmark is created when a record containing the value Locksley is found. After the end of the Recordset has been reached, the Recordset is repositioned to this record by using the Bookmark.

When scrolling through a Recordset, you can use the methods in Table 13.4.

TABLE 13.4 METHODS TO USE WITH A RECORDSET

Method	Use
Move	Moves forward or backward a certain number of records. When a negative number is used, moves backward. Otherwise, moves forward. You can move relative to the current record or relative to a particular bookmark.
MoveFirst	Moves to the first record in a Recordset (calling this method with a forward-only cursor may cause the original SQL query to be re-executed).
MoveLast	Moves to the last record in a Recordset.
MoveNext	Moves to the next record in a Recordset.
MovePrevious	Moves to the previous record in a Recordset.

Be aware that many of the methods and properties for scrolling through a Recordset either do not work or are very inefficient when used with a forward-only cursor. For example, the MovePrevious method is incompatible with a forward-only cursor and will result in an error when used with this cursor type.

> **NOTE**
>
> You can use the MovePrevious method with a forward-only Recordset if you set the Recordset cache size to a value greater than 1. This is not recommended because it is memory intensive.

Whenever possible, you should avoid using the scrolling methods that depend on a rich cursor type. Normally, you can achieve the same results by executing a more carefully designed SQL query instead. For example, to list the records in a Recordset backward, use a SQL ORDER BY clause rather than the ADO MoveLast and MovePrevious methods.

Paging Through a Recordset

There are many situations in which you will need to provide a user with the means to page through the records in a Recordset. Suppose, for example, that you are creating an Active Server Page that displays a list of products for sale. If you are selling hundreds of products, you might want to divide the list of products into multiple pages.

The Recordset object contains several special properties for paging through a Recordset. By using these properties to divide the records in a Recordset into different pages, you can display only portions of a Recordset at a time. Here's a list of these properties:

- AbsolutePage—Sets or returns the current page of records.

- PageCount—Returns the number of pages in a Recordset.

- PageSize—Sets or returns the number of records contained in a single page (the default is 10 records per page).

 To divide a Recordset into pages, use the PageSize property to set the number of records in a page. Next, after opening the Recordset, use the AbsolutePage property to move to a particular page. Listing 13.3 (included on the CD as Paging.asp) is an example of how you can display the records in a table named Titles using multiple pages (see Figure 13.3).

13

WORKING WITH
RECORDSETS

FIGURE 13.3

*A Recordset
divided into
multiple pages.*

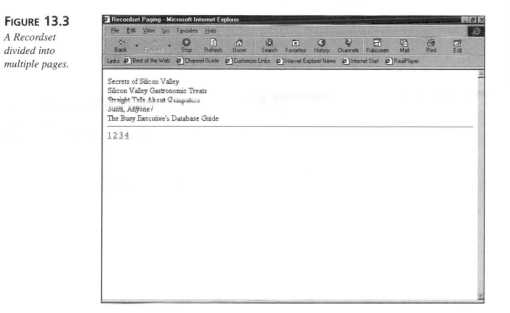

LISTING 13.3 PAGING.ASP

```
<!-- #INCLUDE VIRTUAL="/adovbs.inc" -->
<html>
<head><title>Recordset Paging</title></head>
<body>
<%
DIM currentPage, rowCount, i
currentPage = TRIM( Request( "currentPage" ) )
if currentPage = "" then currentPage = 1
Set Con = Server.CreateObject( "ADODB.Connection" )
Con.Open "FILE NAME=c:\myDataLink.UDL;DATABASE=pubs"
Set RS = Server.CreateObject( "ADODB.Recordset" )
RS.CursorType = adOpenStatic
RS.PageSize = 5
RS.Open "SELECT title FROM Titles ORDER BY title", Con
RS.AbsolutePage = cINT( currentPage )
rowCount = 0
While not RS.EOF and rowCount < RS.PageSize
  Response.Write RS( "title" ) & "<br>"
  rowCount = rowCount + 1
  RS.MoveNext
Wend
Response.Write "<hr>"
for i = 1 to RS.PageCount
  %>
  <a href="Paging.asp?currentPage=<%=i%>"><%=i%></a>
  <%
next
%>
</body>
</html>
```

> **NOTE**
>
> The adovbs.inc file is a text file that contains a long list of constants used with the ADO. This file was installed on your server when you installed Internet Information Server. You can find the adovbs.inc file in the InetPub\iissamples\ ISSamples directory on your Web server.

There are a few things that you should notice about Listing 13.3. First, notice that a variable named rowCount is used to limit the number of records that are displayed on a particular page. If this variable were not used, every page would contain both the records for the page and the records for all the following pages.

Also, notice that the VBScript cINT() function is used to convert the value passed in the URL string to an integer. If you do not do this, the value of the variable might not be correctly interpreted as an integer, and weird errors can result.

Finally, notice that the Recordset is not opened with a forward-only cursor. To use the paging properties, you must use a richer cursor type. Unfortunately, this means that the paging properties can be inefficient. When paging through a Recordset that contains thousands of records, it can take a long time to retrieve and display a page of records.

Limiting the Number of Records Returned in a Recordset

Sometimes, you might not want to retrieve all the records from a SQL query. For example, you might want to retrieve only the first 15 records from a table or the top 10 percent of the records from a table. There are two ways that you can limit the number of records returned in a database query: by using the ADO MaxRecords property or by using the SQL Server TOP keyword. The following script uses the MaxRecords property of the Recordset object to retrieve no more than 15 authors from the Authors table:

```
<%
Set Con = Server.CreateObject( "ADODB.Connection" )
Con.Open "FILE NAME=c:\myDataLink.UDL;DATABASE=pubs"
Set RS = Server.CreateObject( "ADODB.Recordset" )
RS.MaxRecords = 15
RS.Open "SELECT * FROM Authors ORDER BY au_lname", Con
While not RS.EOF
  Response.Write RS( "au_lname" ) & "<br>"
  RS.MoveNext
Wend
%>
```

Notice that the MaxRecords property does not require a rich cursor type. You can use the MaxRecords property when working with a Recordset opened with a forward-only cursor. Also, notice that an ORDER BY clause is included in the SQL query. If the SQL ORDER BY clause is not used, any random set of 15 records is returned. This script retrieves the first 15 authors in order of their last names.

If you are using Microsoft SQL Server 7.0 or Microsoft Access (but not SQL Server 6.5), you can use the TOP keyword to limit the number of records returned. The following script uses the TOP keyword to return the top 15 records:

```
<%
Set Con = Server.CreateObject( "ADODB.Connection" )
Con.Open "FILE NAME=c:\myDataLink.UDL;DATABASE=pubs"
Set RS = Server.CreateObject( "ADODB.Recordset" )
RS.Open "SELECT TOP 15 * FROM Authors ORDER BY au_lname", Con
```

```
While not RS.EOF
   Response.Write RS( "au_lname" ) & "<br>"
   RS.MoveNext
Wend
%>
```

The TOP keyword can also be used to return a certain percentage of records from a database table. The following script retrieves the top 15 percent of records from the Authors table by using the PERCENT keyword:

```
<%
Set Con = Server.CreateObject( "ADODB.Connection" )
Con.Open "FILE NAME=c:\myDataLink.UDL;DATABASE=pubs"
Set RS = Server.CreateObject( "ADODB.Recordset" )
RS.Open "SELECT TOP 10 PERCENT * FROM Authors ORDER BY au_lname", Con
While not RS.EOF
   Response.Write RS( "au_lname" ) & "<br>"
   RS.MoveNext
Wend
%>
```

Updating Records with Native ADO Methods

The discussion of ADO, up to this point, assumes that you will be updating records by executing SQL statements such as the SQL DELETE and UPDATE statements. However, ADO provides you with a choice. Instead of using SQL statements to alter records, you can use native ADO methods. In general, you should avoid using the ADO methods for updating records because they are less efficient than SQL commands. However, in certain situations, they may be more convenient to use. Table 13.5 shows the ADO methods for updating records.

TABLE 13.5—ADO METHODS FOR UPDATING RECORDS

Method	What It Does
AddNew	Adds a new record.
CancelUpdate	Cancels any changes made to a record. It must be used before the Update method is called or before you move to a new record.
Delete	Deletes the current record.
Resync	Used with a forward-only or static cursor to resynchronize a Recordset with the underlying database table after changes have been made.
Update	Saves any changes you make to a record. The Update method is called automatically when you move to a new record.

Table 13.6 shows a list of the ADO properties for updating records.

TABLE 13.6 ADO PROPERTIES FOR UPDATING RECORDS

Property	What It Does
EditMode	This property returns the current editing state. It can have the values adEditNone (no editing in progress), adEditInProgress (current record has been edited but not saved), or adEditAdd (a new record has been added but not saved).
OriginalValue	When a field is updateable, this column contains the original value of the Field in the Recordset before it was changed.
UnderlyingValue	Contains the current value of the column in the database table. The value of this property can differ from the OriginalValue property because the column in the database might have been updated after the Recordset was retrieved.

To add a new record to a database table, you can use the AddNew method like this:

```
<! #INCLUDE VIRTUAL="/adovbs.inc" -->
<%
Set Con = Server.CreateObject( "ADODB.Connection" )
Con.Open "FILE NAME=c:\myDataLink.UDL"
Set RS = Server.CreateObject( "ADODB.Recordset" )
RS.LockType = adLockOptimistic
RS.Open "SELECT  * FROM Webusers WHERE 1<>1", Con
RS.AddNew
RS( "username" ) = "Andrew Jones"
RS( "password" ) = "won't say"
RS.Update
%>
```

This script adds a new record to a database table named WebUsers. It adds a user with the name Andrew Jones and the password won't say.

13

WORKING WITH
RECORDSETS

> **NOTE**
>
> When you execute a SQL string that contains an apostrophe with the Connection object, an error is generated (SQL uses the apostrophe character to mark the beginning and end of a string value). However, no error is generated when you use apostrophes with the native ADO methods for updating Recordsets.

Notice that the table is opened with a SQL query that returns no records. The query requests every record where 1<>1. Because it is metaphysically impossible for 1 to be not equal to itself, no records match the criteria of the query and no records are returned. Because you are only interested in adding a new record, and not retrieving records, opening an empty Recordset saves precious server resources.

Also, notice that the Recordset is opened with optimistic locking. You cannot update a Recordset that uses the default locking type because the default locking type is read-only.

To delete a record, you can use the ADO Delete method like this:

```
<!-- #INCLUDE VIRTUAL="/adovbs.inc" -->
<%
Set Con = Server.CreateObject( "ADODB.Connection" )
Con.Open "FILE NAME=c:\myDataLink.UDL;DATABASE=test"
Set RS = Server.CreateObject( "ADODB.Recordset" )
RS.LockType = adLockOptimistic
RS.Open "SELECT  * FROM Webusers WHERE username='Andrew Jones'", Con
RS.Delete
RS.Update
%>
```

This script retrieves a Recordset that contains all the records from the WebUsers table where the username is Andrew Jones. Next, the ADO Delete method is called to delete the current record. When the Delete method is called, only the current record is deleted. If the Recordset contains hundreds of records where the username is Andrew Jones, only one record would be removed—the first Andrew Jones record.

Finally, to update a Recordset, you can simply assign a new value to a Field. The following example changes the password for Andrew Jones to the value very secret:

```
<!-- #INCLUDE VIRTUAL="/adovbs.inc" -->
<%
Set Con = Server.CreateObject( "ADODB.Connection" )
Con.Open "FILE NAME=c:\myDataLink.UDL;DATABASE=test"
Set RS = Server.CreateObject( "ADODB.Recordset" )
RS.LockType = adLockOptimistic
RS.Open "SELECT  * FROM Webusers WHERE username='Andrew Jones'", Con
RS( "password" ) = "very secret"
RS.Update
%>
```

Batch Updating Records

By default, when you use the native ADO methods to update records, the records are updated in immediate update mode. Every time you make a change, the change is immediately communicated to the database as soon as you call the Update method.

The ADO supports batch updating. When records are updated as a batch, changes to records are transmitted as a group to the underlying database. When updating multiple records, updating records in batch mode is more efficient than updating records in immediate update mode.

To make changes to records using batch mode, you should use a client-side cursor, a batch update locking type, and either a static or keyset-driven cursor. The following script sets all these properties and adds two records to the WebUsers table in batch update mode:

```
<!-- #INCLUDE VIRTUAL="/adovbs.inc" -->
<%
Set Con = Server.CreateObject( "ADODB.Connection" )
Con.Open "FILE NAME=c:\myDataLink.UDL;DATABASE=test"
Set RS = Server.CreateObject( "ADODB.Recordset" )
RS.LockType = adLockBatchOptimistic
RS.CursorType = adOpenStatic
RS.CursorLocation = adUseClient
RS.Open "SELECT  * FROM Webusers WHERE 1 <> 1", Con
RS.AddNew
RS( "username" ) = "Bob"
RS( "password" ) = "secret"
RS.Update
RS.AddNew
RS( "username" ) = "Fred"
RS( "password" ) = "secret"
RS.Update
RS.UpdateBatch
%>
```

When editing records in batch update mode, you can cancel any changes that you have made to the records before you call UpdateBatch by calling CancelBatch. The CancelBatch method cancels any modifications, and the records revert back to their original state.

Retrieving Records into an Array

In certain situations, you'll need to retrieve the records of a Recordset into an array. For example, if you need to alter the data represented by a Recordset, but you don't want to change the records in the Recordset itself, you can change the data in the array instead. To assign the records in a Recordset to an array, you use the GetRows() method of the Recordset object. Here's an example:

```
<%
Set Con=Server.CreateObject("ADODB.Connection")
Set RS=Server.CreateObject("ADODB.RecordSet")
Con.Open "FILE NAME=c:\myDataLink.UDL;DATABASE=test"
```

13

WORKING WITH
RECORDSETS

```
RS.Open "SELECT MyFirstCol, MySecondCol FROM MyTable", Con
MyArray=RS.GetRows()
%>
```

In this script, all the records contained in the Recordset named RS are assigned to the array named MyArray. This array is automatically created and populated by the GetRows() method. The GetRows() method creates a two-dimensional array. The first subscript identifies the field and the second subscript indicates the record number.

The following script can be used to display all the contents of MyArray:

```
<%
FOR i=0 TO UBOUND(MyArray,2)
%>
<BR> First Column:  <%=MyArray(0,i)%>
<BR> Second Column: <%=MyArray(1,i)%>
<%
NEXT
%>
```

The VBScript UBOUND() function is used to determine the size of the second dimension of the array. The FOR...NEXT loop is used to iterate through all its elements. This array represents a Recordset with two columns. When the first index of the array has the value 0, the first column is represented. When the first index of the array has the value 1, the second column is represented.

Working with Disassociated Recordsets

Normally, a Recordset is associated with a particular database connection, and it represents data from a SQL query. However, at its most basic level, a Recordset is nothing more than a container for information. You can create a Recordset and add any data to it that you please. For example, the following script creates a Recordset without ever opening a database connection:

```
<!-- #INCLUDE VIRTUAL="/adovbs.inc" -->
<%
Set RS = Server.CreateObject( "ADODB.Recordset" )
RS.Fields.Append "username", adVarchar, 20
RS.Fields.Append "password", adVarchar, 20
RS.Open
RS.AddNew
RS( "username" ) = "Andrew Jones"
RS( "password" ) = "secret"
RS.Update
%>
<br>Username: <%=RS( "username" )%>
<br>Password: <%=RS( "password" )%>
```

This script creates a Recordset named RS. Next, two Fields named username and password are appended to the Recordset by using the Append method of the Fields collection. Both Fields are VARCHAR fields with a maximum length of 20 characters. After the Recordset contains some fields, it can be opened.

> **NOTE**
>
> When you create a disassociated Recordset, the Recordset is created using a static, client-side cursor with an adLockBatchOptimistic locking type.

All the native ADO methods for updating data can be used on the newly created Recordset. In the preceding script, the AddNew method is used to add a new record to the Recordset.

You can also create a disassociated Recordset by taking a normal Recordset and disassociating it from its database connection. For example, the following script retrieves all the records from the Authors database table, and then severs the database connection by setting the Recordset's ActiveConnection property to Nothing:

```
<!-- #INCLUDE VIRTUAL="/adovbs.inc" -->
<%
Set Con = Server.CreateObject( "ADODB.Connection" )
Con.Open "FILE NAME=c:\myDataLink.UDL;DATABASE=pubs"
Set RS = Server.CreateObject( "ADODB.Recordset" )
RS.CursorLocation = adUseClient
RS.CursorType = adOpenStatic
RS.LockType = adLockBatchOptimistic
RS.Open "SELECT * FROM Authors", Con
RS.ActiveConnection = Nothing
RS( "au_lname" ) = "Jones"
RS.Update
While not RS.EOF
  Response.Write RS( "au_lname" ) & "<br>"
  RS.MoveNext
Wend
%>
```

After the database connection has been severed, the last name of the author in the current record is changed to Jones. Changing the name does not affect the underlying database table because the Recordset is no longer associated with the table. However, when all the author names are displayed, the new last name is displayed as well.

One very useful application of disassociated Recordsets is for caching seldom-changed database data. Database queries are resource intensive. If you retrieve a Recordset once, and then assign the Recordset to an Application variable, you can use the data in the Recordset within all your Active Server Pages without querying the database again.

Creating Persistent Recordsets

A persistent Recordset is a Recordset that has been saved to a disk file. You can use the ADO to create a Recordset, save it to a file, and load the Recordset from the file again. You can even load the Recordset by using a Web site URL.

The Recordset can be saved to a file by using one of two different file formats: Advanced Data TableGram format and XML format. Advanced Data TableGram (ADTG) format is the default format. It's a proprietary format developed by Microsoft. XML, on the other hand, is an open standard supported, among others, by the World Wide Web Consortium (see http://www.w3.org). Here are the two constants used for the file formats:

adPersistADTG: Advanced Data TableGram format. The constant has the value 0.

adPersistXML: XML format. The constant has the value 1.

To save a Recordset to a disk file, you use the Recordset's Save method. Here's an example that saves a Recordset that represents the Authors table to an ADTG file:

```
<!-- #INCLUDE VIRTUAL="/adovbs.inc" -->
<%
Set Con = Server.CreateObject( "ADODB.Connection" )
Con.Open "FILE NAME=c:\myDataLink.UDL;DATABASE=pubs"
Set RS = Server.CreateObject( "ADODB.Recordset" )
RS.CursorLocation = adUseClient
RS.CursorType = adOpenStatic
RS.LockType = adLockBatchOptimistic
RS.Open "SELECT * FROM Authors", Con
RS.Save "c:\inetpub\wwwroot\myfile.rst", adPersistADTG
%>
```

> **NOTE**
>
> You might have to add the adPersistADTG and adPersistXML constants to your adovbs.inc file to use the constants in your Active Server Pages. Add the following two lines to the top of this file:
>
> ```
> Const adPersistADTG = 0
> Const adPersistXML = 1
> ```

This script saves the Authors Recordset to a file with the name myfile.rst. The Recordset is saved using the ADTG format. (Actually, the `adPersistADTG` constant is unnecessary because ADTG is the default format.)

To load the Recordset from the file, you can use a file path, a relative file path, or even a URL. The following example loads the Recordset by using a file path and displays all its records:

```
<%
Set RS = Server.CreateObject( "ADODB.Recordset" )
RS.Open "c:\myfile.rst"
While not RS.EOF
  Response.Write RS( "au_lname" ) & "<br>"
  RS.MoveNext
Wend
%>
```

If you save the Recordset file in a Web directory, you can use a URL to load the file. The following script loads the same Recordset from a URL:

```
<%
Set RS = Server.CreateObject( "ADODB.Recordset" )
RS.Open "http://www.somewhere.com/myfile.rst"
While not RS.EOF
  Response.Write RS( "au_lname" ) & "<br>"
  RS.MoveNext
Wend
%>
```

Persistent Recordsets provide you with a means to easily distribute data from a database table. You can use persistent Recordsets to pass data between Web servers or between a Web server and a client application that uses the ADO.

13

WORKING WITH
RECORDSETS

> **NOTE**
>
> The Save method allows you to save a Recordset to a disk file. The ADO also includes a method for saving a Recordset to a string: the GetString() method. You can use this method to create CSV files from Recordsets on-the-fly. For more information, see the entry for GetString() in your ADO documentation.

Summary

In this chapter, you learned how to use the ADO `Recordset` object within your Active Server Pages. You learned how to retrieve records into a Recordset by executing a SQL query. You also learned how to use different cursor and locking types. Finally, you learned how to work with a number of advanced features of the `Recordset` object.

CHAPTER 14

Working with the Command Object

by Stephen Walther

In this chapter, you will learn how to use SQL stored procedures within your Active Server Pages. In the first part, you will learn how to create and use stored procedures with Microsoft SQL Server. In the second part, you will learn an easy method of executing stored procedures with the Connection object. Finally, you will learn how to gain complete control over all the properties of a stored procedure with the Command object.

Creating Stored Procedures

A Microsoft SQL Server stored procedure is a compiled collection of SQL statements that are stored together as a single-named object within a SQL Server database. A stored procedure can contain one or more standard SQL statements such as the familiar SELECT, INSERT, UPDATE, and DELETE statements. It can also contain Transact-SQL statements.

Transact-SQL is Microsoft's extension to the SQL language. Transact-SQL extends the SQL language into a full-blown programming language by adding support for variables, functions, and control-of-flow language such as conditionals and WHILE loops. By using stored procedures and Transact-SQL, you can migrate many of your Active Server Page scripts to your database server.

Why would you want to do this? Stored procedures offer a number of benefits:

- If you have a complicated set of SQL statements to execute on multiple Active Server Pages, you can place it in a stored procedure and execute the procedure instead. This reduces the size of your Active Server Pages and ensures that the same SQL statements are executed on each page.

- Executing a series of SQL statements in a stored procedure is much more efficient than executing the same series of statements in an Active Server Page. By placing all the statements in a stored procedure, you can avoid multiple trips back and forth between the Web server and database server.

- You can pass values both to and from a stored procedure. This means that stored procedures can be very flexible. The same stored procedure can return very different information, depending on the data passed to it.

- When you pass a collection of SQL statements to the database server, each of the individual statements must be passed. When you execute a stored procedure, on the other hand, only a single statement is passed. By using stored procedures, you can reduce the strain on your network.

- You can configure a table's permissions in such a way that users can modify a table only by using a stored procedure. This can improve the security of the data in your database tables.

- You can execute a stored procedure from within another stored procedure. This strategy enables you to build very complex stored procedures from smaller ones. This also means that you can reuse the same stored procedure for many different programming tasks.

Whenever you need to execute SQL statements in your Active Server Pages, you should carefully consider whether you can place these statements in a stored procedure instead. The benefits listed here are substantial.

How to Create Stored Procedures

You can create a new stored procedure using Microsoft Query Analyzer (formerly known as I/SQL), Microsoft SQL Server Enterprise Manager, or within an Active Server Page script. In all three cases, the stored procedure is actually created with the SQL CREATE PROCEDURE statement.

A SQL stored procedure can contain a single Transact-SQL statement or hundreds of statements (the maximum size of a stored procedure is 128 megabytes). Here's an example that creates a very simple stored procedure:

```
CREATE PROCEDURE getAuthors AS select * from Authors
```

If you execute this statement, a stored procedure named getAuthors is created. This stored procedure retrieves all the rows from the table named Authors.

To create this procedure with Microsoft Query Analyzer, launch this program from the SQL Server 7.0 program group. Connect to your database server and choose the pubs database. Enter the preceding statement and click Execute Query (or F5). The procedure is created (see Figure 14.1).

You can also create this stored procedure with the following Active Server Page script:

```
<!-- #INCLUDE VIRTUAL="/adovbs.inc" -->
<%
Set Con = Server.CreateObject( "ADODB.Connection" )
Con.Open "FILE NAME=c:\myDataLink.UDL;DATABASE=pubs"
Con.Execute "CREATE PROCEDURE getAuthors AS select * from Authors"
%>
```

FIGURE 14.1

Creating a new stored procedure with Microsoft Query Analyzer.

FIGURE 14.1

Creating a new stored procedure with Microsoft Query Analyzer.

After the stored procedure has been created, you can execute it and return a list of authors within Microsoft Query Analyzer. This is a good way to test a stored procedure before you add it to an Active Server Page script. To execute a stored procedure within Query Analyzer, use the EXECUTE statement like this:

```
EXECUTE getAuthors
```

> **NOTE**
>
> When a stored procedure appears as the first line in Microsoft Query Analyzer, you do not need to use the Execute statement to execute the stored procedure—just type in its name. You cannot use this shortcut, however, if a stored procedure appears after other statements. In that case, Query Analyzer will get confused.

The getAuthors stored procedure is very simple. It contains only a single statement that returns a set of rows. A stored procedure becomes more interesting when it includes variables and conditional logic. The following example selects records from one of two tables depending on a random value:

```
CREATE PROCEDURE ranRows
AS
DECLARE @ranValue INT
```

```
SELECT @ranValue = RAND() * 10
IF @ranValue > 5
  SELECT * FROM Authors
ELSE
  SELECT * FROM Titles
```

In this example, a variable named @ranValue is declared with an INTEGER data type (all local SQL variables must begin with the @ character). Next, the RAND() function is used to assign the variable a random value. Depending on this random value, the rows from the Authors or the Titles table are returned.

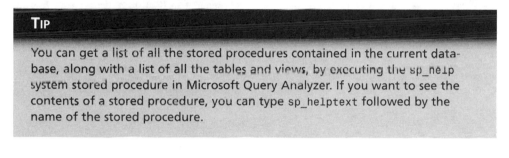

TIP

You can get a list of all the stored procedures contained in the current database, along with a list of all the tables and views, by executing the sp_help system stored procedure in Microsoft Query Analyzer. If you want to see the contents of a stored procedure, you can type sp_helptext followed by the name of the stored procedure.

After it is created, a stored procedure continues to exist in a particular database until you remove it. To delete a stored procedure, you use the SQL DROP PROCEDURE statement like this:

```
DROP PROCEDURE getAuthors
```

Creating Procedures with Parameters

You can pass data back and forth to a stored procedure by using return codes, input parameters, and output parameters. The simplest way to retrieve data from a stored procedure is with a return code. A return code can only contain an integer value.

The following example creates a procedure, named checkAuthor, that uses a return code to indicate whether an author named Green exists:

```
CREATE PROCEDURE checkAuthor
AS
IF EXISTS( SELECT au_lname FROM Authors
  WHERE au_lname = 'Green' )
  RETURN( 1 )
ELSE
  RETURN( 0 )
```

14

WORKING WITH
THE COMMAND
OBJECT

When the RETURN statement is executed in this procedure, the procedure is exited and a return code is passed out of the procedure. The procedure returns the value 1 if the author named Green exists. Otherwise, the procedure returns the value 0.

> **NOTE**
>
> You should not return NULL values in a return code because a NULL value generates an error. You should also be cautious when returning negative integer values because a number of these values are reserved for error codes (-1 through -99). For more information, consult the SQL Server Books Online.

You can execute this procedure in Query Analyzer and view its return code. To do this, execute the following three statements:

```
DECLARE @returnCode INT
EXECUTE @returnCode = checkAuthor
SELECT @returnCode
```

The checkAuthor procedure would be much more useful if it could be used to check for the existence of any author and not just Green. To do this, the procedure must be altered to accept an input parameter:

```
CREATE PROCEDURE checkAuthor
(
  @authorName VARCHAR( 40 )
)
AS
IF EXISTS( SELECT au_lname FROM Authors
  WHERE au_lname = @authorName )
  RETURN( 1 )
ELSE
  RETURN( 0 )
```

This procedure accepts an input parameter named @authorName. The procedure checks whether an author with the name passed as the value of the input parameter exists in the Authors table. If the author exists, the value 1 is returned. Otherwise, the value 0 is returned.

You can execute this stored procedure within Query Analyzer by using a statement like the following:

```
EXECUTE checkAuthor 'Frege'
```

This statement executes the checkAuthor stored procedure with an input parameter that has the value Frege. You can, of course, execute the stored procedure with any value for the input parameter that you please.

To pass data back from a stored procedure, you can use an output parameter. An output parameter, unlike a return code, can have any data type supported by SQL Server. For example, the following stored procedure, named getFirstName, returns the first name of an author:

```
CREATE PROCEDURE getFirstName
(
  @lastName VARCHAR( 40 ),
  @firstName VARCHAR( 40 ) OUTPUT
)
AS
SELECT @firstname = au_fname
FROM Authors
WHERE au_lname = @lastname
```

This procedure accepts an input parameter called @lastName and returns an output parameter called @firstName. Notice that the output parameter is marked as an output parameter with the SQL keyword OUTPUT.

The procedure accepts the last name of an author and returns the author's first name by looking it up in the Authors table. If the author does not exist in the table, the output parameter is passed back with a NULL value (unlike the case of a return code, this does not result in an error).

To execute this stored procedure in Query Analyzer, you must create a variable that can accept the value returned from the output parameter. You can use the following three statements to execute the getFirstName stored procedure and print the output parameter returned:

```
DECLARE @theName VARCHAR( 40 )
EXECUTE getFirstName 'Green', @theName OUTPUT
PRINT @theName
```

Notice that the keyword OUTPUT must also be used when calling the getFirstName stored procedure. When the preceding statements are executed, the output parameter returned from the getFirstName stored procedure is printed to the screen. A single stored procedure can contain a maximum of 1,024 input and output parameters. A parameter can have any data type, including the TEXT and IMAGE data types.

14

WORKING WITH
THE COMMAND
OBJECT

Executing Stored Procedures with the `Connection` Object

The simplest way to execute a stored procedure within an Active Server Page is by using the `Connection` object. You can execute a SQL stored procedure just as you would any other SQL statement. For example, the following Active Server Page script executes a stored procedure named `byRoyalty`:

```
<!-- #INCLUDE VIRTUAL="/adovbs.inc" -->
<%
Set Con = Server.CreateObject( "ADODB.Connection" )
Con.Open "FILE NAME=c:\myDataLink.UDL;DATABASE=pubs"
Set RS = Con.Execute( "byRoyalty 25" )
While not RS.EOF
  Response.Write RS( "au_id" ) & "<br>"
  RS.MoveNext
Wend
%>
```

The `byRoyalty` stored procedure is included in the pubs database (the sample database included with SQL Server). The procedure accepts a single input parameter that represents a certain royalty percentage and returns a list of author IDs for the authors who are receiving that royalty percentage. In the preceding script, the list of author IDs is outputted to the browser by stepping through the Recordset with a `WHILE...WEND` loop.

Instead of executing a stored procedure that returns a Recordset, you can use the `Connection` object to execute a stored procedure that simply adds or updates data in a database table. Consider the following stored procedure:

```
CREATE PROCEDURE addAuthor
(
  @fname VARCHAR( 40 ),
  @lname VARCHAR( 40 )
)
AS
INSERT Authors ( au_fname, au_lname )
  VALUES ( @fname, @lname )
```

This stored procedure accepts two input parameters, an author's first and last name, and inserts the values of the parameters into the Authors table. To execute this stored procedure, you can use the following script:

```
<!-- #INCLUDE VIRTUAL="/adovbs.inc" -->
<%
Set Con = Server.CreateObject( "ADODB.Connection" )
```

```
Con.Open "FILE NAME=c:\myDataLink.UDL;DATABASE=pubs"
Con.Execute "addAuthor 'Andrew', 'Jones' "
%>
```

This script adds the author named `Andrew Jones` to the Authors table by executing the `addAuthor` stored procedure.

When executing a SQL stored procedure, you do not even need to explicitly call the `Connection` object's `Execute` method. In other words, you can call a stored procedure as if it were a native method of the `Connection` object. Here is an example:

```
<!-- #INCLUDE VIRTUAL="/adovbs.inc"  >
<%
Set Con = Server.CreateObject( "ADODB.Connection" )
Con.Open "FILE NAME=c:\myDataLink.UDL;DATABASE=pubs"
Con.addAuthor "Andrew", "Jones"
%>
```

This script accomplishes the very same thing as the previous script. However, notice that the `addAuthor` stored procedure is called as if it were a native method of the `Connection` object.

Executing stored procedures by using the `Connection` object is convenient. However, this method of calling stored procedures has two significant drawbacks. First, when you execute a stored procedure with the `Connection` object, you cannot retrieve return codes or output parameters. You are limited to returning nothing more than database rows.

Second, executing a stored procedure with the `Connection` object is not very efficient. The server must undergo more work to parse the statement and process any parameters (for example, the ADO must make a best guess of the data types of the parameters).

To use stored procedures more efficiently in your Active Server Pages, and to work with return codes and output parameters, you must use the ADO `Command` object. The rest of this chapter discusses the `Command` object in detail.

Executing Stored Procedures with the `Command` Object

The ADO `Command` object can be used to represent any command that you can execute against a data source. However, when using the `Command` object with SQL Server, the most useful application of the object is for executing SQL stored procedures.

You can use the Command object when executing both row returning and non-row returning stored procedures. You can also use the Command object to retrieve return codes and output parameters from a stored procedure. Suppose, for example, that your database contains the following SQL stored procedure named updateHitCount:

```
CREATE PROCEDURE updateHitCount
AS
UPDATE HitCount
  SET Hits = Hits + 1
```

This stored procedure simply adds 1 to a column named Hits in a table named HitCount. You might use this stored procedure, for example, to track the number of times that your Web site has been visited.

You can execute this stored procedure in an Active Server Page by using the Command object. Here's an example:

```
<!-- #INCLUDE VIRTUAL="/adovbs.inc" -->
<%
Set Con = Server.CreateObject( "ADODB.Connection" )
Con.Open "FILE NAME=c:\myDataLink.UDL"
Set MyCommand = Server.CreateObject( "ADODB.Command" )
Set MyCommand.ActiveConnection = Con
MyCommand.CommandType = adCmdStoredProc
MyCommand.CommandText = "updateHitCount"
MyCommand.Execute
%>
```

This script creates an instance of the Command object by using the CreateObject method of the Server object. Next, the Command is associated with an open database connection by using the Command object's ActiveConnection property. The CommandType property is used to indicate that the command will be used to execute a SQL stored procedure. The CommandText property provides the name of the stored procedure in the SQL database that will be executed. Finally, when the Command object's Execute method is called, the stored procedure is executed and the HitCount table is updated.

The preceding script is used to execute a stored procedure that does not return any rows. However, a Command object can also be used with a row returning stored procedure. To return rows from a stored procedure, you use the Command object with the Recordset object. For example, assume that the following SQL stored procedure named getAuthors exists on your database server. This simple, one-line stored procedure returns all the rows from the Authors table:

```
CREATE PROCEDURE getAuthors AS select * from Authors
```

The following script executes this stored procedure and displays the list of all the authors to the browser:

```
<!-- #INCLUDE VIRTUAL="/adovbs.inc" -->
<%
Set Con = Server.CreateObject( "ADODB.Connection" )
Con.Open "FILE NAME=c:\myDataLink.UDL;DATABASE=pubs"
Set MyCommand = Server.CreateObject( "ADODB.Command" )
Set MyCommand.ActiveConnection = Con
MyCommand.CommandType = adCmdStoredProc
MyCommand.CommandText = "getAuthors"
Set RS = MyCommand.Execute()
While NOT RS.EOF
  Response.Write RS( "au_fname" ) & "<br>"
  RS.MoveNext
WEND
%>
```

In this example, a Recordset is returned when the `Execute` method of the `Command` object is called. Because the Recordset is not explicitly created, it is opened with the default forward-only and read-only cursor and locking types.

You might need to open a Recordset with more functionality when using the `Command` object. For example, you might want to return a Recordset that can be updated or you might want a Recordset that supports the ADO paging properties (see "Updating Records with Native ADO Methods" and "Paging Through a Recordset" in Chapter 13). To open a Recordset with a richer cursor or locking type, you must explicitly declare these properties before opening the Recordset. Here's an example that opens a Recordset with a dynamic cursor and an optimistic lock using the `Command` object:

```
<!-- #INCLUDE VIRTUAL="/adovbs.inc" -->
<%
Set Con = Server.CreateObject( "ADODB.Connection" )
Con.Open "FILE NAME=c:\myDataLink.UDL"
Set MyCommand = Server.CreateObject( "ADODB.Command" )
Set MyCommand.ActiveConnection = Con
MyCommand.CommandType = adCmdStoredProc
MyCommand.CommandText = "getAuthors"
Set RS = Server.CreateObject( "ADODB.Recordset" )
RS.CursorType = adOpenDynamic
RS.LockType = adLockOptimistic
RS.Open MyCommand
RS.AddNew
RS( "au_fname" ) = "Andrew"
RS( "au_lname" ) = "Jones"
RS.Update
While NOT RS.EOF
  Response.Write RS( "au_fname" ) & "<br>"
  RS.MoveNext
WEND
%>
```

14

WORKING WITH
THE COMMAND
OBJECT

This script opens a Recordset with the `Command` object that supports optimistic locking and a dynamic cursor type. Next, the author Andrew Jones is added to the database table and all the records are displayed (the new name Andrew will actually be displayed twice because the current record will have this value after the record is first added and after the record is reached in the `WHILE...WEND` loop).

Using Return Code Parameters with the `Command` Object

Whenever you execute a SQL stored procedure, the stored procedure exits with a return code. If everything goes well, a return code of `0` is returned. If everything does not go well, a negative integer between -1 and -99 is returned.

You can cause different return codes to be returned from a stored procedure by using the `RETURN` statement. You can use these return codes for whatever purpose you want. For example, the following stored procedure returns `1` if the author named Green exists in the Authors table and `0` otherwise:

```
CREATE PROCEDURE checkAuthor
AS
IF EXISTS( SELECT au_lname FROM Authors
  WHERE au_lname = 'Green' )
  RETURN( 1 )
ELSE
  RETURN( 0 )
```

You can use the `Command` object to capture the return code from a stored procedure. To do this, an instance of the `Parameter` object must be created. Here is an example:

```
<!-- #INCLUDE VIRTUAL="/adovbs.inc" -->
<%
Set Con = Server.CreateObject( "ADODB.Connection" )
Con.Open "FILE NAME=c:\myDataLink.UDL;DATABASE=pubs"
Set MyCommand = Server.CreateObject( "ADODB.Command" )
MyCommand.ActiveConnection = Con
MyCommand.CommandType = adCmdStoredProc
MyCommand.CommandText = "checkAuthor"
Set MyParam = MyCommand.CreateParameter("ReturnCode", adInteger, _
    adParamReturnValue)
MyCommand.Parameters.Append MyParam
MyCommand.Execute
Response.Write MyCommand( "ReturnCode" )
%>
```

This example creates an instance of the Parameter object named MyParam to capture the return code from the stored procedure. All parameters—including input, output, and return code parameters—are represented in the ADO by the Parameter object. An instance of the Parameter object is created by calling the Command object's CreateParameter method. When using return code parameters, you must supply the following arguments to the CreateParameter method:

- Name—The name of the parameter. The name is used when referring to the parameter within your Active Server Page script. In the preceding example, the name is used when outputting the value of the parameter with the Response.Write statement.

- Type— The data type of the parameter. For return code parameters, the type is always adInteger.

- Direction—Indicates whether the parameter is a return code, input, or output parameter. When used with a return code parameter, the direction is always adParamReturnValue.

After the instance of the Parameter object has been created, you must append the new object to the command's Parameters collection. In the preceding script, this is accomplished by calling the Append method:

```
MyCommand.Parameters.Append MyParam
```

If you are feeling thrifty, instead of creating and appending the Parameter object with two lines of script, you can combine the two steps by using the following statement:

```
MyCommand.Parameters.Append
➡MyCommand.CreateParameter( "returnCode", adInteger,
➡adParamReturnValue)
```

This statement both creates an instance of the Parameter object and adds the new Parameter object to the command's Parameters collection.

You can retrieve a return code parameter from any stored procedure. You can even retrieve a return code from a stored procedure that returns rows. Consider the following stored procedure:

```
CREATE PROCEDURE checkGetAuthors
AS
SELECT * FROM Authors
IF EXISTS( SELECT au_lname FROM Authors
  WHERE au_lname = 'Green' )
  RETURN( 1 )
ELSE
  RETURN( 0 )
```

This stored procedure does two things. It returns all the rows from the Authors table, but it also returns a particular return code. You can display the rows and the return code outputted by this stored procedure with the following script:

```
<!-- #INCLUDE VIRTUAL="/adovbs.inc" -->
<%
Set Con = Server.CreateObject( "ADODB.Connection" )
Con.Open "FILE NAME=c:\myDataLink.UDL;DATABASE=pubs"
SET MyCommand = Server.CreateObject( "ADODB.Command" )
MyCommand.ActiveConnection = Con
MyCommand.CommandType = adCmdStoredProc
MyCommand.CommandText = "checkGetAuthors"
Set MyParam = MyCommand.CreateParameter( "returnCode", _
    adInteger, adParamReturnValue )
MyCommand.Parameters.Append MyParam
SET RS = MyCommand.Execute()
WHILE NOT RS.EOF
  Response.Write RS( "au_fname" )
  RS.MoveNext
WEND
RS.Close
Response.Write MyCommand( "returnCode" )
%>
```

There is one very important limitation when retrieving return codes with procedures that return rows. Before you can access the return code, you must close the Recordset that contains the rows. This means that you can access the return code only after you have finished displaying all the rows. This limitation is inconvenient. For example, it would be nice if there were a way to return the number of rows being returned in the return code parameter and then display all the rows. However, you can't.

Using Input Parameters with the `Command` Object

To pass values to a stored procedure, you use an input parameter. For example, the following stored procedure accepts an input parameter named `@firstLetter` that is used to retrieve all the authors whose last name start with a certain letter:

```
CREATE PROCEDURE getAuthorsByLastName
(
  @firstLetter VARCHAR( 1 )
)
AS
SELECT * FROM Authors
WHERE au_lname LIKE @firstLetter + '%'
```

Suppose you want to display all the authors whose names start with the letter G from the Authors table in an Active Server Page. You can do this with the following script:

```
<!-- #INCLUDE VIRTUAL="/adovbs.inc" -->
<%
Set Con = Server.CreateObject( "ADODB.Connection" )
Con.Open "FILE NAME=c:\myDataLink.UDL;DATABASE=pubs"
SET MyCommand = Server.CreateObject( "ADODB.Command" )
MyCommand.ActiveConnection = Con
MyCommand.CommandType = adCmdStoredProc
MyCommand.CommandText = "getAuthorsByLastName"
MyCommand.Parameters.Append MyCommand.CreateParameter
➥ ("ReturnCode", adInteger, adParamReturnValue)
MyCommand.Parameters.Append MyCommand.CreateParameter
➥("firstLetter", adVarchar, adParamInput, 1)
MyCommand.Parameters("firstLetter") = "g"
SET RS= MyCommand.Execute()
WHILE NOT RS.EOF
  REsponse.WRite RS( "au_lname" ) & "<br>"
  RS.MoveNext
WEND
%>
```

This script creates two parameters: a return code parameter and an input parameter. The input parameter is created by using the CreateParameter method of the Command object. When used with input parameters, this method accepts the arguments in Table 14.1.

TABLE 14.1 THE ARGUMENTS OF THE CreateParameter METHOD TO CREATE AN INPUT PARAMETER

Argument	Use
Name	The name of the parameter. The name is used when assigning a value to the input parameter before the command is executed.
Type	The data type of the parameter. In the preceding script, a varchar parameter is specified by using the adVarChar constant. Other common data types are adInteger for integer and adLongVarChar for text.
Direction	Indicates that the parameter is an input parameter. When used with input parameters, the direction is always adParamInput.
Size	When creating a parameter with a variable length data type, such as a varchar, provides the maximum size of the parameter. You must supply a size when using VARCHAR, but not when using INTEGER parameters.

14

WORKING WITH
THE COMMAND
OBJECT

Using Output Parameters with the `Command` Object

When retrieving a single record from a database table, or calculating a single value, you should use a stored procedure that returns an output parameter. Using an output parameter is always more efficient than using a `Recordset` object to retrieve a single row from a database table.

For example, suppose that you need to retrieve someone's email address from a table when you are supplied only with the person's username. You might be tempted to open a Recordset with a SQL query to find the email address. Don't do it! Use the following stored procedure instead:

```
CREATE PROCEDURE getEmail
(
  @username VARCHAR( 20 ),
  @email VARCHAR( 100 ) OUTPUT
)
AS
SELECT @email = email
FROM Webusers
WHERE username = @username
```

To use this stored procedure in an Active Server Page, you must retrieve the value of the output parameter into an instance of the ADO `Parameter` object. The following script demonstrates how to work with an output parameter:

```
<!-- #INCLUDE VIRTUAL="/adovbs.inc" -->
<%
Set Con = Server.CreateObject( "ADODB.Connection" )
Con.Open "FILE NAME=c:\myDataLink.UDL;DATABASE=pubs"
SET MyCommand = Server.CreateObject( "ADODB.Command" )
MyCommand.ActiveConnection = Con
MyCommand.CommandType = adCmdStoredProc
MyCommand.CommandText = "getEmail"
MyCommand.Parameters.Append MyCommand.CreateParameter
➥ ( "ReturnCode", adInteger, adParamReturnValue)
MyCommand.Parameters.Append MyCommand.CreateParameter
➥ ( "username", adVarchar, _adParamInput, 20)
MyCommand.Parameters( "username" ) = "Andrew Jones"
MyCommand.Parameters.Append MyCommand.CreateParameter
➥ ( "email", adVarchar, adParamOutput, 100)
MyCommand.Execute
Response.Write MyCommand( "email" )
%>
```

This procedure passes an input parameter named username to the stored procedure and retrieves an email address from the email output parameter. An output parameter is created in a similar fashion to an input parameter with the CreateParameter method. Table 14.2 shows the arguments that are used with this method when working with output parameters.

TABLE 14.2 ARGUMENTS OF THE CreateParameter METHOD TO CREATE AN OUTPUT PARAMETER

Argument	Use
Name	The name of the parameter. The name is used when retrieving the value from the input parameter after the command has been executed.
Type	The datatype of the parameter. In the preceding script, a VARCHAR parameter is used for the email parameter by using the adVarChar constant. Other common data types are adInteger for INTEGER and adLongVarChar for TEXT.
Direction	Indicates that the parameter is an output parameter. When used with output parameters, the direction is always adParamOutput.
Size	Creating a parameter with a variable length data type, such as a VARCHAR, provides the maximum size of the parameter. You must supply a size when using VARCHAR, but not when using INTEGER parameters.

In the same way that you can use a return code parameter with a row-returning SQL stored procedure, you can also use an output parameter. If a stored procedure returns rows, you must close the Recordset before you can access the output parameter. Otherwise, you will retrieve an empty value.

Output Parameters and Identity Columns

Microsoft SQL Server supports tables that contain identity columns. An *identity column* is a special type of table column that is guaranteed to always have a unique value. An identity column is normally used to uniquely identify a row of data so that it can be later retrieved.

For example, the following statement creates a table that contains an identity column named au_id:

```
CREATE TABLE Authors (au_id INT IDENTITY, au_name VARCHAR( 50 ) )
```

14

WORKING WITH
THE COMMAND
OBJECT

Whenever a new record is inserted into this table, the au_id column will be automatically incremented so that it will have a new value.

When working with a table that has an identity column, you might need to both insert a new record and retrieve the value of the new record's identity column. Performing this task using only the Recordset and Connection objects is difficult. After you have inserted a new row, it is difficult to identify the row again so that you can retrieve its identity column (that's why you needed the column in the first place).

Fortunately, inserting a record and retrieving its identity column is easy when using stored procedures and the Command object. The following stored procedure, named addAuthor, both inserts the name of a new author and retrieves the value of the identity column of the new row:

```
CREATE PROCEDURE addAuthor
(
  @AuthorName VARCHAR( 50 ),
  @id INT OUTPUT
)
AS
INSERT Authors ( au_name )
  VALUES ( @AuthorName )

SELECT @id = @@IDENTITY
```

This stored procedure uses an input parameter for the author's name and an output parameter for the value of the new row's identity column. The global variable @@IDENTITY contains the value of an identity column whenever a new row is inserted into a table (the variable holds the identity value until another new row is inserted).

The following script inserts the name of a new author into the Authors table and displays the value of the identity column of the new row:

```
<!-- #INCLUDE VIRTUAL="/adovbs.inc" -->
<%
Set Con = Server.CreateObject( "ADODB.Connection" )
Con.Open "FILE NAME=c:\myDataLink.UDL"
SET MyCommand = Server.CreateObject( "ADODB.Command" )
MyCommand.ActiveConnection = Con
MyCommand.CommandType = adCmdStoredProc
MyCommand.CommandText = "addAuthor"
MyCommand.Parameters.Append MyCommand.CreateParameter
➡ ( "ReturnCode", adInteger, adParamReturnValue)
MyCommand.Parameters.Append MyCommand.CreateParameter
➡ ( "AuthorName", adVarchar, adParamInput, 50)
MyCommand.Parameters( "AuthorName" ) = "Andrew Jones"
```

```
MyCommand.Parameters.Append MyCommand.CreateParameter
➥ ( "id", adInteger, adParamOutput )
MyCommand.Execute
Response.Write MyCommand( "id" )
%>
```

Retrieving Parameter Information

You might want to use a stored procedure but don't know the parameters that the procedure requires. For example, you might not know the data types of the parameters or their
sizes. How can you determine this information?

 You can retrieve information about the parameters used in a stored procedure by
using the script in Listing 14.1 (see Figure 14.2). Listing 14.1 is included on the
CD as displayParams.asp.

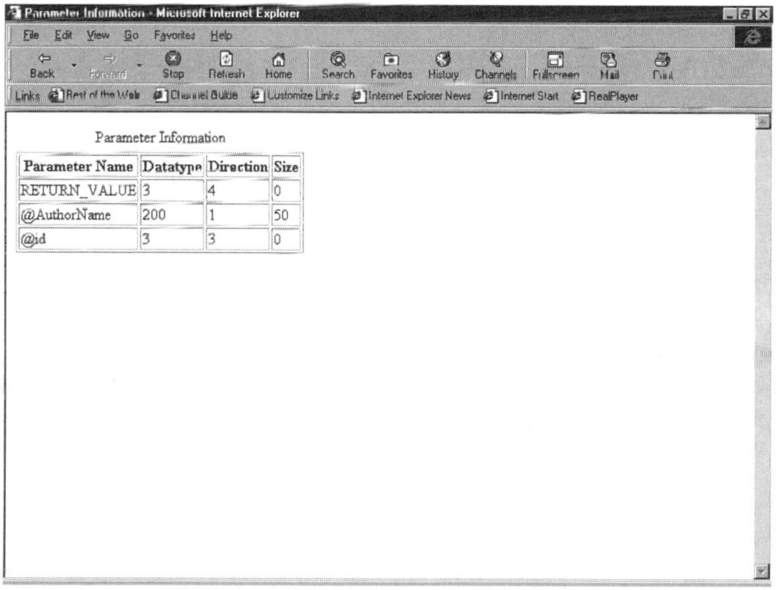

FIGURE 14.2

*Viewing parameter
information.*

Parameter Name	Datatype	Direction	Size
RETURN_VALUE	3	4	0
@AuthorName	200	1	50
@id	3	3	0

Parameter Information

LISTING 14.1   DISPLAYPARAMS.ASP

```
<!-- #INCLUDE VIRTUAL="ADOVBS.inc" -->
<%
Set MyConn=Server.CreateObject("ADODB.Connection")
Set MyCommand=Server.CreateObject("ADODB.Command")
MyConn.Open "FILE NAME=c:\myDataLink.UDL"
Set MyCommand.ActiveConnection=MyConn
MyCommand.CommandType=adCMDStoredProc
```

continues

14

WORKING WITH
THE COMMAND
OBJECT

LISTING 14.1   CONTINUED

```
MyCommand.CommandText="sp_myproc"
MyCommand.Parameters.Refresh
%>
<HTML>
<HEAD><TITLE>Parameter Information</TITLE></HEAD>
<BODY>
<TABLE BORDER=1>
<CAPTION>Parameter Information</CAPTION>
<TR>
 <TH>Parameter Name</TH>
 <TH>Datatype</TH>
 <TH>Direction</TH>
 <TH>Size</TH>
</TR>
<%For Each thing in MyCommand.Parameters %>
<TR>
 <TD><%=thing.name %></TD>
 <TD><%=thing.type %></TD>
 <TD><%=thing.direction %></TD>
 <TD><%=thing.size %></TD>
</TR>
<%
Next
MyConn.Close
%>
</TABLE>
</BODY>
</HTML>
```

This example displays all the parameter information for the procedure named sp_myproc. The name, data type, direction, and size for each parameter is displayed in a table. (The *direction* indicates whether the parameter is an input parameter, output parameter, or return status value.) To display information about another stored procedure, simply substitute the procedure's name for sp_myproc.

The important statement in this example is MyCommand.Parameters.Refresh. When this statement is executed, information about the stored procedure's parameters is retrieved from the database.

This script doesn't return constants. Instead, it returns raw values. To interpret the values returned by this script, you need to examine the ADOVBS include file. In this file, the raw numerical values are associated with the correct constants.

Summary

In this chapter, you learned how to work with SQL stored procedures within your Active Server Pages. You learned how to create and use a stored procedure with Microsoft SQL Server. Next, you learned an easy way to execute stored procedures in your Active Server Pages by using the `Connection` object. Finally, you learned how to use stored procedures with parameters in your Active Server Pages by using the methods and properties of the `Command` object.

14

WORKING WITH
THE COMMAND
OBJECT

CHAPTER 15

Working with Index Server and Full-Text Search

by Stephen Walther

IN THIS CHAPTER

In the previous three chapters, you learned how to use the ActiveX Data Objects (ADO) to work with databases. However, Microsoft designed the ADO (and its silent partner OLE DB) to work with any type of data source, not just a database. In this chapter, you will learn how to use the ADO to query a search server.

This chapter actually describes how to use the ADO with two different search servers. First, you will learn how to use the ADO with Microsoft Index Server. Microsoft Index Server is included with the NT Option Pack, and it is used to index static documents. For example, you can use Index Server to index and perform searches for HTML pages, Microsoft Word documents, and Excel spreadsheets.

The second part of this chapter discusses how to use the ADO with Microsoft Full-Text Search. Microsoft Full-Text Search is integrated into Microsoft SQL 7.0. It is used to index and perform queries against information stored in a database table.

You can use either or both of these search servers to create a standard search page for your Web site. For example, if you visit `http://search.microsoft.com`, you will see the search page displayed in Figure 15.1. After reading this chapter, you will be able to implement the same type of search page using Active Server Pages and the ADO.

FIGURE 15.1

The Microsoft search page.

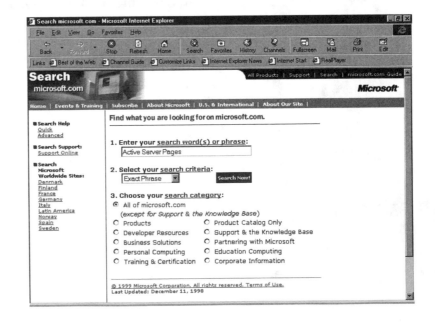

NOTE

Microsoft offers a third search server bundled with Microsoft Site Server. This search server is not discussed in this book. To learn more, visit the Microsoft Site Server Web site at http://www.microsoft.com/siteserver.

Using the ADO with Microsoft Index Server

Microsoft Index Server automatically indexes static documents including HTML pages, Microsoft Word documents, PDF files, Excel spreadsheets, PowerPoint presentations, and plain text files. You can use Index Server to index all the files on your Web site and enable visitors to search for particular documents using a search form.

Index Server will also index Active Server Pages. However, it will only index the static content contained in an Active Server Page. In other words, it will index the source, but not the interpreted content of the page. Index Server will not index, for example, any data the Active Server Page retrieves from a database.

Microsoft Index Server is included with the Windows NT 4.0 Option Pack. You were provided with the option of installing it when you installed IIS. To check whether Index Server is installed on your computer go to Start, Programs, Windows NT 4.0 Option Pack and check whether there is a folder named Microsoft Index Server. If the folder does not exist, you can install Index Server by running the Windows NT 4.0 Option Pack setup program.

After Index Server has been installed, it will constantly work in the background to index all the documents located in your Web server's virtual directories. By default, whenever you add a new virtual directory, Index Server will automatically detect its existence and begin indexing the documents contained in it.

TIP

You can force Index Server to index a directory at any time by using the Index Server Manager. Choose the name of a directory and select Action, Rescan.

Creating a Simple Search Form

 In this section, you will learn how to use the ADO with Index Server to create a simple search page for your Web site. This search page retrieves all the documents that match a search phrase entered in an HTML form (see Figure 15.2). It also lists a brief abstract for each document that is matched. The complete code for the search page is included in Listing 15.1, a little later on, and it is included on the CD as MISsearch.asp.

FIGURE 15.2

The Index Server search page.

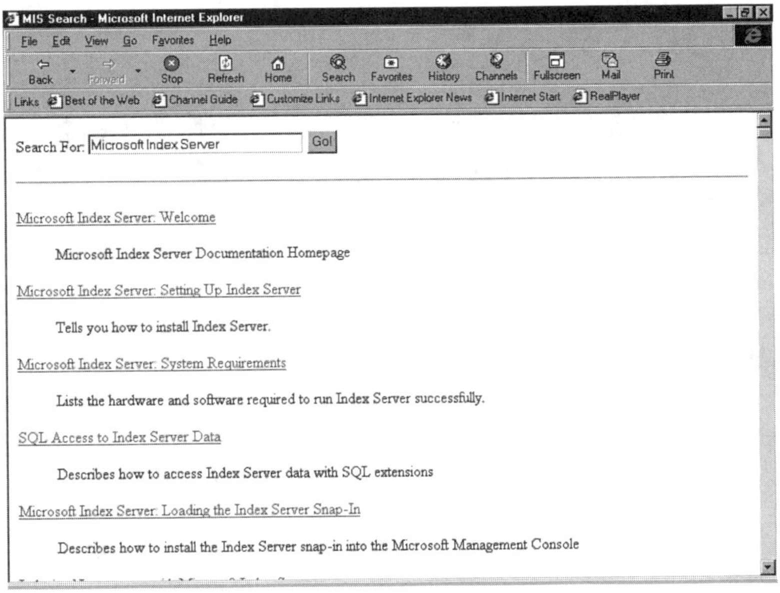

The search page opens a connection to Microsoft Index Server by using the OLE DB Provider for Microsoft Index Server. The following statement is used to open the connection:

```
Con.Open "PROVIDER=msidxs"
```

After the connection is opened, the following statement is executed to perform the actual search:

```
SELECT  Characterization, DocTitle, VPath
FROM  SCOPE() WHERE
FREETEXT(Contents, '" & search & "') > 0
ORDER BY Rank DESC
```

This query has four parts. First, the SELECT statement is used to retrieve a number of the properties of the documents returned by the query. In this example, an abstract

(Characterization), the title (DocTitle), and the full virtual path (VPath) of each document is retrieved. You'll learn more about these properties in a later section, "Searchable Properties."

Next, the FROM clause is used to specify the scope of the search. In this example, every document in every virtual directory enabled for indexing is searched. By default, this means every virtual directory on your Web server.

The WHERE clause uses the FREETEXT predicate to return only those records that match the search phrase entered into the HTML form. The Contents property represents the contents of a document.

Finally, an ORDER BY clause is used to order the results of the query by relevancy. Better matches are listed first. The Rank property contains a value between 0 and 1000 that indicates how closely a particular result matches the search criteria (the higher the number, the better the match).

After this query has been executed, the results are returned in a normal ADO Recordset object. A WHILE...WEND loop is used to display each record in the Recordset one by one.

LISTING 15.1 MISSEARCH.ASP

```
<html>
<head><title>MIS Search</title></head>
<body>
<form method="post" action="MISsearch.asp">
Search For: <input name="search" size=30>
<input type="submit" value="Go!">
</form>
<hr>
<%
search = TRIM( Request( "search" ) )
if search <> "" then
  search = Replace( search, "'", "" )
  set con=server.createobject( "adodb.Connection" )
  con.Open "provider=msidxs"
  mySQL = "SELECT  Characterization, " &_
    " DocTitle, VPATH " &_
    "FROM  SCOPE() " &_
    "WHERE FREETEXT(Contents, '" & search & "') > 0 " &_
    "ORDER BY Rank DESC"
  Set RS = Con.Execute( mySQL )
  if RS.EOF then
    Response.Write "No matches found!"
  else
    WHILE NOT RS.EOF
    %>
```

continues

15

WORKING WITH
INDEX SERVER AND
FULL-TEXT SEARCH

LISTING 15.1   CONTINUED

```
    <p><a href="<%=RS( "VPath" )%>"><%=RS( "DocTitle" )%></a>
    <blockquote>
    <%=Server.HTMLEncode( RS( "Characterization" ) )%>
    </blockquote>
    <%
    RS.MoveNext
    WEND
  end if
end if
%>
```

Restricting the Scope of a Search

You might want to restrict different searches to different groups of documents. For example, your Web site might have one area devoted to customer support and another area devoted to product information. You might want different search pages for each area.

You can restrict the scope of a query by using the SCOPE function. The SCOPE function accepts two arguments. The first argument, the Traversal Type, indicates whether subdirectories of the search directory should also be searched. The Traversal Type can have the value Deep Traversal (search subdirectories) or Shallow Traversal (don't search subdirectories). By default, every subdirectory is searched.

The second argument, the Path, contains a list of the virtual and physical directories to search. You can list multiple directories by separating the path of each directory with a comma. By default, if you do not list any directories, every directory is searched.

The following example restricts the scope of the search query to a virtual directory named ProductInfo. The keywords SHALLOW TRAVERSAL are used to indicate that subdirectories of the ProductInfo directory should not be searched:

```
<%
Set Con=server.CreateObject( "adodb.Connection" )
Con.Open "PROVIDER=msidxs"
mySQL = "SELECT DocTitle FROM " &_
  "SCOPE( 'SHALLOW TRAVERSAL OF ""/ProductInfo"" ' )  " &_
  "WHERE FREETEXT( Contents, 'PART #THX1138' )"
Set RS = Con.Execute( mySQL )
While NOT RS.EOF
%>
<p>Title: <%=RS( "DocTitle" )%>
<%
RS.MoveNext
Wend
%>
```

Searchable Properties

Microsoft Index Server automatically keeps track of several properties of the documents that it indexes. For different types of documents—for example, Microsoft Word and HTML documents—it keeps track of different properties. You can use these properties in your search queries in the same way that you would use a database column name. There are too many properties to list here (consult your Microsoft Index Server documentation to see the full list), but here are some of the more useful ones:

- Access—Indicates the last date and time a document was accessed.
- Characterization—Contains a brief summary of a document. Index Server automatically creates these document summaries while indexing.
- Contents—The contents of a document. You can use this property in a WHERE clause, but you cannot return it within a SELECT list.
- Create—Indicates the date and time the document was created.
- Directory—The physical path of the directory where a document is located.
- DocAuthor—The name of the author of a document.
- DocTitle—The title of a document.
- FileName—The filename of a document.
- HitCount—Number of words matching the search query contained in the document.
- Path—Full physical path of the document.
- Rank—The relevancy rank of the document relative to a search query. It can be a number between 0 and 1000 (the higher the rank, the better the match).
- Size—The size of a document in bytes.
- VPath—The virtual path of a document.
- Write—Indicates the last date and time the document was written.

Suppose, for example, that you want to retrieve a list of only those documents that have a total size of less than 100 bytes. You can perform this query using the Size property:

```
<%
Set con=server.createobject( "adodb.Connection" )
con.Open "provider=msidxs"
mySQL = "SELECT DocTitle, Size " &_
  "FROM  SCOPE()  WHERE " &_
  "Size < 100"
Set RS = Con.Execute( mySQL )
While NOT RS.EOF
%>
```

15

WORKING WITH INDEX SERVER AND FULL-TEXT SEARCH

```
<p>Title: <%=RS( "DocTitle" )%>
<br>Size: <%=RS( "Size" )%>
<%
RS.MoveNext
Wend
%>
```

Creating Custom Searchable Properties

One of the most interesting features of Index Server is its support for the definition of custom properties. For example, you can add a custom property to a group of HTML documents and then perform queries that use the property when searching through the HTML documents.

To add a custom property to an HTML document, you use the HTML <META> tag. The following page has a custom property named myProp:

```
<html>
<head>
<META NAME="myProp" CONTENT="red">
<title>Some Document</title>
</head>
<body>
Hello!
</body>
</html>
```

The <META> tag is added within the <HEAD> tags of an HTML document. In this example, the <META> tag is used to define a property named myProp that has the value red. You can, of course, create a property with any name and value that you please.

After you have added a custom property to an HTML page, you must configure Index Server to recognize the new property. You do this by using the Index Server Manager. Follow these steps:

1. Launch the Index Server Manager and select the folder labeled Properties.

2. The new property should appear in the list of properties in the right-hand frame. If the property does not appear, you can either wait until Index Server catches up with you, or you can force it to rescan the directory that contains the document with the new property. To force a rescan, select the name of the directory and choose Action, Rescan (you might also need to close and restart the Index Server Manager).

3. Select the custom property from the property list and open the property's property sheet. Check the box labeled Cached and then choose the VT_LPWSTR data type for the property (see Figure 15.3).

FIGURE 15.3

Adding a custom property.

4. Select the folder labeled Properties once again, and choose Action, Commit changes.

This series of actions adds the new custom property to the property cache. After you first add a new custom property, the property has the value NULL for every document until the documents are indexed again.

 After Index Server recognizes the custom property, you can use it within your search queries in the same way as you can use the standard properties such as DocTitle and Size. The script in Listing 15.2 (included on the CD as customProp.asp) retrieves all the HTML documents in which the myProp property has the value green.

You should notice the following very strange and unreadable line in the script:

```
Con.Execute "SET PROPERTYNAME 'd1b5d3f0-c0b3-11cf-9a92-00a0c908dbf1'
➥PROPID 'myProp' AS myProp"
```

The purpose of this statement is to associate the custom property with a friendly name that you can use in your queries. The long string of numbers and letters represents the GUID (Globally Unique Identifier) for properties associated with HTML documents.

If you create a new custom property named favColor, for example, then you would use this statement to provide the favColor property with a friendly name (the same GUID is always used for HTML documents):

```
Con.Execute "SET PROPERTYNAME 'd1b5d3f0-c0b3-11cf-9a92-00a0c908dbf1'
➥PROPID 'favColor' AS favColor"
```

15

WORKING WITH
INDEX SERVER AND
FULL-TEXT SEARCH

LISTING 15.2   CUSTOMPROP.ASP

```
<%
Set Con=Server.CreateObject( "adodb.Connection" )
Con.Open "provider=msidxs"
Con.Execute "SET PROPERTYNAME 'd1b5d3f0-c0b3-11cf-9a92-00a0c908dbf1'
➥PROPID 'myProp' AS myProp"
mySQL = "SELECT  DocTitle, myProp " &_
  "FROM  SCOPE() " &_
  "WHERE FREETEXT(myProp, '" & "green" & "') > 0 "
Set RS = Con.Execute( mySQL )
WHILE NOT RS.EOF
%>
<p><%=RS( "DocTitle" )%>
<br><%=RS( "myProp" )%>
<%
RS.MoveNext
WEND
%>
```

Using the ADO with SQL 7.0 Full-Text Search

If you create a database-driven Web site with Active Server Pages, the majority of your data will not be stored in static HTML pages. Instead, the data will be stored in one or more database tables.

For example, imagine that you are building a job Web site for Active Server Pages consultants. You might want to allow visitors to your Web site to submit their resumés through an online form. The most logical and efficient method of storing these resumés is by placing them in a text column of a database table.

This creates a problem when using traditional search servers such as Microsoft Index Server. Because Microsoft Index Server can only be used to index static documents, you cannot use it to index the resumés that have been submitted to the job site. Microsoft Index Server will fail to index the most important data.

Fortunately, Microsoft recognized this problem. To address the problem of indexing data stored in database tables, Microsoft introduced the Full-Text Search service with Microsoft SQL Server 7.0. The Microsoft Full-Text Search service can be used to index and perform queries against the text columns of any SQL 7.0 database table.

Why Is Full-Text Search Necessary?

You might be wondering whether the Full-Text Search service is really necessary. Transact-SQL, the language of SQL Server, already supports character matching through the use of wildcard characters and the LIKE operator. For example, you can use the following SQL statement to retrieve the text of all the resumés that contain the phrase *will work cheap* from a table named Consultants:

```
SELECT resume FROM Consultants
WHERE resume LIKE '%will work cheap%'
```

This statement works perfectly well. It uses the wildcard character % to match a string of any length that precedes or follows the expression. The query will return any resumé that contains an exact match to this phrase.

However, there are two significant drawbacks to using this approach to search through the contents of a database table. First, and most important, the query is not very efficient. If you have a table that contains thousands (or tens of thousands) of resumés, using the LIKE operator in this manner will likely bring your database server to a crawl. SQL Server is simply not designed to handle this type of query efficiently.

Second, the LIKE operator limits you to performing only searches to retrieve exact matches. For example, the LIKE query in the preceding example would not match resumés that contain the phrase *will work very cheap* or *will work very, very cheap*.

Users expect commercial Web sites to support advanced search capabilities such as Boolean searches and fuzzy pattern matching. Users expect to be able to perform the same types of searches that they could perform at Yahoo! or AltaVista. You cannot perform these types of queries with Transact-SQL (or they, at least, would be so complicated and inefficient that they would not be worthwhile).

Microsoft Full-Text Search does not share these deficiencies. It uses its own indexes that are specially designed to handle complex searches. Full-Text Search supports both fuzzy pattern matching and Boolean queries.

Installing and Enabling Full-Text Search

The Full-Text Search Service is bundled with Microsoft SQL 7.0. Although the service is included with all versions of SQL 7.0, it will not work with the Desktop version. You cannot use Full-Text Search with Windows 95/98 or Windows NT Workstation. The service will only work with Windows NT Server.

The Full-Text Search Service is not installed by default when you install SQL Server. During installation, you must choose to perform a Custom Installation and select the

Full-Text Search Service from the menu of installable components. Alternatively, you can install the Full-Text Search Service after you have installed SQL Server by running the setup program again.

After the service has been installed, it will be listed in the SQL Server Service Manager with the name Microsoft Search. Before you can begin using the service, you must enable it by clicking Start/Continue with the service selected (see Figure 15.4).

FIGURE 15.4

Starting the Microsoft Full-Text Search Service.

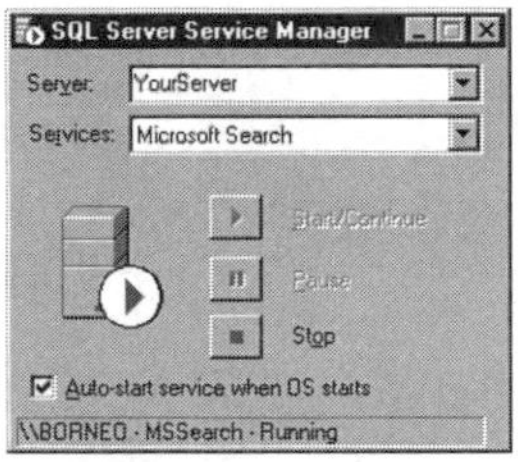

You also have the option of specifying the amount of system resources that the Full-Text Search service should use. To set this option, launch the SQL Server Enterprise Manager, click Support Services, and right-click Full-Text Search to open the Full-Text Search property sheet. Within the property sheet, click the tab labeled Performance and provide a value for System Resource Usage (see Figure 15.5).

FIGURE 15.5

Setting search resource use.

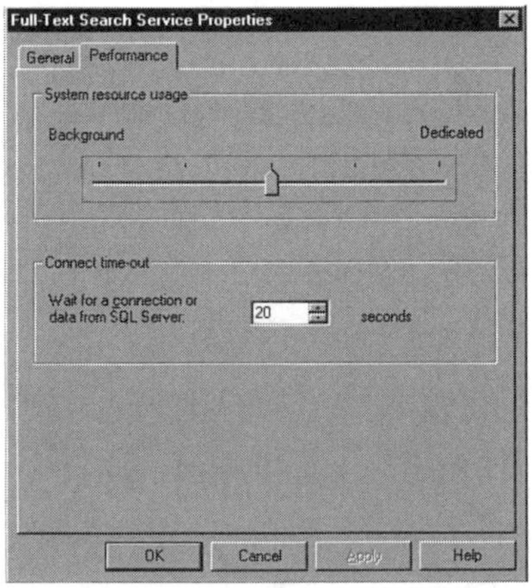

Adding Full-Text Indexing to a Table

You can define and create a full-text index for a table by using either the SQL Server Enterprise Manager or by executing system stored procedures. It's much easier to create an index by using the Enterprise Manager, so this is the method that will be described here.

Before adding support for Full-Text Search to a table, you should be aware that you cannot alter the table after the index has been added. For example, you cannot change any of the table's normal indexes or change the table's columns (however, you can change the data in the table). To make changes to a table with a full-text index, you must drop the full-text index, make the changes, and add the full-text index once again. This makes life difficult in the case of a live Web site because it means that you cannot make table changes without temporarily disabling your Web site's search page.

You should also be aware that you cannot add a full-text index to a table unless the table has a unique, single-column index. To create a unique, single-column index for a table, you can add a primary key to the table. Typically, you define a primary key for an identity column to ensure that all the values in the column are unique.

To create a full-text index for a table, launch the Microsoft Enterprise Manager and select a table. Next, right-click the table and choose Full-Text Index Table, Define Full-Text Indexing on a Table. This series of actions will launch the Full-Text Indexing Wizard (see Figure 15.6). The wizard will lead you through the following steps:

1. Select an Index. Every table that has a full-text index must have a column that has unique values. This column is called the table's Key column. When you perform a full-text query, the value of the Key column can also be returned for all the rows that match the query.

FIGURE 15.6

Creating a full-text index.

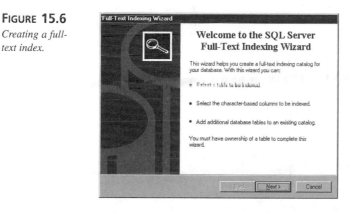

2. Select Table Columns. A full-text index can be created for one or more text columns in a table. For example, you can index VARCHAR, CHAR, and TEXT columns.

3. Select a Catalog. A full-text index is stored in a catalog. You can either create a new catalog or select an existing catalog. Although you can place multiple full-text indexes in the same catalog, you should not do this when indexing large tables.

4. Select or Create Population Schedules. Unlike a normal table index, a full-text index is not updated automatically by SQL Server. If new rows are added to a table or the records in a table are changed, the table's full-text index must be updated. To update a full-text index on a scheduled basis, create a population schedule. You can choose to update the index from scratch every time (a full population) or you can choose to update an index with only new changes (an incremental population). Normally, you should schedule an incremental population.

After you complete the wizard and click Finish, the new full-text index is created in the catalog that you specified. When the index is first created, it is empty. Before you can start using the index, you must populate it.

To populate the index, choose Full-Text Catalog, right-click the name of your catalog, and select Start Population, Full Population. This will begin the population process.

For a large table, it might take a very long time to populate the index for the first time. You can view the population progress in real-time by double-clicking the name of your catalog and watching the item count. Every time a new row in your table has been indexed, the item count will increase by one (see Figure 15.7).

FIGURE 15.7

Viewing the item count.

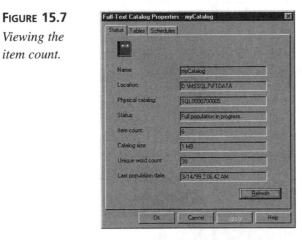

Performing Full-Text Queries

To support full-text queries, two new predicates and two new functions were added to Transact-SQL. By using the CONTAINS predicate and the CONTAINSTABLE function, you can perform Boolean and other types of very precise search queries. By using either the FREETEXT predicate or the FREETEXTTABLE function, you can perform free-form searches.

Using the CONTAINS Predicate

The CONTAINS predicate is very flexible. You can use this predicate to perform any of the following types of searches:

- Boolean searches—In a Boolean search, you can use the words AND, OR, and AND NOT in the search phrase. For example, you can search for all the resumés in a table of resumés that contain the expression *San Francisco* or *Modesto*.

- Exact phrase searches—By placing quotation marks around a search phrase, you can return only those records that exactly match the expression. For example, you can search for *Active Server Pages* and not return records that contain the expression *old book pages*.

- Weighted searches—In a weighted search, you can assign different weights to the terms that appear in the search phrase. For example, in a search for resumés that contain the terms *ASP* and *PERL*, you might assign more importance to *ASP* than *PERL*.

- Inflectional searches—In an inflectional search, the grammatical variations of a search term are also matched. This includes both the plural and singular forms of nouns and different verb tenses. For example, a search for the term *house* would also return rows that contain the term *houses*; a search for the term *open* would also return rows that contain the term *opened*.

- Proximity searches—In a proximity search, you can give a higher rank to matches where the terms in the search phrase appear closer together. For example, you might place a higher value on those resumés where the terms *very* and *cheap* appear close together than on those resumés where the two terms appear farther apart.

For example, suppose you want to execute a query that returns all the records from a table of resumés that contain the words *San Francisco* or *Modesto*. You can perform this search with the CONTAINS predicate using the following statement:

```
SELECT c_resume FROM Consultants WHERE
CONTAINS( c_resume, '"San Francisco" OR "Modesto"' )
```

This statement returns all the resumés from the Consultants table where the column named c_resume contains the words *San Francisco* or *Modesto*. The CONTAINS predicate accepts two arguments. The first argument supplies a list of columns that are searched (you can use * for all columns). The second argument supplies the search phrase.

Here's how the search criteria in the previous example can be used in an Active Server Page script:

```
<!-- #INCLUDE VIRTUAL="/adovbs.inc" -->
<%
Set Con = Server.CreateObject( "ADODB.Connection" )
Con.Open "FILE NAME=c:\myDataLink.UDL"
mySQL = "SELECT c_resume FROM Consultants WHERE " &_
  "CONTAINS( c_resume, '""San Francisco"" OR ""Modesto""' )"
Set RS = Con.Execute( mySQL )
While NOT RS.EOF
  Response.Write RS( "c_resume" ) & "<br>"
  RS.MoveNext
WEND
%>
```

Notice the odd things that must be done with the quotation marks to get this example to work. VBScript uses quotation marks to mark the beginning and end of a string. If you use two quotation marks in a row, however, VBScript will interpret the quotation mark as part of the string.

Using the CONTAINSTABLE Function

You can perform the same types of searches with the CONTAINSTABLE function as you can with the CONTAINS predicate. However, the CONTAINSTABLE function returns a table rather than a set of rows.

The advantage of using the CONTAINSTABLE function is that you can use this function to rank the results returned. The table returned by this function has two columns named Key and Rank. The Key column contains a unique value for each row, and the Rank column contains the relevance ranking of each row. Each row is ranked between the values of 0 and 1000 (the higher the rank the better).

For example, the following query retrieves all the resumés from the Consultants table that contain the word *Active* or *Server* and ranks the results:

```
SELECT Rank, c_resume FROM
Consultants
INNER JOIN
CONTAINSTABLE( Consultants, c_resume, 'Active or Server' )
AS SR
ON c_id = [Key]
ORDER BY Rank DESC
```

This statement is complicated, and it requires some explanation. When a table is returned by the CONTAINSTABLE function, it includes only the Key and Rank columns. If you want to show the records that have been matched, you must join this table with the table that was searched. In the preceding example, the Consultants table is joined with the table returned by CONTAINSTABLE by using the c_id column of the Consultants table and the Key column of the CONTAINSTABLE table.

In the preceding example, the Rank column is used to order the search results returned by the query. For example, if a resumé contains both the words *Active* and *Server*, it will be ranked higher than a resumé that contains only the word *Server*. The rank of each row is outputted along with the actual content of the resumé.

The CONTAINSTABLE function accepts three arguments. The first argument contains the name of the table to be searched. The second argument contains a list of columns to be searched (you can use * for all columns). Finally, the third column contains the actual search phrase.

Using the FREETEXT Predicate

Most people do not use sophisticated search criteria when performing a search at a Web site. People very rarely perform Boolean searches or proximity searches. Typically, they just type a bunch of words and hope for a good match.

The FREETEXT predicate is useful for performing free-form searches. It was designed to match the meaning of the words in a search phrase more than the exact words used. Here is an example of how you can use the FREETEXT predicate to search for all resumés that match *Active Server Pages*:

```
SELECT c_resume
FROM Consultants WHERE
FREETEXT( c_resume, 'Active Server Pages' )
```

You can type just about anything as your search phrase without receiving a syntax error. The FREETEXT predicate will always attempt to find good matches.

If you enter Boolean search criteria, however, the OR, AND, and AND NOT operators will be ignored. You cannot use a FREETEXT predicate to perform the same types of searches that you can perform with the CONTAINS predicate.

Using the FREETEXTTABLE Function

You can perform the same types of searches with the FREETEXTTABLE function as you can with the FREETEXT predicate. However, the FREETEXTTABLE function returns a table instead of a set of matching rows.

The table returned by this function contains two columns named Key and Rank. The Key column uniquely identifies each row in the search results. The Rank column provides a relevancy ranking for each result. Here is an example of how this function can be used:

```
SELECT Rank, c_resume FROM
Consultants
INNER JOIN
FREETEXTTABLE( Consultants, c_resume,
    'Active Server Pages' )
AS SR
ON c_id = [Key]
ORDER BY Rank DESC
```

This statement retrieves the resumés that match the search criterion *Active Server Pages*. The table returned by the FREETEXTTABLE function is joined to the Consultants table by using the c_id and Key columns. The results of this query are ordered according to relevancy by using the Rank column.

The FREETEXTTABLE function accepts three arguments. The first argument contains the name of the table to search. The second argument contains the list of columns to search (or * for all columns). The last argument contains the search phrase.

Here's how you can implement this query in an Active Server Page script:

```
<!-- #INCLUDE VIRTUAL="/adovbs.inc" -->
<%
Set Con = Server.CreateObject( "ADODB.Connection" )
Con.Open "FILE NAME=c:\myDataLink.UDL"
mySQL = "SELECT Rank, c_resume FROM " &_
  "Consultants " &_
  "INNER JOIN " &_
  "FREETEXTTABLE( Consultants, c_resume, " &_
  " 'Active Server Pages' )" &_
  "AS SR " &_
  "ON c_id = [Key] " &_
  "ORDER BY Rank DESC "
Set RS = Con.Execute( mySQL )
While NOT RS.EOF
  Response.Write RS( "c_resume" ) & "<br>"
  RS.MoveNext
WEND
%>
```

Retrieving Index Statistics

If you double-click the name of your search catalog in the SQL Server Enterprise Manager, you can view several statistics about the current state of your full-text index. For example, you can view the item count (the number of table rows that have been indexed), the unique key count (the number of unique words indexed), and the population status (whether a full or incremental population is in progress).

You can retrieve these very same values by using the FULLTEXTCATALOGPROPERTY system stored procedure. The following statement, for example, returns the number of items that have been indexed:

```
SELECT FULLTEXTCATALOGPROPERTY('myCatalog', 'ItemCount')
```

Replace the word myCatalog with the name of your full-text catalog. When you execute this statement, the number of rows that have been indexed in a table is returned.

 You can use the FULLTEXTCATALOGPROPERTY procedure to create a statistics page for your Web site that shows the current status of your full-text index. The script in Listing 15.3 (included on the CD as searchStats.asp) outputs a number of the available statistics to the browser (see Figure 15.8).

FIGURE 15.8

Retrieving search statistics.

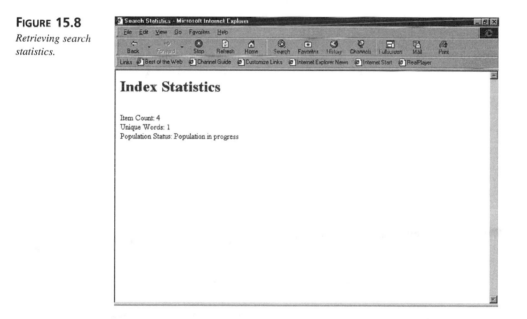

LISTING 15.3 SEARCHSTATS.ASP

```
<html>
<head><title>Search Statistics</title></head>
<body>
<%
Function showPop( thePopStatus )
  SELECT CASE thePopStatus
    CASE "0"
    showPop = "Idle"
    CASE "1"
```

continues

LISTING 15.3   CONTINUED

```
   showPop = "Population in progress"
   CASE "2"
   showPop = "Paused"
   CASE "3"
   showPop = "Throttled"
   CASE "4"
   showPop = "Recovering"
   CASE "5"
   showPop = "Shutdown"
   CASE "6"
   showPop = "Incremental population"
   CASE "7"
   showPop = "Updating Index"
  END SELECT
End Function

Set Con = Server.CreateObject( "ADODB.Connection" )
Con.Open "FILE NAME=c:\myDataLink.UDL;DATABASE=TEST"
mySQL = "SELECT FULLTEXTCATALOGPROPERTY('myCatalog', 'ItemCount') ICount"
Set RS1 = Con.Execute( mySQL )
mySQL = "SELECT FULLTEXTCATALOGPROPERTY('myCatalog',
➥'UniqueKeyCount') UKey"
Set RS2 = Con.Execute( mySQL )
mySQL = "SELECT FULLTEXTCATALOGPROPERTY('myCatalog',
➥'PopulateStatus') PStatus"
Set RS3 = Con.Execute( mySQL )
%>
<h1>Index Statistics</h1>
<br>Item Count: <%=RS1( "ICount" )%>
<br>Unique Words: <%=RS2( "UKey" )%>
<br>Population Status: <%=showPop( RS3( "PStatus" ) )%>

</body>
</html>
```

Using Full-Text Search to Create a Search Page

This section shows an example of how you can create a simple search page using Full-Text Search. This search page allows you to search through a table of resumés for job candidates that match your search criteria. The search page supports both Boolean and free-form searches.

The table used in this example is named Consultants. It can be created with the following SQL statement:

```
CREATE TABLE Consultants (
  c_id INT IDENTITY PRIMARY KEY,
```

```
    c_name VARCHAR( 50 ),
    c_resume TEXT
)
```

This table contains three columns. The first column is an identity column. It is used to uniquely identify each row in the table (you must create a unique column to use full-text search). The second column contains the names of people who have submitted resumés. Finally, the third column contains the actual text of the resumés.

After you create this table, create a full-text index for the table, add some resumés, and populate the index. See the two sections entitled "Installing and Enabling Full-Text Search" and "Adding Full-Text Indexing to a Table," earlier in this chapter, to learn how to do this.

 The complete listing for the search page is contained in Listing 15.4 (included on the CD as search.asp). The search page has a form that contains a text input field and a select list. The select list is used to select whether a free-form or Boolean search should be performed. The results of a search are shown below the form (see Figure 15.9).

FIGURE 15.9
The Full-Text search page.

```
🔍 Search - Microsoft Internet Explorer                                    _ 8 ×
 File  Edit  View  Go  Favorites  Help                                      e
  ⇦  →   ⊗    🔄    🏠    🔍     🔲     🕒    🕮    🔲    🕲    🖨
 Back Forward Stop Refresh Home Search Favorites History Channels Fullscreen Mail Print
 Links 🔲Best of the Web 🔲Channel Guide 🔲Customize Links 🔲Internet Explorer News 🔲Internet Start 🔲RealPlayer

 Search For: [Active Server Pages                              ]
 Search Criteria: [Free text search ▼]  [Search!]
 ─────────────────────────────────────────────────────────────

 24 - Andrew Jones

       I am interested in pursuing a career in Active Server Pages programming. I have worked with a number of
       Internet Startups in the Cambridge area

 24 - Noelle Bermingham

       Active Server Pages consultant located in the San Francisco Bay Area.

 4 - John Orr

       I am active in a number of programming areas. I am currently located in Modesto, California.
```

Notice one peculiar thing about this listing. When the search phrase is retrieved from the HTML form, every apostrophe in the search phrase is removed. If you include apostrophes in your search phrase, it will generate a syntax error when it is submitted to SQL Server.

You should also be aware of the fact that the search page will generate an error if you attempt to do a Boolean search without using a Boolean search phrase. To get around this problem, you need to capture errors using the ON ERROR RESUME next statement and the ERR object. When you perform a free-form search, however, you can type anything you please without receiving an error.

LISTING 15.4   SEARCH.ASP

```
<html>
<head><title> Search </title></head>
<body>
<form method="post" action="search.asp">
Search For:
<input name="search" type="text" size=50>
<br>Search Criteria:
<select name="criteria">
<option value="0">Free text search
<option value="1">Boolean search
</select>
<input type="submit" value="Search!">
<hr>
<%
search = TRIM( Request( "search" ) )
criteria = TRIM( Request( "criteria" ) )
if search <> "" then
  search = Replace( search, "'", "" )
  Set Con = Server.CreateObject( "ADODB.Connection" )
  Con.Open "FILE NAME=c:\myDataLink.UDL"
  mySQL = "SELECT Rank, c_name, c_resume FROM " &_
  "Consultants INNER JOIN "
  if criteria = "0" then
    mySQL = mySQL & "FREETEXTTABLE( Consultants, *, "
  else
    mySQL = mySQL & "CONTAINSTABLE( Consultants, *, "
  end if
  mySQL = mySQL & "'" & search & "' )" &_
  "AS SR " &_
  "ON c_id = [Key] " &_
  "ORDER BY Rank DESC "
Set RS = Con.Execute( mySQL )
if RS.EOF then
  Response.Write "No matches found!"
else
  While NOT RS.EOF
  %>
  <p><%=RS( "Rank" ) %> - <%=RS( "c_name" )%>
  <blockquote><%=RS( "c_resume" )%></blockquote>
```

```
<%
   RS.MoveNext
  WEND
end if
end if
%>
```

Summary

In this chapter, you learned two methods of adding a search page to your Web site. In the first part, you learned how to use Microsoft Index Server to index the static documents on your Web server. You also learned how to use Index Server with the ADO to perform searches. In the second part, you learned how to use Full-Text Search to index and search the data stored in a database table.

Active Server Pages Custom Components

PART

IV

CHAPTER 16

Third-Party Components

by Stephen Walther

IN THIS CHAPTER

There is nothing more exciting to an Active Server Pages developer than the discovery of a new Active Server Page component. Third-party components open new programming possibilities by extending the basic set of intrinsic and installable components included with Internet Information Server.

Do you need to request a page from another Web site? No problem. Several third-party components enable you to use the HTTP protocol to grab a page off another Web site. Do you need to create custom images within your Active Server Page scripts? Again, there are components that allow you to dynamically draw images of any kind within your Web pages. Chances are, if you need to do something within your Active Server Page scripts that is not supported by the default Active Server Page components, someone has written a custom component to do it.

This chapter focuses on three very useful Active Server Page components. In the first part of this chapter, "Graphics Components," you will be introduced to the ShotGraph graphics component. This component enables you to create custom JPEG images on-the-fly. You can use this component to create graphs in response to user queries or dynamically create images with different fonts.

In the second part of this chapter, "File Upload Components," you will learn how to use the Software Artisans SA-FileUp component to easily accept file uploads at your Web site. This component enables you to save file uploads to a file or database or to manipulate the content of the file within your Active Server Pages.

In part three of this chapter, "Networking Components," you will learn how to use a WinSock component to work with both the HTTP protocol and NNTP protocol. Using a WinSock component, you can post form data and retrieve Web pages from other Web sites. A WinSock component can also be used to post and retrieve articles from NNTP compatible news groups.

The fourth part of this chapter, "Other Components," contains a brief survey of some of the more interesting third-party components available to use in your Active Server Pages. In this fourth part, you will not only be presented with a brief description of these components, you will also be provided with a list of valuable resources for finding additional components on the Web.

Graphics Components

 The CD that accompanies this book includes an evaluation copy of the ShotGraph component. The ShotGraph component has a rich set of methods and properties for manipulating JPEG images. Using the ShotGraph component you can

- Dynamically generate images of numerals for a hit counter on your Web page.
- Create pie charts and other graphs in response to user queries.
- Automatically create thumbnail images for a collection of images.
- Display text with any typeface available on your Web server.
- Scale, rotate, and mirror images in response to user actions.

Basically, the ShotGraph component enables you to do just about anything with a JPEG image that you can imagine. In this section, two sample applications of this component will be discussed: You will learn how to use the ShotGraph component to create a hit counter and how to use the component to generate graphs from a database table.

> **NOTE**
>
> The evaluation version of the ShotGraph component included with this book is limited to images with a maximum size of 320×240 pixels. Also, some of its methods and properties are disabled.

Creating a Hit Counter with the ShotGraph Component

Suppose you want to track and display the number of times that the home page of your Web site has been requested. You could display a simple hit counter with the following Active Server Page script (included on the CD as plainHitCounter.asp):

```
<%
Application.Lock
Application( "home_hits" ) = Application( "home_hits" ) + 1
Application.UnLock
 %>
<html>
<head><title>Home Page</title></head>
<body>
Welcome
<p>
This page has been visited <%=Application( "home_hits" )%> times.
</body>
</html>
```

This script uses an application variable to store the number of times that the current page has been accessed. The value of this variable is simply outputted as plain text. As you can see from Figure 16.1, this is not the most exciting way to display this information.

It would be much more interesting to display the number of page requests as an image rather than as plain text. If the number of requests is displayed as an image, you can have complete control over the color and font that are used to display the information. You can use the ShotGraph component to dynamically generate a JPEG image with the following script:

```
<%
Response.ContentType="image/jpeg"
hits = Request.QueryString( "hits" )
width = 150
height = 60
Set g=CreateObject("shotgraph.image")
g.CreateImage width, height, 2
'Yellow color
g.SetColor 0, 255, 255, 0
'Blue color
g.SetColor 1, 0, 0, 255
g.SetBgColor 0
g.FillRect 0, 0, width, height
g.SetBkMode "TRANSPARENT"
g.CreateFont "Comic Sans MS", 1, 40, 0, False, False, False, False
g.SetTextAlign "TA_CENTER","TA_BASELINE"
g.SetTextColor 1
g.TextOut width / 2, height /2, FormatNumber( Hits, 0 )
Response.BinaryWrite g.JpegImage( 90,0,"" )
%>
```

Save the preceding script with the filename myImage.asp (it's included with the CD). When you load this script in your browser, different images are displayed depending on the value you pass with the query string variable named hits. For example, if you enter the URL http://localhost/myImage.asp?hits=2333 in the address bar of your Web browser, then the number 2,333 will be displayed as an image (see Figure 16.2).

FIGURE 16.2

A custom image created with the ShotGraph component.

The image is created by calling the CreateImage method of an instance of the ShotGraph component. The CreateImage method accepts three parameters: the image width, the image height, and the number of colors in the palette of the image. In the preceding example, an image with a two-color palette is created.

The SetColor method is used to set the two colors in the palette. The first parameter of this method specifies the index of the color's palette entry, and the remaining three parameters contain the red, green, and blue (RGB value) of the color.

The CreateFont method is used to specify the font of the text displayed. In the preceding example, the text is displayed with a Comic Sans MS typeface. You can use any font that is currently installed on your computer. The text is actually added to the image by calling the TextOut method.

Finally, the image is outputted by calling the `BinaryWrite()` method of the `Response` object. To display this dynamically created image in an Active Server Page, you can use the normal HTML `<IMG>` tag with the number of hits passed as a query string variable. The following script (included as fancyHitCounter.asp on the CD) correctly displays the image generated by myImage.asp:

```
<%
Application.Lock
Application( "home_hits" ) = Application( "home_hits" ) + 1
Application.UnLock
 %>
<html>
<head><title>Home Page</title></head>
<body>
Welcome, this page has been requested
<p>
<img src="myimage.asp?hits=<%=Application( "home_hits" )%>">
<p>
times!
</body>
</html>
```

Creating Graphs with the ShotGraph Component

One of the most useful applications of the ShotGraph component is for creating graphs. The component can be used to dynamically create graphs from data stored in a database table. In this section, you will learn how to do this.

When you installed SQL Server, by default, a database named Pubs was also installed. This database includes several sample tables that relate to a fictitious publishing company. We will use the table named `Titles` from the Pubs table in our sample application. This table contains a list of book titles and their types (business books, popular computing books, and so on).

The script in Listing 16.1 displays a bar chart that displays the number of books that fall under each category from the `Titles` table (see Figure 16.3). The script performs the following actions:

1. The list of categories and the count of titles under each category is retrieved with the SQL statement `select type, count(*) theCount from titles group by type`.

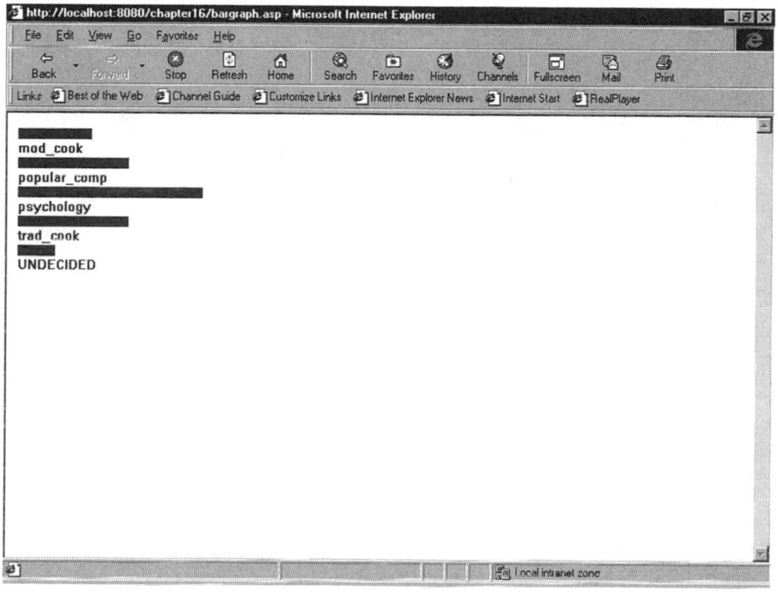

FIGURE 16.3

Bar chart generated with the ShotGraph component.

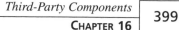

2. The results from the database query are moved to an array with the GetRows() method of the RecordSet object. This is done so that the maximum dimensions of the graph can be determined before drawing it.

3. A count of the number of bars to draw is determined by retrieving the upper bound of the array with the VBScript UBOUND() function.

4. The maximum number of titles under any category is retrieved by stepping through the array. This value is used to calculate the maximum length of any bar in the bar graph so that all the bars can be scaled to fit within the image.

5. An instance of the ShotGraph component is created and an initial blank image is created by calling the CreateImage() method with the image dimensions.

6. The bars are drawn on the image by passing the values of the elements of the array to the Rectangle() method.

7. The JPEG image is outputted to the browser by calling the BinaryWrite() method of the Response object.

LISTING 16.1   DRAWING A BAR GRAPH FROM TABLE DATA (BARGRAPH.ASP)

```
<%
Response.ContentType="image/jpeg"
MySQL = "select type, count(*) theCount from titles group by type"
Set Con = Server.CreateObject( "ADODB.Connection" )
Con.Open "DSN=myDSN;uid=sa;pwd=Secret"
SET RS = Con.Execute( MySQL )
myArray = RS.GetRows

' Get Count of Rows
count = UBOUND( myArray, 2 )

' Get Maximum Value
for i = 1 to count
  if myArray( 1, i ) > maxValue then
     maxValue = myArray( 1, i )
  end if
next

' Create ShotGraph Instance
Set g=CreateObject("shotgraph.image")
g.CreateImage 200, 30 * count, 2
g.SetColor 0, 255, 255, 255
g.SetColor 1, 0, 0, 255
g.SetBgColor 0
g.FillRect 0, 0, 200, 30 * count

' Draw The Bars
g.SetBGColor 1
g.CreatePen "PS_SOLID", 1, 1
ypos = 1
for i = 1 to count
   xpos = cINT( myArray( 1, i ) * ( 190 / maxValue ) )
   g.Rectangle 1, ypos, xpos, ypos + 10
   g.TextOut 1, ypos + 12, myArray( 0, i )
   ypos = ypos + 30
next
Response.BinaryWrite g.JpegImage( 90,0,"" )
%>
```

File Upload Components

In Chapter 3, "Working with HTML Forms," you learned how to use the HTML file upload
button. For example, the following HTML form includes a button that enables users to
select a picture from their local hard drive and upload the picture to your Web site:

```
<HTML>
<HEAD><TITLE> File Upload </TITLE></HEAD>
```

```
<BODY>

<FORM ENCTYPE="multipart/form-data"
ACTION="upload.asp" METHOD=POST>

Please choose a picture to upload:
<BR><INPUT NAME="picture" TYPE=FILE ACCEPT="image/*">
<BR><INPUT TYPE=SUBMIT VALUE="Submit Me!">
</FORM>

</BODY>
</HTML>
```

You can use the methods discussed in Chapter 3 to retrieve and interpret the uploaded information. However, this can be very cumbersome, especially if you must accept multiple file uploads on the same form, or if you want to use multiple form elements. A much better solution is to use a third-party file upload component.

 Several third-party components that you can buy enable you to accept file uploads. You should visit the companion Web site to this book at www.asp-site.com to see a list of some of the most popular ones. One of the easiest components to use is the SA-FileUp component. An evaluation version of this component is included with the CD that accompanies this book.

> **NOTE**
>
> The evaluation version of the Software Artisans SA-FileUp component that accompanies this book limits you to accepting no more than 50 file uploads. To purchase the full version of the SA-FileUp component, visit the Software Artisans Web site at http://www.softartisans.com.

You can use the SA-FileUp component to save an uploaded file to the Web server's hard drive, save the file to a database, or to simply assign the contents of a file to a variable. For example, you can use the following Active Server Page to save to disk a GIF image that was uploaded with the form described above.

```
<%
Set upl = Server.CreateObject("SoftArtisans.FileUp")
%>
<HTML>
<HEAD><TITLE> File Upload </TITLE></HEAD>
<BODY>

<% IF upl.isEmpty THEN %>
```

```
You did not enter a file to upload!
<% ELSE IF upl.ContentDisposition <> "form-data" THEN %>
Your browser does not support file uploads!
<%
ELSE
     upl.Form( "picture" ).SaveAs "c:\temp\theImage.gif"
%>
The image was saved as the file C:\temp\theImage.gif
<%
END IF
END IF
%>


</BODY>
</HTML>
```

This example saves whatever file is uploaded by the user as c:\temp\theImage.gif. Before you can use this example, you must make sure that the Web user has adequate permissions to save a file to this directory. If you are using anonymous access, then you will need to grant the IUSER_MACHINENAME user permission to write to this directory. To change this user's permissions for a directory, right-click the name of the directory and choose Properties, Security, Permissions.

When using the SA-FileUp component, it is important to realize that you can no longer use the Request object in the same page. You must use the Upload component as a replacement for the Request object, even when working with form fields other than the file upload button. For example, if the form described in the previous section were modified to include a form field for the name of the image, you would use the following statement to retrieve the value of this field:

```
imageName = upl.Form( "imageName" )
```

An Example of an Application of File Uploads

Suppose you want to create a Web site that is devoted to pets. You want this site to include a page that enables users to upload photos of their favorite cat, dog, or parakeet. After a user uploads a photo, you want the picture to be automatically displayed for all the world to see.

 To create this page, you can use the SA-FileUp component in conjunction with the File Access component. The Active Server Page in Listing 16.2 enables users to upload photos (in GIF or JPEG format) to a Web site directory named Photos and automatically displays all the pictures in this directory:

> **NOTE**
>
> To learn more about the File Access Component, see Chapter 8, "Working with the File System."

LISTING 16.2   UPLOADING AND DISPLAYING IMAGES (FILEUPLOAD.ASP)

```asp
<%
CONST photoDir = "/photos"
Set upl = Server.CreateObject("SoftArtisans.FileUp")
IF upl.userFileName <> "" AND upl.ContentDisposition = "form-data" THEN
    filename = Server.MapPath( photoDir )  & "\" &
    ➥getFileName( upl.userFileName )
    upl.Form( "photo" ).SaveAs filename
END IF

FUNCTION getFileName( byVal thePath )
    getFileName = RIGHT( thePath,
    ➥LEN( thePath ) - instrREV( thePath, "\" ) )
END FUNCTION

SUB showPhotos
    Set MyFileObject=Server.CreateObject("Scripting.FileSystemObject")
    Set MyFiles=MyFileObject.GetFolder( Server.MapPath( photoDir ) )
    For each thing in MyFiles.Files
    %>
    <IMG SRC="<%=photoDir & "/" & thing.Name %>"><p>
    <%
    Next
END SUB

%>
<HTML>
<HEAD><TITLE> Photos </TITLE></HEAD>
<BODY>

<% showPhotos %>

<FORM ENCTYPE="multipart/form-data"
ACTION="<%=Request.ServerVariables( "SCRIPT_NAME" )%>"
METHOD=POST>
<HR>
Upload a photo:
<INPUT NAME="photo" TYPE=FILE ACCEPT="image/*">
<INPUT TYPE=SUBMIT VALUE="Upload Photo">
</FORM>

</BODY>
</HTML>
```

To use this example, you must change the value of the constant `photoDir` to the name of a directory that can be accessed by your Web server. You also will need to change the permissions of this directory so that the anonymous `IUSR_MACHINENAME` user has permission to write to this directory.

Networking Components

Your server communicates with the rest of the Internet world through sockets. The socket specification was first developed for the Berkeley Software Distribution (BSD) from the University of California at Berkeley for UNIX. WinSock (short for Windows Sockets) is the socket standard used on Windows computers.

WinSock provides an Application Programming Interface (API) for interfacing with the TCP/IP protocol (although it can also be used with other protocols such as IPX/SPX). Because almost all communication across the Internet happens through the TCP/IP protocol, the WinSock API gives you access to the underlying plumbing of the Web. Powerful stuff!

To gain access to the WinSock API through Active Server Pages, you must use a third-party Active Server Page component. Several good WinSock components are available. Two good choices are the w3 Sockets component (currently free at `http://www.dimac.net`) or ServerObjects' ASPSock (available at `www.serverobjects.com`). In this chapter, we will be using the w3 Sockets component in the examples.

What exactly can you do with a WinSock component? In the following pages, you will be presented with two examples. First, you will learn how to use a WinSock component with the HTTP protocol to retrieve and post Web pages. Next, you will learn how to use a WinSock component with the NNTP protocol to access newsgroup articles.

Using WinSock to Communicate with Other Web Sites

Before you can use a WinSock component to retrieve Web pages from other Web sites, you must understand the basics of the HTTP protocol. When a browser sends a request for a Web page, the request looks something like this:

```
GET /example.htm  HTTP/1.1
HOST: www.aspsite.com
ACCEPT: image/gif, image/x-xbitmap, image/jpeg, image/pjpeg, */*
```

The preceding request retrieves the page named example.asp from the Web site at www.aspsite.com. When the server at www.aspsite.com receives this request, it attempts to find the page and then it sends it back across the Internet to the agent that requested it (typically, your browser).

 To request a page with a WinSock component, you simply send an HTTP request like the preceding one through the component. For example, the following Active Server Page script (included on the CD as SocketRequest.asp) retrieves the home page from Yahoo at www.yahoo.com and displays the HTML source (see Figure 16.4):

```
<%
SET mySock = Server.CreateObject("Socket.TCP")
mySock.Host = "www.yahoo.com:80"
theRequest = "GET / HTTP/1.1" & vbCRLF
theRequest = theRequest & "Accept: image/gif, image/x-xbitmap,
➥image/jpeg, image/pjpeg, */*" & vbCRLF
theRequest = theRequest & vbCRLF
mySock.Open()
mySock.SendLine theRequest
mySock.WaitForDisconnect()
Response.Write "<pre>" & Server.HTMLEncode( mySock.Buffer ) & "</pre>"
mySock.Close()
%>
```

FIGURE 16.4

*Page source
from a WinSock
component.*

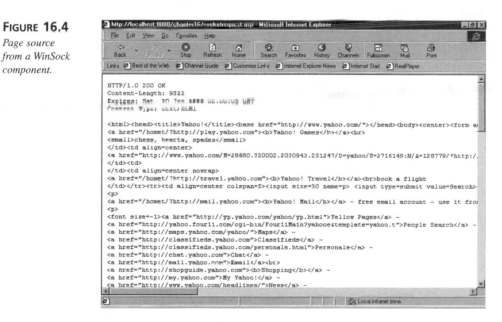

This example uses the w3 Sockets component to interface with the WinSock API. The first line in the script creates an instance of the component. Next, the HOST property is set to www.yahoo.com:80 in order to communicate with the Yahoo server on port 80 (the standard HTTP port). After the socket has connected to the proper port, a request string is built. Finally, the request string is written to the socket with the SendLine() method, and the result of the request is printed to the browser window by displaying the content of the socket's buffer property.

> **NOTE**
>
> See Chapter 24, "Maintaining ASP Web Sites," for a programming example that demonstrates how you can use the WinSock component to automatically check on the status of your Web site.

Posting to a form at another Web site is a similar process to retrieving a Web page. When you post form data, however, you use the HTTP POST method rather than the HTTP GET method. You must also include a CONTENT-TYPE header that indicates the format of the data being posted and a CONTENT-LENGTH header that indicates the size of the data being posted. An HTTP POST looks like this:

```
POST /result.asp HTTP/1.1
Content-type: application/x-www-form-urlencoded
Accept: text/plain
Content-length: 33

username=Andrew+Jones&password=secret
```

Notice that the data being posted is separated from the HTTP headers by two carriage returns and linefeeds. Also, the data is URL encoded. In this example, two form fields are posted. The first form field, which has the name "username", has the value "Andrew Jones" and the second form field, which has the name "password" and has the value "secret". Your browser might use a request like this one when posting the following HTML form:

```
<html>
<head><title>Simple Form</title></head>
<body>
<form method="post" action="result.asp">
<br><input name="username" type="text">
<br><input name="password"
<br><input type="submit" value="Submit">
</form>
</html>
```

You can simulate the posting of the preceding form with the w3 socket component. To post the form information, URL encode the form data and write it to the component. The following script posts the data to a page named result.asp at www.aspsite.com (included on the CD as postRequest.asp):

```
<%
postData = "username=" & Server.HTMLEncode( "Andrew Jones" )
postDate = postDate & "&password=" & Server.HTMLEncode( "secret" )
SET mySock = Server.CreateObject("Socket.TCP")
mySock.Host = "www.aspsite.com:80"
theRequest = "POST  /result.asp HTTP/1.1" & vbCRLF
theRequest = theRequest & "Accept: text/plain" & vbCRLF
theRequest = theRequest & "Content-length: " & len( postData )
theRequest = theRequest & vbCRLF & vbCRLF
theRequest = theRequest & postData
mySock.Open()
mySock.SendLine theRequest
mySock.WaitForDisconnect()
Response.Write mySock.Buffer
mySock.Close ()
%>
```

Using WinSock to Communicate with Network Newsgroups

A WinSock component can also be used to communicate with an NNTP server. NNTP, the Network News Transport Protocol, is the standard protocol used to post and retrieve articles from Internet newsgroups such as microsoft.public.inetserver.iis and alt.collecting.beanie-babies. You can also set up your own NNTP server with the Microsoft NNTP Server included with the Windows NT Option Pack.

The NNTP protocol, like the HTTP protocol, consists of a simple set of human-readable, English commands. For example, to select a particular newsgroup, such as alt.collecting.beanie-babies, you send the command GROUP alt.collecting.beanie-babies to the NNTP server. When the server receives this command, it responds with information about the number of articles in the newsgroup and the first and last article number of the articles in the newsgroup.

The script in Listing 16.3 connects to an NNTP server and requests and displays all the current articles from the alt.news.microsoft newsgroup (see Figure 16.5). The script works by first connecting to an NNTP server located at nntp.domain.com on port 119 (port 119 is the standard port for NNTP). After being connected, the script selects the alt.news.microsoft newsgroup by using the NNTP GROUP command. Next, all the articles in this newsgroup are displayed by using the NNTP ARTICLE and NNTP NEXT commands. The ARTICLE command retrieves the currently selected newsgroup article, and the NEXT command moves to the next available article in the newsgroup.

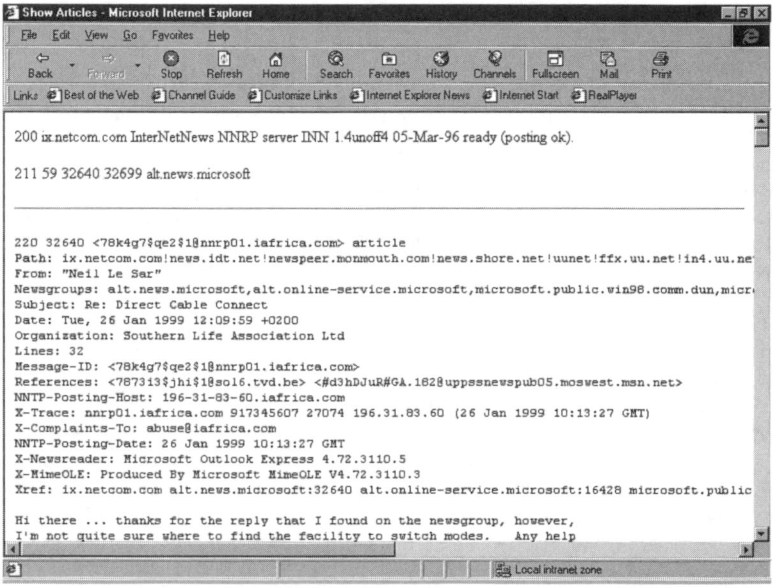

FIGURE 16.5
FIGURE 16.5

List of newsgroups retrieved with the WinSock component.

NOTE

To learn more about the commands in the NNTP protocol, do a search for NNTP protocol at Yahoo (www.yahoo.com). The protocol is defined in RFC 977.

LISTING 16.3 REQUESTING NEWS ARTICLES (REQUESTNEWS.ASP)

```
<html>
<head><title>Show Articles</title></head>
<body>
<%
' Connect To News Server
SET mySock = Server.CreateObject( "Socket.TCP" )
mySock.Host = "nntp.domain.com:119"
mySock.Open
response.write mySock.getLine & "<p>"

' Get Articles From alt.test
mySock.SendLine "GROUP alt.news.microsoft"
result = mySock.getLine
response.write result & "<p>"


' Get Number Of Articles And First And Last
breakit = SPLIT( result )
```

```
numArticles = breakit( 1 )
firstArticle = breakit( 2 )
lastArticle = breakit( 3 )

' Display List Of Articles
while LEFT( result, 3 ) <> "421"
  mySock.SendLine "ARTICLE"
  mySock.WaitFor( vbCRLF & "." & vbCRLF )
  response.write "<hr><pre>" & mySock.buffer & "</pre>"
  mySock.SendLine "NEXT"
  result = mySock.getLine
wend


' Disconnect
mySock.SendLine "QUIT"

mySock.Close()
%>
</body>
</html>
```

Other Components

There are hundreds of third-party components produced both by companies and by single individuals that you can use to extend your Active Server Pages. Better yet, many of these components are free. In this final part of the chapter, several of the more interesting of these components will be described. First, however, here is a list of three of the best resources for finding components on the Web:

- ASPSite (www.aspsite.com)

  The ASPSite is the companion Web site to this book. As I write this, the Component section of the ASPSite contains a list of over 150 components. The components are divided into categories and can be searched.

- ActiveServerPages.com (www.activeserverpages.com)

  This Web site contains an extensive list of Active Server Page components. It's also one of the best general resources on Active Server Pages on the Internet.

- 15seconds (www.15seconds.com)

  15seconds has a section devoted to ASP components. However, it is a much better resource for articles on programming Active Server Pages.

- ServerObjects (`www.serverobjects.com`)

  ServerObjects is the company behind many of the most used Active Server Page components. ServerObjects has components for networking and creating images, as well as many other unique components (some of which will be described next).

File Access Components

In Chapter 8, "Working with the File System," you were introduced to the File Access component. The File Access component enables you to perform basic file manipulation tasks such as reading and writing text files, and copying and moving folders. For the majority of file-related tasks, the File Access component works quite well.

 However, you might have advanced needs that cannot be satisfied by the File Access component. The CD that accompanies this book includes a fully functional version of the Software Artisans SA-FileManager component. This component is fully compatible with the File Access component, plus it has several advanced methods and properties of its own. For example, unlike the File Access component, you can use the SA-FileManager component to encrypt and decrypt files on your hard drive. This feature could be useful for protecting passwords or other sensitive information on your server. The component also has several useful methods for working with binary files. To see the complete documentation for this component, visit the Software Artisans Web site at `http://www.softartisans.com`.

Email Components

In Chapter 10, "Working with Email," you learned how to use the CDO for NTS to send and receive email using the SMTP protocol. However, in its current form, the CDO has some serious limitations. First, the CDO does not support the POP protocol. This means that you cannot use the CDO to retrieve email from multiple mail boxes on a POP server. Second, and more importantly, it does not work well under a heavy load from multiple simultaneous users (if more than one user sends an email message at the same time, one of the email messages might get overwritten and never sent).

To address these limitations, you can buy a third-party email component. For example, the ServerObjects AspPOP3 component enables you to communicate with a POP3 server. Using this component, you can pass the name of your POP3 server, your username, and your password and retrieve all your email messages. To learn more about this component visit `http://www.serverobjects.com`.

If you need to send a lot of email from your Web site, you should investigate either the ServerObjects AspQMail component (www.serverobjects.com) or Flicks Software's ocxQMail (www.flicks.com). Both of these components enable you to spool email so that more email messages can be sent at a time. ocxQMail also has an interesting feature that enables you to automatically send email at scheduled dates. You can use this feature, for example, to send follow-up mail automatically after a user first registers at your Web site.

Banner Advertisement Components

In Chapter 9, "Tracking Page Views and Displaying Advertisements," you learned how to use the Ad Rotator component to display banner advertisements. The Ad Rotator component is limited to displaying images only. Banner advertisements that contain JavaScript are becoming increasingly popular, so this image-only limitation can be serious.

Instead of using the Ad Rotator component, you can use a third-party banner advertisement component such as oceantek's AdShark (http://oceantek.com/adshark/features.html). AdShark can be used to display advertisements that contain images, HTML, JavaScript, and even Java. The component also has extensive logging features for tracking how many times a banner advertisement has been displayed or clicked. Finally, you can use AdShark to limit the display of advertisements by number of impressions, transfers, or date.

Form Validation Components

If you require users to register at your Web site by providing address and credit card information, you should evaluate the Software Artisans SA-Check component. The SA-Check component can be used to prevent users from submitting random information when submitting an HTML form. The component validates address information, including cities, states, countries, zip codes, phone numbers, and email addresses. You can also use the component to check whether a valid credit card number has been entered without performing an actual credit card authorization (the component uses the MOD 10 algorithm to determine whether the credit card number entered is a valid one). Finally, you can use this component to screen out profanity that users may enter into forms at your Web site.

Microsoft Word and Microsoft Excel Components

Sometimes an HTML page is not the most appropriate method to present information to a user. Instead of using an Active Server Page to generate a standard Web page, you can use a third-party component in your Active Server Page script to create either Microsoft Word documents or Excel spreadsheets.

For example, Chili!Soft's Chili!Reports (`www.chilisoft.com`) enables you to dynamically generate a Microsoft Excel spreadsheet from within an Active Server Page and send it over the Web. With Chili!Reports, you can have access to all of Microsoft Excel's functions, formulas, pivot tables, and graphs when creating the spreadsheet.

Sterling Strategic Solutions Productivity ASP component not only generates Microsoft Excel spreadsheets, it also can be used to dynamically create Microsoft Word documents. To see a demonstration of this component, visit `http://www.sterlingweb.com`.

Summary

This chapter has provided you with an overview of what you can do with third-party Active Server Page components. In the first part, you learned how to use the ShotGraph component to dynamically generate JPEG images from within your Active Server Pages. In the second part, you learned how to use Software Artisan's SA-FileUp component to easily accept file uploads to your Web site through a standard HTML form. In the third part, you learned how to use a WinSock component to communicate with both HTTP and NNTP servers. Finally, you were provided with a brief description of some of the more interesting components available for download or purchase off the Internet.

CHAPTER 17

Creating Windows Script Components

by Craig Eddy

IN THIS CHAPTER

Throughout this book, you've learned about using components within your ASP files. These components range from the built-in ASP objects such as Request and Response, to the various third-party components discussed in Chapter 16, "Third-Party Components." Now it's time to learn about building your own components.

Although it's probably possible to find a third-party component to meet just about any need, the use of components can have drawbacks. First and foremost, you have no control over the future direction of the component. Although it may meet your needs today, a component may be changed at any time by its producer into something that is less useful to you. Likewise, you're dependent upon this third-party developer for support, bug fixes, and the like.

The second drawback to using a third-party component is that you probably will not have access to the component's source code. This means that the component will truly be a "black box," whose workings remain inaccessible to you. It also means you won't be able to change any of the component's behavior to make it more closely match your needs.

After you've weighed these drawbacks, you might decide that you have the time, energy, and desire to "roll your own" component. This chapter and the two that follow describe how to use three of the most common methods for creating components that are accessible from ASP code: Windows Script Components, the subject of this chapter, Visual Basic, and Visual C++. Visual Basic and Visual C++ component creation is discussed in Chapters 18 and 19.

In this chapter you'll first learn what a Script Component is and when you would want to use one. Because Script Components aren't currently installed with Internet Information Server or Active Server Pages, you'll need to download and install them. This is covered in "Installing the Script Component Engine," later in this chapter. After you've installed the engine, you're introduced to eXtensible Markup Language (XML), which is the language used to describe a Script Component to the outside world.

After the basics are under your belt, the rest of the chapter describes how to add properties, methods, and script code to your component. You'll even dabble in debugging the component and handling errors which might occur.

What Is a Windows Script Component?

Script Components were originally called scriptlets by Microsoft. The name *scriptlet* implies that we're dealing with a very small script, similar to the analogy of the Java app and Java applet. According to that definition, the name is a misnomer. In fact, a Windows

Script Component can be any size at all. So, just what is a Script Component then? Quite simply, a Windows Script Component is a reusable COM component that you create using any ActiveX scripting language.

From the outside world, a Script Component looks just like any other COM/ActiveX component. In your ASP files, you won't be able to tell the difference between a Script Component and the Ad Rotator installable component. This is the nature of the COM interface: Every COM component appears as a "black box" to the code that utilizes the component's services. The code utilizing the component is known as the *client*, and the component, while being used by the client, is known as a *server*. Your code will use a Windows Script Component just as it would the Ad Rotator component.

This black box nature of COM components is where the similarities between Windows Script Components and other, more traditional, COM components (typically created in Visual C++ or Visual Basic) end, however. The following are the differences between Script Components and compiled components:

- Script Components are typically small and efficient. Although not as efficient as a compiled component because of their interpretive nature, the typical use of a Script Component involves very few lines of code encapsulated into a COM interface.

- Script Components are not compiled in any way, shape, or form. They are created using a simple text editor, some rudimentary XML tags, and script code. Therefore, you can test and modify your component in a very short cycle.

- Script Components require very few runtime support files. These include the Script Component runtime engine (SCROBJ.DLL, more on this later) and the runtime engine for the ActiveX scripting language used within your script. If your Script Component uses VBScript or JScript on your IIS machine, these are already installed. And chances are, if you're using another language, such as Python or PERLScript, you've already installed these as well.

Microsoft first introduced the concept of a scriptlet (now called a Windows Script Component) with Internet Explorer 4.0. This version of the Web browser was capable of displaying not only standard ActiveX controls but also a new type of control called a DHTML scriptlet. These scriptlets utilized Dynamic HTML (DHTML) to provide scripting of the browser's object model and user interface encapsulation (enabling you to create a display object that could be reused in multiple Web pages).

After DHTML scriptlets caught on among Web developers, Microsoft realized that this technology would have a great many applications on the server side as well. Using a server-side Windows Script Component enables an ASP developer to encapsulate often-used script code into a familiar-looking COM package. This encapsulation allows you to easily reuse and maintain your ASP script code.

After a brief introduction to how COM makes server-side Windows Script Components possible, the rest of this chapter discusses how to create and use these components.

Installing the Script Component Engine

Installing support for Windows Script Components and the Script Component Wizard is probably one of the easiest tasks you can undertake with IIS and ASP. After you download the installation files from the Microsoft Web site, simply run the executable. You're now ready to create and use Script Components. (You'll probably want to read the rest of this chapter first, though.) This section describes the installation process.

Downloading and Installing the Engine

The file you need to install the Script Component engine, along with a very helpful reference in the form of an HTML Help file, can be downloaded from Microsoft's Web site. Point your browser to `http://msdn.microsoft.com/scripting` and click on the link labeled Windows Script Components. When you see the link for the Downloads page, click it and then download the appropriate files (the Script Component Wizard is a separate download from the rest of the engine).

After you've downloaded the file to your machine, double-click it to start the installation process. Click your way through the various dialog boxes, and you'll eventually receive a dialog informing you that the installation is complete. Believe it or not, that's all there is to it. Unfortunately, you've got a little more work to do in order to make Script Components work!

What You'll Find when You're Finished

The Windows Script Component and the Script Component Wizard installations consist of the following components:

- The runtime engine, SCROBJ.DLL—This is the interface between your ASP file and the component's script file. This module is responsible for communicating the Script Component's COM interface to the client. This is done by interpreting the component's public interface (as defined in the component's file) and translating it to the automation interface which the client is expecting to see.

- The Script Component Wizard—This simple but powerful wizard assists you in creating the shell of your Script Component. I highly recommend you create all of your Script Components using the wizard. You'll learn more about what the wizard

can do and how to use it in the section "Simplifying Life with the Script Component Wizard." A shortcut to this wizard is placed on your Start menu under Programs, Microsoft Windows Script. Figure 17.1 shows the initial dialog of the wizard.

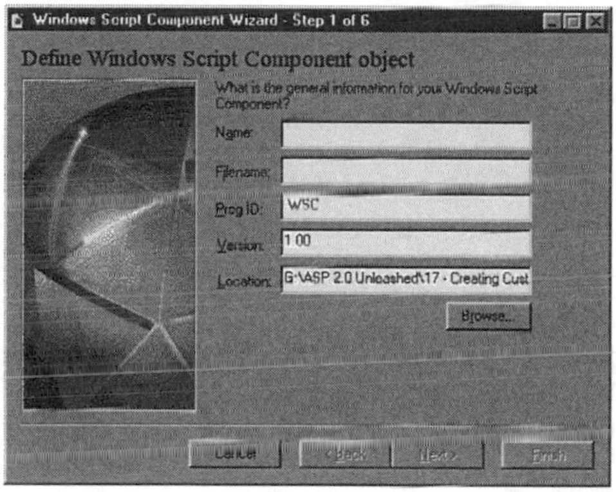

FIGURE 17.1

The initial dialog of the Windows Script Component Wizard.

- A plethora of useful shortcuts when you right-click a .WSC file in Windows Explorer (.WSC is the extension typically used for Windows Script Component files)—Figure 17.2 shows the menu items available. The Open and Edit menu items perform the same task: They open the file in Notepad. The Generate Type Library shortcut will create a type library (.TLB) file for the Script Component. This is used to help development environments such as Visual InterDev and Visual Basic discern what's available within the Script Component. The Register item will register the component with the system, making it available as a COM component, and Unregister will remove this registration information from the system.

FIGURE 17.2

The Windows Explorer shortcut menu for a Windows Script Component file.

Introducing XML

Windows Script Components are not ASP files. They're not HTML files, and they're not JavaScript or VBScript `include` files. Instead, they're files with embedded script code supporting a public interface that is documented using XML.

XML is an acronym for eXtensible Markup Language. An XML file looks similar to an HTML file, but there are many important differences, which we'll discuss in this section. XML files can be used to create a structured document based on a set of rules defined in a document type definition (DTD) file. Script Component files use XML to delineate the various sections of the file, enabling the SCROBJ.DLL module to find the data it needs to register the Script Component and work with its interface.

> **NOTE**
>
> For more information on XML, see Chapter 6, "Interacting with the Client: ASP and Internet Explorer."

How XML and HTML Compare

Although XML and HTML files look similar, there are many important differences which you should be aware of. These differences apply whether you're creating a Script Component file or an XML-structured document that represents a hierarchical database structure.

The biggest difference is that, although HTML allows only a fixed set of markup tags, XML is designed to allow XML authors the flexibility to define their own set of markup tags. The DTD file describes the syntax of the tags that are used in the document. You won't be creating a DTD file for your Script Components because the SCROBJ.DLL file requires a particular structure that the component's file must obey.

There are three other very important differences between XML and HTML that you need to be aware of:

- XML tags are case-sensitive. This includes element types (such as `<method>`) and attribute names (such as `name`). This means that a tag written as `<method name="Initialize"></method>` is very different from the one written as `<METHOD name="Initialize"></method>` (which is an incorrect tag, by the way).

- Attribute values require quotation marks, either single or double. For example, `<script language=JScript>` would be invalid. The correct tag is `<script language="JScript">` or `<script language='Jscript'>`.

- Tags must always be in open and close pairs, as in `<script>` and `</script>`. In HTML there's a simple `<BR>` element that can stand by itself. In XML this is not allowed. You must always have a closing element. For tags that do not have child tags, you can close the tag using `/>`, as in `<method name="Initialize"/>`.

- Reserved characters contained within elements must be inside a section that is designated as being a data section (in XML speak, this is known as being "opaque"). This prevents the XML parser from confusing these reserved characters with valid XML markup. You should create an opaque section around all your script code because it will typically use reserved characters such as `<`, `>`, and `&` This is done by wrapping the script code in a `<![CDATA[` section (which is closed using `]]>`).

Specifying XML Conformance in a Script Component

Because the sole purpose of the XML tags in a Windows Script Component file is to provide the SCROBJ.DLL with the information needed to register and manipulate the component, you are allowed to be lax on the restrictions specified in the previous section. However, if you ever want to edit your component file using an XML editor, you must strictly adhere to the XML rules.

To specify that the component file conforms to the rules of XML, include the `<?XML ?>` element as the very first element in your file. The element has a `version` attribute that specifies which version of XML your component conforms to. The syntax for this element is

```
<?XML version="1.0" ?>
```

If you don't want to have the Script Component file interpreted by the strict rules of XML, simply leave this element out of your file. Leaving this element out enables you to have the variations in tags as HTML allows.

CAUTION

If you leave out the `<?XML ?>` element you must not wrap your script code with a `<![CDATA[` as described in the previous section. Doing so will confuse the parser and cause errors to be reported whenever you register, unregister, or utilize the component.

The Anatomy of a Windows Script Component

Now that you've learned a little about XML and a few of its rules, let's look at the XML portions of a Script Component file. As I said in the previous section, Script Component files are organized as XML documents. This means that they should contain a certain set of elements that describe the component and what functionality it provides. This section describes those elements; further information on each of these elements can be found in the Script Component documentation on the MSDN Web site (`http://msdn.microsoft.com/scripting/default.htm?/scripting/scriptlets/doc/lettitle.htm`).

The `<package>` and `<component>` Elements

If you're familiar with COM programming, you're probably aware that an individual COM component can contain multiple COM classes. The same is true of Script Components. You can have multiple, distinct objects within a single Script Component file. This is accomplished using the `<package>` and `<component>` elements.

The `<package>` element is used to enclose multiple `<component>` elements. Each `<component>` element represents a single Script Component object. If your file contains only a single Script Component object, the `<package>` element is optional.

An example of using these elements together is

```
<package>
<component id="Scriptlet1">
    (component body goes here)
</component>

<component id="Scriptlet2">
    (component body goes here)
</component>
</package> element> element> element> element>
```

Registration Information

The COM automation subsystem of the Windows-based operating systems relies on information stored in the Windows registry to help it locate and evaluate the runtime module of a given COM component. Script Components are not an exception to this rule.

Part of the Script Component's XML structure is a `<registration>` element. This element contains all the information necessary for SCROBJ.DLL to enter the registry information needed to access the Script Component from a COM client. This information is contained in the `progid`, `classid`, `description`, and `version` attributes described next.

An example of the syntax is

```
<registration progid="unleashed.wsc"
     classid="{abb298d0-b213-11d2-8580-00a024166737}"
     version="1.00"
     description="Sample Script Component">
</registration>
```

The `progid` and `classid` Attributes

Both the `progid` and `classid` attributes are used by a COM client to specify which COM server should be instantiated. The COM client will use one or the other of these attributes when it creates the server. Note that you must have at least one of these attributes present in the component's `<registration>` element.

The `progid`, as you can see from the sample syntax, is a string usually composed of two or more words separated by a period. The string typically describes the purpose of the component. You're probably already familiar with PROGIDs because they're used by the ASP Server object's `CreateObject` method. For the preceding example, you'd use the syntax

```
set scptlt = Server.CreateObject("unleashed.wsc")
```

The `progid` attribute is optional, but if you leave it out you must specify a `classid` attribute. Clients will be forced to use the `classid` to identify the Script Component.

The `classid` element specifies a CLSID for the Script Component. A CLSID is a globally unique identifier (GUID) for a COM object. Because they are guaranteed to be unique each time one is generated, GUIDs can be used to uniquely identify a component when it is installed onto multiple machines. Because a `progid` value is in human readable form, it is possible for the name to be duplicated by other components, thus making it impossible for the COM system to know exactly which component to run when the `progid` is specified in a `CreateObject` method call.

Microsoft has a rather complicated format and function to generate CLSIDs that's beyond the scope of this discussion. Suffice it to say, there are tools in Visual Studio, available for free, that will generate CLSID values for you. Likewise, the Script Component Wizard will generate a new CLSID each time you create a Script Component. If you've used the `<OBJECT>` tag in either HTML or an ASP file, you've seen CLSIDs in action.

An example of using the Script Component described above in an ASP file's `<OBJECT>` is

```
<OBJECT id=cmpnt classid="clsid:abb298d0-b213-11d2-8580-00a024166737">
</OBJECT>
```

The `classid` attribute is optional, but you must specify either the `progid` or the `classid`. If you leave out the `classid` attribute, a CLSID will automatically be created each time the Script Component is registered. Although this may seem to be a time-saving mechanism, it's a sure road to problems because your Script Component will have a different CLSID each time it gets registered. This means that any code which uses the `<OBJECT>` tag to create an instance of your Script Component will have to be modified each time the component is registered. Because the Script Component Wizard is kind enough to generate the CLSID values for you, it's best to go ahead and use them!

> **NOTE**
>
> The values for `progid` and `classid` are not case-sensitive. Therefore the `progid` values `Unleashed.WSC` and `unleashed.wsc` both refer to the same Script Component file.

Version and Descriptive Information

In addition to the `progid` and `classid` attributes, you should also specify version and description information for your Script Components.

The `version` attribute is used by COM clients that require a version-dependent instance of the servers they instantiate. This string typically takes the form `n.nn` and should be incremented any time you change the public interface of the Script Component. COM will use the version number to attempt to locate information about the interface that existed for a particular version number. Thus, when a client wants to use a particular version of the interface, the client's code will specify the version number, and COM will attempt to locate the proper implementation of that interface and version. For example, you may use `set x = Server.CreateObject("ADODB.Connection.1.5")` to retrieve version 1.5 of the ADO `Connection` object.

The `description` is used for the type library. It's a string that will help identify the component to object browsers such as the one built in to Visual InterDev and Visual Basic. However, the released version of the type library generator seems to ignore this text altogether. Instead, it opts for a more generic Scriptlet Type Library description for every Script Component.

Executing Script During the Registration Process

Although the SCROBJ.DLL runtime engine is responsible for entering the necessary information describing your Script Component into the Windows registry, there might be occasions when you'll want your component to detect and react to this happening. You can do just that by adding a `<script>` element inside the `<registration>` element.

The runtime engine can call two functions within this scripting section: `Register` and `Unregister`. Here's an example of how this feature might be used:

```
<registration progid="unleashed.wsc"
     classid="{abb298d0-b213-11d2 8580-00a024166737}"
     version="1.00"
     description="Sample Script Component">
<script language="VBScript">
<![CDATA[
function Register()
    MsgBox "Unleashed Script Component registered!"
end function
function Unregister()
    MsgBox "Unleashed Script Component has been unregistered!"
end function
]]>
</script>
</registration>
```

The `<public>` Element

The `<public>` element contains a description of the public interface provided by the Script Component. This includes the properties, methods, and events exposed by the component. The element wraps the `<property>`, `<method>`, and `<event>` elements that specify the individual properties, methods, and events supported by the Script Component. You'll learn about these elements in depth in the upcoming sections, but here's a sample of the syntax:

```
<public>
    <method name="Initialize"/>
    <property name="LastName"/>
    <event name="ItemSaved"/>
</public>
```

The `<implements>` Section

The `<implements>` element enables a component to access additional COM interface handlers. For example, the built-in ASP objects `Request`, `Server`, `Session`, `Application`, and `Response` are made available to your Script Component through a separate interface handler.

The complete syntax for the `<implements>` element is

```
<implements type="COMHandlerName" [id="internalName"] [default=fAssumed]>
handler-specific information here
</implements>
```

The `type` attribute specifies the name of the interface handler to be implemented, `id` is used to create a separate namespace within the Script Component (in cases where the interface handler has a naming conflict with another handler being implemented), and the `default` attribute is used to specify whether the value of `id` is assumed when referencing objects provided by the interface handler. (The default is `true` and, in most cases, you won't specify this attribute.)

To utilize the built-in ASP objects, specify this `<implements>` element in your Script Component:

```
<implements type="ASP" id="ASP"/>
```

Then, within your script code, you can simply reference the built-in objects as if you were coding in an Active Server Page file. That is, simply use code like the following:

```
Session("IsLoggedIn") = 0
```

or

```
sReturn = Server.HTMLEncode(Session("LastName")).
```

For more in-depth details on this element, see the Script Component Documentation on the Microsoft MSDN Web site.

Additional Elements Found in Script Component

Although the preceding elements are the ones that are absolutely necessary for every Script Component to contain, several additional elements might provide some benefit when you are creating your components.

The `<object>` Element

The `<object>` element behaves within a Script Component just as the `<OBJECT>` tag does in both HTML and ASP files: You use it to define and create an instance of an object that will be accessible to your script code. Using an `<object>` element makes the object available globally, and it enables scripting tools such as Visual InterDev to provide statement completion for the object's members.

The syntax of the <object> element is as follows:

```
<object id="objID" [classid="clsid:GUID" ¦ progid="progID"]/>
```

The *objID* value is used to provide a name that scripting code can use to identify the object. This name must be unique throughout the Script Component. The classid and progid elements (you need one or the other of these) specify the CLSID and ProgID for the COM object being created.

The <resource> Element

If you've done any programming in Visual C++ (and perhaps Visual Basic), you've probably used a resource file. This is a file in which you can store data that you'd rather not hard-code into your application, such as strings that should be localized if used in a different language.

The runtime engine provides a getResource function that your script code uses to retrieve the value of a resource. The syntax for this element is as follows:

```
<resource id="resourceID">
    text or numeric value
</resource>
```

An example of using a resource is provided in Listing 17.1.

LISTING 17.1   USING THE <resource> ELEMENT

```
<resource id="errNonDateValue">
    The value passed was not a valid date.
</resource>
<script language="VBScript">
<![CDATA[
Function GetDateInOneWeek(baseDate)
    If IsDate(baseDate) then
        GetDateInOneWeek = DateAdd("w", 1, baseDate)
    Else
        GetDateInOneWeek = getResource(errNonDateValue")
    End If
End Function
]]>
</script> element>> element>
```

The <reference> Element

This is one of the most useful of the other elements. Using the <reference> element, you can provide your Script Component's code with access to the constants provided by another COM component's type library. This is particularly useful if your Script Component accesses Microsoft's ADO object model, which is replete with constant definitions.

The syntax for this element is

```
<reference [object="progID" ¦ guid="typelibGUID"] [version="version"]/>
```

In this element, the `object` attribute specifies the ProgID of the object whose interface is represented by the type library to be referenced. The `guid` attribute specifies the GUID of the type library (each type library has its own unique identifier just like each COM object). You must specify only one of these two attributes. The `version` attribute is used to specify the version number of the type library.

For example, to use the constants associated with the ADO `Connection` object, you can include a reference to the object's type library:

```
<reference object="ADODB.Connection"/>
```

> **NOTE**
>
> The `<reference>` element should appear inside the `<component>` element. If there is more than one Script Component in the package, the type library applies to only the Script Component in whose `<component>` element it is declared.

The `<comment>` Element

The `<comment>` element is used to enclose text within other XML elements that you want ignored by the Script Component runtime engine. Documenting your Script Component is a good reason to use this element.

The syntax is

```
<comment>
    text or data here
</comment>
```

Simplifying Life with the Script Component Wizard

If you've been thoroughly confused by the preceding section, take heart. Using the Windows Script Component Wizard, you can automate the creation of most of the XML in your Script Component file. This will enable you to concentrate on the real work involved: coding the component's properties and methods. This section describes how to use the wizard.

To start the wizard, click on the Start button, select Programs, Microsoft Windows Script, and finally Windows Script Component Wizard. To use the wizard, follow these steps:

1. On the wizard's first dialog, shown in Figure 17.3, you'll enter some basic information about your Script Component. This information will be found in the `<registration>` element of the component file.

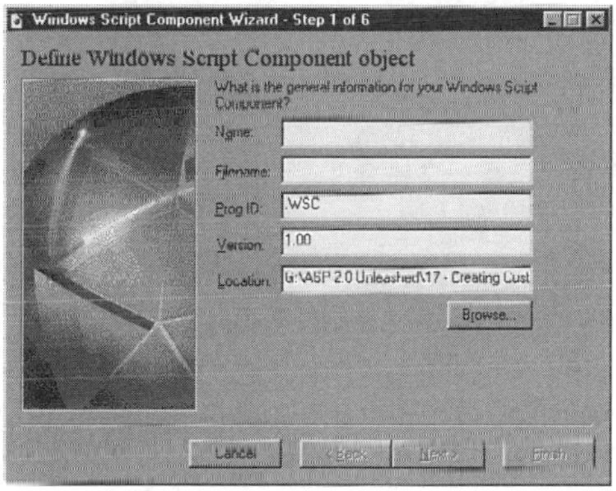

FIGURE 17.3

The initial dialog of the Windows Script Component Wizard.

The Name field will be mapped to the `description` attribute. As you type in this field, the wizard will automatically enter the same text into the Filename and Prog ID fields. You can, of course, override this default text in these fields.

If necessary, change the Version field and the Location, which is where the component's file will be stored. Click Next to continue.

2. On the second dialog, shown in Figure 17.4, specify the characteristics of your Script Component. Using the first set of radio buttons, specify the scripting language you'll use. You can choose VBScript, JScript, or Other, in which case you'll have to enter the language specifier. In your Script Component, you're not limited to using only the language you choose here. The wizard is going to put in some stub code for you utilizing the specified language.

To specify that you want access to the built-in ASP objects, check the box labeled Do You Want Special Implements Support? and select the Support Active Server Pages radio button.

If you want to enable error trapping and debugging support within your Script Component, check the appropriate boxes. You should enable these only while you're developing your component, however, because in production you'll want the component to run in "silent" mode. There are more details on these options in the section titled "Debugging and Error-Handling Techniques." Click Next to continue.

FIGURE 17.4

The Specify Characteristics dialog of the Windows Script Component Wizard.

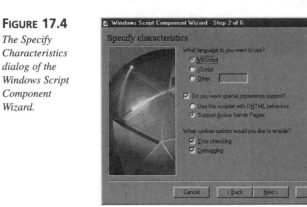

3. The third dialog, shown in Figure 17.5, is where you'll specify the properties that your Script Component provides. In the grid's first column enter the name for the property. The second column, labeled Type, is where you specify whether the property is Read/Write, Read-Only, or Write-Only. Finally, the third column is for specifying an optional default value for the property. This is the value that will be assigned to the property when the Script Component is first created. After you've entered the information about your component's properties, click Next to continue.

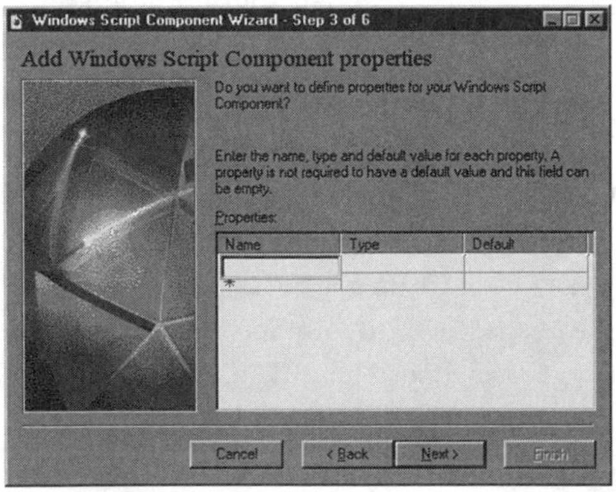

FIGURE 17.5

The Add Windows Script Component properties dialog of the Wizard.

4. On the dialog that appears, tell the wizard what methods your Script Component provides. Methods are intended to be actions that the client code takes on the data contained within the object. Enter the names of the methods in the first column. The second column is where you specify any parameters for each method. Separate parameter names with a comma and remember that there are no type definitions specified for scripting methods. (Everything is passed as a Variant data type,

meaning that the parameter can contain any sort of data.) You should not put the parentheses around the parameter list because the wizard will do this for you. Click Next to continue.

5. The fifth dialog is where you enter any events you want your Script Component to raise. Because Active Server Pages cannot respond to events raised by the objects they instantiate, you'll probably leave this screen blank. If you are designing a component to use with Visual Basic or a similar environment, you enter the names of the events fired by the component in the text box. Click Next to continue.

> **CAUTION**
>
> On the Events dialog, be sure to enter each event's name on a separate line in the text box. The wizard adds event names to the interface using the entire text entered on each line.

6. That's all there is to it! The final dialog displays a summary of the Script Component file that the wizard is about to create. Click the Finish button to have the file created.

The wizard will let you know that it has created the Script Component file. You can then double-click the file to open it in Notepad.

 Listing 17.2 shows a simple Script Component created with the wizard. This code can be found on the accompanying CD as the file unleashed.wsc in the \Source\Chapter17 folder. This Script Component has two properties, LastName and FirstName, and one method, Initialize. Notice that most of the grunt work has been completed already. All that's left is to enter the code to support the properties and methods exposed by the component. This is the subject of the rest of this chapter.

LISTING 17.2 A SKELETON COMPONENT CREATED BY THE WINDOWS SCRIPT COMPONENT WIZARD

```
<?XML version="1.0"?>
<component>

<registration
    description="Unleashed"
    progid="Unleashed.WSC"
    version="1.00"
    classid="{a5a670a0-f128-11d2-a60b-444553540000}"
>
```

continues

LISTING 17.2   CONTINUED

```
</registration>

<public>
    <property name="LastName">
        <get/>
        <put/>
    </property>
    <property name="FirstName">
        <get/>
        <put/>
    </property>
    <method name="Initialize">
        <PARAMETER name="InitFirstName"/>
        <PARAMETER name="InitLastName"/>
    </method>
</public>

<implements type="ASP" id="ASP"/>

<script language="VBScript">
<![CDATA[

dim LastName
dim FirstName

function get_LastName()
    get_LastName = LastName
end function

function put_LastName(newValue)
    LastName = newValue
end function

function get_FirstName()
    get_FirstName = FirstName
end function

function put_FirstName(newValue)
    FirstName = newValue
end function

function Initialize(InitFirstName, InitLastName)
    Initialize = "Temporary Value"
end function

]]>
</script>
</component>
```

Defining a Script Component's Properties

Now that you've seen how to use the Windows Script Component Wizard to do most of the interface work for you, let's take a step back and see why the wizard did what it did.

Property definitions are placed within the `<public>` element (see Listing 17.2 earlier). Using properties, there are two ways you can expose data contained within your component to the outside world. The first way is to simply expose a local (to the component) variable in the `<property>` element. The second way is to wrap the data with property get (for reading the property's value) and put (for assigning a value to the property) functions.

Using Variables as Properties

If you don't care to protect your object's variables from the outside world, you can create a property that's linked directly to an internal variable. Any time the client code modifies the property value, the data stored by the internal variable will be modified as well. And to top it off, your component can't even tell that the data has been changed.

Should these facts not faze you, and you just need a simple way to expose some data as a property, here's the syntax for exposing a local (to the component) variable:

```
<public>
    <property name="LastName"/>
    <property name="FirstName" internalname="strFirstName"/>
</public>
```

The first property definition ties a property named LastName to an internal variable also named LastName. The second definition ties a property named FirstName to an internal variable named strFirstName.

These variables should be defined as global variables within only one of your component's `<script>` tags (assuming you have more than one `<script>` section, which isn't necessarily the case):

```
<script language="VBScript">
Dim strFirstName
Dim LastName
etcetera
</script>
```

Notice that any property defined in this manner is by definition a read/write property. You cannot control access to the property in any manner.

17

CREATING
WINDOWS SCRIPT
COMPONENTS

Using Functions to Define Properties

If the previous section's dire warnings about the dangers of using variables directly as properties didn't sway you, here are a few of the advantages to using functions to return and set property values:

- Your functions can add validation code that verifies data before setting or returning the property's value.
- You can decide whether the property should be read/write, read-only, or write-only.

To use functions for setting or retrieving property values, you'll need to add appropriate `<get>` and `<put>` elements within the property's `<property>` element. The `<get>` element is used to specify the function that will be called whenever the client requests the value of the property. The `<put>` element defines the function that will be called when the client is assigning a value to the property.

To specify a read-only property, simply omit the `<put>` element. For a write-only property, leave out the `<get>` element.

Here's the example from the previous section rewritten to use functions:

```
<public>
    <property name="LastName">
        <get/>
        <put/>
    </property>
    <property name="FirstName">
        <get internalname="getFirstName"/>
        <put internalname="putFirstName"/>
    </property>
</public>
```

For the `LastName` property, we have not specified an `internalname` attribute for either the `<get>` or `<put>` elements. In this case, you must create functions in your script called `get_LastName` and `put_LastName`. The runtime engine prefixes the property's name with `get_` and `put_`.

For the `FirstName` property, we've specified the names of the functions to use. These then must be defined within the script code.

The code of the `get` function must return the value of the property as the return value for the function. In the case of the `put` function, the function must be defined to take a single parameter. The value of this parameter is the value that the client is attempting to assign to the property.

Adding Methods to the Script Component

Methods are much simpler to define than properties. You don't have to worry about whether it's read/write or whether it directly exposes a variable. For a method, you simply place a `<method>` element within the component's `<public>` element. The syntax of this element is

```
<method name="externalName" [internalname="internalName"]>
```

The `externalName` value is the name of the method as it appears to the client code. The value of the optional `internalName` attribute is the name of the function within the component. If the two names are identical, you can omit the `internalName` attribute.

If the method requires any parameters, you specify them within the `<method>` element using one `<parameter>` element for each required parameter as in the following example:

```
<method name="externalName" [internalname="internalName"]>
    <parameter name="parameterName">
</method>
```

Debugging and Error-Handling Techniques

Typically server-side Script Components will run silently. However, while you're developing a Script Component, you might want to run it in debug mode. You'll probably also want some more detailed error messages.

There's an element that you can add to your component file that allows for both of these handy tools. This element's syntax is

```
<?component error="errorvalue" debug="debugvalue"?>
```

By default, any runtime or syntax errors generated by a Script Component will display a very generic error message. If you'd like to turn on more verbose error messages, set the `error` attribute to `True`.

Likewise, by default you cannot use a script debugger (such as Visual InterDev) to debug a running Script Component. If you set the `debug` attribute to `true`, however, you can debug a running Script Component. The debugger will be launched in response to a breakpoint set in the development environment (this is possible in Visual InterDev) or in response to the VBScript `Stop` statement or the JScript `debugger` statement.

Using a Script Component in ASP

Now that you know all there is to know about creating a Script Component, this final section of this chapter will show you how to utilize the component. Of course, if you've made it to this chapter you already know how to use a Script Component in your ASP pages because Script Components are just like any other COM object. Still, there are a few steps necessary to take a Script Component file from the Notepad/design stage to the utilization stage.

Registering the Script Component

Before you can use a new Script Component with any COM client, you must register the Script Component. As mentioned earlier, the registration process simply enters information into the Windows registry that allows the operating system to start up a COM server component.

The registry entries map the component's CLSID and/or ProgID information to the actual implementation of the server. In the case of Script Components the implementation is handled by the SCROBJ.DLL runtime engine which, using further information stored in the registry, reads and parses the appropriate Script Component file.

To register a Script Component, simply right-click the component's file in Windows Explorer and select the Register item from the shortcut menu. That's all there is to it! After the component is registered, you never have to register it again unless something in the <registration> section changes. Likewise, if you make any changes to the script code that implements the component, you don't have to restart IIS in order for the modified code to be used.

If you're moving the component to a new machine, I'd recommend installing the Windows Script Component runtime components as you did on the original machine.

Creating a Type Library File

Another step you'll want to take if you plan to use your Script Component from code you're writing in Visual InterDev is to create a type library. You do this by right-clicking the Script Component's file and selecting Generate Type Library from the shortcut menu. A .TLB file with the same name as the Script Component file is created in the current directory (at the time of this writing, the .TLB file was named scriptlet.tlb but I expect this will be corrected in a future version of the Script Component runtime).

The type library file allows Visual InterDev to determine what properties and methods are supported by the Script Component. With this information in hand, InterDev can provide you with statement completion and IntelliSense, probably the best innovations in programming in a long time!

Creating and Using an Instance of a Script Component

Like any COM component, Active Server Pages provide two ways to create a new instance of a Script Component: with the CreateObject method and with an <OBJECT> tag. If you use the CreateObject route, you'll specify the ProgID value. If you go with the <OBJECT> tag, you'll need the scriptlet's classid value from the <registration> element.

After an instance of a Script Component object is created, you use it just like any other object. You can set or retrieve the values of the object's properties (assuming the property allows the access you're attempting), and you can call the object's methods.

Listing 17.3, available on the accompanying CD as scriptcmp.asp in the \Source\Chapter17 folder, demonstrates a simple Active Server Page that utilizes the Script Component created in this chapter.

LISTING 17.3 A SIMPLE ASP FILE UTILIZING THE SCRIPT COMPONENT

```
<%@ Language=VBScript %>
<object RUNAT=SERVER ID=scptPet
 CLASSID="clsid:a5a670a0-f128-11d2-a60b-444553540000">
</object>
<%
  set scptOwner = server.CreateObject("unleashed.WSC")
  scptOwner.FirstName = "Craig"
  scptOwner.LastName = "Eddy"

  scptPet.FirstName = "Lucy"
  scptPet.LastName = "Eddy"
%>
<HTML><BODY>
<H2>Pet</H2>
First Name: <%=scptPet.FirstName%><br>
Last Name: <%=scptPet.LastName%><p>
<H2>Owner</H2>
First Name: <%=scptOwner.FirstName%><br>
Last Name: <%=scptOwner.LastName%><br>
</BODY></HTML>
```

Summary

This chapter has shown you a powerful and simple way to create real COM components using ActiveX Scripting code. These components are small, easy to maintain, and do not require a compiler or development environment to create them.

The next chapter delves into creating components using Visual Basic. These components are compiled, and you do need to have the Visual Basic development environment present on your system, but you'll be able to accomplish a lot with them.

CHAPTER 18

Creating Custom Components with Visual Basic

by Craig Eddy

IN THIS CHAPTER

Chapter 17, "Creating Windows Script Components," discussed how you can use ActiveX scripting to create server-side components. These components are accessible to your ASP code in the same manner as the built-in `Request` and `Response` objects. The tremendous difference, however, is that *you* get to control what happens in components that you create.

Although the use of ActiveX scripting to create components is indeed powerful and has advantages, using a full-fledged development environment such as Visual Basic or Visual C++ opens a whole world of opportunities. There are, of course, a few drawbacks to creating components using a compiled language, but these are greatly outweighed by the advantages.

This chapter discusses creating components with Visual Basic. Chapter 19, "Creating Custom Components with Visual C++," discusses how to create components with C++. The following topics are covered in this chapter:

- The advantages of using Visual Basic as opposed to scriptlets or Visual C++
- How to create an ActiveX server-side component to be used from your ASP code
- How you can use Visual Basic 6.0's WebClass components to create an entire IIS-based application with Visual Basic

> **NOTE**
>
> This chapter provides enough detail to create custom components with Visual Basic. It does not, however, delve into all the intricacies of coding those components using Visual Basic. This is left to a text on programming with Visual Basic, such as *Sams Teach Yourself Visual Basic 6 in 21 Days* by Greg Perry (ISBN: 0-672-31310-3) or *Developing COM/ActiveX Components with Visual Basic 6* by Dan Appleman (ISBN: 1-56276-576-0).

The Advantages of Visual Basic for Component Development

There are many advantages to using Visual Basic to develop custom components. Although scriptlets provide a quick and efficient means of creating a component, besides the Scriptlet Wizard that Microsoft provides there's no development environment and you're limited to the capabilities of your chosen scripting language.

Likewise, Visual C++ provides a great deal of functionality to your component. Using Visual C++, the sky's literally the limit. You can develop any type of component that does just about any required task at a blinding speed. However, this flexibility comes at the price of complexity. Without a doubt, the C++ language is one of the hardest to master.

Visual Basic provides a great middle ground for component development, especially for server-side components that don't require a user interface. (Visual C++ is by far the language of choice for developing fast user interface–intensive applications.) Here are a few of the advantages of using Visual Basic (all but the last of these apply to either version 5.0 or 6.0):

- It is a simple language that's easy to master.
- Visual Basic makes working with the basic data types extremely easy. Strings in C++ can be very difficult to work with because of the many representations available. Likewise, pointers are a little safer in Visual Basic. In most cases, you won't even realize you're working with a pointer. With Visual C++, you must pay careful attention to those pointer variables.
- Visual Basic provides a full-featured development environment with features such as IntelliSense, statement completion, and integrated database tools.
- The native code compiler uses the same compiler as Visual C++. This means that you can build fast, scalable components.
- The Object Browser lets you see the interfaces exposed by the components that your code references.
- Visual Basic 6.0 introduced the WebClass. This is a special type of project designed to be run on Internet Information Server, version 3.0 or later. A WebClass is a complete IIS application, including the capability to use HTML template files instead of repeated Response.Write code. The second half of this chapter discusses the WebClass in detail.

Developing Server-Side Components

If you've read to this point in the book, you've probably realized that most of the work done by Active Server Pages is actually accomplished by ActiveX components (also called COM components) running on the server (or on another machine if you're using DCOM). The Request and Response objects, which seem to be built in to Active Server Pages, are actually COM components that IIS instantiates for your code.

Using Visual Basic (from version 4.0 on), you can easily create your own set of components. Like the Request and Response objects, these components will be accessible from your Active Server Pages. The only difference is that, although the Request and Response objects appear to be "built-in" components, components that you create will have to be instantiated by your ASP code.

Visual Basic performs much of the grunt work associated with building ActiveX/COM components for you. You just define your component's object model (its set of exposed properties and methods), write the code, and compile. Visual Basic will add all the low-level COM functions for you. These functions are used by the operating system to register your component and invoke its properties and methods. Just as with the scriptlet runtime engine discussed in Chapter 17, using Visual Basic relieves you of the grunt work.

> **NOTE**
>
> More details about building IIS/ASP components with Visual Basic can be found online at
>
> http://msdn.microsoft.com/workshop/server/components/vbmtsiis.asp

Creating the Project

The first step to creating a custom component with Visual Basic is to create a new ActiveX project. Visual Basic is capable of compiling your code into many different types of "executable" files. When you start up the Visual Basic development or select New Project from the File menu, you'll have the capability to create any of these and more types of projects (see Figure 18.1).

FIGURE 18.1

Visual Basic's New Project dialog box.

- Standard Win32 EXEs—These are standard Windows applications.

- ActiveX EXEs—These are ActiveX/COM server components that run "out-of-process," meaning they run in a different process than does the client code that instantiated the component. Although you can access ActiveX EXEs from Active Server Pages, it's not recommended and requires a change to the IIS metabase that allows all executables to be launched from script code running on the server. For more details, see the IIS documentation.

- ActiveX DLLs—These are ActiveX/COM components that run in the same process as the client that instantiated the component. Typically, your custom components will fall into this category.

- IIS applications—This is a special type of application that uses HTML to present its user interface and compiled Visual Basic code to process requests and respond to events from the browser. These are discussed in the second half of this chapter.

- ActiveX controls (OCXs) —These are specialized components that include the additional support needed for host applications to display and manipulate the component in a GUI environment. You can also embed OCX components in a Web page. Typically, OCXs are user-interface components and cannot be created using a call to Server.CreateObject. Therefore, you won't be creating many of these for use in your ASP code.

- ActiveX document DLLs and ActiveX document EXEs—An ActiveX document enables you to display Visual Basic forms within OLE document container applications such as Internet Explorer or Microsoft Office Binder. Although this is a neat idea, it has no application within Active Server Pages and won't be discussed here.

18

CREATING CUSTOM COMPONENTS WITH VB

> **NOTE**
>
> ActiveX DLLs and EXEs are often referred to as *code components* because they are typically used as an invisible component that provides some sort of service through code, as opposed to user interaction.

To create an ASP-accessible component, double-click the ActiveX DLL icon in the Visual Basic New Project dialog. Visual Basic will create a new project with a single class module (see Figure 18.2).

FIGURE **18.2**

The beginnings of an ActiveX DLL component.

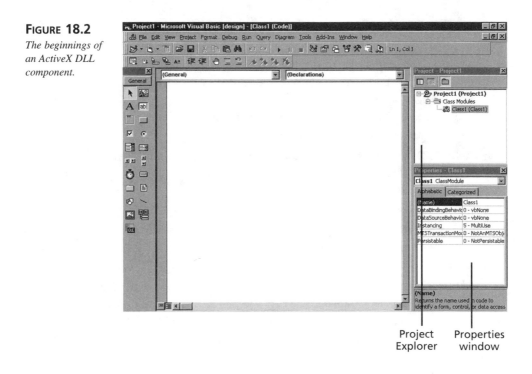

Project
Explorer

Properties
window

The project represents the component. Visual Basic uses a default project name of Project1. You'll, of course, want to change this to something more meaningful. Each class module represents an individual object within the component. The initial class module is named, most imaginatively, Class1. Again, you'll want to change this name.

Where do the project and class names come into play? If you'll recall the syntax of the Server.CreateObject method, you'll remember that it takes a string which is the ProgID of the component to be instantiated. The ProgID is used by the operating system to locate the executable file that will provide the running instance of the component. A ProgID is typically in the form *servername.objectname*. In the case of Visual Basic, the *servername* portion is the project's name and the *objectname* portion is the class name.

So, if you were to leave the Visual Basic default names intact, the ProgID would be Project1.Class1, and the ASP code used to create an instance of this object would be Server.CreateObject("Project1.Class1"). Obviously, this does not even approach self-documenting code, so you'll want to choose project and class names that describe the function and purpose of the component you're creating. To change the names, click on the item (project or class) in the Project Explorer window's tree (if the Project Explorer is not visible, press Ctrl+R). Then click in the (Name) property in the Properties window and change the value. If the Properties window is not visible, press F4.

Accessing the Built-In ASP Objects

One of the best uses for custom components accessed from Active Server Pages is to replace code that's used in multiple ASP files. In order to do this, you'll probably need to access the built-in ASP objects (`Request`, `Response`, `Server`, `Session`, and `Application`). Fortunately, just as with server scriptlets, Visual Basic makes accomplishing this a simple task.

The first step in accessing the built-in objects is to add a reference to the appropriate type libraries to your project. You'll need to reference the Microsoft Active Server Pages Object Library and the Microsoft Transaction Server Type Library. To do so in the Visual Basic development environment, click the Project menu item and select References. The References dialog, shown in Figure 18.3, is displayed.

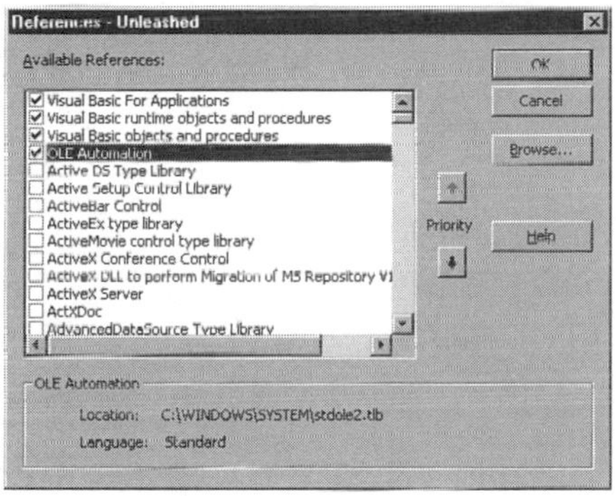

FIGURE 18.3

*The Visual Basic
References dialog
box.*

18

CREATING CUSTOM
COMPONENTS
WITH VB

Scroll the Available References list until you find the Microsoft Active Server Pages Object Library entry. Check the box next to the entry. Then scroll down a little farther until you find Microsoft Transaction Server Type Library and check it. If Active Server Pages and Microsoft Transaction Server are installed, these files will be available in the References list. Click the OK button to save these new selections to the project.

After these type libraries are referenced in the project, you can create instances of the appropriate objects. The first object instance you must create is called `ObjectContext`. This is the Microsoft Transaction Server (MTS) object that houses the running instances of all the built-in ASP objects related to a particular session. There's a global function called `GetObjectContext()` that returns a reference to this `ObjectContext`.

The `ObjectContext` object is a `Collection` object similar to the `Session` and `Application` objects. You access each item in the collection using the item's key value. In the case of the built-in ASP objects, the key values are the names of the objects (`Request`, `Response`, `Server`, `Session`, and `Application`).

So, to retrieve the `Response` object you'd use code similar to the following:

```
Dim objContext as ObjectContext
Dim objResponse as Response

Set objContext = GetObjectContext()
Set objResponse = objContext("Response")
```

Coding the Component

Now that the basics of creating a custom component for use in Active Server Pages have been covered, take a look at the down-to-business details. Like any COM component, custom components created in Visual Basic can have both properties (which represent the data portion of the object) and methods (which represent the action portion of the object).

Visual Basic provides several ways to add properties and methods to your class modules (remember, a class module is where Visual Basic stores the code for a single object within in a component):

- Using the Add Procedure dialog
- Using the Class Builder utility
- Manually typing the property or method routines

The first two methods are discussed in this section. After you know what a property or method looks like in code, you might find it easier to use just the third method.

Adding Properties

The properties of a component represent the data stored by the object. You can think of a property as an attribute of the object. For example, `Color` may be a property for the `Car` object.

Properties can be read/write, read-only, or write-only. This means that you can control access to the object's data by making the property fit into the particular access scheme.

> **NOTE**
>
> I'd recommend against using write-only properties. Very rarely would you want to prevent client code from reading the value of a property. After all, if you have the right to set the value of a property, you surely should have the right to read back that value!

Using Functions to Define a Property

In a Visual Basic class module, properties can be represented by Property Get (for reading the property value) and Property Let (for setting the property value) routines. If you want a property to be read-only, omit the Property Let routine. For a write-only property, omit the Property Get routine.

Adding a property is simple. Open the code window for the class module of the object for which you want to add the property (either double click the class module name in the Project Explorer or click the class module name and then click the View Code button on the Project Explorer). After the code window is active, use the Tools menu and click on the Add Procedure menu item. The Add Procedure dialog box shown in Figure 8.4 appears.

FIGURE 18.4

The Add Procedure dialog box.

18

CREATING CUSTOM COMPONENTS WITH VB

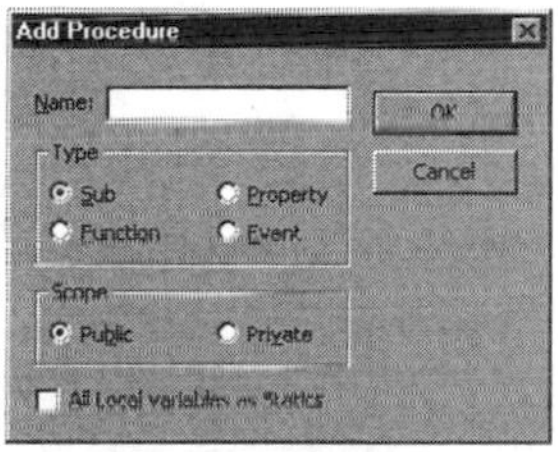

In the Name edit box, enter the name of the property. Don't worry about the Property Get or Property Let portion; Visual Basic will add this in for you. Just enter the name as you want it to appear in your ASP code when you actually use the object.

In the Type radio buttons, select Property. Leave the other Public radio button selected, and set the All Local Variables as Statics check box appropriately. (A static variable maintains its value each time the routine in which it is defined is called; non-static variables are reset to a known default value each time the routine is called.)

Click the OK button, and the appropriate code stubs are added to the class module. Figure 18.5 shows the class module's code window after a property called Name is added with the Add Procedure dialog.

Because the Add Procedure dialog has no place for you to specify the data type of the property, Visual Basic adds the code for a property whose data type is Variant (which can hold practically any type of data but has a lot of overhead associated with it). To set the appropriate data type for the new property, replace the word Variant in both the Property Get and Property Let routines with the appropriate type. For example, the Name property is a string; so wherever you see Variant replace it with String (see Figure 18.6).

FIGURE 18.5
*The class module
with a* Name *property added.*

FIGURE 18.6
*The modified
code, showing the
proper data type
for the* Name
property.

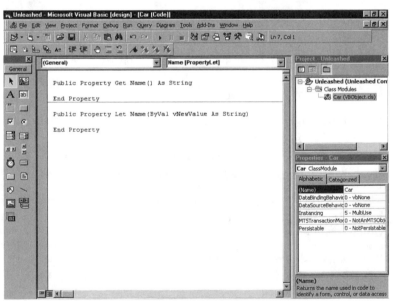

Likewise, the Add Procedure dialog doesn't let you specify the type of access to the property that is allowed (read/write, read-only, write-only). Instead, Visual Basic puts in the routines for both reading and writing the property's value. To make the property read-only, simply delete the code stub for the Property Let routine. For a write-only property, remove the Property_Get routine.

Now all that's left to do is write the actual code for the routines. In most cases, the property value will be stored by a local variable defined in the class module. For the Name property, I'd use a local variable called m_sName. The m_ portion signifies that it's a module-level variable; the s shows that it's a String. The Name portion is a description of the data it contains.

The Property Get routine is actually a Visual Basic function. As you can see in Figure 18.6, the routine has a data type specified for it: Property Get Name() As String. This means that to return the value of the property, somewhere in the routine you'll need to set the return value to the property's value. This is done, in Visual Basic, as in the following example, where you set the name of the function equal to the value to be returned by the function (in this case, the value of the property that is stored locally in the variable m_sName):

```
Name = m_sName
```

For the Property Let routine, the new value that's being assigned to the property is passed using the routine's one-and-only parameter. You'll use this value to set the local variable's value, assuming that the new value passes any and all validation tests for the property.

Listing 18.1 shows the completed code for the Name property.

LISTING 18.1 THE Name PROPERTY'S Get AND Let ROUTINES

```
Private m_sName as String

Public Property Get Name() As String

    Name = m_sName

End Property

Public Property Let Name(ByVal vNewValue As String)
    ' if empty string is passed, raise the
' invalid property value error (error # 380)
    If Len(vNewValue) = 0 Then Err.Raise 380

    m_sName = vNewValue

End Property
```

18

CREATING CUSTOM
COMPONENTS
WITH VB

Using a Public Variable as a Property

There's an easier way to create a property on a Visual Basic object, but the ease comes with a price. If you define a Public variable in the class module's Declarations section, that variable will be exposed as a property to any COM client that instantiates your object. Here's an example:

```
Public Name as String
```

Although this might appear wonderful, there are some drawbacks:

- The property is always a read/write property.
- You cannot perform any validation on the values assigned to the property.
- Your code receives no notification that the value of this Public variable has been changed. This means that if the value of the property affects other data within your object, you won't be able to keep that data up-to-date as this property value changes.

Adding Methods

Adding methods to your object follows the same logic as adding properties. You use the Add Procedure dialog, choosing either Sub or Function from the Type radio buttons.

Here's how you'd add a method called Drive to the Car object:

1. Open the code window of the Car object's class module.
2. Use the Tools, Add Procedure menu item to bring up the Add Procedure dialog.
3. In the Name edit box, enter the name of the method: Drive. Because the Drive method will return a value that indicates whether the car started in motion, select the Function radio button. If the method were not going to return a value, you'd leave the default Sub radio button selected.
4. Because this is a method to be exposed by the Car object, leave the Public radio button selected. Click the OK button to add the code to the class module. Your screen should now resemble Figure 18.7. (The code for the Name property was added in the section "Using Functions to Define a Property," earlier in this chapter.)
5. The Drive method will return a Boolean value indicating success or failure. To code this, change the line defining the method's procedure to read:

```
Public Function Drive() As Boolean
```

FIGURE 18.7

The Car *object with the* Drive *method added.*

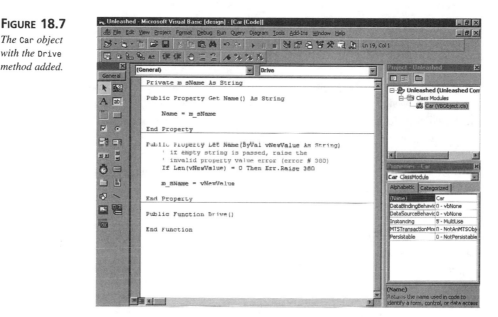

6. Likewise, the method must know how fast to go and whether to go forward or reverse. Assuming an integer rate of speed, and using an optional Boolean parameter to indicated "go forward," change that same line to read

```
Public Function Drive(Speed as Integer, _
Optional Forward as Boolean = True) As Boolean
```

The Optional keyword indicates that the client code does not have to pass the parameter to the method. If the client does not pass this parameter, either a default value (which depends on the data type of the parameter) or the value specified will be placed into the parameter variable when the procedure is executed. This is handled by the COM engine.

7. Now all that's left is writing the code that makes the Car object move. This exercise is left to the reader!

Using the Class Builder Utility

Visual Basic ships with a neat add-in called the Class Builder utility. This add-in is helpful in creating and adding objects to a component and adding the procedure stubs for a component's properties and methods. If you have a collection class within your

18

CREATING CUSTOM
COMPONENTS
WITH VB

component (which is a class that contains a collection of objects defined by another class in your component), the Class Builder will create most of the code needed to make it work.

Let's take a look at some of the features of the Class Builder. Because the Class Builder is an add-in, you must tell Visual Basic to load it. The specific steps required to do so have changed from version 5.0 to version 6.0, but in both versions you first invoke the Add-In Manager from the Add-Ins menu. Next, you select the Class Builder add-in and enable it (version 5.0) or load it (version 6.0). Likewise, some features of the utility have been added with version 6.0, so if you're using 5.0 your screens might look a little different. The basic concepts are identical, however.

The Class Builder window for the Car object is shown in Figure 18.8. Notice that the All tab lists both the Name property and the Drive method.

FIGURE 18.8

The Class Builder utility.

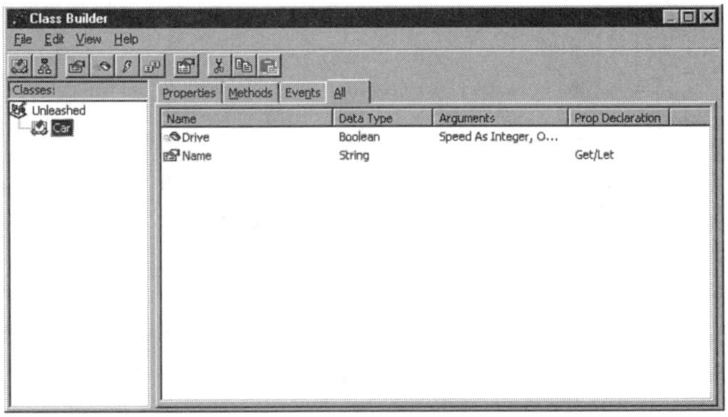

Using the utility you can rename, delete, cut, copy, paste, and view the properties of existing properties and methods. You can also add new properties, methods, events, or enumerations to your object.

> **NOTE**
>
> You won't be able to delete classes that were not created with the Class Builder. Instead, delete the class module from the Visual Basic Project Explorer.

To add a new object, click the project's name in the tree view and then click the Add New Class toolbar button (it's the leftmost button). To add a collection class that is a collection of objects defined in the component, you should first create the class that defines the object to be collected. Then right-click the project's name in the tree view and select New, Collection from the shortcut menu. The Collection Builder dialog (shown in Figure 18.9) will appear.

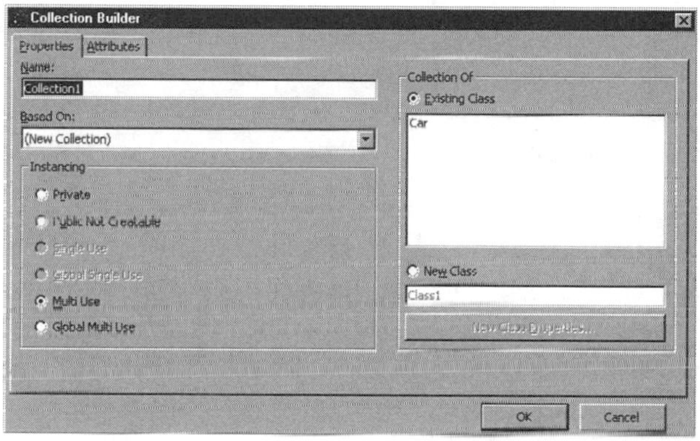

FIGURE 18.9

The Class Builder utility's Collection Builder dialog box.

Specify a good name for the new class and select which of the existing classes the new one collects. In this case, I'm creating a Fleet object that will be a collection of Car objects. I enter Fleet in the Name edit box and select the Car entry in the Existing Class list box. Click OK, and the Collection Builder adds the new collection class to the Class Builder dialog box, as seen in Figure 18.10.

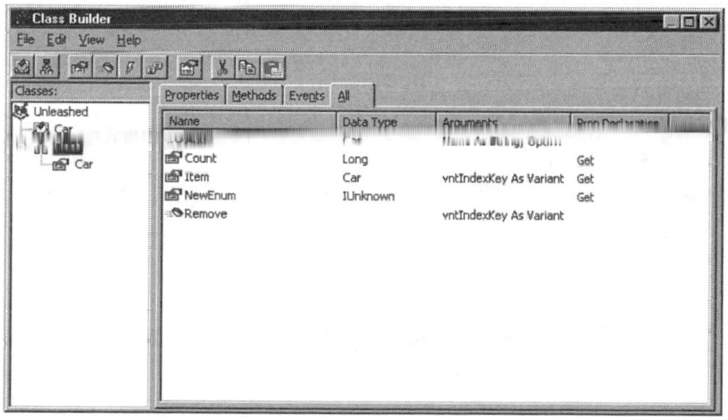

FIGURE 18.10

The Class Builder after adding a collection class.

When you exit the Class Builder after making some changes, you'll be prompted to update the project. If you want your changes to be reflected in the project, allow the Class Builder to modify your code.

18

CREATING CUSTOM
COMPONENTS
WITH VB

Using the Component from ASP

After you've entered the component's code, you must compile it using the Visual Basic File, Make menu item. This will display the Make Project dialog box, where you can specify the name of the component's DLL file and the folder where it will be created. You can also set up some compiler options such as the version number for the component and any compiler switches (such as optimization options). These are available when you click the Options button on the Make Project dialog box.

After you've compiled the component, you can use it in your Active Server Pages. The Visual Basic compiler takes care of all the low-level COM requirements: creating CLSIDs and ProgIDs, registering the component, and so on. If you move the component to another machine, you'll need to register it on that machine (use REGSVR32.EXE with the DLL filename as the only command-line option) and make sure that all the required runtime support is available.

As with all ActiveX/COM components, you can create an instance of a Visual Basic component in your Active Server Pages using either the <OBJECT> tag or the Server.CreateObject() method.

If you use the <OBJECT> tag, you should specify the CLSID for the object. This will improve the performance of your ASP page because the ASP engine will not have to perform the following steps to locate the component. Because Visual Basic generates this GUID for you and doesn't have a place within the development environment to find the value it generated, you must look it up in the Windows registry. Start in the HKEY_CLASS-ES_ROOT hive and search for a key that matches your component's PROGID. The PROGID consists of the project name (Unleashed in the preceding examples), a period, and the class name (Car or Fleet from earlier). When you find the appropriate key, expand its tree item, and you'll see a Clsid key. The default value for this key is the object's CLSID. Figure 18.11 shows the entry on my computer for the Car object. The CLSID is 3171008B-BAB2-11D2-A60B-444553540000, and the PROGID is Unleashed.Car.

The syntax for the <OBJECT> tag is

```
<object id="objID" classid="clsid:GUID"></object>
```

In this syntax, *objID* is the name that you'll use to reference the component in your ASP script code, and the value for *GUID* is the CLSID you found in the registry. For the Car object, the tag would be

```
<object id="myCar"
 classid="clsid:3171008B-BAB2-11D2-A60B-444553540000">
</object>
```

FIGURE **18.11**

*The Registry entry
for the* Car *object.*

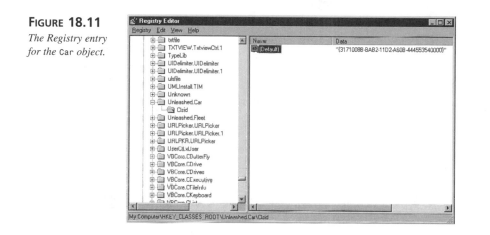

For the CreateObject method, you already know everything you need. The syntax
used is

```
Set myCar = Server.CreateObject("Unleashed.Car")
```

Introducing Visual Basic's WebClass Application

Visual Basic 6.0 introduced a whole new type of Visual Basic application: the IIS application. An IIS application is typically known as a WebClass application, perhaps because
that name has a better ring to it. A WebClass application enables you to use Visual Basic
to write server-side code that responds to requests from the user's browser. Just as with
Active Server Pages, your code can create browser-independent applications.

WebClasses have access to the built-in ASP objects (Response, Request, Server,
Session, and Application). The WebClass code is responsible for returning the HTML
that will be displayed, but this task is eased through the availability of special elements
of the WebClass called HTML template items. These contain HTML code that can be
outputted all at once using a WriteTemplate method.

Any application that you create with Active Server Pages can also be created using a
WebClass in the Visual Basic development environment. This includes the capability to
set break points within your VB code. One additional feature of the WebClass, that's not
available with Active Server Pages, is tag replacement for HTML template items. As
you'll see, an HTML template can contain special tags that will cause the template item's
ProcessTag event to fire in your VB application. This enables you to use a standard

format for a database form (the HTML template) but still be able to change the data dynamically, for example.

Another cool feature of the WebClass is the capability to create and fire both early-bound and late-bound events and have these events raised to the WebClass from the browser. The event code then returns the appropriate response to the browser.

The rest of this chapter discusses IIS applications and the many features available within them. The example built isn't particularly useful, but it demonstrates how to use the more important features of Visual Basic's new WebClass.

> **NOTE**
>
> IIS applications can be run on IIS versions 2.0, 3.0, or 4.0, Peer Web Services for Windows NT Workstation, or the Personal Web Server for Windows 95/98. The built-in ASP objects (`Response`, `Request`, `Server`, `Session`, and `Application`) have differing sets of supported properties and methods among some versions of these server platforms. Be sure to take into account this possibility if your IIS application might be run on a different server platform from the one used to develop it.

Creating a WebClass Application

This section discusses the basics of starting a new IIS application. There are a few things to consider at the start of your application's design, such as state management and which server-side ActiveX server components you'll need to access.

> **NOTE**
>
> Additional information about creating a new IIS application, as well as a list of Microsoft Knowledge-Base articles relating to WebClasses, can be found at
>
> `http://support.microsoft.com/support/kb/articles/q191/0/39.asp`

Creating a New IIS Application

You create an IIS/WebClass application following the same steps you followed to create an ActiveX DLL. If you've just launched Visual Basic from the Windows Start menu, you'll use the New tab of the New Project dialog. If Visual Basic is already running, use the File, New Project menu item to launch the New Project dialog box (shown in Figure 18.12).

FIGURE 18.12

The New Project dialog box.

Double-click the IIS Application icon and Visual Basic will create a new project, complete with some startup code. The project's name will be the default `Project1`. A default WebClass object named `WebClass1` will also be created. This object is where most of your work will take place.

The development environment for a WebClass consists of two parts: the WebClass designer (shown in Figure 18.13) and the code window. The WebClass designer replaces the Visual Basic forms designer that you're probably accustomed to from standard Visual Basic applications. Using this designer, you can add new HTML template WebItems, add Custom WebItem objects, add events to either of these WebItems, and start and stop your local server.

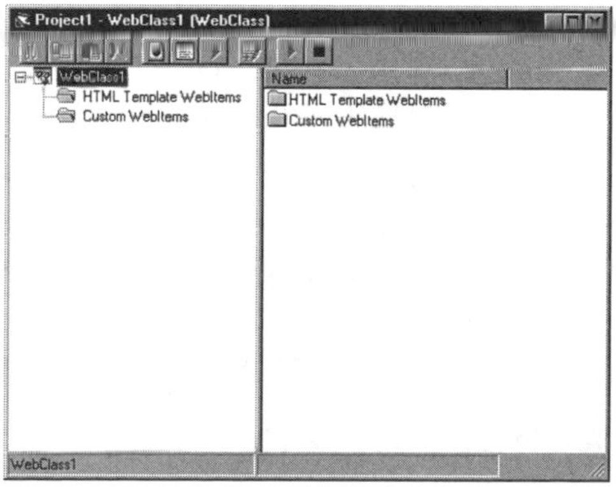

FIGURE 18.13

The WebClass designer.

As you work with the various components of an IIS application, you'll become familiar with the features of the WebClass Designer. To see the code behind an item in the WebClass, simply double-click the item. For example, to see the startup code that Visual Basic adds by default, double-click the WebClass1 entry in the designer's tree pane. The code window for the WebClass appears (see Figure 18.14).

FIGURE 18.14

The WebClass's default code.

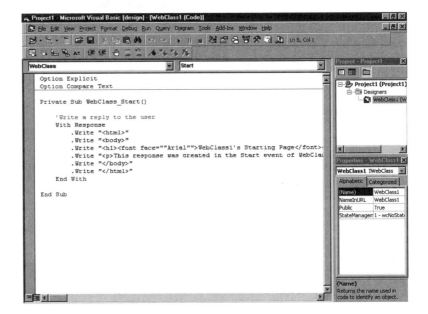

The default code that Visual Basic places into the project is enough to get an IIS application up and running. The WebClass_Start event code is executed when the WebClass object is first instantiated. As you can see from Figure 18.14, the default code uses the Response object to output some simple HTML to the browser.

Before you run the new project, you should save it. Visual Basic will create a new Web on your local Web server and prompt you for a name to associate with this Web (the ASP application name for the virtual Web folder that's created). Also, you must save the project before you add the first HTML template WebItem to the project. Figure 18.15 shows the results of running the default IIS application. Here I named the Web First.

Accessing the Built-In ASP Objects

As you might be able to decipher from the code in Figure 18.14, an IIS application starts its life with access to the built-in ASP objects (Response, Request, Server, Session, and Application). You don't have to do any special work to make them available as you did with a standard ActiveX DLL. Support for them is compiled into the application DLL by the Visual Basic compiler.

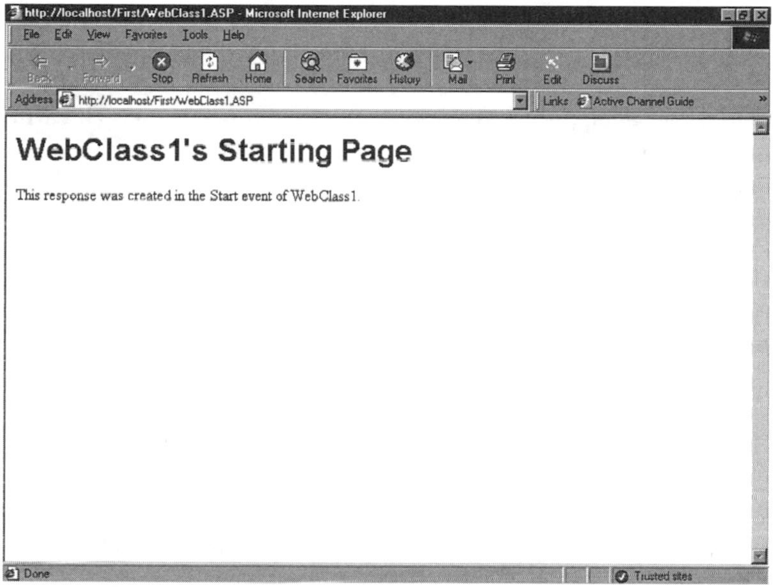

FIGURE 18.15

The output from the default IIS application code.

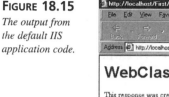

As you can see from the default code, these are the same objects you're used to from ASP scripting. You output HTML to the browser using the `Response.Write()` method, just as in Active Server Page coding. There's one additional feature: the `BrowserType` object. This is the same component as the BrowserType component discussed in Chapter 7, "Generating Dynamic Content from the Server." The BrowserType object is discussed later in this chapter, in the section "Special Features of WebClass Applications."

Accessing Other ActiveX Server Components

As with all types of Visual Basic applications, IIS applications can instantiate other ActiveX components. For example, if you have some custom business logic built into an ActiveX component, you can access that functionality from a WebClass in your project. This functionality can include anything from login verification to custom data formatting.

Whatever the functionality, utilizing it within a WebClass is simple. First, you should create a reference to the external component within your project. Doing so allows the project to use early-bound calls to the component's properties and methods. Using early-bound calls is much more efficient.

To add a reference to an external component, pull up the Visual Basic References dialog box by using the Project, References menu item. The References dialog box allows you to select any of the ActiveX server components that are currently registered on the machine or to register a new component if you have its implementation file (DLL or EXE). To select an already-registered component, locate it in the Available References list box and check the box next to its entry. To register a new component on the system or to locate a component by filename, use the Browse button. This will display the standard File, Open dialog, allowing you to locate and select the component's implementation file.

After you have created a reference to the component, you use it by creating an instance variable to hold the object instances provided by the component. For example, the following creates a new variable named `objMyFleet` of type `Fleet` from the component named `Unleashed`, and it also starts a running instance of the object:

```
Dim objMyFleet as New Unleashed.Fleet
```

After this is accomplished, you can use any of the properties or methods provided by the object.

Maintaining Your Component's State

Another important concept to consider at the start of your IIS application's development is state maintenance. This means you can control how the state of the WebClass is maintained from request to request. An IIS application created in Visual Basic has two possible state maintenance modes: maintained or not maintained. The value is specified using the `StateManagement` property of the `WebClass` object. This property has two values: `wcNoState` or `wcMaintainInstance`.

If you choose to maintain the WebClass's state across requests, you'll use more memory on the server (because the WebClass is kept "alive" in a `Session` object for the entire lifetime of the user's session), but you'll be able to maintain the WebClass's internal (local) variables from request to request. Note that the use of Session objects requires that the browser support cookies, so make sure your users are aware of this necessity. If you choose not to maintain the state, the memory used by the WebClass will be freed as soon as the response is completed, but you won't be able to maintain the values of local variables across different requests.

The operation of `Session` object variables is not affected in any way by the setting of the `StateManagement` property. You can always choose `wcNoState` value and use the `Session` variables to store the data used across requests (just as you do with standard ASP code). However, this goes against the grain of most VB development.

If you choose the `wcMaintainInstance` value and want to unload the current instance to free up memory or terminate its usage, a `ReleaseInstance()` method will accomplish just that task. The application terminates at the end of the procedure in which the `ReleaseInstance()` method is invoked.

Working with WebItems

Now that the basics of IIS applications have been covered, it's time to look at what's necessary to make the application do some serious work. Although the `WebClass_Start` event is perfectly capable of handling a single request, to make a usable application you'll need to add some elements. In an IIS application these elements are called WebItems.

WebItems are used by a WebClass to provide content and events to the browser. Each WebClass can contain many WebItems. The WebItems are stored within the WebClass, not as separate modules within the project. So, you'll find the WebItems you add to a WebClass in the tree pane of the WebClass's designer window. This is also, of course, where you'll add new WebItems to the WebClass.

There are two types of WebItems: the HTML Template WebItem and the Custom WebItem. To add a WebItem to a WebClass, open the WebClass's designer and click either the Add HTML Template WebItem or the Add Custom WebItem toolbar button. If you're adding an HTML Template WebItem, a File Open dialog appears. Use this dialog to navigate to the HTML file you're using as the template for this new WebItem.

Using an HTML Template WebItem

The HTML Template WebItem allows you to associate an HTML file with a WebItem. Before you add the WebItem to the WebClass, you must create the HTML file. You can use any HTML editor (including Notepad) to create the HTML file. The HTML contained within the file can either be a complete HTML document or just a portion of an HTML document that will be inserted into the middle of another HTML document.

When you add a template file to the WebClass and save the project, Visual Basic will make a copy of the template file. If the original file was not located in the project's directory, the file will simply be copied, with the same name, to the project directory. If the original file is in the project's directory, Visual Basic will create a copy and append a number to the original filename. For example, template.htm might be renamed to template1.htm. You should work in the copy of the file from this point on in order to change the appearance of the output.

You use the WebItem's `WriteTemplate()` method to output the template's contents to the response stream. You can place calls to a WebItem's `WriteTemplate()` method anywhere that you're creating a response. The contents of the template file will be added to the response.

You can also transfer the flow of the response stream to a specific WebItem by setting the WebClass-global `NextItem` property to that specific WebItem. After the current procedure exits, the specified WebItem's `Respond` event will fire, allowing the WebItem to write to the `Response` stream. The following code demonstrates this concept:

```
Private Sub WebClass_Start()
    With Response
        .Write "<html>"
        .Write "<body>"
        .Write "<h1><font face=""Arial"">"
        .Write "WebClass1's Starting Page</font></h1>"
        .Write "<p>This response was created in the "
        .Write "Start event of WebClass1.</p>"
    End With
    Set NextItem = Piece      'transfer control to Piece
End Sub

Private Sub Piece_Respond()
    Response.Write "In the Piece_Respond event: "
    Piece.WriteTemplate
End Sub
```

Another extremely useful feature of an HTML Template WebItem is that it can contain replacement tags which will cause the WebItem's `ProcessTag` event to fire when the `WriteTemplate()` method is invoked. This enables you to customize the contents of the response stream within the hard-coded HTML that the template contains. Tag replacement is covered in the section "Special Features of WebClass Applications," later in this chapter.

Adding a Custom WebItem

Custom WebItems don't have an associated HTML file. The Custom WebItem contains event handlers that are invoked either when the WebItem is invoked (through setting the `NextItem` property) or when a specific action takes place in the browser. You can add events to a WebItem at design time or use the `UserEvent` event to generate dynamic events (more on this in the next section).

Because Custom WebItems don't have a template file, the `WriteTemplate()` method is not valid. Instead, you use the `Respond` event or one of the event handlers to programmatically create the response stream.

Responding to Events

Most of the work done by an IIS application takes place within an event handler. Event handlers are invoked in response to actions taken in the browser or when particular elements within the response stream are processed. Four types of events are discussed here: built-in events, template events, custom events, and the UserEvent event.

Events exist on WebClass objects and on both types of WebItems. The standard set of events for both HTML Template and Custom WebItems is the same.

Built-In Events

There are several built-in events for both the WebClass and its constituent WebItems. These are fired in response to system-level events or as the default action when there is no other event handler to handle a request from the current page in the WebClass application. You don't have to do anything to access the code window for these events; they're added automatically by Visual Basic. The built-in events are summarized in Table 18.1.

TABLE 18.1 THE BUILT-IN IIS APPLICATION EVENTS

Object	*Event*
WebClass	Start
	BeginRequest
	EndRequest
	Initialize
	Terminate
	FatalErrorResponse
WebItem	Respond
	UserEvent
	ProcessTag

You've already seen the first event. The Start event is invoked whenever the WebClass application's main page is requested. This is done when requests are made for *ProjectName*.ASP where *ProjectName* is the WebClass's NameInURL property (which defaults to the WebClass's name), or when a WebItem that does not exist is requested.

The BeginRequest and EndRequest event handlers are invoked whenever any request is made of the application. This includes requests for WebItems in addition to the WebClass itself. If you need some centralized processing to take place with every page requested in the application, these are the events to use. The BeginRequest event fires at the start of the request, before any other event handlers are invoked. The EndRequest event is fired after all other event handlers (including the `ProcessTag` events) have finished. This occurs immediately before the Web server returns the contents of the response stream to the browser.

The `Initialize` and `Terminate` events are identical to the `Initialize` and `Terminate` events familiar to ActiveX component programmers. These events fire when an instance of the object is created and destroyed, respectively.

The `FatalErrorResponse` event handler is invoked whenever the WebClass's processing is terminated due to an error. The event handler procedure has a single parameter, `SendDefault as Boolean`, which is used to tell the Web server whether the event has created the appropriate error message.

CAUTION

If you use Visual Basic's built-in `Err.Raise` method to raise errors within your WebClass, the `FatalErrorResponse` event handler will not be invoked unless something has already been written to the response stream.

If the `SendDefault` parameter is set to `False` by your code, then you should create the error message to be returned (using the `Response.Write` method or an HTML Template WebItem's `WriteTemplate` method). The WebClass has a property named `Error` that contains the error number, description, and source. You can use this property to determine which error occurred and inform the browser appropriately. Note that any data that's already been outputted to the response stream (using `Response.Write` or the `WriteTemplate` method) will still be present when the error handler is invoked. You can use the `Response.Clear` method to remove any existing data. Leaving the `SendDefault` parameter set to `True` will cause the default ASP error message to be sent to the browser.

For WebItems, the `Respond` event is invoked whenever the WebItem is requested, and there's not an event handler for the selected element in the current page (more on this in the upcoming "Template Item Events" section). This event is the default event for a WebItem, and the browser response must be created within this event. Otherwise, the application will appear dead in the water! The other two WebItem events from Table 18.1 (`UserEvent` and `ProcessTag`) are discussed in the following sections.

Custom, Early-Bound Events

At design-time, you can create your own events that can be invoked from the browser. Events can be created on either the HTML Template WebItem or a Custom WebItem. Typically, they'll be created on a Custom WebItem.

Custom events are invoked by clicking on hyperlinks within pages generated by other events or WebItems. The WebClass library provides a handy global method named URLFor, which you can use to construct the URL for a WebItem and its events. You'll see how this works in the sample IIS application discussed later.

To create a new event, open the WebClass's designer window. Click the WebItem to which you will add the new event (you cannot add events to the WebClass itself, only its WebItems), and click the Add Custom Event toolbar button (found on the WebClass designer window, not on Visual Basic's toolbar). A new branch representing this new event is added to the WebItem's tree. To rename the event, right-click it in the tree and select Rename on the shortcut menu. To write code for the event handler, double-click the event in the tree or open the WebClass's code window and use the drop-down list boxes at the top of the code window to find the event.

To create a hyperlink that will invoke a particular event, use code similar to

```
Response.Write "<A HREF="
Response.Write URLFor(WebItem, "EventName")
Response.Write ">Invoke Event</A>"
```

Whenever this link is clicked in the browser, the WebClass will attempt to invoke an event named *EventName* in the WebItem specified by *WebItem* (this must evaluate to an object of type WebItem). Notice that the event's name is in quotation marks, meaning you must pass a string for this parameter. If such an event does not exist in the WebItem, the WebItem's UserEvent is invoked (see the next section). If you specify a WebItem that doesn't exist, the URLFor method will generate a runtime error.

The UserEvent Event

Whenever a WebItem is referenced in a URL and an unknown event is specified in the URL, the WebItem's UserEvent handler will be called. This is useful for creating dynamic events that aren't known at design-time, possibly because they are based on data being handled by the WebClass.

You create a link for a UserEvent just as you create a link for an early-bound event:

```
Response.Write "<A HREF="
Response.Write URLFor(WebItem, "EventName")
Response.Write ">Invoke Event</A>"
```

EventName is the name that will be passed to the UserEvent handler. The stub for the UserEvent handler is

```
Private Sub WebItemName_UserEvent(ByVal EventName As String)
```

The EventName parameter passed to the handler is the same value that's provided in the link.

Template Item Events

WebItems present another special kind of event: template item events. Certain properties of certain HTML tags can be controlled using template item events. For example, if you have an <IMG> tag in an HTML template file, the SRC, DYNSRC, LOWSRC, and USEMAP attributes of this tag can all be generated dynamically.

Whenever you add an HTML Template WebItem to your WebClass, and it contains tags with attributes eligible for a template item event (form elements, image tags, hyperlinks, and most other tags that contain a URL reference), the tags and attributes are added to the WebClass designer's list view for the WebItem (see Figure 18.16).

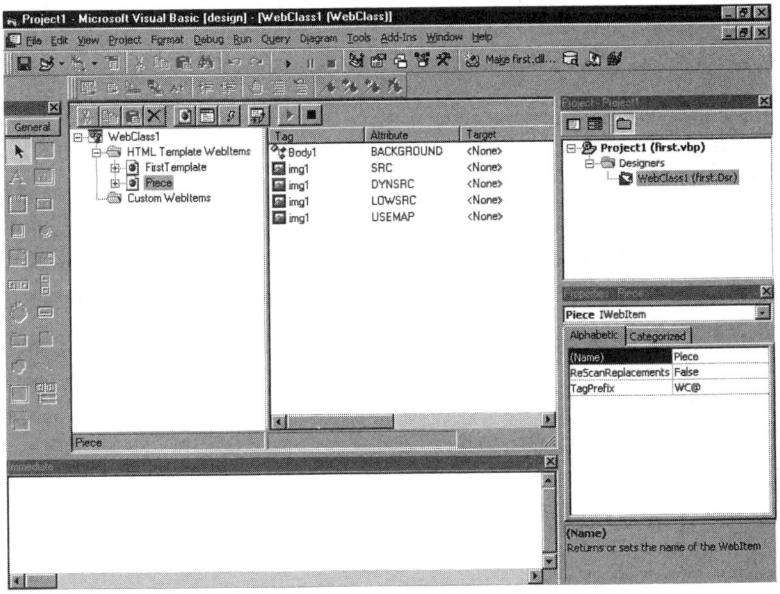

FIGURE 18.16

The WebClass designer with an HTML template having tags eligible for a template item event.

To add an event handler for any of the eligible attributes, double-click the entry in the list view for the attribute, and Visual Basic will open the code window for that event handler. Use the Response.Write() or Response.BinaryWrite() methods to provide the necessary output.

Note that the event is not expecting you to provide the URL for the tag's attribute. Instead, you should return the data that the URL would be expected to describe. For example, for an `<IMG>` tag's SRC attribute, the event is expecting you to write the image data to the output stream:

```
Private Sub Piece_img1Src()

    Response.BinaryWrite LoadResData(101, "custom")

End Sub
```

This code will read the resource file attached to the WebClass project and write the data to the output stream.

Handling Form Input

When you utilize WebClass applications to handle HTML forms, it's really not much different from using Active Server Page scripting (at least as far as code goes). The form's data is contained in either the `Request.QueryString` collection (if the form's METHOD attribute was GET) or the `Request.Form` collection (if the form's METHOD attribute was POST).

In the HTML form's `<FORM>` tag, set the ACTION attribute to an event in one of the WebClass's WebItems, either by hard-coding the URL (if using an HTML template), by using the URLFor method (if using `Response.Write` to output the form), or by using HTML tag replacement discussed later in this chapter (if you're using an HTML template and want to use the URLFor method to create the proper URL). Alternatively, you can simply use a custom WebItem and process the form data in the WebItem's Respond event. In the event handler, simply access the collection that's appropriate for the form's specified method (GET or POST).

 Combining this form data processing with other HTML or Custom Template Web Items makes it very easy to control the flow of the application based on the form's data. For example, you might want to route users to different pages of a registration form, depending on their entries in the form. Using the `Response.Redirect` method or, if you have WebItems for the other pages, you can easily accomplish this task by setting the NextItem property. Listing 18.2 shows a very simple example of how this can be accomplished (this project can be found on the CD in the \Source\Chapter18\Forms directory).

LISTING 18.2   PROCESSING FORM DATA

```
Private Sub WebClass_Start()

    'Write a reply to the user
    With Response
        .Write "<html>"
        .Write "<body>"
        .Write "<h2><font face=""Arial"">"
        .Write "WebClass Form Processing</font></h2>"
        .Write "<form method=post action=" & URLFor(FormSubmit) & ">"
        .Write "Name: <input type=text name=username><p>"
        .Write "Marital Status: <select name=mstatus>"
        .Write "<option value=0 SELECTED>Select status..."
        .Write "<option value=1>Married<option value=2>Single"
        .Write "<option value=3>Other</select><p>"
        .Write "<input type=submit></form>"
        .Write "</body>"
        .Write "</html>"
    End With

End Sub


Private Sub FormSubmit_Respond()

    With Response
        .Write "Hello " & Request.Form("username") & "<br>"

        Select Case Request.Form("mstatus")
        Case 0
            Response.Redirect ("myformclass.asp")
        Case 1
            Set NextItem = WI_Married
        Case 2
            Set NextItem = WI_Single
        Case 3
            Set NextItem = WI_Other
        Case Else
            Response.Redirect ("myformclass.asp")
        End Select

    End With

End Sub

Private Sub WI_Married_Respond()

    Response.Write "Welcome to the Married Folks Forum!"

End Sub
```

```
Private Sub WI_Other_Respond()

    Response.Write "Welcome to the Other Folks Forum!"

End Sub

Private Sub WI_Single_Respond()

    Response.Write "Welcome to the Single Folks Forum!"

End Sub
```

To create this project from scratch, create a new IIS application. Change the WebClass's `Name` and `NameInURL` properties to `MyFormClass`. Next, add four custom WebItems: `FormSubmit`, `WI_Married`, `WI_Single`, and `WI_Other`. Then copy the code from the listing and run the application.

Special Features of WebClass Applications

Now that you've seen the basics of WebClass applications, it's time to take a look at a few of the more advanced features available. This section discusses the `URLData` property, HTML template tag replacement, and the `BrowserType` object.

Persisting Data with the `URLData` Property

In addition to using the `Session` variable object to hold data, you can maintain the state of your application by using the `URLData` property. This property, which is global to the WebClass, is a string that is appended to the URL of every WebItem and event in the application. You can then either use the `Request.QueryString` or the `URLData` property to determine the current state. When you use the `QueryString` property, the key into the collection will be `WCU`. The sample WebClass application (found on the CD at \Source\Chapter18\UnleashedWCProject.vbp) uses the `URLData` property.

Using HTML Template Tag Replacement

Another feature for creating dynamic Web pages is the tag replacement available when using HTML template files. By adding special tags to the HTML file, you can cause the WebItem's `ProcessTag` event handler to be executed. This enables you to replace the contents of the tag with dynamic content. The event handler is defined as

```
Private Sub TemplateItem_ProcessTag(ByVal TagName As String, _
                    TagContents As String, SendTags As Boolean)
```

The `TagName` parameter specifies the name of the tag being replaced. Each HTML template item has a `TagPrefix` property that specifies the string used to identify a replacement tag. The default value is `WC@`. The HTML tag, assuming this default, that you'll use whenever you want to have the `ProcessTag` event handler executed is
`<WC@TagName>TagContents</WC@TagName>`.

The data placed inside the tag's beginning and ending delimiters (represented in the sample tag by `TagContents`) is passed to the event handler in the `TagContents` parameter. This parameter is also an output parameter: The event handler sets the value of this parameter to the data that should be used. This can be plain text or HTML.

The `SendTags` parameter is used to specify whether the tags that caused the `ProcessTag` event are also returned to the browser. The default value is `False`, which means that only the value of the `TagContents` parameter will be sent to the browser. If the `SendTags` parameter is set to `True`, the `<WC@TagName>` and `</WC@TagName>` will also be sent to the browser.

Using the `BrowserType` Object

The final special feature available in WebClass applications is the `BrowserType` object. This object is the same object as discussed in Chapter 7 but is available globally in your WebClass with no code required.

 Listing 18.3 shows how you might use the `BrowserType` object to pass control to a different WebItem depending on the user's browser. This code can be found on the CD in the \Source\Chapter18\BrowserType directory. This WebClass has three custom WebItems added to it: `IEPages`, `NetscapePages`, and `UnknownPages`.

LISTING 18.3   PROCESSING FORM DATA

```
Private Sub WebClass_Start()

    If InStr(BrowserType.Browser, "IE") Then
        Set NextItem = IEPages
    ElseIf InStr(BrowserType.Browser, "Netscape") Then
        Set NextItem = NetscapePages
    Else
        Set NextItem = UnknownPages
    End If

End Sub
```

```
Private Sub IEPages_Respond()

    With Response
        .Write "You're using version " & BrowserType.version
        .Write " of Internet Explorer"
    End With

End Sub

Private Sub NetscapePages_Respond()

    With Response
        .Write "You're using version " & BrowserType.version
        .Write " of Netscape"
    End With

End Sub

Private Sub UnknownPages_Respond()

    With Response
        .Write "You're using version " & BrowserType.version
        .Write " of " & BrowserType.Browser
    End With

End Sub
```

Summary

This chapter covers a lot of ground. You learned how to use Visual Basic (from version 4.0 on) to create COM components that can be accessed from your Active Server Pages. You also learned about an even more useful new class of application introduced with Visual Basic version 6.0: the IIS application. Using IIS applications, you can completely replace all your Active Server Pages with a single VB application.

Chapter 19 discusses how you can use Visual C++ and the Active Template Libraries (ATL) to create small, fast COM components, accessible from your Active Server Pages.

CHAPTER 19

Creating Components with Visual C++

by Craig Eddy

IN THIS CHAPTER

The previous two chapters dealt with creating server-side components using scripting and Visual Basic. This chapter demonstrates how to build such a component using Microsoft's Visual C++ development environment. Specifically, the component will be built using Microsoft's Active Template Library (ATL). For information on Visual C++ and ATL, see Microsoft's MSDN Web site at http://msdn.microsoft.com.

ATL provides the easiest, quickest way to build COM components with Visual C++. The ATL wizards make adding new COM classes, as well as their properties and methods, a piece of cake. If you're dead set on using MFC in your projects, ATL provides for MFC support, and I'll show you how to add this support to your component.

This chapter covers several topics:

- The advantages of using Visual C++ to build server-side components
- Which threading models you should use for your components
- How to create a simple component

Advantages of Using Visual C++

If you read the previous two chapters, you're no doubt aware how easy it is to create components using either scripting or Visual Basic. Either of these two methods can produce a component in seemingly record time, with very little coding on your part. As you'll see in this chapter, developing a COM component in Visual C++ involves a bigger commitment of coding time on your part. So just what makes using Visual C++ such an attractive proposition?

Here's a short list of the advantages of using Visual C++ to develop server-side components:

- Performance—Without a doubt Visual C++ produces the fastest component when compared with scripting (which is completely interpreted) and Visual Basic (which is compiled, but still partially interpreted through the VB "virtual machine"). Additionally, using scripting requires extra overhead to parse and execute the script code. Because a C++ component is compiled, it runs natively.

- Access to more features—Using Visual C++ to develop your component opens up the whole of the operating system. You can directly access the system registry, have greater control over thread execution, and have more options when dealing with reading and writing to I/O devices on the server.

- Leverage existing code—If you have business logic already written with Visual C++, it's a trivial matter to transfer that logic into a server-side component.

- Protection—Keep your code from prying eyes. If you distribute your components to other parties, you'll probably want to protect your intellectual property rights. Using scripting for components makes this impossible. Visual Basic provides a little more code protection, but decompilers are available.

When you use ATL, you gain a few more advantages:

- Smaller, faster components.
- Support for all threading models (although only two are recommended for server-side components).
- Adding support for additional COM interfaces that your component implements is almost trivial.
- A whole slew of additional classes that you can use internally (such as CComBSTR and CComPtr).
- Support for the COM error-handling mechanism.

Threading Models

If you're like me and your background is in developing software to run on desktops, you're probably not used to the reality that a component might be required to service several clients simultaneously. This means that at the exact same moment the component can be running one routine for one client and a completely different routine for another client.

The Windows operating system handles this reality by allowing the component to execute on multiple threads at the same time. This means that the component's code can be going down more than one path at a given moment. Windows gives each thread a specific slice of time in which to operate, and then switches execution to another thread. How your component takes advantage of this multithreaded processing is determined by the threading model that you select when you create a component. There are four different threading models: single, apartment, free, and both.

19

CREATING
COMPONENTS
WITH VISUAL C++

> **NOTE**
>
> For more details on threading and threading models, see http://
> msdn.microsoft.com/msdn-online/workshop/components/com/comthread.asp.

You can use any of these models when you create a component. However, only the apartment and both models will give you acceptable performance in a multiuser Active Server Page environment.

Single-Threaded Components

The single model is by far the worst of all threading models with respect to server-side components. When a single-threaded component is running, every call to one of its methods is executed on a single thread. This means that after one call is made, subsequent calls are blocked from executing until the prior call has completed. Even worse, if many simultaneous users attempt to access the component, a deadlock situation can arise.

If that's not enough to scare you away from single-threaded components, you should also be aware that these components run in the context of the SYSTEM account. This means that the component will have all the permissions associated with the SYSTEM account. Typically you don't want to open this up to your Web browsers.

Free-Threaded Components

The free-threaded model is also not recommended for developing server-side components. First, free-threaded components must be registered with Microsoft Transaction Server (MTS) in order to access the ObjectContext object (used when supporting transactions within a component or Active Script Page). Components that are apartment or both-threaded can access the ObjectContext object without being registered with MTS.

Additionally, free-threaded components, like single-threaded, run in the context of the SYSTEM account.

Apartment-Threaded Components

Apartment-threaded components can be used for components with page or session scope (meaning that the components are used only in a single ASP page or placed in a Session variable). However, when you create an apartment-threaded component at the session level, the entire session is locked into a single thread. This slows access time. If your components run only for the duration of a single page, though, apartment-threading will work fine.

If you attempt to assign an apartment-threaded component to an Application variable, a runtime error will occur. In other words, if Unleashed.ApartmentThreaded is apartment-threaded the following code will cause an error:

```
Set Application("Oops") =
➡Server.CreateObject("Unleashed.ApartmentThreaded")
```

Both-Threaded Components

The both-threading model can be used for any server-side component, regardless of its intended scope. However, to be most efficient the component should create a free-threaded marshaler object. This object is used to make calls between threads without requiring any marshaling or thread switches. The ATL New Object Wizard makes it easy to add this support to your classes (as you'll see when you create a component later in this chapter).

If you create a both-threaded component and do not create a free-threaded marshaler object, you will be able to use the component in an application scope only if the MD_ASP_TRACK_THREADING_MODEL configuration parameter is set to True (1). The default for this parameter is False (0). Otherwise, a runtime error will be generated when you attempt to assign an instance of the component to an application-scope variable. At the session level, a runtime error will not occur, but you will significantly impact performance if you do not create the free-threaded marshaler object.

The disadvantage to using both-threaded components is that you cannot serialize calls to the component. This means that you must build thread safety into your code. Although this can slow down your development time, it might be necessary for session- or application-scoped components.

Creating the Component

Now that you know which threading model to select (both-threading if your component needs to support any scope, apartment-threading if page-scope), take a look at how a component is created using Visual C++ 6.0 and ATL 3.0.

There are three general steps required to create a server-side component with Visual C++ and ATL:

1. Create a new ATL COM project.
2. Add an ATL simple object for each class your component will provide.
3. Add the properties and methods supported by the component's classes.

19

CREATING
COMPONENTS
WITH VISUAL C++

NOTE

The final version of the files for this component can be found on the accompanying CD in the \Source\Chapter19\first folder.

Creating the ATL Project

Creating the new project is the easiest step. Launch Visual C++ from the Windows Start menu, and you'll have an empty workspace. Click File, New and the New dialog box, shown in Figure 19.1, appears.

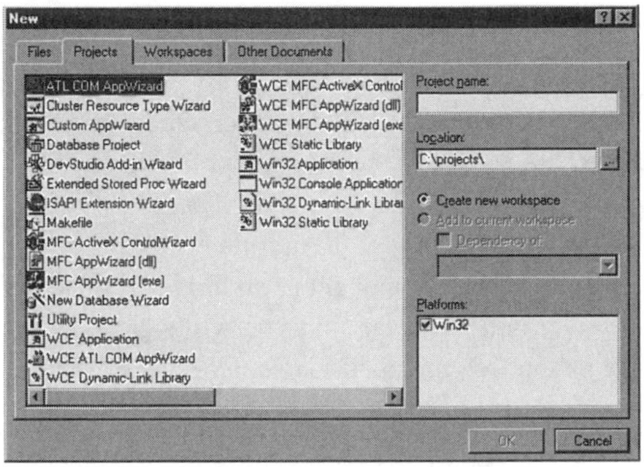

FIGURE 19.1

The Visual C++ New dialog box.

First, make sure that the Projects tab is selected. In the list view on the left side of the dialog, click on ATL COM AppWizard. Enter a name for the project in the Project Name edit box, and make sure that the Location box is appropriate. The wizard will create a subdirectory that's a combination of the Location entry and the Project Name entry (you'll see what I mean as you type in the Project Name edit box).

When you've entered the information, click OK and the wizard will launch, as shown in Figure 19.2.

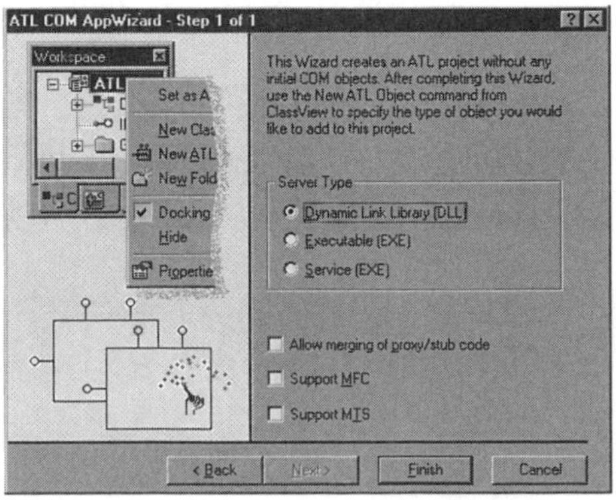

FIGURE 19.2

The ATL COM AppWizard's one and only dialog box.

In general, a server-side component will be implemented as a DLL (because a DLL runs in-process, thus improving performance). Leave the Server Type radio button at its default. If for some reason you need to create an out-of-process component, select the Executable (EXE) option. Note that you might also have some options on the IIS server to set correctly for out-of-process components (for details, see http://msdn.microsoft.com/msdn-online/workshop/server/components/outproc.asp).

If you will be using any of the MFC classes (and there are some handy non-UI classes in MFC) or if you think you might ever need to, check the box labeled Support MFC. You can come back later and add MFC support to the component, but doing so involves some somewhat tedious coding (see Microsoft Knowledge Base article Q173974 for details on how to add MFC support to an ATL project).

If your component will be registered with MTS, check the box labeled Support MTS.

When you're finished, click the Finish button and the wizard will display a dialog that details the project you're about to create. Click OK on this dialog, and the wizard will create the skeleton of your new project.

After its work has been accomplished, the development environment will appear as shown in Figure 19.3 (after expanding the Workspace tree).

FIGURE 19.3

The results of the ATL COM AppWizard's work.

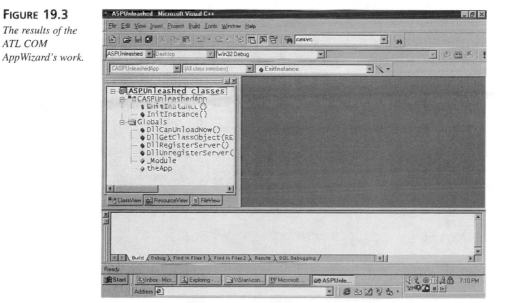

What do you have at this point? The ATL COM AppWizard has created the shell of your component. This shell consists of the code necessary to compile and load the DLL as a COM server. The server can't do anything yet, though, because it contains no COM classes (also known as CoClasses). What you have is the left side of the ProgID parameter that you use when you call the `Server.CreateObject()` method (in the component shown in Figure 19.3, this would be `ASPUnleashedApp`).

Adding a New Class

To complete your component you must add a CoClass. The CoClass is where the component's properties and methods will be implemented. In the ATL world, this is done using the Insert, New ATL Object menu item found on the Visual C++ editor. After you select this menu item, the ATL Object Wizard, shown in Figure 19.4, is launched.

FIGURE 19.4

The ATL Object Wizard.

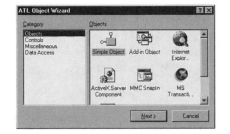

This dialog enables you to add many different types of ATL objects to your project. The Objects category contains items that are implemented as COM objects, such as an MMC Snapin. Under the Controls category you'll find many different ActiveX controls that can be creating using ATL. The Miscellaneous category contains one class, Dialog; and the Data Access category contains classes for creating OLE DB providers and consumers.

Because you're creating a component for use in Active Server Pages, you want to create an ActiveX Server Component, found in the Objects category. Therefore, click ActiveX Server Component, and then click the Next button. The ATL Object Wizard Properties dialog box, shown in Figure 19.5, appears.

FIGURE 19.5

The ATL Object Wizard properties dialog box.

For an ActiveX server component this dialog has three tabs: Names, Attributes, and ASP. The Names tab is where you specify the name for the new class being created. The value that ends up in the CoClass edit box will serve as the right portion of the ProgID used in the call to `Server.CreateObject()`. You can enter this value in the Short Name edit box, and the wizard will fill in all the other boxes for you. Typically, you'll leave the other boxes at the values entered by the wizard, but you can override them. This tab also enables you to use different names for the C++ class (used internally by your code) and the COM CoClass interface (used externally by the COM client, such as an Active Server Page).

When you have satisfactory values, click the Attributes tab, shown in Figure 19.6. On this tab, you specify the various attributes of the CoClass. These attributes include the threading model (discussed earlier in this chapter), the interface method (although ActiveX Server Components can only be dual interface), and whether or not the object can be aggregated. Your choice of threading model is dictated by the scope of the component within your ASP application, but for maximum flexibility choose the Both radio button.

FIGURE 19.6

The Attributes tab of the ATL Object Wizard properties dialog box.

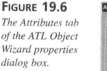

If you want to raise COM-style errors from your object, check the Support IsupportErrorInfo box. This will add the code necessary for your component to use the COM error-handling mechanism.

Because you're using the both threading model, you also want to have a free-threaded marshaler object hanging around. Therefore, check the box labeled Free-Threaded Marshaler. This will instruct the wizard to add all the code required for the free-threaded marshaler.

You use the Support Connection Points check box if your component will raise events to its host. Because an Active Server Page cannot respond to events from a COM component that it instantiates, in most cases, there's no need to check this box.

Finally, the ASP tab (shown in Figure 19.7) contains a few check boxes that the wizard uses to make the built-in (intrinsic) ASP objects available to your object. In order to retrieve the running instances of these built-in objects, you must implement the OnPageStart method. You can uncheck any of the built-in objects that your component doesn't need to access. Doing so will remove the overhead of retrieving and releasing the instances of these objects.

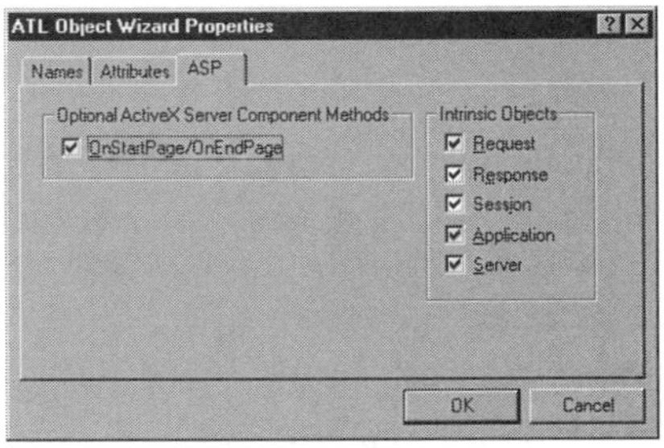

FIGURE **19.7**

The ASP tab of the ATL Object Wizard properties dialog box.

After you're satisfied with the check boxes here, click OK, and the wizard will add the new class to the project and modify the Interface Definition Language (IDL) file to include the newly created CoClass. The IDL file is used to generate the component's type library, a very necessary COM piece. When the wizard finishes, your project will appear similar to Figure 19.8 (with the newly added class expanded in the tree).

NOTE

To learn more about IDL, I'd highly recommend the article "Understanding Interface Definition Language: A Developer's Survival Guide" from the August 1998 issue of *Microsoft Systems Journal*. You can find the article online at http://www.microsoft.com/msj/0898/idl/idltop.htm.

For this project, I used MyClass as the Short Name value on the ATL Object Wizard Properties dialog. The wizard added two items to your workspace: CmyClass, a C++ class, and ImyClass, an interface provided by the object. The IMyClass interface is where the actual properties and methods will be placed for the CoClass (more on this in a minute). The interface is contained within (so to speak) the CMyClass C++ class definition. The interface as created by the wizard provides two methods, OnPageStart and OnPageEnd. These methods are invoked at the start and end of parsing of the Active Server Page that creates an instance of this new object.

FIGURE 19.8

The project after a new ActiveX Server Component object is added.

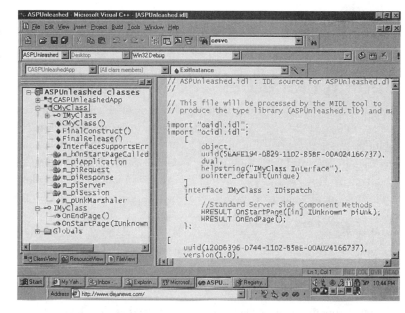

NOTE

If an instance of your component is created using the <OBJECT> tag with an Application scope, the OnPageStart and OnPageEnd methods will not be called because the component's scope extends beyond the current page. In these cases, you should use the MTS GetObjectContext function and retrieve the intrinsic objects this way. If you suspect your component might be used in this way, you'll probably want to put code in to detect the lack of valid pointers to the intrinsic objects and retrieve them using the GetObjectContext methodology. Details can be found in the section "Accessing the Built-In ASP Objects" in Chapter 18, "Creating Custom Components with Visual Basic."

The wizard has also added several class-level variables to hold the instances of the ASP intrinsic objects (m_piApplication, m_piRequest, m_piResponse, m_piServer, and m_piSession), as well as the free-threaded marshaler object (m_pUnkMarshaler). The ASP intrinsic objects are retrieved by code that the wizard has placed inside the OnPageStart method. The free-threaded marshaler is created in the class's FinalConstruct procedure and released in the class's FinalRelease procedure.

19

CREATING
COMPONENTS
WITH VISUAL C++

You could actually compile the project at this point and have an ASP component, which you could create using `Server.CreateObject()`. However, without any properties or methods this object isn't able to do any real work.

Adding Properties and Methods

As with all ActiveX components, the real work is done when properties are set or methods are invoked. Although ATL provides a few simple dialogs for adding properties and methods, the information that you must enter on the dialogs is more detailed than with the Visual Basic Add Procedure dialog (see the section "Coding the Component" in Chapter 18). However, this additional information requirement enables you to fine-tune your component's interface in ways that are not possible with Visual Basic.

Adding a Property

As with Visual Basic, properties are much easier to add than methods. When you add a new property, the ATL Wizard will add several functions to your class's exposed interface, depending on whether the property is read/write, read-only, or write-only.

The write function will be named put_*PropertyName* and the read function will be named get_*PropertyName*. Additionally, if the property's data type is another COM object, there will be a third function named putref_*PropertyName*, which is called when the client code uses `Set object.PropertyName = SomeOtherObjectReference`.

Although the wizard will add the function headers to the class's include file, the stubs to the CPP file, and the proper code to the IDL file, you will need to add the implementation code and probably a member variable to hold the property value within your class.

Here are the steps to add a string property to your class:

1. Using the tree in the Workspace pane, right-click over the interface entry (if you look back at Figure 19.8, it's `IMyClass`) that appears directly beneath the *ProjectName* Classes root entry. A small shortcut menu will appear. Click the Add Property item.

2. The Add Property to Interface dialog, shown in Figure 19.9, appears. This dialog is used to enter information about the new property. First, select the Property Type. You can either select one from the list or enter another COM data type (including other COM interfaces such as `IFontDisp`). With the exception of other COM interfaces, you should stick to the entries in the list. For a string property, select `BSTR`.

3. Next, enter a name for the property in the Property Name edit box. As you make changes in the dialog box, the text in the Implementation frame is modified. This text will be added to the IDL file for the new property.

FIGURE 19.9

The Add Property to Interface dialog.

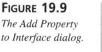

4. If the property takes any parameters, enter those in the Parameters edit box. Most properties do not use parameters.

5. In the Function Type frame, specify the available access to the property. Clear the Get Function check box to make the property write-only. Clear the Put Function check box to make the property read-only.

6. If the property's data type is another COM object and you want to support the Set statement only, click the PropPutRef radio button. If you want to support BOTH Set and standard property value assignment, you'll have to add the put_*PropertyName* function and IDL code manually.

7. Clicking the Attributes button launches the Edit Attributes dialog. On this dialog, you can change some of the interface attributes of the new property. In particular, you should modify the helpstring attribute's value to describe the new property (be sure to leave it wrapped in double quotes). This attribute is displayed as help text in object browsers whenever the property is selected in the object browser.

8. Click OK on the Add Property to Interface dialog, and the wizard adds the necessary support to your project.

9. To get to the implementation of the property, you must expand the class name in the Workspace pane. You'll then see the interface name as a child node. Expand this, and you'll see the entries for the get and put functions for the new property. Double-click the entry, and the code window will load the function. What you see will be similar to what appears in Listing 19.1.

LISTING 19.1   CODE ADDED FOR A NEW STRING PROPERTY

```
STDMETHODIMP CMyClass::get_Name(BSTR *pVal)
{
AFX_MANAGE_STATE(AfxGetStaticModuleState())

// TODO: Add your implementation code here

return S_OK;
}

STDMETHODIMP CMyClass::put_Name(BSTR newVal)
{
AFX_MANAGE_STATE(AfxGetStaticModuleState())

// TODO: Add your implementation code here

return S_OK;
}
```

10. To add a member variable that will hold the property's value, right-click the class name and select the Add Member Variable menu item. The Add Member Variable dialog appears. Enter the data type (CComBSTR in this case) and a name for the variable (using your naming convention, of course). You can control access to the member variable using radio buttons in the Access frame. Click OK and the variable is added to your class.

11. Now you can change your properties implementation code to use the new member variable (see Listing 19.2).

LISTING 19.2   CODE TO SUPPORT THE STRING PROPERTY

```
STDMETHODIMP CMyClass::get_Name(BSTR *pVal)
{
AFX_MANAGE_STATE(AfxGetStaticModuleState())

if (pVal == NULL) return E_POINTER;
*pVal = m_bstrName.Copy();

return S_OK;
}

STDMETHODIMP CMyClass::put_Name(BSTR newVal)
{
AFX_MANAGE_STATE(AfxGetStaticModuleState())
m_bstrName = newVal;
return S_OK;
}
```

Adding a Method

Adding a method to a component follows the same path as adding a property. The biggest difference is that you must manually enter the IDL pieces when you specify the method's parameters. Here are the steps:

1. Using the tree in the Workspace pane, right-click over the interface entry (in Figure 19.8, it's IMyClass) that appears directly beneath the *ProjectName* Classes root entry. A small shortcut menu will appear. Click the Add Method item.

2. The Add Method to Interface dialog appears (see Figure 19.10). Enter the name of the method in the Method Name edit box.

FIGURE 19.10

The Add Method to Interface dialog.

3. After a name is entered, the Attributes button becomes enabled. As with a property, this button displays a dialog for entering and modifying the interface attributes for the method. Click the button to change the helpstring attribute to something resembling the purpose of the method.

4. In the Parameters edit box, enter all the parameters passed to the method, as well as a parameter to handle the return value of the method (should it be required to return a value).

   This is done using IDL notation. For example, [in] long InitialValue, [in, out] long * Multiplier, [out, retval] long* returnValue.

   For the first parameter, [in] specifies that the parameter is passed by value. This means that if any changes are made to the parameter by the method's code, they won't be reflected in the variable the caller passed.

   The second parameter is specified with [in, out] and as a *pointer* (meaning the address of the variable on the caller's side) to a variable. This variable will have any changes bubbled back to the caller. Although scripting languages and Visual Basic will automatically convert a variable to its pointer, any Visual C++ code that uses this method will have to explicitly specify that the address of something should be used.

The final parameter uses [`out`, `retval`] and a pointer to provide the return value. Scripting code does not provide this as a direct parameter, but rather it uses the method name in an assignment, as in x = *object.method*(1, lMultiplier). The C++ code implementing the method would not use `return` *value* to set this parameter but sets it explicitly, as in *returnValue = InitialValue * Multiplier.

5. Click the OK button, and the wizard will add the appropriate code to the IDL file, the class header file, and the class's CPP file. What's placed in the CPP file is shown in Listing 19.3.

LISTING 19.3 CODE ADDED FOR A NEW METHOD

```
STDMETHODIMP CMyClass::GetValue(long InitialValue,
                long *Multiplier, long *returnValue)
{
    AFX_MANAGE_STATE(AfxGetStaticModuleState())

    // TODO: Add your implementation code here

    return S_OK;
}
```

6. All that's left is to add the code to your method.

Removing a Property or Method

Unfortunately ATL does not provide a wizard for removing a property or method. To do that you must remove the references to the property or method in three places. First, remove the implementation code from the class's CPP file. Second, remove the function definitions from the class's header file. Finally, remove the references to the property or method from the IDL file.

Remember that a property can be implemented with more than one function depending on the access allowed. If the property is writable, there will be a put_*PropertyName* and/or a putref_*PropertyName* function and IDL entries for each. If the property is readable, there will be a get_*PropertyName* function and IDL entry.

A Simple Example

You will now develop a simple example that has one property and one method. The component will be used to convert a value to a string that's formatted using the currency settings on the server (as defined by the Regional Settings Control Panel applet). The final version of all the files for this component can be found on the accompanying CD in the \Source\Chapter19\formatter folder.

This component has one property, Value, that's defined as a double. You could use the CURRENCY data type, but allow for a greater range of numbers in case the component's scope expands to include other kinds of formatting. There is one method, FormatAsCurrency. This method has no incoming parameters but will return a string (which in COM is defined using the BSTR data type). The string will be properly formatted for insertion into HTML by using the Server.HTMLEncode() method. The ProgID used for this component will be Unleashed.Formatter.

Here's how to create the component:

1. Start a new ATL COM AppWizard project. Name the project Unleashed. Don't bother with MFC support unless you plan to add to the component using MFC.

2. Use the Insert, New ATL Object menu to add a new ActiveX Server Component class.

3. On the Names tab, enter Formatter in the Short Name edit box.

4. On the Attributes tab, specify Apartment Threaded (unless you plan to store an instance of the component in a session variable, then use Both threading and check the Free-Threaded Marshaler box). Also check the Support ISupportErrorInfo box.

5. On the ASP tab, uncheck the entries for all the intrinsic objects except the Server entry. Click the OK button to add the class.

6. Expand the Workspace pane's tree one level and right-click on the IFormatter entry. Select Add Property from the shortcut menu. Use the double data type and name the property Value. Leave all else at the default, unless you want to change the helpstring attribute (which is found by clicking the Attributes button). Click OK to add the property's definition and supporting functions to the class.

7. Right-click the CFormatter entry in the Workspace pane and select the Add Member Variable menu item. On the Add Member Variable dialog, enter double as the data type and m_dblValue as the variable's name. Click OK.

8. Expand the CFormatter entry in the Workspace pane, then expand its IFormatter entry and double-click the get_Value entry. Change the code for this function and the put_Value function to match Listing 19.4.

LISTING 19.4 CODE FOR THE VALUE PROPERTY

```
STDMETHODIMP CFormatter::get_Value(double *pVal)
{
    if (pVal == NULL) return E_POINTER;

    *pVal = m_dblValue;
```

continues

19

CREATING
COMPONENTS
WITH VISUAL C++

LISTING 19.4   CONTINUED

```
    return S_OK;
}

STDMETHODIMP CFormatter::put_Value(double newVal)
{
    m_dblValue = newVal;

    return S_OK;
}
```

9. Next, add the FormatAsCurency method. Right-click the IFormatter entry and select Add Method from the shortcut menu. Enter FormatAsCurrency in the Method Name edit box. The method's only parameter is its return value, so enter [out, retval] BSTR* returnVal in the Parameters edit box empty. Click OK, and the method is added.

10. Double-click the method's entry in the Workspace tree and enter the code from Listing 19.5.

LISTING 19.5   CODE FOR THE FormatAsCurrency METHOD

```
STDMETHODIMP CFormatter::FormatAsCurrency(BSTR *returnVal)
{
    USES_CONVERSION;

    char pszTemp[MAX_PATH];
    char pszOutput[MAX_PATH] = {0};

    sprintf(pszTemp, "%f", (float)m_dblValue);

    int iRet = GetCurrencyFormat(LOCALE_SYSTEM_DEFAULT,
                        LOCALE_NOUSEROVERRIDE, pszTemp,
                        NULL, pszOutput, MAX_PATH);
    if (iRet) {

        if (m_bOnStartPageCalled) {

            CComBSTR bstrTemp(pszOutput);
            m_piServer->HTMLEncode(bstrTemp, returnVal);

        } else

            *returnVal = ::SysAllocString(A2W(pszOutput));

    } else
        *returnVal = NULL;

    return S_OK;
}
```

If you are unfamiliar with C++ or the BSTR data type, here's the basics of how the method works. The USES_CONVERSION macro sets up some code necessary to call the A2W macro. The GetCurrencyFormat API function is used to format the value. This function requires that the value be placed into a character array, which is done using pszTemp and the sprintf function. The function returns the formatted string into the pszOutput buffer. The LOCALE_SYSTEM_DEFAULT and LOCALE_NOUSEROVERRIDE parameters specify how the format will be read from the Regional settings. The function returns the number of characters placed into the buffer.

If any characters are returned, the code checks to see whether the m_bOnStartPageCalled variable is true. This is the case if the OnStartPage method was invoked (in other words, you're in an ASP environment as opposed to Visual Basic creating an instance of the component), and the pointer to the instance of the built-in Server object is valid. If it is, you can count on the fact that the m_piServer points to an instance of the ASP built-in Server object. Call its HTMLEncode method to make sure the string returned can be displayed within HTML.

If the m_bOnStartPageCalled variable is not true, you cannot use the m_piServer object. Instead, the returnVal pointer variable is set to point at the result of SysAllocString. SysAllocString takes a wchar and converts it to a BSTR, allocating the space necessary to hold the string. The A2W macro converts the char array into a wchar array, which is necessary for SysAllocString.

 Compile the project, and the component is ready to be used. With an ATL COM AppWizard project, the compiler takes care of registering the ActiveX component on your machine. Listing 19.6 shows an Active Server Page that exercises the new component. The file format.asp can be found in the \Source\Chapter19\formatter folder on the accompanying CD. Figure 19.11 shows the output from this page.

LISTING 19.6   THE ASP CODE TO EXERCISE THE NEW COMPONENT

```
<%@ Language=VBScript %>

<HTML><BODY>
The number 234567.2345 formatted with
the Formatter component looks like<br>
<%
    set xFormatter = Server.CreateObject("Unleashed.Formatter")
    xFormatter.Value = 234567.2345
    Response.Write xFormatter.FormatAsCurrency
%>
</BODY></HTML>
```

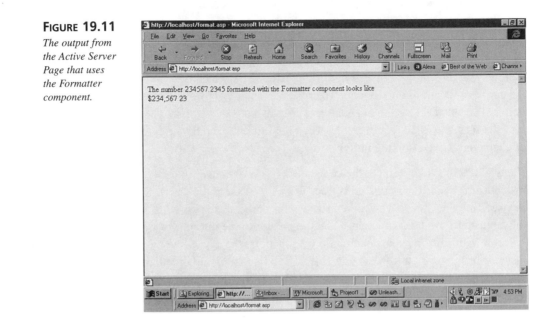

Summary

This chapter discusses the basics of creating Active Server Page components using Visual C++. Creating components with Visual C++ gives you the greatest amount of flexibility and, by far, the fastest components. However, a bit more work must be done on the programmer's part to pull it off. The various threading models are discussed, and you learned that either the apartment or both threading models are ideal for ASP components.

Next, you saw how easy it is to use ATL and its wizards to create a new component, add its properties and methods, and enter the code required to do the actual work. Finally you created a small but useful sample component to convert a number into a currency format based on the server's regional settings.

Creating Multitier Distributed Applications

PART V

IN THIS PART

Understanding Windows DNA

by Christian Gross

IN THIS CHAPTER

CHAPTER 20

Up to this point in the book, all the things shown regarding ASP have been purely mechanical. By mechanical I mean, if you set parameter X and call method Y, something will happen. There have also been some small demos on how these mechanical things can be used to make something happen.

You will now switch gears and think about how to put everything together to build an application that solves problems. This chapter explains what "the vision" is. In Microsoft terms, this means Windows DNA. The explanation of Windows DNA will not be mechanically or technically detailed. Instead, it is intended to give you the big picture. The next section goes into some technical detail about the various services within the vision. And finally, an explanation the role of ASP within the Windows DNA vision is offered.

The Windows DNA Vision

To understand any concept, you must understand its context and how it came to be. Therefore, to understand the vision of Windows DNA, you must understand how the Windows platform has evolved.

- Windows 3.x—The Windows family began in earnest with the release of Windows 3.0. What made this version of Windows popular is the rich user interface. Windows 3.x, however, brought something more important to the table. It brought a common user interface and device driver model. Before Windows, device drivers had to be custom fitted to each DOS application. This was tedious. Applications with custom drivers have custom memory requirements and custom problems. Windows changed all that and made it possible for a customer to ask for Windows device drivers. The user interface and application tasking were good as well, because they possessed the consistency to accomplish certain tasks.

- Windows NT—A problem of Windows 3.x was its lack of stability. Windows NT was a new operating system intended for the Enterprise. In a way, it was a stable Windows 3.x. It included some things, such as integrated networking and server components, that were called services. But the server service aspect was not extensive enough to enable you to write server-side applications, because it did not provide transactions, messaging, and so on.

- Windows 95/98—The Windows family kept on growing with this replacement for Windows 3.x. Windows 95 and 98 are 32-bit operating systems. However, they differ in end user clientele to Windows NT. Windows 95/98 are consumer operating systems. Here the requirement is for devices to auto-configure themselves and make it easier to manage the client machine. This is a formidable task because there are over a hundred million machines running some Windows program.

The focus of Windows 95/98 is to make it easier to navigate the Web and perform the specific tasks.

- Windows NT Option Pack—Windows NT provided the foundation for a stable and scalable operating system. It did not provide the additional Enterprise services required. The NT Windows Option Pack adds that capability. The Option Pack has services (Internet Information Server) IIS, MSMQ (Microsoft Message Queue), MTS (Microsoft Transaction Server), and so on. With the release of the Windows NT Option Pack, the Enterprise development effort was started at Microsoft. It marked the difference between the independent software developer and the Enterprise application developer who requires these services.

- Windows 2000—The release of Windows 2000 brought with it more services, and a more consistent and elegant COM called COM+. Windows 2000 is the operating system that can handle the large tasks at the large enterprises.

What Is Windows DNA?

What is the Windows DNA vision in a nutshell? Windows DNA is the realization of an operating system that exposes various services and facilities that makes it possible to build applications using a logical design process.

This definition is very vague, but yet specific. It says that to build applications you need a logical design process. Too often in the development process, there is a road block because the technology is not yet there. To solve this, the developer creates his own solution or hacks another already developed solution. These hacks or bridge solutions cause problems because they are the weak link. As the application grows in complexity, keeping these weak links working becomes more difficult and tedious.

For example, a previous project of mine involved a brand new application using the Windows platform as user interface. The old application was written using DOS and assembler. The application needed to communicate to a server and did so using a custom socket library. The new application had to work with the DOS, assembler, and socket interfaces. In this application alone, there are three communication mechanisms. Windows DNA solves this by saying the communication is a service called COM, which has one layer and is much easier to plug and play. The cornerstone of Windows DNA is COM and component building.

The Problem that Confronts Windows DNA

The problem that Windows DNA solves is the application. In every corporation there are business processes. Examples include the creation of order forms, issuing of invoices, and the displaying of profit margins. This application will need to work in a multiuser scenario on a network, and preferably on the Internet.

20

UNDERSTANDING
WINDOWS DNA

Therefore, the application will have the following attributes:

- It will interact with the user using a keyboard, screen, or mouse.
- It will potentially use other input devices such as touch screen, pen device, and voice activation.
- It will connect to other machines using networking concepts.
- When multiple machines share data, it must operate in a reliable and consistent manner.
- The application must easily manage itself and its environment.

This is a big change from the Windows API days. In those days, the concern was how to make the user interface cool. The shift in focus is because the computer is a cornerstone of our society. We cannot live without it. People now use computers in a purely utilitarian fashion to get their jobs done. These people have the ability to learn about and interact with the computer, but they do not want to be bothered with the details of installation scripts, command-line parameters, and application crashes. They want things to work.

The Solution: Windows DNA

The Windows DNA platform is a multitiered, distributed application model. (I will talk in detail about the platform in the next section.) It provides a set of services and facilities that are part of the operating system infrastructure. These services combine things like personal computers, mainframes, Internet, client-server, and so on.

Mixing all these technologies, the operating system might become bloated. However, this is not the case because it is possible for you to pick and choose only the services that you require. This is accomplished by picking the right Windows 2000 tier and installing the required services. The guiding principles of Windows DNA are as follows:

- Internet ready—Internet technology such as TCP/IP, HTTP, and FTP, are integrated into the operating system. This makes it possible for applications to assume Internet availability.
- Faster time to market—Developing vertical applications is not simple. A vertical application is very customer tuned. An example is a banking application. To make themselves more productive, banks require custom applications tuned to their environment. These solutions are only applicable in the banking industry and usually apply to only the one customer. If you are able to focus on application writing and not plumbing, you will bring your application to market faster.

- Interoperability—Cross-platform is a complicated issue. There is no easy solution. Another way to achieve almost the same thing is to interoperate. Interoperability uses open protocols and open standards to make sure a solution will work with multiple vendors.

- Less complexity—Having various installations makes things more complicated. Some things are part of the operating system. An example of this is TCP/IP. Because the future is in TCP/IP networking, it makes sense to integrate it into the operating system. This makes the entire installation and support issue less onerous because there are fewer variables to consider. It again enables you to focus on solving the business problem.

- Language tool independence—The basis of the Windows platform is to make it possible for third-party developers to choose their own development environments. They will be able to choose the language that will best solve the business process problem.

- Lowering the total cost of ownership—The last step is to make it simpler to deploy, manage, and iterate the application over time. This can be achieved by simplifying installation and version control processes.

After reading these guiding principles, you might think that Windows DNA is only for the large enterprise that has multiple operating systems and thousands of clients. The answer is that Windows DNA is for both small companies and large companies. It must be, because sometimes a small company will communicate with a large company. When that happens they must both communicate using the same binary language.

Using Internet technologies, it is possible to exchange information with millions of other people and corporate entities. In this scenario, the services must be available 24 hours a day. More than one time zone is involved. In all likelihood, the application will be accessed at all times of the day.

The Services of Windows DNA

Figure 20.1 is the Windows DNA architecture, which is used to build multitier applications. There are three tiers: presentation, business logic, and data. This is not a physical architecture. It represents an abstract concept. It is possible for multiple physical tiers to exist within one of the abstract tiers.

FIGURE 20.1

*Windows DNA
architecture.*

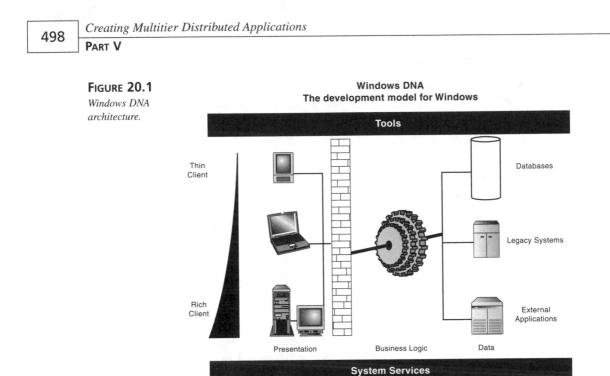

COM Everywhere

The key aspect to creating this architecture is to enable each layer to communicate with the other. This is accomplished by using COM (Component Object Model). It is a binary object model that defines a predefined method of exchanging information. When this model is pervasive, using the various services and communicating between COM objects becomes very simple.

Even though I stated that COM is binary, it is cross-platform. Consider Figure 20.2. A pointer, which is a piece of memory that contains an address where other information is stored, references a vtable. A *vtable* is a segment of memory that contains a series of other pointers. However, this time the pointers point to functions, which implement some desired functionality.

FIGURE 20.2

*COM interface
and implementa-
tion technique.*

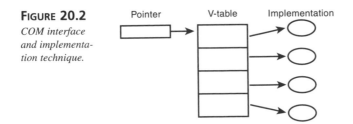

This way of designing COM objects is called separation of interface from implementation. By defining an interface, it is possible to define what the interface is supposed to do. The implementation is a realization of that intention. In the previous chapter where you built some COM objects that were called by ASP, you were doing this implicitly.

COM is cross platform because the interface is a definition that is standard across all platforms. A COM string called BSTR is the same BSTR on an Intel chip, a Sparc chip, and an Alpha chip. What is not cross-platform is the binary implementation because it has been compiled for the platform specified.

A way of achieving both cross-platform interface and implementation is to use a technology like Visual J++ because Java bytecode is cross platform. By using a Microsoft COM-compatible Java virtual machine (VM), you only write the code and compile it once.

So why COM? Besides the technical reasons, currently COM is, by far, the largest component strategy. That is why DNA is based on COM. Breaking compatibility is not a possibility. With COM it is possible to build software components that can be executed and deployed on any of the tiers. The COM runtime provides support for packaging, partitioning, and other multitier issues.

The Presentation Tier

The presentation tier is the tier where the application interacts with the human. This is a necessary tier because humans do not have the capacity to comprehend the bits and bytes on the hard disk in an efficient manner. At this tier, the data is represented in a manner that we can understand. Currently, this manner is largely keyboard, screen, and mouse oriented. But this will change in the future to provide better facilities for the handicapped—voice and gesture facilities.

In the current version of Windows DNA, the focus in the presentation tier is to promote anywhere, anyhow, anytime access. This is made possible using Internet integration such as a browser, dial-up, and networking facilities. This tier is challenging because the types of clients vary dramatically. In the Windows DNA architecture, the client is not only Windows based, but can include UNIX, Macs, and other operating systems.

To be able to support the various platforms, the presentation tier is graded from a rich client to a thin client. Please do not think a thin client means fewer bytes to download because a thin client can include an image that could be several hundred megabytes. The varying parameter is the amount of functionality that can be executed on the client side.

What is Figure 20.3 telling us? It is the abstraction of how to build the presentation tier. On the right side, represented by a series of cogs, are the various technologies. Using the technology, we can build two types of clients (EXE based and page based) Those types of clients can be further subdivided into the four types of clients. These four types vary from a thin client to a rich client.

FIGURE 20.3
Presentation tier details.

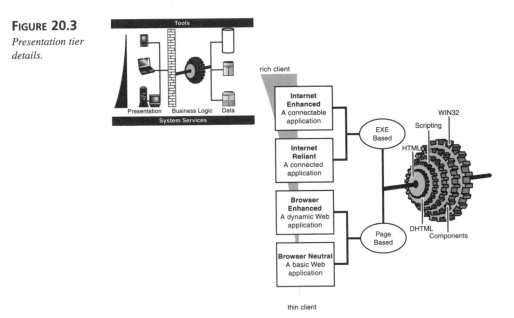

Page-Based Solutions

The thin client is a type of page-based client. This means that the client is connected to the network and downloads the content as it is required. It does not download the entire application, only pages of it.

Specifically, a thin client is thin because it presents a static information set to the presentation tier. You can then fill out a few text boxes, set some check boxes, and submit it for processing. This type of functionality is similar to batch form processing from the mainframe days. The only difference is that the terminal can be anywhere on the Internet. Typically, this type of client is a Web browser. A static Web browser approach will ensure that your application has the broadest support. This type of application is called a *browser-neutral* application. In this solution, the runtime environment is determined by the client. Typical applications include the Web.

If more functionality is required, a dynamic Web application is needed. In this situation, a more advanced set of the Web user interface is used. This makes the application more interactive. However, the cost of this interaction is that fewer Web browsers can decipher the content. For example, it is possible to develop content that will function only on Internet Explorer or Netscape Navigator. The advantage of this extra functionality is a more versatile application. Typical applications would be a Web browser-based intranet or extranet application. Usually in this situation, it is possible to know which browser is used. This will solve the problem best with the benefit of Internet technologies.

EXE-Based Solutions

The next two types of solutions are those that require quite a bit of functionality on the client side. These applications are executable based. This means that some application is installed on the client machine, and it resides on that machine.

An Internet-reliant application uses a mixture of the underlying operating system and the network for content. These applications require the functionality of the operating system because of the complex tasks that are being processed. In this situation, the browser, which might be embedded, does not provide the richness. However, like the browser-based solution, it must be connected to the Internet for its content. An example of this application is a data warehousing application. When sifting through a data warehouse, you typically generate complex pivot tables. These tables can be graphed and compared. From that information, you make some kind of decision. Because of the graphing and complex processing, the operating system graphic subsystem is required. You must be connected to the network because you cannot download the data warehouse onto your desktop. It will not fit because the processing power required is immense.

The last type of rich client is one that can only use the client machine and will never know of the existence of the Internet. The application may be a single-user application that lives in its own world. However, these types of applications are becoming fewer and fewer because most clients want to exchange information. Client applications include Microsoft Word or Microsoft Excel. These applications do not explicitly require the Internet, but can be used for collaboration purposes.

This type of client is also breeding the new hybrid-client application. The hybrid-client application uses the Internet when it needs to, but does so invisibly. The user does not notice the difference. An example is Microsoft Money. This application is installed on the client machine and can, for the most part, live in isolation. But when you want to retrieve your statements from the bank, you must go online. An embedded browser starts up and connects to your bank. From there, it downloads your statements and displays them. During this entire process the user never types in a URL or gives any network commands except when connecting to the Internet. So in other words, the hybrid client made seamless use of the Internet.

20

UNDERSTANDING
WINDOWS DNA

The Various Technologies

In order for you to recognize the various client types, I will outline the core technologies:

- HTML— Hypertext Mark-Up Language, the user interface language of the Web. When only the term HTML is mentioned, typically, it is version 3.2 or more recently version 4.0. Both of these versions are a plain vanilla variety that support forms-based processing. This technology has the broadest reach among all technologies. This technology is typically used in the thin client.

- DHTML— Dynamic HTML is the more advanced Web-browser user interface. Dynamic HTML differs from HTML in that it supports a full-fledged object model. Every part of the user interface can be dynamically addressed, removed, or added. This makes the user interface incredibly powerful. However, fewer browsers support this feature.

- Scripting—Within the DHTML object model, a scripting interface is defined. So it would seem questionable to consider scripting a technology. It is, however, because with scripting it is possible to control any type of client. For example, Microsoft Excel can be scripted to perform certain tasks. Scripting applies to all clients. The major benefit of scripting is that it provides application customizability without requiring complex programming skills.

- Components—DHTML, scripting, and most other things on the client would not be possible without components.

- Win32—The Win32 API is a way of interacting with the operating system. This technology is appropriate for those clients that need special graphics or high performance. The Win32 API is specific to Windows. It is not a similar programming model to HTML or Dynamic HTML.

The Firewall Tier

This tier is not really a tier, but it is a significant security device that must be mentioned. Between the presentation tier and the business logic tier, the firewall tier is erected. A firewall is a security wall that ensures the data on the inside of the firewall is not compromised.

In general architecture, a firewall is only a service within the overall framework. Windows DNA is different than most operating systems, however, in that it moves the security to the business logic tier.

There are several advantages to doing this. The first is that there is a consistent security verification mechanism. Consider the example of a castle. Using current security mechanisms, a rider could ride into the castle as Anonymous. Then depending on the service, a security verification might be required. The problem is that as the rider moves through the castle, he has to keep verifying himself. In addition, consider what happens if a service is not secure. Then a rider could become evil and cause destruction. With each service asking for identification, it is not easily possible to maintain a consistent security policy. When the rider is kicked out of one pub, he should be kicked out of all pubs in the castle. With some security mechanisms, this does not happen.

When you make the firewall a central security authority, anyone accessing any service will be known. He or she will be assigned a specific set of rights and privileges. If those rights are abused, they can be revoked in an easy and consistent manner. In the end, Windows DNA creates a faster and simpler security framework.

The Business Logic Tier

The business logic tier is the heartbeat of your application. It processes and manipulates the data. The business process rules and workflow procedures handle this. This tier is an important tier because most of your time will be spent programming and designing it. On this tier, things that you will be interested in are high-volume processing, transaction support, large-scale deployment, messaging, and possibly the Web. Just looking at the last sentence you will notice that the middle tier is very complex.

The business logic tier has three major services, COM+, MSMQ, and IIS. Of course, there are other services like Microsoft Exchange and Microsoft SQL Server, but they are not part of the Windows 2000 distribution, as shown by Figure 20.4.

Each service performs a specific task. COM+ is responsible for the basic COM and transaction functionality. IIS (Internet Information Server) is responsible for Internet services such as SMTP (Simple Mail Transfer Protocol), FTP (File Transfer Protocol), and HTTP (Hyper-Text Transfer Protocol). MSMQ (Microsoft Message Queue) is responsible for messaging. Each of the services may use other services to create new services. An example would be queued components. They use both COM+ and MSMQ to create a new service.

COM+

The next generation of COM is COM+. It extends COM by adding services that make COM usable for the Enterprise. Am I saying that COM is not usable for the Enterprise? Not at all; COM only provides the framework for components. To be able to make COM components have transaction capabilities additional services are required. This is the purpose of COM+.

Figure 20.4

Architecture of the business logic tier.

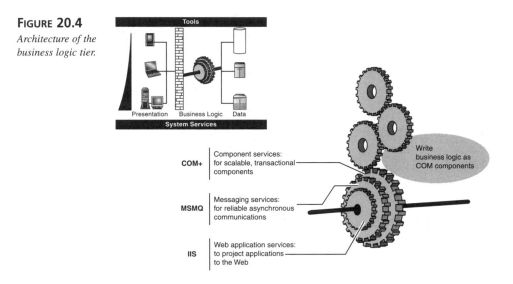

Tracing back the history of COM+ and transaction services, they first came to life in SQL Server. SQL Server 6.5 distributed a service called the DTC (Distributed Transaction Coordinator). This service was responsible for SQL Server transaction management. Then the DTC was re-released with a simpler wrapper called MTS (Microsoft Transaction Server). MTS made it possible to write COM objects that performed business processes and could control a transaction. COM+ takes the transaction aspect and incorporates it into the COM runtime and operating system. MTS could be embedded into the operating system formerly, however an MTS object could bypass MTS. The loopholes are now closed in COM+, and it becomes more consistent and elegant. From a programming point of view, COM+ means that all server-side COM objects can take advantage of transactions to make their applications more reliable.

TIP Integration

COM+ uses OLE transactions to manage the transaction processing environment. But this is specific only to the Windows 2000 platform. Using TIP (Transaction Internet Protocol), it is possible for COM objects to participate in other transaction processing (TP) environments. These transactions can be managed by the TP system. This is different from the previous version in MTS. In that version, the transaction had to be managed by MTS and the DTC.

Enhanced Security

When I discussed the firewall tier, I explained that Windows 2000 enhanced the security model. Quite a bit of that work is part of the COM+ environment. In COM+, security is based in either role-based security or process access permissions. Role-based security is a mechanism in which the user is part of a large group that has a role. Roles can be managers, employees, and so on. Roles make it simpler to manage users that have different security privileges depending on their domain. An example is an accounting person who has high access to the accounting processes but low access to the manufacturing processes. An extension of role-based security in COM+ is the capability to apply security at the method level for the COM objects.

Centralized Administration

In the previous edition of Windows NT, COM components were managed using the MTS Explorer. To manage any DCOM settings, DCOMCNFG was used. In Windows 2000, both of these tools are replaced with the Component Services Explorer. It combines and extends the administration of COM+ objects. Tasks include deployment, management, and monitoring of the COM+ application.

In-Memory Database (IMDB)

One service that is new in Windows 2000 is IMDB. IMDB is an in-memory database that keeps tables in RAM memory. Many applications today require high performance. In those applications much of the data is read-mostly. Examples include the retrieval of a product catalog. This table changes, but very slowly. Most of the time it is read, and it can be cached. This is where IMDB serves its purpose. With it, you can cache the product catalog table, which is now a high-speed access table.

IMDB is not a general service. It serves a specific purpose and functionality that has been determined by the programmer.

Queued Components

DCOM (Distributed COM) is used so that a COM object can be called between two different machines. DCOM is a synchronous protocol. When a call originates from one machine, the receiver must be available. If that receiver is not available, the call will fail, and any operation will also fail. If that operation is executing within the context of a transaction, the transaction will fail also. You must then implement a fail and retry mechanism.

In Windows 2000, an easier solution is to use queued components. Queued components make it possible to call another component on another machine asynchronously. Queued components use MSMQ as the underlying messaging architecture. Therefore, if the connection or call fails, it can retry until it does succeed.

Event Services

In Windows NT 4.x, it is not possible to connect events to components easily . There is a technology called COM connection points, but it is very limiting. What is required is a technology that permits loosely coupled events, where the event receiver can be active or not active.

20

UNDERSTANDING
WINDOWS DNA

This event mechanism is called COM+ events. Using COM+ events, it is possible to make unicast or multicast calls. The receiver of the event connects to the client using a subscription technique.

The publish and subscribe mechanism is one in which the publisher informs the COM+ event services that it has information it wants to distribute. A receiver that is interested in this information indicates its interest to the COM+ event service using a subscription. When the publisher has any information that is changing, COM+ event services will then propagate the changes to the various subscribers.

Dynamic Load Balancing

With the release of Windows 2000, it is possible to dynamically load balance a COM+ object. Dynamic load balancing is the technique of evenly distributing the processing load over a set of machines. Load balancing is a server-oriented process and occurs transparently with respect to the client making the server call.

Internet Services

Various Internet services are provided by the Internet Information Server (IIS). These include

- HTTP—This is the protocol of the Web and serves up Web pages or any content that the Web browser requests.

- FTP—This is the protocol used on the Internet to transfer files. It is specifically geared toward file transfer and is, therefore, more efficient.

- SMTP—This is the protocol used to transfer mail messages from one machine to another. It can be used in conjunction to POP.

What makes IIS special with respect to other Internet servers is its integration with transactions. When a request is made to the IIS, it is a transaction request. By using transactions as a basis for handling requests, all the benefits of COM+ can be realized. This also makes COM+ more flexible when it needs to be dynamically load-balanced or optimized.

To build content for the IIS, it is possible to use ISAPI (Internet Server API) or typically ASP (Active Server Pages). ASP technology is a scripting environment in which logic is executed from scripts. The script language is neutral and totally dynamic. It is used in conjunction with the COM+ object to provide a full-featured business application. ASP can be used to generate DHTML or XML. Although not part of Windows 2000, the process of creating ASP, DHTML, and XML applications can be handled using Visual InterDev.

Messaging Services

Asynchronous messages are handled using Microsoft Message Queue Server (MSMQ). Messaging is a totally different way to write code. It assumes that the connection between the client and server does not exist. It assumes that eventually the operations will be carried out. The eventuality model makes it possible to write applications that function over unreliable networks or in unreliable conditions.

MSMQ is an event-driven architecture. The data is pushed to the server, and the server must react to the event being called. Event driven is nothing new because Windows itself is event driven.

Interoperating with Existing Systems, Applications, and Data

Making Windows 2000 Internet ready was one task. But another very big task is to make it ready to integrate legacy systems. Legacy systems are legacy because they still do the task well enough. Therefore, replacing these systems is not an option. Instead, these system must be integrated into the overall architecture.

Windows 200 provides the capability to integrate various legacy technologies in the following ways:

- MSMQ integration—Messaging integration is provided for MSMQ using various products. To connect from the Windows platform to the MQSeries product, SNA Server can be used. To connect from other platforms (UNIX, MVS, OS/2, and so on) to MSMQ, FalconMQ client from Level8 can be used.

- COM Transaction Integrator—Using this interface, it is possible to extend CICS and IMS transactions as a series of COM objects. In the COM Transaction Integrator, a series of development tools and some business logic wrap the IBM mainframe transaction. The communication to the IBM transaction is handled by Windows SNA server.

- Universal Data Access—This layer has not yet been discussed, but it is the database access layer. By using native drivers, it is possible to connect to resources that reside on the other platform side.

- DCOM on UNIX/Mainframe—This is a technology that makes it possible to write COM objects on platforms other than Windows. Software AG provided the first port to Solaris. That has been extended to include the mainframe platform and currently extends to a full architecture called EntireX iNTegrator.

- TIP/XA-Transaction Integration—There exists several transaction protocol standards. TIP has already been discussed. Another standard is the XA-Protocol. The integration provided is through a resource dispense/manager.

Some Final Words

The business logic tier is a very important tier. It contains by far the largest number of COM objects that provide specific services. This flexibility is required to build world-class Enterprise applications that can receive, process, and send back data from the data tier.

The Data Tier

The last tier is the data tier. It is the resource management tier. In contrast to the business logic tier, there is no processing of data. Instead, the task of managing the huge amount of data is defined. Databases and resources are getting bigger every day, and this task is becoming more and more difficult.

The UDA (Universal Data Format) strategy is a bit different from other vendors. UDA stores and manipulates data. Some data is in a spreadsheet, some in a word processing document, and more yet in a relational database. One way is to create a storage repository that can handle all these data types. In current-day practices, this data is stored through a blob.

But a blob only manages the data as a binary image. It does not ensure relations. For example, if the blob being stored references another document, an invalid reference would not be caught. At the data tier level, this invalid reference means nothing. At the business logic tier, however, it means quite a bit. It could cause a transaction or multiple transactions to be aborted.

A solution is to ensure that the business logic tier writes a correct blob. But this adds extra programming steps that should be part of the data resource. Reference management is a data operation. To add the reference management, an external module to the data repository must be added. This is not optimal.

A better solution would be to say that each resource handles its own data format. But the resource must adhere to a common object model. This makes it possible to manipulate, copy, and reference data in a format neutral manner.

The UDA object model is called OLE DB object model (see Figure 20.5). It is a low-level format that includes the specification of how transactions and rowsets are defined. The OLE DB object is very high speed and low level. This means writing to OLE DB requires quite a bit of legwork. Although it is not part of the Windows 2000 distribution, Visual C++ has a thin template layer on top called OLE DB Consumer Templates. It simplifies OLE DB without making it slower or less efficient.

FIGURE 20.5
Universal data access (UDA).

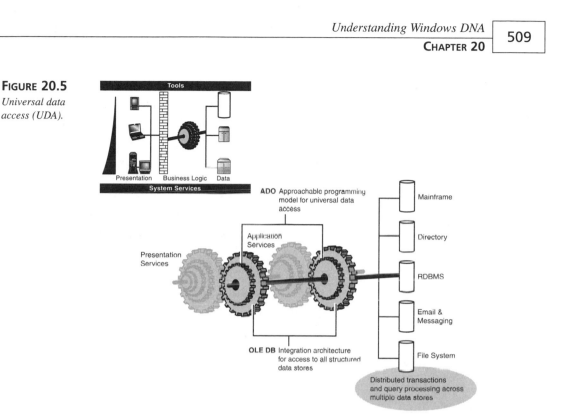

The advantage of the OLE DB object model is that it is not limited. A specific subset must be implemented. Nothing stops a vendor from extending that object model to provide tuned access to their data. This again is like the presentation tier where broad reach must be traded for rich functionality.

Because of the low-level nature of OLE DB, Visual Basic or scripters cannot use it directly. A simplicity model call ADO (Active Data Objects) has been created. This object model is a very small but powerful object that allows access to most of the features of OLE DB. One question that must be answered is how does OLE DB expose a blob? The answer is as other COM objects, but that depends on the implementation of the OLE DB provider. This is why ADO does not need to be big to handle all the various data formats. It is the responsibility of the provider to generate the COM objects.

How ASP Fits into the Vision

The question is how you, as an ASP programmer, will fit into the Windows DNA vision. ASP is a scripting environment that executes on the server side. Therefore, a part of the answer is that your program will reside on the business logic tier. But that is not the only tier, because ASP generates GUI code. This means ASP is indirectly responsible for the

presentation tier. Typically, ASP will generate HTML code. In the case of the thin client, ASP is the presentation tier. But with the DHTML or hybrid client, it generates user interface code that will create some execution logic on the presentation tier. In that case, the processing load is distributed between the presentation and business logic tier. In all these situations, it is assumed that the client is Internet reliant.

Building Web Applications

The process just defined is called *Web application building*. Web applications are different from HTML Web sites in that they perform business logic. This is an important distinction because informational Web sites may use some ASP but produce more information. Examples include the searching of an online catalog. ASP might be used to do the searching, but the client is interested in information.

In Web applications, there is a business process to solve. The business process might be the registration of the client to a conference. It might include the processing of a mortgage online. A Web application typically has multiple steps, and it processes and alters data. This is in contrast to an information Web site where the data is mostly read-only.

In a Web application, there is no reliance on the client. The server does not care where the client is calling from. The server sends all the required HTML content to the client at demand time. The only requirement is that the client has a runtime to process the content sent to it. Typically, the runtime will be an HTML browser.

Your application assumes all the critical steps occur on the server. All the state is kept on the server. In the case of the thin client, the client must always be connected to the network for the duration of the task. However, this architecture has the advantage that, when a new version of the application becomes available, only the server needs updating.

The Web application architecture is outlined in Figure 20.6. The IIS is responsible for catching the HTTP request from a particular client. This request is converted from HTTP to ASP. The ASP request is a script, which has access to the COM environment. In Part II of this book, "Active Server Pages Installable Components," the installable COM objects of ASP were discussed. Part IV, "Active Server Pages Custom Components," showed how to create custom COM objects. In either case, the script has access to service type functionality. A service is different because it does one thing well. In Part II, the example given is the SMTP component. Using it, it is possible for ASP to send feedback information about something that the client has done.

FIGURE 20.6
*Web application
architecture.*

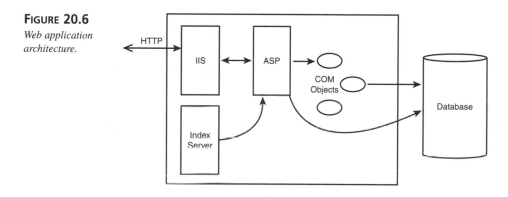

Indexing and Information Retrieval

Although it was possible before, with ASP 2.0 and future release of Index Server, it is now easier to index Web application information. This is important because the end user might want to query a Web site for a specific application. The capabilities and interaction of ASP with Index Server are discussed in Chapter 15, "Working with Index Server and Full-Text Search."

Transaction Services

Now let's broaden the scope and correlate what services Web applications require. I stated that a Windows DNA application solves business processes. Business processes must be fast, reliable, and scalable. The components that have been discussed thus far do not solve any of these problems.

COM+ solves this by making the ASP page part of a transaction. After the ASP page is part of a transaction, it optimizes the business operation. Examples include load balancing for performance and aborting of a transaction for reliability and consistency.

Why is this needed? Consider the example of a Web application accessing two databases on two different machines. The business process is the transferring of money from one account to another. In the first database, the account is debited by an amount X. In the other database, the account is credited by an amount X.

In a real world, one of those operations might fail, and if it does fail, the other must also. Otherwise the balance sheets will be incorrect, and money will either have been created or lost. Thus far, with your ASP database knowledge you would see whether either transaction has failed, and then undo the other transaction. This can be tedious because you must confirm whether the undo has executed successfully.

Using transactions, this undo and consistency check is accomplished automatically. COM+ accomplishes this by making your ASP page and any COM object accessed part of a transaction. If any script or COM object aborts the transaction, all the databases involved will abort as well. It makes it easier to clean up the state.

Messaging Services

The second major service that you require to build Windows DNA type applications is messaging. The ASP Web application is a synchronous process. You make a request to a Web page, and you wait until ASP has finished processing the page. If this process takes a long time, the browser will be waiting for a long time. This is not desirable because the browser may time-out stating that the request could not be fulfilled.

In Figure 20.7 an example messaging flow would be as follows:

1. An HTTP request is received by the IIS server. This starts an ASP script and some processing. During this process, other scripts or COM services/components might be called. All this may be executing within the context of a COM+ transaction.

FIGURE 20.7
Messaging architecture.

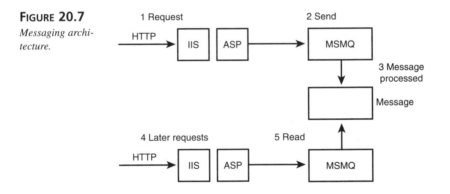

2. At some point in the ASP script, the MSMQ component is called and a message is created. The message is not processed; it is only created and submitted to the MSMQ service. The ASP script continues processing and sends a message back to the client that the message has been sent. At this point, the client and the MSMQ service follow different execution paths. They do not depend on each for information or specific states.

3. The MSMQ service sends the message to the destination. At this point MSMQ has fulfilled its role. Some listening process at the destination processes the message. Most likely the destination process sends a process result message back to MSMQ. MSMQ again does its role and sends the message from the destination back to the place of origination.

4. At some later point in time, the client again issues a request to the IIS server. This request again starts an ASP process.

5. Now instead of generating a message, a processed message is searched for and the contents of it are returned to the client.

When running MSMQ applications, notice that the client must start the request. There is no callback possibility on behalf of the IIS. This process is like polling, but it has the advantage that the process can be started and other tasks can be accomplished in between the various polls. An example of using messaging is the acceptance of a mortgage application. Mortgages typically are not accepted within seconds. The piece of property must be inspected, insurance details must be filled out, and other things must be done before the application can be accepted.

Summary

Windows DNA is an architecture for building business applications. You focus on the business aspect and leave all the system code to the operating system and the underlying database. With Windows DNA, it is also possible to architect a system because the various services are already available. Your role as an ASP programmer is to write scripting code that accesses COM components that execute within transactions. You may write a few COM components, but the focus is on the ASP scripting. For asynchronous processing, you will also use MSMQ to perform batch operations.

In the following chapters you will take the knowledge learned thus far and apply it to building Web applications. Those chapters will focus on how to use transactions and messaging services.

Using ASP with Microsoft Transaction Server

by Steven Banick

IN THIS CHAPTER

Most Web sites are at the mercy of their environment. How many times have you visited a Web site that was not functioning because of a downed database? A programmer's error? Extreme lag? An overburdened server? Today's more complex Web applications often rely on interaction with several different systems to complete an action. Often, if one system is unavailable, the action does not properly complete. You're left with either a partially complete action or a dead Web site. In this chapter, we will discuss Microsoft Transaction Server (MTS) and how it can help you avoid dead-Web site syndrome by examining scalability, fault tolerance, and reliability.

An Introduction to Microsoft Transaction Server

In Chapter 20, "Understanding Windows DNA," you explored the methodology and approach behind the Windows Distributed interNetwork Application architecture. A large piece of the DNA puzzle arrives in the form of Microsoft Transaction Server (MTS). MTS, by name alone, is something of an enigma. If you were to base your understanding of MTS purely on its name, you might deduce that it has something to do with transactions and transactional processing, and leave it at that. Unfortunately, the poorly selected name belies the power and rich feature set that lurk in the belly of the beast.

Through this chapter, you will discover that maybe MTS should have had another name, perhaps Microsoft Component Server or Microsoft Component Manager. Although transactions are a large part of MTS functionality, what MTS provides to a developer is a powerful architectural foundation to manage scalable applications. What exactly does this mean? Let's explore MTS in detail to make this clear.

The Role of MTS

Traditionally, when you are working with distributed applications (Web applications specifically), you are relying on a series of empowered Web pages (ASP pages presumably) and custom-developed logic components. To utilize these components, your Web pages must call upon these components on an as-needed basis. Your components, in turn, must manage themselves and ensure that performance is not impeded through repetitious callings.

Microsoft Transaction Server provides you, as a developer, with a series of features that take over a large part of the drudgery and overhead involved in maintaining distributed applications. Specifically, MTS manages how your application communicates and interacts with components. In Part IV of this book, "Active Server Pages Custom Components," you learned about the Component Object Model (COM) and how to use COM components in your Web application.

Pooling Component Instances and Just-in-Time Activation

When you are working with a Web application, use of components entails a predictable series of steps:

1. The ASP page creates a new instance of the component as an object through instantiation. For example, calling `Set <variable> = Server.CreateObject("<Component">)`.

2. The object/component instance is initialized for the first use.

3. The ASP page calls upon the functionality of the component through the script within the file.

4. After the ASP page is finished using the component, the object instance is destroyed and cleared from memory. This is achieved through either a specific instruction (for example, `Set <variable> = Nothing`), or through expiration of the variable after the completion of processing.

This approach, however, is fraught with pitfalls and problems. The key problem with this approach is its impact on the performance of your Web application. Consider that each time a Web application creates an instance of a component for a user, that component is dedicated to that single user. Also, consider that the instance has a very short life span (typically, one page). This involves a lot of overhead in terms of memory and processing time for each user who is interacting with your Web application. For example, if a single ASP page in your application calls upon a component just once, this means that for every single simultaneous user of your application, the component will be created in memory, used, and then destroyed. Is that efficient?

Matters can be complicated further when you introduce distributed computing. For example, what if your component provides back-end functionality such as a database connection? For each instance of your component, an open connection with your database will be established. If you have 30 simultaneous users accessing your application, that could involve 30 different database connections. So now, not only do you have the overhead involved in creating and disposing of an application, but also the overhead of creating sessions with a database. This impacts not only performance, but also cost—consider the licensing requirements for having many sessions open at the same time. Although this can be partially remedied through thorough design, planning, and reliance on the connection pooling provided by the operating system and database servers, the problem remains.

Pooling Instances

What is the solution here? If you guessed pooling instances of components, you discovered the hidden secret of MTS. Microsoft Transaction Server works around these problems by establishing a persistent context for your components. This context provides your application with a pool of instances for your components. These instances may be shared among users and even applications, minimizing the need to create a single instance of a component for each user. This concept is illustrated in Figure 21.1.

FIGURE 21.1

Applications refer to a context object, which in turn references instances within MTS.

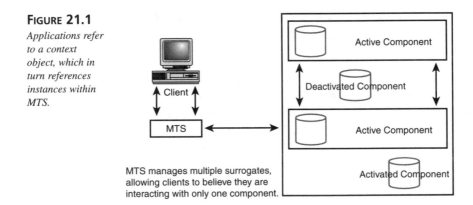

MTS manages multiple surrogates, allowing clients to believe they are interacting with only one component.

After an application is finished using a component, it can release its object context, which in turn can free the component instance within MTS. MTS manages several instances at a time, and cannot, in fact, remove the instance within MTS right away because another user or application might be referencing it. The key principle to understand here is that your application does not directly reference the component instance—instead, it references the context for the object within MTS. MTS itself determines what instance of the component is available for use or if a new instance must be created to meet the demands of the object context.

Understanding State and Context

Components under the management of MTS benefit from other features that otherwise would require complex programming. One important feature of MTS is state. State and behavior are closely related. A component's behavior should be consistent throughout its lifetime (from activation through to deactivation). You can look at behavior as the underlying code or actions behind the component. The volatility in components comes out of *state*. State refers to the data or non-permanent nature of a component. State can present distinct problems when you are working with components under the guidance of MTS.

Because your application might not always be working with the same instance of a component every time the object context is called upon, the same state information might not be available, or worse—different state data may be there. This concept is shown in Figure 21.2.

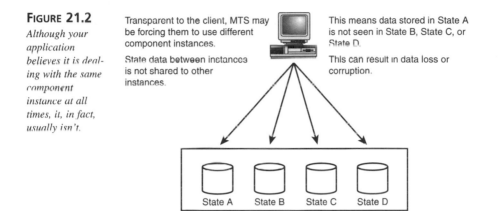

FIGURE 21.2
Although your application believes it is dealing with the same component instance at all times, it, in fact, usually isn't.

Transparent to the client, MTS may be forcing them to use different component instances.

State data between instances is not shared to other instances.

This means data stored in State A is not seen in State B, State C, or State D.

This can result in data loss or corruption.

State A   State B   State C   State D

Ideally, your components are stateless, enabling MTS to destroy and re-create components as the need arises. As ideal as that might be, there often is the need to create components that retain data between calls and interactions with your application. That's where MTS and state come into play. MTS provides developers with four repositories for state data that can be managed in a controlled fashion. These four methods are

- Client state storage—All state information is stored in the client application, enabling the component to act much like a stateless object. Each interaction with the component involves the exchange of state information between MTS and the client application.

- Object state storage—When you follow the traditional path of storing data inside a component, you are working with object state storage in MTS. This should be used with caution, however, because it impedes MTS from managing your components (just-in-time activation and deactivation). When MTS does deactivate the component, all state information that the object held is lost. This is equivalent to setting the object variable to nothing to remove its reference. These components also do not scale well, so they should be avoided if possible.

- Database state storage—Realistically, most systems rely on a database for permanent data storage and some sense of durability for information. Components that use database state storage rely on OLE DB or ODBC linkage to a datasource to store component state information, enabling it to retrieve and store data as needed.

This path is ideal when you are not burdening your component with temporary data in order not to increase the load on your database and slow access.

- Shared property manager—The final method for storing state information, the shared property manager acts as a central resource or dispenser that can be used to share and store data for components. Using a hierarchical approach to property storage, the property manager avoids conflicts between components and data.

Caching and JIT Activation

You just read about object context, instances, and state. The next important piece to the MTS puzzle is caching. As mentioned, MTS maintains a "pool" of component instances that are accessed by object contexts within your applications. The current release of MTS has rudimentary support for caching of components, and future versions will fully support the caching of components within MTS for quick reactivation. In the current MTS (2.0), components will be cached as long as an application is using them. In fact, components are held in cache for approximately three minutes after the application references end. When a component is cached, new instances of the component can be quickly created through just-in-time (JIT) activation. JIT allows MTS (and your applications) to improve performance for new instances of a component, as opposed to starting fresh each time. JIT activation is shown in Figure 21.3.

FIGURE 21.3

Just-in-time activation enables you to "resurrect" deactivated components very quickly.

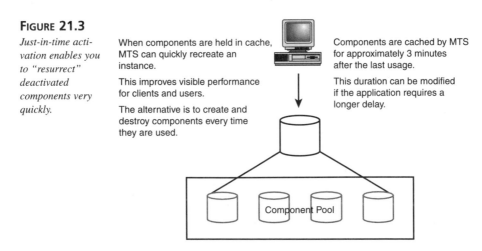

When components are held in cache, MTS can quickly recreate an instance.

This improves visible performance for clients and users.

The alternative is to create and destroy components every time they are used.

Components are cached by MTS for approximately 3 minutes after the last usage.

This duration can be modified if the application requires a longer delay.

Component Pool

Process Isolation

Another benefit of adding persistent context for components is process isolation. Microsoft prides itself on the principle that Windows NT is a robust operating system that isolates programs from one another to improve stability. At the lowest level, this is achieved through process isolation, allowing programs to say, "This is my island; stay away." Component context provides your Web applications with the same staying power by limiting one component instance from another. See Figure 21.4 to see an illustration of process isolation within MTS.

FIGURE 21.4

Process isolation adds a level of reliability and stability to your applications.

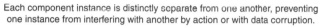
Each component instance is distinctly separate from one another, preventing one instance from interfering with another by action or with data corruption.

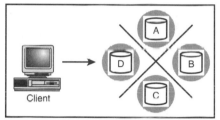

Understanding Transactions

We live in a world of transactions. Everything you do has a beginning state and an end state, signifying the start and finish of any action that you carry out. Unfortunately, all too often, developers don't keep that beginning-middle-end workflow in mind when they develop Web applications. In a perfect world, every action started would finish in its entirety. However, as any Web developer knows, we do not live (or work) in a perfect world.

Microsoft Transaction Server (MTS) was developed to bring transactional control to the Windows platform. Transactional control is nothing new to the computing industry. Transaction servers such as CICS and Tuxedo have been available on other platforms for more years than anyone cares to count. The trick comes down to understanding what a transactional server does. The role of a transactional server is to encapsulate individual actions into a larger operation, with clearly defined "go/no go" milestones. Look at it another way in the following example.

When you go to a bank to transfer money from your savings account to your checking account, you are carrying out a transaction (literally). This transaction is, in fact, several different actions, grouped together into one unit, the actual transaction. Follow the steps behind this transaction:

1. You request the transfer by indicating the source account (your savings account) and the destination account (your checking account). You also indicate the amount to be transferred between the two accounts.

2. The bank first checks the balance in your savings account to ensure that you do indeed have sufficient funds to carry out the transfer.

3. Upon confirmation that your savings account has sufficient funds, the bank confirms that your checking account exists for the transfer.

4. Verifying that the destination account exists, the bank transfers the requested amount of money from your savings account to your checking account.

5. The bank then checks the balance in the checking account to confirm that the money has indeed been transferred from your savings account.

6. After the confirmation is given, the bank debits your savings account the transferred moneys, lowering the balance in your source account.

7. The transaction is complete, and a confirmation is given to you in the form of a receipt.

In breaking the money transfer into seven steps, the transaction has seven unique milestones, or "go/no go" states. If any of these seven milestones returns an error (such as insufficient money to carry out the transfer in step 2), the transaction is aborted and no money is transferred. If there were a problem with the actual money transfer in step 4, step 5 would indicate that the transfer was not successful, so no money should be removed from your source (savings) bank account.

In this context, a transaction provides security of data, ensuring that all the proper steps in the overall process have been completed successfully before the operation can be deemed a success. If for any reason the process has failed, no changes are committed, and the action is aborted.

Understanding ACID

For a transaction to be considered a success, you rely on a commonly agreed-upon baseline that establishes a completed series of actions. Typically, this means that each action that is part of the transaction is completed successfully (although this might not always be the case). In the world of transactional processing, the acronym *ACID* is applied to successful transactions. ACID (Atomic, Consistent, Isolated, Durable) means

- Atomic—To be considered an atomic transaction, the transaction must have each action complete successfully, or the transaction is not considered complete.

- Consistent—A consistent transaction ensures that all data it manages will not disrupt the overall integrity of the environment (such as a database).

- Isolated—Isolated transactions imply that the results of executing all the actions that comprise the transaction will give the same result as executing each of the actions one at a time, one after another.

- Durable—Durable transactions are transactions that have their results stored to a durable device (such as a hard disk drive or a database) before the transaction is considered a success.

When you look to apply the ACID rules to your transactions, you should always keep in mind that these guiding principles are there to ensure the integrity of your application. If you do not subscribe to these principles, you face the risk of unsuccessful transactions damaging the integrity of your application or operating environment.

Commit and Abort

Transactions can have one of two outcomes: success or failure. In transactional processing terms, a success is referred to as a *commit*. This implies that the sum of the actions within your transaction will be committed to the operating environment, such as a database. On the other hand, a transaction failure is called an *abort*. This implies that all the actions that were carried out by your transaction are discarded, and the operating environment is rolled back or left unscathed by the actions of the failed transaction. MTS uses these two events (commit and abort) to determine the course of action after a transaction is completed.

The commit and abort events are called upon using the `SetComplete` methods for a commit, or the `SetAbort` method for an abort. Programmatically, you may also prevent MTS and the DTC from allowing a transaction to commit or abort. This might be required when your application is manipulating data or carrying out its own actions. The `DisableCommit` method prevents MTS, DTC, and RMs from committing a transaction until the `EnableCommit` method is called.

Distributed Transactions

An important concept to recognize is that MTS is not limited to managing transactions on your local server. MTS fully supports transactions that span multiple systems, even networks, provided the transport methods are present (such as Microsoft Message Queuing Services, discussed in the next chapter). Typically your transactions will interact with an external server, such as a database running Microsoft SQL Server or Oracle. To manage distributed transactions, MTS relies on a separate service called the distributed transaction coordinator (DTC). DTC is installed as part of Microsoft SQL Server and MTS.

DTC (as its name implies) coordinates transactions between systems through resource managers (RM). Database systems, such as Microsoft SQL Server, implement an RM that works with DTC to manage transactions. The process is fairly simple on a high level:

1. Your application (the client) communicates with its context object within MTS, and instantiates a transaction.

2. The context object communicates with your component and begins the process of a transaction.

3. MTS then calls upon the DTC to span the transaction to another system, such as a database server.

4. DTC communicates with the RM for the external system (the database) regarding the transaction.

5. After MTS determines that the transaction was successful, it communicates a commit event to the DTC and the RM. Alternatively, if the transaction was a failure, an abort event is communicated to the DTC and the RM.

6. Dependent on the event that was communicated to the RM, it either carries out the changes required (on a commit), or cancels the actions and rolls back to a state before the transaction began (an abort).

Using DTC, MTS can span across multiple systems as long as the external services offer a DTC-compatible RM.

COM+ and the Future of MTS

Just as COM has evolved over several years from its humble beginnings in OLE, it continues to evolve into an increasingly powerful platform: COM+. Microsoft bills COM+ as the next evolutionary step for the Component Object Model, including integration and enhancement with the MTS foundation. COM+ is a core feature of Windows 2000 and acts as the foundation for most of the new operating system's advanced features. COM+ features include

- Dynamic load balancing to improve scalability of your components and component-based applications.

- An in-memory database to improve the performance of your components.

- The capability to include publish and subscribe events and queued components, enabling easier integration with multiple components.

- A simplified programming model that integrates MTS and COM.

> **NOTE**
>
> For more information on COM+ and the improvements it brings as part of Windows 2000, visit the Microsoft COM Web site at
> http://www.microsoft.com/com.

MTS and Components

To use your components with MTS, you are not forced to make changes to your code. Realistically, however, to recognize the benefits of MTS your components should adopt the "best practices" for component design. In this section, you will develop a basic component and place it under the control of MTS. This section also discusses the basics of managing your components under MTS. The following section opens the doors to accessing MTS-aware components within your ASP pages.

Creating an MTS Component

For this example, you will be creating a simple MTS component using Visual Basic. You will be focusing on the details of making your components MTS aware. If you are looking for an introduction to creating components, you should flip to Chapter 18, "Creating Custom Components with Visual Basic." The instructions in this section should also provide you with the information you can take back to other programming languages, such as C++.

Begin with a plan for your component and establish its features. For this example, your component will read in parameters passed to it by the calling application (such as an ASP page), carry out some internal logic, and then return a value. Based on the parameters passed to it, the component will determine whether the transaction was a success or a failure.

To develop the component, open Visual Basic (version 5.0 or higher) and follow these steps:

1. Create a new ActiveX DLL project from the New Project dialog box.
2. Right-click the Class1 class module in the Project Explorer and choose Properties from the context menu.
3. In the Name property, enter a name of ValidateData for the class name.
4. Right-click your project in the Project Explorer and choose Project Properties from the context menu. This opens the Project Properties dialog box, shown in Figure 21.5.
5. In the Project Name text box, enter MTSValidate as the new project name. This is now the name of your component.
6. In the Project Description text box, enter a brief description for this component: Validate data passed by the client application.

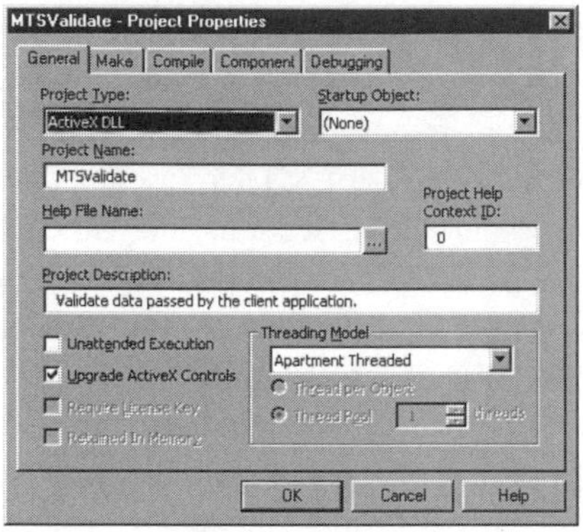

FIGURE **21.5**

The Project Properties dialog box is used to define attributes to your entire Visual Basic project.

NOTE

The Visual Basic project file mtsvalidate.vbp is located on the accompanying CD-ROM. It includes references to the complete code listings for the component you are developing.

The next step is to add the COM code. To do so, we will use the VB Class Builder, a utility included with Visual Basic. This utility is accessible from the Add-Ins menu; however, you might have to install it if you did not do so when you installed Visual Basic. After you have opened the Class Builder from the Add-Ins menu, follow these steps:

1. Click the Add New Method to Current Class button on the toolbar. This opens the Method Builder dialog box, shown in Figure 21.6.

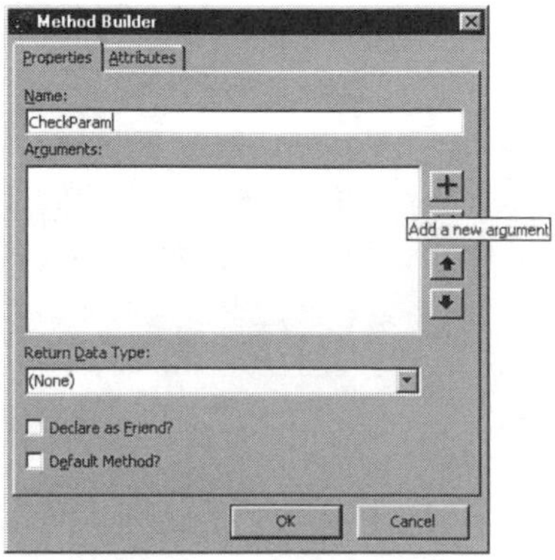

FIGURE **21.6**

The Method Builder dialog box simplifies adding methods to your component.

2. In the Name text box, enter CheckParam for the method name.

3. Now it is time to add arguments for this method. Click the Add a New Argument button (the + button) to open the Add Argument dialog box, shown in Figure 21.7.

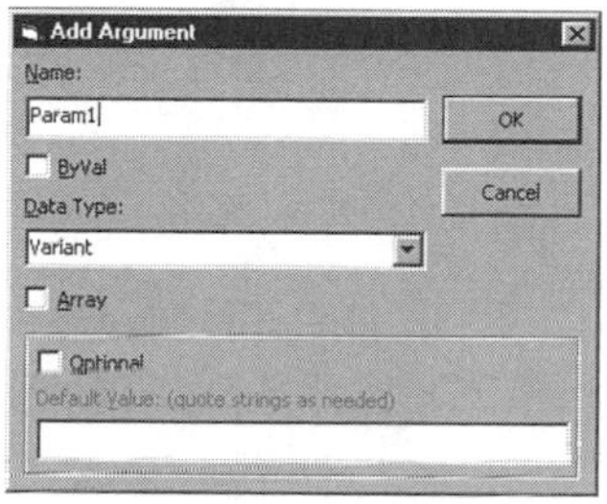

FIGURE 21.7

*For your example,
you will be using
simple Variant
data types for
your arguments.*

4. In the Name text box, enter Param1 as the argument name.

5. Click the OK button to add your new argument.

6. Repeat steps 3–5 and add a second argument named Param2.

7. For the Return Data Type list box, select String.

8. Select the Default Method check box to identify this method as the one to use if no method is specified when calling this component.

9. Click the Attributes tab at the top to switch to the second page of the dialog box, shown in Figure 21.8.

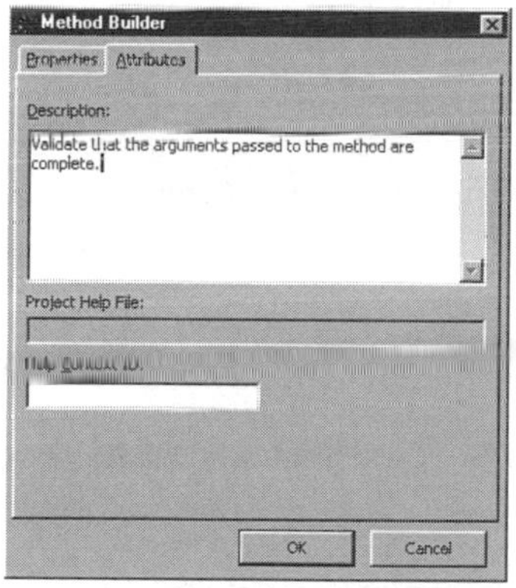

FIGURE 21.8

*The Attributes tab
lets you describe
the method.*

10. In the Description text box, enter the following as the method description:
    Validate that the arguments passed to the method are complete.

11. Click OK to commit your changes to this method. Your new method appears in the Class Builder.

12. From the menu bar, choose File, Update Project to add your changes to the ValidateData class file.

13. Exit the Class Builder Utility by choosing File, Exit from the menu bar.

Your class module should now contain the following two lines of code:

```
Public Function CheckParam(Param1 As Variant, Param2 As Variant)
➥As String
End Function
```

Before you can add the code for the `CheckParam` method you must add a reference to the Microsoft Transaction Server type library. This will enable Visual Basic and our component to access MTS functionality. To do so, follow these steps:

1. From the menu bar, choose Project, References. This opens the References dialog box, as shown in Figure 21.9.

FIGURE 21.9

To use MTS in your component, you must reference the MTS type library.

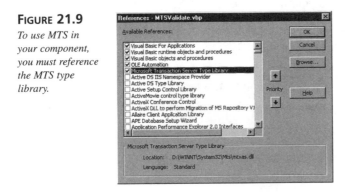

2. Locate the MTS type library in the list: Microsoft Transaction Server Type Library.
3. Select the check box for the MTS type library to identify that it will be used for this project.
4. Click the OK button to add this reference and return to the Visual Basic Editor.

Now add the code for this function. Replace the Function declaration code with the code in Listing 21.1.

LISTING 21.1 THE `MTSValidate.CheckParam` METHOD CODE

```
1 Public Function CheckParam(Param1 As Variant, Param2 As Variant)
  ➥As String
2    Dim objContect As ObjectContext
3    Set objContext = GetObjectContext()
4    If Param1 <> Param2 Then
5        objContext.SetComplete
6    Else
7        objContext.SetAbort
8    End If
9 End Function
```

This (very) simple component will read two parameters passed through the Param1 and Param2 arguments. If the two arguments do not match (that is, they are each unique), the component calls the SetComplete method in line 5, identifying that the transaction was successful. If the two values are the same, however, the SetAbort method is called (line 7) to declare the transaction a failure.

> **NOTE**
>
> This is obviously a very simple example of MTS at work within a component. Undoubtedly you can think of better applications of MTS in your own work!

To finalize this step, you will compile your component in the form of an ActiveX DLL, ready for use by MTS. To compile, follow these steps:

1. From the menu bar, choose File, Make MTSValidate.dll. This opens the Make Project dialog box.
2. Click the Options button to open the Project Properties dialog box, shown in Figure 21.10.

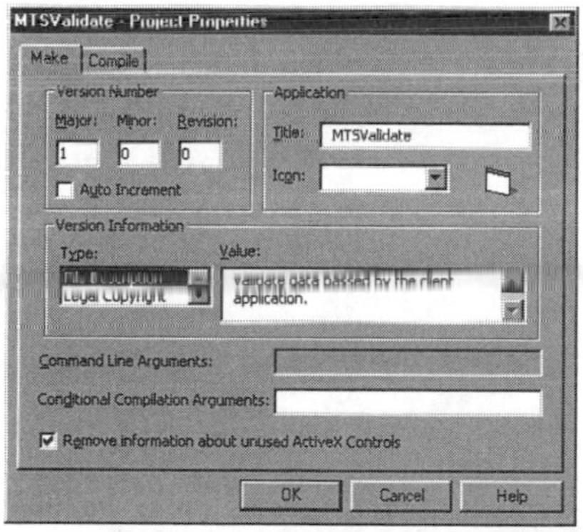

FIGURE 21.10
The Project Properties dialog box at compile time is a subset of the Project Properties dialog box at design time.

3. In the Type list box, locate the File Description item and select it.
4. In the Value text box, enter a description for this component: Validate data passed by the client application. You will use this description to identify your component in project references.
5. Click the OK button to return to the Make Project dialog box.
6. Click the OK button to compile your new component.

> **NOTE**
>
> If you plan to compile your component more than once, you should enable Binary Compatibility in the Project Properties dialog box. Binary compatibility ensures that your ActiveX DLL is registered using the same information in the Windows registry, as opposed to creating a new registration each time. Without binary compatibility enabled, changes to your component will not be recognized by applications that are referencing the old instance of your component.

Packaging Components with the MTS Explorer

Before you can use your component in your applications, you must make MTS aware of the component. When you introduce a new component to MTS, you are *packaging* the component for use. MTS packages might in fact contain multiple components and act as a logical grouping. You probably will use packages to house all the components related to a single application. Packaging takes place in the Microsoft Transaction Server Explorer (MTS Explorer), which is based on the Microsoft Management Console (MMC). The MTS Explorer is installed when you install MTS on your system.

To package your component, follow these steps:

1. Open the MTS Explorer from the Start menu.

2. Expand the folder list in the Console Root to display your computer (MyComputer) and the PackagesInstalled folder, as shown in Figure 21.11.

FIGURE 21.11

Packages act as logical groupings of components.

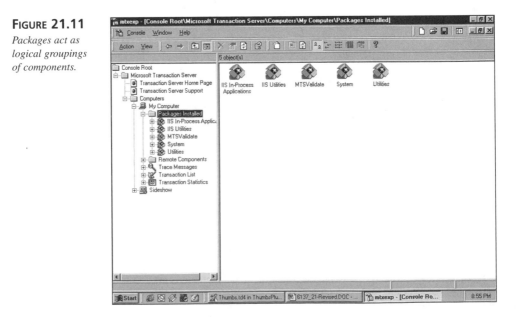

3. Right-click the PackagesInstalled folder and choose New, Package from the context menu. This opens the first screen of the Package Wizard, shown in Figure 21.12.

FIGURE 21.12

Adding new packages to MTS is achieved through the Package Wizard.

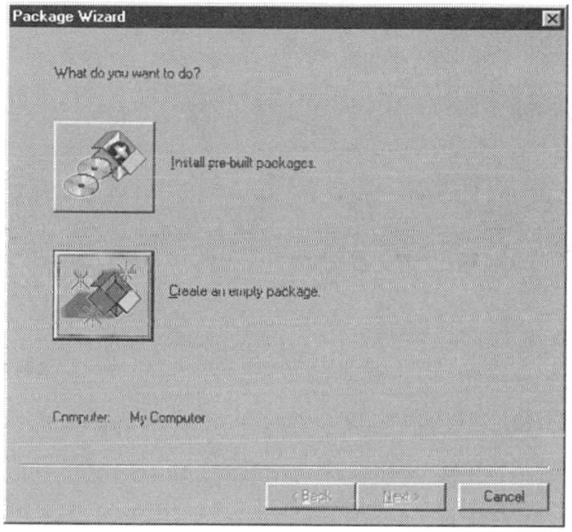

4. Because you are building a new package, click the Create an Empty Package button. This moves you to the second page of the wizard, shown in Figure 21.13.

FIGURE 21.13

Each step of the wizard prompts you for information on your package.

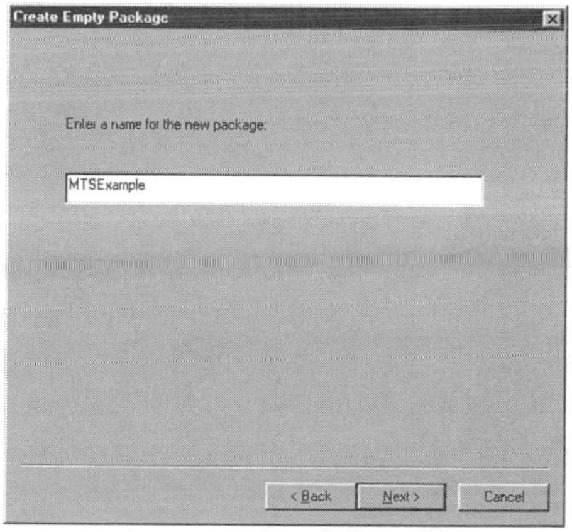

5. In the Create Empty Package dialog box, enter a name for the new package: MTSExample and click the Next button to advance to the next screen, shown in Figure 21.14.

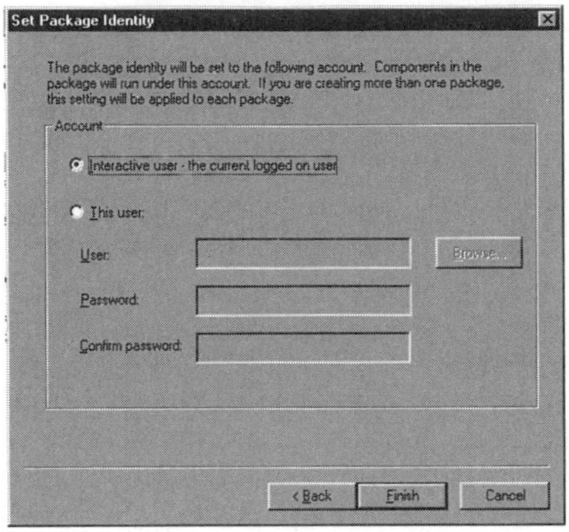

FIGURE 21.14

When your components are running from an ASP page, the top option will force components to run as the IUSR_ machinename user.

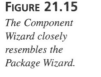

6. The third page of the wizard, Set Package Identity, is used to define what system user account will be used to execute components within this package. For this example, choose Interactive User—The Current Logged on User.

7. Click the Finish button to add the new package. The MTSExample package appears under the PackagesInstalled folder in the console.

After a package has been created, you must add the actual `MTSValidate` component for MTS. Follow these instructions to do so:

1. Expand the MTSExample package folder in the console to display the Components subfolder.

2. Right-click the Components folder and choose New, Component from the context menu. This opens the Component Wizard dialog box, shown in Figure 21.15.

FIGURE 21.15

The Component Wizard closely resembles the Package Wizard.

3. This page offers two choices: Install New Component(s) and Import Component(s) That Are Already Registered. We are going to assume that this is a new component, so click the Install New Component(s) button.

NOTE

The two options provided achieve the same goal under different circumstances. The Install New Component(s) button is used to install a component that has not been registered on the same system that MTS is running under. The second option, Import Component(s) That Are Already Registered, is used to add a component that has already been registered with the operating system as a COM server. If you are packaging the component on the same system on which you developed it, you can choose the second option. More commonly, however, you will be installing a component on a separate server from your development workstation. This is when you should choose the first option. For this example, assume it's a clean server.

---

4. The second page of the wizard appears, Install Components (as shown in Figure 21.16). Click on the Add Files button to open the Select Files to Install dialog box.

FIGURE 21.16
You can install multiple components at once.

5. Using the standard file dialog box, locate your copy of the MTSValidate.dll file and click the Open button. Your component is added to the list, as shown in Figure 21.17.

FIGURE 21.17

*Your selected
components reveal
details in the
bottom pane.*

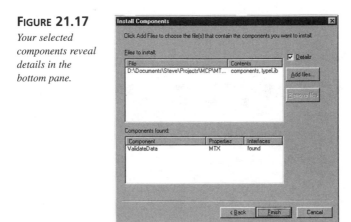

6. Click the Finish button to add the component.

After a component is installed as part of a package, it is available for use under MTS and your applications. There is one step remaining, however. To operate under a transaction, MTS must be instructed on how to treat your component and transaction support. Transactional support comes in four forms for components:

- Requires a transaction—The component must have a transaction to function. If the component is called within a transaction, it will use the parent transaction. If no transaction is present, the component will create a new one.

- Requires a new transaction—Regardless of whether the component was called within a transaction, the component will create a new transaction for itself.

- Supports transactions—The component will use an existing transaction if one is present, however it will not create a new transaction if there isn't one.

- Does not support transactions—The component does not support and will not be included in any transactions.

To define how MTS will treat your component, follow these steps:

1. Right-click your MTSValidate.ValidateData component under the Components folder in the console.

2. Choose Properties from the Context menu. This opens the MTSValidate.ValidateData Properties dialog box, as shown in Figure 21.18.

FIGURE 21.18
You can use this tab to describe your component in MTS.

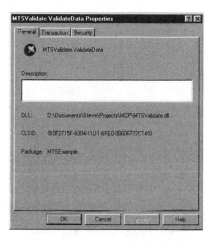

3. Click the Transaction tab at the top of the dialog box, as shown in Figure 21.19.

FIGURE 21.19
Transaction support can take one of four forms.

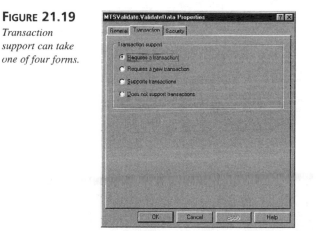

4. Choose the Requires a Transaction radio button. This instructs MTS that your component requires a transaction to function.

5. Click the OK button to commit your changes.

Your component is now available to MTS and your applications!

Using MTS to Increase ASP Scalability and Performance

Adding MTS to the mix of your Web applications and components provides you with a great deal of flexibility, scalability, and power. Using MTS, you can add fault tolerance to your Web applications by ensuring that components are available and managed efficiently, that actions occur as expected (ensuring integrity), and that your Web application can be scaled to handle multiple servers, many more users, and a distributed environment.

> **NOTE**
>
> We will be discussing another level of scalability and reliability that you can introduce to your Web applications in Chapter 22, "Using ASP with Microsoft Message Queue Server."

In this section, you will see two different methods of incorporating MTS into your Web applications:

- Creating transactional Active Server Pages
- Calling on MTS-aware components in ASP

Each of these methods can be combined in your own Web applications to create powerful application platforms.

Creating Transactional Active Server Pages

Although MTS is ideally suited for use with custom-developed components, ASP and Web application developers can take advantage of the flexibility and power of MTS very easily. Inclusion of MTS in your Web pages is very simple; however, it does require you to understand the transactional approach and take care in designing your script logic. The four steps to creating transactions within your ASP pages are

1. Declare your page as transactional, so that it falls under MTS control.
2. Develop the scripts that will be part of the transaction.
3. Define the success or failure of a transaction and script the "milestone" points.
4. Create the transaction events to deal with successful and failed transactions.

21

USING ASP WITH
MTS

The Sample Transactional Application

In this chapter, you will be creating a simple transactional application that will retrieve input from the user with a form and store it in the database. For this example, you will be using the Pubs database sample included with Microsoft SQL Server 6.5 and 7.0. If you are not using Microsoft SQL Server or do not have the Pubs database, you can create the single table you will use with the SQL script shown in Listing 21.2. This SQL script is also found on the companion CD as storesdb.sql.

LISTING 21.2   THE STORES DATABASE SQL SCRIPT

```
Create Table dbo.stores
(
    stor_id char(4) Not Null,
    stor_name varchar(40) Null,
    stor_address varchar(40) Null,
    city varchar(20) Null,
    state char(2) Null,
    zip char(5) Null
)
Go
Alter Table dbo.stores Add Constraint
    UPK_storeid Primary Key Clustered
(
    stor_id
)
Go
```

This script creates the stores database with six columns (stor_id, stor_name, stor_address, city, state, zip) and sets the stor_id column as the primary key for the table.

NOTE

If you are using Microsoft SQL Server, you can use the Query Analyzer to carry out this script. If you are using another vendor's database server, refer to your database documentation for instructions on executing SQL scripts.

Create a file DSN from the ODBC control panel for the Pubs database (or the database that holds your newly created table). Additionally, before proceeding, ensure that your Web server username (IUSR_*machinename*) has both select (read) and insert (write) access to this table.

Declaring Your Page as Transactional

Integrating MTS into your pages is actually a very easy task. When working with MTS, you are declaring that your page is transactional and that all scripts are run under the same transaction context. MTS manages the details of creating the transaction and monitoring whether the actions succeed or fail. In MTS parlance, a successful transaction is called a commit, whereas a failure is called an abort. To declare your page as transactional, the @TRANSACTION directive must be the first line of the page. The @TRANSACTION directive appears as follows:

```
<% @TRANSACTION = value %>
```

The *value* refers to how your page interacts with MTS. The possible values are listed in Table 21.1.

TABLE 21.1   @TRANSACTION VALUES

@TRANSACTION Value	Description
Requires_New	This value starts a new transaction for this page.
Required	This page uses an existing transaction, if available; otherwise it starts a new transaction.
Supported	This page does not start a new transaction; however, it will support transactions spanned from another page.
Not_Supported	This page does not support transactions.

NOTE

Your ASP pages may have only one @ directive line. You may combine your directives on one line, if required. For example

```
<% @TRANSACTION = Required LANGUAGE = VBSCRIPT %>
```

TIP

Only the pages that require transactional processing must include the @TRANS-ACTION declaration. The rest of your Web application does not need to declare transactional processing support, and in fact, to avoid performance problems, they should not.

Creating the Transaction Scripts

Behind the scenes, your ASP pages still contain the same scripts they always have. MTS is used to augment and improve your scripts, but they do not necessarily directly change your code. You can take almost any existing ASP page and add support for transactions without altering your code to any great degree. The transaction scripts are the logic behind your page and the code that takes place when required.

For this example, you will create a simple script to determine whether to update a database with information provided in a form. Your scripts will take data from a form and store it in a database if the transaction is successful (more on this in a later section). To begin, you will create another page for your sample, called form.htm (found on the companion CD-ROM). This will be the page that will input the data using a simple HTML form. Follow these steps to create form.htm:

1. Create a new file, named form.htm, which you will use for the HTML form.

2. In your editor, insert the code shown in Listing 21.3 for the file.

LISTING 21.3 THE FORM.HTM PAGE

```
1  <HTML>
2  <HEAD>
3  <TITLE>Transaction Form</TITLE>
4  </HEAD>
5  <BODY>
6  <FONT FACE="Arial">
7  <H1>Transaction Example: Step 1</H1>
8  <HR SIZE=1 NOSHADE>
9  <P ALIGN="LEFT">
10     This form will be used to insert data into a database if the
11     transaction is successful. If the transaction fails, the user
12     will receive a warning message that the action was not successful.
13 </P>
14 <HR SIZE=1 NOSHADE>
15 <FORM action="transaction.asp" method=POST>
16 <TABLE BORDER="0" ALIGN="CENTER">
17 <TR>
18 <TD>
19     Store Name
20 </TD>
21 <TD>
22 <INPUT type="text" name=txtName size=20 maxlength=20>
23 </TD>
24 </TR>
25 <TR>
26 <TD>
```

continues

LISTING 21.3 CONTINUED

```
27      Telephone
28 </TD>
29 <TD>
30      <INPUT type="text" name=txtTelephone size=12 maxlength=12>
31 </TD>
32 </TR>
33 <TR>
34 <TD>
35      Street Address
36 </TD>
37 <TD>
38      <INPUT type="text" name=txtAddress size=40 maxlength=40>
39 </TD>
40 </TR>
41 <TR>
42 <TD>
43      City
44 </TD>
45 <TD>
46      <INPUT type="text" name=txtCity size=20 maxlength=20>
47 </TD>
48 </TR>
49 <TR>
50 <TD>
51      State
52 </TD>
53 <TD>
54      <INPUT type="text" name=txtState size=2 maxlength=2>
55 </TD>
56 </TR>
57 <TR>
58 <TD>
59      Zip Code
60 </TD>
61 <TD>
62      <INPUT type="text" name=txtZipCode size=5 maxlength=5>
63 </TD>
64 <TR>
65 <TD COLSPAN=2 ALIGN="CENTER">
66      <INPUT type="submit" value="Submit" name=btnSubmit>
67 </TD>
68 </TR>
69 </TABLE>
70 </FORM>
71 <HR SIZE=1 NOSHADE>
72 <P ALIGN="LEFT">
73 This page pushes information to the <U>transaction.asp</U>
   ➥page for processing.
```

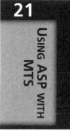

```
74 </P>
75 </FONT>
76 </BODY>
77 </HTML>
```

3. Save your changes to form.htm.

4. Save your changes to transaction.asp.

Listing 21.3 is straightforward and very simple. Lines 15–70 encompass the form that will feed information to our transactional page, transaction.asp, as indicated by the action in line 15.

The next step is for you to create your transaction script in the transaction.asp page shown in Listing 21.4. This file is also found on your CD-ROM.

LISTING 21.4   THE TRANSACTION SCRIPT FOR TRANSACTION.ASP

```
1 <%@TRANSACTION=Required Language=VBScript%>
2 <HTML>
3 <HEAD>
4 <TITLE></TITLE>
5 </HEAD>
6 <BODY>
7 <FONT FACE="Arial">
8 <H1>Transaction Example: Step 2</H1>
9 <HR SIZE=1 NOSHADE>
10 <P ALIGN="LEFT">
11 This page takes the information provided by <U>form.htm</U> and
12 inserts it into the database for storage.
13 </P>
14 <HR SIZE=1 NOSHADE>
15 <%
16 Dim strStoreID, strName, strAddress, strCity, strState, strZipCode
17 Dim objDBConn, strSQLText
18 strStoreID = Request.Form("txtTelephone")
19 strName = Request.Form("txtName")
20 strAddress = Request.Form("txtAddress")
21 strCity = Request.Form("txtCity")
22 strState = Request.Form("txtState")
23 strZipCode = Request.Form("txtZipCode")
24 strStoreID = right(strStoreID, 4)
25 %>
26 <TABLE ALIGN="CENTER">
27 <TR>
28     <TD>
29     <B>Name</B>:
30     </TD>
31     <TD>
```

continues

LISTING 21.4   CONTINUED

```
32      <%= strName %> (<%= strStoreID %>)
33      </TD>
34 </TR>
35 <TR>
36      <TD>
37      <B>Address</B>:
38      </TD>
39      <TD>
40      <%= strAddress %><BR><%= strCity %>, <%= strState %><BR>
41      <%= strZipCode %>
42      </TD>
43 </TR>
44 </TABLE>
45 <HR SIZE=1 NOSHADE>
46 <%
47 strStoreID = "'" & strStoreID & "',"
48 strName = "'" & strName & "',"
49 strAddress = "'" & strAddress & "',"
50 strCity = "'" & strCity & "',"
51 strState = "'" & strState & "',"
52 strZipCode = "'" & strZipCode & "'"
53 strSQLText = "INSERT INTO stores (stor_id, stor_name,
   ➥stor_address," &
54 "city, state, zip) VALUES (" & strStoreID & strName & strAddress & _
55 strCity & strState & strZipCode & ")"
56 Set objDBConn = Server.CreateObject("ADODB.Connection")
57 objDBConn.Open "FILE NAME="d:\PubDB.dsn"
58 objDBConn.Execute strSQLText
59 objDBConn.Close
60 %>
61 Store added to the database!
62 <HR SIZE=1 NOSHADE>
63 <P ALIGN="LEFT">
64 Based on the data from <U>form.htm</U>, this page inserts the values
65 into the database on a successful transaction.
66 </P>
67 </FONT>
68 </BODY>
69 </HTML>
```

There isn't a great deal to this page. Lines 18–23 retrieve the form data from the form.htm page and store it to local variables. On line 24, you truncate the telephone number provided by the user to give a unique store ID to be used in the database. Lines 47–52 format the local variables to create the SQL query that will be used to insert the values into the database as a new record. Finally, lines 56–59 create a database connection and execute the query, closing the connection when it is complete. In line 57, you should replace the path to the PubsDB.DSN to your own file DSN for the Pubs database.

You can test these pages by opening the form.htm page in your Web browser and filling in sample data. After you click the Submit button, you should be presented with a page similar to the one shown in Figure 21.20.

FIGURE 21.20

After a successful database update, you should see a page like this one.

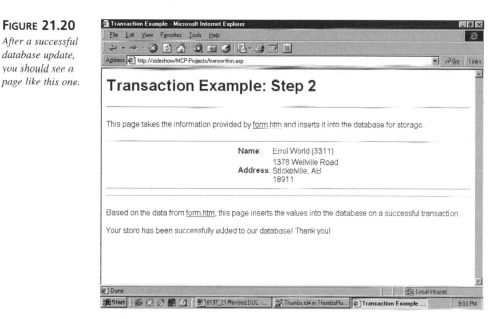

Now, try submitting the same information again by pressing the reload/refresh button in your Web browser. This time you should receive an error at the bottom of the page that looks like this:

```
Microsoft OLE DB Provider for ODBC Drivers error '80040e14'
[Microsoft][ODBC SQL Server Driver][SQL Server]Violation of PRIMARY KEY
constraint 'UPK_storeid'. Cannot insert duplicate key in object 'stores'.
/MCP-Projects/transaction.asp, line 70
```

This error indicates that the script attempted to insert a duplicate entry into the database. Specifically, it attempted to insert duplicate data into a primary key column (storeid). This is where the next step comes in: determining whether the transaction was a success or a failure.

Deciding to Commit or Abort

As you read earlier, MTS classifies a transaction as either a success (a commit) or a failure (an abort). Based on the workflow and logic in your scripts, you can determine whether a transaction is successful and, if it does not succeed, explicitly declare that the transaction is a failure. Typically, your scripts will be relying on the results from another script or component to determine the next course of action. For example, your script may call upon a banking component or function to carry out the transaction's prerequisite activities. The component, if successful, returns a value of 0; whereas, if it is a failure, it returns a 1. After your script has determined that the action was unsuccessful, it can declare the transaction a failure by calling the `ObjectContext.SetAbort` method.

> ## CAUTION
>
> Currently, transactional pages only truly support database transactions. If the transaction is a failure and results in an abort, MTS will roll back the changes. This does not apply directly to file system changes or application/session variables. You can, however, work around this shortcoming through well-thought-out scripting. More on this in "Writing the Transaction Events," later in this chapter.

In the example, you've already seen what would constitute a failed transaction. When you attempted to submit duplicate data into the database, you were greeted with a nasty (but altogether not uncommon) error message. You can use MTS to determine whether the update was successful, and if it wasn't, to display a friendly (or about as friendly as possible) error message. You can also use MTS to trap if the database is not available, saving your users the grief of attempting to submit to an unavailable database.

With the example, you can look at several small "milestones" that can be considered a "go/no go" for your transaction. These milestones can be an opportunity to test for a failure and to abort the transaction if needed. In your transaction.asp page, here are two (but not necessarily all) of the opportunities you have to check for a problem:

- Lines 18–24 of Listing 21.4—These lines assume there is a value present from the form. What if the form submitted blank information or data in the incorrect format?
- Line 62—This is where the actual SQL query takes place to insert the data into the database. What if this action failed?

Using scripting, you can build conditional checks into your page to determine whether everything is proceeding according to plan. If something goes awry, you can declare the transaction a failure and abort the processing. If everything is proceeding nicely, you can leave the transaction to continue until the next check.

For this example, begin by checking if there is data coming from the form. Presumably, you would use input validation in the form itself; however, there is always the possibility

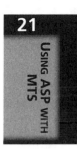

that a user accidentally arrived on the page without the proper data. Add a conditional check for this possibility:

1. Open the transaction.asp page in your editor.
2. Locate Lines 18–24 in Listing 21.4 where form fields are retrieved and replace them with the code in Listing 21.5.

LISTING 21.5 DETERMINE WHETHER THE FORM FIELDS ARE COMPLETE

```
 1 strStoreID = Request.Form("txtTelephone")
 2 strName = Request.Form("txtName")
 3 strAddress = Request.Form("txtAddress")
 4 strCity = Request.Form("txtCity")
 5 strState = Request.Form("txtState")
 6 strZipCode = Request.Form("txtZipCode")
 7 If strStoreID = "" or strName = "" or strAddress = "" or _
 8 strCity = "" or strState = "" or strZipCode = "" Then
 9     ObjectContext.SetAbort
10 Else
11     strStoreID = right(strStoreID, 4)
12 End If
```

3. Save your changes to transaction.asp.

Here, insert a simple check on lines 7 and 8 to verify that the form fields are not empty. If they are, call the `ObjectContext.SetAbort` method to consider the transaction a failure. If the form fields have values, proceed by truncating the telephone number to create the unique ID for the store.

Finally, determine whether the SQL query was completed successfully. To do so, check the `Count` property of the `Connection` object's `Errors` collection. This simple check determines whether an error occurred when the database action took place. Follow these steps:

1. In the transaction.asp file, locate line 62 from Listing 21.4, where the query is executed. Replace the line with the code shown in Listing 21.6.

LISTING 21.6 DETERMINE WHETHER THE DATABASE CONNECTION IS WORKING

```
1 If objDBConn.Errors.Count > 0 Then
2     ObjectContext.SetAbort
3 End If
```

2. Save your changes to the transaction.asp page.

> **NOTE**
>
> You will probably want to use more robust error checking than this simple example, but this demonstrates the point nicely.

Now that your conditional checks are complete, what happens when you re-run the script with duplicate data? Not a great deal. The next and final step that you must complete is the code for the transaction events.

Writing the Transaction Events

The last step in the sample transactional application is adding the transaction events. There are two transaction events that you can define in the form of subroutines:

- OnTransactionCommit—Executed if the transaction was successful.
- OnTransactionAbort—Executed if the transaction was a failure, as trapped by your conditional checks or a custom component.

You can use the transaction events to execute post-transaction scripts, rollback data, or (as in our example) simply display a message to the user. To complete the example, follow these steps:

1. Locate line 65 of Listing 21.4 in your transaction.asp page. This is the line that indicates that the store was successfully submitted. Replace this line with the code shown in Listing 21.7.

LISTING 21.7 ADDING THE TRANSACTION EVENTS

```
1 <%
2 Sub OnTransactionCommit()
3    Response.Write("Your store has been successfully added to our
     ➥database! Thank you!")
4 End Sub
5 Sub OnTransactionAbort()
6    Response.Write("A problem occurred when we tried to add your store
     ➥to our database:<BR>")
7    Response.Write("<B>Error:</B> Please <A HREF=""form.htm"">try again
     ➥</A>.")
8 End Sub
9 %>
```

2. Save your changes to the transaction.asp page.

When you test your pages now, you should receive one of two messages at the bottom of the transaction.asp page, depending on the transaction. If the transaction was successful and the database was updated, you should see a line that reads

```
Your store has been successfully added to our database! Thank you!
```

However, if the transaction failed due to any of your conditional checks, you should see two lines that read

```
A problem occurred when we tried to add your store to our database:
Error: Please try again.
```

Congratulations! You've created your first transactional Web application!

Using MTS Components Within ASP

In Part II of this book, "Active Server Pages Installable Components," and in Part IV, "Active Server Pages Custom Components," you experimented with components on the server side. This section builds on those experiences by calling upon your own MTS component within an ASP page. You developed a component and added it to MTS earlier in this chapter, and you will now move on to the next step of calling on that component in an ASP page. The key difference between this component usage and the usage discussed in previous chapters is the introduction of the MTS events.

When you developed your transactional ASP pages, you relied on two events: OnTransactionCommit and OnTransactionAbort. These same events will be used in the example here, with one difference: the transaction events are being called from your custom component. Remember that your component compares two arguments and determines whether they match. If they are unique, the transaction is a success. If they match, however, the transaction is aborted. Begin by creating a simple HTML page with a form that will be used to start the transaction:

1. Create a new Web page named component-form.htm.
2. Insert the code in Listing 21.8 into your new page.

LISTING 21.8 THE COMPONENT-FORM.HTM PAGE

```
1 <HTML>
2 <HEAD>
3 <TITLE>Component Form</TITLE>
4 </HEAD>
5 <BODY>
6 <FONT FACE="Arial">
7 <H1>Component Example: Step 1</H1>
8 <HR SIZE=1 NOSHADE>
```

continues

LISTING 21.8   CONTINUED

```
 9 <P ALIGN="LEFT">
10     This form will be used to select two values that will be given to
11     our component. If the values are unique, the transaction will
12     succeed. If they match, the transaction will fail.
13 </P>
14 <HR SIZE=1 NOSHADE>
15 <FORM action="component.asp" method=POST>
16 <TABLE BORDER="0" ALIGN="CENTER">
17 <TR>
18 <TD>
19     Parameter 1
20 </TD>
21 <TD>
22     <SELECT name=selParam1>
23         <OPTION>Red</OPTION>
24         <OPTION>Blue</OPTION>
25         <OPTION>Green</OPTION>
26     </SELECT>
27 </TD>
28 </TR>
29 <TR>
30 <TD>
31     Parameter 2
32 </TD>
33 <TD>
34     <SELECT name=selParam2>
35         <OPTION>Red</OPTION>
36         <OPTION>Blue</OPTION>
37         <OPTION>Green</OPTION>
38     </SELECT>
39 </TD>
40 </TR>
41 <TR>
42 <TD COLSPAN=2 ALIGN="CENTER">
43     <INPUT type="submit" value="Submit">
44 </TD>
45 </TR>
46 </TABLE>
47 </FORM>
48 <HR SIZE=1 NOSHADE>
49 <P ALIGN="LEFT">
50 This page pushes information to the <U>component.asp</U> page for
51 processing.
52 </P>
53 </FONT>
54 </BODY>
55 </HTML>
```

3. Save the changes made to component-form.htm.

NOTE

The component-form.htm page can be found on the CD-ROM.

The component-form.htm page, like the transactional ASP example, is a very simple form that will push data to an ASP page. In this case, you are relying on two drop-down boxes (`selParam1` and `selParam2`) to pass two values (colors). These values are pushed to the component.asp page, as the action defined in line 15. This page is shown in Figure 21.21.

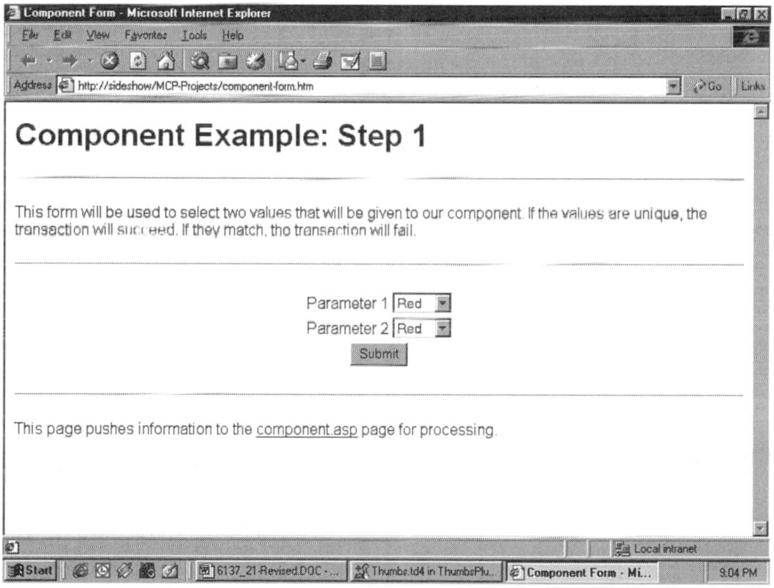

FIGURE 21.21
The component-form.htm page will be used to push color values to the component.

The next step is to create the component.asp page (located on the CD-ROM) that will take the form values and pass them to your MTS component. To do so, follow these steps:

1. Create a new ASP page in your editor named component.asp.
2. Insert the code in Listing 21.9 into the component.asp page.

LISTING 21.9 THE COMPONENT.ASP PAGE

```
 1 <%@TRANSACTION=Required Language=VBScript %>
 2 <HTML>
 3 <HEAD>
 4 <TITLE>Component Example</TITLE>
 5 </HEAD>
 6 <BODY>
 7 <FONT FACE="Arial">
 8 <H1>Component Example: Step 2</H1>
 9 <HR SIZE=1 NOSHADE>
10 <P ALIGN="LEFT">
11 This page takes the information provided by <U>form.htm</U> and
12 inserts it into the database for storage.
13 </P>
14 <HR SIZE=1 NOSHADE>
15 <%
16     On Error Resume Next
17     Dim strParam1, strParam2
18     Dim objMTSValidate
19   strParam1 = Request.Form("selParam1")
20   strParam2 = Request.Form("selParam2")
21   If strParam1 = "" or strParam2 = "" Then
22       ObjectContext.SetAbort
23   End If
24 %>
25 <TABLE ALIGN="CENTER">
26 <TR>
27 <TD>
28     <B>Parameter 1</B>:
29 </TD>
30 <TD>
31     <%= strParam1 %>
32 </TD>
33 </TR>
34 <TR>
35 <TD>
36     <B>Parameter 2</B>:
37 </TD>
38 <TD>
39     <%= strParam2 %>
40 </TD>
41 </TR>
42 </TABLE>
43 <HR SIZE=1 NOSHADE>
44 <%
45 Set objMTSValidate = Server.CreateObject("MTSValidate.ValidateData")
46 CheckParam = objMTSValidate.CheckParam(strParam1, strParam2)
47 %>
48 <%
49 Sub OnTransactionCommit()
```

```
50      Response.Write("<B>The values were unique</B> - the transaction
     ➥ was successful!")
51 End Sub
52 Sub OnTransactionAbort()
53      Response.Write("<B>The values were the same</B> - the transaction
     ➥ failed.")
54 End Sub
55 %>
56 <HR SIZE=1 NOSHADE>
57 <P ALIGN="LEFT">
58 Based on the data from <A HREF="component-form.htm">
59 component-form.htm</A>, this page
60 calls on the <U>MTSValidate</U> component to compare values and
61 determine if the transaction succeeded or failed.
62 </P>
63 </FONT>
64 </BODY>
65 </HTML>
```

3. Save the changes to your new page.

Let's examine what is going on in the component.asp page. On line 1, you are creating a transaction for the page and its components. The component will not create a new transaction, so it will use the page's transaction for its activity. Lines 19–23 read in the form values from the component-form.htm page and ensure that they are not empty. If either value is empty (as unlikely as that might be), the transaction is automatically aborted by calling `ObjectContext.SetAbort` on line 22. Another possibility to consider is a user accessing the component.asp page directly without using the form, leaving the field values empty. Always plan ahead!

The real action begins on line 45, where a new instance of the MTS component is being made, courtesy of your `MTSValidate.DataValidate` MTS component. Line 46 calls on the component by passing the two form values as the required arguments. Internally to the component, it reads the two values and determines whether the transaction is a success (the values are unique) or if it is a failure (the values match). After the component makes that determination, it calls either the `SetCommit` or `SetAbort` methods. These events "bubble up" to the ASP page and are intercepted by the `OnTransactionCommit` event on lines 49–51 or the `OnTransactionAbort` event on lines 52–54.

Open the component-form.htm page in a Web browser and see what happens. If the transaction was successful, a page like the one shown in Figure 21.22 should appear in your Web browser.

FIGURE 21.22
Because the values do not match, the component has declared the transaction a success.

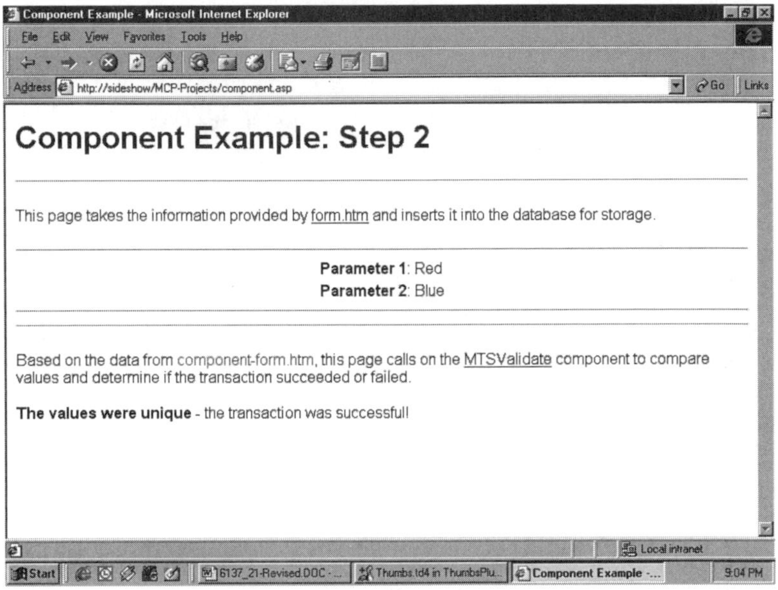

If it failed, however, you will see a page like the one shown in Figure 21.23.

FIGURE 21.23
This time, however, the colors matched so the component declared the transaction a failure.

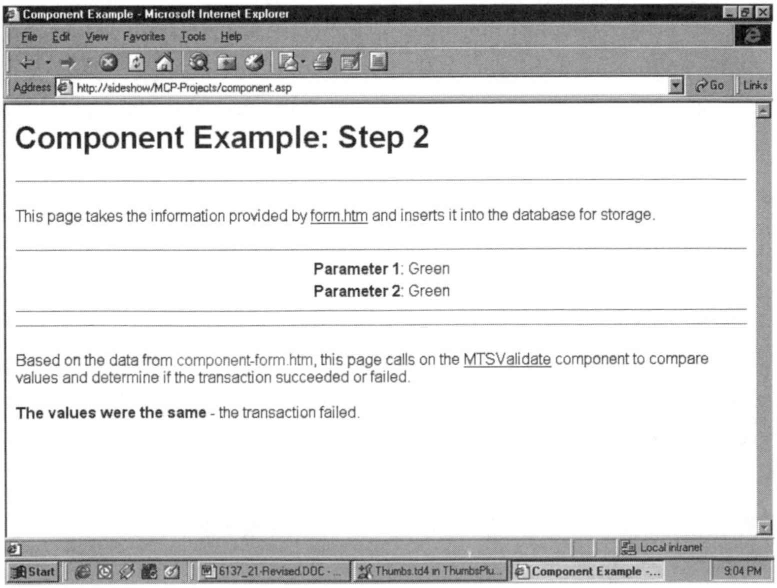

Notice how the page loads very quickly after the first usage. This is thanks to MTS component caching, allowing the page to reference the object context as opposed to an actual component instance, which must be created and destroyed. If you leave this example for a while (approximately three minutes) and no one accesses the page, MTS must reactivate the components again.

Summary

Microsoft Transaction Server opens an entirely new world of component development and extensibility to your Web applications. Using MTS you can improve your application's performance, stability, and scalability without relying on complex manual coding. MTS is a cornerstone of the new COM+ that makes its debut in Windows 2000 and provides an excellent evolutionary path for your Web applications to follow. In Chapter 22, "Using ASP with Microsoft Message Queue Server," you will learn how to integrate an additional layer of flexibility and fault tolerance into your applications.

Using ASP with Microsoft Message Queue Server

by Steven Banick

In This Chapter

CHAPTER

22

There comes a time in a Web application's life when it must communicate over a network with different systems. Traditionally, these inter-system communications relied on programmed fail-safes for fault tolerance. Microsoft Message Queuing Services (MSMQ) enables your applications to communicate across heterogeneous networks and systems, even if they are temporarily offline. Using MSMQ, your applications will no longer have to wait diligently for a response from a system that might not be available—instead, you can use MSMQ to process communication requests and move along to the next important step. MSMQ is ideally suited for applications that operate similar to email—you want the message to get there, but it doesn't necessarily have to arrive just this very second. For example, you may use MSMQ within an ASP page to communicate with your remote database server, a distant billing system, or perhaps a legacy scheduling application.

Why Use MSMQ?

MSMQ is a set of services that you can use to add fault tolerance and scalability to communications in your Web applications. Although not required for MSMQ, the combination of MTS and MSMQ provide your Web applications with increased flexibility and reliability when dealing with communication. MTS manages the finalities of "Did this action succeed? Did it fail?" MSMQ manages the important details of "Did this request get received by the service that needs it?" Consider a typical large or enterprise-level Web application. More times than not, the Web server communicates with one or more data sources, such as a database or a customized processing system. Each time the Web application communicates with the database or processing system, a request is sent and the Web application waits for a response. If, for any reason, the system or database is unavailable, the Web application hits an unavoidable snag and dies.

MSMQ introduces a new level of fault tolerance to Web applications that was previously known only to large-scale business servers and mainframes, such as financial transaction systems. Using MSMQ, your Web applications need no longer directly manage communication with other systems. Instead, your Web applications call upon the messaging services of MSMQ to manage the details of sending and receiving messages to the specified system. Your application now only worries about creating the message to be sent and understanding the message that is received. As long as you have established a common language among all your applications, they can utilize MSMQ for their communications. Figure 22.1 illustrates this concept.

FIGURE 22.1
MSMQ removes the chore of inter-system communication from your application.

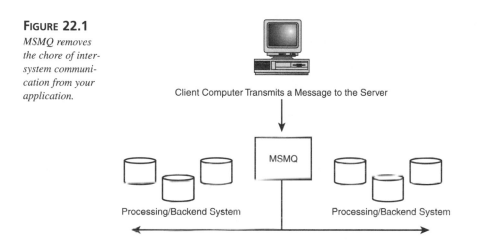

Client Computer Transmits a Message to the Server

MSMQ

Processing/Backend System   Processing/Backend System

22

USING ASP WITH MSMQ

Sending and Receiving Applications

In the world of MSMQ, there are two kinds of applications: sending and receiving. A sending application can be considered the instigator of a messaging transaction. The sending application starts the process of communication by transferring a message to the MSMQ services. This message is then retrieved for processing by the receiving application after it is aware that a message is waiting. Think of this in terms of everyday surface mail:

1. You are sending a letter to your dear old grandmother. You, as the sending application, prepare your message ("Hi Granny! I miss you!") and seal the envelope.

2. Content with your message, you send it via the postal carrier for delivery. The postal carrier, acting as the messaging transport, manages the intricate details of getting your letter from your location to your grandmother's. This is the role of MSMQ.

3. Your grandmother, knowing that new mail arrives on her doorstep every day at 2 p.m., checks for any new arrivals. She sees your letter on her step and quickly snatches it. She tears the envelope wide open and weeps openly at the sentimental message.

It is the role of MSMQ to brave the elements to deliver the sending application's electronic message to the waiting hands of the receiving application. The key understanding is that the receiving application must regularly check for new messages, otherwise (much like old credit card bills) the message might sit untouched for quite some time. Figure 22.2 illustrates the concept of sending and receiving applications.

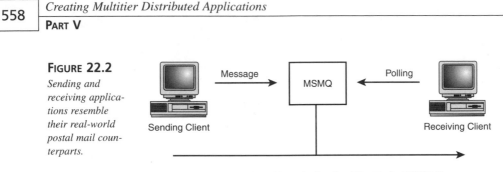

FIGURE 22.2
Sending and receiving applications resemble their real-world postal mail counterparts.

Messages are transferred from the Sending Client to the MSMQ Server.

MSMQ also has the capability to define priorities and attributes to messages. Your application can treat certain communications with more importance than others. Using MSMQ, you can assign attributes to your messages that instruct your applications to manage them differently. Messages can also be treated differently within MSMQ itself and its own approach for delivery. In the case of the postal example, you have the option of sending your letter normal surface mail, express mail, and even certified mail. MSMQ provides much the same functionality to your applications when a simple message transmission is not enough.

Message Queues

Without some form of organization behind it, MSMQ would have a myriad of messages coming from sending applications and a chaotic delivery system for receiving applications. To bring order to the fray, MSMQ uses the concept of *message queues*. A message queue is like a television channel—each channel has its own unique content and provides a distinction between itself and the other channels out there (well, one would hope so). As a developer, you create message queues that will be used as a common communications channel between your sending and receiving applications. It provides the common ground between the two applications. Message queues are stored within the MSMQ database within a Microsoft SQL Server on the MSMQ servers and an internal data store for clients (more on this in a bit).

Message queues are independent groupings of messages based on your application needs. For example, your application might require an incoming orders pool for messages and an outgoing orders pool for responses. Each of these pools can be implemented as message queues, enabling your application to target specific queues for messages it is looking for. The alternative is to have one central message pool that your application must search through to find the type of message it wants.

There are no real limits to the number of message queues that you can create with MSMQ. You can define separate message queues for your application's different processes, ensuring the integrity of communications. As part of the message transmission and reception process, your applications specify a message queue to use. Figure 22.3 illustrates message queues and how they pertain to sending and receiving applications.

FIGURE 22.3

Message queues are independent channels for application communication.

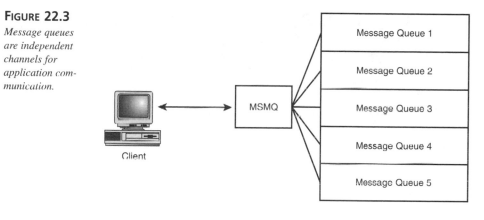

Communicating Across the Network with MSMQ

The significant advantage of using MSMQ over your own application communication routines is its robustness. MSMQ can manage messaging across networks and multiple servers to deliver your message. Essentially, MSMQ opens your Web applications to a world of distributed computing. Take, for example, an airline order processing system. The airline customer service and sales staff can make orders and plan trips via a Web application using a standard Web browser. Orders can be submitted to the Web application server using COM components that are managed by Microsoft Transaction Server (see Chapter 21, "Using ASP with Microsoft Transaction Server" for more information on MTS). These components, acting as the application server, might require processing to be handled by an external system, such as a database. This is where MSMQ comes into play.

Assuming that there is an application on the remote server waiting to receive messages (such as a customized component or an intelligent processing system), MSMQ can ensure that the message is received. The Web application server, using the MSMQ objects, can transmit a message to a prescribed message queue (for example, Orders). MSMQ then manages the details of delivery across the network, enabling the Web application to continue on to the next step. After the processing system has received the message via MSMQ, it can transmit a reply to the Web application system via a different message queue. The Web application server, monitoring for new messages, then informs the customer service representative of the new message (a confirmed order, for example).

> **TIP**
>
> Not every application can behave properly in this sort of environment. If your Web application relies on an immediate return of information, you can still use the reliability of MSMQ to deliver messages; however, your application will still require fail-safe/fault-tolerance routines in case of an outage. If your application can survive without immediate feedback from the remote system, MSMQ provides you with more freedom. It depends entirely on your Web application architecture and its needs.

Delivery Assurance

An important part of MSMQ is the concept of *delivery assurance*. MSMQ, in some ways, is a transaction server. It uniquely identifies each message in its queuing services and ensures its delivery. If the message is not properly transmitted to the remote MSMQ client, the message is resent. MSMQ works on the principle that the message must be completely received and subsequently acknowledged to consider the transmission a success. This ensures that no messages are lost or duplicated. Loosely put, MSMQ determines whether the message arrives or it doesn't—there is no half way about it.

MSMQ uses two different message delivery methods: *express* and *recoverable*. Express delivery is, by and large, the standard way to send messages. Express relies on the recipient receiving the message on the first delivery—that is, MSMQ does not store the message for retransmission in the event of a failure. Express is the most efficient way to deliver messages because it requires fewer resources. Recoverable delivery, on the other hand, requires more resources than express. Recoverable delivery adds the layer of protection that many applications require. A copy of the message is stored by the MSMQ server for recovery in the event of a failure somewhere in the message delivery. Figure 22.4 shows this concept at work.

MSMQ Servers

Behind the scenes, MSMQ relies on servers. There are several different kinds of MSMQ servers:

- Primary Enterprise Controller (PEC)—The PEC is analogous to the Primary Domain Controller (PDC) in a Windows NT network. One PEC must be present for each network where MSMQ is used. It acts as the centralized administrator for the certification keys that are used by MSMQ to authenticate messages. The PEC also acts as an MSMQ routing server.

FIGURE 22.4

MSMQ: When it absolutely, positively has to get there over a network.

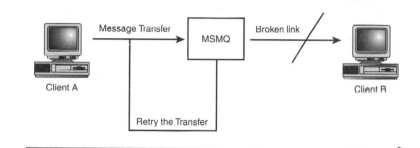

22

USING ASP WITH MSMQ

> **NOTE**
>
> MSMQ supports digital certificates much like Internet Information Server. Using these digital certificates, messages can be digitally signed to ensure the validity of the message. I won't be discussing digital certificates in this chapter; however, if you are interested in knowing more, you can look the Microsoft Message Queue Server section of the Windows NT 4.0 Option Pack documentation.

- Primary Site Controller (PSC)—Each additional site, a logical grouping of MSMQ clients and servers outside your PEC, requires a PSC. The PSC also acts as an MSMQ routing server and contains a copy of all queues and computers that are part of the network.

- Backup Site Controller (BSC)—Analogous to a Backup Domain Controller (BDC) in a Windows NT network, the BSC provides a layer of redundancy for the PEC and PSC, should either of them fail. The BSC maintains a read-only copy of all queue and computer information and can act as an MSMQ routing server.

- MSMQ routing server—MSMQ Routing Servers are used to support dynamic message routing and intermediate message forwarding. Using an MSMQ routing server, your networks can use different protocols to link different clients in your network.

- MSMQ connector server—All MSMQ servers can act as an MSMQ connector server. MSMQ connector servers enable MSMQ-based applications to communicate with non-MSMQ clients, such as external message queuing services. Development of an MSMQ connector server requires use of the MSMQ SDK.

> **NOTE**
>
> Each MSMQ server requires a SQL Server database to store all messaging and network information.

Each MSMQ server type is used to deliver information in your network to different computers. Figure 22.5 illustrates the uses of the different kinds of MSMQ servers.

FIGURE 22.5

MSMQ Primary Enterprise Controllers coordinate all other MSMQ servers.

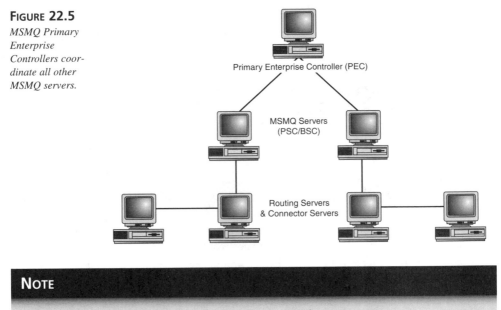

> **NOTE**
>
> We'll be discussing installing MSMQ later in this chapter.

Independent and Dependent Clients

Whereas the MSMQ server manages the storage and delivery of messages in a queue, MSMQ clients are the end-to-end users of the system. Each computer that will interact with MSMQ must be configured as an MSMQ client. MSMQ supports two types of clients:

- Independent clients—These are the clients that utilize the most flexibility and power available with MSMQ. Independent clients maintain their own message

store and are able to queue their own messages if they are unable to communicate with an MSMQ server for delivery. After the MSMQ server is available, the local message queue is transferred to the server. Independent clients are designed around fault tolerance and ensuring message delivery.

- Dependent clients—These are essentially "dumb" MSMQ clients with no local storage. Dependent clients rely on the MSMQ servers available for message delivery and reception. If the server is not available, any messages being transferred are lost.

NOTE

Why would anyone use a dependent client? Several reasons could make a dependent client more appealing. First, if your application messages are not of a critical nature, the overhead of maintaining an independent client might not be required. Second, If your application uses its own fault-tolerance features, you might not need to use the independent client features to retry messages when a server is not available.

TIP

Your ASP page can be a dependent or independent client. This is determined by the MSMQ installation on your Web server. You will learn more about installation later in the chapter.

Figure 22.6 illustrates the differences between independent and dependent clients.

FIGURE 22.6

An independent client maintains its own message store, whereas dependent clients are at the mercy of their MSMQ servers.

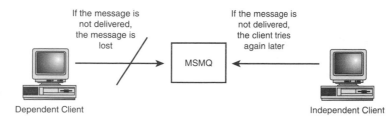

Public, Private, and Transactional Queues

As you learned earlier, message queues are much like a channel on television. These individual channels have unique properties. MSMQ via ASP supports three kinds of message queues, each suited for a unique purpose.

- Public queue—A public queue is accessible by all MSMQ clients. This queue is displayed in Active Directory by the MSMQ servers for all clients to see.

- Private queue—When you need to have a queue that is not publicly visible to all MSMQ clients, you can use private queues. Private queues do not have any security restrictions on them, per se. Instead, they are invisible to all clients. This means that you need to know the name of the queue to access it. Because the queue is not listed in Active Directory, this turns out to be a performance benefit.

- Transactional queue—When you are working with MTS and transactions, the transactional queue is likely to be your best choice. A transactional queue contains transactional messages, which cannot be sent using a standard message queue. Although MTS is not required to use transactional queues (MSMQ relies on DTC to manage them), they can be used cooperatively to extend your MTS transactions.

> **NOTE**
>
> A fourth kind of queue, private message only queue, is accessible via Visual Basic and Visual C++.

Anatomy of a Message

Messages in MSMQ are not complex. Most messages are plain text, providing simplicity and ease of transport. Messages are broken into two distinct parts:

- Message label—The message label is much like the title or header of a Web page or document. The label is used to identify the message and can contain special text to indicate the type of message being sent.

- Message body—This is the core content of the message itself. This is what constitutes the body of a letter, for example. The message you are sending through MSMQ is typically found in the body, using the label as an identifier.

> **NOTE**
>
> MSMQ supports several kinds of message contents, ranging from simple strings and numeric values to objects, arrays, and files. In this chapter, I will be demonstrating the basics of string messages. For more information on other data types, please refer to the MSMQ documentation.

Installing and Configuring MSMQ Services

MSMQ acts as part of the Windows NT operating system, as a service available to applications. The installation of MSMQ is not a difficult task; it does, however, require some understanding of the options involved. Installation of MSMQ can be carried out for either MSMQ servers or MSMQ clients, as I discussed earlier in this chapter.

Requirements for MSMQ

MSMQ is available in two forms: standard and enterprise. The standard version of MSMQ is available as part of the Windows NT 4.0 Option Pack. The enterprise version of MSMQ is part of Windows NT 4.0 Enterprise Edition. The enterprise version of MSMQ includes the core features of MSMQ in addition to four additional capabilities:

- No limit to the number of users connected to MSMQ.
- Capability to connect to other vendor-message queuing systems, such as IBM MQSeries.
- Automatic rerouting to avoid failed networks in multiple network environments.
- Automatic least-cost routing between servers when multiple networks are available.

This chapter focuses on the Standard edition of MSMQ. If you are looking for information on the Enterprise edition, you should visit the Message Queue Overview and Resources Web page at

```
http://www.microsoft.com/ntserver/appservice/exec/overview/
➥MSMQ_Overview.asp
```

Requirements for MSMQ Servers

Earlier in this chapter you read about the different kinds of MSMQ servers available. To install an MSMQ server, you must be running Windows NT 4.0 Server or Windows NT 4.0 Server Enterprise Edition.

Each enterprise network requires at least one primary enterprise controller (PEC) server. This server houses the master copy of the MSMQ information store or database. All MSMQ servers require a Microsoft SQL Server 6.5 or higher database.

Requirements for MSMQ Clients

Any system running Microsoft Windows 9x or Windows NT can be installed as an MSMQ client. As I mentioned earlier, there are two kinds of MSMQ clients: dependent and independent. Ideally, you should ensure that any system that might not have a guaranteed network connection to an MSMQ server is installed as an independent client.

Installing an MSMQ Server

Installing an MSMQ server takes place in the Windows NT 4.0 Option Pack. Each enterprise network requires one primary enterprise controller, so that should be your first step. Additional servers may be primary site controllers, backup site controllers, or standalone MSMQ servers. To install a PEC, follow these steps:

1. Open the Windows NT 4.0 Option Pack setup and choose to Add/Remove components.

2. Locate and select the Microsoft Message Queue check box in the Components list box.

3. Click the Show Subcomponents button to open the Microsoft Message Queue dialog box, shown in Figure 22.7.

FIGURE 22.7

All MSMQ components are installed from the Windows NT 4.0 Option Pack setup.

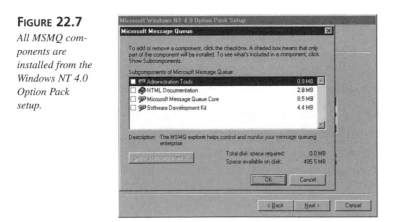

4. Select all four check boxes: Administration Tools, HTML Documentation, Microsoft Message Queue Core, and the Software Development Kit.

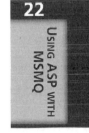

> **NOTE**
>
> The SDK also includes information and files that you can use if you want to develop for MSMQ using Visual Basic, Visual C++, or a similar high-level language.

5. Click the OK button to commit your changes and return to the components list box.

6. Click the OK button to return to the Windows NT 4.0 Option Pack dialog box.

7. Click the Next button to advance to the next screen, shown in Figure 22.8.

FIGURE 22.8

After you set up a PEC, you can install other MSMQ servers on your network.

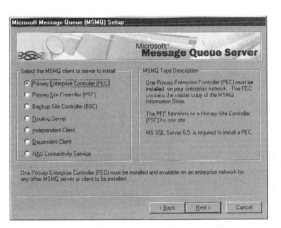

8. This screen enables you to choose the type of server (or client) you want to install. Select the Primary Enterprise Controller (PEC) radio button.

9. Click the Next button to configure your PEC. The next page appears, as shown in Figure 22.9.

10. In the MSMQ Primary Enterprise Controller Name panel, enter the name of your enterprise. This could be your Windows NT domain name or another distinguishing name.

11. In the MSMQ Site Controller Name panel, enter the name of your MSMQ site. This is typically your local area network or a grouping of machines.

12. Click the Next button to advance to the screen shown in Figure 22.10.

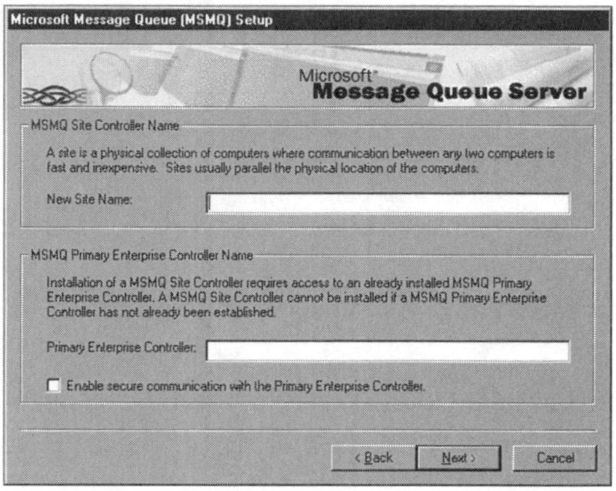

FIGURE 22.9

Installing a PEC creates a master MSMQ information store and a primary site controller.

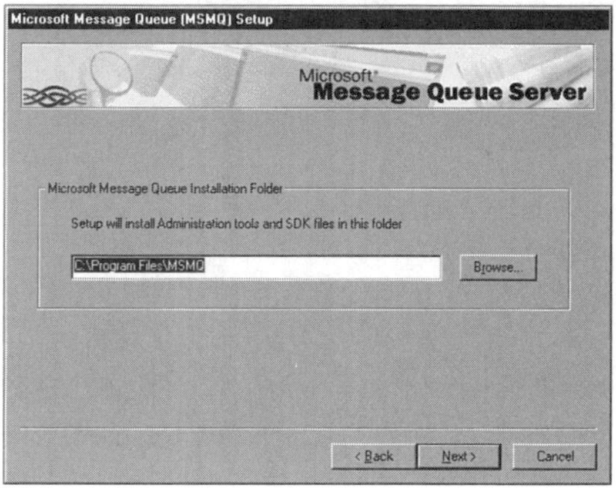

FIGURE 22.10

Use this dialog to specify the installation location for the MSMQ files.

13. At this step, specify the installation path for the MSMQ files. Optionally, you may click on the Browse button to select an existing folder.

14. Click the Next button to begin the installation. The Windows NT 4.0 Option Pack setup proceeds to copy the MSMQ files to your system. After the copy is complete, the dialog box shown in Figure 22.11 appears.

15. At this point you can specify the directory location where the MSMQ database and database log files are stored. You may also additionally specify the starting sizes of the two databases. Click the Continue button to accept the defaults.

16. The MSMQ Connected Networks dialog box appears, shown in Figure 22.12. This dialog box is used to specify the names of networks your server is connected to. Click the Add button to continue.

FIGURE 22.11

This dialog box specifies the data-base size for the MSMQ information store.

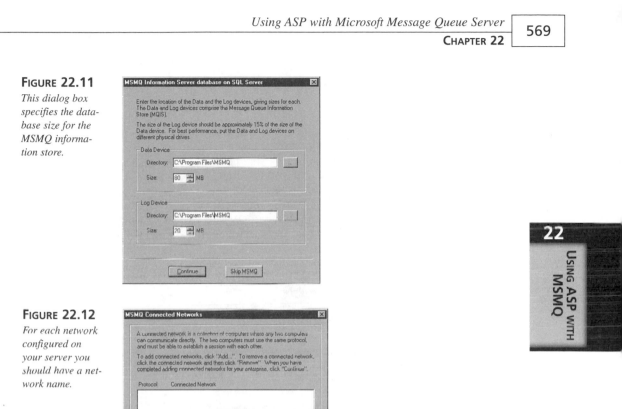

FIGURE 22.12

For each network configured on your server you should have a net-work name.

17. The New Connected Network dialog box, shown in Figure 22.13, is used to add the name of a network to your MSMQ installation. Enter a name for your network in the Connected Network Name field. For example, if your network spans your sales office, you could enter Sales Office.

FIGURE 22.13

You can specify a network name and protocol.

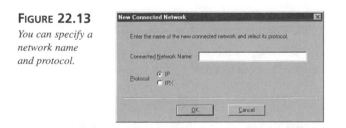

18. Specify the Protocol your network uses: IP or IPX. Select the radio button of the appropriate protocol.

19. Click the OK button to continue.

20. After you have finished adding network names for each installed network, click the Continue button. The next step is to assign network names to your installed networks.

21. If you have multiple IP networks specified on your server, the IP Addresses Assigned to Connected Networks dialog box appears (see Figure 22.14). Select your networks from the top panel and select a network name from the Connected Network drop-down box.

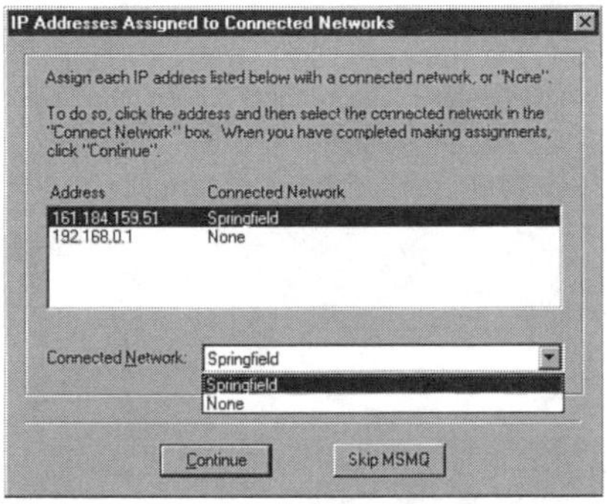

FIGURE 22.14

Network names are used to reference physical connected networks for your server.

> **NOTE**
>
> Each IP address bound to your server's interface cards will appear in this list. You might have multiple IP addresses that are physically part of the same connected network, whereas others may link disparate connections from other locations.

22. When you are finished, click the Continue button.

23. The Windows NT 4.0 Option Pack setup will complete the configuration of MSMQ, leaving you only to click the Finish button.

> **TIP**
>
> Installing the other MSMQ server types is similar to installing a PEC.

Installing MSMQ Clients

The steps involved in installing an MSMQ client are not nearly as involved as those for an MSMQ server. Remember that there are two different kinds of clients you can install (independent and dependent). That being said, the installation process for both clients is identical:

1. Open the Windows NT 4.0 Option Pack setup and choose to Add/Remove components.

2. Locate and select the Microsoft Message Queue check box in the Components list box.

3. Click the Show Subcomponents button to open the Microsoft Message Queue dialog box, shown in Figure 22.7.

4. Select all four check boxes: Administration Tools, HTML Documentation, Microsoft Message Queue Core, and Software Development Kit.

5. Click the OK button to commit your changes and return to the components list box.

6. Click the OK button to return to the Windows NT 4.0 Option Pack dialog box.

7. Click the Next button to advance to the next screen, shown in Figure 22.15.

FIGURE 22.15
You can choose one of two client types for MSMQ.

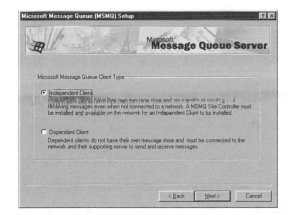

8. Select the type of client you want to install: Independent Client or Dependent Client.

9. Click the Next button to advance to a screen similar to the one shown in Figure 22.16.

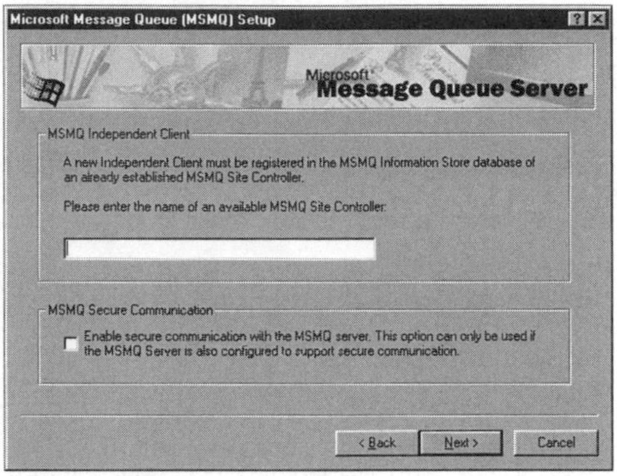

FIGURE 22.16

In this case, you're installing an independent client; however, the screens are the same for dependent clients.

10. In the top pane, enter the name of your MSMQ site controller computer. This is the server that you installed in the last section.

11. Click the Next button to instruct the MSMQ setup to locate the server, as shown in Figure 22.17.

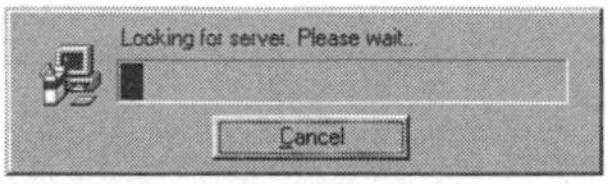

FIGURE 22.17

A progress indicator is displayed as your system attempts to contact the site controller.

12. After the server has been found, you are taken to the screen shown in Figure 22.10 to specify the directory for your MSMQ files. Enter the directory path for your MSMQ files and click the Next button to start the installation.

13. After the installation is complete, click the Finish button to close the Windows NT 4.0 Option Pack setup.

> **NOTE**
>
> Remember that you should only choose to install a dependent client when you have a reasonable assurance that your client will always be able to reach the server, or your messages are not critical to the functionality of your application.

Using Active Server Pages to Queue Messages

With the basics of MSMQ under your belt, you're now ready to leap into raw MSMQ development. Incorporating MSMQ into your Web applications requires more planning than actual coding. Careful design is the key to success with MSMQ. To familiarize yourself with MSMQ and ASP, you will now create a sample order processing Web application. In this example, you will use a simplified architecture based on one system acting as both the MSMQ server and client. If you have an additional machine available, you can expand these instructions to use both machines. This example assumes you have an MSMQ server (likely a primary enterprise controller) installed.

> **NOTE**
>
> Your MSMQ server can act as an MSMQ client.

Understanding MSMQ Components

At the heart of communications with MSMQ are the MSMQ components. These components are much like any other component you would use in your ASP pages or alternatively in a program created in another language, such as Visual Basic. Ten different MSMQ components are installed, each providing access to the MSMQ API (Application Programming Interface). Later in this section, you will experiment with a few of these components in your ASP example. The following is a brief description of each component:

- MSMQQuery—Used to query the MSMQ Information Store (MQIS) for any existing message queues. Results from queries are returned to MSMQQuery in an MSMQQueueInfos object.

- MSMQQueueInfos—Used to select a public queue from a collection of queues returned by MSMQQuery.

- MSMQQueueInfo—Used for queue management, creating and deleting queues, and changing queue properties.

- MSMQQueue—Used to explore the contents of a message queue, much like a recordset for a database.

- MSMQEvent—Used to implement events to queues for queue actions, such as message arrival, errors, and other events.

- MSMQMessages—Used to create MSMQ messages for a message queue.

- MSMQCoordinatedTransactionDispenser—Used to establish a DTC transaction object, returned as an MSMQTransaction object.

- MSMQTransaction—Used to commit or terminate transactions within a message queue, based on a DTC transaction object or an internal transaction.

- MSMQTransactionDispenser—Used to create an internal (non-DTC) transaction object that can be used to send and receive messages.

- MSMQApplication—Used to determine the machine identifier of a computer (client or server).

> **NOTE**
>
> For programming references for each of the components, refer to the Windows NT 4.0 Option Pack documentation.

Using MSMQ in Your ASP Pages

Now that you have an MSMQ server (and client) installed, you are ready to begin using MSMQ within your Web applications. In this section, you will create a basic MSMQ example through ASP, using the MSMQ components. This sample is designed around development when the client and the server are the same machine.

> **NOTE**
>
> If you're feeling ambitious, you could adapt this example to work with a separate client and server. I'll leave that for you to work on another day, however, and concentrate on the basics.

Planning the Communication

At the heart of this example is a simplified order processing system for a new airline, SpudAir. SpudAir is a regional airline with a modest budget and limited time to implement an order-processing system. You have been asked to create a simple order system

for the SpudAir sales staff to process flight requests. The SpudAir process for ordering is very simple:

1. The SpudAir sales representative receives a request from a customer for a seat on an available flight. The sales representative searches the online database of flights and locates an available seat for the customer.

2. The sales representative completes an online form in the order-processing system, requesting the seat be reserved for the customer in the internal SpudAir reservation system.

3. The request is sent electronically to the reservation system flagging the seat as reserved.

4. The reservation system reserves the seat and returns a message to the sales representative to indicate that the seat has been reserved.

5. The sales representative informs the customer that his seat has been reserved and proceeds to charge the customer the flight costs.

For this example, you will create a simple model of this process.

Creating the Message Queue

The first step in creating your processing system is to create the message queues used by the Web application. Looking at the process used by SpudAir, you can identify a message queue that can be created, Reservation Request. To begin, follow these steps:

1. Open the Microsoft Message Queue Explorer. The MSMQ Explorer is shown in Figure 22.18.

2. Locate the Sites folder in the left panel. Click it to expand to the MSMQ site that you created when you installed MSMQ.

3. Expand your MSMQ site to display your MSMQ server.

4. Right-click your MSMQ server. From the context menu, choose New, Queue. The Queue Name dialog box appears, as shown in Figure 22.19.

5. Enter the name of your new queue. For this example, use ReservationRequest.

6. Click OK to commit your changes and create the message queue. Your new message queue is added to the list of queues, as shown in Figure 22.20.

With your message queues created, you're ready to move on to sending messages via ASP pages.

FIGURE 22.18

The Microsoft Message Queue Explorer is the MSMQ administrative console.

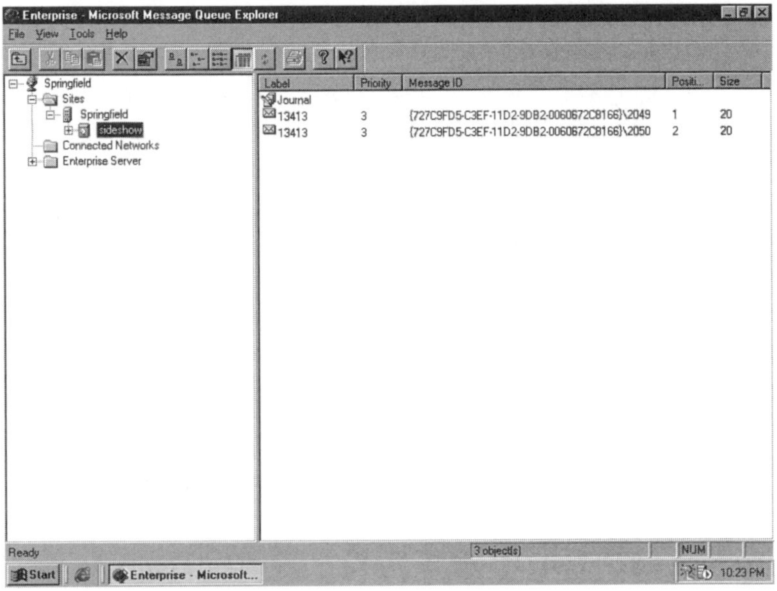

FIGURE 22.19

The Queue Name dialog box enables you to create a transactional queue.

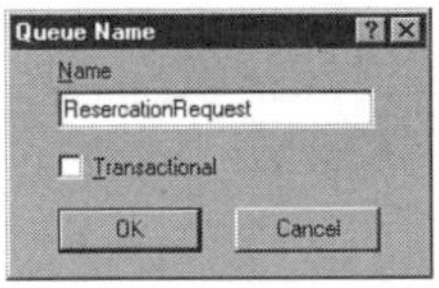

FIGURE 22.20

Each queue appears in the hierarchical list, much like folders in the Windows Explorer.

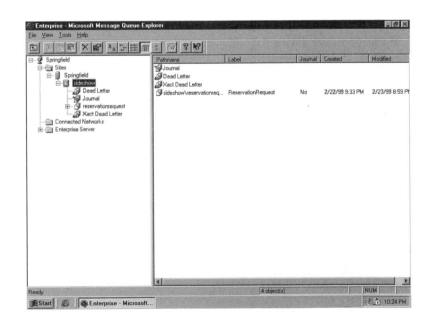

Sending a Message

Before you can send a message to a queue, a line of communication with the MSMQ server must be established. This is called opening a queue. Begin by creating the Web page that will open the queue:

1. Create a new ASP page in your editor called msmq.asp.

2. Copy the contents of Listing 22.1 into your new msmq.asp page.

LISTING 22.1   THE MSMQ.ASP PAGE

```
1  <%@ Language=VBScript %>
2  <HTML>
3  <HEAD>
4  <TITLE>MSMQ Example: Step 2</TITLE>
5  </HEAD>
6  <BODY BGCOLOR="White">
7  <FONT FACE="Arial,Helvetica,Sans-Serif">
8  <H1>Open an MSMQ Public Queue</H1>
9  <P ALIGN="LEFT">
10 This page creates the connection to the MSMQ message queue for all
11 activity. </P>
12 <HR SIZE=1 NOSHADE>
13 <%
14 set objMSMQ = Server.CreateObject ("MSMQ.MSMQQueueInfo")
15 objMSMQ.PathName = ".\ReservationRequest"
16 objMSMQ.Label = "ReservationRequest"
17 On Error Resume Next
18 objMSMQ.Create
19 On Error Goto 0
20 set objMessageQueue = objMSMQ.Open (2, 0)
21 %>
22 <HR SIZE=1 NOSHADE>
23 </FONT>
24 </BODY>
25 </HTML>
```

3. Save the changes to msmq.asp.

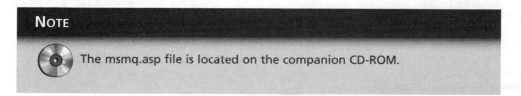

> **NOTE**
>
> The msmq.asp file is located on the companion CD-ROM.

22

USING ASP WITH
MSMQ

This brief listing begins your work with the MSMQ objects. On line 14, you create an instance of the MSMQ.MSMQQueueInfo object which allows you to open the ReservationRequest queue. Lines 15 and 16 reference the queue itself. Notice the objMSMQ.PathName property in line 15, where referencing a queue is much like referencing a physical directory in your file system. In lines 17–19, you are creating the message queue as a fail-safe. In fact, you actually created the queue in the last series of steps; however, you can choose to re-create it to ensure it exists. If the queue exists, as it should, this command is not executed. Finally, on line 20, you actually open the queue for sending a message. As you can see in line 20, two parameters are passed: Access and ShareMode. The values are shown in Table 22.1 and Table 22.2.

TABLE 22.1 OPEN Access PARAMETER VALUES

Constant	Value	Description
MQ_PEEK_ACCESS	0	Read-only access to the queue.
MQ_SEND_ACCESS	1	Write-only access to the queue.
MQ_RECEIVE_ACCESS	2	Read/Write access to the queue.

TABLE 22.2 OPEN ShareMode PARAMETER VALUES

Constant	Value	Description
MQ_DENY_NONE	0	Queue is available to everyone.
MQ_DENY_RECEIVE_SHARE	1	Restricted access to the queue.

> **NOTE**
>
> For more information on the parameters, refer to the Windows NT 4.0 Option Pack documentation.

Open the page in a Web browser, and you'll notice there isn't much to look at. The rest is coming.

The next step is to compose and send the message itself. To do so, you will rely on a form to push the message contents to your msmq.asp page. Follow these instructions:

1. Create a new page in your editor named msmq-form.htm.

2. Insert the code found in Listing 22.2 into your new page.

LISTING 22.2   THE MSMQ-FORM.HTM PAGE

```
1 <HTML>
2 <HEAD>
3 <TITLE>MSMQ Form</TITLE>
4 </HEAD>
5 <BODY>
6 <FONT FACE="Arial">
7 <H1>MSMQ Example: Step 1</H1>
8 <HR SIZE=1 NOSHADE>
9 <P ALIGN-"LEFT">
10 This form will be used to submit a message to the
11 ReservationRequest message queue.
12 </P>
13 <HR SIZE=1 NOSHADE>
14 <FORM action="msmq.asp" method=POST>
15 <TABLE BORDER="0" ALIGN="CENTER">
16 <TR>
17 <TD>
18 Customer Seating Position
19 </TD>
20 <TD>
21 <INPUT type="text" name=txtLabel size=5 maxlength=5>
22 </TD>
23 </TR>
24 <TR>
25 <TD>
26 Customer Name
27 </TD>
28 <TD>
29 <INPUT type="text" name=txtBody size=50 maxlength=50>
30 </TD>
31 </TR>
32 <TR>
33 <TD COLSPAN=2 ALIGN="CENTER">
34 <INPUT type="submit" value="Submit">
35 </TD>
36 </TR>
37 </TABLE>
38 </FORM>
39 <HR SIZE=1 NOSHADE>
40 <P ALIGN="LEFT">
41 This page pushes information to the <U>msmq.asp</U> page for
42 processing.
43 </P>
44 </FONT>
45 </BODY>
46 </HTML>
```

22

USING ASP WITH
MSMQ

   3. Save the changes you have made to msmq-form.htm.

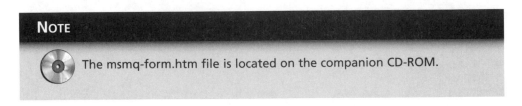

NOTE

The msmq-form.htm file is located on the companion CD-ROM.

This simple page will push the contents of a form to the msmq.asp page, as shown in line 14. The form is comprised of two text boxes, txtLabel and txtBody.

The next step is to alter your msmq.asp page to retrieve the message body and label from the msmq-form.htm page and send the message to the MSMQ message queue. To do so, follow these instructions:

1. Open the msmq.asp page in your editor for the changes.

2. Locate the beginning of the ASP scripting block on line 10 and the end of the scripting block on line 18.

3. Select the entire scripting block and replace it with the code found in Listing 22.3.

LISTING 22.3 THE UPDATED MSMQ.ASP SCRIPTING BLOCK

```
1 <%
2 On Error Resume Next
3 Dim objMSMQ, objMsgQueue, objMessage, strCaption, strBody
4 strLabel = Request.Form("txtLabel")
5 strBody = Request.Form("txtBody")
6 set objMSMQ = Server.CreateObject ("MSMQ.MSMQQueueInfo")
7 objMSMQ.PathName = ".\ReservationRequest"
8 objMSMQ.Label = "ReservationRequest"
9 objMSMQ.Create
10 On Error Goto 0
11 set objMsgQueue = objMSMQ.Open (2, 0)
12 If objMsgQueue.IsOpen Then
13 Set objMessage = Server.CreateObject("MSMQ.MSMQMessage")
14 objMessage.Body = strBody
15 objMessage.Label = strLabel
16 objMessage.Send objMsgQueue
17 End If
18 objMsgQueue.Close
19 %>
```

4. Save the changes you have made to the msmq.asp page.

In lines 4–5, the text box values passed from the msmq-form.htm page are stored to string variables using the Request object. With the message body and labels assigned to variables, the message is ready to be sent. The process begins with the creation of the `objMessage` object in line 13, which is an `MSMQ.MSMQMessage` object. Lines 14–15 define the message by assigning the body and label, respectively. To send the message, line 16 calls the `objMessage.Send` function. Finally, on line 18, the message queue connection is closed.

After you have submitted a few messages, open the MSMQ Explorer and click the ReservationRequest queue. You will notice each of your messages appears in the right panel, identified by a unique number. This is shown in Figure 22.21.

FIGURE 22.21

Each message in the queue can be opened using the MSMQ Explorer.

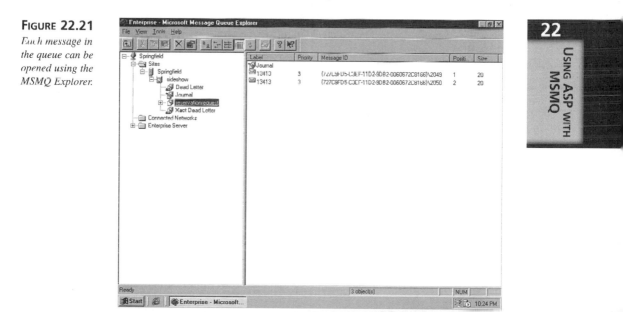

Receiving a Message

The final piece of the MSMQ puzzle is to receive the message. For this step, you will create a third page that will retrieve and display the contents of the message queue. MSMQ supports three methods for reading messages from a message queue: synchronously, asynchronously, and using a cursor (much like a database). ASP, however, only supports the first method—synchronously. This means that execution of your script is blocked until a message is available or your script times out when trying to connect to the MSMQ server.

To create the new page to read the message queue contents, follow these steps:

1. Create a new page in your editor named msmq-read.asp.
2. Insert the code found in Listing 22.4 into your new page.

LISTING 22.4—THE MSMQ-READ.ASP PAGE

```
1 <HTML>
2 <HEAD>
3 <TITLE>MSMQ Read</TITLE>
4 /HEAD>
5 <BODY>
6 <FONT FACE="Arial">
7 <H1>MSMQ Example: Step 3</H1>
8 <HR SIZE=1 NOSHADE>
9 <P ALIGN="LEFT">
10 This page reads the waiting messages in the ReservationRequest
11 message queue and returns it to the screen.
12 </P>
13 <HR SIZE=1 NOSHADE>
14 <%
15 set objMSMQ = Server.CreateObject("MSMQ.MSMQQueueInfo")
16 objMSMQ.PathName = ".\ReservationRequest"
17 set objMessageQueue = objMSMQ.Open(1,0)
18 Do While True
19 Set objMessage = objMessageQueue.Receive(false, true, 1000)
20 If objMessage Is Nothing Then Exit Do
21 Response.Write("Customer: " & objMessage.Body & "<BR>")
22 Response.Write("Seat: " & objMessage.Label & "<BR> <BR>")
23 Loop
24 %>
25 <HR SIZE=1 NOSHADE>
26 <P ALIGN="LEFT">
27 This page pulls the message information from the message queue.
28 </P>
29 </FONT>
30 </BODY>
31 </HTML>
```

3. Save the changes you have made to the msmq-read.asp page.

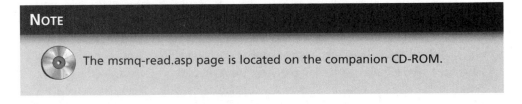

NOTE

The msmq-read.asp page is located on the companion CD-ROM.

In lines 15–17, you establish a read connection to the message queue, ReservationRequest. Subsequently, you create the `objMessage` object, which represents the message itself in line 19, and assuming that the message is not void of content, you write the contents of the message body and label to the screen. This is carried in a

`Do While...Loop` to display all waiting messages in the message queue. A sample is shown in Figure 22.22.

FIGURE 22.22

Each message in the queue is displayed to the visitor.

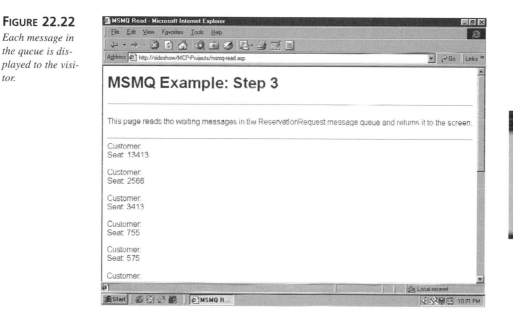

If there are no messages in the queue (for example, if after viewing the page, you refresh it before placing more messages into the queue), the page will appear to have hung. This is the synchronous reading into the message queue by MSMQ, waiting for either a message to become available or the connection to time out. A well-designed Web application would use Microsoft Transaction Server to ensure that the communication could be achieved, and if it couldn't, it would ensure that the user does not experience a delay or error message.

Summary

The simple example in this chapter illustrates just how easy it is to incorporate MSMQ into your Web applications. By using MSMQ to manage your process communications, your Web applications gain a new level of independence and fault tolerance. You also reduce the complexity required to code your own messaging system. MSMQ is ideally suited to a distributed networking environment and multiple systems sharing information or requests. An ideal example of this is the banking world, where financial messages and requests absolutely must be transferred completely or not at all. Using the power of message queuing services, financial institutions can rely on the architecture behind the message system to manage the fine details of passing data. This enables developers to concentrate on the task at hand: working with the information after it has been received.

Advanced Topics

PART
VI

CHAPTER 23

Securing Your Web Site

by Stephen Walther

IN THIS CHAPTER

Every Web site developer must worry about the problem of security. If your Web site hosts confidential information such as credit card numbers, business documents, or passwords, you have a responsibility to protect this information. Failure might have dire consequences, both for your business and for the users of your Web site.

This chapter focuses on two problems of security. In the first part of this chapter, you will learn how to protect the security of your data while it is being transmitted. If someone enters a password or credit card number at your Web site, you must prevent the wrong people from accessing this data as it travels across the Internet or your local network. This first part of this chapter will explain how to use the Secure Sockets Layer to provide a secure channel of communication and will cover some techniques for using the Secure Sockets Layer in your Active Server Pages.

> **NOTE**
>
> Several serious security holes in Internet Information Server have been uncovered. For example, it was discovered that any user could view the ASP source for a page by appending a period at the end of the address for a page. Using this method, anyone could view secret information such as database passwords. Microsoft has posted patches to fix these problems at the Microsoft Web site. To view the latest security updates and download the latest patches, go to `http://www.microsoft.com/security`.

The rest of this chapter focuses on the problem of password protection in your Web site. Two different approaches to this problem are discussed. You will learn how to password protect Active Server Pages by using database security and by using Windows NT security.

Encryption, Authentication and Data Integrity with SSL

The Secure Sockets Layer (SSL) is a protocol, originally developed by Netscape, for transmitting information securely across an unsecure network. SSL is the only existing method for sending private information across the Internet that works with the majority of current browsers. SSL provides a technical solution to three distinct security problems: encryption, authentication, and data integrity.

> **NOTE**
>
> The Microsoft Internet Information Server and Internet Explorer (versions 3.0 and higher) also support the Private Communication Technology Protocol (PCT). Microsoft developed PCT as a more efficient version of SSL.

Encryption

When you enter information into an HTML form and submit it at a Web site, the information is transmitted from your browser to the Web site's server. As the information travels across the Internet, it typically passes through several intermediate connections. In theory, the data entered into the form can be intercepted and read.

The problem is analogous to the situation a general faces when he must send a message containing secret plans across enemy territory. As the messenger travels across the unknown territory, he could be captured, and the enemy could steal and read the secret plans.

The proper solution, for both the general and for the person entering information into the HTML form, is to encrypt the message before it is sent across hostile territory. Even if the message is captured, the privacy of the information is protected—unless, of course, the secret code is cracked.

SSL encrypts information as it passes back and forth between a Web server and a Web browser. The information is encoded using a publicly known encryption algorithm and a secret session encryption key. The number of bits in the session key determines the strength of the encryption.

When you installed IIS, by default you installed a version of IIS that supports a 40-bit session encryption key. However, you have the option of upgrading IIS to use a stronger 128-bit session encryption key. Although messages encrypted with the 40-bit key have been cracked, messages encrypted with the 128-bit key are considered unbreakable with current technology.

Why not always use the 128-bit key? There are two reasons. First, communicating using a 128-bit key can be significantly slower than using the 40-bit key. The longer the key, the more work the server and browser must perform to encrypt and decrypt the messages passed back and forth.

There are also legal restrictions on using the longer 128-bit key. The United States government has classified 128-bit SSL as munitions. This means that it is illegal, with

23

SECURING YOUR
WEB SITE

certain exceptions, to export any program that supports this stronger encryption outside the United States. This applies to both Web servers and Web browsers.

Normally, if you install a 128-bit session key on your Web server, your Web server will automatically negotiate the highest level of encryption to use for securing communication. If someone communicates using a browser with a 40-bit key, your server will automatically use this level of encryption. However, you can also configure IIS to reject browsers that do not support the stronger 128-bit key.

> **NOTE**
>
> To install the stronger 128-bit version of SSL, you will need to get the Microsoft Encryption Pack. Call Microsoft at 1-800-260-6579. After you have the stronger encryption installed, you cannot continue to install the normal Windows NT Service Packs. See Microsoft Knowledge Base Article Q159709 for more information.

Authentication

If you visit a Web site that appears to be Amazon.com in every way, you might feel safe providing your credit card information to buy a book. However, a clever thief could create a Web site that was indistinguishable from Amazon.com and steal your credit card information.

To return to the example of the general sending a message across enemy territory, imagine that the enemy decides to impersonate the intended recipient of the secret plans. The general and the imposter decide on a secret code, and the messenger delivers the message encoded with the secret code. However, the messenger has delivered the secret plans to the imposter.

To prevent one Web site from pretending to be another, SSL can be used to authenticate a Web site. When you install SSL on your Web server, you must install a server certificate. This certificate is used to verify your Web site's identity in much the same way as your driver's license or passport is used to verify your personal identity. A server certificate contains information about your organization, your Web site, and the issuer of the certificate.

To work as a digital ID, a server certificate must be signed by a certificate authority. A certificate authority acts as a trusted third party that verifies the identity of a Web site for its users. Whenever you open a page using SSL, the information from the server certificate is included. For example, using Internet Explorer, you can view the certificate information for the home page of the Microsoft site. Enter `https://www.microsoft.com` into the address bar of your browser and click File, Properties, and then the button labeled Certificates (see Figure 23.1).

FIGURE 23.1

A server certificate for a Microsoft site.

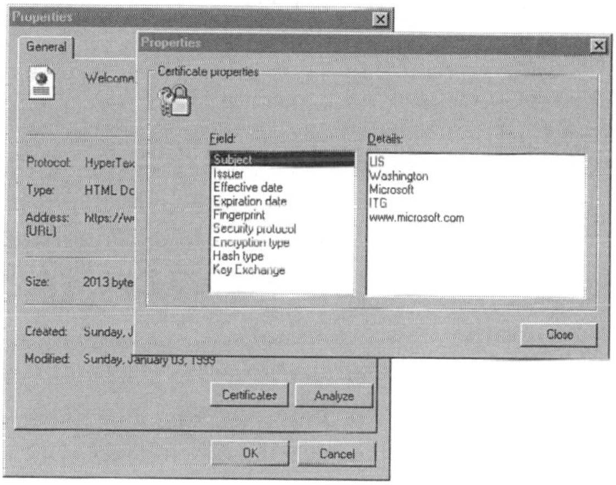

Instead of using a third-party certificate authority, you can also issue and sign your own certificates using Microsoft Certificate Server. In other words, you can be your own certificate authority. Being your own certificate authority is valuable when you need to authenticate multiple computers in your own organization to members of your organization. However, if your Web site is public, you should use a third-party certificate authority such as Verisign because a server certificate is only as trustworthy as its issuer.

SSL version 3.0 also supports client certificates. Client certificates work in exactly the same way as server certificates except they are used to authenticate Web browsers rather than Web servers. Both Microsoft Internet Explorer (version 3.0 and higher) and Netscape Navigator (version 3.0 and higher) support client certificates. You can get a client certificate from a certificate authority, or you can use Microsoft Certificate Server to issue your own.

Data Integrity

Imagine that a malicious individual decides to alter a message as it is transmitted across the Internet. This individual does not read the message or prevent the message from being transmitted. The message is simply vandalized.

To return to the example of the general, suppose that the messenger successfully delivers the general's secret plans to the intended recipient. Without the messenger's knowledge, however, the secret plans have been switched while the messenger was crossing the enemy terrain. The wrong plans have been delivered.

SSL protects the integrity of data as it crosses the Internet. When messages are transmitted with SSL, they include a message authentication code (MAC). This code is used to detect whether a message has been altered. In other words, when you use SSL, you know that the message received is the same as the message sent.

How Secure Is SSL?

How safe is SSL? Can you use SSL to safely transmit credit card information or private business documents across the Internet? All the major commercial Web sites on the Internet that accept credit card information currently use SSL. For example, Amazon.com has accepted credit card information from over 4.5 million customers using SSL.

The real answer is that you do not have much choice. If you want to convey private information across the Internet without forcing your Web site's users to download special programs such as Wallets, ActiveX components, or Java applets, then you must use SSL. SSL is the only method of sending private information that is supported by the majority of browsers.

Configuring Your Server to Use SSL

Configuring your server to use SSL is a straightforward process. However, if you are planning to use a server certificate from a third-party certificate authority, you should be warned that it can be a long process. Receiving a server certificate can take as long as eight weeks. It can also be an expensive process. VeriSign, for example, currently charges $349.00 for a server certificate and you must pay $249.00 each additional year that the certificate is renewed.

There are three main steps involved in installing SSL. First, you must generate a certificate request file and an encryption key pair file using Microsoft Key Manager. Next, you must apply for a server certificate at a third-party certificate authority by providing it with your certificate request file. Finally, after you receive your server certificate, you must install it by using Microsoft Key Manager.

Generating a Certificate Request File

To create a certificate request file—also called a certificate signing request (CSR)—open Microsoft Key Manager by launching the Internet Service Manager and clicking the Key Manager icon. Within Key Manager choose Key, Create New Key. This starts a wizard that will guide you through the task of creating the certificate request file (see Figure 23.2).

FIGURE 23.2

The Microsoft Key Manager.

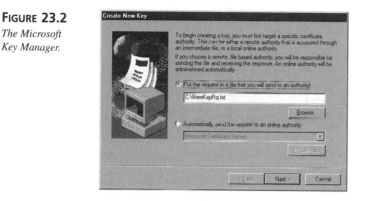

To create the certificate request file, supply the following information:

- Request File—When you complete the wizard, your certificate request file will be stored on your hard drive with this name.
- Key Name—You can supply any name here. This name is used to identify the key.
- Password—You will need to use this password when installing your signed server certificate after you receive it from your certificate authority.
- Key Size—By default, the Key Size will be 512 bits long. If you are using the domestic version of IIS, the key size will be 1024 bits long. The Key Size refers to the strength of the server certificate, not the strength of the session key used to encrypt messages.
- Organization—The name of the owner of your domain name. Usually, the Organization is the name of your company.
- Organizational Unit—The name of your department or business unit.
- Common Name—Your fully qualified domain name. For example, www.aspsite.com. You should not include the protocol (HTTP://).
- Country/Region—The two-letter ISO country code for your country. For example, US for the United States or CA for Canada. The wizard provides a link to a list of these country codes.
- State/Province—The full name of your state or province. For example, California.
- Locality—The name of your city or town. For example, San Francisco.
- Your Name—Your full name.

23

SECURING YOUR WEB SITE

- Email Address—Your email address.
- Phone Number—Your phone number.

After you supply this information to the wizard, a certificate request file will be saved to your hard drive. A broken key will appear in Key Manager signifying that a certificate request file has been generated, but the certificate has not been installed. If you're curious, here's an example of a certificate request file:

```
Webmaster: webmaster@aspsite.com
Phone: 5555555555
Server: Microsoft Key Manager for IIS Version 4.0

Common-name: www.aspsite.com
Organization Unit: aspsite
Organization: aspsite
Locality: San Francisco
State: California
Country: US

-----BEGIN NEW CERTIFICATE REQUEST-----
MIIBMjCB3QIBADB4MQswCQYDVQQGEwJVUzETMBEGA1UECBMKQ2FsaWZvcm5pYTEW
MBQGA1UEBxMNU2FuIEZyYW5jaXNjbzEQMA4GA1UEChMHYXNwc2l0ZTEQMA4GA1UE
CxMHYXNwc2l0ZTEYMBYGA1UEAxMPd3d3LmFzcHNpdGUuY29tMFwwDQYJKoZIhvcN
AQEBBQADSwAwSJBBBMTmq5mQcckNBNngyeUMR81BYgr11AWaTJMJBpsEZXduZXZB
2eho4xwmv5IfYQMjpi59Rtp75y4/WzGZ9Vhki2kCAwEAAaAAMA0GCSqGSIb3DQEB
BAUAA0EAKO+oilJMXLV3BxyymCg8MaXwdY2a2eM31aptIwh65iffoRVMqR3psUGA
+Zh/zqrnwa5NtYiQgSnJq37rZI1Owg==
-----END NEW CERTIFICATE REQUEST-----
```

Applying for a Server Certificate

After you have generated a certificate request file, you can apply for a server certificate from a certificate authority. Here is a list of three of the more popular ones:

- VeriSign Inc. (http://www.verisign.com)
- GTE CyberTrust Solutions (http://www.cybertrust.gte.com)
- Thawte Consulting (http://www.thawte.com)

For example, to apply for a VeriSign server certificate, go to http://www.verisign.com and choose Secure Server ID. You will need to provide VeriSign with identifying information about your organization such as your Dun and Bradstreet DUNS number, your articles of incorporation, or your business license. After you have provided this information, you can submit your certificate request file through an online form. After your information is verified, you will receive an email message that contains instructions for downloading your new server certificate.

Installing Your Server Certificate

The last step in preparing your server to use SSL is to actually install the server certificate. To install the server certificate, launch the Microsoft Key Manager once again and choose Key, Install Key Certificate. Open your server certificate file from your hard drive and supply the same password as you used when you generated the certificate request file. Next, specify the IP address and port to use with SSL. When you have finished, an icon of a completed key should appear within Microsoft Key Manager.

A server certificate only lasts for a preset period of time. In the right frame of the Microsoft Key Manager, you can view the exact date when your certificate will expire. To continue using SSL, you must request a new server certificate before this date.

> **NOTE**
>
> If you must transfer your certificate to a new server, you can use Microsoft Key Manager to create a backup copy of your certificate. Select Key, Export Key, Backup File. You can then load the certificate on the new server by selecting Key, Import Key, Backup File. The new server must have exactly the same Internet domain name as the original server (The IP address can be different).

Using SSL in Active Server Pages

After you have configured your server to use SSL, you can request any page from your Web site securely. To retrieve a Web page using SSL, use an address of the form `https://www.yourdomain.com/page.asp` rather than the normal `http://www.yourdo-main.com/page.asp`. This will work for any page at your Web site.

You can force users to use SSL when requesting pages from your Web site. Open the property page for a directory or single page within the Internet Service Manager and choose the Directory Security or the File Security tab. Next, click the Edit button under Secure Communications and choose Require Secure Channel When Accessing This Resource (see Figure 23.3). If you want to require 128-bit SSL, click the button labeled Encryption Settings and choose Require 128-Bit Encryption.

FIGURE 23.3

Requiring SSL when requesting a Web page.

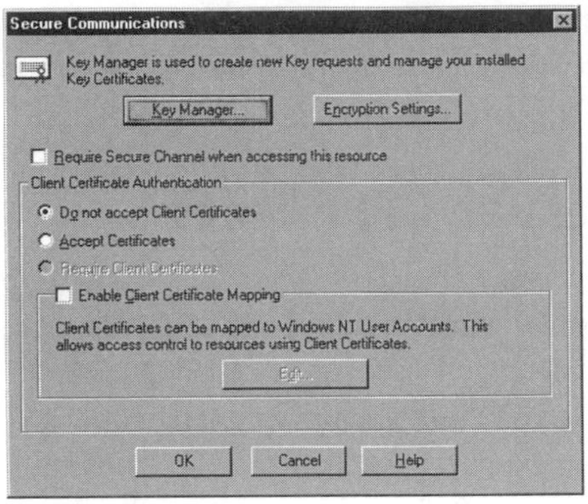

When requesting credit card information, it is a good idea to provide both a secure and an unsecure version of the form for collecting the information. Even though SSL is as old as Netscape 1.0, strangely enough, there are some browsers that still do not support it. To enable users to choose between the two versions of the same page, simply provide two different links:

```
<a href="https://www.yourdomain.com/pay.asp">Pay Now (secure version)</a>
<a href="http://www.yourdomain.com/pay.asp">Pay Now (unsecure version)</a>
```

Within the pay.asp page itself, you can detect whether or not the page is being requested using SSL. If a user is requesting a page unsecurely, you might want to warn him. Here is an example of a subroutine that detects and reports the security status of an Active Server Page (see Figure 23.4):

```
<%
SUB securityStatus
    IF Request.ServerVariables( "SERVER_PORT_SECURE" ) <> "1" THEN
        %>
        <table width=100% cellpadding=4 cellspacing=0
        bgcolor="lightyellow" border=1 align=center>
        <tr>
            <td><b>This Page Is Not Secure</b></td>
        </tr>
        </table>
        <%
    ELSE
        %>
        <table width=100% cellpadding=4 cellspacing=0
        bgcolor="lightgreen" border=1 align=center>
        <tr>
            <td>
            <b>This Page Is Secure</b>
            <br>Issuer:
            <%=Request.ServerVariables( "CERT_SERVER_ISSUER" )%>
```

```
            <br>Subject:
            <%=Request.ServerVariables( "CERT_SERVER_SUBJECT" )%>
            <br>Encryption Key Size:
            <%=Request.ServerVariables( "CERT_KEYSIZE" )%>
            <br>Certificate Key Size:
            <%=Request.ServerVariables( "CERT_SECRETKEYSIZE" )%>
            </td>
        </tr>
        </table>
        <%
    END IF
END SUB
%>
```

FIGURE 23.4

Security status.

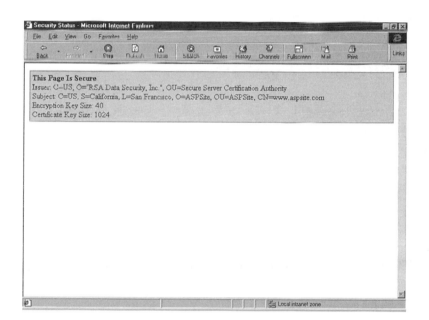

23

SECURING YOUR
WEB SITE

This subroutine uses the SERVER_PORT_SECURE server variable from the ServerVariables collection to determine whether the page is requested using SSL. If the page is requested using SSL, several properties of the secure connection are reported, such as the certificate, encryption key size, and the name of the issuer of the certificate.

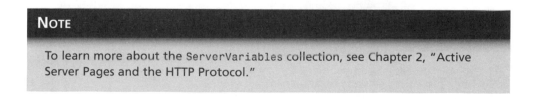

NOTE

To learn more about the ServerVariables collection, see Chapter 2, "Active Server Pages and the HTTP Protocol."

Password Protecting Your Web Site

Suppose you need to create a Web site that requires users to register before they can access password protected areas. For example, you might be developing an online store where visitors must register before they can purchase any products. Or, you might be creating a job site where members must first log in before they can view the current listing of job opportunities.

There are two approaches that you can take to password protect Web pages using Active Server Pages. You can create a custom password system using database security or you can use Windows NT security.

Using Database Security

One solution to the problem of password protecting Web pages is to use database security. Before a user can access a restricted area, his or her username and password are checked against a database table. In the following two sections, you will learn how to create a registration form and a standard INCLUDE file that you can use to password protect sections of your Web site.

The Registration Form

The registration form is used to gather three pieces of information: the user name, a password, and the user's cookie preference (see Figure 23.5). The decision of whether or not to use a cookie for identification purposes must be left in the hands of the user because there are situations in which it would be dangerous to automatically identify a user by a cookie. If more than one person is using the same browser, then the wrong person might be authenticated by the cookie. (For example, if the person is browsing the Internet at the public library.) The registration form is included in Listing 23.1 (register.asp available on the CD).

FIGURE 23.5

The registration form.

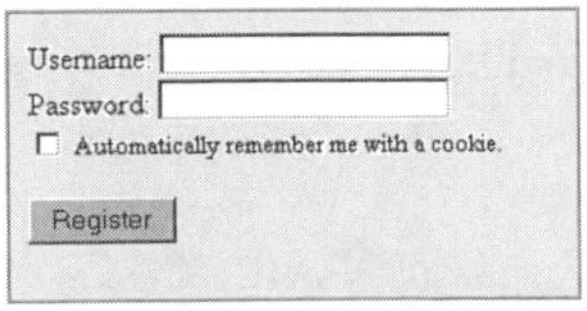

Username: [   ]
Password: [   ]
☐ Automatically remember me with a cookie.

[Register]

LISTING 23.1   USER REGISTRATION FORM—REGISTER.ASP

```asp
<%
function checked( byVal val1, byVal val2 )
     if val1 = val2 then checked = " checked"
end function

username = TRIM( Request( "username" ) )
password = TRIM( Request( "password" ) )
remember = Request( "remember" )
%>
<html>
<head><title>Register</title></head>
<body>
<font face="Arial">Register</font>
<p>
<center>
<table width=300 cellpadding=10 cellspacing=0
 bgcolor="#eeeeee" border=1>
<tr>
     <td>
     <form method="post" action="register2.asp">
     <input name="formscript" type="hidden"
      value="register.asp">
     Username:
     <input name="username" size=20 maxlength=20
      value="<%=Server.HTMLEncode( username )%>">
     <input name="username_req" type="hidden"
      value="You must enter a username">
    <br>Password:
     <input name="password" size=20 maxlength=20
      value="<%=Server.HTMLEncode( password )%>">
     <input name="password_req" type="hidden"
      value="You must enter a password.">
     <br><input name="remember" type="checkbox"
     value="1" <%=checked( remember, "1" )%>>
     <small>Automatically remember me with a cookie.</small>
     <p><input type="submit" value="Register">
     </form>
     </td>
</tr>
</table>
</body>
</html>
```

The real work of registration happens when the user submits the registration form and arrives at register2.asp (see Listing 23.2). The file, register2.asp, uses the validateForm INCLUDE file discussed in Chapter 3, "Working with HTML Forms," to verify whether the user has entered both a username and a password. Next, a

SQL stored procedure named `addUser` is executed to add the new registration information to a table named Users. If the table already contains the username, an error is passed back from the stored procedure by using a return parameter (this prevents two users from having the same username). Finally, the script adds a cookie with the username and, if the user has so selected, another with the user's password.

Here are the SQL statements used to create the Users table for holding the registration information:

```
create table users (
    userID INT NOT NULL IDENTITY(0,1),
    username VARCHAR( 20 ),
    password VARCHAR( 20 ),
    remember BIT,
    secretkey INT default ( RAND() * 1000 )
    )
go

grant all on users to public
```

> **NOTE**
>
> A SQL batch file for creating the Users table and all the stored procedures discussed in this section is included on the CD with the name security.sql.

Notice that the table includes an identity column for a unique user ID. The identity column automatically assigns each user a unique identifying number. The table also contains a secretkey column that automatically generates a random number. The purpose of this column will be explained in the next section.

The following SQL statements are used to create the `addUser` SQL stored procedure:

```
create procedure addUser
(
    @username varchar(20),
    @password varchar(20),
    @remember bit
)
AS
if exists( select username from users
    where username = @username )
    begin
        return( 10 )
    end
```

```
insert users
    (
    username,
    password,
remember
    ) VALUES (
    @username,
    @password,
    @remember
    )
go
grant all on addUser to public
```

The If exists statement is used to check whether a user with the username already exists. If a match is found, the stored procedure is exited with the return code of 10. Otherwise, the new registration information is inserted into the Users table.

LISTING 23.2   ADD NEW REGISTERED USER—REGISTER2.ASP

```
<!-- #INCLUDE FILE="validateform.asp" -->
<!-- #INCLUDE FILE="adovbs.inc"    >
<%
username = TRIM( Request( "username" ) )
password = TRIM( Request( "password" ) )
remember = Request( "remember" )

' Ready Database Connection
Set Con = Server.CreateObject( "ADODB.Connection" )

Con.Open "FILE NAME=c:\myDataLink.UDL"

' Convert Remember To Bit
if remember = "" then
  remember = 0
else
  remember = 1
end if

' Add New User
Set CMD = Server.CreateObject( "ADODB.Command" )
CMD.ActiveConnection = Con
CMD.CommandType = adCmdStoredProc
CMD.CommandText = "addUser"
CMD.Parameters.Append CMD.CreateParameter
➥( "returnStatus",adInteger, adParamReturnValue )
CMD.Parameters.Append
➥CMD.CreateParameter( "username",adVarChar,
➥adParamInput, 20, username )
```

23

SECURING YOUR
WEB SITE

continues

LISTING 23.2   CONTINUED

```
CMD.Parameters.Append
➥CMD.CreateParameter( "password",adVarChar,
➥adParamInput, 20, password )
CMD.Parameters.Append
➥CMD.CreateParameter( "remember",adBoolean,
➥adParamInput,, remember )
CMD.Execute
returnStatus = cINT( CMD( "returnStatus" ) )
CMD.ActiveConnection = Nothing
SET CMD = Nothing

' Check For Name Already Registered
if returnStatus = 10 then
    errorMSG = "The username " & username & " is already registered."
    errorForm
end if

'  Add Cookies
    Response.Cookies( "username" ) = username
    Response.Cookies( "username" ).Expires = "July 31, 2000"
    Response.Cookies( "username" ).Domain =
    ➥Request.ServerVariables( "SERVER_NAME" )
    Response.Cookies( "username" ).Path = "/"
    Response.Cookies( "username" ).Secure = FALSE
if remember = "1" then
    Response.Cookies( "password" ) = password
    Response.Cookies( "password" ).Expires = "July 31, 2000"
    Response.Cookies( "password" ).Domain =
    ➥Request.ServerVariables( "SERVER_NAME" )
    Response.Cookies( "password" ).Path = "/"
    Response.Cookies( "password" ).Secure = FALSE
end if
%>
<html>
<head><title>Register</title></head>
<body>
<font face="Arial">Thank you for registering!</font>
</body>
</html>
```

The Security INCLUDE File

For each page that you want to password protect, you will need to include the Security INCLUDE file at the top of the page by using the Active Server Pages #INCLUDE directive. The Security INCLUDE file will prevent a user from viewing a page unless the user has logged in (see Listing 23.3).

LISTING 23.3   SECURITY INCLUDE FILE—SECURITY.ASP

```
<%
'''''''''''''''''''''
'   Security INCLUDE file
'''''''''''''''''''''
sub requestPassword( byVal MSG )
     %>
     <html>
     <head><title>Login</title></head>
     <body>
     <font face="Arial">Login</font>
     <center>
     <%=MSG%>
     <table width=400>
     <tr>
         <td>
         <form method="post"
          action="<%=Request.ServerVariables( "SCRIPT_NAME" )%>">
         username:
         <input name="username" size=20
          maxlength=20 value="<%=Server.HTMLEncode( username )%>">
         <br>password:
         <input name="password" size=20
          maxlength=20 value="<%=Server.HTMLEncode( password )%>">
         <p><input type="submit" value="Login">
         </form>
         </td>
     </tr>
     <tr>
         <td><a href="register.asp">Click here to register</a></td>
     </tr>
     </table>
     </center>
     </body>
     </html>
     <%
     response.End
end sub

userKey = TRIM( Request( "k" ) )
username = TRIM( Request( "username" ) )
password = TRIM( Request( "password" ) )

' Ready Database Connection
Set Con = Server.CreateObject( "ADODB.Connection" )
Con.Open "FILE NAME=c:\myDataLink.UDL"

if userKey <> "" then
     divider = INSTR( userkey, "p")
```

23

SECURING YOUR
WEB SITE

continues

LISTING 23.3 CONTINUED

```
        userID = LEFT( userKey, divider - 1 )
        secretKey = RIGHT( userKey, LEN( userKey ) - divider )
        Set CMD = Server.CreateObject( "ADODB.Command" )
        CMD.ActiveConnection = Con
        CMD.CommandType = adCmdStoredProc
        CMD.CommandText = "checkKey"
        CMD.Parameters.Append CMD.CreateParameter
        ➥ ( "returnStatus",adInteger, adParamReturnValue )
        CMD.Parameters.Append CMD.CreateParameter
        ➥ ( "userID",adInteger, adParamInput, , userID )
        CMD.Parameters.Append CMD.CreateParameter
        ➥ ( "secretKey",adInteger, adParamInput, , secretKey )
        CMD.Parameters.Append CMD.CreateParameter
        ➥ ( "newsecretKey",adInteger, adParamOutput  )
        CMD.Execute
        returnStatus = cINT( CMD( "returnStatus" ) )
        newsecretKey = CMD( "newsecretKey" )
        CMD.ActiveConnection = Nothing
        SET CMD = Nothing
        if returnStatus <> 0 then
        ➥requestPassword "You must login to access this page.<p>"
        k = "k=" & userID & "p" & newsecretKey
        formK = "<input name=""k"" type=""hidden"" value="""
        ➥& userID & "p" & newsecretKey & """>"
else
        if username <> "" and password <> "" then
        Set CMD = Server.CreateObject( "ADODB.Command" )
        CMD.ActiveConnection = Con
        CMD.CommandType = adCmdStoredProc
        CMD.CommandText = "checkPassword"
        CMD.Parameters.Append CMD.CreateParameter
        ➥ ( "returnStatus",adInteger, adParamReturnValue )
        CMD.Parameters.Append CMD.CreateParameter
        ➥ ( "username",adVarchar, adParamInput, 20, username )
        CMD.Parameters.Append CMD.CreateParameter
        ➥ ( "password",adVarchar, adParamInput, 20, password )
        CMD.Parameters.Append CMD.CreateParameter
        ➥ ( "userID",adInteger, adParamOutput  )
        CMD.Parameters.Append CMD.CreateParameter
        ➥ ( "newsecretKey",adInteger, adParamOutput  )
        CMD.Execute
        returnStatus = cINT( CMD( "returnStatus" ) )
        userID = CMD( "userID" )
        secretKey = CMD( "newsecretKey" )
        CMD.ActiveConnection = Nothing
        SET CMD = Nothing
        if returnStatus = 20 then requestPassword
        ➥ "You did not enter a registered user name.<p>"
        if returnStatus = 10 then
```

```
➥requestPassword "You did not enter a valid password.<p>"
k = "k=" & userID & "p" & secretKey
formK = "<input name=""k"" type=""hidden"" value=""" &
➥userID & "p" & secretKey & """">"
else
requestPassword "You must login to access this page.<p>"
end if
end if
%>
```

> **NOTE**
>
> The CD-ROM that accompanies this book includes two sample files, securepage.asp and securepage2.asp, that demonstrate how the Security INCLUDE file can be used to password protect multiple Active Server Pages.

If someone requests a page that contains the Security INCLUDE file, a form will be displayed that asks for a registered username and password. If a username and password are entered, they are checked against the Users database table with the checkpassword stored procedure (see Listing 23.4).

LISTING 23.4   CHECK USER PASSWORD—CHECKPASSWORD

```
create procedure checkpassword
(
    @username varchar( 20 ),
    @password varchar( 20 ),
    @userID INT OUTPUT,
    @newsecretKey INT OUTPUT
)
AS
select @userID = userID from Users
    where username = @username
    and password = @password

if @userID is not NULL
    begin
        select @newsecretKey = RAND() * 1000
        update Users set secretKey = @newsecretKey
            where userID = userID
    end
    else
    begin
```

23

SECURING YOUR
WEB SITE

continues

LISTING 23.4   CONTINUED

```
        if exists( select userID from Users
                   where username = @username )
        begin
          return( 10 )
        end
        else
        begin
          return( 20 )
        end
     end
go

grant all on checkpassword to public
```

The `checkpassword` stored procedure verifies that the username and password entered exist in the Users table. If a registered username and password have been entered, the stored procedure generates a new secretKey for the user.

The Security INCLUDE file builds a userKey every time a user accesses a protected page. The userKey contains a combination of a userID and secretKey. For example, the userKey for the user with userID 12 and the secretKey 512 would look like this:

```
12p512
```

What is the purpose of this userKey? If someone accesses multiple password-protected Web pages at your Web site, it is a bad idea to pass the username and password through each page. The problem is that the password will be displayed in the address bar of the browser window. Anyone looking over the user's shoulder will be able to view the secret password.

Instead of passing the username and password through each of the password-protected pages, you should pass the userKey. A new userKey is automatically generated whenever the user accesses a password-protected page, so even if someone manages to momentarily view a userKey, it will change as soon as another password-protected page is requested.

After the userKey is generated, you can include it in any links or forms in the body of the page by using either the `K` or the `formK` variable. For example, to pass the userKey in a link, you would use the following syntax:

```
<a href="securepage2.asp?<%=k%>">Next Page</a>
```

To pass the userKey in a form, you use the `formK` variable. Here is an example of a form that includes the userKey:

```
<form method="post" action="securepage2.asp">
<%=formK%>
<input type="submit" value="Next Page">
</form>
```

The Security INCLUDE file uses the `checkKey` stored procedure to check whether a userKey is valid (see Listing 23.5). The `checkKey` stored procedure uses the SQL If exists statement to determine whether the userID and secretKey passed to the stored procedure exist in the table. The stored procedure also automatically creates a new randomly generated secret key.

LISTING 23.5 CHECK RANDOM KEY—CHECKKEY

```
create procedure checkKey
(
    @userID int,
    @secretKey int,
    @newsecretKey int OUTPUT
)
AS

if exists( select userID from Users
    where userid = @userID
    and secretKey = @secretKey )
    begin
      select @newsecretKey = RAND() * 1000
      update Users set secretKey = @newsecretKey
          where userID = @userID
    end
    else
    begin
      return( 10 )
    end
```

When a user registers using the registration form described in the previous section, he or she is given the option to be automatically identified by a cookie. Because the Security INCLUDE file never explicitly references the Cookies collection, you might be wondering how this feature is supported. The answer is that when `Request( "password" )` is used instead of `Request.Form( "password" )` or `Request.QueryString( "password" )`, the whole Request collection is searched. Because the Cookies collection is part of the Request collection, `Request( "password" )` will find the password even if it is passed to the page by a cookie.

Using Windows NT Security

In this final part of the chapter, you will learn a second method of password protecting files and directories within your Web site. This part will explain how to integrate your Web site's security with Windows NT security. You will learn how to protect your Active Server Pages by using Windows NT user accounts, groups, and file permissions.

> **NOTE**
>
> To utilize Windows NT security, you must be using the Windows NT operating system with the NTFS file system. If your Web server is currently installed on a server using the FAT file system, you can convert to NTFS by running the CON-VERT command (look up "convert" under Windows NT Help). However, after you convert to NTFS, you cannot convert back to FAT.

Under the NTFS file system, every file and directory has an associated set of permissions. These permissions determine who can do such things as read, execute, or delete a file. To see the permissions for a file, right-click the filename and choose Properties, Security, Permissions. The dialog box in Figure 23.6 appears.

FIGURE 23.6

The File Permissions dialog box.

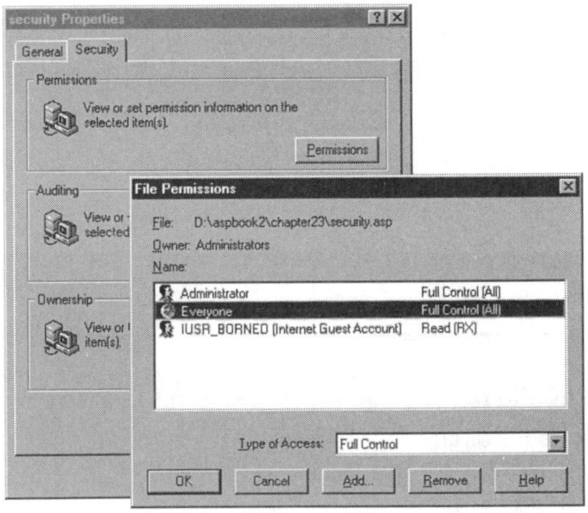

The File Permissions dialog box displays a list of user accounts and groups with their associated access permissions for the file. For example, in Figure 23.6, the Administrator user account is shown as having Full Control of the file. This means that if you are logged on to the computer using the Administrator account, you have permission to do anything to the file, including delete it.

You can change the access permissions for any user account or group by clicking on an entry and selecting new permissions from the group of radio buttons. To make it impossible for anyone logged in under the Administrator account to delete a particular file, for example, simply remove the Administrator account's Delete permissions for the file.

You can also completely remove any user account or group from having any permission to access a file. To do this, select the user account or group name and click the button labeled Remove. To add a user account or group, click the button labeled Add.

> **NOTE**
>
> To create new user accounts or groups, you can use the Windows NT User Manager. You can also work with user accounts and groups within your Active Server Pages by using the Active Directory Service Interfaces (ADSI). See Chapter 11, "Working with the Active Directory Service Interfaces," to learn how to do this.

Whenever someone requests a Web page from your Web site, they are accessing the page under a certain user account. By default, this user account is the IUSR_*computername* account. For example, if the name of your computer is Plato, then the name of the anonymous Internet user account would be IUSR_Plato.

Just as with any other account, you can set the IUSR_*computername* account's permissions to access a file. To prevent an anonymous user from accessing a file on your server over the Internet, you can remove the IUSER_*computername*'s Read permission for the file. You can also prevent an Internet user from accessing any file in a directory by changing the user account's permissions for the whole directory.

If an anonymous Internet user attempts to view an Active Server Page without sufficient permissions, a login dialog box will appear. Using the login dialog box, the anonymous user can identify himself as a particular user in your domain. After the user has logged in and is no longer using the anonymous IUSER_*computername* account, the person will continue to be identified by his or her user account for the rest of time that he or she accesses your Web site.

Using Windows NT security's user accounts, groups, and file permissions, you can create a very fine-grained level of security for your Web site. You can create as many user accounts and groups for your Web site as you need (a domain can support thousands of user accounts and groups), and you can set the permissions for each file and directory on an individual basis.

Authentication Methods

In the previous section, you learned how to set permissions for accessing directories and files within the Windows NT Operating System. You can also control access through the Internet Service Manager. You can set access for individual files, directories, or even complete Web sites.

To use the Internet Service Manager to control access to a file, directory, or Web site, open the property sheet for the object and choose the tab labeled Directory Security or File Security. Next, click the button labeled Edit under Anonymous Access and Authentication Control (see Figure 23.7).

FIGURE 23.7

Security status.

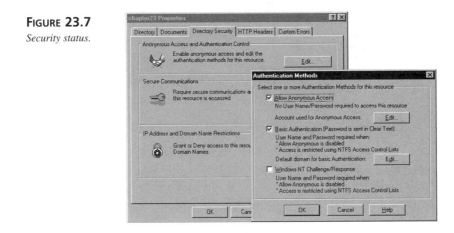

When users access your Web site without logging in, they are accessing your Web site under the anonymous user account. As discussed in the previous section, by default this anonymous account is the IUSER_*computername* account. To prevent anonymous access from unauthenticated Internet users, deselect the check box labeled Allow Anonymous Access. If you prevent anonymous access for a directory, a login dialog box will appear whenever someone attempts to access a file within the directory.

If you choose to allow anonymous access, you can select the user account used for unauthenticated visitors by choosing Edit and entering the username for the anonymous user account. By default, the anonymous user account is the IUSER_*computername* account. However, you can choose whatever user account you please.

If Enable Automatic Password Synchronization is selected, the anonymous user account and Windows NT user account that corresponds to it will automatically have the same password. If you do not select this option, you will bear the responsibility of synchronizing the two passwords in both the Internet Service Manager and the Windows NT User Manager.

The Internet Information Server supports two types of authenticated access. You can allow either Basic Authentication or Windows NT Challenge/Response, or both. This selection determines how usernames and passwords are transmitted across the Internet when users log in with the login dialog box.

After a user logs in, the username and password are included as an HTTP header whenever the user requests pages from the Web site. The username and password will continue to be included with each HTTP request until the user shuts down his or her browser or the user is forced to authenticate once again.

If you select Basic Authentication, the username and password will be sent in uuencoded form. For example, after a user has been authenticated with Basic Authentication, an HTTP request will look something like this:

```
GET /somedir/somepage.asp
Host: www.aspsite.com
HTTP/1.0
Connection: Keep-Alive
Authorization: Basic QWRtaW5pa3RyYYRvcjpudXQ5MHRyYWU
Accept: image/gif, image/x-xbitmap, image/jpeg, image/pjpeg, */*
```

The Authorization header contains the authentication information. In this example, the keyword Basic indicates that Basic Authentication is being used, and the uuencoded string that follows the keyword actually contains the username and password.

> **NOTE**
>
> By default, when users log in using Basic Authentication, they must include a domain name with their username. For example, they must log in using a string of the form domain\username rather than just a username. Typically, this is not what you will want. You can use the Edit button next to the check box for Basic Authentication to supply a default domain name so that users will not have to supply a domain name when logging in.

Uuencoding offers only a very minimal level of privacy. A hacker could decode the preceding string using any number of publicly available uuencoders/decoders (search Yahoo! for "uuencode" to obtain a list of these utilities). In other words, the username and password in the preceding request might as well be plain text. Basic Authentication is not a very secure method for transmitting usernames and passwords.

The Internet Information Server also supports a second authentication method called Windows NT Challenge/Response (also referred to as NTLM authentication). Windows NT Challenge/Response offers a far greater level of security.

If a user logs in using Windows NT Challenge/Response, the username and password are never actually transmitted across the Internet. The Windows NT Challenge/Response authentication process involves the following steps:

1. A user requests a page that requires Windows NT Challenge/Response authentication.

2. The server sends a random value back to the browser.

3. The browser sends three values back to the server: the username, the domain name, and a token. The token contains the password encrypted through a hash function using the random value the server provided.

4. The server sends the username, domain name, and random value to the domain controller.

5. The domain controller has information about all the usernames and passwords for the domain. It uses its copy of the password and the random value to encrypt a token representing the username and domain name. This token is sent back to the server.

6. The server compares the token it received from the domain controller (step 5) to the token it received from the browser (step 3). If the two tokens match, the user is authenticated.

Notice that throughout this complicated series of interactions, the server never receives the user's password in unencrypted form. The unencrypted password is not sent between the browser and server or the server and domain controller. Therefore, there is no step where the password can be stolen off the network.

Unfortunately, Windows NT Challenge/Response Authentication has three serious limitations. First, only Internet Explorer (versions 2.0 and greater) natively supports this form of authentication. If your site's users are using the Netscape browser, they cannot use Windows NT Challenge/Response Authentication without downloading and installing additional software (Microsoft Authentication Proxy for Netscape Navigator, which is available for free download at the Microsoft site). If you need to use a method of authentication that is widely supported, then you have no choice but to use Basic Authentication.

Second, Windows NT Challenge/Response Authentication does not work with proxy servers. Again, if you are using a proxy server, you have no choice but to use Basic Authentication.

> **WINDOWS 2000 NOTE**
>
> Internet Information Server 5.0 also supports a new authentication method named Digest Authentication. Like Windows NT Challenge/Response Authentication, when using Digest Authentication, passwords are not sent over the Internet. However, unlike Windows NT Challenge/Response Authentication, Digest Authentication is compatible with proxy servers. Digest Authentication only works with Internet Explorer (version 4.0 and higher).

Finally, Windows NT Challenge/Response Authentication does not work when resources need to be accessed from multiple servers. For example, if you have an Active Server Page on one server that must access a resource on another server, such as a file or Microsoft Access MDB file, then Windows NT Challenge/Response Authentication will fail. This limitation does not apply if IIS is running on the domain controller. This limitation also does not apply when using Basic Authentication.

You can enable both Windows NT Challenge/Response and Basic Authentication. If a browser does not support Windows NT Challenge/Response, it will automatically use Basic Authentication.

Retrieving Usernames and Passwords

After a user has been authenticated, you can retrieve the user's authentication information. If the user has been authenticated using Basic Authentication, you can retrieve both the username and password. In the case of Windows NT Challenge/Response Authentication, you can retrieve only the username.

The following script uses variables from the server variables collection to retrieve the username and password (authinfo.asp on the CD):

```
<%
authMethod = Request.ServerVariables( "AUTH_TYPE" )
username = Request.ServerVariables( "AUTH_USER" )
password = Request.ServerVariables( "AUTH_PASSWORD" )
%>
<html>
<head><title>Authentication Info</title></head>
</body>
<br><b>Username:</b> <%=username%>
<br><b>Password:</b> <%=password%>
<br><b>Authentication method:</b> <%=authMethod%>
</body>
</html>
```

23

SECURING YOUR WEB SITE

In this example, the AUTH_TYPE server variable has the value BASIC or NTLM depending on the authentication method. The AUTH_USER variable contains the username. If you are using Windows NT Challenge/Response Authentication, this variable will also contain the domain name. Finally, in the case of Basic Authentication (but not Windows NT Challenge/Response), the AUTH_PASSWORD variable contains the user's password.

Dynamic Authentication with Active Server Pages

Whenever someone requests a page that requires authentication, the server responds by sending the status code 401 Not Authorized in the response. This status code prompts the browser to open the login dialog box. You can take advantage of this method to force authentication within your Active Server Page scripts.

Suppose, for example, that you want to password protect pages only during certain hours of the day. Imagine that your Web site hosts documents that you want to restrict to internal use during business hours. If anyone wants to access a document between 8:00am and 6:00pm, they must enter a password. After hours, on the other hand, you want to make the documents available to anyone on the Internet.

 You can password protect an Active Server Page during particular hours of the day by using the following script (dynamicpassword.asp on the CD):

```
<%
if hour( time ) > 8 AND hour( time ) < 14  then
  username = TRIM( Request.ServerVariables( "AUTH_USER" ) )
  if username = "" then
    Response.Status = "401 Not Authorized"
    Response.addHeader "WWW-Authenticate", "Basic Realm=""YourDomain"""
    %>
    You cannot access this page until after 6:00pm.
    <%
  Response.End
  end if
end if
%>
<html>
<head><title>Business Document</title></head>
</body>
This is an interesting business document.
</body>
</html>
```

In this script, if the AUTH_USER server variable does not have a value and it is during business hours, the login dialog box is forced to appear. Notice that a header is also included with the response. The header is used to specify the default domain so that the user does not have to enter it. You should replace "*YourDomain*" with your Windows NT domain name.

Summary

In this chapter, you learned how to secure your Web site. In the first part, you learned how to use SSL to protect the privacy of your data as it is transmitted across the Internet and your local network. In the rest of this chapter, you learned two methods for password protecting sections of your Web site. You learned how to create a standard Security INCLUDE file to password protect your Web pages with database security. You also learned how to integrate your Web site's security with Windows NT Security.

23

SECURING YOUR WEB SITE

Maintaining ASP Web Sites

by Stephen Walther

IN THIS CHAPTER

CHAPTER 24

Maintaining a large Web site can be tedious and time consuming. You must constantly monitor the Web site to ensure that one or another of its parts has not ceased functioning. At any moment, for whatever reason, the Internet Information Server might crash, your database might run out of disk space, or someone might decide to unplug the power cord for your Web server from the wall socket.

Users expect a public Web site to be available at any moment of the day, on any day of the week—Web sites do not get vacations or have the weekend off. Unless you have the resources to have someone sit next to your servers 24 hours a day, you must develop methods to automatically monitor your Web site. In this chapter, you will learn how to do this.

In the first part of this chapter, you will learn how to use Windows Scripting Host to create scripts that run independently of the Web server. Windows Scripting Host can be used to automate many common administrative and monitoring tasks. For example, you can use Windows Scripting Host to automatically back up your Web site files on a daily basis or to automatically check the status of your Web site at scheduled times throughout the day.

The topic of the second part of this chapter is the Windows Task Scheduler. The Task Scheduler provides a graphical user interface (GUI) for the DOS AT command. You can use the Task Scheduler to schedule the execution of Windows Scripting Host scripts.

The final part of this chapter provides some tips on how to effectively monitor your Web site. You will learn how to automatically detect and report errors in your Active Server Page scripts and use the Internet Information Server's Custom Errors feature.

Using Windows Scripting Host

Windows Scripting Host (WSH) is bundled with Internet Information Server in the Windows NT Option Pack. WSH will be included as a standard part of Windows 2000 when this operating system is finally released. You can use WSH to run either VBScript or JScript scripts from within Windows or from the DOS command line.

 A WSH script looks very much like an Active Server Page script. Here is a simple script that prints Hello World! 52 times (included on the CD as hello.vbs):

```
    for i = 1 to 52
  Wscript.Echo "Hello World!"
next
```

If you enter this script into Notepad and save it with the filename hello.vbs, you can run it from a DOS prompt by typing cscript hello.vbs. The file extension .vbs is important because it tells WSH that you are attempting to run a VBScript script. To run a JavaScript script, you must use the extension .js.

Notice three things about this simple script. First, standard VBScript statements are used. WSH uses the same VBScript scripting engine as Active Server Pages. This means that you can use VBScript in a WSH script in exactly the same way as you would within an Active Server Page (this applies to JScript as well).

Second, the script delimiters <% and %> are not used. Script delimiters are unnecessary because a WSH script consists of nothing but script. You cannot intersperse HTML in a WSH script in the same way as you can with an Active Server Page script.

The third thing to notice about the script is the method of printing `Hello World!`. In the preceding script, the `Echo()` method of the `WScript` object is used to print the message. You cannot use the `Response` object to print the message as you would with an Active Server Page file. In fact, you cannot use any of the intrinsic Active Server Page objects within a WSH script such as the `Application`, `Session`, or `Request` objects. On the other hand, you can use ActiveX components such as the ADO, File Access object, or the CDO for NTS (you'll see how later in this chapter).

Executing Windows Scripting Host Scripts

You can execute a WSH script in one of two ways. If you want the script to print its results within a DOS command prompt window, you should use the `cscript` command. Alternatively, you can choose to run the WSH script under Windows by using the `wscript` command. When you execute a script using `wscript`, the results of the script are displayed in a Windows dialog box. Figure 24.1 shows the results of running the hello.vbs script with the `wscript` command. To make the dialog box disappear, you must click OK 52 times, once for each time `Hello World!` is displayed.

FIGURE 24.1

The dialog box from Wscript.

Both the `cscript` and `wscript` commands accept several useful optional parameters. You can suppress any output from a script by using the `//B` parameter. When running WSH scripts from the Task Scheduler (described in the section, "Using the Windows Task Scheduler"), you should use this parameter to prevent your server screen from being cluttered with open dialog boxes. To run a wscript script such as the hello.vbs script with the //B parameter type

```
wscript hello.vbs //B
```

If the hello.vbs script displays any output, the output will be suppressed.

A second useful optional parameter is the //T parameter. The //T parameter limits the time that a script will run to a preset number of seconds. This parameter is useful for keeping control over runaway scripts. For example, if a script gets caught in a never-ending WHILE...WEND loop, the //T parameter can force the script to halt after a certain number of seconds. The following command limits the execution time of the hello.vbs script to two seconds:

```
cscript hello.vbs //T:2
```

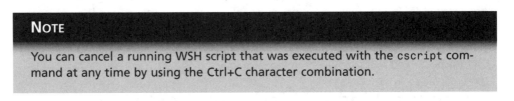

NOTE

You can cancel a running WSH script that was executed with the cscript command at any time by using the Ctrl+C character combination.

Table 24.1 lists the parameters that can be used when running WSH scripts:

TABLE 24.1 WINDOWS SCRIPTING HOST PARAMETERS

Parameter	Action
//I	Interactive Mode: Display user prompts and do not suppress errors (default).
//B	Batch Mode: Do not display user prompts and suppress errors.
//T:*nn*	The number of seconds the script is allowed to run.
//logo	Display a logo when script is run (default).
//nologo	Prevent display of logo when script is run.
//H:Cscript	Registers Cscript as the default scripting language.
//H:Wscript	Registers Wscript as the default scripting language.
//S	Saves the current command-line options.
//?	Displays parameter help.

Within a WSH script, you can halt the execution of the script by using the QUIT() method of the WScript object. Using WScript.QUIT() has the same effect as using

`Response.End` from within an Active Server Page. In the following example, the message
`I am never seen!` is never displayed:

```
WScript.Echo "Hello!"
WScript.Quit
WScript.Echo "I am never seen!"
```

Using ActiveX Components Within Windows Scripting Host

Almost any ActiveX component that can be used in an Active Server Page can be used in
a WSH script. For example, you can query a database by using the ADO, send email by
using the CDO for NTS, or access the file system by using the File Access object. To
create an instance of an ActiveX object within a WSH script, you must use
`WScript.CreateObject`. For example, the following script uses the ADO to retrieve and
display the names of all the authors from the authors table in the sample Pubs database
included with SQL Server:

```
Set Con = WScript.CreateObject( "ADODB.Connection" )
Con.Open "DSN=MyDSN;UID=username;PWD=secret"
MySQL = "select au_fname, au_lname from authors"
Set RS = Con.Execute( MySQL )
while not RS.EOF
  wscript.echo RS( "au_fname" ) & " " & RS( "au_lname" )
  RS.MoveNext
wend
```

Notice that the script looks exactly the same as a normal Active Server Page script except
that `WScript.CreateObject` is used instead of `Server.CreateObject` to create an
instance of an ActiveX object, and `WScript.Echo` is used instead of `Response.Write` to
output to the display.

> **NOTE**
>
> You cannot include other files within a WSH script. There is no equivalent to the
> Active Server Page #INCLUDE directive. This is a serious limitation of WSH, and it
> is my fervent hope that Microsoft decides to include a method to do this in the
> next version of WSH. One of the consequences of this limitation is that there is
> no method to include the ADO constants file (adovbs.inc) within a WSH script.
> To use the ADO constants, you must either copy this file into your WSH file or
> use the raw values of the constants within your script. Neither solution is partic-
> ularly elegant.

24

MAINTAINING
ASP WEB SITES

Accepting Command-Line Parameters

You can execute a WSH script with command-line parameters. Command-line parameters provide you with a method to pass values to a script. For example, the following script sends an email message to a different address depending on the value of the command-line parameter passed to the script when it is executed (included on the CD as commandline.vbs):

```
' Sendmail.vbs
Set Args = WScript.Arguments
if Args.Count > 0 then
  email = Args( 0 )
  SET myMail = WScript.CreateObject("CDONTS.Newmail")
  myMail.From = "admin@yoursite.com"
  myMail.To = email
  myMail.Subject = "Hello from WSH!"
  myMail.Body = "This message was sent from WSH."
  myMail.Send
  SET myMail = Nothing
else
  WScript.Echo "You must enter an email address"
end if
```

This script uses the Arguments property of the WScript object to retrieve the parameters passed to the script when it is executed. You can use the Count property to check whether any parameters were actually passed. In this example, the email address is set to the first parameter passed to the script. The following statement sends an email to the address billg@microsoft.com:

```
cscript sendmail.vbs billg@microsoft.com
```

Using Windows Scripting Host with IIS Admin

One of the most useful applications of WSH is for automatically configuring and monitoring your IIS Web site. You can use WSH with the IIS Admin objects to manipulate any of the properties of your Web server. For example, Listing 24.1 displays a list of all your Web sites and displays each Web site's current status (included on the CD on showStatus.vbs).

LISTING 24.1   DISPLAYING A LIST OF WEB SITES AND THEIR STATUS

```
Set ADsObj = GetObject( "IIS://localhost/W3SVC")
for each key in ADsObj
  if isNumeric( key.Name ) then
```

```
        wscript.echo "=============="
        wscript.echo "Server: " & key.ServerComment
        wscript.echo "State: " & showState( key.ServerState )
   end if
next


function showState( theState )
   select case theState
      case 1
         showState = "Starting..."
      case 2
         showState = "Started"
      case 3
         showState = "Stopping..."
      case 4
         showState = "Stopped"
      case 5
         showState = "Pausing..."
      case 6
         showState = "Paused"
      case 7
         showState = "Continuing"
   end select
end function
```

Using the Windows Task Scheduler

Microsoft Windows NT includes a command for running tasks at scheduled times: the AT command. For example, you can use the AT command to run a script or program once a day or only on Sundays. The AT command works perfectly well, but it's not much fun to use it in its raw form. A better option is to use the Windows Task Scheduler, which provides a more user-friendly interface to the AT command (see Figure 24.2).

The Windows Task Scheduler is not included with the Windows NT Option Pack. The Task Scheduler is an additional component of Internet Explorer. If you do not have the Task Scheduler installed on your computer (check under Administrative Tools from your Start bar), you can download it by visiting the Internet Explorer section of the Microsoft site at http://www.microsoft.com/windows/ie.

Using the Task Scheduler is straightforward. To create a new task, click the icon labeled Add Scheduled Task. Clicking this icon will start a wizard that will lead you, step-by-step, through the process of creating a new task. You will be asked to choose the application to run and to select the times when you want the task to be run.

24

MAINTAINING ASP WEB SITES

FIGURE 24.2
*The Windows Task
Scheduler.*

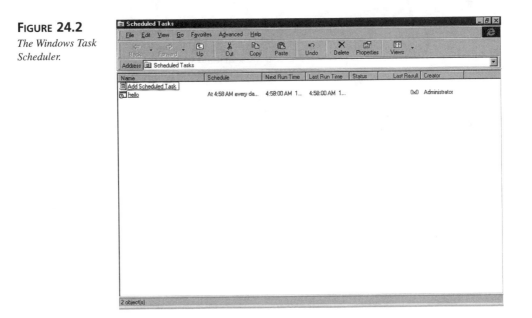

If you want to schedule a task to run more than once a day, say every five minutes, you will have to open the Advanced Schedule Options property sheet for the task. You can open this property sheet by either selecting Open Advanced Properties of This Task from within the Task Scheduler Wizard or by right-clicking on a scheduled task, choosing the tab labeled Schedule, and clicking the button labeled Advanced.

After you have scheduled a task, the task will execute at the times you specified, even when the Windows Task Scheduler is not open on your desktop. The Task Scheduler keeps a log of its activities in a text file named SchedLog.txt located in the Winnt directory. The log can be opened with Notepad or by choosing Advanced, View Log from within Task Scheduler.

The Task Scheduler is very useful for running Windows Scripting Host scripts. For example, if you want to automatically back up all the files on your Web server every evening, you can schedule the following WSH script to run every evening at 11:00 p.m.:

```
Set fs = WScript.CreateObject( "Scripting.FileSystemObject" )
fs.CopyFolder "c:\inetpub\wwwroot", "c:\wwwrootbackup"
```

This simple two-line script creates an instance of the File Access object and copies all the files and subfolders from the wwwroot directory to a directory named wwwrootbackup. You can use a similar script to back up or move the log files from your Web server to another machine on a nightly basis. (If your Web site has a lot of traffic, the log files can quickly overwhelm your hard drive.)

Another useful application of the Task Scheduler is to check the status of your Web site. In Chapter 16, "Third-Party Components," you learned how to use a WinSock component to request HTML pages from any Web site. Instead of using a WinSock component to retrieve a Web page from another Web site, you can use the component to attempt to retrieve pages off your own Web site. If a page cannot be retrieved, you will know that something has gone wrong.

To check the status of a page, you should embed a hidden string within the page. For example, the string "Good Page" can be hidden within a page by using the HTML comment characters like this:

```
<!-- Good Page -->
```

 If you attempt to request a page that contains this hidden string, and the string cannot be found, you know that there is an error in the page or that the Web server is not functioning correctly. Listing 24.2 uses the w3 Sockets WinSock component to request the default.asp page and check for the existence of the hidden string (included on the CD as checksite.vbs).

LISTING 24.2 CHECKING YOUR WEB SITE

```
YourSite = "www.yourdomain.com"
YourPage = "/default.asp"
CheckFor = "Good Page"

SET mySock = WScript.CreateObject("Socket.TCP")
mySock.Host =  YourSite & ":80"
theRequest = "GET " & YourPage & " HTTP/1.0" & vbCRLF
theRequest = theRequest & "Accept: image/gif,
➥image/x-xbitmap, image/jpeg, image/pjpeg, */*" & vbCRLF
theRequest = theRequest & vbCRLF
mySock.Open()
mySock.SendLine theRequest
mySock.WaitForDisconnect()

if INSTR( mySock.Buffer, CheckFor ) > 0 then
  wscript.echo "Everything's fine!"
else
  wscript.echo "Could not retrieve " & YourPage
end if
mySock.Close()
```

This script attempts to retrieve the /default.asp page from the www.yourdomain.com Web site. If the page is retrieved, the content of the page is searched for the string "Good Page". If this string cannot be found, an error is reported.

Instead of simply displaying an error, you can use the CDO for NTS to automatically send an email message. If you schedule this script with the Task Scheduler to run every five minutes, you will know immediately whenever your Web site develops errors or fails, even if you are taking a vacation in Borneo.

> **TIP**
>
> Instead of having error messages emailed to your email account, you can also have them emailed to a pager. Several pager networks support email to pager gateways that enable you to send a text message to a pager with a normal email message.

Monitoring the Performance of Your Web Site

Administrating a Web site is difficult. Normally, you are completely blind to what the users of your Web site are doing or seeing. If an anonymous user of your Web site requests an Active Server Page and receives an error, you will never know.

In this final part of this chapter, you will learn two valuable methods for monitoring the performance of your Web site. First, you will learn how to use the Microsoft Transaction Server to automatically detect and respond to errors in your Active Server Page scripts. Next, you will learn how to use the IIS Custom Errors feature to display more user-friendly error messages.

Capturing Errors with MTS

The current version of Microsoft VBScript includes a very limited set of properties and methods for handling runtime errors. All of these properties and methods are contained in the VBScript `Err` object. Whenever an error occurs, the content of the error is stored in this object.

When used with the `ON Error Resume Next` statement, the `Err` object can be used to detect errors at crucial points in your Active Server Page scripts. For example, the following script captures an error and displays it within the browser window:

```
<%
On Error Resume Next

' This is an error
```

```
Request.blah

if Err <> 0 then
  response.Write "Error Detected! <br>"
  response.Write Err.Description
  Err.Clear
end if
%>
```

The first line of the script, the `On Error Resume Next` statement, has the single purpose of hiding errors. When a script contains this statement, the display of errors is suppressed.

The `Err` object always contains the current error. When the preceding script is executed, the `Err` object will contain the error `Object doesn't support this property or method` because the `Request` object does not support the `Blah` method.

The `Description` property is used to display the error and the `Clear` method is used to reset the `Err` object. After you have detected an error, you should clear the `Err` object so that future errors in the script can also be detected.

The VBScript error handling features leave a lot to be desired. The problem is that the `Err` object is not very useful for detecting and automatically responding to unanticipated errors. Unless you are willing to check the `Err` object after each and every statement in your Active Server Page script, you cannot use the `Err` object to respond to every possible error.

For example, consider the following simple script:

```
<%
On Error Resume Next

' This is the first error
myObj.blah
' This is the second error
Request.blah

if Err <> 0 then
  response.Write "Error Detected! <br>"
  response.Write Err.Description
  Err.Clear
end if
%>
```

This script is the same as the previous one except it contains two errors. However, the first error will never be captured by the `Err` object. If you execute this script, only the second error will be displayed. This is true because the `Err` object is checked only after the second error and not checked after the first one.

24

MAINTAINING ASP WEB SITES

VBScript would be a better language if it included an `On Error GoTo Some Subroutine` statement. Using this imagined statement, you could automatically handle an error no matter where it occurs in your script. But VBScript doesn't contain this statement, so an alternative must be found.

Fortunately, there is an alternative. You can achieve the same goal by using transactional Active Server Pages with Microsoft Transaction Server. The following Active Server Page captures a runtime error no matter where it occurs in the script:

```
<%@ TRANSACTION=Required %>

sub OnTransactionAbort()
        response.Write "Error!, Error!"
end sub

<html>
<head><title>TransError</title></head>
<body>

<%
Response.blah
%>

</body>
</html>
```

The `TRANSACTION` directive in the first line of this page causes the whole page to work as a transaction. If an error occurs in the page, the `OnTransactionAbort()` subroutine is automatically called. In the case of the preceding script, the subroutine simply prints out `Error!, Error!`.

> **NOTE**
>
> To learn more about using Microsoft Transaction Server, see Chapter 21, "Using ASP with Microsoft Transaction Server."

 You can get fancier with the `OnTransactionAbort()` subroutine. Instead of simply using the subroutine to display an error message, you can display an error page and automatically email the error message to your email account. Listing 24.3 provides an example of how to do this (included on the CD as transError.asp).

LISTING 24.3 MONITORING YOUR WEB SITE WITH ASP

```asp
<%@ TRANSACTION=Required %>
<%
response.buffer = TRUE

sub OnTransactionAbort()
    response.clear
    %>
    <html>
    <head><title>Error</title></head>
    <body>
    An error was encountered.
    </body>
    </html>
    <%
    SET objMail=Server.CreateObject("CDONTS.Newmail")
    objMail.From    = "error@yourdomain.com"
    objMail.To        = "webmaster@yourdomain.com"
    objMail.Subject = "!!Error At Web Site!!"
    objMail.Body    = "On " & now() &_
        ", the following error was " &_
        "generated in page " &_
        Request.ServerVariables( "SCRIPT_NAME" ) &_
        ": " & vbnewline & vbnewline &_
        err.Description
    objMail.Importance = 2
    objMail.Send
    Set objMail = Nothing
end sub
%>
<html>
<head><title>TransError</title></head>
<body>

<%
Response.blah
%>

</body>
</html>
```

Notice that the Active Server Page is buffered before it is displayed by using the BUFFER property of the Response object. If there is an error, the buffer is cleared so that the user will never see the raw error message on the screen. A custom error page is displayed instead.

If an error is encountered, an email message is sent to the webmaster@yourdomain.com email account. The email contains the time the error was generated, the page where the error occurred, and the description of the error (see Figure 24.3).

FIGURE 24.3

The emailed error message.

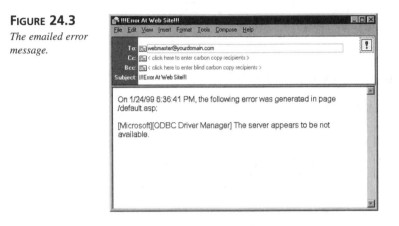

By using transactional Active Server Pages, you can efficiently monitor your Web site. Because a copy of the error is sent to your email inbox, you will automatically know whenever a problem with an Active Server Page develops, and you will have enough information to modify it.

Using IIS Custom Errors

In the previous section, you learned how to monitor your Web site for errors that might appear in your Active Server Page scripts. However, there is a second type of error that can cause problems for the users of your Web site. If someone requests a page that does not exist on your Web server, by default, they will receive the confusing error message displayed in Figure 24.4.

There are many reasons why a user might request a nonexistent page. Someone might mistype the address of one of your Web pages, a search engine might list outdated links to your Web site, or you might have a bad link from another page within your Web site. In any case, the error message displayed in the figure is ugly. If possible, you should avoid displaying it.

Internet Information Server version 4.0 enables you to display custom error messages. Instead of displaying the default 404 Not Found error for a missing page, you can redirect the user to another Active Server Page or display a static HTML page. You can even use the Custom Errors feature to automatically detect the existence of broken links from within your Web site or from other Web sites.

FIGURE **24.4**

404 Not Found error.

To use custom errors, launch the Internet Service Manager, open the property sheet for your Web site, and choose the tab labeled Custom Errors. You will see a list of status codes that are returned by your server when it cannot satisfy a page request.

To create a custom error message for `404 Page Not Found` errors, select the entry for 404 errors and click the button labeled Edit Properties. Next, select URL from the Message Type box and enter the path of an Active Server Page script on your server, for example `/notfound.asp`.

After you have a custom error page configured, whenever someone requests a page from your Web site that does not exist, they will be redirected to your custom error page. Both the error message and the path of the original page requested by the user are passed in the query string. For example, if someone requests a page named doesnotexist.asp, and you have enabled custom error redirection to a page named notfound.asp, the notfound.asp page will be requested as if the user typed

```
http://www.yourdomain.com/notfound.asp;
➥404;http://www.yourdomain.com/doesnotexist.asp
```

Within the notfound.asp page itself, you can retrieve the query string and determine the page that was originally requested. If you record this information by writing it to a file with the File Access component or by having it emailed to you, you can automatically

24

MAINTAINING
ASP WEB SITES

monitor your Web site for broken links. For example, the following script retrieves the error and automatically records it to a file named badlinks.txt:

```
<%
theError = Request.ServerVariables( "QUERY_STRING" )
addLog theError
SUB addLog( byVal theLogged )
    Set MyFS = Wscript.CreateObject( "Scripting.FileSystemObject" )
    Set MyFile = MyFS.OpenTextFile( "c:\badlinks.txt\", 8, TRUE )
    MyFile.WriteLine NOW() & " - " & theLogged
    MyFile.Close
    SET MyFile = Nothing
    SET MYFS = Nothing
END SUB
%>
```

The most useful application of custom errors is for detecting and responding to the Page Not Found error because this error is, by far, the most common one. However, custom errors can also be used with other types of server errors such as 500 errors (for internal server errors) or 401 and 403 errors (for unauthorized access errors). To see a complete list of these errors, refer to your Internet Information Server documentation.

Summary

In this chapter, you learned several valuable methods for maintaining your Active Server Page Web site. In the first part, you learned how to use Windows Scripting Host to create scripts that can be used to perform configuration and maintenance chores. In the second part, you learned how to use the Task Scheduler to automatically execute scripts at preset times. Finally, in the last part, you learned how to use transactional Active Server Pages and the Internet Information Server's Custom Errors feature to monitor your Web site for errors.

CHAPTER 25

Maximizing Active Server Pages Performance

by Stephen Walther

IN THIS CHAPTER

Successful public Web sites tend to grow quickly. When your Web site first goes live on the Internet, receiving a few hundred visitors a day can be an exciting event. Within a few months, however, traffic can climb to thousands or even tens of thousands of unique visitors each day. If you are not prepared, your initial feeling of excitement can quickly be replaced by fear.

If your Web site has not been designed to handle the traffic, horrible things will happen. Your Active Server Page scripts can grind to a halt. You'll begin to receive timeout and deadlock errors from your database server. Your Web server will refuse to grant additional user connections or will return SERVER TOO BUSY errors. Finally, overwhelmed and out of memory and processor capacity, your Web server can simply crash.

Designing a scalable Web site is difficult. The difficulty results from the number of factors that determine Web site performance. You must carefully choose the right hardware, establish the right network connection and, most important, design your Active Server Page scripts to scale.

This chapter focuses on the last problem of scalability. In this chapter, you will learn how to maximize the performance of your Active Server Page Web site by optimizing your HTML pages, your database access, and your Active Server Page scripts. You will also learn how to test the scalability of your Web site by using Microsoft InetMonitor.

Optimizing HTML Pages

The end product of your Active Server Page scripts is almost always an HTML page. An HTML page and the images it contains are the things that are actually transported across the network and presented to the user. A badly designed HTML page can have a very profound effect on the performance of your Web site. In the following sections, you will learn some tips for creating more efficient HTML pages.

Optimizing Images

The single biggest factor that determines the performance of an HTML page is the number and size of the images it contains. Images slow down the display of an HTML page in three ways. First, typically images contain a lot of data. The size of a single image in an HTML page can dwarf the total size of the HTML code for the page. The more bytes in an image, the longer it takes the image to cross the network and render in a browser.

Second, a browser must make a separate request for each image that an HTML page contains. For example, if a page contains five images, the browser must perform five separate requests to the server. Satisfying these requests places more work on the server.

Finally, if the browser does not know the dimensions of an image, the rendering of the page must be delayed or repeated again when the complete image is received. A browser cannot determine the layout of a page until it receives information about the dimensions of all the page elements.

Web sites that receive heavy traffic usually avoid using images. When images are used, they are very carefully optimized. For example, the home page of Yahoo!, the Web site that receives the most traffic on the Internet, currently contains only one image that is not an advertisement. Astonishingly, this single image—the Yahoo! banner logo—contains less than 5,000 bytes (and it's a big image).

You should avoid using images in your Web pages whenever possible. Web designers often feel pressure from associates and investors to include images. However, look at the most successful Web sites on the Internet—such as Yahoo!, eBay, and Amazon—and count the number of images they use. Even Wired, which was once famous for including pages full of images, has become very frugal in its use of images.

When you do decide to include images, you should follow these tips:

- Choose the appropriate image format. Two image formats are commonly supported on the Internet: GIF and JPEG. These two image formats use different compression algorithms to reduce the size of an image. Normally, you should use JPEG images for photographs or other images that contain significant color variation. GIF images are better suited for images that contain sharp lines such as icons or Web-site banners. Using the wrong image format can have a dramatic effect on the size of the image.

- Decrease the size of the image's color palette. A GIF image can use a color palette that contains anywhere from 2 colors to 256 colors. It's important to understand that an image may be using a 256 color palette, even if the image itself actually uses only 2 colors. Most paint programs (such as JASC's Paint Shop Pro) enable you to decrease the size of an image's color palette. If you are not using the extra colors, decreasing the color depth can save you hundreds of bytes, resulting in a faster-loading image.

- Progressively render the image. Both the GIF and JPEG image formats support images that are progressively rendered. When an image is progressively rendered, the browser begins displaying the image even before it receives the complete image information. This has the psychological effect of causing the image to appear to load faster. To progressively render a GIF image, choose to save the image in inter-laced format. To progressively render a JPEG image, choose to save the image with progressive encoding.

- Always include the image height and width attributes. A browser cannot lay out an HTML page until it has information about the size of all its elements. You can speed up the rendering of a page by including the WIDTH and HEIGHT attributes of the <IMG> tag. If the browser is provided with the width and height of the image, it can create an empty placeholder in the page with the proper dimensions while the image is being downloaded.

- Combine separate images into one. A browser must make a separate request for each image contained in an HTML page. If you combine multiple images into a single image, the browser does not need to make as many requests. Also, when the images are combined, they can be compressed more effectively.

- Always include alternative text for an image. Some Web surfers, tired of slow-loading images, have elected to turn off the display of images in their Web browsers. And, strangely enough, there are still some people using the text-only Lynx browser to surf the Internet. If you use the ALT attribute of the HTML <IMG> tag to provide alternative text for your images, these users can still make sense of your Web pages.

Avoiding Frames

Frames make life easier for a Web-site designer. Using frames, you can easily divide a Web page into different areas of content. For example, you can use one frame to contain a navigation page and a second frame to include the actual content of the page. Although frames provide an easy method of laying out a page, they also have an adverse effect on the performance of your Web site. The problem with frames is that Web browsers must make a separate request for each page in a frame. Satisfying these separate requests places a greater load on your Web server.

In almost all situations, you can avoid the use of frames by using HTML tables instead. For example, if you want to include a common navigation area in all the pages in your Web site, you can use the Active Server Pages #INCLUDE directive to add the content to a table cell on each page. From a user's perspective, the page may look exactly the same as if it were divided into separate frames.

Using Tables Effectively

There are many situations in which you will need to display a list of records from a database table. For example, you might be displaying a list of favorite Web sites, a list of products for sale, or a list of messages in a newsgroup. When displaying a list of records, it is tempting to display the list in a single table like this:

```
<table width="100%">
<% while not RS.Eof %>
```

```
<tr>
    <td><%=RS( "website_name" )%></td>
    <td><%=RS( "website_address" )%></td>
</tr>
<%
RS.MoveNext
wend
%>
</table>
```

This Active Server Page fragment displays the records from a recordset by displaying a separate table row for each record. If the recordset contains a lot of records, however, the resulting page might be rendered very slowly. The problem is that a browser will normally wait until the whole table is completed before rendering any part of a table. In other words, the first record will not be displayed until after the last record is outputted to the browser and the closing </table> tag is sent.

One way to get around this problem is to use separate tables for displaying each row in the Recordset. A browser will render the separate tables immediately. Therefore, even if you are displaying a very large Recordset, the user will be able to view each record as soon as it is outputted. Here is a modified script that displays records in separate tables:

```
<% while not RS.Eof %>
<table width="100%" border=0>
<tr>
    <td><%=RS( "website_name" )%></td>
    <td><%=RS( "website_address" )%></td>
</tr>
</table>
<%
RS.MoveNext
wend
%>
```

If you make the columns in each table the same width and hide the borders by using BORDER=0, the separate tables will appear to be one big table. However, the page will be rendered faster.

Optimizing Database Performance

If you are creating a database-driven Web site, you must devote a significant amount of time to monitoring and tuning your database and testing the efficiency of your SQL statements. Even minor adjustments can have dramatic effects on the speed of your Web site. In the following sections, you will learn some methods for making your database access faster.

25

MAXIMIZING ASP
PERFORMANCE

> **NOTE**
>
> This chapter assumes that you are using Microsoft SQL Server (version 6.5 or 7.0). If you want to create a scalable Web site, do not even consider using Microsoft Access. Microsoft Access is a desktop database and not a client/server database. This means that it was not designed to support the large number of simultaneous users that even a modest public Web site receives. For example, Microsoft Access does not support advanced multiuser locking, transaction logs, or efficient indexing.

Measuring Database Performance

To effectively tune your database, you must have a method of measuring its current performance. Microsoft SQL Server includes several utilities for monitoring activity on your database and timing the speed of its queries.

Timing the Execution of SQL Queries

To measure the speed of execution of your SQL queries, you can use Microsoft ISQL/w (in the case of Microsoft SQL Server 6.5) or Microsoft Query Analyzer (in the case of Microsoft SQL Server 7.0). Either one of these utilities will show each of the steps that SQL Server follows to execute your query and the time required for each step.

To time the execution of a SQL statement with Query Analyzer, launch the program from the SQL Server program group and choose Query, Current Connection Options. Next, select the option labeled Show Stats Time. After this option is selected, whenever you execute a query using Query Analyzer, statistics for the query will be displayed along with the results of the query.

To view query statistics using ISQL/w with Microsoft SQL Server 6.5, launch ISQL/w from the SQL Server program group and choose Query, Set Options. Next, select the option labeled Show Stats Time. Either utility will display the same information. For example, after executing the SQL statement select count(*) from orders in Query Analyzer, the following statistics and results are displayed:

```
SQL Server Execution Times:
   CPU time = 0 ms,  elapsed time = 0 ms.
SQL Server parse and compile time:
   CPU time = 0 ms, elapsed time = 0 ms.
```

- - - - - - - - - - -

830

```
(1 row(s) affected)

SQL Server Execution Times:
   CPU time = 0 ms,  elapsed time = 6 ms.

SQL Server Execution Times:
   CPU time = 10 ms,  elapsed time = 8 ms.
SQL Server parse and compile time:
   CPU time = 0 ms, elapsed time = 0 ms.

SQL Server Execution Times:
   CPU time = 0 ms,  elapsed time = 0 ms.
```

The execution time for each step is shown in milliseconds. In this example, you can see that it took SQL Server less than a millisecond to parse and compile the statement and approximately 8 milliseconds to execute the complete query.

Viewing the Query Execution Plan

Normally, knowing the execution time of a query will provide you with enough information to rewrite a query to make it more efficient. Simply keep experimenting until your query executes really, really fast. However, if needed, both ISQL/w and Query Analyzer can provide you with a step-by-step analysis of the plan that SQL Server follows to execute your query, including any indexes it uses.

To view the execution plan for a query using ISQL/w, choose Query, Set Option. Next, select the option labeled Show Query Plan. After you have chosen this option, ISQL/w will display the execution plan for a query whenever it displays the results of a query (see Figure 25.1).

To view a query plan using Query Analyzer, choose Query, Show Execution Plan. After executing a query, you can view the steps SQL Server followed to execute the query by choosing the tab labeled Execution Plan at the bottom of the screen (see Figure 25.2). To view detailed information on any of the steps, hover your mouse over the icon used to represent the step.

Using Profiler

Microsoft SQL 7.0 includes a very useful utility called Profiler. Using Profiler, you can create traces to monitor the actual queries that are executed on your database server. For example, you can create a trace to record the slowest running queries or the queries that most often result in database deadlocks. A trace can be viewed in real-time, or it can be recorded to a file or database table for later analysis.

25

MAXIMIZING ASP PERFORMANCE

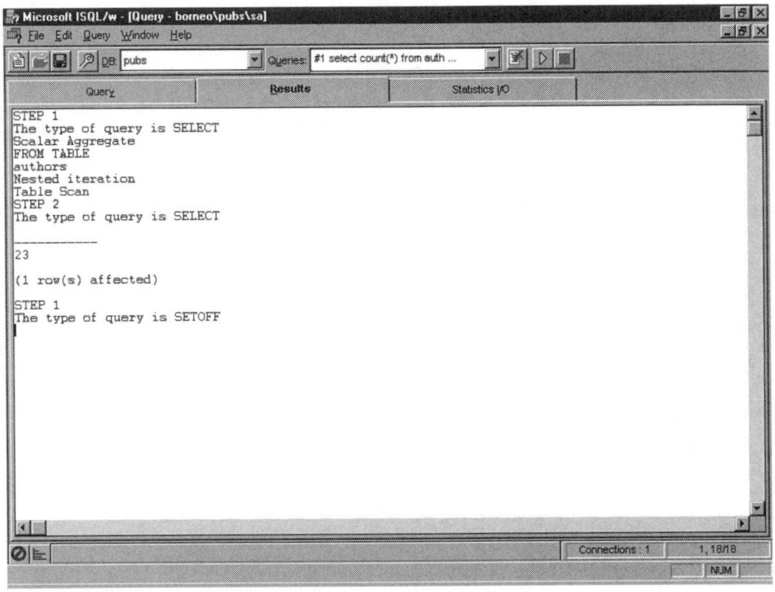

FIGURE 25.1

*A query plan dis-
played with
ISQL/w.*

FIGURE 25.2

*A query plan
shown using the
Query Analyzer.*

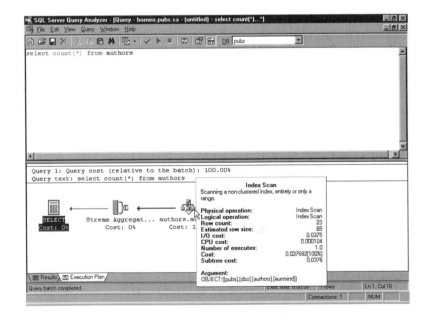

Here's how you can use Profiler to identify the slowest executing queries on your database server.

1. Launch Profiler from the SQL Server program group and choose Tools, Create Trace Wizard.

2. Select the name of your database server and choose the selection labeled Find the Worst Performing Queries.

3. Next, choose the name of the database that you want to monitor and select the minimum amount of time for bad queries. For example, if you want to identify any query that requires more than one second to execute, enter 1000 milliseconds.

After you have saved the trace, the screen shown in Figure 25.3 appears. This screen lists every query running more than one second as soon as it happens.

FIGURE 25.3

The profiler.

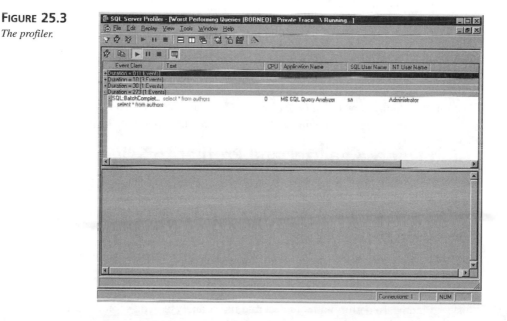

Using Indexes

Your choice of indexes for your database tables has the greatest impact on the performance of your queries. When executing queries, you typically want to do everything possible to avoid a table scan. Table scans are bad because they force SQL Server to begin at the first row of a table and read each row to find the rows that match the query's search criteria. For example, to perform a table scan of a database table that contains 1,000,000

25

MAXIMIZING ASP
PERFORMANCE

rows, SQL Server must read each and every row—a very slow process. When SQL Server uses an index, it can avoid reading the rows one by one.

SQL Server supports two types of indexes: clustered and non-clustered indexes. Each type of index is better at retrieving a certain type of data. A clustered index works most effectively when retrieving a range of values. For example, if you want to retrieve a list of all employees whose salaries fall in the range of $20,000 to $30,000 dollars from a database table that includes a salary column, adding a clustered index to this column would be very effective. A database table can have only one clustered index.

A nonclustered index works well when a table column has a high percentage of very different values. For example, if you need to quickly retrieve a single person's name from a table that contains a column for employee names, adding a nonclustered index to the column would be a good choice. A database table can have as many nonclustered indexes as you need.

Because indexes have such a dramatic impact on performance, you should experiment as much as possible with using different indexes on your database tables. After adding or removing an index, use ISQL/w or Query Analyzer to test the speed of typical queries against the table with the index. You should consider that adding too many indexes to a table might actually slow down operations, such as table updates and insertions, because the indexes for a table must be updated whenever the data in a table is updated.

Using Query Analyzer and Profiler to Select Indexes

Query Analyzer can be used to suggest indexes for a table. To use Query Analyzer to suggest an index, enter a SQL query (or batch) into the top pane of Query Analyzer and select Query, Perform Index Analysis. Query Analyzer will display its index suggestions in the bottom results pane (see Figure 25.4).

Query Analyzer will inspect only the query you entered to suggest an index for a table. If several different types of queries are made against the same table, Query Analyzer might not suggest the optimal set of indexes. Furthermore, Query Analyzer will never suggest a clustered index. To perform a more accurate index analysis, you should use the Profiler.

The Profiler includes a special wizard named the Index Tuning Wizard. Using the Index Tuning Wizard, you can determine the best indexes for a table, including clustered indexes, based on actual SQL Server workloads.

Before you can use the Index Tuning Wizard, you should first create a trace to gather information about the types of queries executed on your database server. To create a trace that can be used with the Index Tuning Wizard, launch the Profiler and select File, Open, Trace Definition. Next, choose the trace named Sample 1 — TSQL and select the option labeled Capture to File. After you save the trace to your hard drive, Profiler will start saving information about the queries being executed.

FIGURE 25.4

Index suggestions from the Query Analyzer.

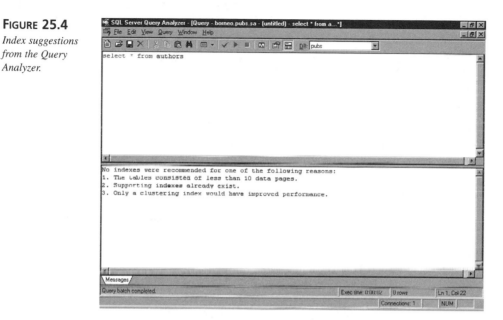

You should run the trace long enough to capture a representative sample of the activity on your database. After you are satisfied that a sufficient amount of information has been collected, you can stop the running trace by choosing File, Stop Traces. Next, launch the Index Tuning Wizard by selecting Tools, Index Tuning Wizard.

The Index Tuning Wizard will ask for the name of your trace file and ask you to select the database tables to tune. After you have supplied this information, the Index Tuning Wizard will make its suggestions for new Indexes. You may choose to allow the wizard to automatically make the index changes for you.

Keeping Statistics Up-to-Date

SQL Server maintains statistics on the distribution of values in the columns of a database table. It uses these statistics to determine the indexes to use for retrieving information from a table when executing a query. These statistics are automatically updated. However, they can become inaccurate if the data in a table undergoes any type of dramatic change. If the statistics for a table become outdated, SQL Server will start to make poor choices when choosing query execution plans.

You can forcibly update the statistics for all the tables in a database, a single table, or a single index for a table at any time. To update the statistics for all the user-defined tables in a database, execute the sp_updatestats system stored procedure. To update the statistics for all the indexes of a single table, execute the UPDATE STATISTICS statement with the name of the table. Finally, the following statement can be used to update the statistics for only the index named OrderDate in the table named Orders:

```
Update Statistics Orders OrderDate
```

Instead of updating statistics manually, you can use the Database Maintenance Plan Wizard to automatically update statistics for your database on a periodic basis. To run the Database Maintenance Plan Wizard, choose Tools, Maintenance Plan from within SQL Enterprise Manager.

Using Stored Procedures

Executing SQL stored procedures from within your Active Server Page scripts is almost always more efficient than executing equivalent SQL query strings. If you want to boost the performance of your Web site's database access, replace all your query strings with calls to stored procedures.

A stored procedure executes faster than a SQL string because a stored procedure is parsed and compiled only once, when it is first executed. In contrast, each and every time a SQL query string is executed, SQL Server must create a new query plan. To learn how to use SQL stored procedures in your Active Server Page scripts, see Chapter 14, "Working with the Command Object."

Selecting Cursors and Locking Types

When retrieving records from a database table, make sure that you choose the proper cursor and locking type. If you do not specify a particular cursor type when opening a Recordset, SQL Server will return the records by using the Default Result Set cursor. The Default Result Set cursor is a SQL Server specific cursor type that is very efficient. When a Default Result Set cursor is used, all the data is immediately sent from the database server without any additional requests from the client.

There is almost never a compelling reason to use a richer type of cursor in an Active Server Page. Dynamic cursors, in particular, should be avoided at all costs. Dynamic cursors exhibit the worst performance of any cursor type. For more information on selecting cursors, see Chapter 13, "Working with Recordsets."

Optimizing Active Server Pages

By using a few simple tricks, you can dramatically increase the performance of your Active Server Pages. In the following sections, you will learn several valuable methods for measuring the performance of your Active Server Pages and tuning your Active Server Pages to run faster by using server resources more effectively.

Measuring Active Server Page Performance

There are two approaches that you can take to measuring the execution speed of your Active Server Pages. If you are interested only in the amount of time that it takes for your Web server to process a complete Active Server Page, you can use Internet Information Server's Extended Logging properties. To time different sections of your Active Server Page scripts, you can use JScript to create a special timer script.

You can log the total time taken to process a page by using W3C Extended Logging and enabling the Time Taken extended property. To do this, launch the Internet Service Manager and open the property sheet for your Web site. Next, choose the tab labeled Web Site and make sure that logging is enabled and that W3C Extended Log File Format is selected. Next, click the button labeled Properties and choose the tab labeled Extended Properties. At the very least, both the URI Stem and Time Taken properties should be enabled (see Figure 25.5).

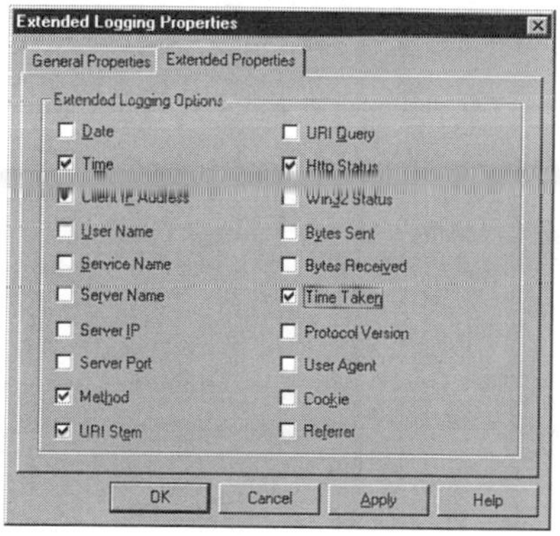

FIGURE 25.5

Enabling the Time Taken extended property

> **NOTE**
>
> There is a bug in the current version of IIS 4.0 that causes the Time Taken property to record the wrong value. Before using the Time Taken extended log property, make sure that you have the latest service packs installed. For more information see Microsoft Knowledge Base Articles Q191256 and Q197817.

After you have enabled the Time Taken property, you can measure the performance of your Active Server Pages by examining your Web site's log files. The Time Taken property is recorded to your log file as a certain number of milliseconds.

 If you need to time different sections of script within an Active Server Page, you can use the JScript Date object. You must use the JScript scripting language, rather than VBScript, to measure time because VBScript does not contain objects or functions that have an accuracy greater than a single second. This is not a limitation however, because you can freely mix a JScript script within a VBScript script. Listing 25.1 demonstrates how you can add a timer function to an Active Server Page (included on the CD as timer.asp).

LISTING 25.1   ADDING A TIMER TO AN ACTIVE SERVER PAGE

```
<script language="JScript" runat="server">
// Timer Function
startTime = new Date();
function showTime()
{
  thisTime = new Date();
  Response.Write( "<hr> elapsed: " )
  Response.Write(  thisTime.getTime() - startTime.getTime() )
  Response.Write( " ms<hr>" )

}
</script>

<html>
<head><title>Timer</title></head>
<body>
<%
for i = 0 to 100
  Response.Write i & " of 100 <br>"
  showTime()
next
%>
</body>
</html>
```

This script uses the JScript `Date` object to return the current time. Whenever the JScript `showTime()` function is called, the elapsed time since the Active Server Page was loaded is displayed. The JScript `getTime()` function returns the number of milliseconds since Midnight, January 1, 1970 (the birth of the JavaScript Universe). Notice that the JScript `showTime()` function is called within the middle of a VBScript script.

Using Application Variables to Avoid Database Access

Imagine that you are an online merchant with a list of products to sell. Imagine further that you do not change your product list very often, maybe once a day or every few days. You might be tempted to store your list of products in a database table and retrieve the product list from this table whenever a customer visits your Web site. For example, the following Active Server Page could be used to show all your products:

```
<html>
<head><title>My Products</title></head>
<body>
<%
Set con = Server.CreateObject( "ADODB.Connection" )

Con.Open "FILE NAME=c:\myDataLink.UDL"
mySQL = "select product_name, product_desc from products"
Set RS = Con.Execute( mySQL )
while not RS.Eof
  %>
  <%=RS( "product_name" ) %> - <%=RS( "product_desc" )%> <p>
  <%
RS.MoveNext
wend
%>
</body>
</html>
```

This page retrieves the name and description of each of your products from a database table named `products`. Each record from the `product` table is outputted to the browser window.

If the list of products does not change often, this Active Server Page would not be a very efficient method of displaying the information. Accessing a database is always a costly operation in terms of server resources. In the example, the very same information is retrieved from the database table over and over again.

Because the product information does not change often, it would be better to retrieve the product list only once and store the list as an array in memory. To do this, the following script can be added to the `Application_OnStart` event of the Global.asa file:

```
Sub Application_OnStart
    Set con = Server.CreateObject( "ADODB.Connection" )

Con.Open "FILE NAME=c:\myDataLink.UDL"
    mySQL = "select product_name, product_desc from products"
    Set RS = Con.Execute( mySQL )
    Application.Lock
    Application( "products" ) = RS.GetRows()
    Application.UnLock
    RS.Close
    Set RS = Nothing
    Set Con = Nothing
End Sub
```

This script loads the list of products from the database table and assigns the list to an `Application` variable array named `products`. Because the script is contained in the `Application_OnStart` subroutine, whenever the Web service is started, the list of products is automatically pulled from the table and assigned to this array.

After the list of products is contained within a variable in memory, the list of products can be displayed on a page without retrieving the list of products once again from the database. For example, the following script displays the list of products from the `products` Application array:

```
<html>
<head><title>My Products</title></head>
<body>
<%
for i = 0 to UBOUND( Application( "products" ), 2  )
  %>
  <%=Application( "products" )(0, i) %> -
  <%=Application( "products" )(1, i )%> <p>
  <%
next
%>
</body>
</html>
```

Retrieving the list of products from memory is much more efficient than retrieving the same list from a database table over and over again.

Avoiding Session Variables

Although using Application variables can make a Web site more efficient, using Session variables almost always makes a Web site less efficient. The problem with Session variables is that a new instance of a Session variable is created for each new visitor to a Web site. Even worse, usually the memory that a Session variable occupies is not reclaimed until at least 20 minutes after a user leaves.

There is rarely a compelling reason to use Session variables. In almost all cases, you can replace Session variables with form or query string variables. Or, in the worst case scenario, you can always use a cookie. To learn more about avoiding Session variables, see Chapter 5, "Working with Sessions."

If you do not plan to use Session variables in your Active Server Pages, you should disable Sessions for your Web site. You can disable Session variables on a page-by-page basis by using the `EnableSessionState` Active Server Page directive. If you include the following line at the very top of a page, Session variables will be disabled for the page:

```
<% EnableSessionState = FALSE %>
```

You can also elect to disable Session variables for your whole Web site by using the Internet Service Manager. To do this, launch the Internet Service Manager, open the property sheet for your Web site, choose the tab labeled Home Directory, and click the button labeled Configuration in the section labeled Application Settings. Next, select that tab labeled App Options and deselect the option labeled Enable Session State (see Figure 25.6).

FIGURE 25.6

How to disable session state.

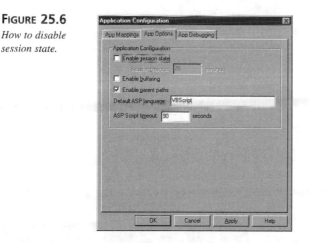

Do Not Buffer Your Active Server Pages

Buffering your Active Server Pages, by using the `Buffer` property of the `Response` object, is generally a bad idea. When an Active Server Page is buffered, none of the page

is outputted until all the page is rendered. Especially in the case of large HTML pages, a buffered page can create a very noticeable delay.

By default, page buffering is turned off for your Web site. You can turn buffering on or off for a complete Web site by using the Internet Service Manager. To do this, launch the Internet Service Manager, open the property sheet for your Web site, choose the tab labeled Home Directory, and click the button labeled Configuration in the section labeled Application Settings. Next, select the tab labeled App Options and either select or deselect the option labeled Enable Buffering (see Figure 25.7).

FIGURE 25.7

How to configure page buffering.

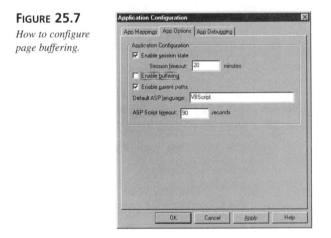

Capacity Planning

In this final part of this chapter, you will be given a brief overview of Microsoft's InetMonitor. Microsoft's InetMonitor tool was designed to allow you to monitor and test the capacity of your overall Web site. The tool has two components. Using the monitor component, you can capture information about the typical behavior of the visitors to your Web site. Using the simulation component, you can simulate hundreds or even thousands of simultaneous users and test how well your Web site performs under heavy user traffic.

NOTE

InetMonitor 3.0 is included with the Microsoft BackOffice Resource Kit (second edition). At the moment, you can also download it directly from the Microsoft Web site at http://www.microsoft.com/msdownload.

> **NOTE**
>
> Microsoft has a second capacity analysis tool named the Web Capacity Analysis Tool (WCAT). You can download WCAT directly from the Microsoft Web site (search for "WCAT" at `http://www.microsoft.com/search`) or purchase it with the Internet Information Server Resource Kit.

There are two tricks involved in installing InetMonitor. First, you must find the hidden documentation after the program is installed. The documentation is hidden in a Microsoft Word document in the same directory where the program was installed (by default, c:\InetMonitor).

Also, before you can use InetMonitor to perform Web capacity tests, you must calibrate your hard drive. You can skip this step while you are getting familiar with the program and perform the calibration at a later date. Refer to either the online help for InetMonitor or the Microsoft Word document to learn how to do the calibration.

One of the greatest strengths of InetMonitor is that it is easy to use. To start monitoring your Web site, choose Monitoring, Monitor Server and enter the name of your server. As soon as you have selected your server, all the services that your server supports—for example IIS, SMTP, or NNTP—will appear in the left window of the screen. To view the properties of your Web server, click on the IIS service. After you have done this, you can monitor several aspects of your Web server's performance by selecting the different tabs.

For example, under the Profiles tab, you can view a profile of your Web service and a profile of a typical user of your Web site (see Figure 25.8). InetMonitor tracks such information as the number of Active Server Page requests a typical user performs in a second and the number of errors a typical user receives.

The most interesting application of InetMonitor is for simulating load on your Web server. InetMonitor is very flexible. You can create custom scripts to simulate any type of user activity. The scripting language supports cookies, different forms of user authentication, and both the HTTP 1.0 and HTTP 1.1 protocol.

To create a simulation, you must first create a script that contains a list of actions for the simulated user. For example, suppose that your Web site contains three pages named test1.asp, test2.asp, and test3.asp, all located in the root directory. The following command script requests each of these page in turn:

```
GET url:/test1.asp
GET url:/test2.asp
GET url:/test3.asp
```

Enter this simple script into Notepad and save it anywhere on your hard drive. To run the simulation, choose the simulation view from InetMonitor by selecting View, Simulation View. You will see the screen that appears in Figure 25.9. Enter the name of your Web server in the box labeled Target Server, the path to the script file you just saved in the box labeled Command Script, and the number of users that you want to simulate in the box labeled Number of Users. To start the simulation, choose Simulation, Run Simulation.

FIGURE 25.8

The InetMonitor program.

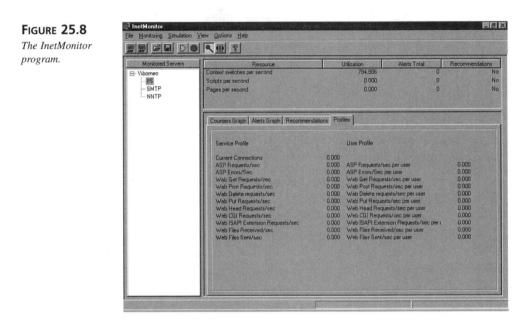

As the simulation runs, you can view such statistics as the number of user connections, page gets, and errors in real-time (as seen in Figure 25.8). You can also decide to log the simulation to a text file by selecting Monitoring, Log Active.

After you have run a simulation, you may receive recommendations from InetMonitor on how you can improve the performance of your Web server. For example, the program might suggest installing more memory or a faster processor.

FIGURE 25.9

Simulating traffic with InetMonitor.

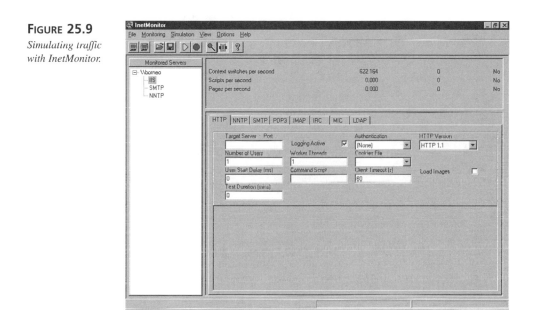

Summary

In this chapter, you learned several valuable techniques for measuring the capacity of your Web site and improving its performance. You learned how to optimize HTML pages, database access, and your Active Server Page scripts. Finally, you were introduced to InetMonitor, a tool that can be used to perform very sophisticated Web-site capacity testing.

CHAPTER 26

Future Directions: Windows 2000, IIS 5.0, and Active Server Pages

by Stephen Walther

IN THIS CHAPTER

The next release of Windows NT, Windows 2000, will include several important new features for the Active Server Pages developer. Windows 2000 includes new versions of the Internet Information Server, VBScript, JScript, the ActiveX Data Objects, and, most important, it includes a new version of Active Server Pages.

Many of these new software releases are available now. You can download release versions of VBScript 5.0 and JScript 5.0 from the Microsoft Web site (`http://msdn.microsoft.com/scripting`). The new version of the ActiveX Data Objects (ADO 2.0) is included with MDAC 2.0 (`http://www.microsoft.com/data`). Finally, computer server vendors, such as Dell (`http://www.dell.com`), will soon be including the Beta 3.0 release of Windows 2000 preinstalled on specially ordered servers.

> **NOTE**
>
> For more information on Windows 2000, see the Microsoft Windows 2000 Web site at `http://www.microsoft.com/windows2000`.

The purpose of this chapter is to provide an overview of the most important enhancements to Internet Information Server, VBScript, and Active Server Pages included with Windows 2000. Some of these changes will profoundly affect the way you program Web sites. (This is a very significant upgrade.) Even if you are not planning on immediately upgrading to Windows 2000, you should become familiar with its new features so that you can start preparing your Web site for the future.

> **NOTE**
>
> The information in this chapter is based on beta versions of Windows 2000, IIS 5.0, and Active Server Pages. The final release versions might differ from what is described here.

A Look at Windows 2000 and IIS 5.0

Internet Information Server version 5.0 looks very much like Internet Information Server 4.0. This is because IIS 4 was really a peek into Windows 2000 with the Microsoft

Management Console idea in its first practical use. Appearances notwithstanding, Microsoft has improved Internet Information Server in four important areas.

- It has improved the performance of IIS by adding the capability to compress pages as they are transmitted from the server.

- It has enhanced IIS security features by adding a new authentication protocol and adding new security wizards.

- Internet Information Server has an improved capability to recognize Active Server Pages.

- Finally, Microsoft has added new remote authoring features to IIS by implementing the Distributed Authoring and Versioning Protocol (DAV).

HTTP Compression

The less information that needs to be transmitted from a server to a browser, the faster the information will get there. IIS 5.0 includes an option that enables you to compress Web pages before they are sent to a browser. This feature works only with compression-enabled browsers (in other words, Microsoft Internet Explorer 5.0 and not Netscape). A browser that cannot accept compressed files will still work when IIS has HTTP compression enabled; it just won't receive compressed files.

You can choose to compress only static HTML pages, only Active Server Pages, or both. If you enable compression, you must enable it for your whole Web site. You cannot choose to allow compression in the case of some directories and not others.

Here's how HTTP compression works in the case of static pages. When someone requests a page from your Web site, IIS 5.0 checks whether the browser accepts compressed files. If the browser does accept compressed files, the server looks in a special compression directory to see whether the requested file already exists in compressed form. If the file already exists, the server sends it. Otherwise, if this is the first time that the file has been requested, the server will send an uncompressed version of the requested file and create a compressed version in the compression directory for the next time the page is requested.

HTTP compression works a little differently in the case of Active Server Pages. Because an Active Server Page is assumed to be different every time it is generated, IIS 5.0 will never store a copy of a compressed Active Server Page in the compression directory. Instead, the server will recompress the Active Server Page and send it each time it is requested.

Clearly, HTTP compression works much better with static HTML files than it does with Active Server Pages. If you enable compression for Active Server Pages, you can place a significant load on your computer's processor because the processor must work to compress an Active Server Page every time it is requested. For this reason, it might make sense to compress HTML files only.

To enable HTTP compression, launch the Internet Services Manager and open the property sheet for your Web site. Next, choose WWW Service and click the button labeled Edit. Finally, under the tab labeled Service, choose the compression options you want enabled (see Figure 26.1).

FIGURE 26.1

Enabling HTTP compression.

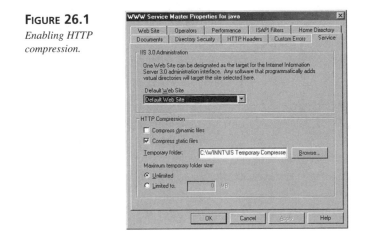

How effective is HTTP compression? To get a sense of how much it can reduce the size of a file, you can compare the original size of a file to the size of the compressed file in the compression directory. (By default, this is located at WINNT/IIS Temporary Compressed Files.) For example, a file that contains nothing but 1,000 X's in a row contains exactly 1,000 bytes. After the file is compressed by IIS 5.0, however, the file contains only 38 bytes. This is an easy case, however, because compression algorithms are particularly effective when used to compress long sequences of the same data.

As another test, I downloaded a typical page from the Internet. The original file was 50,573 bytes, and the compressed version had only 13,048 bytes. In other words, the compressed version of the page is only 26% of the original size. Not bad.

You can compare the size of the compressed and uncompressed versions of pages on your Web site to determine whether you should use compression. When experimenting, remember to monitor the performance of your Web server's processor. To monitor the performance of your server, use the Windows 2000 System Monitor (the replacement for the Performance Monitor on Windows 2000).

IIS 5.0 Security

IIS 5.0 includes two significant security enhancements. First, a new authentication method, Digest Authentication, has been added. Digest Authentication is similar to Windows NT Challenge/Response Authentication, except that it works when used with proxy servers and firewalls. Like Windows NT Challenge/Response Authentication, passwords are never sent across the network in plain text. Also, like Windows NT/Challenge Response Authentication, this authentication method works only with Microsoft Internet Explorer. (Windows NT Challenge/Response Authentication works with Internet Explorer version 2.0 or later, and Digest Authentication works only with Internet Explorer version 5.0.)

IIS 5.0 also contains new security wizards for requesting and installing certificates (the Certificate Wizard), managing certificate trust lists (the CTL Wizard), and configuring file and directory permissions (the Permissions Wizard). The Permissions Wizard is particularly useful. You can use this wizard to coordinate the NTFS file permissions for your Web page files with IIS security.

The Permissions Wizard includes two templates for setting up the two most common types of Web servers. Using the Public Access Internet/Intranet Web Site template, you can automatically grant all public users read-only permission for your Web site files and give administrators complete control. Using the Secure Internet Web Site Template, you can restrict access to only authenticated users. To start the Permissions Wizard, launch the Internet Services Manager, select your Web site, and choose Action, Task, Permissions Wizard (see Figure 26.2).

FIGURE 26.2

The Permissions Wizard.

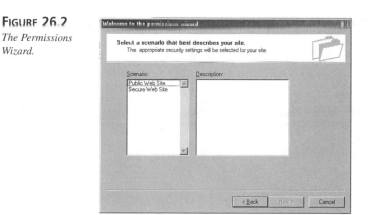

Scriptless Active Server Pages

When creating a Web site, I always make every page an Active Server Page by saving every page with the extension .asp. I do this even in the case of static HTML pages that contain no Active Server Page scripts. I create every page as an Active Server Page because I know that there is a possibility that I may be forced to add scripts to the page in the future. I worry that converting an HTML page to an Active Server Page by changing the .htm extension to .asp may result in breaking links with search engines or with other pages within the Web site.

This behavior has always made me uneasy. IIS 4.0 must work harder to process an Active Server Page because it must submit every page with the .asp extension to the Active Server Pages engine (asp.dll), regardless of whether the page includes scripts or not. So, making every page an Active Server Page results in a slightly less efficient Web site.

IIS 5.0 has relieved my anxiety. IIS 5.0 is smart enough to detect whether a page actually includes any Active Server Page scripts. If a page does not include any scripts, it is sent to the browser much more quickly. So, there is no longer a compelling reason not to make every page an Active Server Page.

Distributed Authoring and Versioning

Distributed Authoring and Versioning (DAV) is an extension of the HTTP protocol that enables users to manipulate files and directories on a Web server over the Internet. You can use DAV to perform such operations as moving, copying, and deleting files and folders. DAV also supports file locking so that multiple users can access and make changes to files on a Web server without overwriting each other's changes.

DAV provides much of the same functionality as the protocol used by Microsoft FrontPage to edit Web pages over the Internet, except that the DAV standard is an open standard. The specification is provided in an Internet Engineering Task Force (IETF) Internet Draft (see `http://www.ietf.org/`). Because it is an open IETF standard, the DAV standard is expected to be supported by a wide range of Web clients and servers (not just Microsoft). Microsoft currently supports DAV in Internet Explorer 5.0 and it will support DAV in Office 2000.

New in VBScript 5.0

Windows 2000 includes a new release of VBScript (VBScript version 5.0). This new release of VBScript includes new features for dynamically controlling program

execution, working with classes and objects, using regular expressions, and hiding source code. You can use these new features in both Active Server Page and Windows Scripting Host scripts.

Dynamically Executing Code

A new statement has been added to VBScript that enables VBScript code to be executed at runtime. Using the Execute statement, you can execute any string that contains valid VBScript code.

For example, the following script assigns all the items in the Form collection of the Request object to local VBScript variables:

```
<%
for each thing in Request.Form
  Execute thing & " ="" " & Request.Form( thing ) & " "" "
next
%>
```

If a form that contains a text field named Password is submitted to an Active Server Page that contains this script, then the value of the form field will be automatically assigned to the local VBScript variable named password.

The string that is passed to the EXECUTE statement may contain multiple VBScript statements. Each statement must be separated by a colon. For example, this script assigns two values to a variable named myvar:

```
<%
theCode = "myvar=3:myvar=67"
Execute theCode
%>
```

After this script is executed, the variable will have the value 67.

 It is important to realize that you can use any normal VBScript code with the EXECUTE statement, including any code that refers to Active Server Page objects. The following Active Server Page (included on the CD as formExecute.asp) contains an HTML text area that enables users to enter a script. When the form is submitted, the script is executed (see Figure 26.3):

```
<!-- FormExecute.asp -->
<%
On Error Resume Next
theCode = Request( "theCode" )
theCodeArray = Split( theCode, vbCRLF )
theScript = Join( theCodeArray, ":" )
%>
<html>
```

```
<head><title>Form Execute</title></head>
<body>
<% Execute theScript %>

<form method="post" action="FormExecute.asp">
<textarea name="theCode"
  cols=60 rows=10><%=theCode%></textarea>
<br><input type="submit" value="Execute!">
</form>

</body>
</html>
```

FIGURE 26.3

The form for executing scripts.

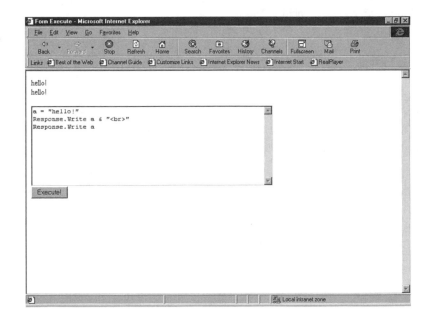

This script retrieves the script entered into the text area and breaks it into an array using the VBScript SPLIT() function. Next, the JOIN() function is used to add the pieces of the script back together, with colons acting as dividers between each statement. Finally, the script is executed with the EXECUTE statement.

> **CAUTION**
>
> Do not use a script like this one on a public Web site because it opens several very serious security holes. For example, someone could decide to execute a script that uses the File Access component to delete all the files from your Web server's hard drive.

Dynamically Evaluating Code

The `Execute` statement, described in the previous section, enables you to execute VBScript code at runtime. In certain circumstances, however, you might want to evaluate an expression rather than execute it. To evaluate the value of an expression, you can use the new VBScript `EVAL()` function. For example, the following script outputs the value `TRUE` because 1 is, in fact, less than 2:

```
<%
result - EVAL( "1 < 2 " )
Response.Write result
%>
```

Working with Classes

If you are a fan of object-oriented programming or familiar with Visual Basic, then you should be happy to discover that VBScript 5.0 supports classes. A *class* is a custom-defined object that contains custom properties and methods. You can use classes to more efficiently structure your code and control the ways in which variables are read and modified.

For example, within your Active Server Page scripts, you might need to track and update information about the visitors to your Web site. To do this, you can define a class that represents a Web user:

```
<%
Class WebUser
  Private Username, Password
  Public Default Property Get theUsername
    theUsername = username
  End Property
  Public Property Get checkPassword( thePassword )
    if thePassword = Password then
      checkPassword = TRUE
    else
      checkPassword = FALSE
    end if
  End Property
  Public SUB addWebuser( theUsername, thePassword )
    Username = theUsername
    Password = thePassword
  END SUB
END CLASS
%>
```

This class defines one method and two properties. The `addWebUser()` method is used to initialize the `Username` and `Password` variables. The `checkPassword` property checks whether a password is valid. Finally, the default property of the class returns the user-name.

To use this class in a script, you must first create an instance of it by using the NEW statement. After you have created an instance of the class, you can treat it in exactly the same way as you would any other Active Server Page object:

```
<%
' Create an instance of the class
Set aUser = new WebUser
' Add a new user
aUser.addWebuser "Andrew Jones", "secret"
' Check the password
Response.Write "Is 'dodgy' the right password?"
Response.Write aUser.CheckPassword( "dodgy" )
' Display the username
Response.Write "<br>" & aUser
%>
```

Notice that the last statement in the script returns the username without specifying a property. This works because the default property of the WebUser class is the username.

Why use classes? The main advantage of a class is that it provides a method of controlling how the values of variables can be accessed and changed. A class can shield variables from unintended modifications.

In the preceding example, the Password variable was declared as a Private variable. This means that the only way that this variable can be read or changed is by calling the methods and properties of the WebUser class. Because the WebUser class does not include a property for returning the value of the Password variable, the information is kept private.

Working with Objects

VBScript 5.0 includes a new statement for working with objects, the WITH statement. Normally, when working with objects, you must supply the object's name whenever you call one of its properties or methods. For example, suppose that you need to insert multiple records into a database table with the Connection object:

```
<%
Set Con = Server.CreateObject( "ADODB.Connection" )

Con.Open "FILE NAME=c:\myDataLink.UDL"
Con.Execute "insert ( aNumber ) values ( 1 )"
Con.Execute "insert ( aNumber ) values ( 2 )"
Con.Close
%>
```

Every time you call the Execute method, you must refer to the Connection object. If you use the WITH statement, however, you can declare a default object and omit the object's name:

```
<%
Set Con = Server.CreateObject( "ADODB.Connection" )
With Con

  .Open "FILE NAME=c:\myDataLink.UDL"
  .Execute "insert ( aNumber ) values ( 1 )"
  .Execute "insert ( aNumber ) values ( 2 )"
  .Close
End With
%>
```

Every method and property call that appears between the WITH and END WITH statements uses the Con object. The sole purpose of the WITH statement is to save you some typing.

Parsing Strings with Regular Expressions

One of the main reasons for the popularity of the PERL scripting language is its support for regular expressions. Regular expressions can be used to perform complicated string-manipulation tasks such as pattern matching and string replacement. With the new release of VBScript, you can now brag to your PERL friends that VBScript supports regular expressions. VBScript 5.0 supports basic, regular-expression pattern matching with two new objects: the RegExp and the Match object.

You can use regular expressions to validate information entered into an HTML form. For example, you can use a regular expression to check whether a user entered a real email address, social security number, or phone number by matching the information the user entered against a string pattern defined by a regular expression.

A regular expression contains a sequence of special characters that define a pattern. For example, the regular expression "r[ao]t" matches the string "rat", the word "rot", but not the string "rut". When a list of characters are enclosed in brackets in a regular expression, any character in that list is matched.

Here is an example of how you can use this regular expression in an Active Server Page:

```
<%
myString = "The rat ate the rotting cheese."
Set myRegExp = New RegExp
myRegExp.Global = TRUE
myRegExp.Pattern = "r[ao]t"
Set myMatches = myRegExp.Execute( myString )
for each thing in myMatches
```

```
  Response.Write thing & "<br>"
next
%>
```

This script creates an instance of the RegExp object. Two properties of this object are set. First, the Global property is used to indicate whether the whole string should be searched or whether the search should end after the first match is found. The Pattern property is used to assign the regular expression to the RegExp object.

After the RegExp object has been initialized, the Execute method is called to return any matches. The matches are assigned to the myMatches object (an instance of the Match object). The FOR...EACH loop is used to walk through the collection contained in myMatches and output the matching patterns to the browser window. In this case, the two strings "rat" and "rot" are displayed.

Regular expressions are very powerful. The implementation of regular expressions in VBScript 5.0 includes special characters for matching word boundaries, for matching whitespace characters, and for matching repeating character sequences.

Hiding Code with Microsoft Script Encoder

Recently, Microsoft released the first version of Microsoft Script Encoder (http://msdn.microsoft.com/scripting). This utility can be used to protect the source code for your Active Server Page scripts.

> **TIP**
>
> The company ServerObjects produces a tool similar to the Microsoft Script Encoder utility named AspCodeLock. It uses a component to dynamically decrypt encoded Active Server Page files completely in memory. For more information, visit http://www.serverobjects.com.

One of the advantages of Active Server Page scripts is that you can create a script without compiling it. The disadvantage is that if you distribute your scripts, everyone is able to view your source code. Microsoft Script Encoder solves this problem by translating Active Server Page scripts into a form that cannot be read by human eyes.

Here is an example of an Active Server Page before it has been encoded:

```
<html>
<head><title>Secret</title></head>
<body>
<%
```

```
' All this information is confidential
Set Con = Server.CreateObject( "ADODB.Connection" )
Con.Open "DSN=MyDSN;UID=sa;PWD=popcorn"
%>
</body>
</html>
```

Here is an example of the same script after it has been encoded:

```
<%@ LANGUAGE = VBScript.Encode  %>
<html>
<head><title>Secret</title></head>
<body>
<%#@~^kAAAAA==@#@&B~zV^PY4kk~k      0GDslOrKxPbdP1Wx6r[+
Ybls@#@&j[]Y~ZKUP{PjnM\+. ;DnlDn}4%[]mD`PrbG6f~R/W      xn^DkW
 EP*@#@&;GUR}w[]x-J9jg'\XQj1pj(9{/lIKqfxwK21W.     J@#@&^#~@%>
</body>
</html>
```

To use the Microsoft Script Encoder, open a DOS prompt and run the utility named
screnc.exe from the command line. For example, to encode the file named secret.asp to a
file named supersecret.asp, use the command

```
screnc secret.asp supersecret.asp
```

After an Active Server Page has been encoded, you can use it on your Web site in the
normal way. Because an Active Server Page is executed on the server, encoding an
Active Server Page presents no browser compatibility problems. However, if your script
contains client-side scripts, it will work only with Internet Explorer 5.0.

CAUTION

Microsoft warns that the Microsoft Script Encoder only prevents casual viewing
of your source code. A determined individual could decode your encoded files.
Do not use Microsoft Script Encoder to protect genuinely private information.

Enhancements to ASP Built-In Objects

The version of Active Server Pages included with IIS 5.0 includes several substantial
changes to the built-in ASP objects. The new version of Active Server Pages includes
better methods for controlling program execution, better error handling, and enhanced

Session and Application objects. The new program execution features are particularly important and will be described in detail in the following sections.

Controlling Program Execution

Suppose you need to conditionally display one of two different Active Server Pages depending on the information that a user submits in an HTML form. Previous to IIS 5.0, there really were only two ways to do this: you could use the Redirect method of the Server object to redirect the user to another Active Server Page, or you could display one of two Active Server Pages included with the #INCLUDE directive. Both of these methods have serious drawbacks.

The Redirect method of the Response object works by sending an HTTP header back to the Web browser to tell the browser to request another page. This method of retrieving another page is slow because the browser must make two requests to get one page. Even worse, some browsers will ignore the instruction to automatically retrieve the new page and will display an Object Has Moved message instead.

The method of including multiple Active Server Pages in a single Active Server Page with the #INCLUDE directive also has its problems. When you include multiple pages in an Active Server Page, IIS will insert all the included pages before performing any script processing. This means that you will end up with bloated Active Server Pages stealing valuable server memory.

Fortunately, Microsoft has provided a very elegant solution with IIS 5.0. Actually, it has provided two good solutions. Using the new Transfer method of the Server object, you can redirect a user to a new page on the server rather than on the browser. Using the new Execute method of the Server object, you can execute a script in one Active Server Page from within another Active Server Page.

Better Page Redirection

The new Transfer method of the Server object has exactly the same effect as the Redirect method without any of the Redirect method's shortcomings. The Transfer method redirects a user to another Web page without forcing the Web browser to request a new page. All the action takes place on the Web server.

For example, suppose that you want to require a user to enter his or her username and password before a page can be accessed. Here is an example of a simple HTML form that requests this information:

```
<html>
<head><title>Simple Form</title></head>
```

```
<body>

<form method="post" action="result.asp">
<br>Enter your name:
<input name="username">
<br>Enter your password:
<input name="password">
<input type="submit" value="Okay">
</form>

</body>
</html>
```

This HTML form is posted to an Active Server Page named result.asp. Within result.asp, you can check whether a username and password were actually submitted and, if not, you can automatically redirect the user back to the original page. Here is how you can do this:

```
<%
username = TRIM( Request( "username" ) )
password = TRIM( Request( "password" ) )
if username - "" or password = "" then
  Server.Transfer "form.asp"
end if
%>
<html>
<head><title>Thanks</title></head>
<body>

Thanks for entering your username and password!

</body>
</html>
```

In this example, the Transfer method of the Server object is used to transfer the user back to the original HTML form if a username and password were not submitted. When the Transfer method is called, the execution of the current script is stopped. The rest of the Active Server Page will never be seen, and the new page will be displayed instead.

Another significant advantage of the Transfer method over the Redirect method is that the contents of the Request collection are not lost when transferring between pages. For example, when the form information is submitted to the result.asp page, and the user is transferred back to the form.asp page, the original information that the user submitted is still available within the form.asp page. This means that you can automatically re-enter all the form information:

```
<%
username = TRIM( Request( "username" ) )
```

```
password = TRIM( Request( "password" ) )
%>
<html>
<head><title>Simple Form</title></head>
<body>

<form method="post" action="result.asp">
<br>Enter your name:
<input name="username" value="<%=username%>">
<br>Enter your password:
<input name="password" value="<%=password%>">
<input type="submit" value="Okay">
</form>

</body>
</html>
```

The preceding script is a modified version of the original form.asp page. Both the user-name and password fields are assigned values from the Request collection. If a user submits the form with a username, but forgets to enter a password, the user will be transferred back to this page; and the username that was originally entered will automatically appear once again.

NOTE

You might be curious as to what happens if you use the Transfer method to transfer an Active Server Page back to itself. Does the Active Server Page get caught in an infinite loop? Does the computer begin to melt? Actually, the script transfers back to itself a total of 115 times and then stops. You can test this strange result with the following Active Server Page named myself.asp:

```
<%
response.write application( "count" ) & "<br>"
application( "count" ) = application( "count" ) + 1
server.transfer "myself.asp"
%>
```

There are a limited set of circumstances in which it would make more sense to use the Response.Redirect method rather than the Response.Transfer method. You cannot use the Response.Transfer method to redirect a user to a Web page on another Web site. The Transfer method can only transfer a user to another page on the same Web server.

Also, you cannot use the Transfer method to transfer a user to another Active Server Page application. You can transfer to a page that exists in another Active Server Page

application, but you will not gain access to any of the application variables of the second application.

In general, you should avoid the `Redirect` method in favor of the `Transfer` method whenever possible. The `Transfer` method is faster and, because the `Transfer` method executes only on the server, the method is compatible with every browser.

Executing Active Server Pages

IIS 5.0 includes a second method for transferring execution of a script from one Active Server Page to another. You can use the `Execute` method of the `Server` object to execute a script in one Active Server Page from within another Active Server Page. Consider the following Active Server Page named Active1.asp (included on the CD as Active1.asp):

```
<!-- Active1.asp -->
<html>
<head><title>Messages</title></head>
<body>

Executing another script:
<% Server.Execute "active2.asp" %>
<br>All Done!

</body>
</html>
```

This Active Server Page executes a second Active Server Page named Active2.asp (included on the CD as Active2.asp). When the Active2.asp script is executed, a message is outputted to the browser window three times. After Active2.asp is finished executing, the remainder of Active1.asp is displayed (see Figure 26.4).

```
<!-- Active2.asp -->
<%
for i = 1 to 3
  Response.Write "<br>hello from Active2!"
next
%>
```

You might be surprised to learn that script variables are not passed between the two scripts. If a variable is assigned a value in Active1.asp, then the value of the variable cannot be retrieved from within Active2.asp. If you need to pass a variable between the two scripts, then you must use an Application variable or a Session variable, or pass the value within a query string. For example, the following script passes a message from outer-script.asp to innerscript.asp:

```
<!-- outerscript.asp -->
<html>
<head><title>Messages</title></head>
<body>

Executing another script:
<%
Application( "message" ) = "hello!"
Server.Execute "innerscript.asp" %>
<br>All Done!

</body>
</html>
```

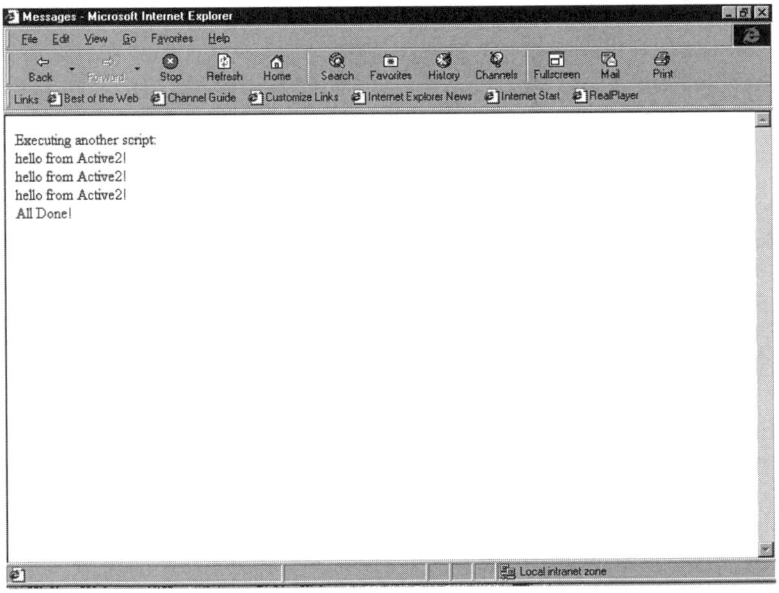

FIGURE 26.4

The output of Active1.asp.

The message `"hello!"` is passed within an Application variable when the script named innerscript.asp is called. When the script is executed, the value of the Application variable is correctly displayed.

```
<!-- innerscript.asp -->
<%=Application( "message" )%>
```

> **NOTE**
>
> You can be more careless with your use of Application variables with IIS 5.0 than you were with them in previous versions of IIS. Unlike previous versions of IIS, IIS 5.0 includes two methods for removing Application variables from memory. Using the `Remove` method of the Application object, you can remove a single Application variable, and using the `RemoveAll` method, you can remove all of them. Similar methods exist for the `Session` object.

Enhancements to ASP Installable Components

Microsoft claims that the performance of the Active Server Page components, included with IIS 5.0, has been significantly enhanced so that they are more scalable. Other than this upgrade in performance, only minor changes have been made to the components. Microsoft has added a single new component with this release of IIS: the Logging Utility component.

Logging Utility Component

The Logging Utility component enables you to access your Web server's log files from within your Active Server Page scripts. If you need to generate custom statistics on how your Web site is being used, this component can be very valuable.

For example, if you are displaying banner advertisements on your Web site, you can use this component to retrieve and display the number of times that a banner advertisement was viewed on a certain day. If you need to improve the performance of your Web site, the Logging Utility component can retrieve statistics on your site's slowest running Active Server Pages. Finally, the component can be used to gather information about the pages on your Web site that are visited the most often.

There are two important restrictions on using the Logging Utility component. First, it will work only with the four log file formats included with Active Server Pages. It will not work with ODBC logging (logging to the database), and it will not work with custom log file formats developed by third-party companies.

Also, to use the Logging Utility component, you must be authenticated on your Web server. In other words, you cannot access an Active Server Page that uses the component under the anonymous user account. To prevent anonymous access for a file, launch the

Internet Services Manager, open the property sheet for the file, select the tab labeled File Security, and disable the Allow Anonymous Access option.

Summary

This chapter provided a brief overview of some of the important new features of Windows 2000, IIS 5.0, VBScript 5.0, and Active Server Pages. In the first part of this chapter, you learned about the new features of IIS 5.0 that provide HTTP compression, new security options, scriptless Active Server Pages, and Distributed Authoring and Versioning. In the second part, you learned about the new features and extensions to VBScript 5.0. In the third part, you learned about the new program-flow-control features of the Active Server Page Server Object. Finally, in the last part, you were provided with a brief discussion of the new component included with Active Server Pages: the Logging Utility component.

Active Server Pages Sample Applications

PART
VII

Creating a Discussion Forum

by Stephen Walther

IN THIS CHAPTER

CHAPTER 27

For more than a year now, the companion Web site to this book (www.aspsite.com) has hosted a discussion forum devoted to programming with Active Server Pages. This forum has been very active. One of the most popular questions posted at this forum, not surprisingly, concerns how the discussion forum itself was written. In this chapter, all the secrets of the ASPSite discussion forum will be revealed. In the following pages, you will learn how to create your own discussion forum that you can incorporate into your Web sites.

The discussion forum described in this chapter has many advanced features:

- It supports multiple discussion areas. For example, the forum at the ASPSite includes separate areas devoted to programming with ADO, SQL, JScript, and VBScript.

- It supports threaded discussions. If someone posts a question, multiple people can post replies to the same question, and each reply appears directly beneath the original question.

- It makes extensive use of frames. The list of discussion areas, the list of messages, and the current message all appear within a single page in separate frames (see Figure 27.1). This makes it easier to navigate through all the messages.

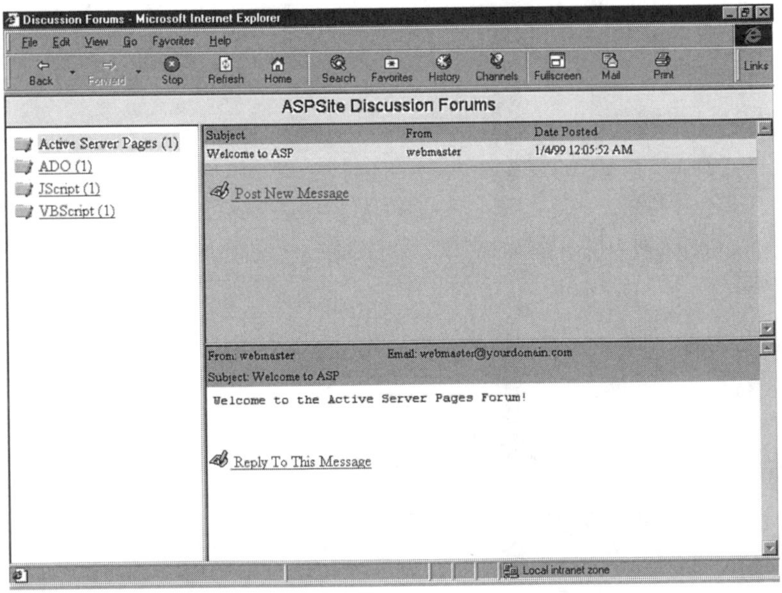

FIGURE 27.1

The discussion forum.

- The discussion forum uses only server-side Active Server Page scripts. Because it does not rely on any special features of a browser, the discussion forum is compatible with any browser that supports frames.

Overview of the Project

Like any programming project, the discussion forum involved several programming challenges. Two problems, in particular, had to be overcome: the problem of synchronizing the content of different frames and the problem of creating threaded discussions.

Synchronizing Frames

The discussion forum contains three HTML frames that must be synchronized. The left frame, named forumlist, contains a list of forum areas. When someone clicks on a particular forum area, the other two frames must display messages from the selected forum. The top frame, named messagelist, contains a list of messages. When someone clicks on a message, the bottom frame, named message, must display the body of the message.

Synchronizing the content of these frames presented a problem. Normally, when you click on a hypertext link, only one page is loaded. However, in the discussion forum, when you click on either the name of a forum area or a message in the list of messages, the content of more than one frame must be updated.

For example, the messages in the discussion forum are displayed in two frames. The top frame displays a list of messages, and the bottom frame displays the body of the currently selected message. Whenever someone selects a new message to view by clicking on a message in the top frame, the top frame changes so that the current message is highlighted (the background color is changed), and the bottom frame changes to display the body of the selected message (see Figure 27.2).

One solution to this problem of synchronizing multiple frames is to use a client-side language such as JavaScript. For example, the following JavaScript statement can be used to change the content of one frame from within another frame:

```
<script language="Javascript">
    parent.message.location.href="message.asp?m=2";
</script>
```

This statement loads the page named message.asp into the frame named message. If this script is included in the top frame in the discussion forum, the bottom message frame should automatically synchronized with the currently selected message. In the preceding statement, the ID of the message to be displayed is passed as a URL variable.

FIGURE 27.2

Synchronizing frames.

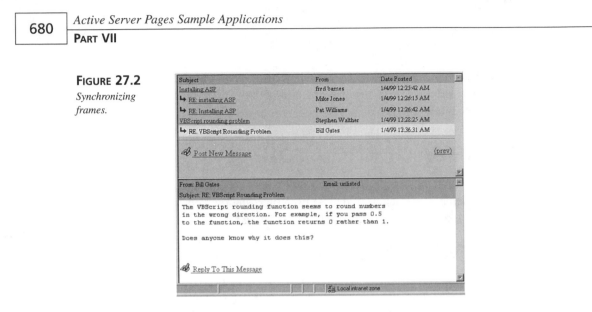

However, using a client-side language has a significant disadvantage. Not all browsers fully support JavaScript, and when a browser doesn't, the error can be ugly. Active Server Pages scripts, on the other hand, do not depend on any features of a browser.

The discussion forum does not use JavaScript to synchronize the content of the frames. Instead, the frames are coordinated by reloading the frameset file that contains the frames. Here is a simplified version of the frameset file that contains the messagelist and message frames:

```
<!-- Messages Frameset File -->
<% messageID = TRIM( Request( "m" ) ) %>
<html>
<head><title>Messages</title></head>
<frameset rows="*,*" >
    <frame name="messagelist" src="messagelist.asp?m=<%=messageID%>" >
    <frame name="message" src="message.asp?m=<%=messageID%>">
</frameset>
</html>
```

When a user clicks on a link in the messagelist frame, the link reloads its parent frameset file. Here is an example of a link that might appear in the messagelist frame:

```
<a href="messages.asp?f=ADO&m=21" target="messages">
Setting Cursor Types?</a>
```

When the messages frameset file is reloaded with this link, both the messagelist frame and the message frame are also reloaded. The ID of the current message is passed to both these frames through the m URL variable. In other words, multiple frames are updated at once from a single hypertext link.

This method of updating and synchronizing the content of multiple frames is compatible with all browsers that support frames. This approach is used in the discussion forum both to coordinate the list of messages with the selected message and to coordinate the list of forums with the messages of the selected forum.

> **NOTE**
>
>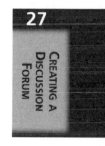
>
> You can use the method of changing the frameset file described in this section to simulate dynamic #INCLUDEs. You cannot assign a variable to the Active Server Pages #INCLUDE directive, but you can assign a variable to the SRC attribute of a frame within an Active Server Page script. Here is a sample script that randomly displays different pages within two frames (included on the CD as dynamicframe.asp):
>
> ```
> <%
> randomize
> if rnd()  > 0.5 then
>     framesrc = "http://www.microsoft.com"
> else
>     framesrc = "http://www.netscape.com"
> end if
> %>
> <html>
> <frameset rows="*,*">
> <frame src="<%=framesrc%>">
> <frame src="<%=framesrc%>">
> </frameset>
> </html>
> ```

Creating Threaded Discussions

The second challenge in building the discussion forum was to find a way to efficiently store and display a threaded discussion. The problem with threaded discussions is that new replies can be posted within the middle of the list of messages at any time. For example, someone could post a message on July 16, 1999, and someone else could post a reply to this message a year later. The fact that messages may receive replies means that messages cannot be stored and displayed in the same order in which they are posted.

All the messages are stored in a single table named messages. This table includes columns for the author of the message, the subject of the message, the entry date of the message, and the actual body of the message. The table also contains a column that represents the order number of the message. The order number of the message determines the order in which the messages are displayed.

One approach to handling new replies to messages is to simply update the order number of the messages whenever a new reply is posted. For example, if a reply were posted to message 32, the order number of all the messages with an order number greater than 32 would be increased by one, and the new reply would be stored with the order number 33. Using this method, there would be a one-to-one correspondence between the order number of each message and the order in which the message is displayed.

The problem with this approach is that it is very database intensive. If a new reply is posted to a message that appears in the middle of the list of messages, then half the messages would have to be updated with new order numbers. If the discussion forum contained hundreds of messages, the database could become quickly overwhelmed.

Our forum takes a different approach. Whenever a new reply to a message is posted, the reply is stored with the same order number as the original message. For example, all the replies to the message with order number 32 also have the order number 32. The entry date of the message is then used to display the replies in the correct order.

The advantage of this method of storing messages is that it is not very database intensive. When a new reply is posted, none of the other messages must be updated. Each reply is associated with the proper message, and the correct order of the messages is preserved.

Building the Discussion Forum

To use the discussion forum, you will need to copy all the Active Server Pages for the forum from this chapter's directory on the CD-ROM that accompanies this book to a directory on your server. Your Web server must be able to access this directory.

After you have copied all the files, make two changes to the Active Server Page file named forumfuncs.asp. First, you will need to change the #INCLUDE directive at the top of this file to point to the location of the ADOVBS.INC file on your server (the ADOVBS.INC file was automatically installed on your server when you installed IIS).

You will also need to change the database connection string used with the discussion forum. The database connection string is set by a constant named dbCon that appears at the top of forumfuncs.asp. Supply a valid Data Link filename for the database that you will use to store the discussion forum messages.

27

CREATING A
DISCUSSION
FORUM

NOTE

For more information on creating connection strings see Chapter 12, "Working with Connections and Data Sources."

 Finally, you will need to install the database table and stored procedures used for the discussion forum. To do this, load the SQL script named installforums.sql from the CD into Microsoft ISQL/w or Microsoft Query Analyzer, choose a database, and execute the script. When you execute the script, a default set of forums is automatically created.

To view the discussion forum, load the file named forums.asp into your Web browser. If everything is installed correctly, the discussion forum should appear as it does in Figure 27.3.

FIGURE 27.3

The installed discussion forum.

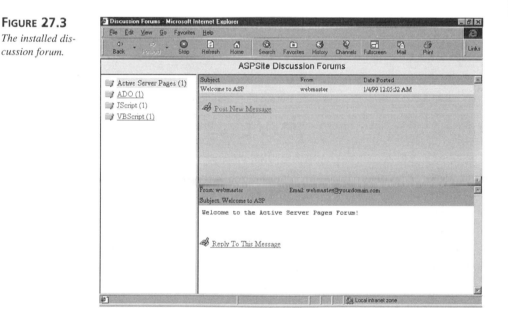

Relationship Between the Discussion Forum Files

 The discussion forum is composed of 10 distinct Active Server Page files, all of which are available on the CD. The relationship between these files is complex, so this section presents a brief overview of how all the files are related.

- forum.asp—The file that you load into your browser to view the discussion forum. forum.asp is a frameset file that defines two frames. The top frame contains top-bar.asp. The bottom frame contains the frameset file named content.asp.

- topbar.asp—This file displays the banner that appears at the top of the screen. The logo ASPSite Discussion Forums is displayed. You can change this logo to anything you please.

- content.asp—This file is a frameset file that includes the forumlist.asp frame and the messages.asp frameset file. When a new message is posted, this frameset file is reloaded so that all its child frames will also be reloaded.

- forumlist.asp—This file is used to display a list of all the forum areas. It is described in more detail in the section titled "Displaying the List of Forums," later in this chapter.

- messages.asp—A frameset file that defines the messagelist.asp frame and the message.asp frame. When a new message is selected, this file is reloaded so that both of its child frames will be reloaded with the right message selected.

- messagelist.asp—Displays a list of messages for the currently selected forum area. It is described in more detail in the section titled "Displaying the List of Messages," later in this chapter.

- message.asp—Used to display the actual body of a message. It is described in more detail in the section titled "Displaying the Message Body," later in this chapter.

- post.asp—Contains the form for posting a new message. It is described in more detail in the section titled "Posting a New Message," later in this chapter.

- reply.asp—Contains the form for posting a reply to a message. It is described in more detail in the section titled "Replying to a Message," later in this chapter.

- forumfuncs.asp—Contains all the common functions and subroutines used by the other files.

The Messages Table

The discussion forum uses a single database table, named messages, to store all the messages posted to any of the forum areas. This table is created with the following SQL CREATE TABLE statement:

```
CREATE TABLE dbo.messages (
    m_id int IDENTITY (1, 1) NOT NULL ,
    m_forumName varchar (30) NOT NULL ,
    m_subject varchar (30) NOT NULL ,
    m_username varchar (30) NOT NULL ,
    m_email varchar (70) NOT NULL ,
    m_entrydate datetime NOT NULL default getDATE() ,
    m_message text NULL ,
    m_ordernum int NULL ,
    m_reply bit NOT NULL
)
```

The m_id column is used to assign each message a unique message ID (it's an identity column). The m_forumName column is used to specify the forum where the message should appear, the m_ordernum column determines the display order of the message, and the m_reply column indicates whether or not the message is a reply.

The m_entrydate column contains the date and time when the message was entered into the messages table. Notice that the column has a default value of getDATE(). The SQL getDATE() function automatically assigns the current date and time to the column.

The actual content of the message is contained in the m_subject, m_username, m_email, and m_message columns, which correspond to the subject of the message, the author of the message, the email address of the author of the message, and the message body.

Displaying the List of Forums

The left frame of the discussion forum lists all the available areas for discussion. When you click on any of the links in this frame, the messages that correspond to the discussion area are displayed. The Active Server Page file named forumlist.asp is used to display the list of forums.

The list of forums is retrieved by using the following SQL stored procedure:

```
create procedure getForums
as
select m_forumname, count( m_id ) theCount
from messages
group by m_forumname

order by m_forumname
```

This stored procedure retrieves the name of each forum from the messages table. A count of the number of messages for each forum is also retrieved.

If you want to add a new forum, you simply add a message to the messages table with the new forum name. For example, the following SQL statement adds a new forum named Other Topics:

```
insert messages (
     m_forumName,
     m_username,
     m_email,
     m_subject,
     m_message,
     m_ordernum,
     m_reply
     ) values (
     'Other Topics',
     'webmaster',
     'webmaster@yourdomain.com',
     'Welcome to Other Topics',
     'Welcome to other topics!',
     0,
     0
     )
```

To remove a forum, delete all the messages in the messages table with the forum name. To change the name of the forum, update the forumName column with the new forum name.

When the discussion forum is first loaded, the default forum area is automatically selected. The default forum is determined by a constant named defaultForum that appears at the top of the content.asp file. If you change the names of the forum areas, you should also change this constant.

Displaying the List of Messages

The top frame in the discussion forum displays a list of the messages that correspond to the current forum. The messages are listed by subject, author, and entry date. No more than 15 messages are displayed at a time.

When the discussion forum is first loaded in a browser, the message ID of the last message posted to the default forum is automatically retrieved. This is accomplished with the following SQL stored procedure:

```
CREATE PROCEDURE getLastMessage
(
     @forumName varchar( 30 ),
     @lastMessage int OUTPUT
```

```
)
AS
declare @maxOrderNum int, @maxDate datetime
select @maxOrderNum = max( m_ordernum )
from messages
where m_forumName = @forumName

select @maxDate = max( m_entrydate )
from messages
where m_ordernum = @maxOrderNum
and m_forumName = @forumName

select @lastmessage = m_id from messages
where m_ordernum = @maxOrdernum
and m_entrydate = @maxDate
and m_forumName = @forumName
```

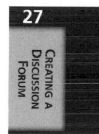

This procedure is more complicated than you might expect because the last message might not have the highest message ID. If a reply were posted to an earlier message in the forum, the message ID of the last message would be less than the message ID of the reply. To get around this problem, the MAX() SQL aggregate function is used to retrieve the message ID with the latest entry date and the highest order number in the current forum.

After a message ID has been retrieved, the Active Server Page file named messagelist.asp is used to display the list of messages. The list of messages are retrieved from the messages table by using the following SQL stored procedure:

```
create procedure getMessages
(
    @forumName varchar( 30 ),
    @messageID int
)
as
declare @messageOrder int

select @messageOrder = m_ordernum
from messages
where m_id = @messageID

select
    m_id,
    m_ordernum,
    m_username,
    m_subject,
    m_entrydate,
    m_reply
    from messages
    where m_forumName = @forumName
```

```
and m_ordernum > ( @messageOrder - 6 )
and m_ordernum < ( @messageOrder + 16 )
order by m_ordernum, m_entrydate
```

Two parameters are passed to this stored procedure, the name of the current forum and the current message ID. The stored procedure retrieves the message order number from the message ID and selects all the messages that have an order number close to this order number.

More than one message in the messages table can have the same order number. For example, all the replies to a message will have the same order number as the original post. This means that the getMessages stored procedure can return any number of messages.

Two subroutines, named getMessages and showMessages, located in the forumfuncs.asp file are used to actually display the list of messages. The getMessages subroutine places all the messages retrieved from the getMessages SQL stored procedure into an array. This is accomplished with the GetRows() method of the RecordSet object:

```
theArray = RS.getRows()
```

The list of messages is transferred from a Recordset to an array so that only 15 messages at a time will be displayed. The getMessages subroutine finds the index number of the currently selected message by iterating through the contents of the array. After the currently selected message is found, the first message to display is determined by subtracting 4 from the index position of the currently selected message. The following script finds the index of the first message to display:

```
for k = 0 to UBOUND( theArray, 2 )
    if cLNG( theArray( m_id, k ) ) = cLNG( theMessageID ) then
        theFirstMessage = k - 4
        if theFirstMessage < 0 then theFirstMessage = 0
        exit for
    end if
next
```

After the index number of the first message has been found, the list of 15 messages is displayed with the showMessages subroutine. The showMessages subroutine displays the messages in a table. All the messages except the currently selected message are displayed with the default background color. The currently selected message is displayed with a gray background.

Each message in the list, except for the selected message, is displayed as a link. The link contains a URL variable for the forum name and a URL variable for the message ID. Here is an example:

```
<a href="messages.asp?f=ADO&m=21" target="messages">
Setting Cursor Types?</a>
```

When you click on the link, the messages frameset is reloaded, and the whole process of displaying the list of messages is started once again.

Displaying the Message Body

The bottom frame of the discussion forum displays the body of the currently selected message. The bottom frame displays an Active Server Page named message.asp. The following script is used to retrieve the message from the messages table:

```
' ' ' ' ' ' ' ' ' ' ' ' '
'   Retrieve The Message
' ' ' ' ' ' ' ' ' ' ' ' '
MyCQL = "select * from messages where m_id=" & messageID
Set RS = Server.CreateObject( "ADODB.RecordSet" )
RS.Open MySQL, Con, adOpenStatic
```

> **TIP**
>
> Notice that the default forward-only cursor is *not* used to retrieve the message. Instead, a static cursor is opened. When retrieving text columns, you should not use a forward-only cursor because, occasionally, the content of a text column will be truncated.

The body of the message is displayed with the following script:

```
<table width="100%" cellpadding=4 border=0>
<tr>
    <td>
    <pre><%=Server.HTMLEncode( RS( "m_message" ) )%></pre>
    </td>
</tr>
</table>
```

The <PRE> tag is used to preserve carriage returns and spaces in the original message. Without the <PRE> tag, the message appears without its original spacing as a single long line. The HTMLEncode() method of the Server object is used to prevent any HTML code from being displayed. If the message is not HTML encoded before being displayed, and if the original message contains any special HTML characters, the message can become garbled.

Posting a New Message

When a new message is posted, the form in Figure 27.4 appears. When this form is submitted, the SQL stored procedure in Listing 27.1 is used to add the new message to the database. This procedure uses the SQL INSERT statement to add the new message to the messages table. Next, it creates a unique order number for the new message by finding the maximum existing order number and adding one. Each new post to a discussion forum area is, therefore, guaranteed to have a unique order number.

FIGURE 27.4

Posting a new message.

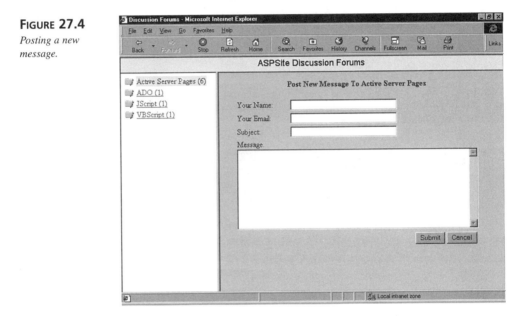

LISTING 27.1 POST NEW MESSAGE—POSTMESSAGE

```
create procedure postMessage
(
    @forumName varchar( 30 ),
    @subject varchar( 30 ),
    @username varchar( 30 ),
    @email varchar( 70 ),
    @newMessageID int OUTPUT
)
as
declare @maxOrderNum int

insert messages (
    m_forumName,
    m_subject,
```

```
        m_username,      m_email,
        m_reply
        ) values (
        @forumName,
        @subject,
        @username,
        @email,
        0
        )

select @newMessageID = @@IDENTITY

select @maxOrderNum = max( m_ordernum ) + 1
from messages
where m_forumName = @forumName

update messages set m_ordernum = @maxOrderNum
where m_id = @newMessageID
```

Replying to a Message

When you reply to a message, the form in Figure 27.5 appears. Replying to a message is similar to posting a message. The main difference between the two is that the order number of a reply is assigned the same order number as the original post. This ensures that the proper replies are associated with the proper posts. New replies are added to the database table with the SQL stored procedure in Listing 27.2.

FIGURE 27.5

A reply to a message

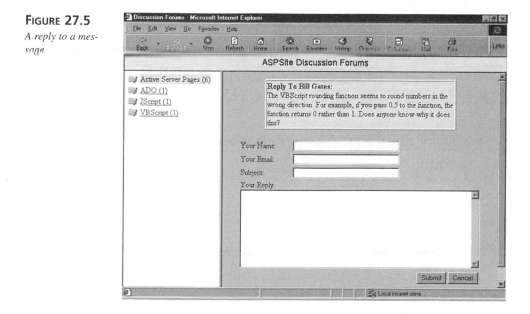

LISTING 27.2   POSTING A REPLY—POSTREPLY

```
create procedure postReply
(
     @forumName varchar( 30 ),
     @subject varchar( 30 ),
     @username varchar( 30 ),
     @email varchar( 70 ),
     @newMessageID int OUTPUT,
     @reply integer
)
as
insert messages (
     m_forumName,
     m_subject,
     m_username,        m_email,
     m_reply
     ) values (
     @forumName,
     @subject,
     @username,
     @email,
     1
     )

select @newMessageID = @@IDENTITY

select @reply = m_ordernum
from messages
where m_id = @reply

update messages set m_ordernum = @reply
where m_id = @newMessageID
```

Extending the Discussion Forum

Several useful features could be added to the discussion forum described in this chapter. It would be nice, for example, if whenever someone posts a new reply to a message, an email message containing the new reply would be sent to the author of the original message and everyone else who replied to the message.

In Chapter 10, "Working with Email," you learned how to use the CDO for NTS to send email messages from within an Active Server Page. You can also use the CDO for NTS to automatically send email messages from the discussion forum. To do this, use the sendMail subroutine described in the section titled "Sending Email with the CDO for NTS," in Chapter 10.

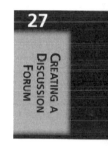

Another useful feature that you can add to your discussion forum is syntax highlighting. When someone posts a message that contains an Active Server Page script in a forum at the ASPSite, the script automatically appears with a yellow background (in the same way as it would appear in Microsoft's Visual InterDev). This is accomplished by automatically inserting Cascading Style Sheet <SPAN> tags within the body of the message. Here is the function that performs the replacement:

```
function highlight( byVal theMessage )
    pos =INSTR( theMessage,"&lt;%")
    if pos > 0 then endpos = INSTR( 1, theMessage ,"%&gt;" )
    while ( pos > 0 and endpos > pos )
    theMessage = Replace( theMessage, "&lt;%",
    ➥"<SPAN CLASS=""yellow"">!lt;%", 1, 1)
    theMessage = Replace( theMessage, "%&gt;", "%!gt;</SPAN>", 1, 1)
    pos = INSTR( theMessage, "&lt;%")
    if pos > 0 then endpos = INSTR(1, theMessage, "%&gt;" )
    wend
    theMessage = Replace( theMessage, "!lt;", "&lt;")
    theMessage = Replace( theMessage, "!gt;", "&gt;")
    highlight = theMessage
end function
```

This function replaces every occurrence of the HTML encoded string "<%" with the HTML encoded string "<SPAN CLASS="yellow"><%" and every occurrence of the HTML encoded string "%>" with the string "</SPAN>". If the following style rule is added to the head of the document, any script enclosed in the script delimiters will appear with a yellow background:

```
<STYLE>
.yellow {background: yellow}
</STYLE>
```

 An example of an Active Server Page that uses this function is included with the CD that accompanies this book (highlight.asp).

I'm sure that several other useful features can be added to the discussion forum. If you think of one, please do not hesitate to visit the forums at the ASPSite (www.aspsite.com) and post a message about it.

Summary

In this chapter, you learned how to create a complete discussion forum using nothing but Active Server Pages. This discussion forum has many advanced features such as message threading and multiple synchronized frames.

CHAPTER 28

Creating an Online Store

by Jeff Spotts

IN THIS CHAPTER

One of the many ways in which use of the Internet has exploded in recent years is in the area of electronic commerce. Web surfers can now order goods from a rapidly growing number of online stores. Many businesses have discovered that they can offer their products for sale through Web sites, as more and more consumers turn to the Internet for their shopping needs. In fact, a number of businesses offer products for sale via the Internet only, and have no need for physical locations that customers can visit!

In this chapter, you will explore the use of Active Server Pages to create an online store. You will develop a site that can be used by a business to sell its products through the Internet.

The site you will create in this chapter will be quite generic and simple. It's meant as a starting point to use if you choose to develop a site for your business. A full-blown online store can be as simple as your sample application or complex enough to take a full team of developers weeks or even months to create. It could, in fact, be the subject of a book of its own.

> **NOTE**
>
> If you would like to see the sample site in action, visit
> `http://www.aspsite.com/aspstore`. Here you will find the complete ASP
> Unleashed Online Store sample application as described in this chapter.

Navigating the Online Store

The ASP Unleashed Online Store application consists of a series of Active Server Pages that are designed to work in harmony. When a user visits the site, he will begin with default.asp, the "front page" of your online store site. It will present the user with the basic information necessary to navigate your entire site from this start page.

From the start page, the user can search for items by keyword. There are also links to the user's shopping cart, as well as to other helpful areas such as Customer Service and a Help page. The start page may also contain time-sensitive featured products, giving the user the opportunity to add certain items to his shopping cart directly from the application's home page.

Creating the Site Location

It's really quite a simple task to set up the environment that will contain the online store site. On your Web server, create a virtual directory that will contain all the site's ASP files, as well as a few support files. Your sample application's virtual directory is named ASPStore. The site is, therefore, accessible by navigating to `http://servername/asp-store`. Because this will be a standalone ASP application, you will also need to create a Web application named ASPStore.

> **NOTE**
>
> See Chapter 4, "Working with Active Server Pages Applications" to learn more about creating Active Server Pages applications.

> **TIP**
>
> If you would like to set up the sample Online Store application on your own Web server, all necessary files are included on the book's companion CD. To set it up, follow the instructions presented in the setup.htm file located in this chapter's folder on the CD.

Preparing the Database

Your online store application will serve as a two-way conduit for information to and from the end user. The initial function of the site will be to display information about your products to the user. The user will, in turn, send back to the site information concerning products he or she wants to order.

For your sample site, you will create a relational database containing three tables:

- A `Products` table will store information concerning the products that you sell.
- An `Orders` table will contain a record for each order placed by a customer.
- An `Order Details` table will contain a record for each item in each order. Records in this table represent line items related to order records in the `Orders` table.

Because of its wide availability, Microsoft Access was chosen as the database platform for your demonstration. As you will see, however, the database will be accessed using ActiveX Data Objects (ADO) via ODBC, so the actual database platform is irrelevant to the application. You will see how to establish a "generic" connection to the database that can be easily modified for different platforms.

> **CAUTION**
>
> Although use of a Microsoft Access database is fine for development, it is not appropriate for a Web site that will receive even moderate traffic. Before moving your online store application into a production environment, you should consider the use of a more robust client/server database engine (for example, Microsoft SQL Server).

The Products Table

The Products table stores the names, descriptions, prices, and other information concerning the products that your store will have available for sale. It will contain the following fields:

- ItemID—A numeric field containing a long integer which serves as a record identifier.

- ItemProductNumber—A text field containing an identifier such as a catalog number or UPC code that is unique for each product.

- ItemName—A text field containing the name of the product.

- ItemDescription—A longer text field that allows for a more complete description of the product.

- ItemPictureFile—The name of a graphics file that will be used to retrieve a picture of the product for display on the Web pages. The graphic files are assumed to be stored in a folder named Products under the application's Images folder.

- ItemRegularPrice—A currency field containing the regular price of the product.

- ItemSalePrice—If the product currently has a sale or special price, it will be contained in the field. Otherwise, this field will contain 0.

- BeginSpecial—A date/time field that contains the first date that this product is to be displayed in the "Today's Featured Products" section of your application's main page.

- EndSpecial—A date/time field that contains the last date that this product is to be displayed in the "Today's Featured Products" section of your application's main page.

The Orders Table

A record will be added to the Orders table for each order entered by a customer. It will contain the following fields:

- OrderID—A numeric field containing an automatically incrementing long integer that serves as a record identifier.

- OrderDate—A date/time field containing the date on which the order was completed.

- OrderTime—A date/time field containing the time at which the order was completed.

- CustomerName—A text field containing the name of the customer who placed this order.

- CustomerAddress—A text field containing the address of the customer who placed this order.

- CustomerCity—A text field containing the city of the customer who placed this order.

- CustomerState—A text field containing the state of the customer who placed this order.

- CustomerZIP—A text field containing the ZIP code of the customer who placed this order.

- CustomerPhone—A text field containing the telephone number of the customer who placed this order.

- OrderAmount—A currency field containing the total dollar amount of the order.

- PaymentMethod—A text field containing the name of the credit card used to pay for the order.

- PaymentAccount—A text field containing the account number of the credit card used to pay for the order.

- ExpDate— A text field containing the expiration date of the credit card used to pay for the order.

The Order Details Table

Each time an order is placed, one record is added to the Orders table; in addition one record is added to the Order Details table for each item requested in that order. This sets up an effective one-to-many relationship between the two tables.

- OrderID—This numeric field contains a long integer identifying the record from the Orders table to which this detail record is related.

- ProductNumber—This text field contains the product number (from the Products table) identifying the product that is represented by this detail record.

- Quantity—A numeric field representing the quantity of this product that was ordered.

- Price—A currency field containing the regular or sale price of the product being purchased at the time the order was placed.

Storing the Data

After you have created the database, it should be accessible to the Web server via an ODBC connection. For the sample site, set up a System Data Source Name (DSN) of ASPStore; this ODBC connection will be used to connect to the database. In the upcoming section titled "Global.asa," you will see how the online store's data connection is stored as a system variable whenever a session begins.

> **NOTE**
>
> See Chapter 12, "Working with Connections and Data Sources" for more information about creating a database connection.

Common Elements

To ensure a consistent look and feel throughout the application, I have designed two include files that will give each page in the site a standard header and footer. By using these include pages, it will be easy to make modifications to the tops and bottoms of each page in the application.

HEADER.INC

HEADER.INC, shown in Listing 28.1, is included near the beginning of each page, somewhere near the `<html>` tag. Before the HTML Include tag is implemented, however, ASP code in each page sets the values of two variables that will be used by HEADER.INC. sPageHead is used to set the page's title inside the `<head>` tag; sPageCaption specifies the page's caption inside a blue bar that resembles a newspaper dateline just below the logo on each page.

In the upper-left corner of each page, HEADER.INC places a logo for the entire site; this logo acts as an `<a href>` link to default.asp, the main page of the application. There are also navigation links in the upper-right corner to two commonly accessed pages in the site.

LISTING 28.1 HEADER.INC

```
<head>
<title><% = sPageHead %></title>
</head>

<body>
<table border="0" width="100%">
  <tr>
    <td width="70%"><a href="default.asp">
    <img src="images/OnlineStore.gif"
      alt="ASP Unleashed Online Store Home" border="0"></a></td>
    <td valign="top">
      <table bgcolor="#dc143c" border="0" width="100%">
        <tr>
          <td bgcolor="#87cefa" align="center">
          <font face="Verdana,Arial" size=-1>
          <a href="default.asp">Online Store Home</a>
          </font></td>
        </tr>
        <tr>
          <td bgcolor="#87cefa" align="center">
          <font face="Verdana,Arial" size=-1>
          <a href="shopcart.asp">Shopping Cart</a>
          </font></td>
        </tr>
      </table>
    </td>
  </tr>
</table>
<table border="0" width="100%">
  <tr>
    <td bgcolor="#0000FF" align="center">
    <font face="Verdana,Arial" color="#ffffff">
    <b><% = sPageCaption %></font></b></td>
  </tr>
</table>
```

FOOTER.INC

Similar to HEADER.INC, FOOTER.INC is designed to give the bottom of each page in the application a consistent look. It consists of a series of helpful links, followed by site copyright information. The include directive for FOOTER.INC is to be placed just before the closing </body> and </html> tags in each page. FOOTER.INC is shown in Listing 28.2.

LISTING 28.2   FOOTER.INC

```
<br><table border="0" width="100%">
  <tr align="center">
    <td bgcolor="#33ccff">
      <font face="Verdana, Arial" color="#ffff33" size="-1">
      <a href="help.asp">Help</a></font></td>
    <td bgcolor="#33ccff">
      <font face="Verdana, Arial" color="#ffff33" size="-1">
      <a href="shopcart.asp">Shopping Cart</a></font></td>
    <td bgcolor="#33ccff">
      <font face="Verdana, Arial" color="#ffff33" size="-1">
      <a href="custsvc.asp">Customer Service</a></font></td>
    <td bgcolor="#33ccff">
      <font face="Verdana, Arial" color="#ffff33" size="-1">
      <a href="feedback.asp">Feedback</a></font></td>
  </tr>
</table>
<br>
<hr align="CENTER" size="2" color="#0000FF">
<div align="center"><font face="Arial" color="#808080" size=-2>
The ASP Unleashed Online Store web site was created by
<a href="mailto:jspotts@bigfoot.com">Jeff Spotts</a>.
Copyright &copy; 1999 Jeff Spotts. All Rights Reserved.
</font>
</div><hr align="CENTER" size="2" color="#0000FF">
```

Global.asa

I have created a Global.asa file, shown in Listing 28.3, that sets up session variables to be used throughout the application. This task is performed by placing code in the Global.asa file's `Session_OnStart` sub procedure; this code is executed whenever a user establishes a session with the server.

> **NOTE**
>
> See Chapter 4, "Working with Active Server Pages Applications," and Chapter 5, "Working with Sessions," to learn more about using the Global.asa file and session variables.

LISTING 28.3   GLOBAL.ASA

```
<SCRIPT LANGUAGE=VBScript RUNAT=Server>
Sub Session_OnStart
  dim sItemNums(0), nItemQtys(0)
```

```
    sItemNums(0) = ""
    nItemQtys(0) = 0

    session("CartItemNumArray") = sItemNums
    session("CartItemQtyArray") = nItemQtys
    session("DBLogin") = "DSN=ASPStore"
    session("shipbasecharge") = 4.50
    session("shipitemcharge") = 1.25

End Sub
</SCRIPT>
```

Global.asa establishes the following variables for each session:

- `Session("CartItemNumArray")` is an array that will contain item numbers identifying products that the user adds to his shopping cart.

- `Session("CartItemQtyArray")` is another array that will contain the quantities of the respective products that the user adds to his shopping cart.

- `Session("DBLogin")` contains the login information needed to connect to the application's main data source. Assuming that an ODBC connection has been established on the server, the DSN will be part of this variable.

- `Session("shipbasecharge")` and `Session("shipitemcharge")` contain the shipping charges for orders placed from your online store. The first variable represents the per-order charge; the second represents the per-item charge. That is, the total shipping charge for each order will be the base charge plus the per-item charge multiplied by the number of items shipped.

The first two variables, `Session("CartItemNumArray")` and `Session("CartItem-Cession("CartItemQtyArray")`, will be used to pass the contents of the user's shopping cart from page to page. The other three variables, `Session("DBLogin")`, `Session("shipbasecharge")`, and `Session("shipitemcharge")`, are established here so that they can be changed easily if necessary.

The Online Store's Portal

As the home page of the application, default.asp is the first screen that your users see when they hit the site. This portal page should, therefore, be eye-catching, but simple enough not overwhelm the user. Default.asp is illustrated in Figure 28.1.

Your customers can immediately begin shopping in one of two ways as soon as they see this page. First, a text box on the left side offers them the opportunity to type keywords on which to search for products. Second, a list of currently featured items is presented

near the bottom; Add to Cart buttons next to each item give the user the opportunity for
quick product selection.

FIGURE **28.1**

*The Online Store's
main page should
be aesthetically
pleasing to users.*

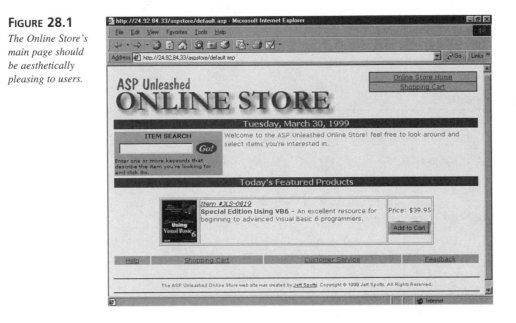

Default.asp

Aside from the header and footer include files described earlier, default.asp, as shown in
Listing 28.4, also contains pointers to two other include files:

- ADOVBS.INC, provided by Microsoft, allows VBScript applications easy access to
  predefined ADO constants.
- PROCS.INC contains a sub procedure and a function that will be used by multiple
  pages within the application. By storing this code in an include file that is brought
  into pages as required, you can reduce duplicated code.

The two main programming features of interest in default.asp are the <form> that allows
the user to input search keywords, and an area of ASP code that selects and displays featured products from the database.

LISTING **28.4**   DEFAULT.ASP

```
<!--#INCLUDE FILE="adovbs.inc"-->
<!--#INCLUDE FILE="procs.inc"-->

<%
```

```
      sPageHead = "ASP Unleashed Online Store Home Page"
      sPageCaption = formatdatetime(now,vblongdate)
      session("redirectto") = "default.asp"
      session("salecomplete") = false
%>
<html>
<!--#INCLUDE FILE="header.inc"-->

<table border="0" width="100%">
  <tr>
    <td width="30%">
      <table border="0" width="100%" bgcolor="#c0c0c0" cellspacing="0">
        <tr>
          <td align="center" bgcolor=#66ccff>
          <font face="Verdana,Arial" size=-1>
          <strong>ITEM SEARCH</strong></font></td>
        </tr>
        <tr>
          <td align="center">
            <table border="0">
              <tr>
                <form action="prodsearch.asp" method="POST">
                <td><input type="Text" name="txtSearch" size="20"
                  maxlength="100"></td>
                <td><input type="image" src="images/go.gif" border="0"
                  alt="Click to begin search"></td>
                </form>
              </tr>
            </table>
          </td>
        </tr>
        <tr>
          <td><font face="Verdana,Arial" color="#000000" size="-2">
          Enter one or more keywords that describe the item you're
          looking for and click Go.</font></td>
        </tr>
      </table>
    </td>
    <td valign="top">
      <font face="Verdana,Arial" color="#008000" size="-1">
      Welcome to the ASP Unleashed Online Store! feel free to look around
      and select items you're interested in.</font>
    </td>
  </tr>
</table>

<%
  set dbMain = server.createobject("ADODB.Connection")
  dbMain.open session("dblogin")
```

continues

LISTING 28.4 CONTINUED

```
 Set rsProducts = Server.CreateObject("ADODB.Recordset")

 sSQL = "SELECT * FROM products WHERE beginspecial <= #" & date() & _
   "#" & " AND endspecial >= #" & date() & "#"
 rsProducts.open sSQL, dbMain, adopenstatic, adlockpessimistic, adcmdtext
%>

<% if not rsproducts.eof then %>
<table border="0" width="100%">
  <tr>
  <td bgcolor="#0000FF"><font face="Verdana,Arial" color="#ffff00">
    <p align="center"><b>Today's Featured Products</b></p></font></td>
  </tr>
</table>
<br>
<table width="75%" border="1" align="center">
<%
  rsproducts.movefirst
  do while not rsproducts.eof
    WriteProductRow
    rsProducts.movenext
  loop
%>
</table>
<% end if %>
<!--#INCLUDE FILE="footer.inc"-->
</body>
</html>
```

Preparing a Search

The <form> included in default.asp contains an input text box, txtSearch, that allows the user to input a keyword that matches the name, item number, or description of a product he is looking for. A Go image submits the form to its destination, Prodsearch.asp, which in turn performs the actual search and displays the results. Prodsearch.asp is discussed later in this chapter.

Displaying Specials

In the latter lines of default.asp, a SQL statement is constructed that looks for records in the main database's Products table in which the current date is between the record's beginspecial and endspecial fields. This SQL statement is, in turn, used to create a Recordset, rsProducts, containing records that meet those criteria. The Recordset's EOF property is examined to determine whether any matching records were found. If so, a table is created to display the products.

After the table is created, the following lines of code are executed:

```
rsproducts.movefirst
do while not rsproducts.eof
  WriteProductRow
  rsProducts.movenext
loop
```

This code loops through the records in the `rsProducts` Recordset, calling a sub procedure named `WriteProductRow` each time through. `WriteProductRow` is not visible in
default.asp. It is included in PROCS.INC, as discussed previously.

Displaying a Product

The purpose of `WriteProductRow`, as seen in Listing 28.5, is to create, in an already-
defined table, one row displaying the specific product represented by the current record
of the `rsProducts` Recordset. This row contains the following cells:

- A picture of the product, if available. This picture is created by referencing the
  name of a picture file obtained from the `Products` table's `ItemPictureFile` field.

- An informational cell containing the product's item number, name, and description.
  Each of these elements is formatted using font variations to make them easy to
  identify.

- A pricing cell that displays the product's current price. If the product has a sale
  price (which is obtained from the `ItemSalePrice` field), the regular price is reported as well for comparison purposes. This cell also contains a link to shopcart.asp
  with a querystring that tells shopcart.asp to execute in Add mode, as well as another querystring to pass the item number.

LISTING 28.5   PROCS.INC

```
<%
'PROCS.INC
Sub WriteProductRow
  'Write a table row for the current record of rsProducts
  response.write "  <tr>" & vbcrlf

  'First cell for picture
  sTemp = trim("" & rsproducts("itempicturefile"))
  if sTemp = "" then
    sTemp = "Picture Not Available"
  else
    sTemp = "<img src='images\products\" & sTemp & "' border=0 alt=''>"
  end if
```

continues

Listing 28.5   CONTINUED

```
response.write "    <td align='center'>"
response.write "<font face='Verdana, Arial' color='#008000' size='-1'>"
response.write sTemp & "</font></td>" & vbcrlf

'Second cell for Item #, name, description
response.write "    <td valign='top'>"
response.write "<font face='Verdana, Aria' color='#000000' size='-1'>"
response.write "<i><u>Item #" & rsProducts("itemproductnumber")
response.write "</u></i></font><br>"
response.write "<font face='Verdana, Arial' color='#0000ff' size='-1'>"
response.write "<b>" & rsProducts("itemname") & "</b> - "
response.write "<font face='Verdana, Arial' color='#008000' size='-1'>"
response.write rsProducts("itemdescription") & "<br><br>"
response.write "</font></td>" & vbcrlf

'Third cell for price and "add to cart" link
if rsproducts("itemsaleprice") > 0 then
  sTemp = "SALE: " & formatcurrency(rsProducts("itemsaleprice")) & _
    "<br>(Regular " & _
      formatcurrency(rsProducts("itemregularprice")) & ")"

else
  sTemp = "Price: " & formatcurrency(rsProducts("itemregularprice"))
end if
response.write "    <td align='center' valign='middle' nowrap>"
response.write "<font face='Verdana, Arial' color='#0000ff' size='-1'>"
response.write sTemp & "<br><br>"
response.write "<a href='shopcart.asp?mode=add&itemno="
response.write rsproducts("itemproductnumber") & "'></font>"
response.write "<img src='images/addtocart.jpg' border='0'></a></td>"
response.write vbcrlf

response.write "  </tr>"  & vbcrlf

End Sub

Function RemoveQuotes(s)
  dim i, s2
  s = trim(s)

  if len(s) = 0 then
    RemoveQuotes = ""
    exit function
  end if

  s2 = ""
  for i = 1 to len(s)
    if mid(s,i,1) = "'" then
      s2 = s2 & "''"
```

```
    else
       s2 = s2 & mid(s, i, 1)
    end if
  next
  RemoveQuotes = s2
End Function
%>
```

Shopcart.asp is a page where a product is added to a user's shopping cart. It is discussed in detail in the section "The Application's Busiest Page," later in this chapter.

Searching for Products

If the user types information into default.asp's text box and clicks the Go button, the form's destination, prodsearch.asp (see Listing 28.6), is loaded and executed. This page is responsible for performing a product search based on the keyword information that the user entered while viewing default.asp. If one or more matching products are located, each is displayed using the WriteProductRow sub procedure stored in Procs.inc, which was discussed in the previous section. The result of a typical product search is illustrated in Figure 28.2.

FIGURE 28.2

A user who has performed a keyword search is presented with product matches.

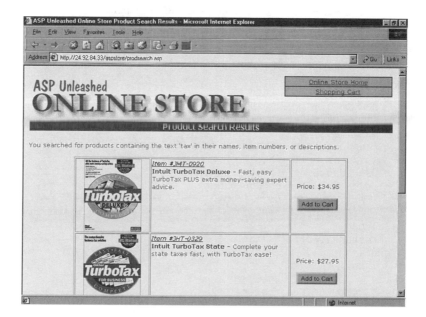

LISTING 28.6   PRODSEARCH.ASP

```
<!--#INCLUDE FILE="adovbs.inc"-->
<!--#INCLUDE FILE="procs.inc"-->
<%
    sPageHead = "ASP Unleashed Online Store Product Search Results"
    sPageCaption = "Product Search Results"


%>
<html>

<!--#INCLUDE FILE="header.inc"-->

<br><font face="Verdana,Arial" color="#008000" size="-1">
You searched for products containing the text
'<% = request.form("txtSearch")%>'
in their names, item numbers, or descriptions.
<br><br>
<%
  set dbMain = server.createobject("ADODB.Connection")
  dbMain.open session("dblogin")
  Set rsProducts = Server.CreateObject("ADODB.Recordset")

  sSearch = RemoveQuotes(request.form("txtSearch"))
  sSQL = "SELECT * FROM products WHERE itemproductnumber LIKE '%" & _
    sSearch & "%' OR itemname LIKE '%" & _
    sSearch & "%' OR itemdescription LIKE '%" & _
    sSearch & "%'"
 rsProducts.open sSQL, dbMain, adopenstatic, adlockpessimistic, adcmdtext

  if rsproducts.eof then
    response.write "No products matching that criteria were found."
    response.write vbcrlf
  else
    response.write "<table width='75%' border='1' align='center'>"
    response.write vbcrlf
    rsproducts.movefirst
    do while not rsproducts.eof
      WriteProductRow
      rsProducts.movenext
    loop
    response.write "</table>" & vbcrlf
  end if
%>

<!--#INCLUDE FILE="footer.inc"-->
</body>
</html>
```

Notice that this code calls a function named RemoveQuotes. This function, contained in Procs.inc (shown earlier in Listing 28.5), is used to modify text strings that were input by the user, replacing each single quote with a pair of single quotes. This effectively allows the user to input a search criteria that itself contains single quotes without causing problems for the SQL WHERE clause.

After constructing a SQL statement containing the user's criteria, a Recordset containing matching records is created. If the Recordset's EOF property is True, the user is told that there are no matching records. If, however, there are matching records, then the user is presented with a table containing all matching records. As was the case with default.asp, each product has a link to shopcart.asp. Also, as in default.asp, the table row for each product is written using the WriteProductRow sub procedure that is included from Procs.inc.

For a discussion of more efficient ways to search the database, see Chapter 15, "Working with Index Server and Full-Text Search."

The Application's Busiest Page

Shopcart.asp, shown in Listing 28.7, is your online store application's workhorse page. As you will see when you examine the ASP code, shopcart.asp is designed to run in one of several modes; each of these is described in the following sections. Figure 28.3 shows shopcart.asp in action.

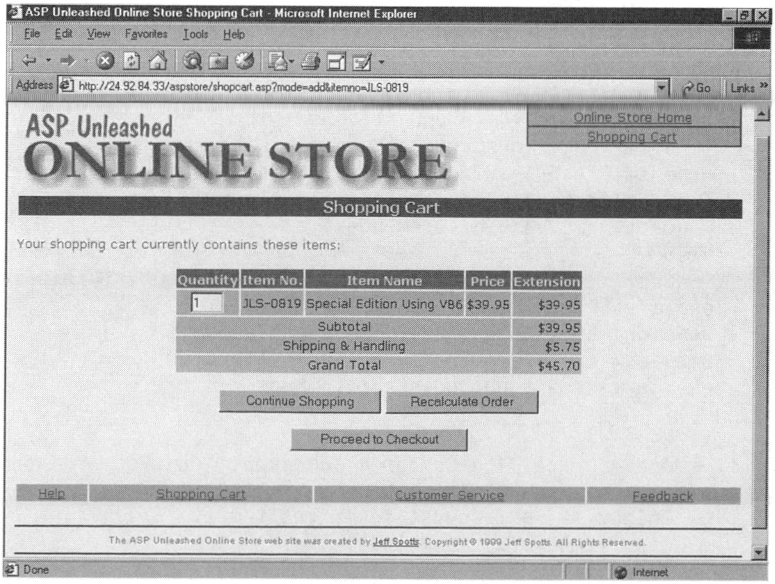

FIGURE 28.3

Shopcart.asp is being used in Add mode to add an item to the user's shopping cart.

LISTING 28.7   SHOPCART.ASP

```
<!--#INCLUDE FILE="adovbs.inc"-->
<%
  sCartItemNums = session("cartitemnumarray")
  nCartItemQtys = session("cartitemqtyarray")
  nNumCartItems = ubound(sCartItemNums)

  'Determine the mode of this page's operation. If we got here from a
  ' link that had a "mode" querystring of "add", mode is add:
  sMode = request.querystring("mode")

  'Or, we could have gotten here from a form:
  select case request.form("cmdSubmit")
    case "Proceed to Checkout"
      sMode = "checkout"
    case "Recalculate Order"
      sMode = "recalc"
    case "Continue Shopping"
      sMode = "continue"
  end select

  if sMode = "add" then
    nThisItemIndex = 0
    sItemNo = ucase(request.querystring("itemno"))
    if nNumCartItems > 0 then
      for i = 1 to nNumCartItems
              if ucase(scartitemnums(i)) = sItemNo then
          nThisItemIndex = i
          exit for
        end if
      next
    end if
    if nThisItemIndex = 0 then
      nThisItemIndex = nNumCartItems + 1
      redim Preserve sCartItemNums(nThisItemIndex)
      redim Preserve nCartItemQtys(nThisItemIndex)
      sCartItemNums(nThisItemIndex) = sItemNo
      nCartItemQtys(nThisItemIndex) = 1
    else
      nCartItemQtys(nThisItemIndex) = nCartItemQtys(nThisItemIndex) + 1
    end if
    session("cartitemnumarray") = sCartItemNums
    session("cartitemqtyarray") = nCartItemQtys
    nNumCartItems = ubound(sCartItemNums)
  end if

  if sMode = "recalc" or sMode = "checkout" or sMode = "continue" then
    for i = 1 to nNumCartItems
      nThisQty = int(request.form("txtItemQty" & i))
      nCartItemQtys(i) = nThisQty
```

```
    next
    session("cartitemnumarray") = sCartItemNums
    session("cartitemqtyarray") = nCartItemQtys
  end if

  'Move to another page based on mode.
  '  If mode is "add" or "recalc", we stay here.
  '  If mode is "continue", we move back to the main page so the user
  '     can shop more.
  '  If mode is "checkout", we stay here but change the mode th
  select case sMode
    case "continue"
      response.redirect("default.asp")
  end select

  set dbMain = server.createobject("ADODB.Connection")
  dbMain.open session("dblogin")

  if sMode = "checkout" then
    sPageHead = "ASP Unleashed Online Store Checkout"
    sPageCaption = "Checkout"
  else
    sPageHead = "ASP Unleashed Online Store Shopping Cart"
    sPageCaption = "Shopping Cart"
  end if
%>
<html>

<!--#INCLUDE FILE="header.inc"-->

<br>
<font face="Verdana,Arial" color="#008000" size="-1">
<% if sMode = "checkout" then %>
<form action="submitorder.asp" method="POST">
<% else %>
<form action="shopcart.asp" method="POST">
<% end if %>
<%
  if nNumCartItems = 0 then
    response.write "There are no items in your shopping cart.<br>"
  else
    if sMode = "checkout" then
%>
Your order is ready to submit. Please provide the following information
and click the "Submit Order" button.
<br><br>
<table align="center" border="0">
  <tr bgcolor="#c0c0c0">
```

continues

LISTING 28.7   CONTINUED

```
    <th colspan="2" align="center"><font face="Verdana,Arial" size="-1">
    Customer Information</td>
</tr>
<tr>
  <td align="right"><font face="Verdana,Arial" size="-1">Name:</td>
  <td><font face="Verdana,Arial" size="-1">
    <input type="Text" name="txtCustomerName" size="30" maxlength="30">
    </td>
</tr>
<tr>
  <td align="right"><font face="Verdana,Arial" size="-1">Address:</td>
  <td><font face="Verdana,Arial" size="-1">
    <input type="Text" name="txtAddress" size="30" maxlength="30"></td>
</tr>
<tr>
  <td align="right"><font face="Verdana,Arial" size="-1">
    City/State/ZIP:</td>
  <td><font face="Verdana,Arial" size="-1">
    <input type="Text" name="txtCity" size="25" maxlength="30">
    <input type="Text" name="txtState" size="4" maxlength="4">
    <input type="Text" name="txtZIP" size="7" maxlength="7"></td>
</tr>
<tr>
  <td align="right"><font face="Verdana,Arial" size="-1">
    Daytime Phone:</td>
  <td><font face="Verdana,Arial" size="-1">
    <input type="Text" name="txtPhone" size="15" maxlength="15"></td>
</tr>
<tr>
  <td align="right"><font face="Verdana,Arial" size="-1">
    Payment Method:</td>
  <td><font face="Verdana,Arial" size="-1">

    <input type="Radio" name="optPaymentType" value="visa">
      Visa 
    <input type="Radio" name="optPaymentType" value="mc">
      Mastercard 
    <input type="Radio" name="optPaymentType" value="amex">
      American Express
  </td>
</tr>
<tr>
  <td align="right"><font face="Verdana,Arial" size="-1">
    Account Number:</td>
  <td><font face="Verdana,Arial" size="-1">
    <input type="Text" name="txtAcctNo" size="20" maxlength="20"></td>
</tr>
<tr>
  <td align="right"><font face="Verdana,Arial" size="-1">
```

```
        Expiration (mm/yyyy):</td>
      <td><font face="Verdana,Arial" size="-1">
        <input type="Text" name="txtExpDate" size="10" maxlength="7"></td>
    </tr>
</table>
<%
    else
      response.write "Your shopping cart currently contains these items:"
    end if
%>
<br><br>
<table align="center" border="0">
  <tr bgcolor="#ff0066">
    <th><font face="Verdana,Arial" color="#ffff33" size="-1">
      Quantity</font></td>
    <th><font face="Verdana,Arial" color="#ffff33" size="-1">
      Item No.</font></td>
    <th><font face="Verdana,Arial" color="#ffff33" size="-1">
      Item Name</font></td>
    <th><font face="Verdana,Arial" color="#ffff33" size="-1">
      Price</font></td>
    <th><font face="Verdana,Arial" color="#ffff33" size="-1">
      Extension</font></td>
  </tr>
<%
  cSubTotal = 0
  nNumItems = 0
  for i = 1 to nNumCartItems
    Set rsProducts = Server.CreateObject("ADODB.Recordset")
    sSQL = "SELECT * FROM products WHERE itemproductnumber = '" & _
      sCartItemNums(i) & "'"
    rsProducts.open sSQL, dbMain, adopenstatic, _
      adlockpessimistic, adcmdtext
%>
  <tr bgcolor="#99ccff">
<%
  sTemp = "<input type='Text' name='txtItemQty" & i & "' value='" & _
    nCartItemQtys(i) & "' size='3'>"
  nNumItems = nNumItems + nCartItemQtys(i)
%>
    <td align="center">
      <font face="Verdana,Arial" color="#000000" size="-1">
      <% = sTemp %></font></td>
    <td align="center">
      <font face="Verdana,Arial" color="#000000" size="-1">
      <% = rsProducts("itemproductnumber") %></font></td>
    <td><font face="Verdana,Arial" color="#000000" size="-1">
      <% = rsProducts("itemname") %></font></td>
<%
```

28

CREATING AN
ONLINE STORE

continues

LISTING 28.7 CONTINUED

```
  if rsProducts("ItemSalePrice") > 0 then
    cPrice = rsProducts("ItemSalePrice")
  else
    cPrice = rsProducts("ItemRegularPrice")
  end if
%>
    <td align="center">
       <font face="Verdana,Arial" color="#000000" size="-1">
      <% = formatcurrency(cPrice) %></font></td>
<%
  cExtension = nCartItemQtys(i) * cPrice
  cSubTotal = cSubTotal + cExtension
%>
    <td align="right">
      <font face="Verdana,Arial" color="#000000" size="-1">
      <% = formatcurrency(cExtension) %></font></td>
  </tr>
<% next %>
  <tr bgcolor="#c5c5c5">
    <td align="center" colspan="4">
      <font face="Verdana,Arial" size="-1">Subtotal</font></td>
    <td align="right"><font face="Verdana,Arial" size="-1">
      <% = formatcurrency(cSubTotal) %></font></td>
  </tr>
<% cShipping = 4.50 + (1.25 * nNumItems) %>
  <tr bgcolor="#c5c5c5">
    <td align="center" colspan="4">
     <font face="Verdana,Arial" size="-1">Shipping & Handling</font></td>
    <td align="right"><font face="Verdana,Arial" size="-1">
      <% = formatcurrency(cShipping) %></font></td>
  </tr>
<% cTotal = cSubTotal + cShipping %>
  <tr bgcolor="#66ff00">
    <td align="center" colspan = "4">
      <font face="Verdana,Arial" size="-1">Grand Total</font></td>
    <td align="right"><font face="Verdana,Arial" size="-1">
      <% = formatcurrency(cTotal) %></font></td>
  </tr>
</table>
<br><div align="center">

<input type="Submit" name="cmdSubmit" value="Continue Shopping">
<input type="Submit" name="cmdSubmit" value="Recalculate Order">
<br><br>
<% if sMode = "checkout" then %>
<input type="Submit" name="cmdSubmit" value="Submit Order">
<% else %>
<input type="Submit" name="cmdSubmit" value="Proceed to Checkout">
```

```
<% end if %>
</div></form>
<% end if %>

<!--#INCLUDE FILE="footer.inc"-->
</body>
</html>
```

General Construction of Shopcart.asp

Shopcart.asp consists of several ASP routines mixed with standard HTML. Near the top of the page, the current operating mode is determined by examining how the page was loaded. If the page was loaded using a mode querystring, Add mode is invoked. Otherwise, the page may have been loaded from a form that uses one of a group of Submit buttons named cmdSubmit. By looking at the value of `Request.Form("cmdSubmit")`, shopcart.asp can determine which mode should be in effect. At various points in the page, different pieces of code are executed depending on the current mode of operation.

All modes include an HTML form; in most modes, the form's action destination is shopcart.asp itself. The main reason for this recursion is that, if the user modifies the quantity of one or more items in his shopping cart, you have the opportunity to execute code in shopcart.asp to modify the shopping cart session variables before redirecting to another page.

If you have spent much time visiting online store sites, you might have noticed that when a user views his shopping cart, he can change item quantities; however, if he does so, he must click a special button to save the quantity changes. I find this to be counterintuitive, especially for users who are not particularly computer literate. The method you have implemented in shopcart.asp eliminates this need.

Add Mode

Usually, the first time shopcart.asp is invoked is when the user has clicked on an Add to Cart link next to a product that he would like to purchase. The Add to Cart link passes two querystrings to shopcart.asp, as in this example:

```
<a href='shopcart.asp?mode=add&itemno=LMS-0218'>
```

When shopcart.asp executes, the querystring mode=add triggers Add mode. This, in turn, causes the code block beginning with

```
if sMode = "add"
```

to execute. This code block looks through the sCartItemNums array, which is being passed throughout the session as part of the user's shopping cart, to see if the item number represented by the itemno querystring is already in the array. If the item number is in the array, the quantity of that item is increased; otherwise, the array is extended to include the item.

After this addition to the shopping cart has been performed, most of the rest of the ASP code is skipped because it applies to the other modes. The rest of shopcart.asp then displays the current contents of the user's shopping cart, as you saw in Figure 28.3.

Displaying the Shopping Cart

Near the bottom of shopcart.asp is a block of code that displays the contents of the user's shopping cart. It does this by using a mixture of ASP code and regular HTML, and it should be fairly straightforward to follow by examining the code. As it spins through the items contained in the arrays that represent the shopping cart, it locates each item in the database, displays the information for that item, and calculates a running subtotal. After all items in the shopping cart have been displayed, shipping charges are calculated (based on the Session variables shipbasecharge and shipitemcharge described in the Global.asa section earlier in this chapter) and displayed. Finally, the order total is displayed.

Continue Mode

Continue mode comes into play when the user clicks the Continue Shopping button. This submits shopcart.asp's form back to shopcart.asp itself, as described earlier. Code is executed that reacts to any quantity changes that the user made and updates the shopping cart session variables. The user is then redirected back to default.asp to continue shopping.

Recalculate Mode

Recalculate mode is really not necessary, but is provided as a means for the user to be able to immediately see the results of any quantity changes he made. Recalculate mode works much like Continue mode in that the same shopping cart update code is executed. However, instead of redirecting the user back to default.asp, Recalculate mode allows the rest of shopcart.asp to execute, which effectively shows the user his updated, recalculated shopping cart.

Checkout Mode

When the user clicks the Proceed to Checkout button, shopcart.asp is reloaded in Checkout mode. This mode is similar to Recalculate mode, with two fundamental differences.

The first difference comes in the definition of the form itself. All other modes use shopcart.asp as the form's `action` destination. Checkout mode directs the form to a different page, submitorder.asp. As you will see in the upcoming section "Finalizing the Order," this page will actually finalize the customer's order and will add it to the database.

The second difference is that when shopcart.asp is executed in Checkout mode, the user is presented with a series of text boxes to allow him to enter his order shipping and payment information. This information will be used by submitorder.asp when completing the order.

Figure 28.4 depicts shopcart.asp in Checkout mode.

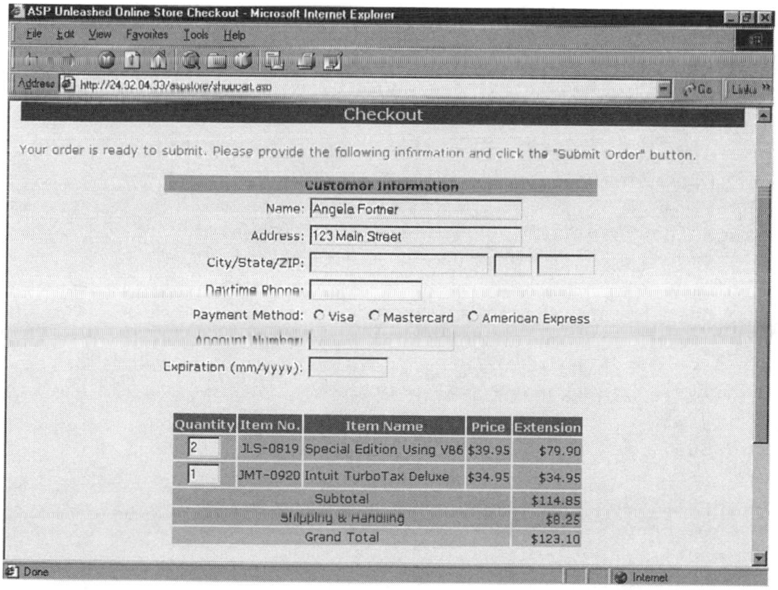

FIGURE 28.4
When the user is ready to check out, he may enter his shipping and payment information.

Finalizing the Order

After the user has entered his shipping and payment information on shopcart.asp, he will click the Submit Order button to invoke submitorder.asp (see Listing 28.8). This page is responsible for adding the order information to the database and will provide a summary of the order that the user may print.

LISTING 28.8   SUBMITORDER.ASP

```
<!--#INCLUDE FILE="adovbs.inc"-->
<%
  dim sErrorString
  sErrorString = ""
  dim cItemPrice(99), sItemName(99)
  dim cOrderTotal
  cItemPrice(0) = 0
  sItemName(0) = ""
  cOrderTotal = 0

  if session("salecomplete") = true then
    session("salecomplete") = false
    response.redirect "default.asp"
  end if

  sCartItemNums = session("cartitemnumarray")
  nCartItemQtys = session("cartitemqtyarray")
  nNumCartItems = ubound(sCartItemNums)

  for i = 1 to nNumCartItems
    nThisQty = int(request.form("txtItemQty" & i))
    nCartItemQtys(i) = nThisQty
  next
  session("cartitemnumarray") = sCartItemNums
  session("cartitemqtyarray") = nCartItemQtys

Sub CheckErrors(sField, sItemName)
  if trim(request.form(sField)) = "" then
    sErrorString = sErrorString & "The " & sItemName & _
      " field cannot be blank.<br>"
  end if
End Sub

  CheckErrors "txtCustomerName","Customer Name"
  CheckErrors "txtAddress","Customer Address"
  CheckErrors "txtCity","City"
  CheckErrors "txtState","State"
  CheckErrors "txtZIP","ZIP"
  CheckErrors "txtPhone","Telephone"
  CheckErrors "optPaymentType","Payment Type"
  CheckErrors "txtAcctNo","Account Number"
  CheckErrors "txtExpDate","Expiration Date"

  if sErrorString = "" then
```

```
set dbMain = server.createobject("ADODB.Connection")
dbMain.open session("dblogin")

Set rsProducts = Server.CreateObject("ADODB.Recordset")
for i = 1 to nNumCartItems
  sSQL = "SELECT * FROM products WHERE itemproductnumber = '" & _
    sCartItemNums(i) & "'"
  rsProducts.open sSQL, dbMain, adopenstatic, _
    adlockpessimistic, adcmdtext
  if rsProducts("itemsaleprice") > 0 then
    cItemPrice(i) = rsProducts("itemsaleprice")
  else
    cItemPrice(i) = rsProducts("itemregularprice")
  end if
  sItemName(i) = rsProducts("itemname")
  cOrderTotal = cOrderTotal + (nCartItemQtys(i) * cItemPrice(i))
  nNumItems = nNumItems + nCartItemQtys(i)
  rsProducts.close
next
cShipping - session("shipbasecharge") + _
  (nNumItems * session("shipitemcharge"))
cOrderTotal = cOrderTotal + cShipping

dbMain.BeginTrans

Set rsOrders = Server.CreateObject("ADODB.Recordset")
sSQL = "SELECT * FROM orders"
rsOrders.open sSQL, dbMain, adOpenStatic, adlockpessimistic, adcmdtext

rsOrders.addnew
rsOrders("orderdate") = date()
rsOrders("ordertime") = time()
rsOrders("customername") = request.form("txtCustomerName")
rsOrders("customeraddress") - request.form("txtAddress")
rsOrders("customercity") = request.form("txtCity")
rsOrders("customerstate") = request.form("txtState")
rsOrders("customerzip") = request.form("txtZIP")
rsOrders("customerphone") = request.form("txtPhone")
rsOrders("orderamount") = cOrderTotal
rsOrders("paymentmethod") = request.form("optPaymentType")
rsOrders("paymentaccount") = request.form("txtAcctNo")
rsOrders("expdate") = request.form("txtExpDate")

rsOrders.update
rsorders.movelast
nOrderID = rsorders("orderid")
rsOrders.close

Set rsOrderLines = Server.CreateObject("ADODB.Recordset")
```

continues

LISTING 28.8   CONTINUED

```
    sSQL = "SELECT * FROM orderdetails WHERE orderid = " & nOrderID
    rsOrderLines.open sSQL, dbMain, adOpenStatic, _
      adlockpessimistic, adcmdtext

  for i = 1 to nNumCartItems
    rsOrderLines.addnew
    rsOrderLines("orderid") = nOrderID
    rsOrderLines("productnumber") = sCartItemNums(i)
    rsOrderLines("quantity") = nCartItemQtys(i)
    rsOrderLines("price") = cItemPrice(i)
    rsOrderLines.update
  next
  dbMain.CommitTrans

    session("salecomplete") = true
 end if

  sPageHead = "ASP Unleashed Online Store Order Confirmation"
  sPageCaption = "Order Confirmation"

%>
<html>

<!--#INCLUDE FILE="header.inc"-->
<font face="Verdana,Arial" color="#008000" size="-1">
<%
  if sErrorString = "" then

    response.write "Order # " & nOrderID & " has been entered. Use " & _
      " your browser's PRINT function to print a copy of this order." & _
      "<br><br>"
  sSQL = "SELECT * FROM orders WHERE orderid = " & nOrderID
    rsOrders.open sSQL, dbMain, adOpenStatic, adlockpessimistic, adcmdtext
%>
<table align="center" border="0">
  <tr>
    <td valign="top">
      <table border="0">
        <tr>
          <td align="center" bgcolor="#808080">
            <font color="#ffffff"><b>Order # <% = nOrderID %>
            </b></font></td>
        </tr>
        <tr>
          <td align="center" bgcolor="#3300ff">
            <font color="#ffffff"><b>Order Date <% = date() %>
            </b></font></td>
        </tr>
      </table>
```

```
        </td>
        <td>
          <table align="center" border="0">
            <tr bgcolor="#c0c0c0">
              <th colspan="2" align="center">
                <font face="Verdana,Arial" size="-1">
                Customer Information</td>
            </tr>
            <tr>
              <td align="right"><font face="Verdana,Arial" size="-1">
                Name:</td>
              <td><font face="Verdana,Arial" size="-1" color="#0000ff">
                <% = rsOrders("customername") %></td>
            </tr>
            <tr>
              <td align="right"><font face="Verdana,Arial" size="-1">
                Address:</td>
              <td><font face="Verdana,Arial" size="-1" color="#0000ff">
                <% = rsOrders("customeraddress") %></td>
            </tr>
            <tr>
              <td align="right"><font face="Verdana,Arial" size="-1">
                City/State/ZIP:</td>
              <td><font face="Verdana,Arial" size="-1" color="#0000ff">
                <% = rsOrders("customercity") & ", " %>
                <% = rsOrders("customerstate") %>
                <% = " " & rsOrders("customerzip") %></td>
            </tr>
            <tr>
              <td align="right"><font face="Verdana,Arial" size="-1">
                Daytime Phone:</td>
              <td><font face="Verdana,Arial" size="-1" color="#0000ff">
                <% = rsOrders("customerphone") %></td>
            </tr>
            <tr>
              <td align="right"><font face="Verdana,Arial" size="-1">
                Payment Method:</td>
<%
        select case rsOrders("paymentmethod")
          case "visa"
            sTemp = "Visa"
          case "mc"
            sTemp = "MasterCard"
          case "amex"
            sTemp = "American Express"
        end select
%>
              <td><font face="Verdana,Arial" size="-1" color="#0000ff">
                <% = sTemp %></td>
```

continues

LISTING 28.8   CONTINUED

```
            </td>
          </tr>
        </table>
      </td>
</table>
<br><br>

<table align="center" border="0">
  <tr bgcolor="#ff0066">
    <th><font face="Verdana,Arial" color="#ffff33" size="-1">
      Quantity</font></td>
    <th><font face="Verdana,Arial" color="#ffff33" size="-1">
      Item No.</font></td>
    <th><font face="Verdana,Arial" color="#ffff33" size="-1">
      Item Name</font></td>
    <th><font face="Verdana,Arial" color="#ffff33" size="-1">
      Price</font></td>
    <th><font face="Verdana,Arial" color="#ffff33" size="-1">
      Extension</font></td>
  </tr>
<%
  cSubTotal = 0
  nNumItems = 0
  for i = 1 to nNumCartItems
%>
  <tr bgcolor="#99ccff">
    <td align="center">
      <font face="Verdana,Arial" color="#000000" size="-1">
      <% = nCartItemQtys(i) %></font></td>
    <td align="center">
      <font face="Verdana,Arial" color="#000000" size="-1">
      <% = sCartItemNums(i) %></font></td>
    <td><font face="Verdana,Arial" color="#000000" size="-1">
      <% = sItemName(i) %></font></td>
    <td align="center">
      <font face="Verdana,Arial" color="#000000" size="-1">
      <% = formatcurrency(cItemPrice(i)) %></font></td>
<%
  nNumItems = nNumItems + nCartItemQtys(i)
  cExtension = nCartItemQtys(i) * cItemPrice(i)
  cSubTotal = cSubTotal + cExtension
%>
    <td align="right">
      <font face="Verdana,Arial" color="#000000" size="-1">
      <% = formatcurrency(cExtension) %></font></td>
  </tr>
<% next %>
  <tr bgcolor="#c5c5c5">
```

```
      <td align="center" colspan="4">
        <font face="Verdana,Arial" size="-1">Subtotal</font></td>
      <td align="right"><font face="Verdana,Arial" size="-1">
        <% = formatcurrency(cSubTotal) %></font></td>
  </tr>
<%
  cShipping = session("shipbasecharge") + _
    (nNumItems * session("shipitemcharge"))
%>
  <tr bgcolor="#c5c5c5">
    <td align="center" colspan="4">
     <font face="Verdana,Arial" size="-1">Shipping & Handling</font></td>
    <td align="right"><font face="Verdana,Arial" size="-1">
      <% = formatcurrency(cShipping) %></font></td>
  </tr>
<% cTotal = cSubTotal + cShipping %>
  <tr bgcolor="#66ff00">
    <td align="center" colspan = "4">
      <font face="Verdana,Arial" size="-1">Grand Total</font></td>
    <td align="right"><font face="Verdana,Arial" size="-1">
      <% = formatcurrency(cTotal) %></font></td>
  </tr>
</table>

<div align="center"><font face="Verdana,Arial" size="+1">
<br>Thank you for your order!</font></div>
<% else %>
The following errors error(s) occurred while processing the information
you provided:<br><br>
<font face="Courier New" color="#000000">
<% = sErrorString %>
</font>
<br><br>Please press your browser's BACK button and correct this
information, then reoubmit your order.
<% end if %>
<br>
<%
  if session("salecomplete") = true then
    redim sItemNums(0)
    redim nItemQtys(0)
    sItemNums(0) = ""
    nItemQtys(0) = 0
    session("CartItemNumArray") = sItemNums
    session("CartItemQtyArray") = nItemQtys
    session("salecomplete") = false
  end if
%>
<!--#INCLUDE FILE="footer.inc"-->
</body>
</html>
```

Starting the Process

After setting up some variables, submitorder.asp contains an interesting piece of code:

```
if session("salecomplete") = true then
  session("salecomplete") = false
  response.redirect "default.asp"
end if
```

This code is a safety feature to keep the user from accidentally resubmitting the same order if he reloads submitorder.asp for some reason. As you will notice later in the code, the session variable `salecomplete` is set to `True` after the order has been completed and entered into the database. The preceding code checks the value of `session("salecomplete")`; if it is `True`, the order has been completed, and the rest of the code on this page should not be executed. The user will be redirected to default.asp in that case.

After that matter is dealt with, submitorder.asp executes the shopping cart recalculation code found in `SHOPCART.ASP` in case the user changed any of the product quantities in the text boxes in shopcart.asp before clicking the Submit Order button.

Checking for Errors

Next, submitorder.asp checks to make sure that there was an entry in each of the text boxes at the top of shopcart.asp. Here is a golden opportunity to customize the online store application for your company's situation. You may, for example, want to give the user the opportunity to log in or otherwise extract his user information from a customer database. Also, depending on how your company's order processing system is set up, you should somehow verify the validity of the customer's credit card information before continuing.

In our example, if the user has left any of the text boxes blank, he is informed which ones caused problems and instructed to go back to complete the information.

Entering the Order

After the information provided by the user has been verified, you are ready to finalize the order by adding one record to the `Orders` table, plus one record to the `Order Details` table for each product that the user ordered. This is accomplished by spinning through the shopping cart session variables and using standard ADO techniques to add the appropriate records.

Depending on your business, you will probably need to develop some type of interface to the database to extract order information as orders are entered. After your organization has been somehow notified of new orders, processing of the orders can begin.

Displaying the Order

After the order information has been entered, a summary of the order (including the newly generated order ID number and the order date) is presented in a format that the user can print. This is accomplished in a manner similar to the way the shopping cart is presented in shopcart.asp. Figure 28.5 shows a completed order displayed by submitorder.asp.

FIGURE 28.5

The user has completed his order and may print a copy for his records.

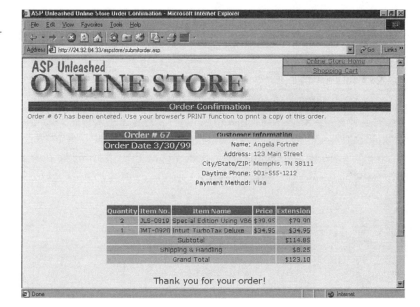

Cleaning Up

Finally, the last bit of code in submitorder.asp resets the shopping cart session variables. This is done in order to empty the shopping cart in case the user decides to shop some more. He doesn't want to buy the same items twice!

Opportunities for Improvement

As discussed previously, this sample application is designed to be generic. As you develop your site, you should take advantage of several areas in which you can improve and customize the site for your business. Some of the main areas that can be customized include the following:

- Introduction of the capability to log in to the system. This will save the user the trouble of retyping his information each time he places an order.

- Addition of an Order Status function. As you interface this application into your shipping system, you may be able to update the order's status in the Orders table. In this case, the user should be able to look up an order he has placed to see if and how it has shipped.

- Addition of a procedure to verify the user's credit card information.

- Automatic notification of newly placed orders to your company's shipping or processing department.

Summary

In this chapter, you have seen how to develop a fundamental online store site. You have seen how to use ASP code in harmony with HTML and learned some site flow principles to make a site that is both functional and easy for the user to navigate. You have also been presented with some ideas for customizing the site to make it work for your particular business.

Creating a Job Site

by Stephen Walther

IN THIS CHAPTER

In this chapter, you will be provided with a real-life programming application of Active Server Pages. You will learn how to create the ASP Job Site, an online job site for Active Server Pages consultants and employers. This programming application enables Active Server Pages consultants to post their resumés and search for job opportunities. Employers can use the site to advertise job listings and search through the resumés.

The ASP Job Site illustrates how to create a database-driven Web site using Active Server Pages. All the data for both the resumés and job listings are stored entirely within a SQL Server database. This programming application also illustrates how to work with form data. You will learn how to use Active Server Pages to collect and redisplay information entered into HTML forms.

> **NOTE**
>
> You can view a functioning version of the ASP Job Site by visiting
> `http://www.aspsite.com/aspjobsite`.

Overview of the Job Site

The ASP Job Site consists of 10 Active Server Pages. Each of these pages will be discussed in later sections, one by one. However, before getting into the details of how each page works, here is a quick overview of the function of each page:

- default.asp—This page is the home page for the ASP Job Site. It provides a menu of the other pages and introduces visitors to the Web site.
- postresume.asp—This page enables visitors to enter their resumés by filling out an HTML form.
- postresume2.asp—This page inserts a new resumé into the database and thanks visitors for submitting their resumés.
- postjob.asp—This page enables employers to enter a new job listing by filling out an HTML form.
- postjob2.asp—This page inserts a new job listing into the database and thanks the visitor for submitting the job listing.
- searchresumes.asp—This page enables employers to search through all the current resumés.
- resumedetail.asp—This page displays a complete resumé by retrieving it from the database.

- searchjobs.asp—This page enables consultants to search through all the current job listings.

- jobdetail.asp—This page displays a complete job listing by retrieving it from the database.

- jobsitefuncs.asp—This file contains all the common subroutines and functions used by the other pages in the ASP Job Site.

Installing the Job Site

 Before reading the rest of this chapter, you should install the ASP Job Site on your Web server. To install the ASP Job Site, copy (to a directory on your server) all the files located in the directory named Chapter29 on the CD that accompanies this book. This directory must be accessible from your Web server. For example, you can copy the files to a directory named JobSite located under the root directory of your Web Server (typically, wwwroot).

You should also grant either script or execute permissions for the directory where the Job Site files are located. To do this, launch the Internet Service Manager and open the property sheet for the directory. Next, click the tab labeled Directory and check either the box labeled Script or the box labeled Execute.

 After you have copied the files to your Web server, you will need to create two database tables named Resumes and Jobs. These are the tables where the data for the resumés and job listings are stored. The Chapter29 directory includes a file named maketables.sql that will automatically create these tables for you. Load the maketables.sql file into Microsoft Query Analyzer (or ISQL/w, if you are using SQL 6.5) and execute the file.

The maketables.sql file creates the tables by executing the SQL statements contained in Listing 29.1.

LISTING 29.1   MAKETABLES.SQL

```
CREATE TABLE [dbo].[Jobs] (
    [job_id] [int] IDENTITY (1, 1) NOT NULL ,
    [fname] [varchar] (100) NULL ,
    [lname] [varchar] (100) NULL ,
    [phone] [varchar] (20) NOT NULL ,
    [email] [varchar] (80) NOT NULL ,
    [state] [varchar] (5) NULL ,
    [country] [varchar] (5) NULL ,
    [bdesc] [varchar] (100) NULL ,
```

continues

29

CREATING A JOB SITE

LISTING 29.1 CONTINUED

```
    [perman] [varchar] (3) NULL ,
    [contract] [varchar] (3) NULL ,
    [job] [text] NULL ,
    [expires] [datetime] NULL ,
    [entrydate] [datetime] NOT NULL DEFAULT getDATE()
)
GO

CREATE TABLE [dbo].[Resumes] (
    [resume_id] [int] IDENTITY (1, 1) NOT NULL ,
    [fname] [varchar] (100) NULL ,
    [lname] [varchar] (100) NULL ,
    [phone] [varchar] (20) NULL ,
    [email] [varchar] (80) NULL ,
    [state] [varchar] (5) NULL ,
    [country] [varchar] (5) NULL ,
    [bdesc] [varchar] (100) NULL ,
    [perman] [varchar] (3) NULL ,
    [contract] [varchar] (3) NULL ,
    [resume] [text] NULL ,
    [expires] [datetime] NULL ,
    [entrydate] [datetime] NOT NULL DEFAULT getDATE()
)
GO
```

After you have added the tables, you can configure the ASP Job Site to access them. All the files use a global constant named `connectionstring` to open the database connection. This constant is defined in the first line of the file named jobsitefuncs.asp. It appears like this:

```
CONST connectionstring =
➥ "PROVIDER=SQLOLEDB;UID=sa;PWD=secret;DATABASE=test"
```

Replace the values given to the UID and PWD parameters with valid security information for your database. Next, change the name of DATABASE to a database located on your server (it should be the same database where you created the Jobs and Resumes tables).

Creating the Job Site

 The following sections provide detailed information on how each of the files in the ASP Job Site work. Because many files are too long to list in their entirety in this chapter, I strongly suggest that you use a text editor to open the files from the CD while you read this chapter. All the files are located in the Chapter29 directory on the CD.

Displaying the Home Page

The home page of the ASP Job Site is contained in the file named default.asp. The purpose of the home page is to welcome new visitors and provide a menu of links to the other pages (see Figure 29.1). It also displays statistics on the number of current resumés and job listings.

FIGURE 29.1

The home page of the ASP Job Site.

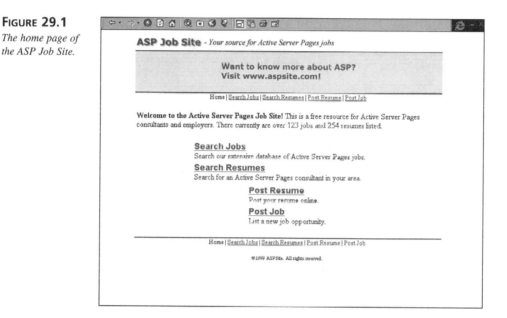

The HTML content included at both the top and bottom of the page is generated by two subroutines named displayHeader and displayFooter. The same subroutines are used to create the header and footer for all the pages in the ASP Job Site. Both subroutines are located in the jobsitefuncs.asp file, which is included in every page using the ASP INCLUDE directive.

The header includes an advertisement. This advertisement is generated by using the Ad Rotator component. The component enables you to randomly display different advertisements with different frequencies. To learn more about the Ad Rotator component, see Chapter 9, "Tracking Page Views and Displaying Advertisements."

Both the header and footer include a navigation bar that displays the links to the other pages in the ASP Job Site. The name of every page, except for the current page, appears as a hypertext link. The navigation bar enables users to easily get to any page, and it also displays information about the page where the user is currently located. The navigation bar is created by the subroutine in Listing 29.2.

29

CREATING A JOB SITE

LISTING 29.2   ASP JOB SITE NAVIGATION BAR

```asp
Sub displayNavbar( byVal currentPage )
  if currentPage = "Home" then
  %>
  Home ¦
  <%
  else
  %>
  <a href="default.asp">Home</a> ¦
  <%
  end if
  if currentPage = "Search Jobs" then
  %>
  Search Jobs ¦
  <%
  else
  %>
  <a href="searchjobs.asp">Search Jobs</a> ¦
  <%
  end if
  if currentPage = "Search Resumes" then
  %>
  Search Resumes ¦
  <%
  else
  %>
  <a href="searchresumes.asp">Search Resumes</a> ¦
  <%
  end if
  if currentPage = "Post Resume" then
  %>
  Post Resume ¦
  <%
  else
  %>
  <a href="postresume.asp">Post Resume</a> ¦
  <%
  end if
  if currentPage = "Post Job" then
  %>
  Post Job
  <%
  else
  %>
  <a href="postjob.asp">Post Job</a>
  <%
  end if
End Sub
```

Listing 29.2 consists of a long series of conditionals. When the subroutine is called, the name of the current page is passed. If the name of a page does not equal the name of the current page, a hypertext link to the page is displayed. Otherwise, the name of the page is displayed as plain text. The home page of the ASP Job Site displays statistics on the current number of resumés and job listings posted. These statistics are displayed with the script in Listing 29.3.

LISTING 29.3   DISPLAYING RESUMÉ AND JOB STATISTICS

```
' Get resume and job statistics
if Application( "statupdate" ) = ""
➥OR Application( "statupdate" ) < NOW() then
  Set Con = Server.CreateObject( "ADODB.Connection" )
  Con.Open connectionstring
  mySQL = "SELECT COUNT(*) numresumes FROM Resumes"
  SET RS = Con.Execute( mySQL )
  Application( "resumes" ) = RS( "numresumes" )
  mySQL = "SELECT COUNT(*) numjobs FROM Jobs"
  SET RS = Con.Execute( mySQL )
  Application( "jobs" ) = RS( "numjobs" )
  Application( "statupdate" ) = DATEADD( "h", 1, NOW() )
end if
```

The script in Listing 29.3 requires some explanation. The statistics on the number of resumés and jobs listed are retrieved from the database by opening a database connection and executing two SQL COUNT(*) queries. This is an expensive operation. Performing database operations is one of the slowest things you can do in an Active Server Page.

To avoid the two database queries each time someone requests the home page, the statistics are stored in two application variables. The application variables are updated only once an hour. Because it is assumed that the statistics will not change often, no one will be the wiser, and you will have avoided putting an unnecessary load on your database server.

Every time the statistics are updated, the application variable named statupdate is set to an hour in the future. The script will be skipped as long as the current time is less than the time stored in the statupdate variable. Therefore, the statistics are updated only once an hour.

Entering a Resumé

The two Active Server Pages named postresume.asp and postresume2.asp enable a user to enter a resumé and save it to the database. The postresume.asp page displays the HTML form for the resumé. When the user submits the form, the postresume2.asp page actually adds the form data to the database table named Resumes.

The HTML form generated by postresume.asp is shown in Figure 29.2. It allows users to enter their contact information such as their names, email addresses, and phone numbers. It also enables users to pick their states and countries from two HTML select lists. The lists of states and countries are added to the form by including the files named states.inc and countries.inc. These files simply contain a list of states and countries.

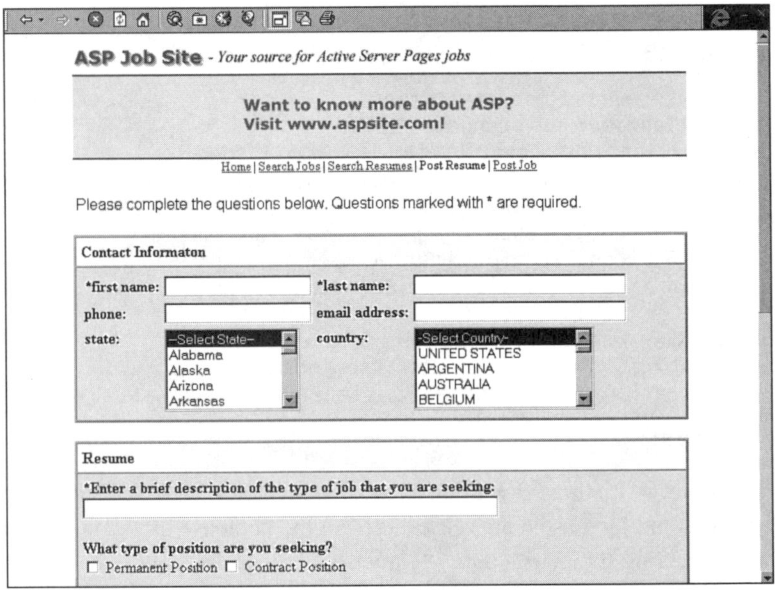

FIGURE 29.2
The form for entering resumés.

The form also enables users to specify the length of time their resumés should be listed. A user can choose to display his or her resumé anywhere from one week to eight weeks. After this time, the resumé will no longer appear in search results.

Finally, the form includes a large text area where the user can enter the actual text of a resumé. The user can enter a resumé using either plain text or text formatted with HTML tags.

When a user submits the form, the form data is sent to postresume2.asp. This page performs three actions. First, it checks whether all the required form fields are completed. This is accomplished with the script in Listing 29.4.

LISTING 29.4 CHECK FOR REQUIRED RESUMÉ FIELDS

```
' Check For Required Fields
if TRIM( Request( "fname" ) ) = "" then
  errorForm "postresume.asp", "You must enter your first name."
end if
```

```
if TRIM( Request( "lname" ) ) = "" then
  errorForm "postresume.asp", "You must enter your last name."
end if
if TRIM( Request( "bdesc" ) ) = "" then
  errorForm "postresume.asp", "You must enter a brief description."
end if
if TRIM( Request( "resume" ) ) = "" then
  errorForm "postresume.asp", "You must enter a resume."
end if
```

The script in Listing 29.4 retrieves the values of each of the required form fields and checks whether each value is equal to a zero length string. If the value is equal to a zero length string, the errorForm subroutine is called.

The errorForm subroutine is located in the jobsitefuncs.asp file. This subroutine displays an error message and dumps all the form fields into hidden form variables (see Figure 29.3). When a user clicks the Return button, all the original data that the user entered into the resumé form is passed back to the form to be redisplayed.

FIGURE 29.3

The error form that appears when submitting a resumé.

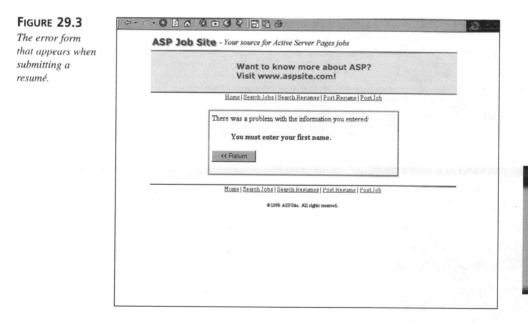

Next, if a user has entered all the required fields, the postresume2.asp page will attempt to add the form data to the database table named Resumes. This is accomplished with the script in Listing 29.5.

LISTING 29.5   ADDING RESUMÉ DATA TO THE DATABASE

```
' Ready Database Connection
Dim Con
Set Con = Server.CreateObject( "ADODB.Connection" )
Con.Open ConnectionString

' Check Whether Resume was already submitted
mySQL = "SELECT * FROM Resumes " &_
   "WHERE lname='" & fixQuotes( Request( "lname" ) ) & "' " &_
   "AND bdesc='" & fixQuotes( Request( "bdesc" ) ) & "' " &_
   "AND expires > getDate()"
Set RS = Server.CreateObject( "ADODB.Recordset" )
RS.Open mySQL, Con, adOpenStatic, adLockOptimistic
if not RS.EOF then
   errorForm "default.asp", "You have already submitted your resume."
end if

' Enter Resume Into Database
RS.AddNew
for each field in Request.Form
  RS( field ) = Request.Form( field )
next
RS.Update
RS.Close
Set RS = Nothing
Set Con = Nothing
```

Notice that the script in Listing 29.5 actually accomplishes two tasks. First, it checks whether the same resumé was already submitted. Web site users have an obnoxious tendency to hit the Refresh button on their Web browsers after they have submitted a form. Unless you take action, this results in duplicate data being submitted to the database (the same Active Server Page is executed twice).

To get around this problem, the script in Listing 29.5 checks whether a resumé with the same last name and brief description already exists in the database. If the same resumé information has already been submitted, the errorForm subroutine is called, and an error form is displayed.

The script in Listing 29.5 uses a trick to add the form data to the database. The names of the columns in the Resume table are exactly the same as the names of the HTML form fields. Taking advantage of this fact, the data is added to the database table by iterating through the contents of the Form collection. Using this trick, you can easily add data to a database table from an HTML form, no matter how many fields are contained in the form.

Entering a Job Listing

The two Active Server Pages named postjob.asp and postjob2.asp enable users to add a job listing to the ASP Job Site. These two pages are almost identical to the postresume.asp and postresume2.asp pages discussed in the previous section. However, the form data is added to the database table named Jobs rather than the Resumes table.

The postjob.asp page generates the form shown in Figure 29.4. This form enables an employer to enter contact information and enter the actual text of the job listing. The same two files, states.inc and countries.inc, are used to create the HTML select lists for the states and countries.

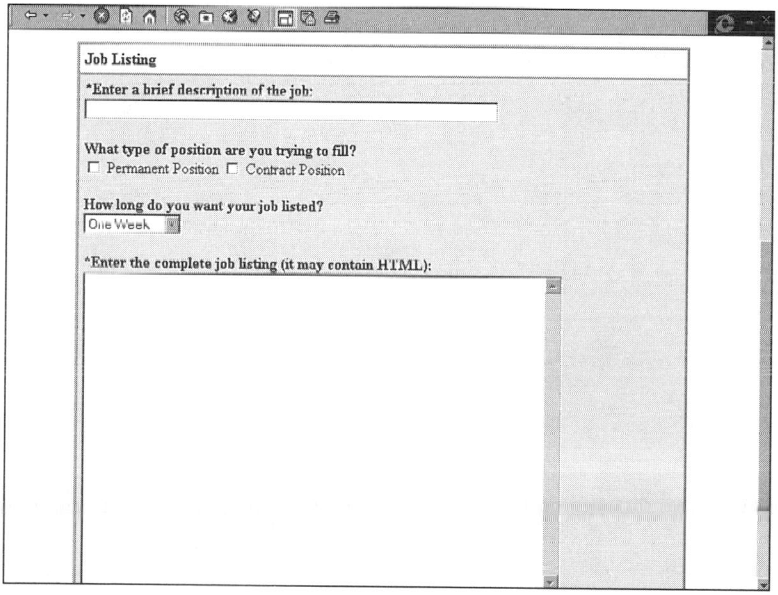

FIGURE 29.4

The form for entering a job listing.

The form also enables users to specify the amount of time that their job listings should be listed. A user can choose to display a job listing anywhere from one week to eight weeks. After this time, the job listing will no longer appear in the search results.

When the postjob.asp page is submitted, the form data is sent to the postjob2.asp page. This page performs three actions. It checks whether all the required form fields have been completed, it checks whether the same job listing has already been entered, and it enters the data into the Jobs database table.

Searching Through the Resumés

The Search Resumes page is contained in the file named searchresumes.asp. This page enables potential employers to search through all the resumés. A user can search the resumés by state or country, by the type of position (contract or permanent), or by entering keywords (see Figure 29.5).

FIGURE 29.5

The page for searching resumés.

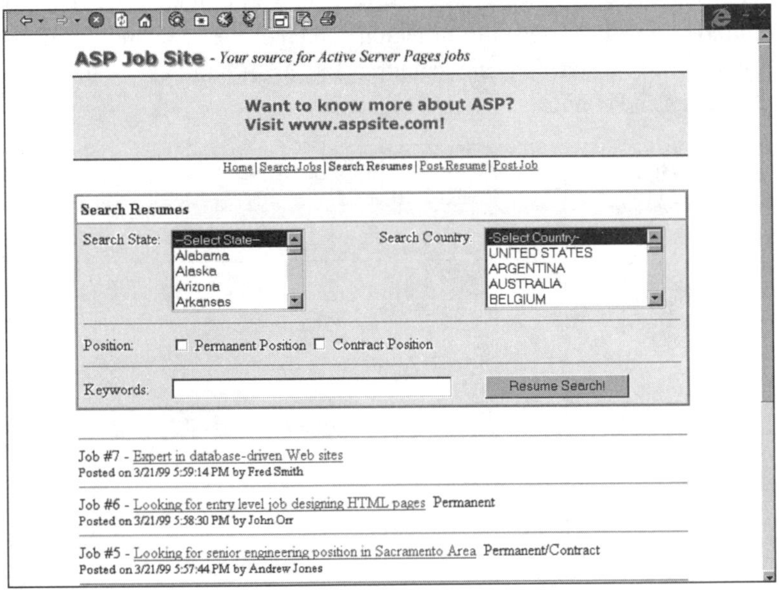

When a user submits the Search Resumes form, the data is sent to the same Active Server Page (the page posts to itself). The Search Resumes page detects that the form was submitted by checking for the existence of the hidden form field named doSearch. This field is hidden in the Search Resumes form. If this hidden form field has a value, then a database query is executed. The database query is constructed with the script in Listing 29.6.

LISTING 29.6   CONSTRUCTING THE SEARCH RESUMÉS QUERY

```
' Get Search Criteria
state = TRIM( Request( "state" ) )
country = TRIM( Request( "country" ) )
perman = TRIM( Request( "perman" ) )
contract = TRIM( Request( "contract" ) )
keywords = TRIM( Request( "keywords" ) )

' Create Search String
```

```
mySQL = "SELECT * FROM Resumes WHERE expires>getDATE() "
if state <> "??" then
  mySQL = mySQL & "AND state='" & state & "' "
end if
if country <> "???" then
  mySQL = mySQL & "AND country='" & country & "' "
end if
if perman <> "" AND contract = "" then
  mySQL = mySQL & "AND perman = 'Yes' "
end if
if contract <> "" AND perman = "" then
  mySQL = mySQL & "AND contract = 'Yes' "
end if
if keywords <> "" then
  mySQL = mySQL & "AND bdesc LIKE '%" & fixQuotes( keywords ) & "%' "
end if
mySQL = mySQL & "ORDER BY entrydate DESC"
```

The script in Listing 29.6 retrieves the values from the form fields submitted by the Search Resumes form and assigns these values to local variables. Next, it constructs a valid SQL query string. For example, if a user chooses to restrict the resumé search by state, then the clause AND state='*state name*' is added to the SQL query.

The query also prevents outdated resumés from being displayed. This is accomplished with the clause that reads WHERE expires>getDATE(). The expires column contains the date when the resumé expires. Because the SQL getDATE() function returns the current data and time, this clause will prevent any resumé from being displayed that has expired before the current date and time.

> **NOTE**
>
> Resumés continue to take up space in the database after they expire. You can either manually delete the expired resumés every so often, or you can create a SQL Server job that will do this automatically.

Notice that the query uses the SQL LIKE operator to match the keywords entered in the search. As discussed in Chapter 15, "Working with Index Server and Full-Text Search," the LIKE operator is not the most efficient method of performing a search. If you are using Microsoft SQL Server version 7.0, you should use a full-text query rather than the LIKE operator. For details on how to configure your database server to perform full-text queries, see Chapter 15.

29

CREATING A JOB
SITE

After the SQL query has been constructed, it is executed and the results of the query are displayed. The resumés that match the query are shown as a list in order of the date that they were submitted (they are ordered with the `entrydate` column of the `Resume` table). The full text of each resumé is not displayed. Instead, the brief description field for each resumé is listed as a hypertext link. Each hypertext link refers to the Resume Detail Active Server Page. When a user clicks on any of the links, the Resume Detail page shows the complete resumé.

Displaying a Complete Resumé

The Resume Detail page is contained in the file named resumedetail.asp. The page displays all the resumé data, including contact information and the complete text of the resumé (see Figure 29.6).

FIGURE 29.6

Displaying the details of a resumé.

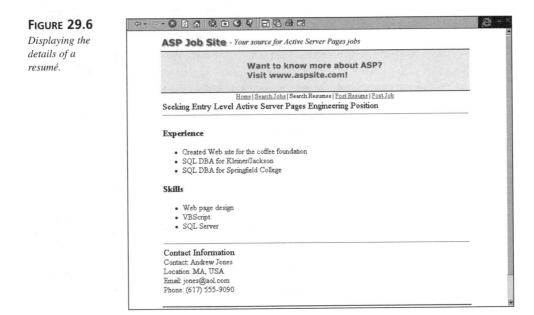

The only way to get to this page is by performing a resumé search and clicking on one of the links shown in the search results. Each link has a URL variable named `id` that uniquely identifies the resumé. The `id` variable is taken from the `resume_id IDENTITY` column in the Resumes table.

The Resume Detail page knows which resumé to display by using the `id` variable. When the Resume Detail page is requested, it retrieves the `id` variable from the `QueryString` collection. Next, it retrieves the correct resumé from the Resumes table by using the `id` variable to match the `resume_id` column.

The text of the resumé can contain HTML content. On the other hand, it might contain only plain text. This creates problems for formatting the text of the resumé. HTML ignores whitespace characters such as carriage returns and spaces. If you simply output the content of a resumé, all the spacing entered by the user when the resumé was submitted will be lost.

The function in Listing 29.7 is used to output the text of a resumé.

LISTING 29.7   FORMATTING HTML AND PLAIN TEXT OUTPUT

```
FUNCTION formatText( ByVal theText )
  if INSTR( theText, ">" ) > 0 then
theText = Replace( theText, "<table", "<x", vbtextcompare )
    theText = Replace( theText, "</table",  "<x", vbtextcompare )
    theText = Replace( theText, "<tr", "<x", vbtextcompare )
    theText = Replace( theText, "</tr", "<x", vbtextcompare )
    theText = Replace( theText, "<td", "<x", vbtextcompare )
    theText = Replace( theText, "</td", "<x", vbtextcompare )
formatText = theText
  else
    theText = Replace( theText, vbCRLF&vbCRLF, "<p>" )
    theText = Replace( theText, vbCRLF, "<br>" )
    formatText = theText
  end if
END FUNCTION
```

The function in Listing 29.7 checks whether the text of the resumé contains a > character. If the text contains the > character, the function assumes that the text includes HTML formatting. There is a danger here. If the text of the resumé contains the HTML <table>, <tr>, or <td> tags, displaying the resumé will corrupt the appearance of the Resume Detail page. This will happen because the Resume Detail page itself displays the text of the resumé within an HTML table. To prevent the Resume Detail page from being corrupted, each of these potentially dangerous tags are replaced.

If a user has entered a resumé without using HTML formatting, special care must be taken to display the resumé with the correct formatting. Unless special precautions are taken, all the carriage returns that the user originally entered when submitting the resumé will be lost, and the resumé will appear as one long, unreadable paragraph.

The formatText function translates carriage returns (which will not appear in HTML) into the HTML <p> and <br> tags. Two carriage returns in a row are translated into the <p> tag, which creates a paragraph break. A single carriage return is translated into the <br> tag, which creates a line break. Notice that this process will not completely reproduce the original formatting, but it's the best you can do using standard HTML.

29

CREATING A JOB SITE

> **NOTE**
>
> You might be wondering why the HTML <pre> tag is not used to preserve the spacing of the resumé in the formatText function. The <pre> tag was introduced to display preformatted text. It preserves all the original spacing. However, the disadvantage of the <pre> tag is that it does its job too well. The <pre> tag prevents word-wrapping. If someone enters a long resumé without entering any carriage returns, the text will word-wrap while it is being entered into the HTML form, but it will not word-wrap when redisplayed with the <pre> tag.

Searching Through the Job Listings

The Search Jobs Active Server Page, included in the file named searchjobs.asp, is almost exactly the same as the Search Resumes page. However, the Search Jobs page is used to search through the job listings contained in the Jobs table rather than the resumés in the Resumes table. The Search Jobs page appears in Figure 29.7.

FIGURE 29.7

The page for searching through job listings.

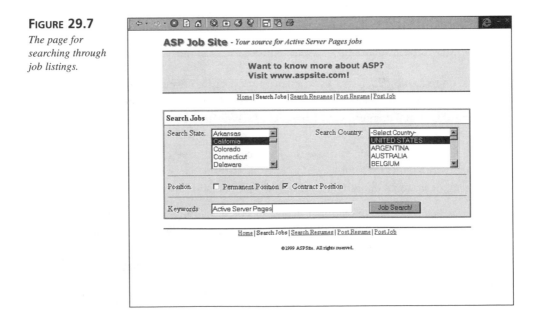

You can use the Search Jobs page to search for job listings by state or country. You can also restrict your search to display only permanent or contract jobs. Finally, you can search through the job listings by entering keywords.

NOTE

Job listings continue to take up space in the database after they expire. You can either manually delete the expired job listings every so often, or you can create a SQL Server job that will do this automatically.

When you submit the Search Jobs HTML form, the form data is posted back to the Search Jobs page. A SQL query string is constructed from the search criteria posted, and the results from the query are displayed. The search results appear as a list of brief descriptions of each job. Each brief description is a link to the Jobs Detail page.

Displaying a Complete Job Listing

The Job Detail page is contained in the file named jobdetail.asp. The purpose of this page is to display all the data for a particular job listing. The Job Detail page appears in Figure 29.8.

FIGURE 29.8
Displaying the details of a job listing.

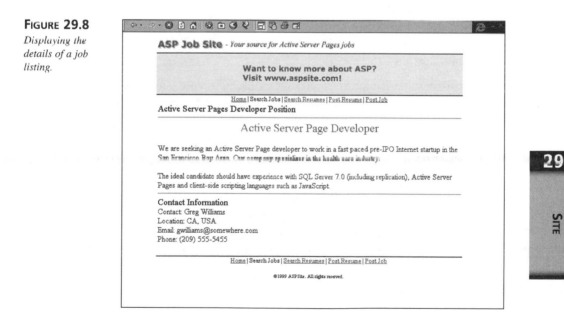

The Job Detail page functions exactly like the Resume Detail page. When someone clicks a hypertext link from the results of a job search, the link takes the person to the Job Detail page. The link includes a query string variable named id that uniquely identifies the job listing. The value of this variable corresponds to the `job_id` IDENTITY column in the `Jobs` database table.

The data for the Job Detail page is retrieved from the database table named `Jobs`. The correct row from the table is retrieved by matching the `id` variable to the value of the `job_id` column for the row.

The text of the job listing is formatted with the `formatText` function. The function removes any `<table>`, `<tr>`, or `<td>` tags from the contents of the job listing. It also replaces carriage returns with HTML `<p>` and `<br>` tags.

Extending the Project

As it stands, the ASP Job Site works as a fully functional Web site. You could take the same code and, with a few changes in the text, create a job site for cooks, dentists, or even refrigerator repair men. However, any Web site can be improved, and this section contains some suggestions for how the ASP Job Site can be extended.

One problem with the ASP Job Site is that it does not allow users to update a resumé or job listing after it has been submitted. For example, if an employer fills a position, there is no way for the employer to take down a job listing. The job listing will continue to appear until it expires.

To allow users to update information that they have posted, a username and password system must be added to the job site. This addition would be necessary to prevent malicious individuals from making unwanted changes to other users' resumés or job listings. To learn more about password protecting Active Server Pages, see Chapter 23, "Securing Your Web Site."

Another problem with the ASP Job Site, as it's currently implemented, is that it does not enable users to remain anonymous. If you post your resumé, you must include your phone number or email address to allow potential employers to contact you. Employers must also include contact information when they post a job listing.

There are a number of ways that you can extend the ASP Job Site to allow users to remain anonymous. First, you could allow users to respond to a job listing or resumé online. For example, an employer could list a job anonymously, and then read through the replies to the listing to decide whom to contact. The replies could be stored in a database table.

A second way to provide anonymity would be to send messages back and forth for users by using the CDO for NTS. For example, if a job candidate wants to contact an employer, the candidate could enter a message into an HTML form. Immediately after the form is submitted, the message is sent to the employer by using the CDO for NTS to mail an email message. Using this scheme, neither the employer nor the job candidate would ever see each other's email address. To learn how to use the CDO for NTS to send email, see Chapter 10, "Working with Email."

Summary

In this chapter, you learned how to create a fully functional Job site using nothing but Active Server Pages scripts. You learned how to collect information from an HTML form and store the information in a database. You also learned how to create search forms that can be used to perform custom queries.

Appendixes

APPENDIX A

Frequently Asked Questions About Active Server Pages

IN THIS APPENDIX

This appendix addresses the questions that are most frequently posted on the Active Server Pages newsgroups and the ASPSite (the companion Web site to this book at www.aspsite.com). When appropriate, references are provided to specific chapters in this book where more information can be found. For updated information, please visit http://www.aspsite.com/answers.

Installation Questions

Which Operating Systems Support Active Server Pages?

Active Server Pages runs natively on Microsoft Windows NT Server 4.0, Microsoft Windows NT Workstation 4.0 with Peer Web Services, and Windows 95/98 with the Personal Web Server.

Using Chili!Soft's Chili!ASP (see http://www.chilisoft.com), you also can use Active Server Pages with SUN Solaris and IBM AIX. Chili!ASP enables Active Server Pages to run on Apache servers, Netscape Enterprise and FastTrack servers, the Lotus Domino Go Webserver, and O'Reilly Website Pro.

For more information on installing Active Server Pages, see Chapter 1, "Building Active Server Pages."

How Do I Get the Latest Version of Internet Information Server and Active Server Pages?

You can download the latest version of Active Server Pages and Internet Information Server at the Microsoft Web site. Go to http://www.microsoft.com/iis and select Downloads. Download the Windows NT Server 4.0 Option Pack. You will be provided with the option of downloading either the Windows NT or Windows 95/98 version of the Option Pack.

For more information on installing Active Server Pages, see Chapter 1, "Building Active Server Pages."

How Do I Get the Latest Version of the ActiveX Data Objects (ADO)?

The latest version of the ActiveX Data Objects (ADO) is available at the Microsoft Web site. Go to http://www.microsoft.com/data and download the Microsoft Data Access Components (MDAC).

For more information on the Microsoft Data Access Components, see Chapter 12, "Working with Connections and Data Sources."

General Scripting Questions

How Do I Add a Quotation Mark to a VBScript String?

There are two ways to add a quotation mark to a VBScript string:

```
myVar = "He said, ""Hello!"" "
myVar = "He said, " & CHR( 34 ) & "Hello!" & CHR( 34 )
```

The first method uses two quotation marks in a row to create a single quotation mark. The second method uses the ASCII value of the quotation mark character.

How Can I Break a Single VBScript Statement into Multiple Lines?

You can break a single VBScript statement into multiple lines by using the _ underscore character. For example, the string in the following statement is broken into several lines of code by using the &_ character combination:

```
myVar = "When in the Course of human events, " &_
    "it becomes necessary for one people to " &_
    "dissolve the political bands which have " &_
    "connected them with another, and to assume " &_
    "among the powers of the earth, the separate " &_
    "and equal station to which the Laws of " &_
    "Nature and of Nature's God entitle them, " &_
    "a decent respect to the opinions of " &_
    "mankind requires that they should declare " &_
    "the causes which impel them to the separation. "
```

What Is the Proper Method of Comparing Strings in VBScript?

When you compare two strings with the identity operator, the comparison is case sensitive. For example, the following statement returns the value `false`:

```
<%= "apple" = "APPLE" %>
```

There are two methods of performing a case-insensitive comparison of two strings:

```
<%= StrComp( "apple", "APPLE", vbTextCompare )%>
<%= UCASE( "apple" ) = UCASE( "APPLE" ) %>
```

The first method uses the VBScript `StrComp` function with the `vbTextCompare` constant. The second method forces both strings into uppercase.

You should be aware that several other VBScript string functions, such as the `InStr` and `Replace` functions, are also case sensitive. To perform case-insensitive comparisons with these functions, you must use the `vbTextCompare` constant.

How Can I Re-enable Errors After Using ON ERROR RESUME NEXT?

The VBScript `ON ERROR RESUME NEXT` statement suppresses errors in your script. If you include the statement outside any functions or subroutines, the statement will apply to every statement that follows it (otherwise, it will apply only within the function or subroutine). To re-enable the reporting of errors, use the `ON ERROR GOTO 0` statement like this:

```
<%
ON ERROR RESUME NEXT
' The following error is ignored
fakeOBJ.Blah
ON ERROR GOTO 0
' The following error is reported
fakeOBJ2.Blah
%>
```

For more information on detecting errors in your Web site, see Chapter 24, "Maintaining ASP Web Sites."

How Can I Prevent My Script from Timing Out?

By default, an Active Server Page script will stop executing and time out after 90 seconds. If you have a long running script, the script may stop executing too early. You can extend the amount of time a script is allowed to run by using the `ScriptTimeout` property of the `Server` object. Here's an example:

```
<% Server.ScriptTimeout = 200 %>
```

This statement changes the timeout period to 200 seconds.

When Do I Need to Explicitly Convert a Variable to a Particular Data Type?

If you are comparing numbers or dates and times and there is a danger that VBScript might interpret the values as strings, you should use one of the VBScript conversion functions. For example, suppose an HTML form contains two input boxes for two numbers, and you execute the following script:

```
<%
firstNum = Request( "firstNum" )
secondNum = Request( "secondNum" )
%>
<%=firstNum > secondNum %>
```

If you enter 32 for the first number and 223 for the second number into the form, the script will output the wrong result. The script will return the value TRUE because the string 32 is greater than the string 223, even though the number is not. To force an integer comparison, rather than a string comparison, use a script like this:

```
<%
firstNum = CInt( Request( "firstNum" ) )
secondNum = CInt( Request( "secondNum" ) )
%>
<%=firstNum > secondNum %>
```

The CInt function converts a value to the Integer subtype (also see the CDate, CCur, IsNumeric, and IsDate functions).

When Should I Pass a Variable by Value and When by Reference?

When you pass a variable by value to a subroutine or function, a new instance of the variable is created. Any changes made to the value of the variable do not affect the value of the original variable. On the other hand, when you pass a variable by reference, changes made to the variable do affect the value of the original variable. Here's an example:

```
<%
SUB addOne( ByVal fvar, ByRef svar )
  fvar = fvar + 1
  svar = svar + 1
END SUB
firstvar = 0
secondvar = 0
addOne firstvar, secondvar
%>
```

After this script is executed, the variable named firstvar has the value 0 and the variable named secondvar has the value 1.

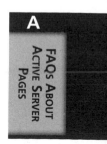

How Can I Add a Space Between the Output of Two Variables?

For some mysterious reason, when you output two variables in a row in an Active Server Page, any spaces that appear between the variables will disappear. For example, the following script outputs `"AndrewJones"` rather than `"Andrew Jones"`:

```
<%
fname = "Andrew"
lname="Jones"
%>
<%=fname%> <%=lname%>
```

The easiest way to get around this problem is to use a script like the following:

```
<%
fname = "Andrew"
lname="Jones"
%>
<%=fname & " " & lname%>
```

Does Active Server Pages Support Dynamic Includes?

Some server-side scripting environments, such as Cold Fusion, support dynamic includes. A dynamic include enables you to use a variable for the name of the file to include in a page. Active Server Pages does not support dynamic includes. The following script will not work:

```
<%
myFile = "firstpage.asp"
%>
<!-- #INCLUDE FILE="<%=myFile%>" -->
```

This include directive will attempt to include a file named `"<%=myFile%>"`, which probably does not exist. The problem is that all server-side directives, including the `#INCLUDE` directive, are processed before Active Server Page scripts. If you must dynamically include different pages within an Active Server Page, consider using a script like the following:

```
<%
myFile = "firstpage.asp"
if myFile = "firstpage.asp" then
%>
<!-- #INCLUDE FILE="firstpage.asp" -->
<%
```

```
end if
if myFile = "secondpage.asp" then
%>
<!-- #INCLUDE FILE="secondpage.asp" -->
<%
end if
if myFile = "thirdpage.asp" then
%>
<!-- #INCLUDE FILE="thirdpage.asp" -->
<%
end if
%>
```

This script conditionally displays one of three different pages. The version of Active
Server Pages bundled with IIS 5.0 will include better methods for dynamically including
files. See Chapter 26, "Future Directions: Windows 2000, IIS 5.0, and Active Server
Pages," for more information.

How Do I Use the `Option Explicit` Statement in an Active Server Page?

The `Option Explicit` statement forces you to declare all your variables. Using this
statement can make it easier to program complicated Active Server Pages because mis-
spelled variable names will generate errors.

You must use the `Option Explicit` statement before any other VBScript statement or
HTML content in a script. If you don't, you'll receive an error like the following:

```
Microsoft VBScript compilation error '800a0400'
Expected statement
/test.asp, line 5
Option Explicit
^
```

Here's an example that uses the `Option Explicit` statement correctly:

```
<Option Explicit %>
<html>
<head><title>My Page</title></head>
<body>
<%
DIM myVar
myVar = "Hello!"
%>
</body>
<html>
```

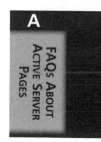

Session and Application Variables Questions

Why Do Session Variables Sometimes Fail to Work?

Session variables depend on browser cookies. If a browser does not support cookies, or a user has turned off cookies or the user's cookie file is corrupted, Session variables will not work. For some suggestions on avoiding Session variables, see Chapter 5, "Working with Sessions."

How Can I Remove an Application Variable?

The current version of Active Server Pages, included with IIS 4.0, does not contain a method for removing Application variables. After you create one, it remains in memory until the Internet Service is stopped, the Global.asa file is changed, or the current application is unloaded.

The version of Active Server Pages included with IIS 5.0, on the other hand, includes two new methods for removing Application variables: the `Remove` and `RemoveAll` methods. For more information on IIS 5.0, see Chapter 26, "Future Directions: Windows 2000, IIS 5.0, and Active Server Pages."

File Questions

How Do I Detect Whether a File Exists?

You can check whether a file exists by using the `FileExists` method of the `FileSystemObject`. The following script detects whether a file named test.txt exists:

```
<%
Set fs = Server.CreateObject( "Scripting.FileSystemObject" )
if fs.FileExists( "c:\test.txt" ) then
  Response.Write "File Exists!"
else
  Response.Write "No File!"
end if
%>
```

To learn more about the `FileSystemObject` see Chapter 8, "Working with the File System."

How Can I Automatically Display a List of Files in a Directory?

You can display a list of files in a folder by using the `FileSystemObject` and the `Folder` object like this:

```
<%
Set fs = Server.CreateObject( "Scripting.FileSystemObject" )
Set folder = fs.GetFolder( "c:\myfolder" )
For Each thing In folder.Files
  Response.Write thing.name & "<br>"
Next
%>
```

This script lists the names of all the files in a folder named myfolder located on the c: drive. For more information see Chapter 8, "Working with the File System."

Image Questions

How Can I Store an Image in a Database Table?

Although you can store an image in a SQL Server BLOB column, it is almost always better to store the URL of an image in a database table rather than the image itself. (Storing an image in a database table places unnecessary work on your database server.) For example, the following script displays several images in a row by retrieving the URL of each image from a database table named `myImages`:

```
<%
Set Con = Server.CreateObject( "ADODB.Connection" )
Con.Open "FILE NAME=c:\myDataLink.UDL"
mySQL = "SELECT image_URL from myImages"
Set RS = Con.Execute( mySQL )
While Not RS.EOF
%>
<img src="<%=RS( "image_URL" )%>">
<%
RS.MoveNext
Wend
%>
```

How Can I Dynamically Generate a Graph or Image in an Active Server Page?

Several third-party Active Server Pages components enable you to dynamically create custom images. One of the best of these components is the ShotGraph

component included on the CD-ROM that accompanies this book. For more information, see Chapter 16, "Third-Party Components."

Browser Questions

How Do I Detect the Type of Browser a Person Is Using to Visit My Web Site?

The USER-AGENT header indicates the type of browser. The following script captures the value of the USER-AGENT header from the ServerVariables collection and displays it:

```
<%
browserType = Request.ServerVariables( "HTTP_USER_AGENT" )
Response.WRite browserType
%>
```

For more information on the ServerVariables collection, see Chapter 2, "Active Server Pages and the HTTP Protocol."

How Can I Detect the Page From Which a Person Originated?

The REFERER header contains the URL of the last page the person visited. This header can be retrieved from the ServerVariables collection. The following script displays the value of the REFERER header:

```
<%
browserType = Request.ServerVariables( "HTTP_REFERER" )
Response.WRite browserType
%>
```

For more information on the ServerVariables collection, see Chapter 2, "Active Server Pages and the HTTP Protocol."

ActiveX Data Objects Questions

Why Do I Sometimes Receive an Error When Using the Connection Object to Execute a SQL String?

Consider the following script. It retrieves a user's first name from an HTML form and inserts it into a database table:

```
<%
firstname = Request( "firstname" )
mySQL = "INSERT myTable ( firstname ) VALUES "
mySQL = mySQL & "('" & firstname & "')"
Set Con = Server.CreateObject( "ADODB.Connection" )
Con.Open "FILE NAME=c:\myDataLink.UDL"
Con.Execute mySQL
%>
```

Suppose, however, that the user entered a single quote when entering a first name. For example, the user entered the name O'Reilly. Because SQL uses a single quote to mark the beginning and end of a string value, the single quote would generate an error.

Before entering a string into a database table with the Connection object, you must first translate any single quotes into two quotes in a row. The following script avoids errors caused by a quotation mark:

```
<%
FUNCTION fixQuotes( theVar )
  fixQuotes = REPLACE( theVar, "'", "''" )
END FUNCTION
firstname = Request( "firstname" )
firstname = fixQuotes( firstname )
mySQL = "INSERT myTable ( firstname ) VALUES "
mySQL = mySQL & "('" & firstname & "')"
Set Con = Server.CreateObject( "ADODB.Connection" )
Con.Open "FILE NAME=c:\myDataLink.UDL"
Con.Execute mySQL
%>
```

In this example, the fixQuotes function replaces any single quote with two quotes. Doubling the quotes enables you to enter single quotes into a database table.

How Do I Retrieve a TEXT Field in an Active Server Page?

If you do not take special precautions when retrieving a TEXT field from a database table, the value of the TEXT field might be truncated. If you are using a forward-only cursor type, you should list the TEXT field as the very last field in your select list. Alternatively, consider using a richer cursor type when opening a Recordset that contains a TEXT field. The following script will correctly retrieve and display a TEXT field:

```
<!-- #INCLUDE VIRTUAL="/adovbs.inc" -->
<%
Set Con = Server.CreateObject( "ADODB.Connection" )
Con.Open "FILE NAME=c:\myDataLink.UDL"
Set RS = Server.CreateObject( "ADODB.RecordSet" )
```

```
RS.CursorType = adOpenDynamic
RS.Open "Select TextColumn FROM mytable", Con
%>
```

This script opens a Recordset with a dynamic cursor. For more information about Recordset cursors see Chapter 13, "Working with Recordsets."

Why Does `RecordCount` Always Return the Value `-1`?

The `RecordCount` property returns the number of rows in a Recordset after it has been opened. You cannot use this property with a forward-only cursor when using SQL Server (it will always return `-1`). To use this property, open a Recordset with a richer cursor type like this:

```
<!-- #INCLUDE VIRTUAL="/adovbs.inc" -->
<%
mySQL = "SELECT * FROM WebUsers"
Set Con = Server.CreateObject( "ADODB.Connection" )
Con.Open "FILE NAME=c:\myDataLink.UDL"
Set RS = Server.CreateObject( "ADODB.Recordset" )
RS.CursorType = adOpenDynamic
RS.Open mySQL, Con
Response.Write RS.RecordCount
%>
```

This script opens a Recordset with a dynamic cursor. For more information about Recordset cursors see Chapter 13, "Working with Recordsets."

Why Do I Receive an Error Whenever I Try to Update the Value of a Field in a Recordset?

By default, when you open a Recordset, it is opened with a forward-only cursor and read-only lock type. To update a Recordset, you must open a Recordset that is not read-only. Here is an example:

```
<!-- #INCLUDE VIRTUAL="/adovbs.inc" -->
<%
Set Con = Server.CreateObject( "ADODB.Connection" )
Con.Open "FILE NAME=c:\myDataLink.UDL"
Set RS = Server.CreateObject( "ADODB.Recordset" )
RS.LockType = adLockOptimistic
RS.Open "SELECT  * FROM Webusers WHERE 1<>1", Con
RS.AddNew
RS( "username" ) = "Andrew Jones"
RS( "password" ) = "won't say"
RS.Update
%>
```

This script opens a Recordset with an optimistic locking type and adds a new record to a table named Webusers.

How Can I Limit the Number of Rows Returned by a Database Query?

If you are using Microsoft SQL 7.0 or Microsoft Access, you can use the SQL TOP keyword to limit the number of records returned. Otherwise, if you are using Microsoft SQL 6.5, use the MaxRecords property of the Recordset object like this:

```
<%
Set Con = Server.CreateObject( "ADODB.Connection" )
Con.Open "FILE NAME=c:\myDataLink.UDL;DATABASE=pubs"
Set RS = Server.CreateObject( "ADODB.Recordset" )
RS.MaxRecords = 15
RS.Open "SELECT * FROM Authors ORDER BY au_lname", Con
While not RS.EOF
  Response.Write RS( "au_lname" ) & "<br>"
  RS.MoveNext
Wend
%>
```

For more information see Chapter 13, "Working with Recordsets."

How Do I Retrieve the Value from a SQL Statement That Uses COUNT(*), MAX, MIN, or @@IDENTITY?

There are two methods that you can use to retrieve the value from a SQL function or a SQL global variable. You can either use an alias for the value or refer to the value by its ordinal position in the Recordset. The following example displays the value returned from SQL COUNT(*) using both methods:

```
<%
mySQL = "SELECT COUNT(*) theCount from Authors"
Set Con = Server.CreateObject( "ADODB.Connection" )
Con.Open "FILE NAME=c:\myDataLink.UDL;DATABASE=pubs"
SET RS = Con.Execute( mySQL )
Response.Write RS( "theCount" )
Response.Write RS( 0 )
%>
```

The first Response.Write statement uses the alias theCount. The second Response.Write statement uses the ordinal position of the value.

How Do I Retrieve an Output Parameter from a SQL Stored Procedure Within an Active Server Page Script?

To retrieve an output parameter or a return code, you must use the ADO Command and Parameter objects. See Chapter 14, "Working with the Command Object."

Form and Query String Questions

How Can I Accept File Uploads in an HTML Form?

 See Chapter 3, "Working with HTML Forms," for an example of how you can accept and work with file uploads from an HTML form with Active Server Page scripts. See Chapter 16, "Third-Party Components," for a discussion of the Software Artisan's SA-FileUP component, which is included on the CD-ROM that accompanies this book.

What Causes the Value of a Form Field to Become Truncated?

HTML uses quotation marks to mark the beginning and end of a value. So, if a variable contains quotation marks in its value, the value of the variable will be truncated when displayed. For example, the HTML form in the following script will not display correctly:

```
<%
myVar = "He said, ""Hello!"""
%>
<form method="post" action="page.asp">
<input name="myfield" type="text"
  value="<%=myVar%>">
<input type="submit" value="Enter">
</form>
```

Instead of displaying the string He said, "Hello!" as the value of the form element, the value He said, appears. Every character after and including the " is cut off. To get around this problem, HTML encode the string before displaying it, like this:

```
<%
myVar = Server.HTMLEncode( "He said, ""Hello!""" )
%>
<form method="post" action="page.asp">
```

```
<input name="myfield" type="text"
  value="<%=myVar%>">
<input type="submit" value="Enter">
</form>
```

For more information on working with HTML forms, see Chapter 3, "Working with HTML Forms."

How Can I Include Spaces or Other Special Characters in a Query String?

To include spaces or other special characters—such as periods and quotation marks—in a query string, URL encode the query string. The following example correctly encodes a query string before displaying it:

```
<%
myVar = Server.URLEncode( "He said, ""Hello!""" )
%>
<a href="page.asp?qvar=<%=myVar%>">Go</a>
```

For more information on using query strings, see Chapter 2, "Active Server Pages and the HTTP Protocol."

Questions About Active Server Pages Web Sites

Do Any Internet Service Providers Host Active Server Pages?

Several good Internet service providers host sites that use Active Server Pages and SQL Server. Two examples are Bitshop (www.bitshop.com) and Data Return (www.dataretun.com). Both companies enable you to administer an Active Server Page site remotely using Microsoft Visual InterDev and Microsoft SQL Server Enterprise Manager.

What Good Web Sites Have Information on Active Server Pages?

The number of good Web sites that have information on Active Server Pages is growing quickly. Here is a list of some of the Web sites that I visit on a weekly basis:

www.aspsite.com	The companion Web site to this book.
www.15seconds.com	This Web site has thousands of pages of information on Active Server Pages.

www.activeserverpages.com	This Web site has a great component section and several interesting articles.
www.asphole.com	This Web site contains lists of components and articles related to Active Server Pages.
www.swynk.com	Good site for information on Active Server Pages and SQL Server.
www.microsoft.com/iis	Microsoft's Internet Information Server site.

APPENDIX B

ASP Objects and Components Reference

This appendix provides a quick reference for the Active Server Page objects and installable components. This reference is not intended to be comprehensive. For more information on each object and component, consult the Microsoft online documentation (available at `http://localserver/iishelp` on a server with IIS installed).

ASP Built-In Objects

You can use any of the following Active Server Pages built-in objects without explicitly declaring them in your Active Server Page scripts.

The `Application` Object

The `Application` object can be used to store and retrieve information that can be shared by all users of an application. For more information on the `Application` object, see Chapter 4, "Working with Active Server Pages Applications."

Collections	
`Contents(key)`	Contains data and objects with application scope not declared with the `<object>` tag
`StaticObjects(key)`	Contains objects with application scope declared with the `<object>` tag

Methods	
`Lock`	Prevents other users from accessing the `Application` collection
`Unlock`	Enables other users to access the `Application` collection

Events	
`OnEnd`	Triggered by stopping the Web server, modifying the Global.asa file, or unloading the application
`OnStart`	Triggered by the first request for a Web page in the application

The `ObjectContext` Object

The `ObjectContext` object is used to control Active Server Page transactions. For more information on the `ObjectContext` object, see Chapter 21, "Using ASP with Microsoft Transaction Server."

Methods

SetAbort	Explicitly aborts a transaction
SetComplete	Overrides any calls to the SetAbort method

Events

OnTransactionAbort	Triggered by Aborted transaction
OnTransactionCommit	Triggered by Completed transaction

The Request Object

The Request object represents all information sent in a request from a browser to your server. For more information on the Request object, see Chapter 2, "Active Server Pages and the HTTP Protocol."

Collections

ClientCertificate(*key*)	Contains values from client-certificate
Cookies(*key*)	Contains values from browser cookies
Form	Contains values from HTML form fields
QueryString	Contains values from query string
ServerVariables	Contains values from headers and environmental variables

Method

BinaryRead(*count*)	Retrieves raw content of HTML form

Property

TotalBytes	The number of bytes in the browser request

The Response Object

The Response object represents all information that is sent from your server to a browser. For more information on the Response object see Chapter 2, "Active Server Pages and the HTTP Protocol."

Collection

Cookies(*key*)	Enables you to add a cookie to a browser

Methods

AddHeader *name, value*	Adds new header to a browser
AppendToLog	Adds an entry to the IIS log file

continues

Methods

BinaryWrite *data*	Writes non-string information in the response
Clear	Clears the buffered response
End	Ends processing of a script
Flush	Sends all contents of the buffer
Redirect *URL*	Redirects a browser to a new page
Write *variant*	Sends a string to a browser.

Properties

Buffer	Buffers an Active Server Page
CacheControl	Controls caching by proxy servers
CharSet(*Charsetname*)	Character set to use on current page
ContentType	Specifies the content type of the response
Expires	Controls caching by browsers using relative time
ExpiresAbsolute	Controls caching by browsers using absolute time
IsClientConnected	Indicates whether a browser is still connected
PICS(*PICSLABEL*)	Adds a PICS rating to a page
Status	Specifies the status line returned by server

The Server Object

The Server object enables the use of various utility functions on the server.

Methods

CreateObject(*progID*)	Creates an instance of an object
HTMLEncode(*string*)	Converts a string to use special HTML characters
MapPath(*path*)	Converts a virtual path to a physical path
URLEncode(*string*)	Converts a string to URL-encoded form

Property

ScriptTimeout	The number of seconds a script is allowed to run before being terminated

The Session Object

The Session object represents the information about a particular user session. For more information on the Session object see Chapter 5, "Working with Sessions."

Collections

Contents(*key*)	Contains data and objects with session scope declared without using the <object> tag
StaticObjects(*key*)	Contains objects with session scope declared using the <object> tag

Method

Abandon	Ends a user session after the current page is processed

Properties

CodePage	Specifies the server code page
LCID	Specifies the location identifier
SessionID	A unique identifier for the user session
Timeout	The time in minutes before a session terminates

Events

OnEnd	Triggered by the user not requesting a page longer than the Session Timeout period
OnStart	Triggered by the first request for a Web page by the user

ASP Installable Components

Before using any of the following installable components in your Active Server Page scripts, you must explicitly declare an instance of the component. A sample declaration is provided for each component.

The Ad Rotator Component

The Ad Rotator component enables you to display banner advertisements with different frequencies. For more information on the Ad Rotator component see Chapter 9, "Tracking Page Views and Displaying Advertisements." To create an instance of the Ad Rotator component use

```
<% Set MyAd=Server.CreateObject("MSWC.AdRotator") %>
```

Method	
GetAdvertisement (*Rotator Schedule File*)	Displays an advertisement on a page

Properties	
Border(*size*)	Displays a border around the advertisement with a size in pixels
Clickable(*boolean*)	Specifies whether an advertisement is a hyperlink
TargetFrame(*frame*)	The HTML frame where the advertisement should be displayed

Files	
Redirection File	When you click an advertisement, you're sent to this page
Rotator Schedule File	Text file that lists the properties of the advertisements

The Browser Capabilities Component

The Browser Capabilities component enables you to detect the features of a Web browser. For more information on the Browser Capabilities component see Chapter 7, "Generating Dynamic Content from the Server." To create an instance of the Browser Capabilities component use

```
<% Set MyBrow=Server.CreateObject("MSWC.BrowserType") %>
```

File	
Browscap.ini	Text file that contains information about browsers

The Content Linking Component

For more information on the Content Linking component see Chapter 7, "Generating Dynamic Content from the Server." To create an instance of the Content Linking component use

```
<% Set myLink=Server.CreateObject("MSWC.NextLink") %>
```

Methods

GetListCount(*Content Linking List File*)	Returns total number of pages in the Content Linking List File
GetListIndex(*Content Linking List File*)	Returns the position of the current page in the Content Linking List File
GetNextDescription (*Content Linking List File*)	Returns the description of the next page in the Content Linking List File
GetNextURL(*Content Linking List File*)	Returns the URL of the next page in the Content Linking List File
GetNthDescription (*Content Linking List File, index*)	Returns the description of the page with the index in the Content Linking List File
GetNthURL (*Content Linking List File, index*)	Returns the URL of the page with the index in the Content Linking List File
GetPreviousDescription (*Content Linking List File*)	Returns the description of the previous page in the Content Linking List File
GetPreviousURL (*Content Linking List File*)	Returns the URL of the previous page in the Content Linking List File

File

Content Linking List File	Text file containing a list of pages

The Content Rotator Component

The Content Rotator component enables you to display HTML strings with different frequencies. For more information on the Content Rotator component see Chapter 7, "Generating Dynamic Content from the Server." To create an instance of the Content Rotator component use

```
<% Set myContent=Server.CreateObject("IISSample.ContentRotator") %>
```

Methods

ChooseContent(*Content Schedule File*)	Returns an HTML string from the Content Schedule File
GetAllContent(*Content Schedule File*)	Returns all HTML strings from the Content Schedule File

File

Content Schedule File	Text file that contains a list of HTML strings

The Counters Component

The Counters component enables you to create one or more counters to track information such as the number of visits to a Web site. For more information on the Counters component see Chapter 9, "Tracking Page Views and Displaying Advertisements." To create an instance of the Counters Component include the following HTML code in the Global.asa file:

```
<OBJECT RUNAT=SERVER SCOPE=Application ID=myCounter
PROGID="MSWC.Counters"></OBJECT>
```

Methods	
Get(*counter*)	Returns the value of a counter
Increment(*counter*)	Adds one to the value of a counter
Remove(*counter*)	Removes a counter
Set *counter*, *number*	Sets counter to equal a certain numeric value

File	
Counters.txt	This text file contains all the individual counters

The Lookup Table Component

The Lookup Table component enables you to cache information in an object that can be created with page, session, or application scope. For more information on the Lookup Table component see Chapter 4, "Working with Active Server Pages Applications." To create an instance of the Lookup Table component with page scope use the following:

```
<% SET myLookup = Server.CreateObject( "IISSample.LookupTable" )%>
```

To create an instance of the Lookup Table component with application scope add the following code to the Global.asa file:

```
<OBJECT RUNAT=SERVER SCOPE=Application ID=myLookup
PROGID="IISSample.LookupTable"></OBJECT>
```

Methods	
Count	Returns the number of key/value pairs that exist in the Lookup table.
LoadValues*filepath*, *format*	Loads key/value pairs into the component from a file. See the values for *format*.
LoadValuesEx*filepath*, *format*, *period*	Loads key/value pairs into the component from a file on a periodic basis. See the values for *format*. The value for *period* is specified in seconds.

Methods

LookupValue(*key*)	Returns the value for a specific key.
Key(*index*)	Returns the key located at the index position.
KeyExists(*key*)	Returns True if the specified key exists in the Lookup Table.
ReadLock	Locks the Lookup Table until the ReadUnlock method is called.
ReadUnlock	Releases a lock created by calling ReadLock.
Value(*index*)	Returns the value of the key located at the index position.

File

Lookup Table File	Text file that stores the key/value pairs. Each key/value pair is separated by a comma. To create multiline values, use \ at the end of a line as a continuation character.

Format

0	String keys and string values.
1	String keys and integer values.
2	Integer keys and string values.
3	Integer keys and integer values.
10	String keys and string values (ignore duplicate keys).
11	String keys and integer values (ignore duplicate keys).
12	Integer keys and string values (ignore duplicate keys).
13	Integer keys and integer values (ignore duplicate keys).

The NewMail Object

The NewMail object enables you to send email from an Active Server Page. For more information on the NewMail object see Chapter 10, "Working with Email." To create an instance of the NewMail object use

```
<%SET myMail = Server.CreateObject("CDONTS.Newmail")%>
```

Methods

AttachFile(*file path*)	Attaches a file to an email message
AttachURL(*file path*, *URL*)	Attaches a file to an email message with an associated URL
Send	Sends an email message

Properties

Bcc	The email address used for sending a blind carbon copy of the email message
Body	The text of the email message
BodyFormat	Specifies whether the email message contains HTML or plain text
Cc	The email address used for sending a carbon copy of the email message
ContentBase	Sets the base URL for all URLs included in the email message
ContentLocation	Sets an absolute or relative path for all URLs included in the email message
From	The email address of the sender of the email message
Importance	The priority of the email message
MailFormat	The encoding format of the email message
Subject	The subject line of the email message
To	The email address of the recipient of the email message

The Page Counter Component

The Page Counter component enables you to track the number of times that a page has been requested. For more information on the Page Counter component see Chapter 9, "Tracking Page Views and Displaying Advertisements." To create an instance of the Page Counter component use

```
<% Set myCNT=Server.CreateObject("IISSample.PageCounter")%>
```

Methods

Hits([*Web Page Path*])	Returns the number of times a page has been requested
PageHit()	Updates the number of times the current page has been requested
Reset([*Web Page Path*])	Resets to zero the number of times a page has been requested

File

Hit Count Data File	Text file that stores the number of requests that each page has received

VBScript Reference

In This Appendix

This appendix contains a quick reference of all the VBScript statements, functions, operators, and objects. Many of the VBScript functions use constants. See the end of this appendix for a list of these constants.

For more information on VBScript, consult the Microsoft VBScript online documentation included with the Windows NT Option Pack or visit the Microsoft Windows Script Technologies Web site at `http://msdn.microsoft.com/scripting`.

Statements

Call

`[Call]` *name* `[`*argumentlist*`]`

This statement transfers control to a function or subroutine. Using `Call` when calling a function or subroutine is always optional. However, if the optional `Call` keyword is used, *argumentlist* must be enclosed in parentheses.

Class

```
Class name
[statements]
End Class
```

Defines a class, assigning a name, variables, properties, and methods.

Const

`[Public | Private] Const` *constantname=expression*

This statement is used to declare a constant. You can declare multiple constants within a single line by separating each constant assignment with a comma.

Dim

`Dim` *varname*`[(`*[subscripts]*`)][,` *varname*`[(`*[subscripts]*`)]]` . . .

This statement creates a new variable and allocates storage space.

Do...Loop

Syntax 1:

```
Do [{While | Until} condition]
[statements]
[Exit Do]
[statements]
Loop
```

Syntax 2:

```
Do
[statements]
[Exit Do]
[statements]
Loop [{While ¦ Until} condition]
```

Both forms of the statement repeat `statements` while `condition` is TRUE or until it becomes TRUE.

Erase

```
Erase array
```

This statement erases `array`, reinitializing elements of fixed-size arrays and recovering storage space of dynamic arrays.

Execute

```
Execute statement
```

Executes a statement at runtime. The statement can contain multiple statements divided by colons.

Exit

```
Exit Do
```

This statement exits a `Do...Loop` statement.

```
Exit For
```

This statement exits a `For...Next` or `For Each...Next` loop.

```
Exit Function
```

This statement exits a function.

```
Exit Sub
```

This statement exits a subroutine.

For...Next

```
For counter = start To end [Step step]
[statements]
[Exit For]
[statements]
Next
```

This loop repeats a group of *statements* the number of times designated by the loop counter.

For Each...Next

```
For Each element In group
[statements]
[Exit For]
[statements]
Next [element]
```

For each element in the array or collection, this loop repeats the group of *statements*.

Function

```
[Public ¦ Private] Function name [(arglist)]
[statements]
[name = expression]
[Exit Function]
[statements]
[name = expression]
End Function
```

This statement defines a Function, assigning a name, arguments, and code.

If...Then...Else

Syntax 1:

```
If condition Then statements [Else elsestatements]
```

Syntax 2:

```
If condition Then
statements
[ElseIf condition-n Then
[elseifstatements]] . . .
[Else
[elsestatements]]
End If
```

Both forms of the statement conditionally execute groups of statements.

On Error

```
On Error Resume Next
```

When an error occurs, this statement executes the statement immediately following the statement that caused the runtime error, or executes the statement immediately following the most recent call out of the procedure containing the `On Error Resume Next` statement. To re-enable the reporting of errors, use `On Error Goto 0`.

Option Explicit

`Option Explicit`

This statement forces the explicit declaration of all variables using the `Dim`, `Private`, `Public`, or `ReDim` statements. It must appear before any other statement or content in the Active Server Page.

Private

`Private varname[([subscripts])]|, varname[([subscripts])]] . . .`

This statement creates private variables (variables available only to the script in which they were declared) and allocates storage space.

Property Get

```
[Public [Default]| Private] Property Get name [(arglist)]
[statements]
[[Set] name = expression]
[Exit Property]
[statements]
[[Set] name = expression]
End Property
```

Defines a property procedure that returns the value of a property for a class.

Property Let

```
[Public | Private] Property Let name ([arglist,] value)
[statements]
[Exit Property]
[statements]
End Property
```

Defines a property procedure that sets the value of a property for a class.

Property Set

```
[Public | Private] Property Set name([arglist,] reference)
[statements]
[Exit Property]
[statements]
End Property
```

Defines a property procedure that sets a reference to an object for a class.

Public

```
Public varname[([subscripts])][, varname[([subscripts])]] . . .
```

This statement creates public variables (variables available to all procedures in all scripts in all projects) and allocates storage space.

Randomize

```
Randomize [number]
```

This statement gives the Rnd function's random-number generator a new seed value. If you use this statement without supplying a number, the system timer is used for the seed value. If you do not use Randomize before using the RND() function, the same sequence of numbers will be generated every time RND() is called.

ReDim

```
ReDim [Preserve] varname(subscripts) [, varname(subscripts)] . . .
```

This statement revises dimension subscripts, sizing or resizing a dynamic array. Preserve protects data in the existing array.

Rem

Syntax 1:

```
Rem comment
```

Syntax 2:

```
' comment
```

Both forms of this statement keep comments from being parsed. If Rem follows other statements on a line, it must be separated by a colon.

Select Case

```
Select Case testexpression
[Case expressionlist-n
[statements-n]] . . .
[Case Else expressionlist-n
[elsestatements-n]]
End Select
```

This statement executes statements paired with any *expressionlist* that matches *testexpression*. If *testexpression* doesn't match any *expressionlist*, the statements paired with Case Else are executed.

Set

```
Set objectvar = {objectexpression ¦ Nothing}
```

This statement sets the object reference for the variable or the property. Nothing dissociates objectvar from any specific object.

Sub

```
[Public ¦ Private] Sub name [(arglist)]
[statements]
[Exit Sub]
[statements]
End Sub
```

This statement defines a subroutine, assigning a name, arguments, and code.

While...Wend

```
While condition
[statements]
Wend
```

This loop continues to execute the series of statements as long as condition is TRUE.

With

```
With object
[statements]
End With
```

With enables you to perform a series of statements with a single object without explicitly referring to the object in every statement.

Functions

Abs(number)

This function returns an absolute value.

Array(arglist)

This function creates an array.

Asc(string)

This function returns the ANSI code for the first letter in string.

AscB(*string*)

This function returns the first byte in *string*.

AscW(*string*)

This function returns the first Unicode character code in *string*.

Atn(*number*)

This function returns the arctangent.

CBool(*expression*)

This function converts to variant of subtype Boolean.

CByte(*expression*)

This function converts to variant of subtype Byte.

CCur(*expression*)

This function converts to variant of subtype Currency.

CDate(*date*)

This function converts to variant of subtype Date.

CDbl(*expression*)

This function converts to variant of subtype Double.

Chr(*charcode*)

This function converts the ANSI character code to the corresponding keyboard character.

ChrB(*charcode*)

This function converts the character code to a single byte.

ChrW(*charcode*)

This function converts the Unicode character code to the corresponding keyboard character.

CInt(*expression*)

This function converts to variant of subtype Integer.

CLng(*expression*)

This function converts to variant of subtype Long.

Cos(*number*)

This function returns the cosine.

CreateObject(*servername.typename*)

This function creates an Automation object. Within an Active Server Page, use the CreateObject method of the Server object instead of this function.

CSng(*expression*)

This function converts to variant of subtype Single.

CStr(*expression*)

This function converts to variant of subtype String.

Date

This function returns the date according to the system.

DateAdd(*interval,number,date*)

This function adds the time interval to *date*. The *interval* argument accepts the following values:

Setting	Description
yyyy	Year
q	Quarter
m	Month
y	Day of Year
d	Day
w	Weekday
ww	Week of Year
h	Hour
n	Minute
s	Second

DateDiff(*interval,date1,date2[, firstdayofweek[,firstweekofyear]]*)

This function returns the number of intervals between two dates. See the later section "Date and Time Constants" for values of *firstdayofweek* and *firstweekofyear*. The *interval* argument accepts the values shown in the following table:

Setting	Description
yyyy	Year
q	Quarter
m	Month
y	Day of year
d	Day
w	Weekday
ww	Week of year
h	Hour
n	Minute
s	Second

DatePart(*interval,date[,firstdayofweek[, firstweekofyear]]*)

This function returns the designated part of the date. See the later section "Date and Time Constants" for values of *firstdayofweek* and *firstweekofyear*. The *interval* argument accepts the values shown in the following table:

Setting	Description
yyyy	Year
q	Quarter
m	Month
y	Day of year
d	Day
w	Weekday
ww	Week of year
h	Hour
n	Minute
s	Second

DateSerial(*year*,*month*,*day*)

This function converts to variant of subtype Date.

DateValue(*date*)

This function converts to variant of subtype Date.

Day(*date*)

This function returns a number representing the day of the month according to the argument.

Exp(*number*)

This function raises e to the power of *number*.

Eval(*expression*)

This function evaluates the expression and returns the result.

Filter(*InputStrings*,*Value*[,*Include*[, *Compare*]])

This function creates a new array according to the filter criteria. See the later section "Comparison Constants" for values of *Compare*. *InputStrings* must be a one-dimensional array of strings. *Value* is the string to search for.

Fix(*number*)

This function converts to integer (for a negative number, this function rounds the number up).

FormatCurrency(*Expression*[,*NumDigitsAfter Decimal*[,*IncludeLeadingDigit*[,*UseParensFor NegativeNumbers*[,*GroupDigits*]]]])

This function formats an expression as currency. See the later section "Tristate Constants" for values of *IncludeLeadingDigit*, *UseParensForNegativeNumbers*, and *GroupDigits*.

FormatDateTime(*Date*[,*NamedFormat*])

This function formats dates and times. See the later section "Date Format Constants" for values of *NamedFormat*.

FormatNumber(*Expression*[,*NumDigitsAfter Decimal*[,*IncludeLeadingDigit*[,*UseParensFor NegativeNumbers*[,*GroupDigits*]]]])

This function formats numbers. See the later section "Tristate Constants" for values of *IncludeLeadingDigit*, *UseParensForNegativeNumbers*, and *GroupDigits*.

FormatPercent(*Expression*[,*NumDigitsAfter Decimal*[,*IncludeLeadingDigit*[,*UseParensFor NegativeNumbers*[,*GroupDigits*]]]])

This function formats percentages. See the later section "Tristate Constants" for values of *IncludeLeadingDigit*, *UseParensForNegativeNumbers*, and *GroupDigits*.

GetLocale

This function returns the current locale (as a 32-bit integer) without setting a new one. The locale determines the formatting of currencies and dates.

GetObject([*pathname*][,*class*])

This function returns the specified *Automation* object from the specified file.

Hex(*number*)

This function returns the hexadecimal value of *number*.

Hour(*time*)

This function returns the hour according to the *time* argument.

InputBox(*prompt*[,*title*][,*default*][,*xpos*][, ypos*][,*helpfile*,*context*])

This function prompts and returns user input. Don't use this with Active Server Pages!

InStr([*start*,]*string1*,*string2*[,*compare*])

This function returns the first appearance of *string2* within *string1*. See the later section "Comparison Constants" for values of *compare*.

InStrB([*start*,]*string1*,*string2*[,*compare*])

This function returns the byte position of the first appearance of *string2* within *string1*. See the later section "Comparison Constants" for values of *compare*.

InStrRev(*string1*,*string2*[*start*[,*compare*]])

This function returns the first appearance of *string2* within *string1* starting from the end of the string. See the later section "Comparison Constants" for values of *compare*.

Int(*number*)

This function returns an integer (for a negative number, it rounds the number down).

IsArray(*varname*)

This function determines whether the variable is an array.

IsDate(*expression*)

This function determines whether *expression* can be converted to date format.

IsEmpty(*expression*)

This function determines whether the variable has been initialized.

IsNull(*expression*)

This function determines whether *expression* is null.

IsNumeric(*expression*)

This function determines whether *expression* is a number.

IsObject(*expression*)

This function determines whether *expression* is an Automation object.

Join(*list*[,*delimiter*])

This function joins substrings in an array separated by the character indicated by *delimiter*. It's the opposite of the Split function.

LBound(*arrayname*[,*dimension*])

This function returns the lower limit of the array dimension. It always returns zero with the current version of VBScript.

LCase(*string*)

This function converts a string to lowercase.

Left(*string*,*length*)

This function returns the left string portion of the designated length.

LeftB(string, bytes)

This function returns the left string portion of the designated number of bytes.

Len(*string*¦*varname*)

This function returns the length of the string or the byte size of the variable.

LenB(*string*)

This function returns the number of bytes used to represent the string.

LoadPicture(*picturename*)

This function loads a picture object.

Log(*number*)

This function returns the natural logarithm of the number.

LTrim(*string*)

This function removes extra leading spaces.

Mid(*string*,*start*[,*length*])

This function returns a string portion of the designated length.

MidB(*string,start*[*,bytes*])

This function returns a string portion of the designated number of bytes.

Minute(*time*)

This function returns the minute according to the *time* argument.

Month(*date*)

This function returns the month represented by the number.

MonthName(*month*[*,abbreviate*])

This function returns the month represented by the name.

MsgBox(*prompt*[*,buttons*][*,title*][*helpfile,context*])

This function prompts the user to choose a button and indicates which button the user has chosen. See the later section "MsgBox Constants" for *button* and return values. Don't use this in an Active Server Page!

Now

This function returns the current date and time according to the system.

Oct(*number*)

This function returns the octal value of *number*.

Replace(*expression,find,replacewith*[*,start*[*,count*[*,compare*]]])

This function replaces the designated substring *find* with the substring *replacewith* the designated number of times. See the later section "Comparison Constants" for values of *compare*.

Right(*string,length*)

This function returns the right string portion of the designated length.

RightB(*string,bytes*)

This function returns the right string portion of the designated number of bytes.

Rnd([*number*)])

This function generates a pseudo-random number.

Round(*number*[,*numdecimalplaces*])

This function rounds *number*.

RTrim(*string*)

This function removes extra right spaces.

ScriptEngine

This function returns the name of the scripting language in use.

ScriptEngineBuildVersion

This function returns the name of the script engine in use.

ScriptEngineMajorVersion

This function returns the major version number of the script engine in use.

Second(*time*)

This function returns the second of the minute according to the *time* argument.

SetLocale(*lcid*)

This function returns the current locale and sets the new locale specified by *lcid*. After the locale is set, currencies and dates are formatted according to the locale.

Sgn(*number*)

This function returns the sign of *number*.

Sin(*number*)

This function returns the sine of *number*.

Space(*number*)

This function creates a string with the specified number of spaces.

Split(*expression*[,*delimiter*[,*count*[, *compare*]]])

This function splits a string and converts it into an array. It's the opposite of the Join function. See the later section "Comparison Constants" for values of *compare*.

Sqr(*number*)

This function returns the square root of the specified number.

StrComp(*string1*,*string2*[,*compare*])

This function performs a string comparison. See the later section "Comparison Constants" for values of *compare*.

StrReverse(*string1*)

This function reverses the characters of a string.

String(*number*,*character*)

This function creates a string with *character* repeated the specified number of times.

Tan(*number*)

This function returns the tangent of *number*.

Time

This function returns the current time according to the system.

TimeSerial(*hour*,*minute*,*second*)

This function returns Date Variant.

TimeValue(*time*)

This function returns Date Variant containing time.

Trim(*string*)

This function removes extra spaces at left and right.

TypeName(*varname*)

This function returns the subtype by name. See the later section "VarType Constants" for return values.

UBound(*arrayname*[,*dimension*])

This function returns the upper bound of the array dimension. If no dimension is specified, the first dimension is assumed.

UCase(*string*)

This function converts the string to uppercase.

VarType(*varname*)

This function returns the subtype by value. See the later section "VarType Constants" for return values.

Weekday(*date*,[*firstdayofweek*])

This function returns the day of the week by number. See the later section "Date and Time Constants" for values of *firstdayofweek*.

WeekDayName(*weekday*,*abbreviate*, *firstdayofweek*)

This function returns the day of the week by name. See the later section "Date and Time Constants" for values of *firstdayofweek*.

Year(*date*)

This function returns the year according to the argument.

Operators

+ Operator

```
result = expression1 + expression2
```

Sum. This operator can also be used for string concatenation but & is less ambiguous.

And Operator

```
result = expression1 And expression2
```

Logical conjunction. This operator also performs bitwise comparison, returning digit 1 only where both expressions have digit 1.

& Operator

```
result = expression1 & expression2
```

String concatenation.

/ Operator

```
result = number1/number2
```

This operator divides two numbers and returns a floating-point number.

Eqv Operator

```
result = expression1 Eqv expression2
```

Logical equivalence. This operator also performs bitwise comparison, returning digit 1 only where bits in the two expressions are identical.

^ Operator

```
result = number^exponent
```

This operator raises a *number* to the power of *exponent*.

Imp Operator

result = expression1 Imp *expression2*

Material implication. This operator also performs bitwise comparison. The following table illustrates logical implication:

expression1	*expression2*	*result*
TRUE	TRUE	TRUE
TRUE	FALSE	FALSE
TRUE	NULL	NULL
FALSE	TRUE	TRUE
FALSE	FALSE	TRUE
FALSE	NULL	TRUE
NULL	TRUE	TRUE
NULL	FALSE	NULL
NULL	NULL	NULL

The following table illustrates the bitwise comparison associated with the Imp operator:

expression1	*expression2*	*result*
0	0	1
0	1	1
1	0	0
1	1	1

\ Operator

result = number1\number2

This operator divides two numbers and returns an integer.

Is Operator

result = object1 Is *object2*

This operator checks whether two variables refer to the same object and returns TRUE or FALSE.

Mod Operator

result = number1 Mod *number2*

This operator divides two numbers and returns only the remainder.

* Operator

result = number1*number2

Multiplication.

- Operator

result = number1-number2

Subtraction.

-number

Sign of number.

Not Operator

result = Not expression

Logical negation. This operator also performs bitwise negation.

Or Operator

result = expression1 Or expression2

Logical disjunction. *result* is TRUE if either expression is TRUE or both expressions are TRUE. The Or operator also performs bitwise comparison, returning digit 0 only where both expressions have the digit 0. Elsewhere the digit 1 is returned.

Xor Operator

result = expression1 Xor expression2

Logical exclusion. *result* is TRUE if one and only one expression is TRUE. The Xor operator also performs bitwise comparison, returning the digit 1 only where one and only one expression has the digit 1. Elsewhere the digit 0 is returned.

Objects

The Dictionary Object

The Dictionary object can be used to store key/value pairs. To use the Dictionary object in an Active Server Page script, you must declare an instance of the object like this:

```
<% Set myDict = Server.CreateObject( "Scripting.Dictionary" )%>
```

C

VBSCRIPT
REFERENCE

Methods

Add *Key*, *Item*

This method adds *Key* and associated *Item* to a Dictionary object.

Exists(*Key*)

This method checks whether the specified *Key* already exists in the Dictionary object and returns either TRUE or FALSE.

Items

This method returns all *Items* in the Dictionary object as an array.

Keys

This method returns all existing *Keys* in the Dictionary object as an array.

Remove(*Key*)

This method removes *Key* and its associated item from the Dictionary object.

RemoveAll

This method removes all keys and their associated items from the Dictionary object.

Properties

CompareMode

This property specifies how items in the Dictionary should be compared. See the later section "Comparison Constants" for possible values.

Count

This property counts items in the Dictionary object (read-only).

Item(*Key*)

This property returns the item associated with the designated *Key* in the Dictionary object or associates a new value with the key.

Key(*Key*)

This property sets the specified *Key* in the Dictionary object.

The Err Object

The Err object contains information about runtime errors and enables you to raise custom errors. You do not need to create an instance of this object to use it in your scripts.

Methods

Clear

This method explicitly clears the Err object of all property settings.

Raise(*number, source, description, helpfile, helpcontext*)

This method returns a runtime error. *number* identifies the type of error. VBScript errors are numbered in the range 0–65535. *source* indicates the object or application that originally generated the error.

Properties

Description

This property returns or sets a brief description of an error.

HelpContext

This property sets or returns the identifier for a topic within the Help file that's appropriate for the Err object.

HelpFile

This property sets or returns the fully qualified path to the Help file that's appropriate for the Err object.

Number

This property returns a number identifying the error or, if *errornumber* is included, associates the error with either a VBScript error number or an SCODE error value.

Source

This property identifies the source of the error, usually by class name or programmatic ID of the object or the application that generated the error.

The Match Object

The Match object represents the properties of a match that results from calling the Execute method of the RegExp object. You never explicitly create an instance of the Match object.

Properties

FirstIndex

This property returns the position where the first match occurs in the string passed to the Execute method of the RegExp object.

C

VBSCRIPT
REFERENCE

Length

This property returns the length of the match.

Value

This property returns the actual value of the match.

The `Matches` Collection

The `Matches` collection contains all the `Match` objects returned by calling the `Execute` method of the `RegExp` object.

Properties

Count

This property returns the number of `Match` objects in the `Matches` collection.

Item(*key*)

This property returns the `Match` object specified by *key*.

The `RegExp` Object

The `RegExp` object enables you to perform regular expression pattern matching. To use the `RegExp` object in an Active Server Page, you must declare an instance of it like this:

```
<% Set myReg = Server.CreateObject( "VBScript.RegExp" ) %>
```

Methods

Execute(*string*)

This method performs pattern matching against the *string* using the pattern set with the `Pattern` property.

Replace(*string1, string2*)

This method replaces the text in *string1* with the text in *string2* according to the pattern set with the `Pattern` property.

Test(*string*)

This method returns TRUE if *string* matches the pattern set with the `Pattern` property.

Properties

Global

If this property is assigned the value TRUE, every match is returned. Otherwise, only the first match is returned.

IgnoreCase

If this property is assigned the value TRUE, then a case-insensitive pattern match is performed.

Pattern

This property is used to set or return the regular expression pattern that is used when performing matches. The pattern can contain any of the regular expression characters in the following table:

Character	Description
\	Matches special characters such as the newline character (\n) or escapes regular expression character (\\)
^	Matches the beginning of input
$	Matches the end of input
*	Matches the character that immediately precedes it if it appears zero or more times
+	Matches the character that immediately precedes it if it appears one or more times
?	Matches the character that immediately precedes it if it appears zero times or one time
.	Matches any single character except the newline character
(pattern)	Matches the pattern in the parentheses and remembers the match in the Matches collection
x|y	Matches either character x or character y
{n}	Matches the character that immediately precedes it if it appears exactly n times
{n,m}	Matches the character that immediately precedes it if it appears at least n times and at most m times
[xyz]	Matches any one of the characters in the brackets
[^xyz]	Matches any character not in the brackets
[a-z]	Matches any character in the range of characters
[^a-z]	Matches any character not in the range of characters
\b	Matches a word boundary

continues

Character	*Description*
\B	Matches a nonword boundary
\d	Matches a numeral
\D	Matches any non-numeric character
\f	Matches form feed character
\n	Matches newline character
\r	Matches carriage return character
\s	Matches whitespace
\S	Matches nonwhitespace character
\t	Matches a tab character
\v	Matches a vertical tab character
\w	Matches any word character or underscore
\W	Matches any nonword character
\(*num*)	Matches previously remembered pattern if it appears *num* times
n	Matches ASCII character (*n* represents an ASCII character as an octal escape value)
\x*n*	Matches ASCII character (*n* represents an ASCII character as a hexadecimal escape value)

Constants

In the following sections, the constants (left column of each table) can be used in place of the values (in the center column).

Color Constants

Constant	*Value*	*Description*
vbBlack	&h00	Black
vbRed	&hFF	Red
vbGreen	&hFF00	Green
vbYellow	&hFFFF	Yellow
vbBlue	&hFF0000	Blue
vbMagenta	&hFF00FF	Magenta
vbCyan	&hFFFF00	Cyan
vbWhite	&hFFFFFF	White

Comparison Constants

Constant	Value	Description
vbBinaryCompare	0	Binary comparison
vbTextCompare	1	Textual comparison
vbDatabaseCompare	2	Comparison based on information in the database

Date and Time Constants

Constant	Value	Description
vbSunday	1	Sunday
vbMonday	2	Monday
vbTuesday	3	Tuesday
vbWednesday	4	Wednesday
vbThursday	5	Thursday
vbFriday	6	Friday
vbSaturday	7	Saturday
vbFirstJan1	1	Week of Jan 1 (default)
vbFirstFourDays	2	First week of the year that has at least four days
vbFirstFullWeek	3	First full week of the year
vbUseSystem	0	Use the date format of the computer's regional settings
vbUseSystemDayOfWeek	0	Use the first day of the week according to the system settings

Date Format Constants

Constant	Value	Description
vbGeneralDate	0	Display the date and/or time according to the system settings
vbLongDate	1	Display the date in long date format
vbShortDate	2	Display the date in short date format
vbLongTime	3	Display the time in long time format
vbShortTime	4	Display the time in short time format

MsgBox Constants

These constants are used with the MsgBox function to specify buttons and icons displayed in the message box and to identify the default icon.

Constant	Value	Description
vbOKOnly	0	Show only the OK button.
vbOKCancel	1	Show OK and Cancel buttons.
vbAbortRetryIgnore	2	Show Abort, Retry, and Ignore buttons.
vbYesNoCancel	3	Show Yes, No, and Cancel buttons.
vbYesNo	4	Show Yes and No buttons.
vbRetryCancel	5	Show Retry and Cancel buttons.
vbCritical	16	Show Critical Message icon.
vbQuestion	32	Show Warning Query icon.
vbExclamation	48	Show Warning Message icon.
vbInformation	64	Show Information Message icon.
vbDefaultButton1	0	The first button is the default.
vbDefaultButton2	256	The second button is the default.
vbDefaultButton3	512	The third button is the default.
vbDefaultButton4	768	The fourth button is the default.

The constants in the following table specify modality:

Constant	Value	Description
vbApplicationModal	0	The current application won't continue until the user responds to the message box.
vbSystemModal	4096	No applications will continue until the user responds to the message box.

The constants in the following table identify which button has been pressed:

Constant	Value	Description
vbOK	1	OK button
vbCancel	2	Cancel button
vbAbort	3	Abort button
vbRetry	4	Retry button
vbIgnore	5	Ignore button
vbYes	6	Yes button
vbNo	7	No button

String Constants

Constant	Value	Description
vbCr	Chr(13)	Carriage return
vbCrLf	Chr(13) & Chr(10)	Combination carriage return and line feed
vbFormFeed	Chr(12)	Form feed
vbLF	Chr(10)	Line feed
vbNewLine	Chr(13) & Chr(10) or Chr(10)	Newline character appropriate for platform
vbNullChar	Chr(0)	Character of value 0
vbNullString	string having value 0	Null string
vbTab	Chr(9)	Horizontal tab
vbVerticalTab	Chr(11)	Vertical tab

Tristate Constants

Constant	Value	Description
TristateTrue	-1	True
TristateFalse	0	False
TristateUseDefault	-2	Use the default setting

VarType Constants

Constant	Value	Description
vbEmpty	0	Uninitialized (default)
vbNull	1	Contains no valid data
vbInteger	2	Integer subtype
vbLong	3	Long subtype
vbSingle	4	Single subtype
vbDouble	5	Double subtype
vbCurrency	6	Currency subtype
vbDate	7	Date subtype
vbString	8	String subtype
vbObject	9	Object
vbError	10	Error subtype

continues

C

VBSCRIPT
REFERENCE

Constant	Value	Description
vbBoolean	11	Boolean subtype
vbVariant	12	Variant (only used for arrays of variants)
vbDataObject	13	Data access object
vbDecimal	14	Decimal subtype
vbByte	17	Byte subtype
vbArray	8192	Array

SQL Reference

IN THIS APPENDIX

This appendix provides a brief reference for the Microsoft SQL Server statements and stored procedures that you will find yourself using most often while programming Active Server Pages. However, SQL is a complicated language, and this appendix cannot even begin to cover all its nuances. The syntax of many of the SQL statements and functions has been simplified in this appendix. To learn everything you'd ever need to know about using SQL with Microsoft SQL Server, rush to your local bookstore and buy *Microsoft SQL Server 7.0 Unleashed* by Greg Mable, et al. (1999, Sams Publishing, ISBN 0-672-31227-1).

SQL Statements

The following SQL statements enable you to create and remove database tables and stored procedures, retrieve data from a database table, modify table data, and grant permissions on database objects.

SELECT

```
SELECT [TOP [PERCENT]] select_list
FROM table_source
WHERE search_condition
ORDER BY order_by_expression
```

The SELECT statement is used to retrieve one or more rows from a database table. Instead of listing particular column names in the *select_list*, you can also use * as a wildcard character to represent all columns.

Examples

- Using SELECT to retrieve all the columns and all the rows from the Authors table:

  ```
  SELECT * FROM Authors
  ```

- Using SELECT to retrieve the last name of the author who has the first name Andrew:

  ```
  SELECT au_lname
  FROM Authors
  WHERE au_fname = 'Andrew'
  ```

- Using SELECT to retrieve a list of publishers and book titles. The results are ordered by the name of the publisher:

  ```
  SELECT pub_name, title
  FROM publishers,titles
  WHERE publishers.pub_id = titles.pub_id
  ORDER BY pub_name
  ```

- Using SELECT to retrieve the names of the first 10 authors from the Authors table in order of the last name.

```
SELECT TOP 10 au_fname, au_lname
FROM Authors
ORDER BY au_lname
```

INSERT

```
INSERT table_name ( column_list )
VALUES ( value_list )
```

The INSERT statement is used to insert one or more rows into a database table (Microsoft Access uses INSERT INTO).

Examples

- Using INSERT to add a new username and password to a Passwords table.

```
INSERT Passwords ( username, password )
VALUES ( 'Andrew', 'Jones' )
```

- Using INSERT with SELECT to insert multiple rows into the newPasswords table from the oldPasswords table:

```
INSERT newPassword ( username, password )
SELECT username, password
FROM oldPasswords
```

UPDATE

```
UPDATE table_name
SET column_name = value
WHERE search_condition
```

The UPDATE statement is used to update one or more rows in a database table.

Examples

- Using UPDATE to change the password in every row in a table named Passwords where the username column has the value Andrew Jones:

```
UPDATE Passwords
SET password = 'secret'
WHERE username = 'Andrew Jones'
```

- Using UPDATE to change the values of multiple columns all at once:

```
UPDATE Passwords
SET username = 'Bill Gates',
    password = 'Billions'
WHERE username = 'Andrew Jones'
```

D

SQL REFERENCE

DELETE

```
DELETE table_name
WHERE search_condition
```

The DELETE statement is used to delete one or more rows from a database table.

Example

- Using DELETE to remove all the rows from the Passwords table in which the pass-word column has the value secret:

```
DELETE Passwords
WHERE password = 'secret'
```

TRUNCATE TABLE

```
TRUNCATE TABLE table_name
```

This statement efficiently removes all the rows from a table.

Example

- Using TRUNCATE TABLE to remove all the rows from the Passwords table:

```
TRUNCATE TABLE Passwords
```

CREATE TABLE

```
CREATE TABLE table_name
( column_name data_type [,...n] )
```

The CREATE TABLE statement is used to create a new database table. See the later section, "SQL Server Data Types," for a list of data types that you can use when defining the columns for a table.

Examples

- Using CREATE TABLE to create a table named Passwords that contains usernames and passwords:

```
CREATE TABLE Passwords
( username VARCHAR( 50 ), password VARCHAR( 50 ) )
```

- Using CREATE TABLE to create a table with an IDENTITY column:

```
CREATE TABLE WebUsers
( user_id INT IDENTITY, username VARCHAR( 50 ) )
```

- Using CREATE TABLE to create a table with a column with a default value of the current data and time:

```
CREATE TABLE WebUsers
```

```
(
  username VARCHAR( 50 ),
  entrydate DATETIME DEFAULT GETDATE()
)
```

CREATE PROCEDURE

```
CREATE PROCEDURE procedure_name
[ @parameter_name data_type [OUTPUT] ]
[,...n]
AS
sql_statement [,...n]
```

The CREATE PROCEDURE statement is used to create a new SQL Server stored procedure.

Examples

- Using CREATE PROCEDURE to create a new stored procedure that retrieves all the rows from the Passwords table:

```
CREATE PROCEDURE getPasswords
AS
SELECT * FROM Passwords
```

- Using CREATE PROCEDURE to create a new stored procedure that accepts an input parameter and returns an output parameter:

```
CREATE PROCEDURE getUsername
(
  @password VARCHAR( 50 ),
  @username VARCHAR( 50 ) OUTPUT
)
AS
SELECT @username = username
FROM Passwords
WHERE password = @password
```

GRANT

```
GRANT ALL ¦ permission
ON table ¦ stored_procedure
TO security_account
```

The GRANT statement assigns permissions to use a database object to a database user or role.

Examples

- Using GRANT to give SELECT permission to the database user named WebUser for the table named Passwords:

```
GRANT SELECT ON Passwords TO WebUser
```

- Granting all permissions on a table named `Passwords` to the `public` role.

  ```
  GRANT ALL ON Passwords TO public
  ```

DROP TABLE

```
DROP TABLE table_name
```

This statement permanently removes a database table.

Example

- Using `DROP TABLE` to permanently remove a table named `Passwords`:

  ```
  DROP TABLE Passwords
  ```

DROP PROCEDURE

```
DROP PROCEDURE procedure_name
```

This statement permanently removes a stored procedure.

Example

- Using `DROP PROCEDURE` to permanently remove a stored procedure named `getPasswords`:

  ```
  DROP PROCEDURE getPasswords
  ```

EXECUTE

```
EXECUTE
[@return_code = ] procedure_name
[@parameter = value ¦ @variable [OUTPUT] ]
[,...n]
```

The `EXECUTE` statement is used to run a SQL stored procedure.

Examples

- Using `EXECUTE` to execute the `getPasswords` stored procedure:

  ```
  EXECUTE getPasswords
  ```

- Using `EXECUTE` to execute a stored procedure named `getValue` that returns a return code:

  ```
  DECLARE @returnCode INT
  EXECUTE @returnCode = getValue
  SELECT @returnCode
  ```

- Using EXECUTE to execute a stored procedure that has both an input parameter and an output parameter:

```
DECLARE @password VARCHAR( 20 )
EXECUTE getPassword 'Andrew Jones', @password OUTPUT
SELECT @password
```

USE

```
USE database_name
```

The USE statement is used to specify the database in which subsequent SQL statements will be executed.

Example

- In this example, the USE statement switches the database to the master database. The sp_help statement is used to display all the objects in the database.

```
USE Master
sp_help
```

SQL Functions

All the following functions can be used with the SELECT statement. The majority of these functions can be used to retrieve summary information about the data stored in a table column.

GETDATE

```
GETDATE()
```

This function returns the current date and time.

Example

- Using GETDATE() to display the current date and time:

```
SELECT GETDATE()
```

AVG

```
AVG( column_name )
```

The AVG function is used to retrieve the average value for a table column.

Example

- Using AVG to return the average number of times that all users have visited a Web site.

```
SELECT AVG( user_numvisits )
FROM WebUsers
```

COUNT

```
COUNT( * ¦ column_name )
```

The COUNT function is used to retrieve either a count of the number of rows in a database table or a count of the number of rows in which a certain column has a value.

Examples

- Using COUNT to return the number of rows in a table named WebUsers:

```
SELECT COUNT(*)
FROM WebUsers
```

- Using COUNT to return the number of rows in a table named WebUsers where the username column does not have a NULL value:

```
SELECT COUNT( username )
FROM WebUsers
```

MAX

```
MAX( column_name )
```

The MAX function is used to retrieve the maximum value for a table column.

Example

- Using MAX to return the maximum number of times that any user has visited a Web site:

```
SELECT MAX( user_numvisits )
FROM WebUsers
```

MIN

```
MIN( column_name )
```

The MIN function is used to retrieve the minimum value for a table column.

Example

- Using MIN to return the minimum number of times that any user has visited a Web site:

```
SELECT MIN( user_numvisits )
FROM WebUsers
```

SUM

```
SUM( column_name )
```

The SUM function is used to add the values of a column.

Example

- Using SUM to return total number of times that a Web site has been visited:

```
SELECT SUM( user_numvisits )
FROM WebUsers
```

SQL Global Variables

The following two global variables can be used with the SELECT statement.

@@IDENTITY

The SQL Server global @@IDENTITY variable contains the value of an IDENTITY column after a row has been inserted.

Example

- This example assumes that the table named WebUsers has an IDENTITY column named user_id. After a row is inserted into the table, the value of the IDENTITY column for the new row is returned with the @@IDENTITY variable:

```
INSERT WebUsers ( username ) VALUES ( 'Andrew Jones' )
SELECT @@IDENTITY
```

@@ROWCOUNT

This variable contains a value representing the number of rows that the last statement affected.

D

SQL REFERENCE

Example

- This example displays the number of rows that were modified by an UPDATE statement using the @@ROWCOUNT variable:

```
UPDATE Passwords
SET username = 'Bill Gates'
WHERE password = 'Billions'
SELECT @@ROWCOUNT
```

SQL Server Stored Procedures

The following two system stored procedures can be used to retrieve information about the objects in a database.

sp_help

```
sp_help [table_name ¦ procedure_name ]
```

The sp_help system stored procedure is used to display information on database objects. When used without a table or procedure name, it lists the properties of all the objects in the current database.

Examples

- Using sp_help to display information about the WebUsers table (Returns information including the table columns, indexes and constraints):

```
sp_help WebUsers
```

- Using sp_help to display information about the stored procedure named getAuthors (Returns information including the date and time the procedure was created):

```
sp_help getAuthors
```

sp_helptext

```
sp_helptext procedure_name
```

The sp_helptext system stored procedure can be used to display the SQL statements that constitute a SQL stored procedure.

Examples

- Using sp_helptext to display the contents of the getAuthors stored procedure:

```
sp_helptext getAuthors
```

- Using `sp_helptext` to display the contents of the `sp_helptext` system stored procedure:

```
USE master
sp_helptext sp_helptext
```

SQL Server Data Types

You can use any of the data types in Tables D.1–D.6 when defining table columns or local variables:

TABLE D.1   CHARACTER DATA TYPES

Data Type	Description
CHAR	Fixed-length character data with a maximum size of 8,000 characters.
VARCHAR	Variable-length character data with a maximum size of 8,000 characters.
TEXT	Variable-length character data with a maximum size of 2,147,483,647 characters.
NCHAR	Unicode fixed-length character data with a maximum size of 4,000 characters.
NVARCHAR	Unicode variable-length character data with a maximum size of 4,000 characters.
NTEXT	Unicode Variable-length character data with a maximum size of 1,073,741,823 characters.

TABLE D.2   NUMERIC DATA TYPES

Data Type	Description
BIT	Has the value 0 or 1.
INTEGER	Integer data between −2,147,483,648 and 2,147,483,647.
SMALLINT	Integer data between −32,768 and 32,767.
NUMERIC	Fixed precision and scale numeric data between $-10^{38}-1$ and $10^{38}-1$.
DECIMAL	Same as NUMERIC
FLOAT	Floating precision data type between $-1.79E + 308$ through $1.79E + 308$.
REAL	Floating precision data type between $-3.40E + 38$ through $3.40E + 38$.

TABLE D.3   DATE AND TIME DATA TYPES

Data Type	Description
DATETIME	Can have a value between January 1, 1753, and December 31, 9999 (accurate to 3.33 milliseconds)
SMALLDATETIME	Can have a value between January 1, 1900, through June 6, 2079 (accurate to one minute)

TABLE D.4   MONEY DATA TYPES

Data Type	Description
MONEY	Can have a value between –922,337,203,685,477.5808 and 922,337,203,685,477.5807.
SMALLMONEY	Can have a value between –214,748.3648 and 214,748.3647.

TABLE D.5   BINARY DATA TYPES

Data Type	Description
BINARY	Fixed-length binary data with a maximum size of 8,000 bytes.
VARBINARY	Variable-length binary data with a maximum size of 8,000 bytes.
IMAGE	Variable-length binary data with a maximum size of 2,147,483,647 bytes.

TABLE D.6   MISCELLANEOUS DATA TYPES

Data Type	Description
CURSOR	Used with stored procedures that have a reference to a cursor as an OUTPUT parameter.
TIMESTAMP	Provides a database-wide unique identifier.
UNIQUEIDENTIFIER	Provides a Globally Unique Identifier (GUID).

INDEX

Symbols

& (ampersand), 49, 797
' (apostrophe), 337
@ (at) symbol, 144
**/ \ (division operators),
  797-798**
^ (exponential operator), 797
**> (greater than sign), 11,
  15-17, 619**
*** (multiplication operator),
  799**
% (percent sign) 11, 15, 619
**/? (question mark) parame-
  ter, 620**
**" " (quotation marks), 66,
  418, 753**
+ (sum operator), 797
- (subtraction operator), 799
1.xx-5.xx status codes, 43
15 seconds, 409
**404 Page Not Found error,
  631**

A

Abandon method, 112, 771
**aborting transactions,
  309-310, 522-523, 543-546**
Abs(number) function, 785
AbsolutePage property, 333
**AbsolutePosition property,
  330-331**
ACCEPT attribute, 78-79
Access, *see* Microsoft Access
**access control lists (ACLs),
  281**

account names, 270
**AccountDisabled property,
  266**
**AccountExpirationDate prop-
  erty, 267**
ACID, *see* MTS
**ACLs (access control lists),
  281**
ACTION attribute, 465

Active Directory (AD), 250
  domains, 251-252
  LANs, 251
  locality (L), 251
  names, 251
  organizational units (OU), 251
  scalability, 250
  state/province (ST), 251
  trust relationships, 251
  see also ADSI
Active Server Pages, *see* ASP
**Active Template Library
  (ATL), 472**
ActiveX
  components, 8, 18, 439
    external, 458
    IIS applications, 457-458
    WSH scripts, 621
  controls, 164, 441
  creating projects, 440-442
  DLLs, 441, 529-530
  EXEs, 441
  IIS applications, 441
  naming, 442
  object instances, 621
  ProgID, 442
  see also ADO
ActualSize property, 323
Ad Rotator component, 19
  advertisements, 209-210
  files, 772
  methods, 210
  properties, 772
adding
  classes, 478-481
  COM code, 526-527
  components, 8, 428
  discussion forum, 686
  disk files to Recordsets, 343
  event handlers, 464
  headers, 769
  keys, 800
  links, 177, 179
  maketables.sql file, 731-732
  methods, 428, 448, 485-489
  MTS type library references,
    528-529
  objects, 254, 450

  to Online Store shopping cart,
    711-715, 717-718
  properties, 444, 482-484,
    486-489
  quotation marks, 753
  records, 336-337
  scripts, 11-13, 15
  spaces between variables, 756
  text to images, 397
  users, 241, 243-244
addresses
  DHTML, 129, 131
  pages, 31
  servers, 54
  submitting, 411
addWebUser() method, 663
adLock values, 328
**ADO (ActiveX Data Objects),
  20**
  ADOMD, 288
  ADOX, 288, 301-302, 310
  ADSI, 277-280
  Command object, 289
  connections, 289-291, 308-310
  constants, 311
  downloading, 290, 752
  Recordset object, 289
adOpen constants, 326
**adovbs.inc file, 311, 326, 334,
  704**
adPersistADTG constant, 342
AdShark, 411
**ADSI (Active Directory
  Services Interface), 248**
  accessing, 252
  ADO, 277-280
  authentication, 256
  domains, 261-262
  Exchange Server, 274-275
  groups, 263-264
  IADs interface, 253, 256
  LDAP, 252
  namespaces, 252, 255
  NDS, 252
  nodes, 255
  NT services, 269-272
  objects, 253-254
  print queues, 272-273

Other Related Titles

Installing the CD-ROM

If you have AUTOPLAY turned on, your computer will automatically run the CD-ROM interface. If AUTOPLAY is turned off, follow these directions:

1. Insert the CD-ROM into your CD-ROM drive.
2. From the Windows desktop, double-click the My Computer icon.
3. Double-click the icon representing your CD-ROM drive.
4. Double-click the icon titled START.EXE to run the interface.